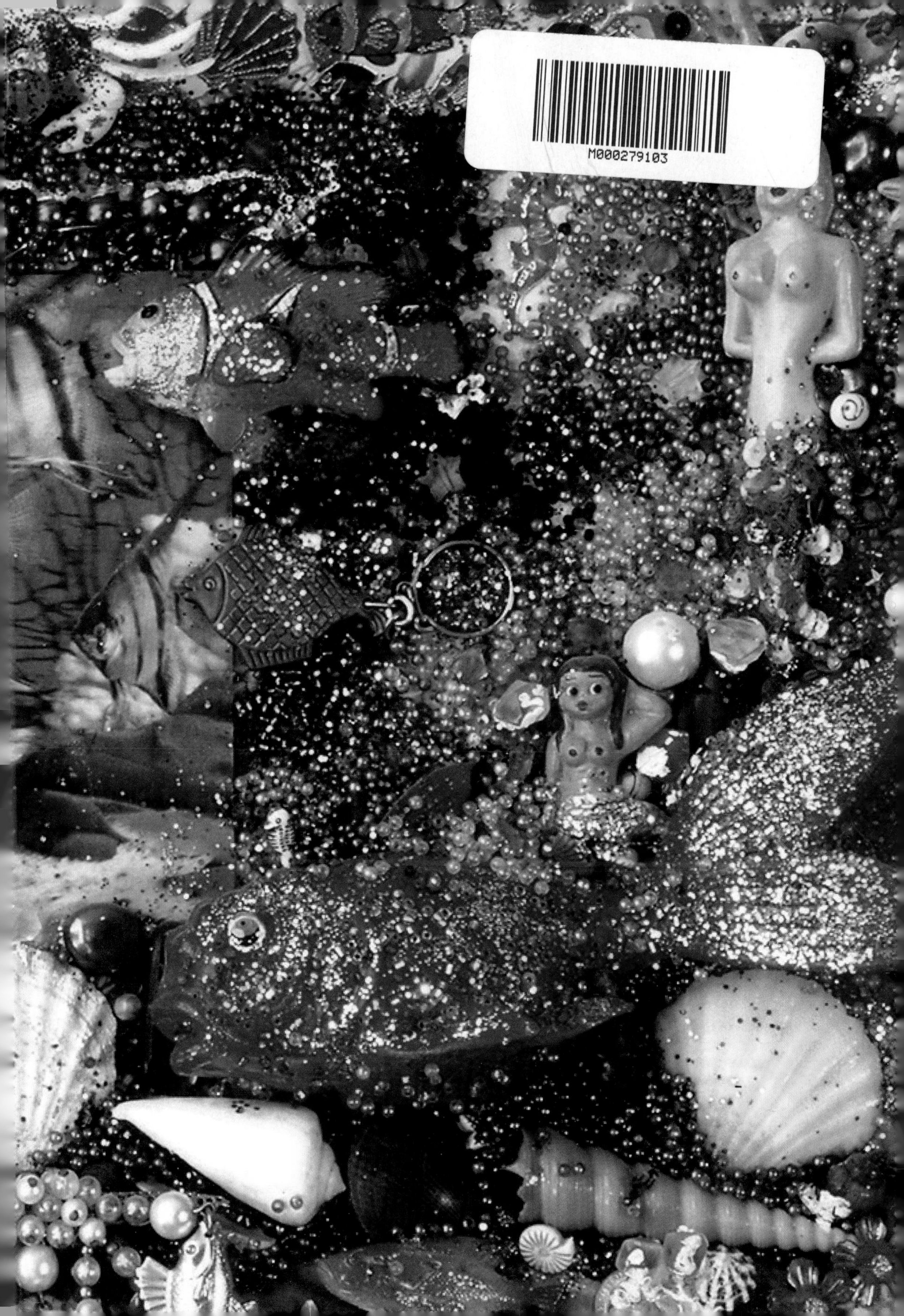

BC-BN

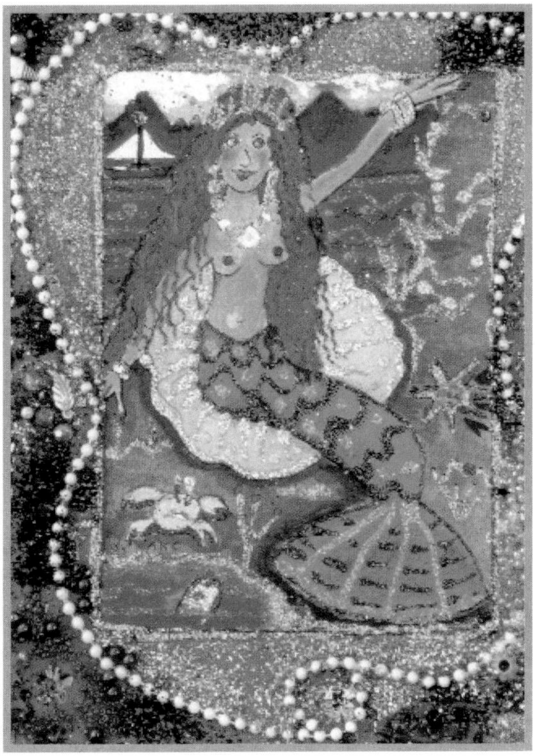

Dedication
This book is in memory of my
dear friend Sherry Dashiell
who gave me so much love

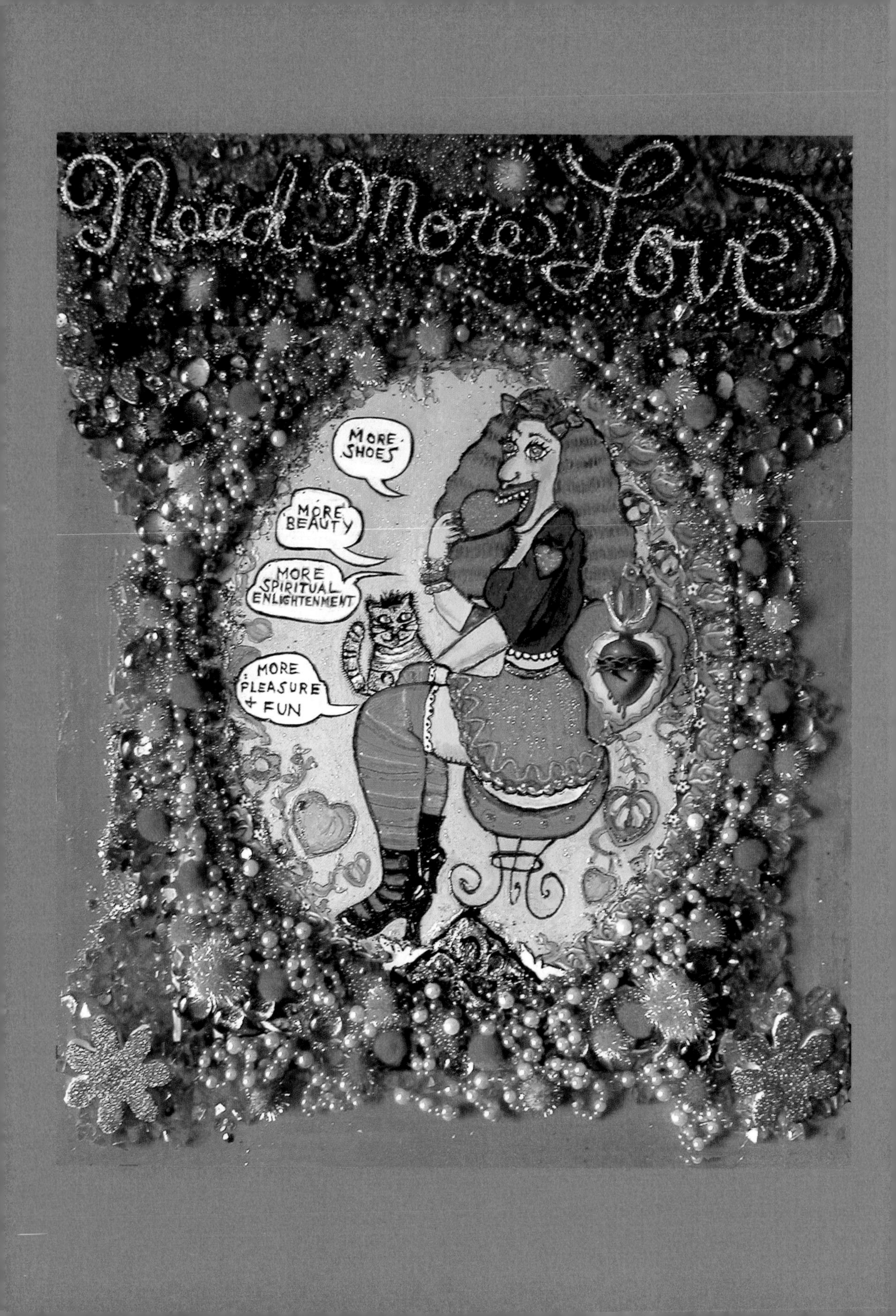
Need More Love
MORE SHOES
MORE BEAUTY
MORE SPIRITUAL ENLIGHTENMENT
MORE PLEASURE + FUN

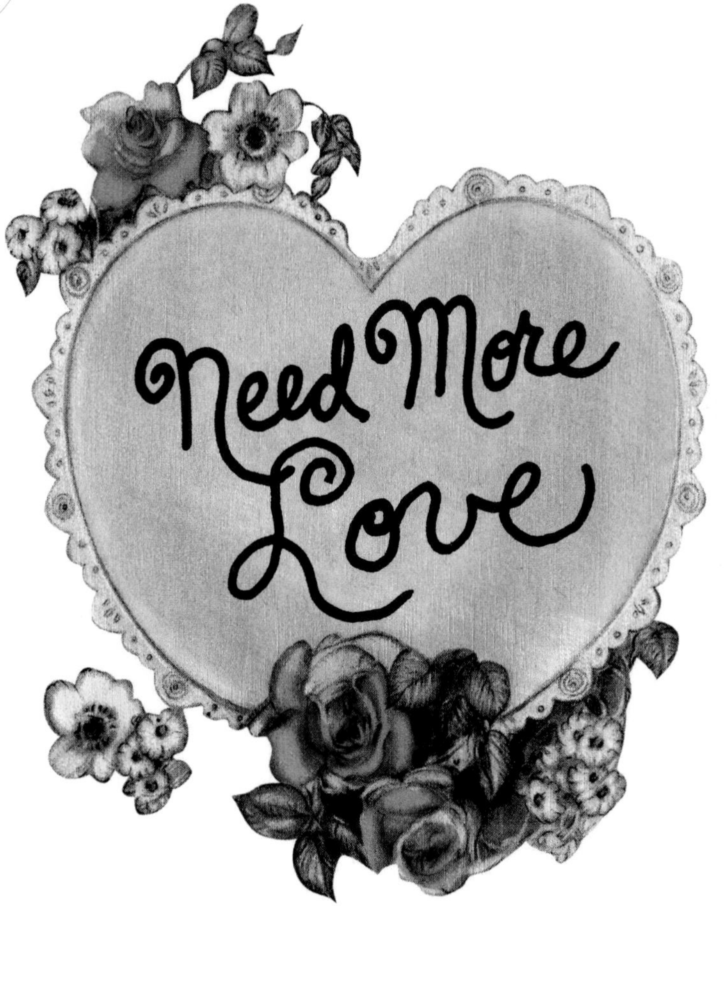
Need More
Love

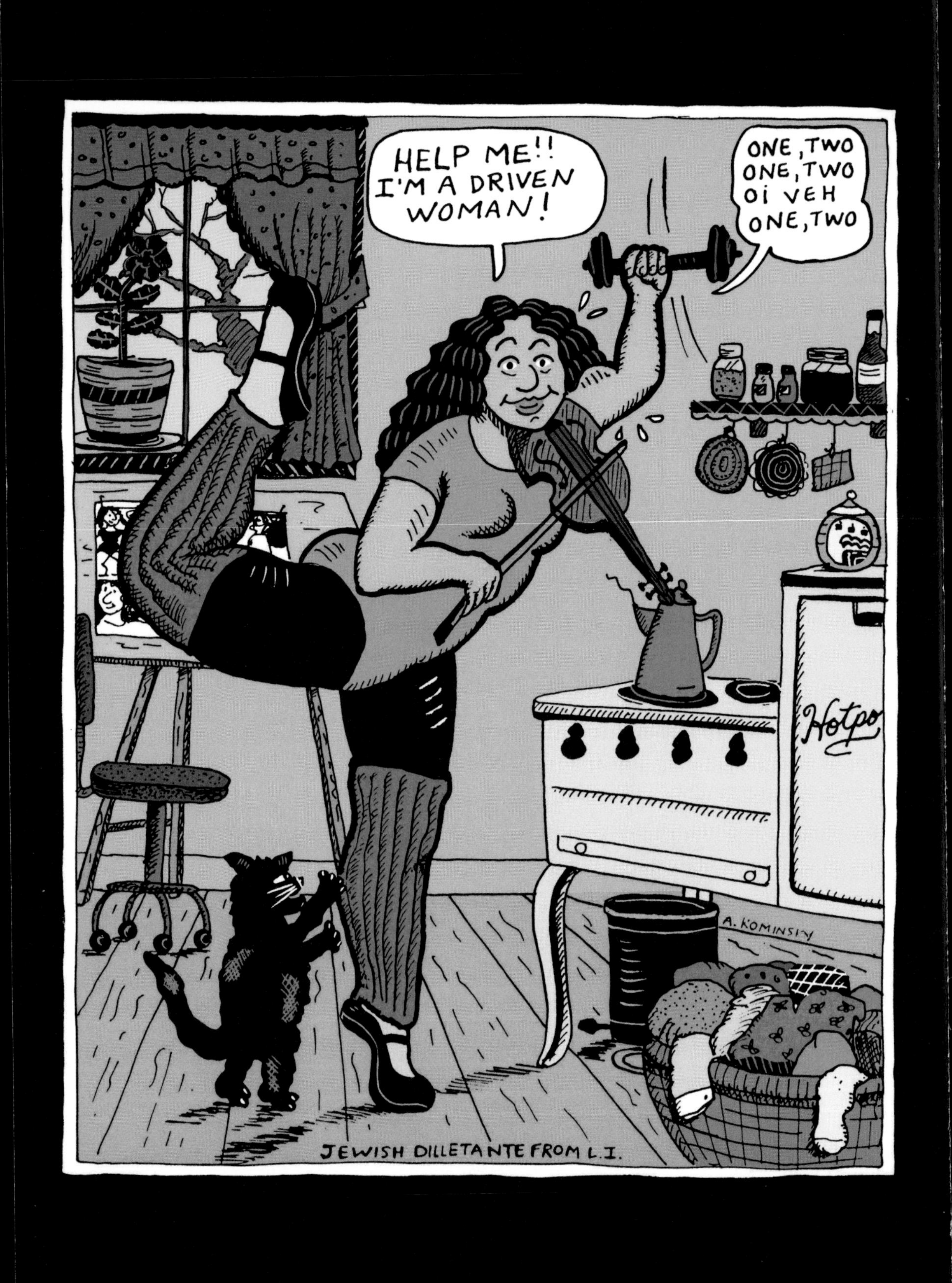
HELP ME!! I'M A DRIVEN WOMAN!
ONE, TWO ONE, TWO Oi VEH ONE, TWO
Hotpo
A. KOMINSKY
JEWISH DILLETANTE FROM L.I.

Aline Kominsky Crumb

MQP

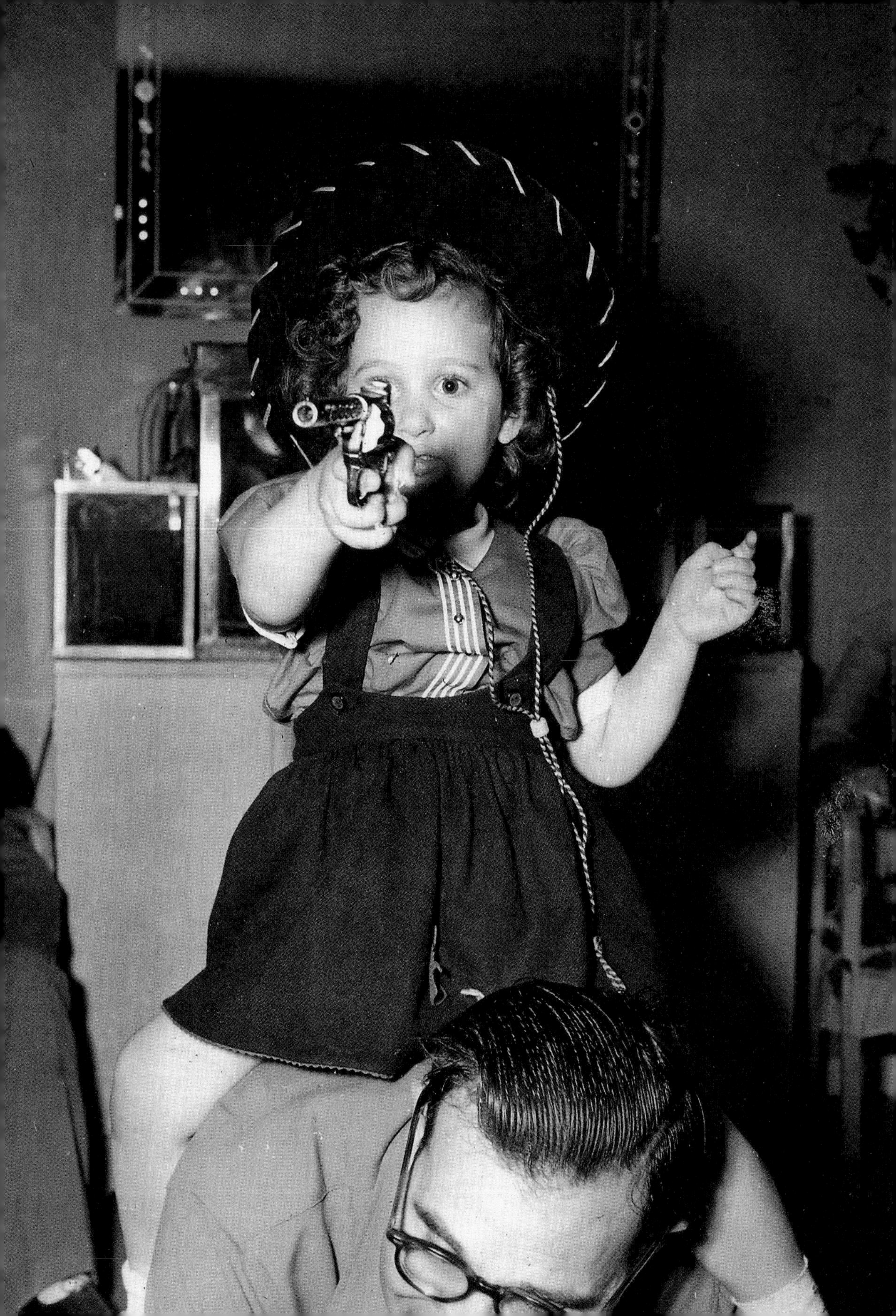

Need More Love

contents

Introduction

People ask "Why the title *Need More Love*?" Well, obviously that is what I find lacking in human relationships and society in general. Look at the nightmarish world we live in … don't we need more compassion and empathy? Yes, it's true, I admit it, I'm one of those ageing baby-boomer love children who dream of a kinder, gentler, more peaceful world … but more specifically, when you read my story, it will become clear to you that I didn't get enough tender loving care myself (boo-hoo!) as a little kid.

I've spent my life making up for that and I've done a pretty good job. I have been the partner and muse to my famous husband (not an unsatisfying role.) I have been an artistic inspiration as well as a collaborator for many of Robert's best stories. We have raised Sophie, a powerful Amazon, whom I often refer to as my Zen Mistress … And we have helped each other FEEL more love!

I have so far had an adventurous and richly fulfilling life and, now that I'm in my fifties, I feel so full of love that I am bursting with the desire to share it with you!

My artistic career began when I was eight years old and I have never stopped working. I began painting, spent years drawing comics and now I do it all. Living with a more famous artist has perhaps affected the public's perception of me as a serious artist, but it hasn't touched my drive or inspiration to produce "Ahrt!" This book is my chance to flaunt my accomplishments in one intense volume that tells it all!

So get ready to laugh and cry and thrill your eyeballs … and most of all to share some LOVE!

Aline Kominsky Crumb

ALINE
RELAXING
AT
HOME

CHAPTER ONE
Post-War Jerks

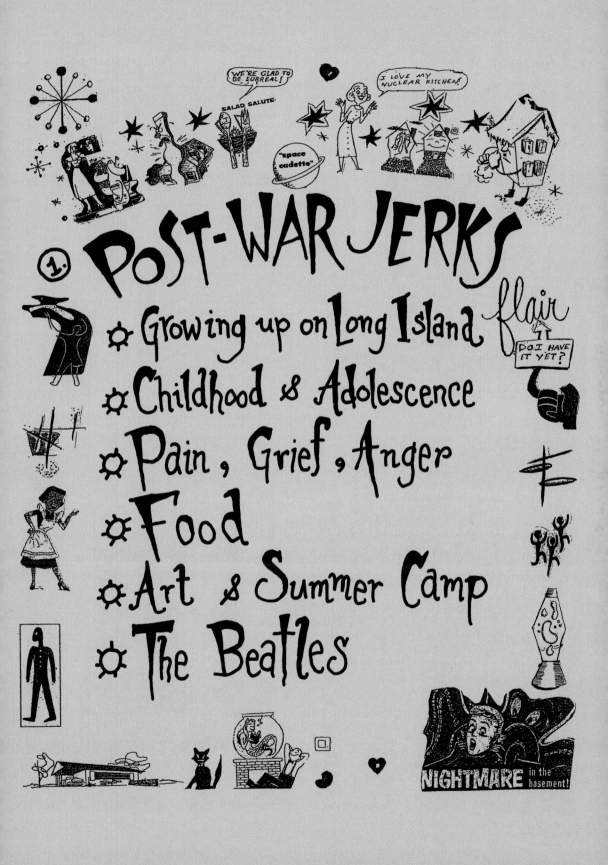

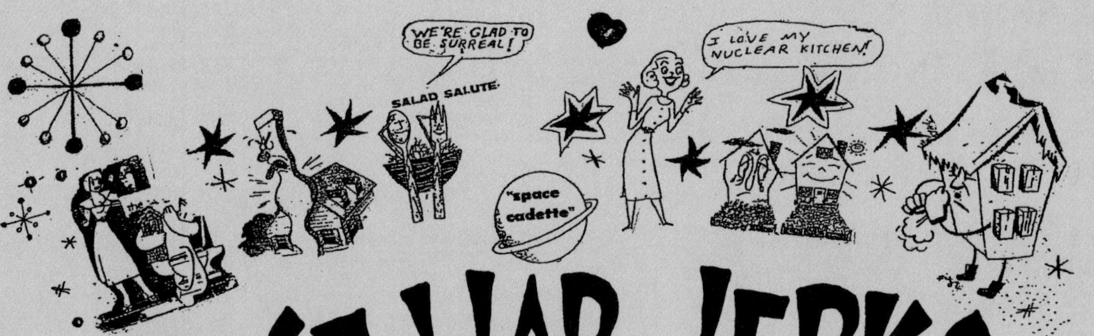
WE'RE GLAD TO BE SURREAL!
SALAD SALUTE
"space cadette"
I LOVE MY NUCLEAR KITCHEN!

1. POST-WAR JERKS

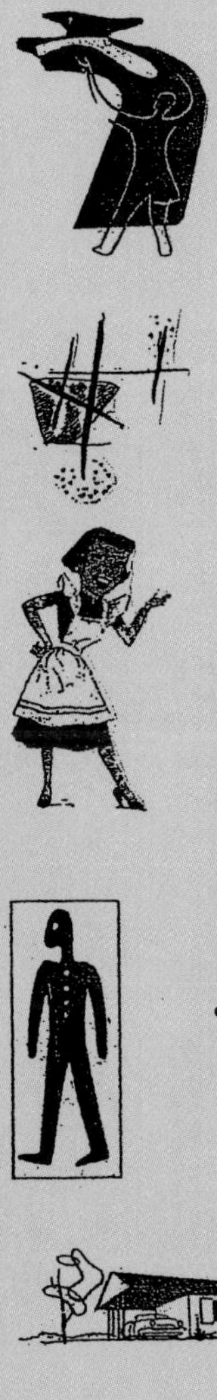

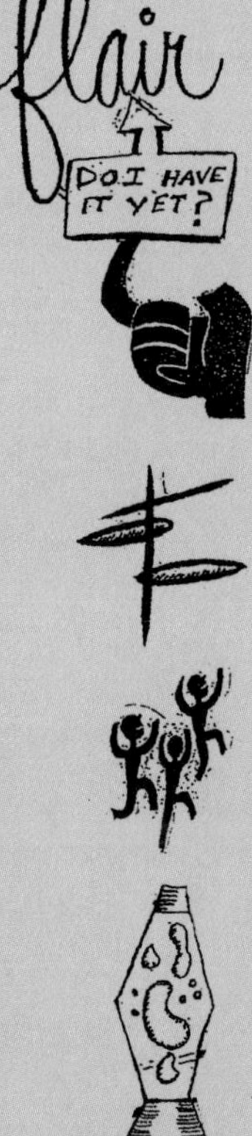
flair
DO I HAVE IT YET?

- Growing up on Long Island
- Childhood & Adolescence
- Pain, Grief, Anger
- Food
- Art & Summer Camp
- The Beatles

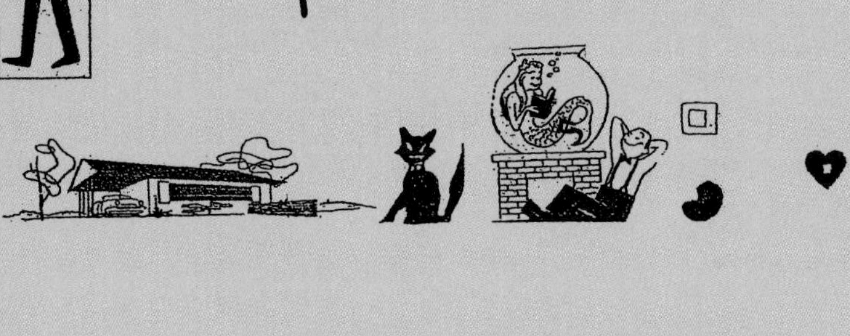

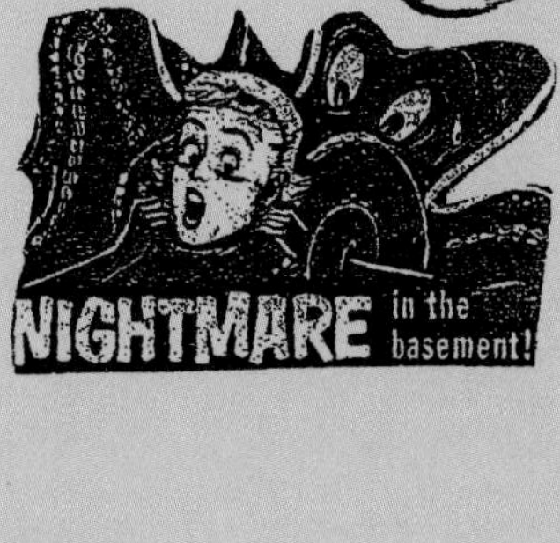
NIGHTMARE in the basement!

Growing up on Long Island

I was born in Long Beach, Long Island, New York, in August 1948. My mother, Annette, went into labor on my grandfather Joe's yacht so they had to go to a hospital that had a dock on the water. Long Beach was also where my grandfather and my father had their double-loser Sinclair gas station and Studebaker-Nash car dealership (both companies went bankrupt.)

Long Beach was the home of several big mob families. Remember *The Godfather* and *Goodfellas*? I'm sure my father would have loved to have been a cool gangster, but he was too much of a loser to succeed even as a criminal. He died when I was 19 so I never had a chance to talk to him. My mother erased him from our existence by selling our house and getting rid of all our possessions, and she never talked about him again. Forty years later, it's still uncomfortable to mention him in her presence.

In my comics I've reconstructed my impressions and stories from a selective albeit drug-damaged memory bank … here are recurring themes of sleaziness, out of control materialism, upward striving, tension, financial problems, selfishness and misery … not an atypical post-war jerk family atmosphere!

America in the 1950s presented an image of prosperity, efficiency, cleanliness, wholesomeness and order, full of well-adjusted, clean-cut productive stress-free citizens. Thanks to modern conveniences, they enjoyed lots of leisure time for Bar-B-Ques with Mom and Dad, Sis and Bro, Spot the Dog, and a few like-minded friendly happy pals.

For my family, and as it turns out for many others, reality was filled with overwhelming pressure to succeed, stress-induced alcoholism, pill-popping, constant fighting and lots of verbal and sometimes even physical abuse—particularly toward us innocent kids. In fact, for most of my generation, growing up in the 1950s in the U.S., and perhaps more so on Long Island, was a horrible nightmare. The bizarre visual and cultural world of the 1950s added a surreal aura to the atmosphere. Objects and motifs from this period still attract and somehow terrify me!

Page 8: **Me on my uncle Dave's back, Far Rockaway, New York, 1951**
Right: My father Arnie, Paris 1946, sitting on an Army jeep in front of the Eiffel Tower
This was probably the high point of his short life.

Annette and Arnie—my parents—came from Belle Harbor and Brooklyn. Remember Woody Allen's *Radio Days*? The neighborhood looked like that. My mother's family was quite prosperous and owned a big, beautiful house that had been built in the 1920s. Her family was neurotic, continually yelling and overeating, but they still held on to old-fashioned family values. They kept a Kosher home, and were clannish, always surrounded by scores of relatives and hangers on for dinner. They suffocated us kids with clinging guilt-inducing love, but still a lot of love!

My father's family was a total mystery. I barely knew them when I was growing up. There were dark secrets hinting at drug use and suicide, which was highly unusual for a Jewish family during this period. The one story that my father would tell over and over was how much he had loved Paris during the war. He had been a photographer for the American Army newspaper the *Stars and Stripes*.

Dad had planned to stay in Paris after the war to study photography at the Sorbonne—it's easy to see from the wartime photos of Arnie at this time that this was the high point of his life. Sad to say, but the handsome devil in these shots turned into a miserable schlub. When his GI buddies returned home and he stayed on, his mother was so furious she sent him a telegram saying that she was deathly ill and that he better return immediately.

Arnie met Annette, who became pregnant with me almost immediately. Et voilà! The end of Arnie's dream, the beginning of his voyage to hell.

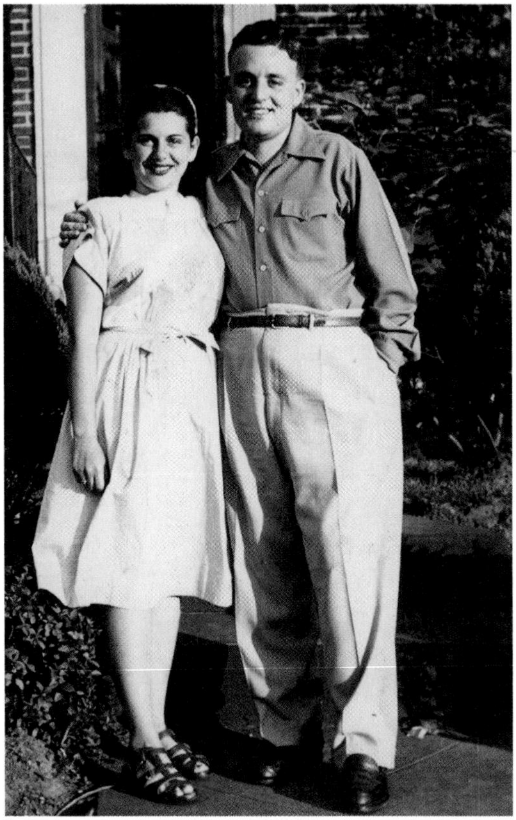

Above: **Hyde Park, New York, 1947**
My parents are just engaged.

Below: **Painting, set in Belle Harbor, New York, 1947**
Granma Fanny enticing her son-in-law with a plate of goodies.

Right: **Painting, set in Belle Harbor, New York, 1947**
"The Proposal."

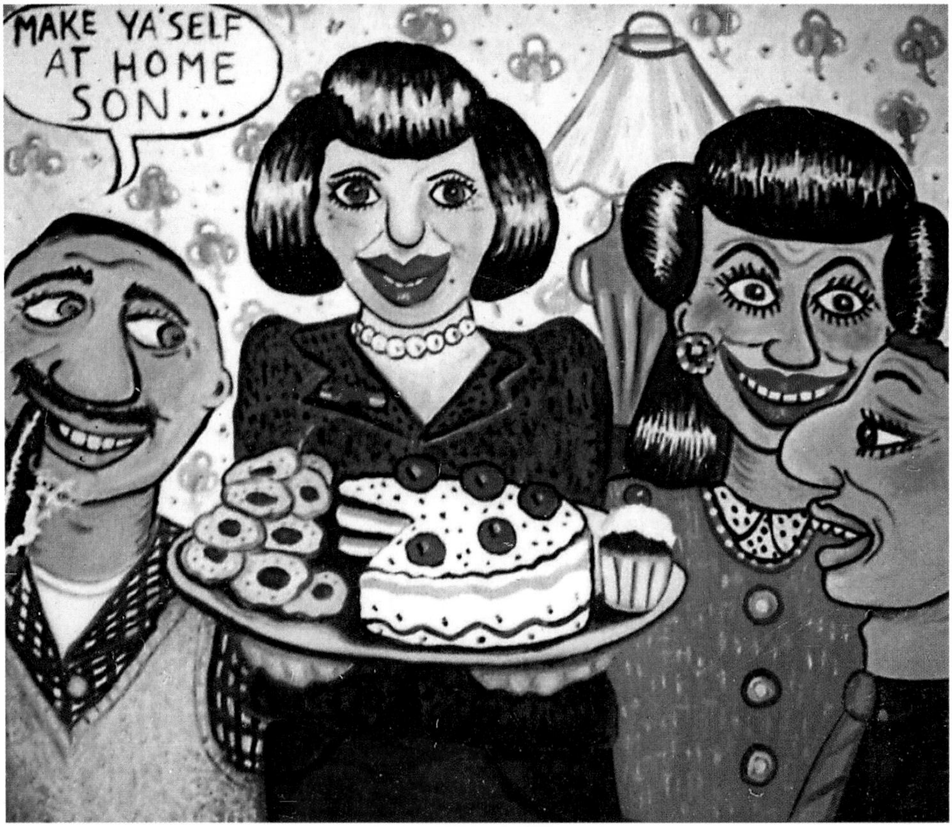
MAKE YA'SELF AT HOME SON...

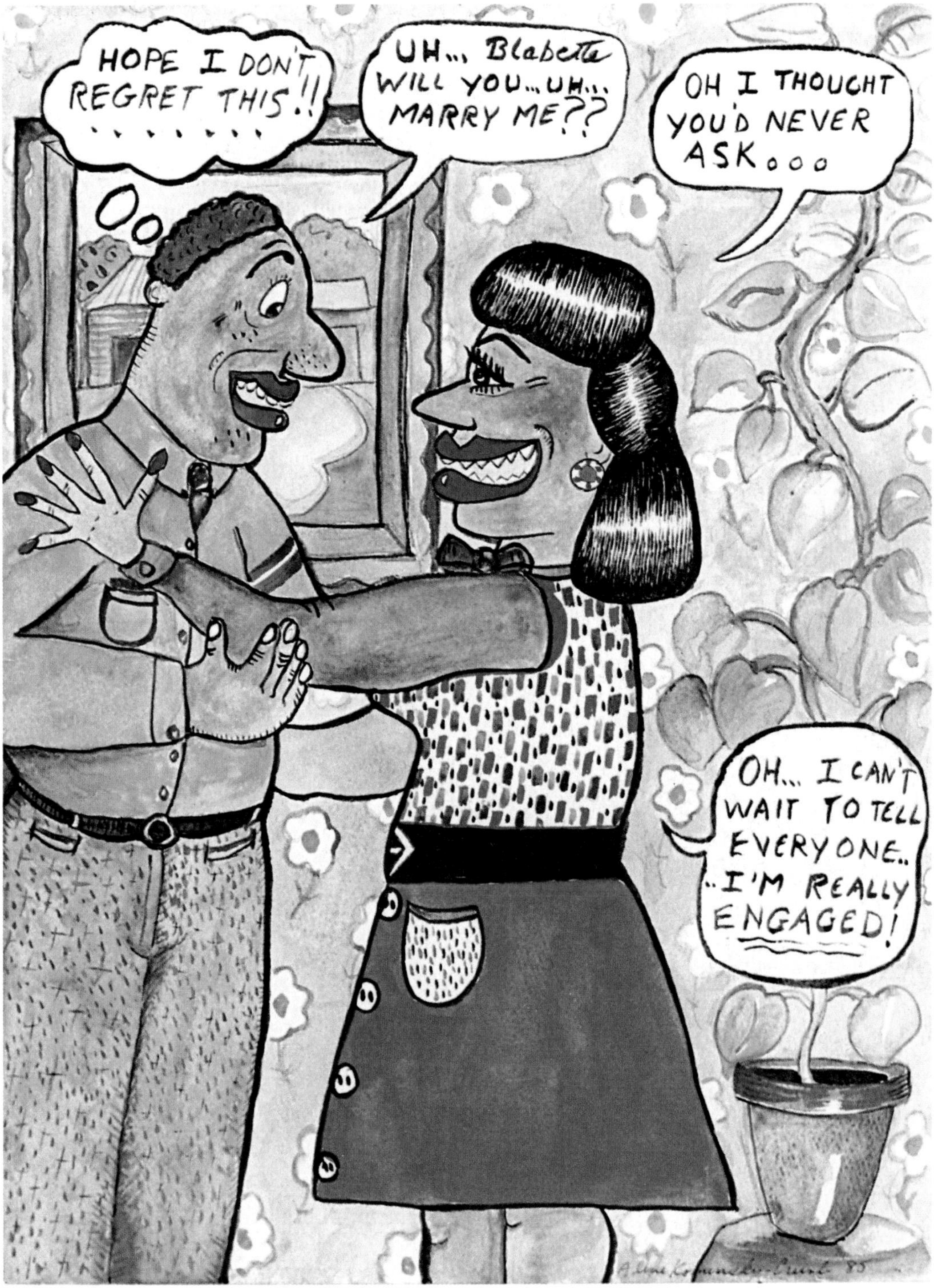
HOPE I DON'T REGRET THIS!! ....
UH... Blabette WILL YOU...UH... MARRY ME??
OH I THOUGHT YOU'D NEVER ASK...
OH... I CAN'T WAIT TO TELL EVERYONE.. ..I'M REALLY ENGAGED!

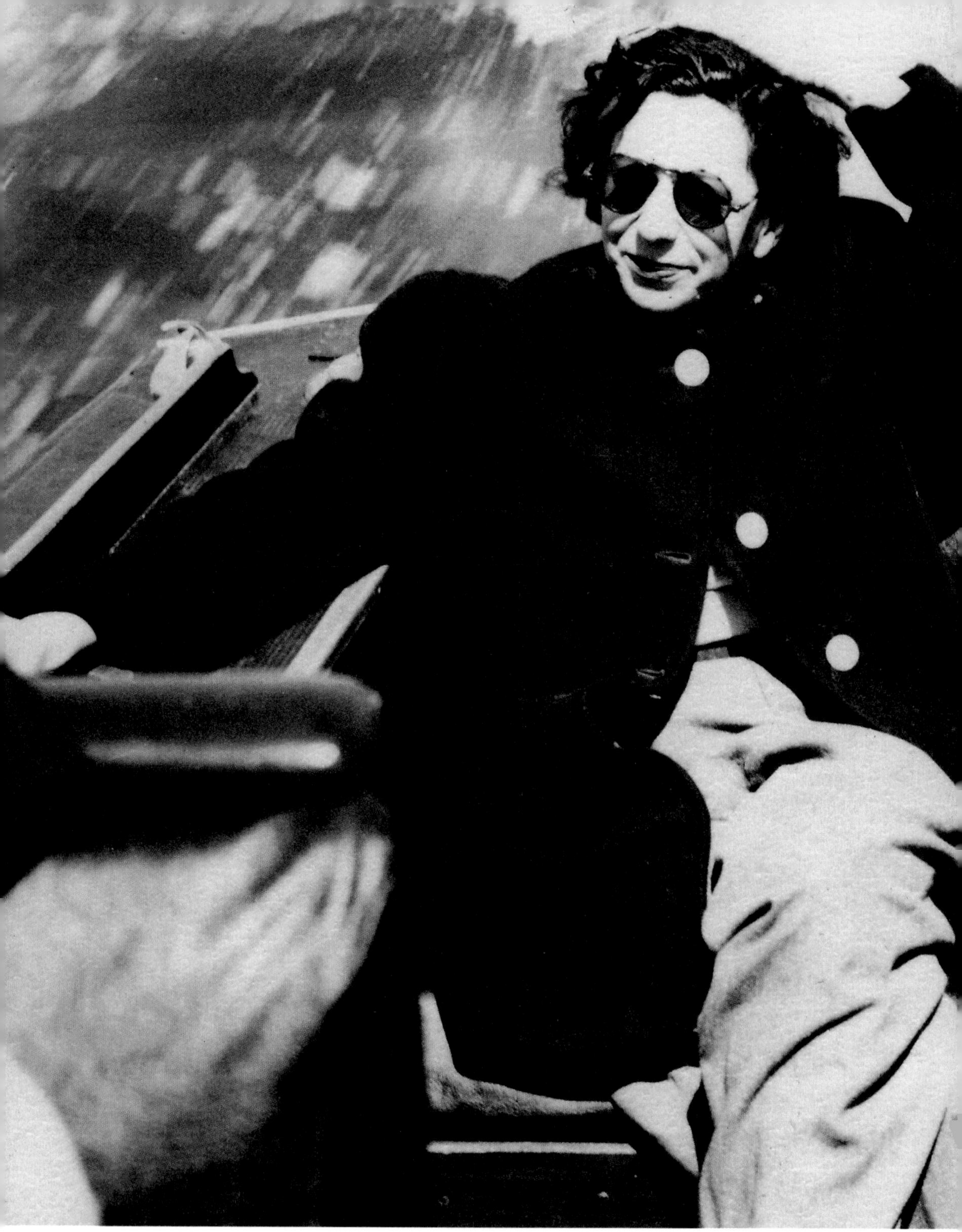

Above: **The "Gawgeous Grannies" on my grandfather Joe's yacht *The Wishmaker,* 1946**
It was on this boat that my mother went into labor with me one year later.

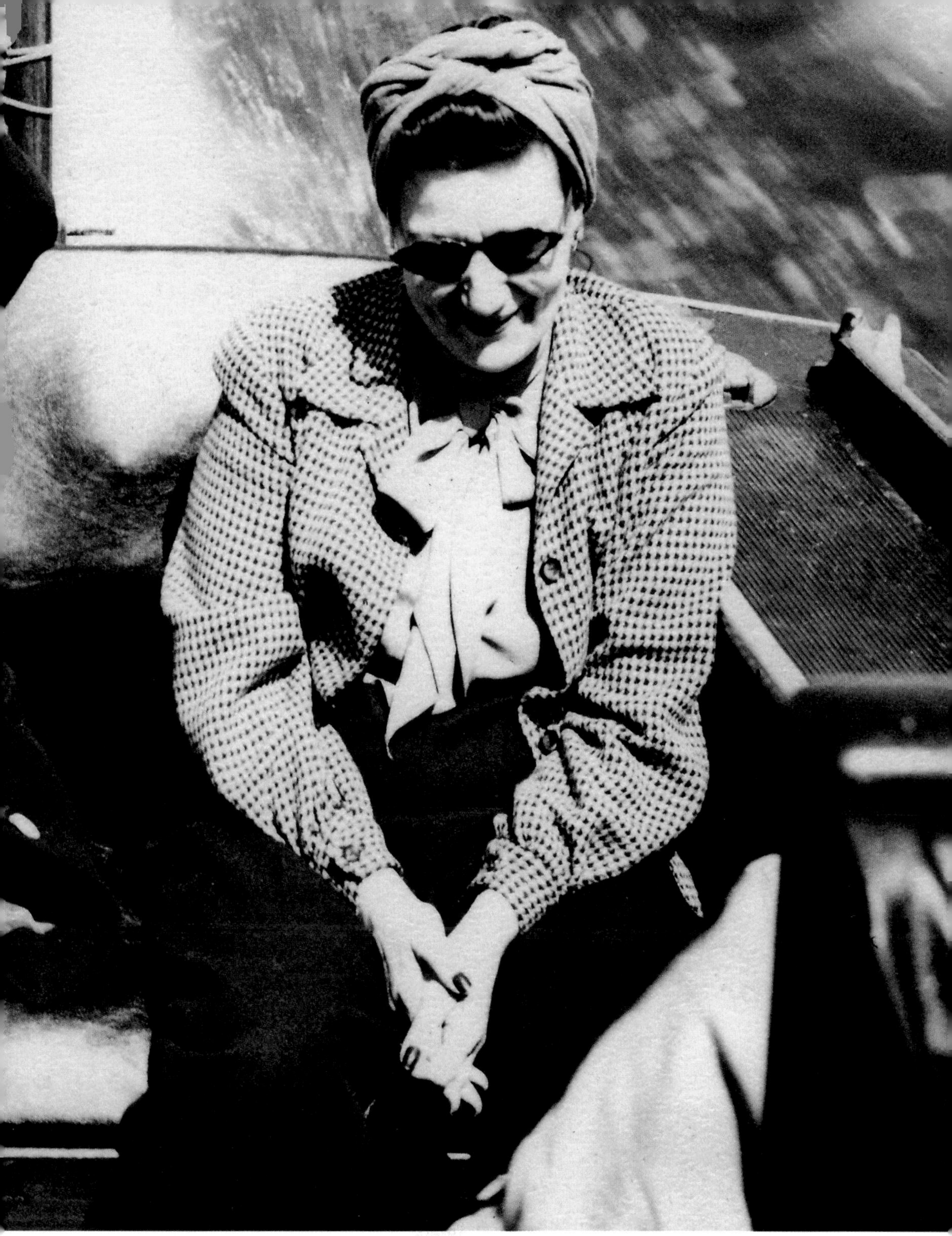

Next page: **My parents (left of the picture) on honeymoon, Miami, Florida, 1947.**
The fishing seems good but dad looks miserable. He's already starting to get chubby.

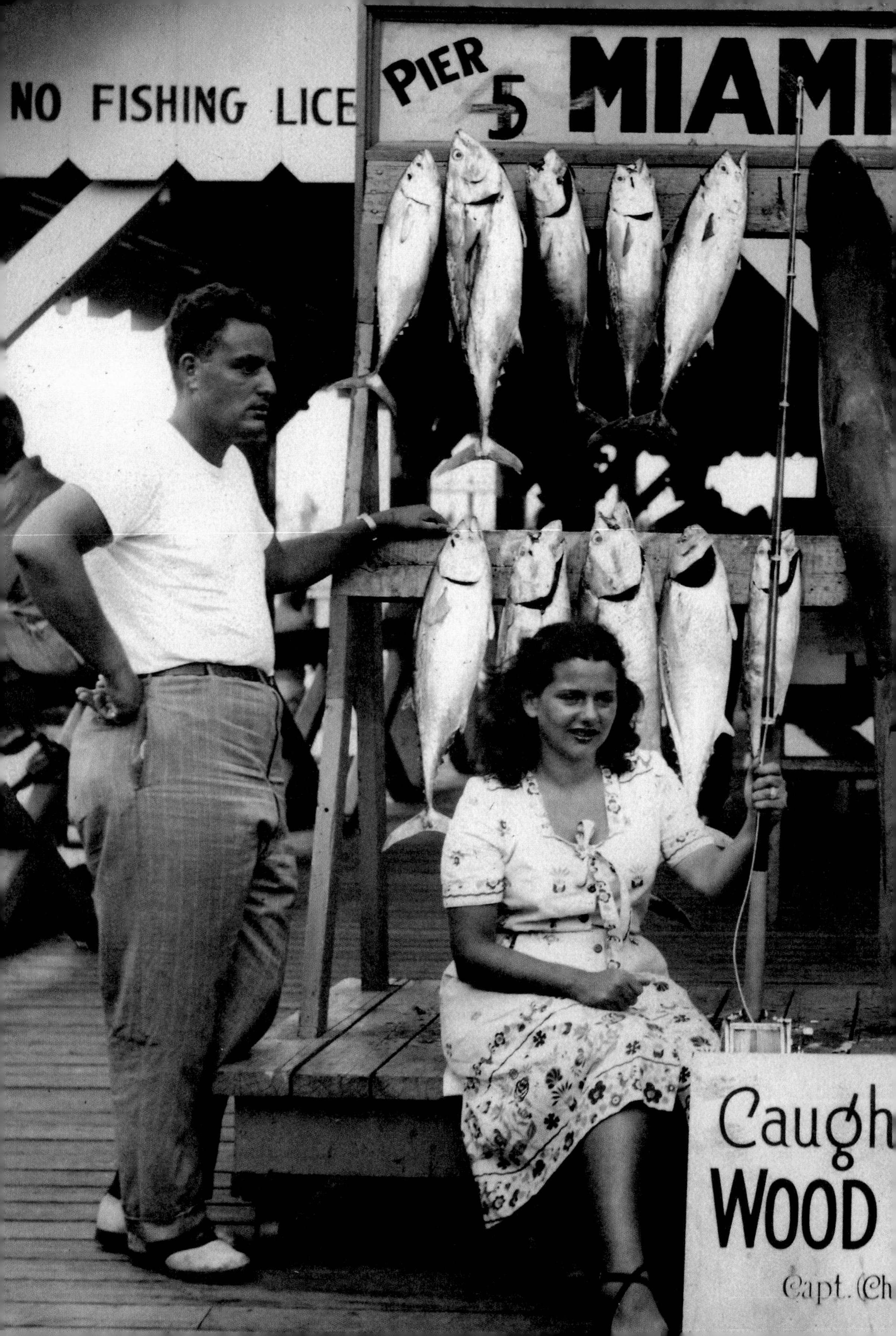
NO FISHING LICE
PIER 5
MIAMI
Caugh
WOOD
Capt. (Ch

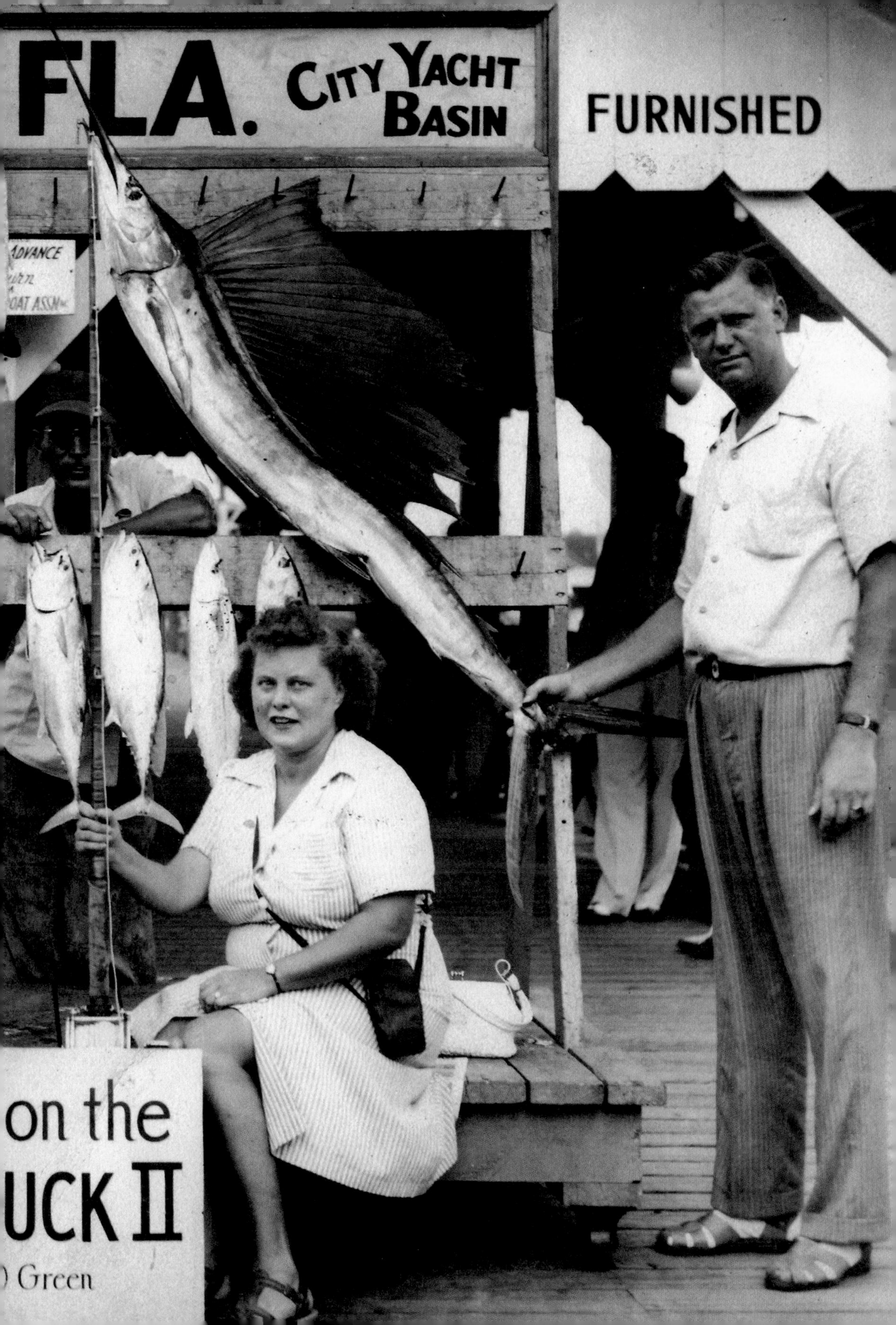
FLA.
CITY YACHT BASIN
FURNISHED
on the
UCK II
Green

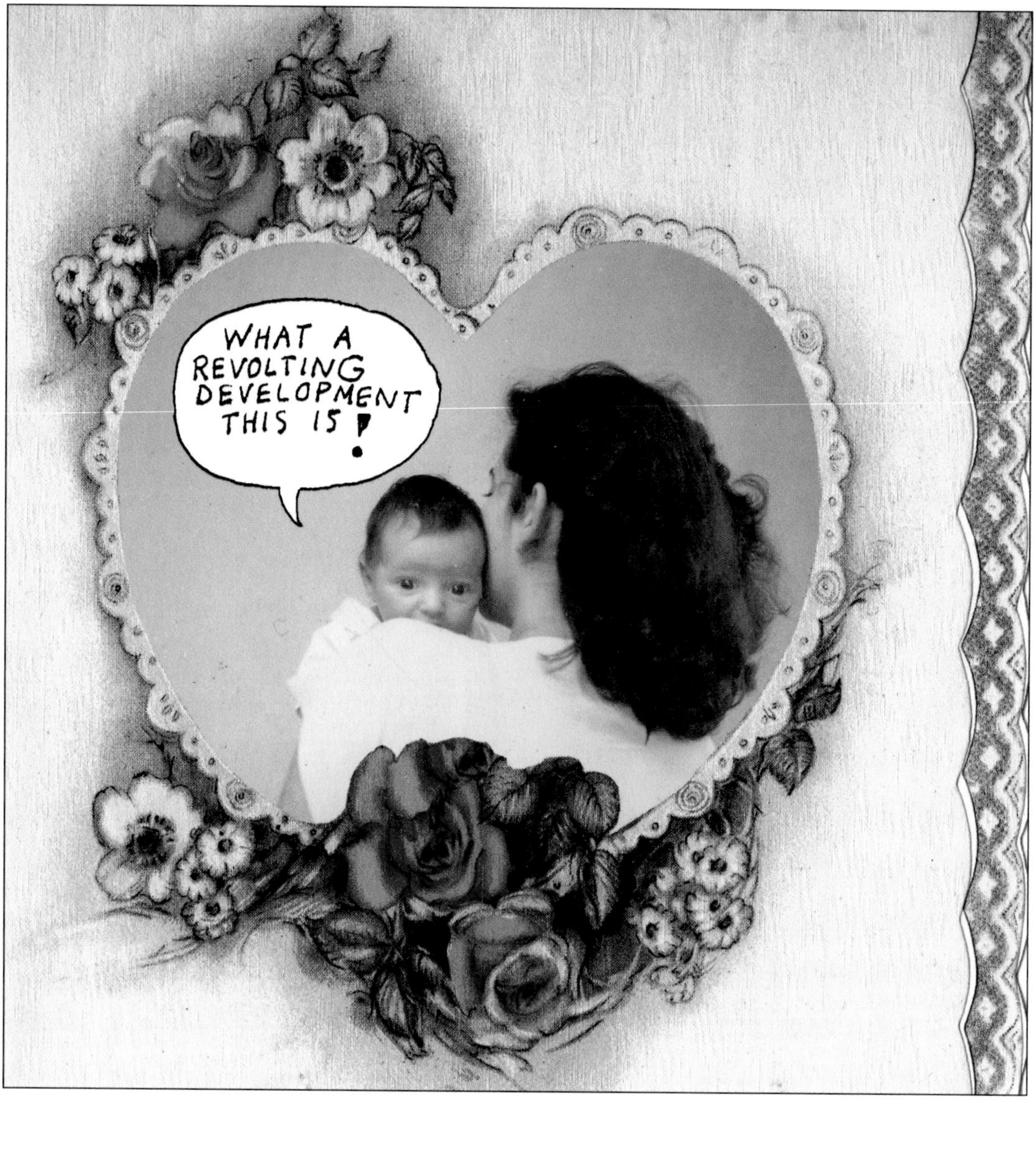
WHAT A REVOLTING DEVELOPMENT THIS IS!

Mr. and Mrs.

Arnold Goldsmith

announce the birth of a daughter

Aline Ricky

seven pounds, fifteen ounces

on Sunday August 1, 1948

Residence: 13-24 Caffrey Ave.
Far Rockaway, N. Y.

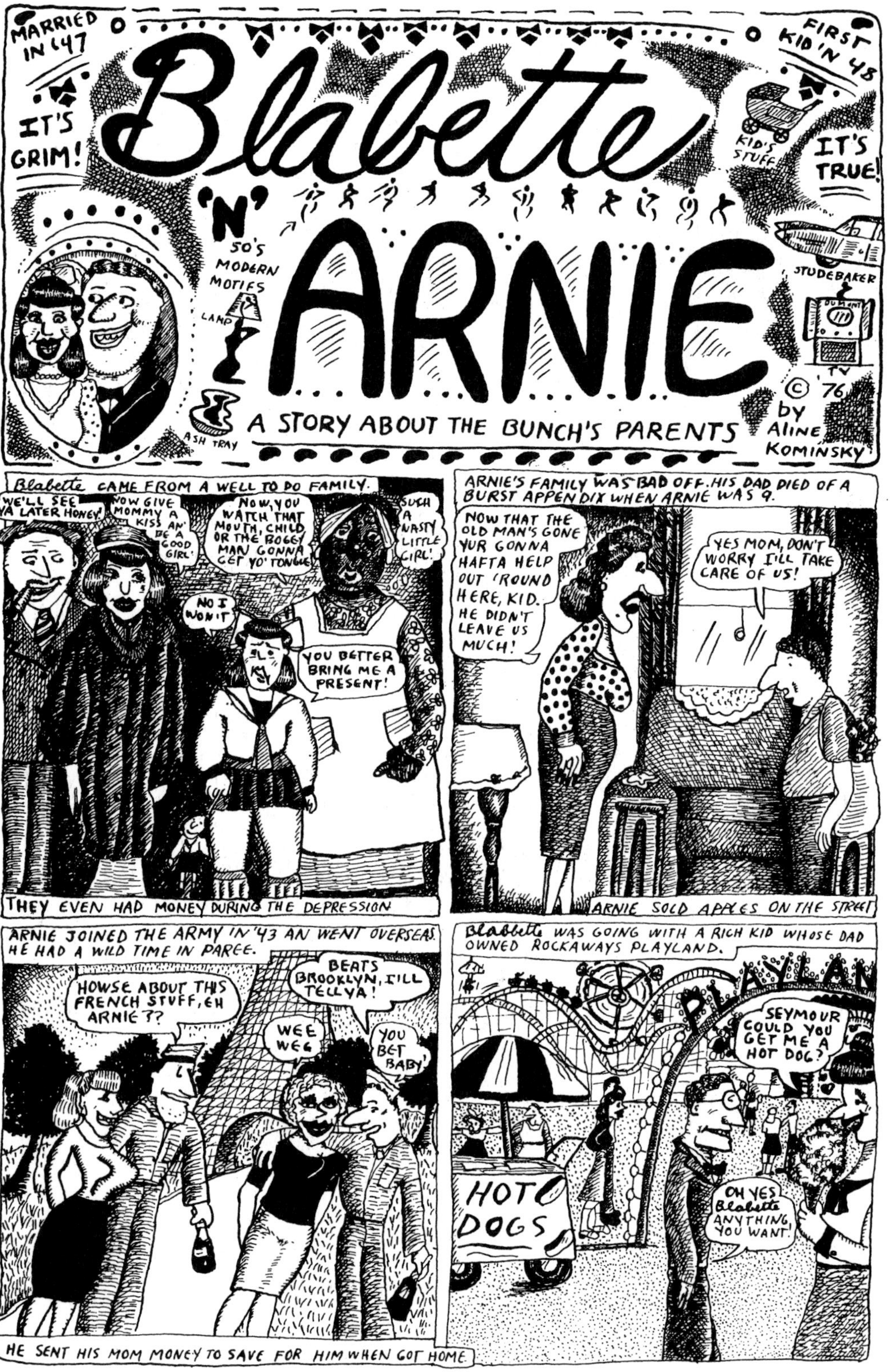
MARRIED IN '47
IT'S GRIM!
Blabette
'N'
ARNIE
50's MODERN MOTIFS
LAMP
ASH TRAY
A STORY ABOUT THE BUNCH'S PARENTS
FIRST KID 'N 48
KID'S STUFF
IT'S TRUE!
STUDEBAKER
DUMONT
TV
© '76 by Aline Kominsky
Blabette CAME FROM A WELL TO DO FAMILY.
WE'LL SEE YA LATER HONEY!
NOW GIVE MOMMY A KISS AN' BE A GOOD GIRL!
NOW, YOU WATCH THAT MOUTH, CHILD OR THE BOGGY MAN GONNA GET YO' TONGUE!
SUCH A NASTY LITTLE GIRL!
NO I WON'T!
YOU BETTER BRING ME A PRESENT!
THEY EVEN HAD MONEY DURING THE DEPRESSION
ARNIE'S FAMILY WAS BAD OFF. HIS DAD DIED OF A BURST APPENDIX WHEN ARNIE WAS 9.
NOW THAT THE OLD MAN'S GONE YUR GONNA HAFTA HELP OUT 'ROUND HERE, KID. HE DIDN'T LEAVE US MUCH!
YES MOM, DON'T WORRY I'LL TAKE CARE OF US!
ARNIE SOLD APPLES ON THE STREET
ARNIE JOINED THE ARMY IN '43 AN WENT OVERSEAS. HE HAD A WILD TIME IN PAREE.
HOWSE ABOUT THIS FRENCH STUFF, EH ARNIE??
BEATS BROOKLYN, I'LL TELLYA!
WEE WEE
YOU BET BABY!
HE SENT HIS MOM MONEY TO SAVE FOR HIM WHEN GOT HOME.
Blabette WAS GOING WITH A RICH KID WHOSE DAD OWNED ROCKAWAYS PLAYLAND.
PLAYLAN
SEYMOUR COULD YOU GET ME A HOT DOG?
HOT DOGS
OH YES Blabette ANYTHING YOU WANT!

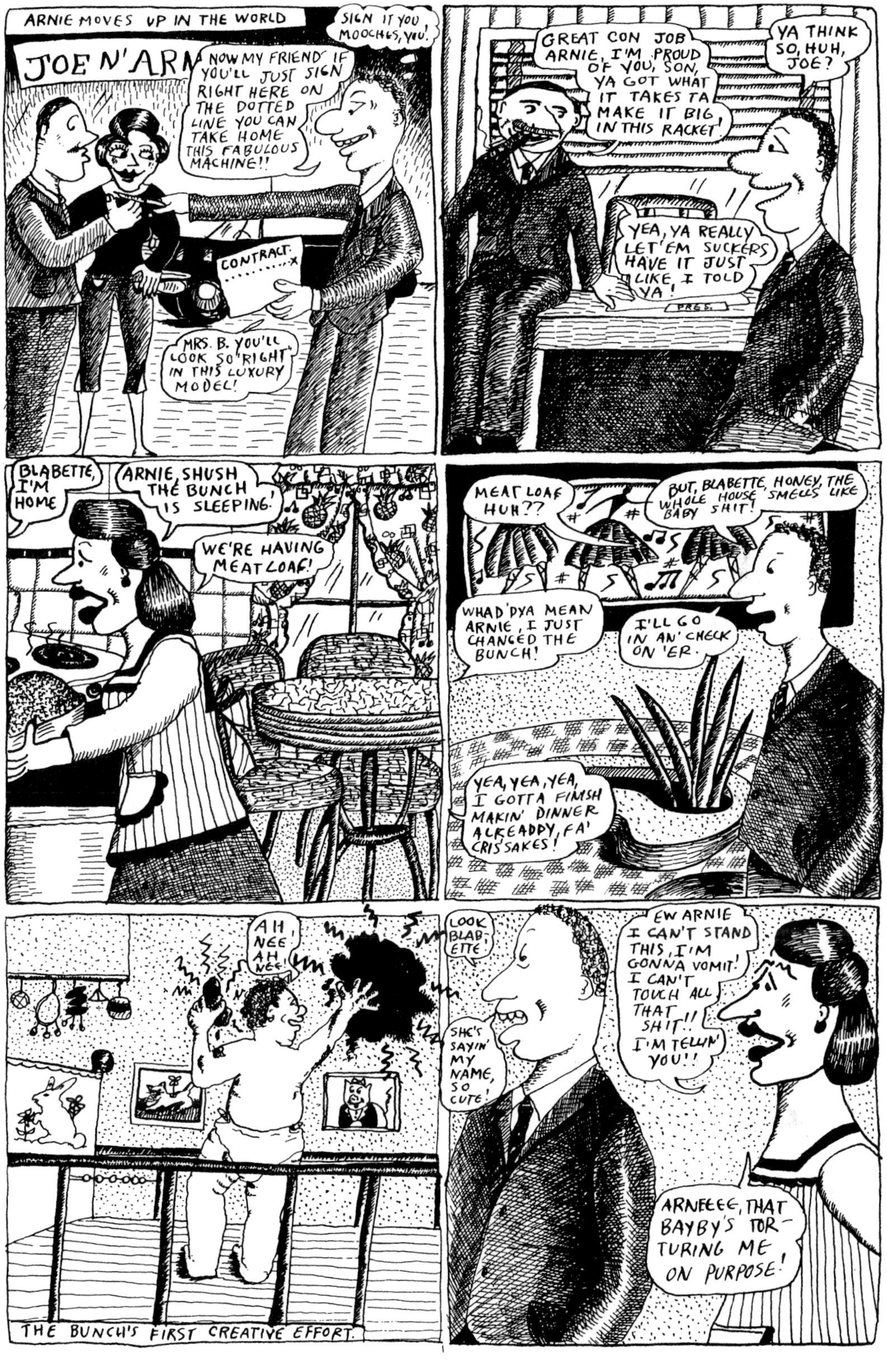
ARNIE MOVES UP IN THE WORLD
JOE N'ARN
SIGN IT YOU MOOCHES, YOU!
NOW MY FRIEND IF YOU'LL JUST SIGN RIGHT HERE ON THE DOTTED LINE YOU CAN TAKE HOME THIS FABULOUS MACHINE!!
CONTRACT
MRS. B. YOU'LL LOOK SO "RIGHT" IN THIS LUXURY MODEL!
GREAT CON JOB ARNIE, I'M PROUD OF YOU, SON, YA GOT WHAT IT TAKES TA MAKE IT BIG IN THIS RACKET!
YA THINK SO, HUH, JOE?
YEA, YA REALLY LET'EM SUCKERS HAVE IT JUST LIKE I TOLD YA!
PRES.
BLABETTE, I'M HOME
ARNIE, SHUSH THE BUNCH IS SLEEPING.
WE'RE HAVING MEAT LOAF!
MEAT LOAF HUH??
BUT, BLABETTE, HONEY, THE WHOLE HOUSE SMELLS LIKE BABY SHIT!
WHAD'DYA MEAN ARNIE, I JUST CHANGED THE BUNCH!
I'LL GO IN AN' CHECK ON 'ER.
YEA, YEA, YEA, I GOTTA FINISH MAKIN' DINNER ALREADDY, FA' CRIS'SAKES!
AH NEE AH NEE
LOOK BLAB-ETTE
SHE'S SAYIN' MY NAME, SO CUTE!
EW ARNIE I CAN'T STAND THIS, I'M GONNA VOMIT! I CAN'T TOUCH ALL THAT SHIT!! I'M TELLIN' YOU!!
ARNEEEE, THAT BAYBY'S TOR-TURING ME ON PURPOSE!
THE BUNCH'S FIRST CREATIVE EFFORT.

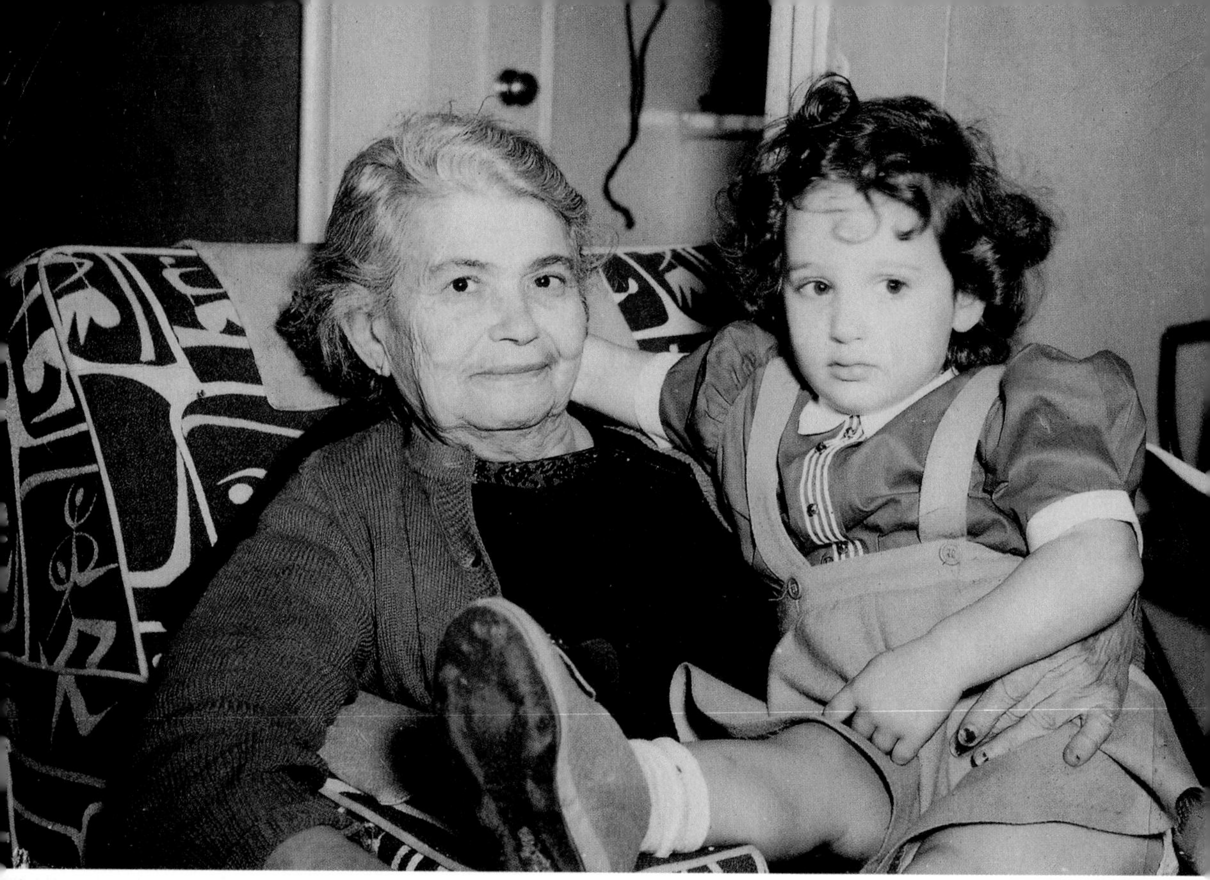

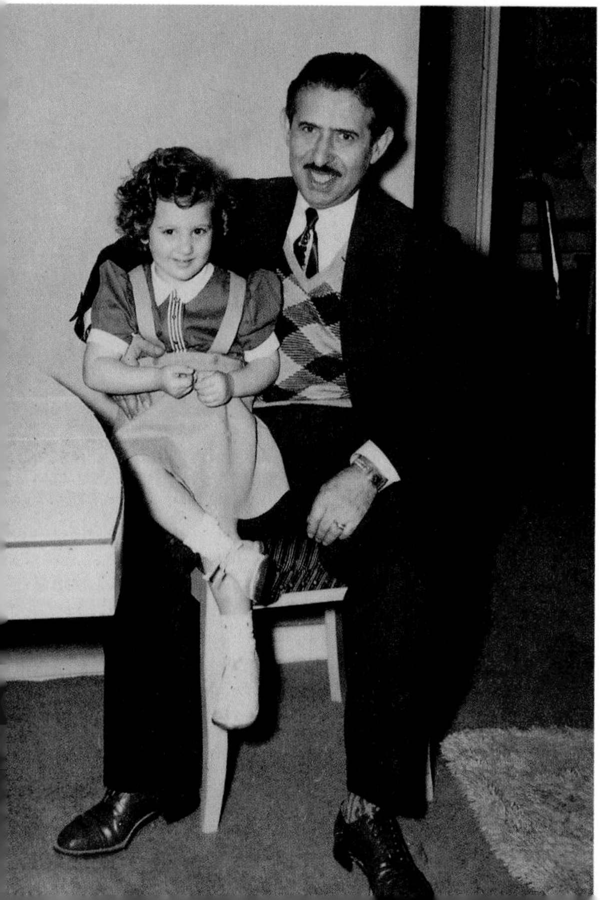

Above: **Far Rockaway, New York, 1951**
Me aged three, sitting on my great-grandmother Sophie's lap.

Left: **Far Rockaway, New York, 1951**
Same day, with me sitting on Granpa Joe's knee.

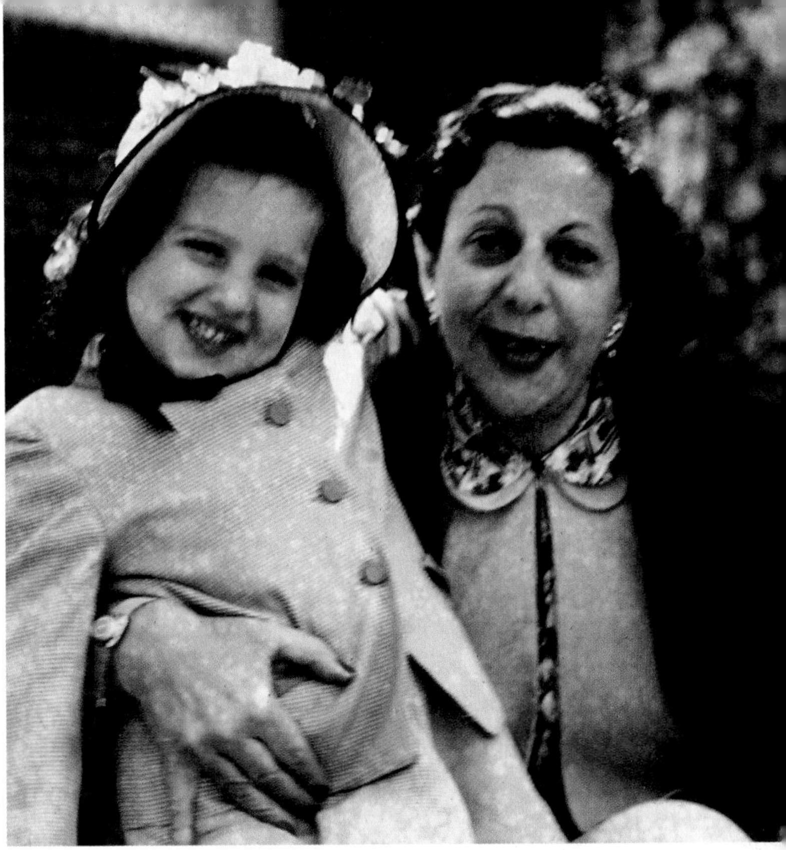

Right: **In Grandma Fanny's arms, 1951**
I'm wearing a straw bonnet for Passover
Below: **Far Rockaway, New York, 1951**
Sitting on my dad's lap. looking very much like Arnie's daughter.

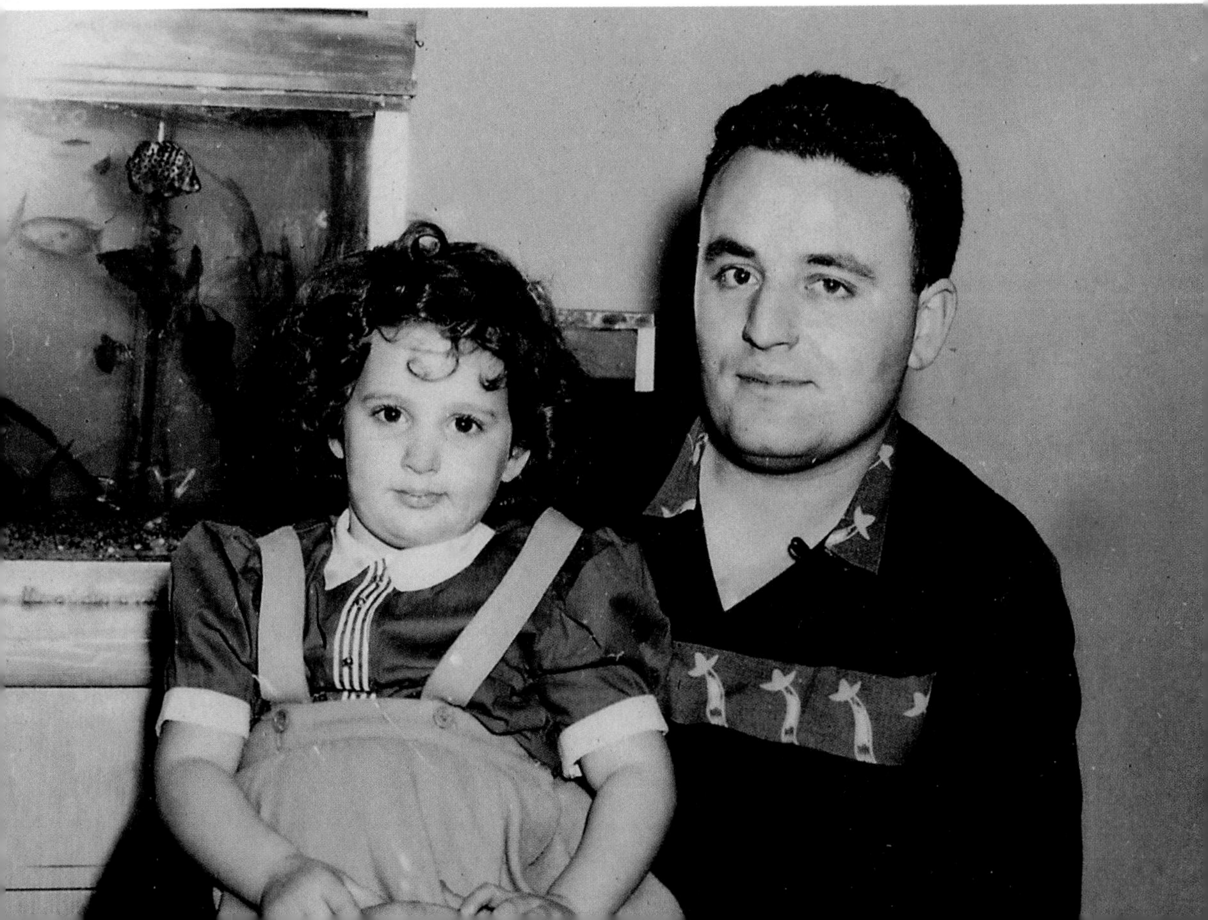

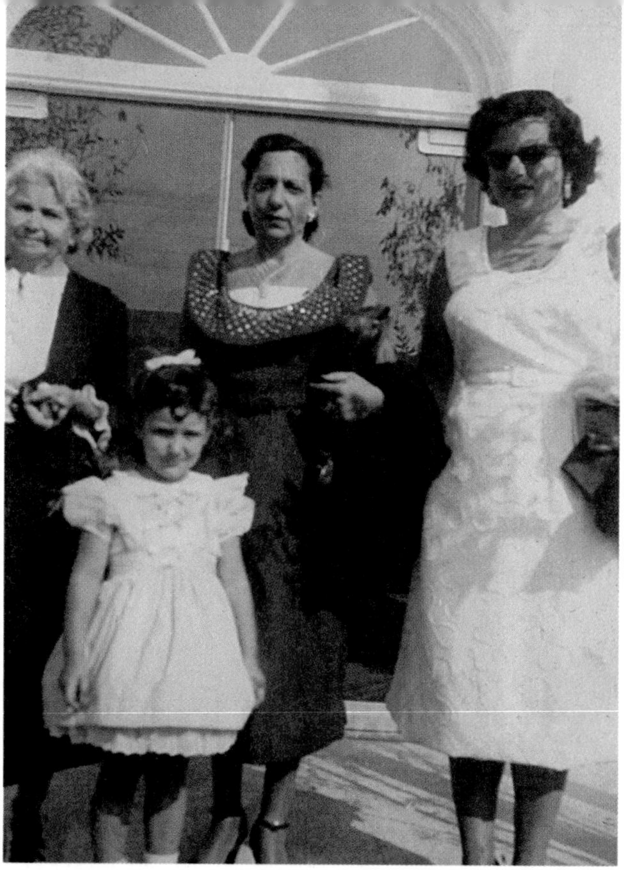

Left: **Far Rockaway, New York, 1952**
Four generations. I'm aged four.

Below: **Far Rockaway, New York, 1952**
At home posing with my aunt Ruthie, my blimpie mom, and Grandma Fanny in our very 1950s apartment.

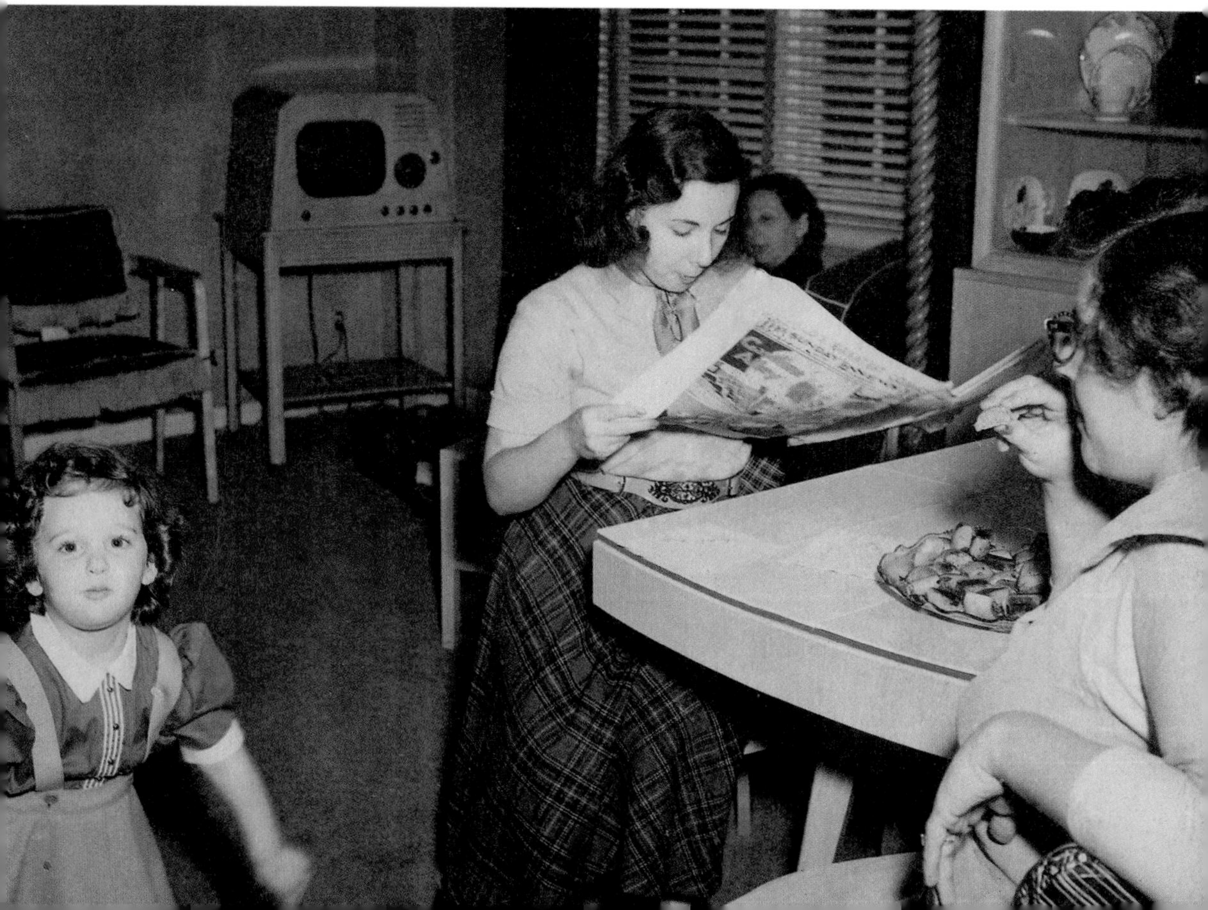

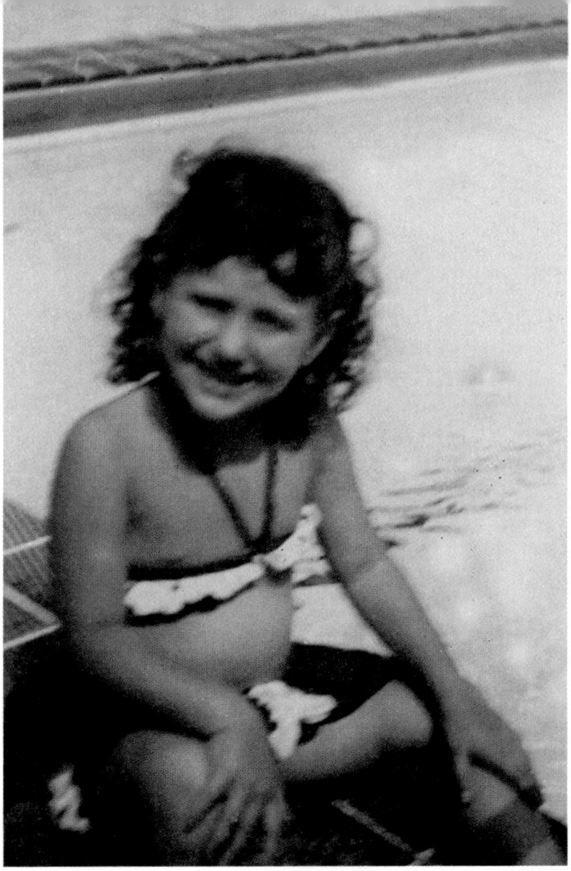

Right: **Miami Beach, 1952**
Me looking very "Hollywood" in my two-piece bathing suit.

Below: **Belle Harbor, New York, 1951**
Me with my mom and grandma at my grandparents' house.

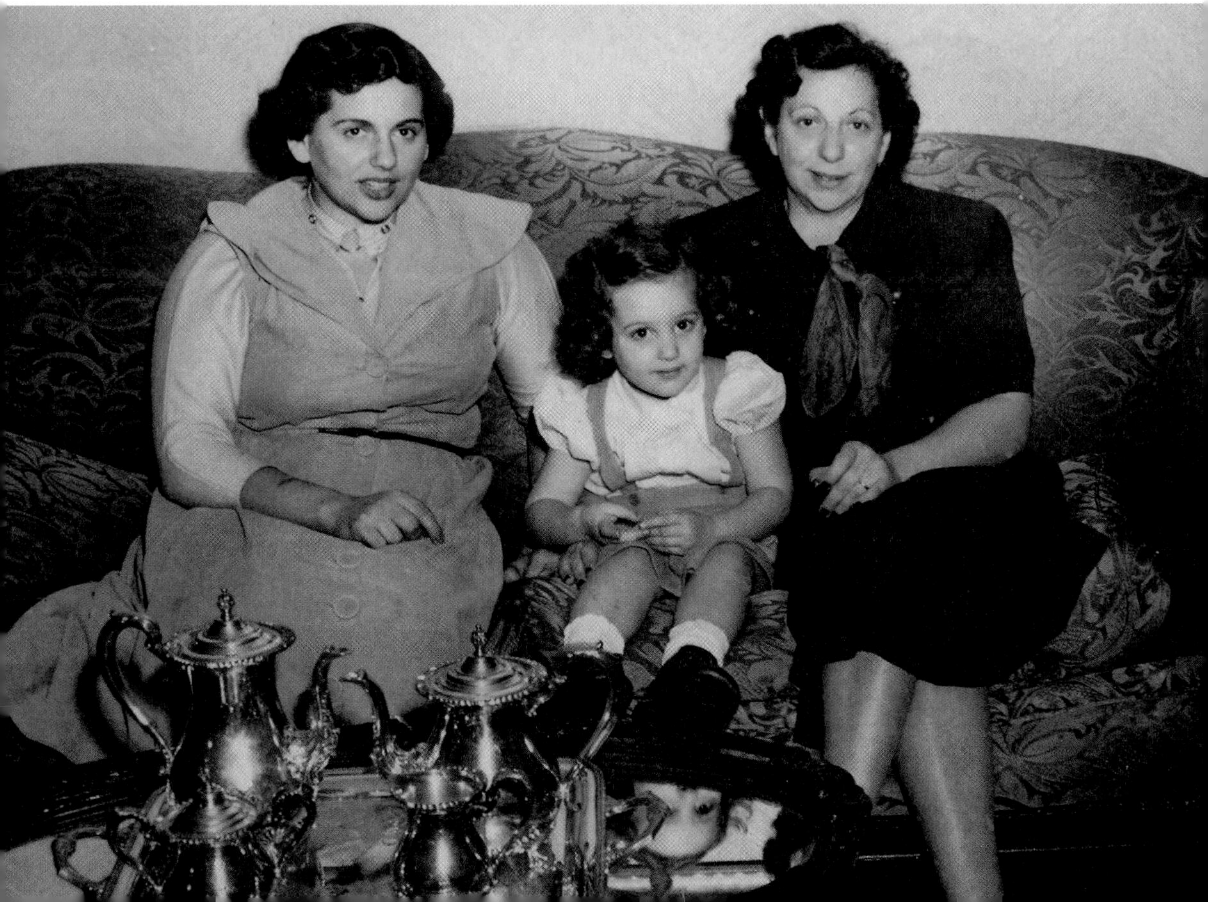

Getting socially mobile

I have happy memories of my early childhood. I spent most of my time at my grandparents' house with my relatives, especially my great-grandmother Sophie. I still love everything from the 1920s because I associate these things with this early childhood period of warmth, protection, and security.

My brother Alex, or Akkie as he was called as a kid, was born five years after me. Unfortunately for him, my parents decided to move to Woodmere, a town about forty minutes away from the family home, where they had bought a horrible, sterile, 1950s modern tract house, built on a defunct golf course.

To them, this represented a big move up in the world: away with the old-fashioned neighborhood and boring familiar stuff, and on to a cool, new suburban life! It was at this point that my parents' relationship started to deteriorate. The financial and social pressure to keep up was monstrous in

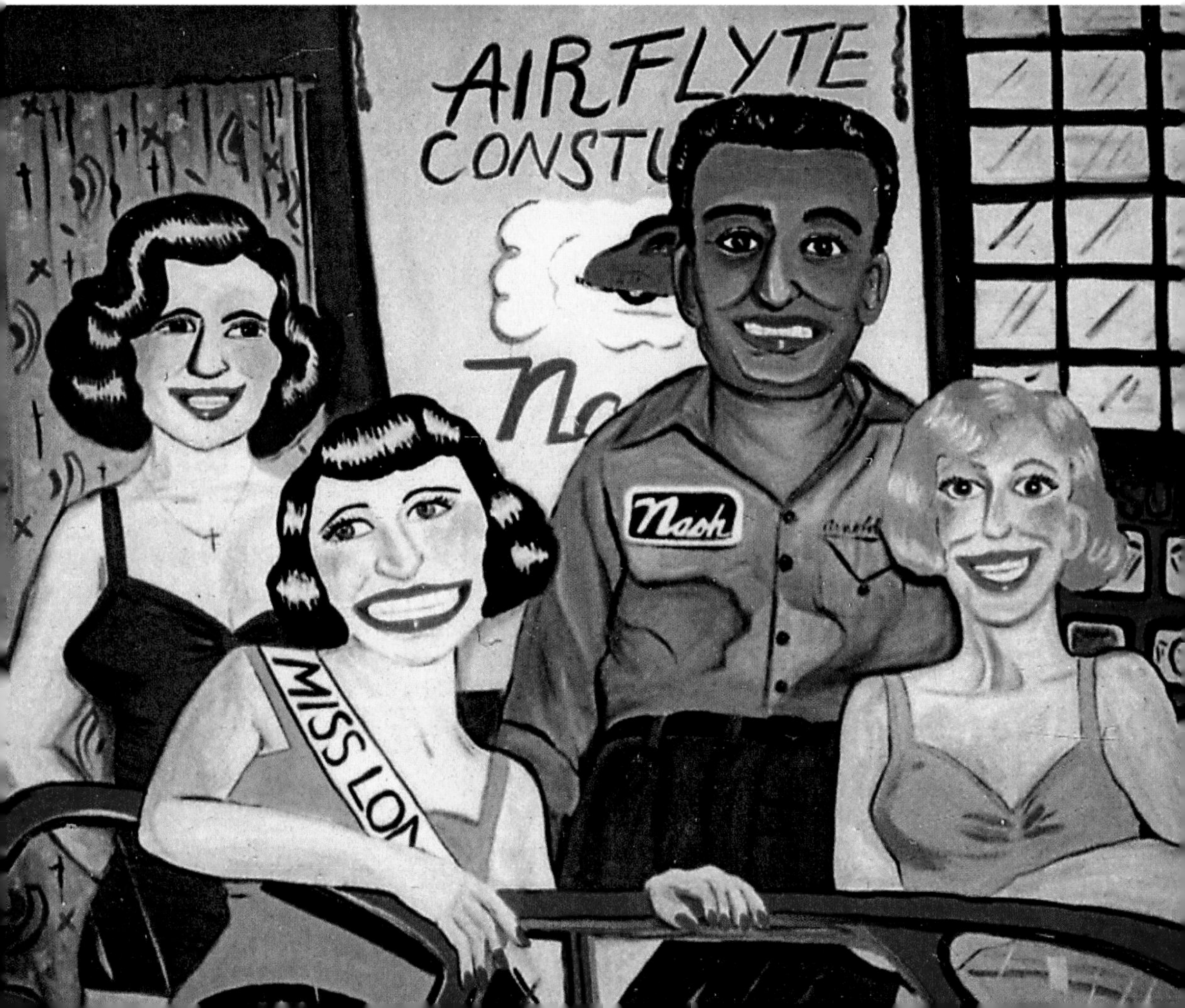
AIRFLYTE
CONST
Nash
MISS LO

the Five Towns. This neighborhood on the south shore of Long Island, comprising Inwood, Lawrence, Cedarhurst, Woodmere and Hewlett, was known for gangsters and "JAPs"—Jewish American princesses. Money was sacred, material prosperity was worshipped.

An education was seen merely as a way to make more money. The ultimate for Jewish boys was to go to medical school and become doctors, or gods as far as everyone was concerned. For us girls, a good education was the way to land a rich husband and secure a "better life," meaning a large, showy new house, a big brand new car, the right schools, summer camps and beach and country clubs, the absolute latest fashion ("It's what they're wearing deah dahling!"), and every beauty treatment available— including a nose job, fairly routine in this socioeconomic group.

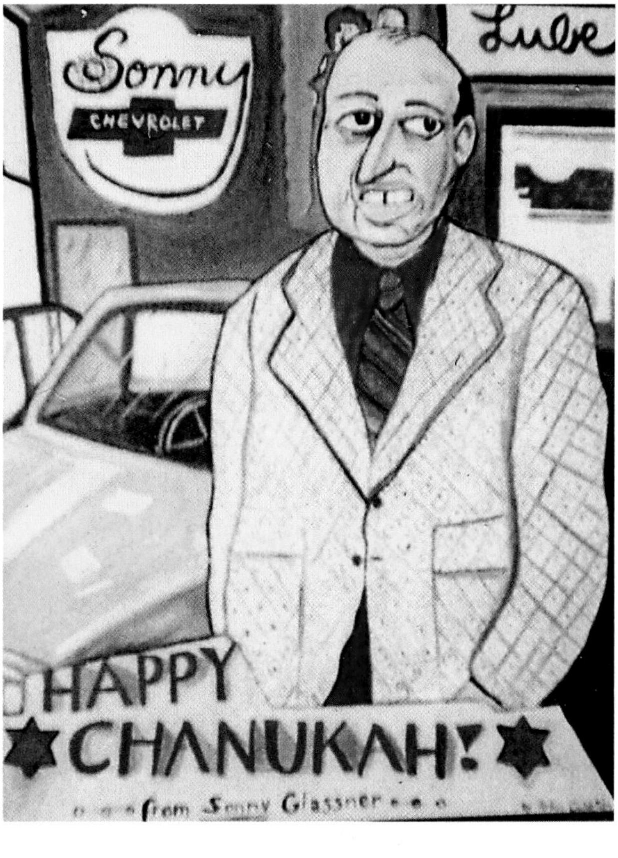
Sonny
CHEVROLET
Lube
HAPPY
CHANUKAH!
from Sonny Glassner

Left: **Painting based on my father's loser car dealership in Long Beach, New York**
He was so thrilled to pose with beauty contest winners. His life was soon to decline rapidly when his business went under.

Right: **Painting of Sonny the Car Dealer**
I copied this image from a sleazy ad I found in the Yellow Pages.

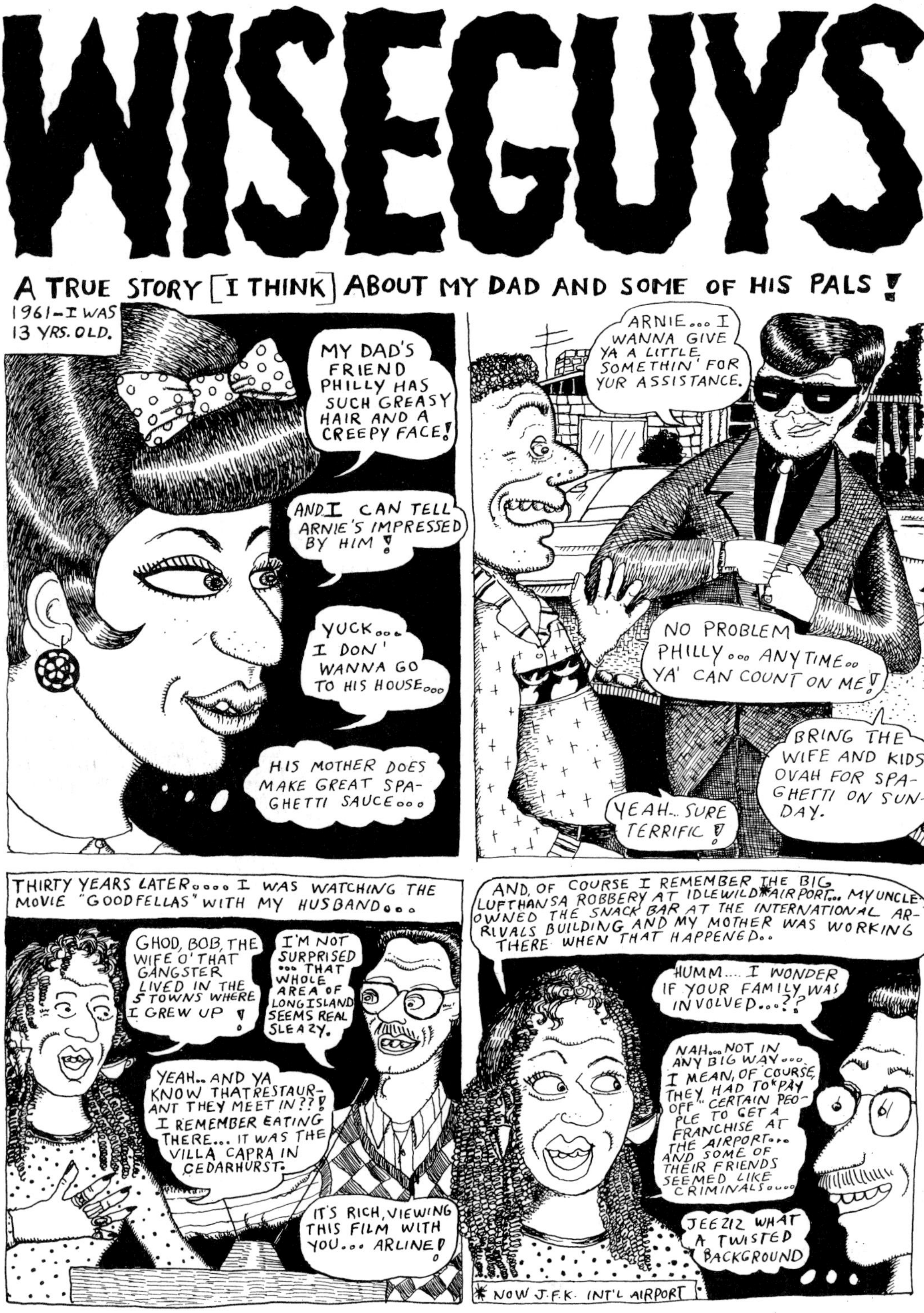
WISEGUYS
A TRUE STORY [I THINK] ABOUT MY DAD AND SOME OF HIS PALS!
1961 – I WAS 13 YRS. OLD.
MY DAD'S FRIEND PHILLY HAS SUCH GREASY HAIR AND A CREEPY FACE!
AND I CAN TELL ARNIE'S IMPRESSED BY HIM!
YUCK... I DON' WANNA GO TO HIS HOUSE...
HIS MOTHER DOES MAKE GREAT SPA-GHETTI SAUCE...
ARNIE... I WANNA GIVE YA A LITTLE SOMETHIN' FOR YUR ASSISTANCE.
NO PROBLEM PHILLY... ANYTIME.. YA' CAN COUNT ON ME!
BRING THE WIFE AND KIDS OVAH FOR SPA-GHETTI ON SUN-DAY.
YEAH.. SURE TERRIFIC!
THIRTY YEARS LATER.... I WAS WATCHING THE MOVIE "GOODFELLAS" WITH MY HUSBAND...
GHOD, BOB, THE WIFE O' THAT GANGSTER LIVED IN THE 5 TOWNS WHERE I GREW UP!
I'M NOT SURPRISED ... THAT WHOLE AREA OF LONG ISLAND SEEMS REAL SLEAZY.
YEAH.. AND YA KNOW THAT RESTAUR-ANT THEY MEET IN??! I REMEMBER EATING THERE... IT WAS THE VILLA CAPRA IN CEDARHURST.
IT'S RICH, VIEWING THIS FILM WITH YOU... ARLINE!
AND, OF COURSE I REMEMBER THE BIG LUFTHANSA ROBBERY AT IDLEWILD* AIRPORT.. MY UNCLE OWNED THE SNACK BAR AT THE INTERNATIONAL AR-RIVALS BUILDING AND MY MOTHER WAS WORKING THERE WHEN THAT HAPPENED..
HUMM.... I WONDER IF YOUR FAMILY WAS INVOLVED...??
NAH... NOT IN ANY BIG WAY... I MEAN, OF COURSE, THEY HAD TO "PAY OFF" CERTAIN PEO-PLE TO GET A FRANCHISE AT THE AIRPORT... AND SOME OF THEIR FRIENDS SEEMED LIKE CRIMINALS....
JEEZIZ WHAT A TWISTED BACKGROUND...
* NOW J.F.K. INT'L AIRPORT

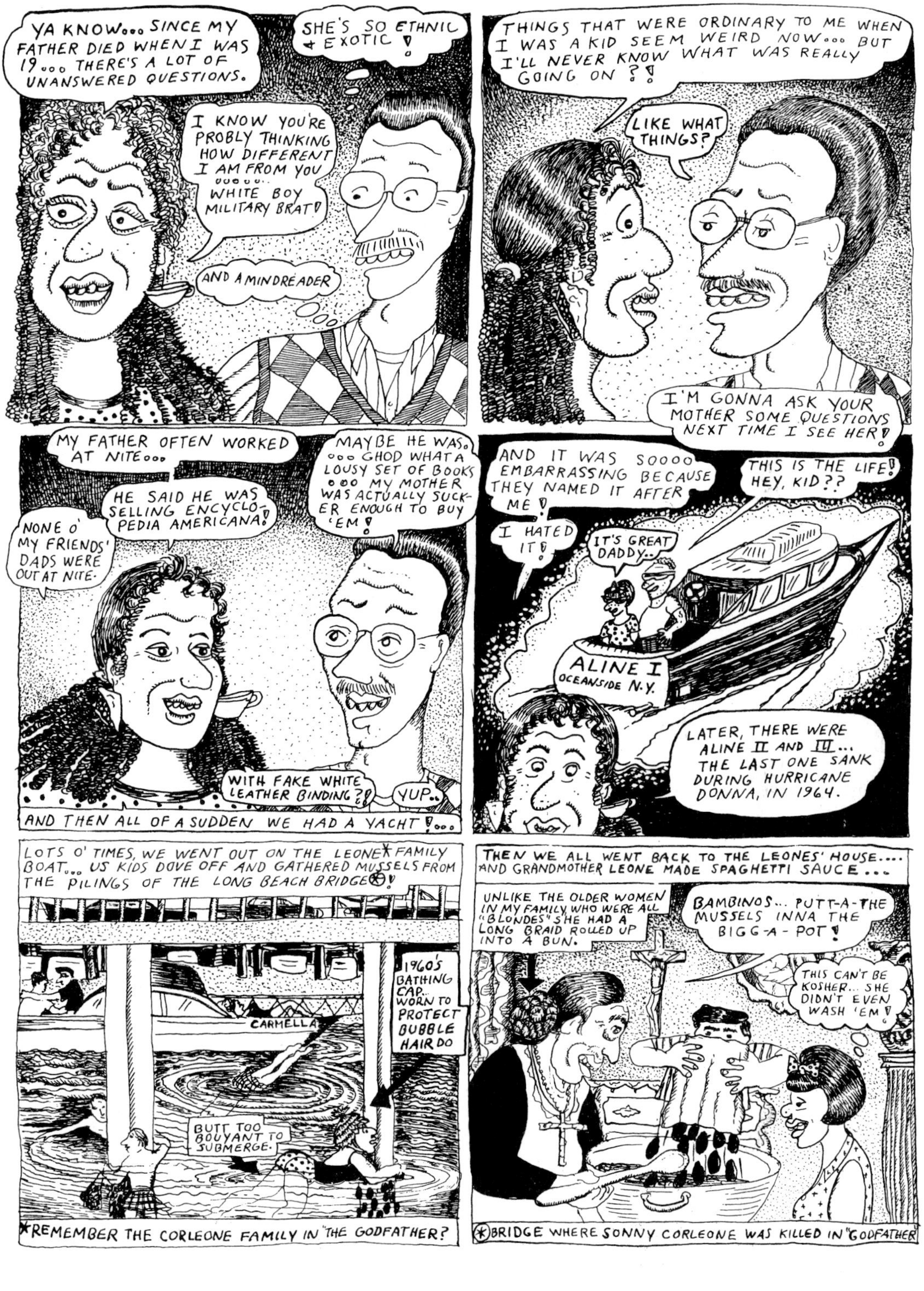

YA KNOW... SINCE MY FATHER DIED WHEN I WAS 19... THERE'S A LOT OF UNANSWERED QUESTIONS.
SHE'S SO ETHNIC + EXOTIC!
I KNOW YOU'RE PROBLY THINKING HOW DIFFERENT I AM FROM YOU ..... WHITE BOY MILITARY BRAT!
AND A MINDREADER
THINGS THAT WERE ORDINARY TO ME WHEN I WAS A KID SEEM WEIRD NOW... BUT I'LL NEVER KNOW WHAT WAS REALLY GOING ON ?!
LIKE WHAT THINGS?
I'M GONNA ASK YOUR MOTHER SOME QUESTIONS NEXT TIME I SEE HER!
MY FATHER OFTEN WORKED AT NITE...
HE SAID HE WAS SELLING ENCYCLOPEDIA AMERICANA!
NONE O' MY FRIENDS' DADS WERE OUT AT NITE.
MAYBE HE WAS... GHOD WHAT A LOUSY SET OF BOOKS ... MY MOTHER WAS ACTUALLY SUCKER ENOUGH TO BUY 'EM!
WITH FAKE WHITE LEATHER BINDING?!
YUP..
AND THEN ALL OF A SUDDEN WE HAD A YACHT!...
AND IT WAS SOOOO EMBARRASSING BECAUSE THEY NAMED IT AFTER ME!
I HATED IT!
THIS IS THE LIFE! HEY, KID??
IT'S GREAT DADDY..
ALINE I
OCEANSIDE N.Y.
LATER, THERE WERE ALINE II AND III... THE LAST ONE SANK DURING HURRICANE DONNA, IN 1964.
LOTS O' TIMES, WE WENT OUT ON THE LEONE* FAMILY BOAT... US KIDS DOVE OFF AND GATHERED MUSSELS FROM THE PILINGS OF THE LONG BEACH BRIDGE(*)!
CARMELLA
1960'S BATHING CAP... WORN TO PROTECT BUBBLE HAIR DO
BUTT TOO BOUYANT TO SUBMERGE.
*REMEMBER THE CORLEONE FAMILY IN "THE GODFATHER?
THEN WE ALL WENT BACK TO THE LEONES' HOUSE.... AND GRANDMOTHER LEONE MADE SPAGHETTI SAUCE...
UNLIKE THE OLDER WOMEN IN MY FAMILY WHO WERE ALL "BLONDES" SHE HAD A LONG BRAID ROLLED UP INTO A BUN.
BAMBINOS... PUTT-A-THE MUSSELS INNA THE BIGG-A-POT!
THIS CAN'T BE KOSHER... SHE DIDN'T EVEN WASH 'EM!
(*)BRIDGE WHERE SONNY CORLEONE WAS KILLED IN "GODFATHER

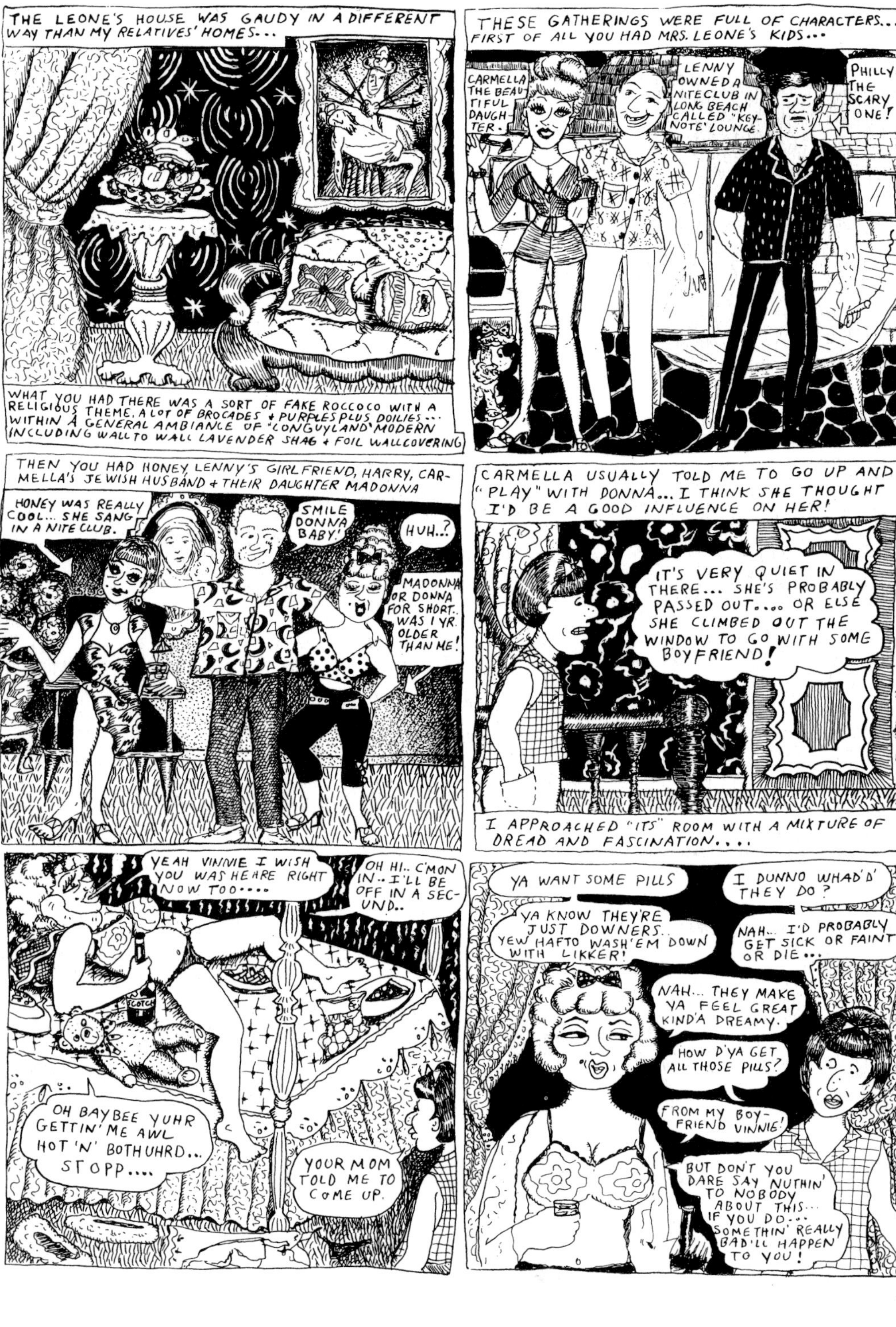

THE LEONE'S HOUSE WAS GAUDY IN A DIFFERENT WAY THAN MY RELATIVES' HOMES...
WHAT YOU HAD THERE WAS A SORT OF FAKE ROCCOCO WITH A RELIGIOUS THEME, A LOT OF BROCADES + PURPLES PLUS DOILIES... WITHIN A GENERAL AMBIANCE OF "LONGUYLAND" MODERN INCLUDING WALL TO WALL LAVENDER SHAG + FOIL WALLCOVERING
THESE GATHERINGS WERE FULL OF CHARACTERS.... FIRST OF ALL YOU HAD MRS. LEONE'S KIDS...
CARMELLA THE BEAUTIFUL DAUGHTER.
LENNY OWNED A NITECLUB IN LONG BEACH CALLED "KEY-NOTE" LOUNGE.
PHILLY.. THE SCARY ONE!
THEN YOU HAD HONEY, LENNY'S GIRLFRIEND, HARRY, CARMELLA'S JEWISH HUSBAND + THEIR DAUGHTER MADONNA
HONEY WAS REALLY COOL... SHE SANG IN A NITE CLUB.
SMILE DONNA BABY!
HUH..?
MADONNA OR DONNA FOR SHORT. WAS I YR. OLDER THAN ME!
CARMELLA USUALLY TOLD ME TO GO UP AND "PLAY" WITH DONNA... I THINK SHE THOUGHT I'D BE A GOOD INFLUENCE ON HER!
IT'S VERY QUIET IN THERE... SHE'S PROBABLY PASSED OUT... OR ELSE SHE CLIMBED OUT THE WINDOW TO GO WITH SOME BOYFRIEND!
I APPROACHED "ITS" ROOM WITH A MIXTURE OF DREAD AND FASCINATION....
YEAH VINNIE I WISH YOU WAS HEARE RIGHT NOW TOO....
OH HI.. C'MON IN.. I'LL BE OFF IN A SECUND..
OH BAYBEE YUHR GETTIN' ME AWL HOT 'N' BOTHUHRD... STOPP....
YOUR MOM TOLD ME TO COME UP.
SCOTCH
YA WANT SOME PILLS
I DUNNO WHAD'D' THEY DO?
YA KNOW THEY'RE JUST DOWNERS.. YEW HAFTO WASH'EM DOWN WITH LIKKER!
NAH... I'D PROBABLY GET SICK OR FAINT OR DIE...
NAH... THEY MAKE YA FEEL GREAT KIND'A DREAMY.
HOW D'YA GET ALL THOSE PILLS?
FROM MY BOY-FRIEND VINNIE!
BUT DON'T YOU DARE SAY NUTHIN' TO NOBODY ABOUT THIS... IF YOU DO... SOMETHIN' REALLY BAD'LL HAPPEN TO YOU!

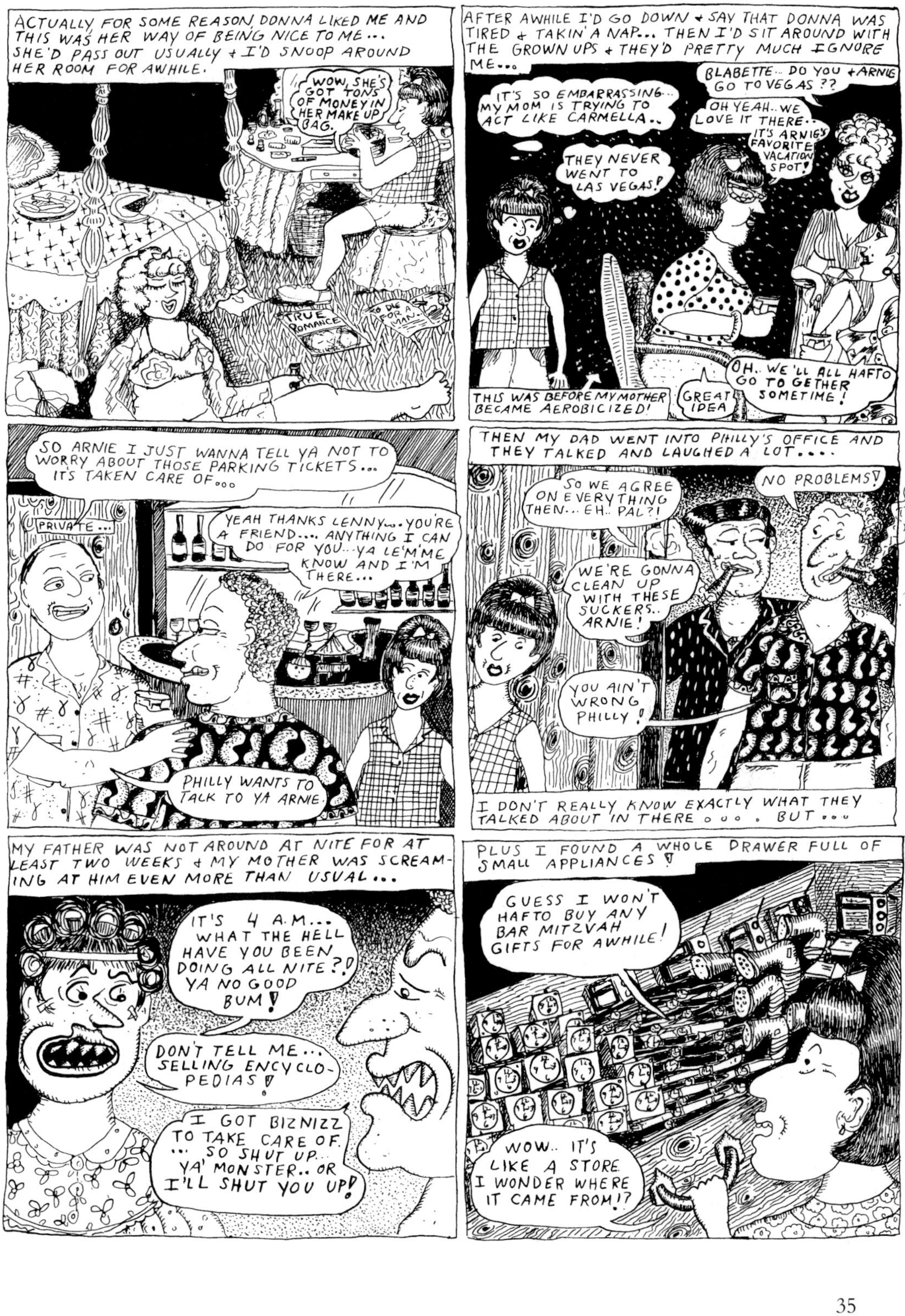
ACTUALLY FOR SOME REASON DONNA LIKED ME AND THIS WAS HER WAY OF BEING NICE TO ME... SHE'D PASS OUT USUALLY + I'D SNOOP AROUND HER ROOM FOR AWHILE.
WOW, SHE'S GOT TONS OF MONEY IN HER MAKE UP BAG.
TRUE ROMANCE
TO DIE FOR A MAN
AFTER AWHILE I'D GO DOWN + SAY THAT DONNA WAS TIRED + TAKIN' A NAP... THEN I'D SIT AROUND WITH THE GROWN UPS + THEY'D PRETTY MUCH IGNORE ME...
IT'S SO EMBARRASSING... MY MOM IS TRYING TO ACT LIKE CARMELLA..
BLABETTE... DO YOU + ARNIE GO TO VEGAS??
OH YEAH.. WE LOVE IT THERE..
IT'S ARNIE'S FAVORITE VACATION SPOT!
THEY NEVER WENT TO LAS VEGAS!
OH.. WE'LL ALL HAFTO GO TOGETHER SOMETIME!
GREAT IDEA
THIS WAS BEFORE MY MOTHER BECAME AEROBICIZED!
SO ARNIE I JUST WANNA TELL YA NOT TO WORRY ABOUT THOSE PARKING TICKETS... IT'S TAKEN CARE OF...
PRIVATE...
YEAH THANKS LENNY.... YOU'RE A FRIEND.... ANYTHING I CAN DO FOR YOU... YA LE'M'ME KNOW AND I'M THERE...
PHILLY WANTS TO TALK TO YA ARNIE.
THEN MY DAD WENT INTO PHILLY'S OFFICE AND THEY TALKED AND LAUGHED A LOT....
SO WE AGREE ON EVERYTHING THEN... EH.. PAL?!
NO PROBLEMS!
WE'RE GONNA CLEAN UP WITH THESE SUCKERS.. ARNIE!
YOU AIN'T WRONG PHILLY!
I DON'T REALLY KNOW EXACTLY WHAT THEY TALKED ABOUT IN THERE... BUT...
MY FATHER WAS NOT AROUND AT NITE FOR AT LEAST TWO WEEKS + MY MOTHER WAS SCREAMING AT HIM EVEN MORE THAN USUAL...
IT'S 4 A.M... WHAT THE HELL HAVE YOU BEEN DOING ALL NITE?! YA NO GOOD BUM!
DON'T TELL ME... SELLING ENCYCLOPEDIAS!
I GOT BIZNIZZ TO TAKE CARE OF. ... SO SHUT UP.. YA' MONSTER.. OR I'LL SHUT YOU UP!
PLUS I FOUND A WHOLE DRAWER FULL OF SMALL APPLIANCES!
GUESS I WON'T HAFTO BUY ANY BAR MITZVAH GIFTS FOR AWHILE!
WOW.. IT'S LIKE A STORE. I WONDER WHERE IT CAME FROM!?

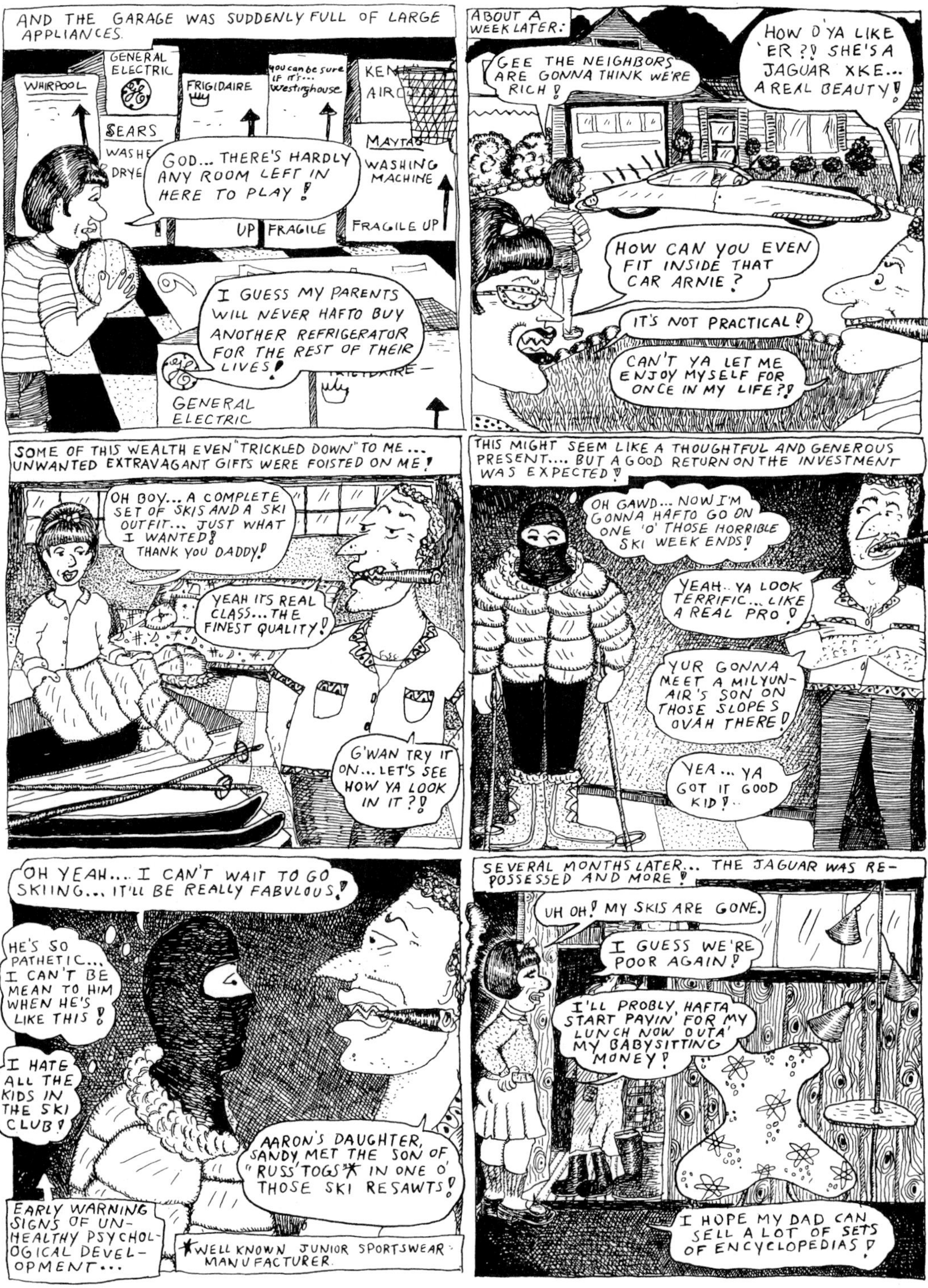
AND THE GARAGE WAS SUDDENLY FULL OF LARGE APPLIANCES.
WHIRPOOL
GENERAL ELECTRIC
FRIGIDAIRE
you can be sure if it's... Westinghouse
SEARS
MAYTAG
WASHING MACHINE
UP FRAGILE
FRAGILE UP
GOD... THERE'S HARDLY ANY ROOM LEFT IN HERE TO PLAY!
I GUESS MY PARENTS WILL NEVER HAFTO BUY ANOTHER REFRIGERATOR FOR THE REST OF THEIR LIVES!
GENERAL ELECTRIC
ABOUT A WEEK LATER:
GEE THE NEIGHBORS ARE GONNA THINK WE'RE RICH!
HOW D'YA LIKE 'ER?! SHE'S A JAGUAR XKE... A REAL BEAUTY!
HOW CAN YOU EVEN FIT INSIDE THAT CAR ARNIE?
IT'S NOT PRACTICAL!
CAN'T YA LET ME ENJOY MYSELF FOR ONCE IN MY LIFE?!
SOME OF THIS WEALTH EVEN "TRICKLED DOWN" TO ME... UNWANTED EXTRAVAGANT GIFTS WERE FOISTED ON ME!
OH BOY... A COMPLETE SET OF SKIS AND A SKI OUTFIT... JUST WHAT I WANTED! THANK YOU DADDY!
YEAH ITS REAL CLASS... THE FINEST QUALITY!
G'WAN TRY IT ON... LET'S SEE HOW YA LOOK IN IT?!
THIS MIGHT SEEM LIKE A THOUGHTFUL AND GENEROUS PRESENT.... BUT A GOOD RETURN ON THE INVESTMENT WAS EXPECTED!
OH GAWD... NOW I'M GONNA HAFTO GO ON ONE 'O' THOSE HORRIBLE SKI WEEK ENDS!
YEAH.. YA LOOK TERRIFIC... LIKE A REAL PRO!
YUR GONNA MEET A MILYUN-AIR'S SON ON THOSE SLOPES OVAH THERE!
YEA... YA GOT IT GOOD KID!..
OH YEAH... I CAN'T WAIT TO GO SKIING... IT'LL BE REALLY FABULOUS!
HE'S SO PATHETIC... I CAN'T BE MEAN TO HIM WHEN HE'S LIKE THIS!
I HATE ALL THE KIDS IN THE SKI CLUB!
AARON'S DAUGHTER, SANDY MET THE SON OF "RUSS' TOGS"* IN ONE O' THOSE SKI RESAWTS!
EARLY WARNING SIGNS OF UN-HEALTHY PSYCHOLOGICAL DEVELOPMENT...
*WELL KNOWN JUNIOR SPORTSWEAR MANUFACTURER.
SEVERAL MONTHS LATER... THE JAGUAR WAS RE-POSSESSED AND MORE!
UH OH! MY SKIS ARE GONE.
I GUESS WE'RE POOR AGAIN!
I'LL PROBLY HAFTA START PAYIN' FOR MY LUNCH NOW OUTA' MY BABYSITTING MONEY!
I HOPE MY DAD CAN SELL A LOT OF SETS OF ENCYCLOPEDIAS!

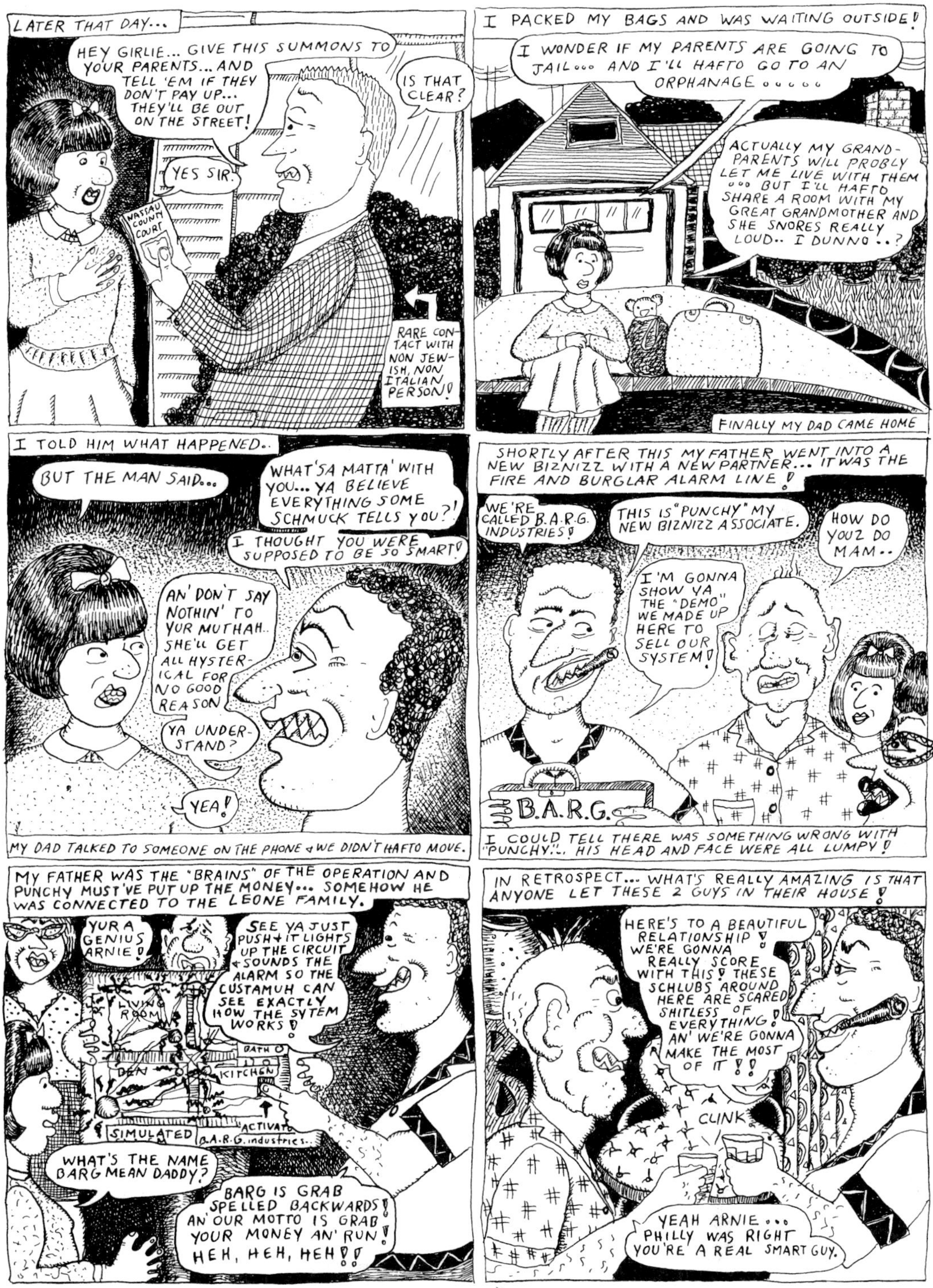
LATER THAT DAY...
HEY GIRLIE... GIVE THIS SUMMONS TO YOUR PARENTS... AND TELL 'EM IF THEY DON'T PAY UP... THEY'LL BE OUT ON THE STREET!
IS THAT CLEAR?
YES SIR.
NASSAU COUNTY COURT
RARE CONTACT WITH NON JEWISH, NON ITALIAN PERSON!
I PACKED MY BAGS AND WAS WAITING OUTSIDE!
I WONDER IF MY PARENTS ARE GOING TO JAIL... AND I'LL HAFTO GO TO AN ORPHANAGE......
ACTUALLY MY GRANDPARENTS WILL PROBLY LET ME LIVE WITH THEM... BUT I'LL HAFTO SHARE A ROOM WITH MY GREAT GRANDMOTHER AND SHE SNORES REALLY LOUD.. I DUNNO..?
FINALLY MY DAD CAME HOME
I TOLD HIM WHAT HAPPENED..
BUT THE MAN SAID...
WHAT'SA MATTA' WITH YOU... YA BELIEVE EVERYTHING SOME SCHMUCK TELLS YOU?!
I THOUGHT YOU WERE SUPPOSED TO BE SO SMART!
AN' DON'T SAY NOTHIN' TO YUR MUTHAH.. SHE'LL GET ALL HYSTERICAL FOR NO GOOD REASON
YA UNDERSTAND?
YEA!
MY DAD TALKED TO SOMEONE ON THE PHONE & WE DIDN'T HAFTO MOVE.
SHORTLY AFTER THIS MY FATHER WENT INTO A NEW BIZNIZZ WITH A NEW PARTNER... IT WAS THE FIRE AND BURGLAR ALARM LINE!
WE'RE CALLED B.A.R.G. INDUSTRIES!
THIS IS "PUNCHY" MY NEW BIZNIZZ ASSOCIATE.
HOW DO YOUZ DO MAM..
I'M GONNA SHOW YA THE "DEMO" WE MADE UP HERE TO SELL OUR SYSTEM!
B.A.R.G.
I COULD TELL THERE WAS SOMETHING WRONG WITH "PUNCHY".. HIS HEAD AND FACE WERE ALL LUMPY!
MY FATHER WAS THE "BRAINS" OF THE OPERATION AND PUNCHY MUST'VE PUT UP THE MONEY... SOMEHOW HE WAS CONNECTED TO THE LEONE FAMILY.
YUR A GENIUS ARNIE!
SEE YA JUST PUSH & IT LIGHTS UP THE CIRCUIT & SOUNDS THE ALARM SO THE CUSTAMUH CAN SEE EXACTLY HOW THE SYTEM WORKS!
LIVING ROOM
BATH
DEN
KITCHEN
SIMULATED
ACTIVATE
B.A.R.G. industries.
WHAT'S THE NAME BARG MEAN DADDY?
BARG IS GRAB SPELLED BACKWARDS! AN' OUR MOTTO IS GRAB YOUR MONEY AN' RUN! HEH, HEH, HEH!!
IN RETROSPECT... WHAT'S REALLY AMAZING IS THAT ANYONE LET THESE 2 GUYS IN THEIR HOUSE!
HERE'S TO A BEAUTIFUL RELATIONSHIP! WE'RE GONNA REALLY SCORE WITH THIS! THESE SCHLUBS AROUND HERE ARE SCARED SHITLESS OF EVERYTHING! AN' WE'RE GONNA MAKE THE MOST OF IT!!
CLINK
YEAH ARNIE... PHILLY WAS RIGHT YOU'RE A REAL SMART GUY.

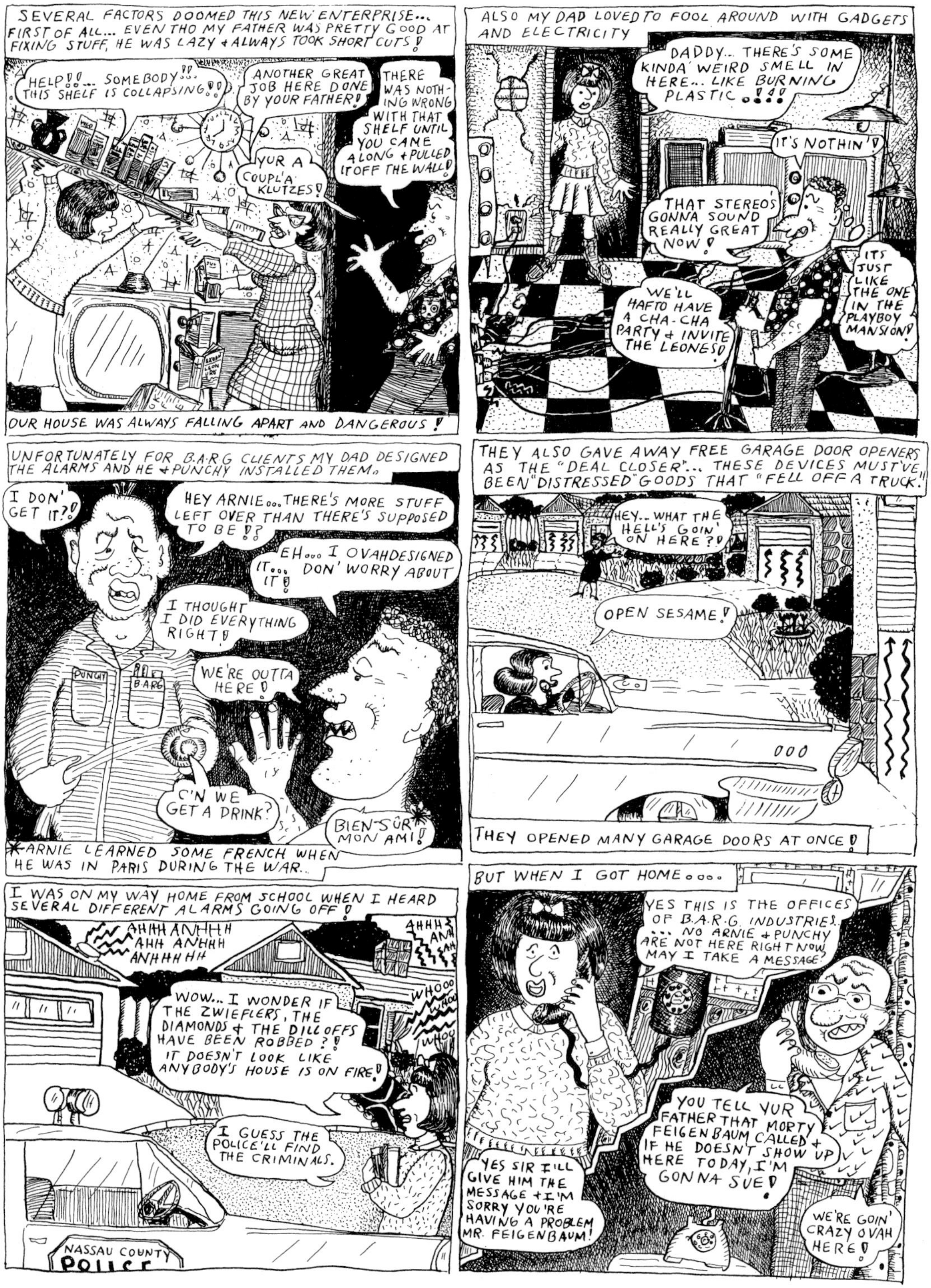
SEVERAL FACTORS DOOMED THIS NEW ENTERPRISE... FIRST OF ALL... EVEN THO MY FATHER WAS PRETTY GOOD AT FIXING STUFF, HE WAS LAZY & ALWAYS TOOK SHORT CUTS!
HELP!!... SOMEBODY!! THIS SHELF IS COLLAPSING!!
ANOTHER GREAT JOB HERE DONE BY YOUR FATHER!
THERE WAS NOTHING WRONG WITH THAT SHELF UNTIL YOU CAME ALONG & PULLED IT OFF THE WALL!
YUR A COUPL'A KLUTZES!
OUR HOUSE WAS ALWAYS FALLING APART AND DANGEROUS!
ALSO MY DAD LOVED TO FOOL AROUND WITH GADGETS AND ELECTRICITY
DADDY... THERE'S SOME KINDA' WEIRD SMELL IN HERE... LIKE BURNING PLASTIC...!!
IT'S NOTHIN'!
THAT STEREO'S GONNA SOUND REALLY GREAT NOW!
WE'LL HAFTO HAVE A CHA-CHA PARTY & INVITE THE LEONES!
ITS JUST LIKE THE ONE IN THE PLAYBOY MANSION!
UNFORTUNATELY FOR B.A.R.G CLIENTS MY DAD DESIGNED THE ALARMS AND HE & PUNCHY INSTALLED THEM.
I DON' GET IT?!
HEY ARNIE... THERE'S MORE STUFF LEFT OVER THAN THERE'S SUPPOSED TO BE!?
EH... I OVAHDESIGNED IT... DON' WORRY ABOUT IT!
I THOUGHT I DID EVERYTHING RIGHT!
WE'RE OUTTA HERE!
PUNCHY
B.A.R.G
C'N WE GET A DRINK?
BIEN SÛR MON AMI!*
*ARNIE LEARNED SOME FRENCH WHEN HE WAS IN PARIS DURING THE WAR...
THEY ALSO GAVE AWAY FREE GARAGE DOOR OPENERS AS THE "DEAL CLOSER"... THESE DEVICES MUST'VE BEEN "DISTRESSED" GOODS THAT "FELL OFF A TRUCK"!
HEY... WHAT THE HELL'S GOIN' ON HERE?!
OPEN SESAME!
THEY OPENED MANY GARAGE DOORS AT ONCE!
I WAS ON MY WAY HOME FROM SCHOOL WHEN I HEARD SEVERAL DIFFERENT ALARMS GOING OFF!
AHHH ANHHH AHH ANHHH ANHHHHH
AHHH
WHOOO WHOO WHOO
WOW... I WONDER IF THE ZWIEFLERS, THE DIAMONDS & THE DILLOFFS HAVE BEEN ROBBED?! IT DOESN'T LOOK LIKE ANYBODY'S HOUSE IS ON FIRE!
I GUESS THE POLICE'LL FIND THE CRIMINALS.
NASSAU COUNTY POLICE
BUT WHEN I GOT HOME....
YES THIS IS THE OFFICES OF B.A.R.G. INDUSTRIES... NO ARNIE & PUNCHY ARE NOT HERE RIGHT NOW, MAY I TAKE A MESSAGE?
YOU TELL YUR FATHER THAT MORTY FEIGENBAUM CALLED & IF HE DOESN'T SHOW UP HERE TODAY, I'M GONNA SUE!
YES SIR I'LL GIVE HIM THE MESSAGE & I'M SORRY YOU'RE HAVING A PROBLEM MR. FEIGENBAUM!
WE'RE GOIN' CRAZY OVAH HERE!

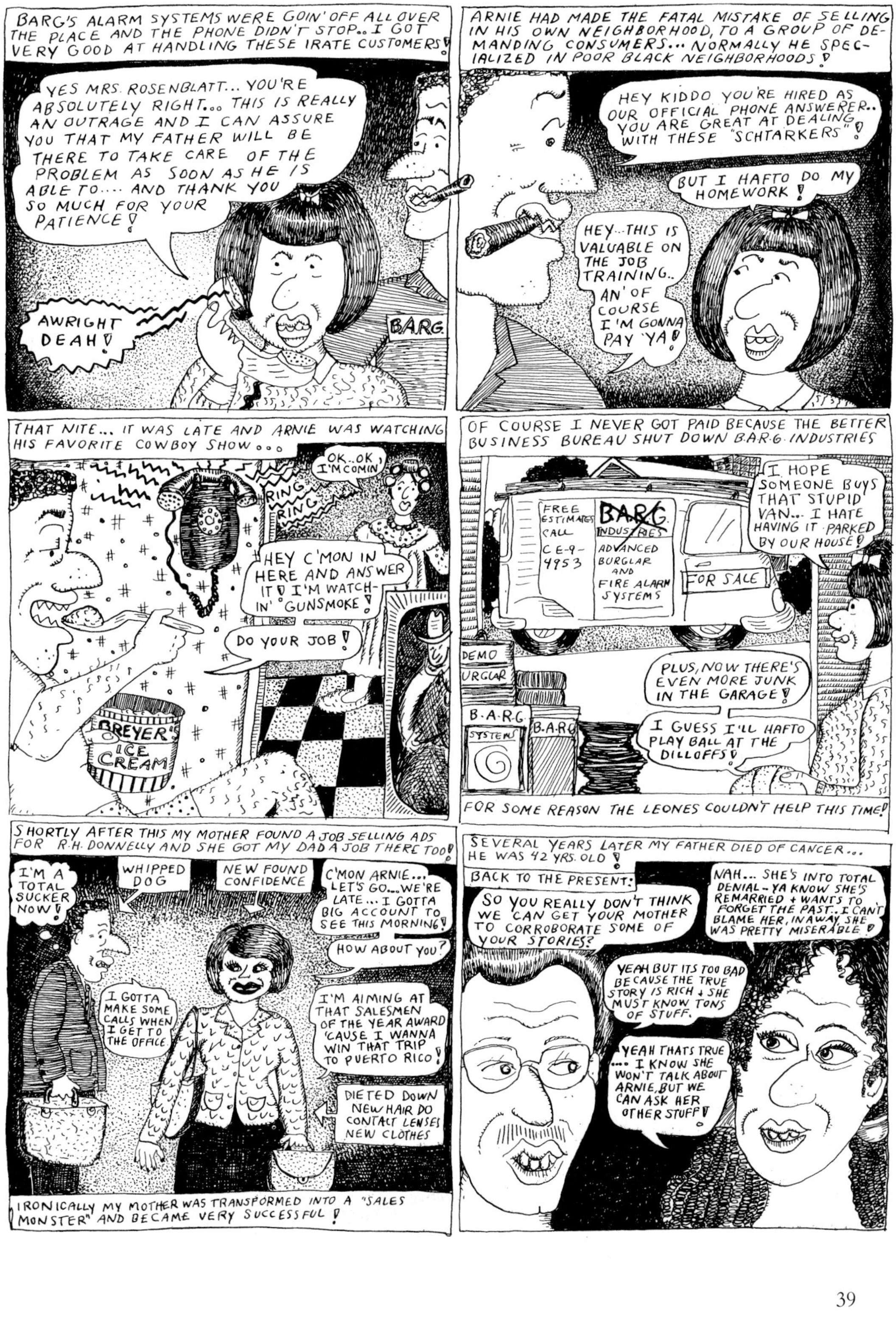
BARG'S ALARM SYSTEMS WERE GOIN' OFF ALL OVER THE PLACE AND THE PHONE DIDN'T STOP.. I GOT VERY GOOD AT HANDLING THESE IRATE CUSTOMERS!
YES MRS. ROSENBLATT... YOU'RE ABSOLUTELY RIGHT... THIS IS REALLY AN OUTRAGE AND I CAN ASSURE YOU THAT MY FATHER WILL BE THERE TO TAKE CARE OF THE PROBLEM AS SOON AS HE IS ABLE TO.... AND THANK YOU SO MUCH FOR YOUR PATIENCE!
AWRIGHT DEAH!
B.A.R.G.
ARNIE HAD MADE THE FATAL MISTAKE OF SELLING IN HIS OWN NEIGHBORHOOD, TO A GROUP OF DEMANDING CONSUMERS... NORMALLY HE SPECIALIZED IN POOR BLACK NEIGHBORHOODS!
HEY KIDDO YOU'RE HIRED AS OUR OFFICIAL PHONE ANSWERER.. YOU ARE GREAT AT DEALING WITH THESE "SCHTARKERS"!
BUT I HAFTO DO MY HOMEWORK!
HEY...THIS IS VALUABLE ON THE JOB TRAINING.. AN' OF COURSE I'M GONNA PAY YA!
THAT NITE... IT WAS LATE AND ARNIE WAS WATCHING HIS FAVORITE COWBOY SHOW...
OK..OK I'M COMIN
RING RING
HEY C'MON IN HERE AND ANSWER IT! I'M WATCHIN' GUNSMOKE!
DO YOUR JOB!
BREYER'S ICE CREAM
OF COURSE I NEVER GOT PAID BECAUSE THE BETTER BUSINESS BUREAU SHUT DOWN B.A.R.G. INDUSTRIES
FREE ESTIMATES CALL CE-9-4953
BARG INDUSTRIES ADVANCED BURGLAR AND FIRE ALARM SYSTEMS
FOR SALE
I HOPE SOMEONE BUYS THAT STUPID VAN... I HATE HAVING IT PARKED BY OUR HOUSE!
PLUS, NOW THERE'S EVEN MORE JUNK IN THE GARAGE!
I GUESS I'LL HAFTO PLAY BALL AT THE DILLOFFS!
DEMO
URGLAR
B.A.R.G. SYSTEMS
B.A.R.G
FOR SOME REASON THE LEONES COULDN'T HELP THIS TIME!
SHORTLY AFTER THIS MY MOTHER FOUND A JOB SELLING ADS FOR R.H. DONNELLY AND SHE GOT MY DAD A JOB THERE TOO!
I'M A TOTAL SUCKER NOW!
WHIPPED DOG
NEW FOUND CONFIDENCE
C'MON ARNIE... LET'S GO...WE'RE LATE... I GOTTA BIG ACCOUNT TO SEE THIS MORNING!
HOW ABOUT YOU?
I GOTTA MAKE SOME CALLS WHEN I GET TO THE OFFICE
I'M AIMING AT THAT SALESMEN OF THE YEAR AWARD 'CAUSE I WANNA WIN THAT TRIP TO PUERTO RICO!
DIETED DOWN NEW HAIR DO CONTACT LENSES NEW CLOTHES
IRONICALLY MY MOTHER WAS TRANSFORMED INTO A "SALES MONSTER" AND BECAME VERY SUCCESSFUL!
SEVERAL YEARS LATER MY FATHER DIED OF CANCER... HE WAS 42 YRS. OLD!
BACK TO THE PRESENT:
SO YOU REALLY DON'T THINK WE CAN GET YOUR MOTHER TO CORROBORATE SOME OF YOUR STORIES?
NAH... SHE'S INTO TOTAL DENIAL - YA KNOW SHE'S REMARRIED + WANTS TO FORGET THE PAST.. I CAN'T BLAME HER, IN A WAY, SHE WAS PRETTY MISERABLE!
YEAH BUT ITS TOO BAD BECAUSE THE TRUE STORY IS RICH + SHE MUST KNOW TONS OF STUFF.
YEAH THATS TRUE ... I KNOW SHE WON'T TALK ABOUT ARNIE, BUT WE CAN ASK HER OTHER STUFF!

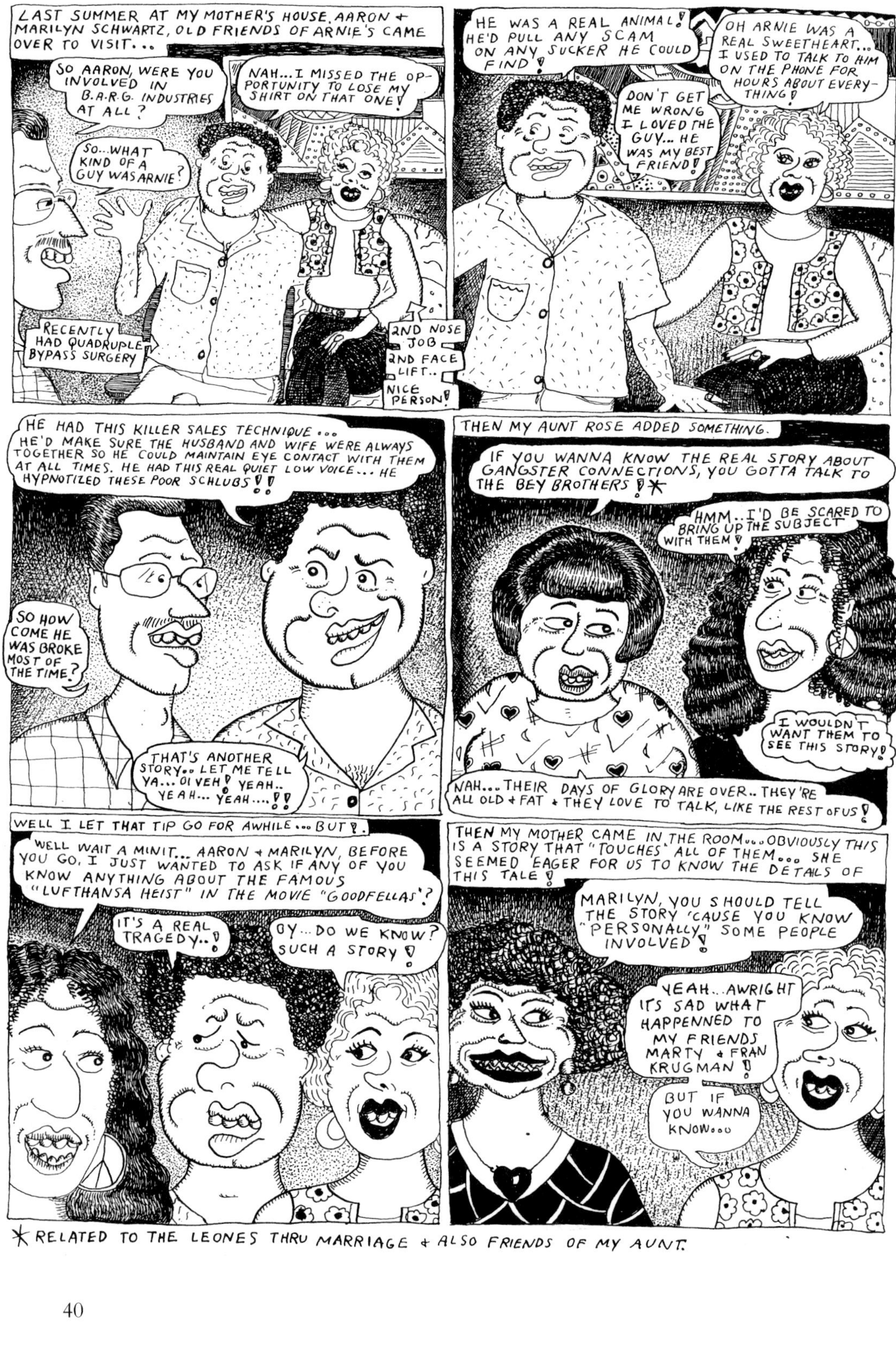
LAST SUMMER AT MY MOTHER'S HOUSE, AARON + MARILYN SCHWARTZ, OLD FRIENDS OF ARNIE'S CAME OVER TO VISIT...
SO AARON, WERE YOU INVOLVED IN B.A.R.G. INDUSTRIES AT ALL?
NAH... I MISSED THE OPPORTUNITY TO LOSE MY SHIRT ON THAT ONE!
SO... WHAT KIND OF A GUY WAS ARNIE?
RECENTLY HAD QUADRUPLE BYPASS SURGERY
2ND NOSE JOB
2ND FACE LIFT..
NICE PERSON!
HE WAS A REAL ANIMAL! HE'D PULL ANY SCAM ON ANY SUCKER HE COULD FIND!
DON'T GET ME WRONG I LOVED THE GUY... HE WAS MY BEST FRIEND!
OH ARNIE WAS A REAL SWEETHEART... I USED TO TALK TO HIM ON THE PHONE FOR HOURS ABOUT EVERYTHING!
HE HAD THIS KILLER SALES TECHNIQUE... HE'D MAKE SURE THE HUSBAND AND WIFE WERE ALWAYS TOGETHER SO HE COULD MAINTAIN EYE CONTACT WITH THEM AT ALL TIMES. HE HAD THIS REAL QUIET LOW VOICE... HE HYPNOTIZED THESE POOR SCHLUBS!!
SO HOW COME HE WAS BROKE MOST OF THE TIME?
THAT'S ANOTHER STORY.. LET ME TELL YA... OI VEH! YEAH.. YEAH... YEAH....!!
THEN MY AUNT ROSE ADDED SOMETHING.
IF YOU WANNA KNOW THE REAL STORY ABOUT GANGSTER CONNECTIONS, YOU GOTTA TALK TO THE BEY BROTHERS!*
HMM.. I'D BE SCARED TO BRING UP THE SUBJECT WITH THEM!
I WOULDN'T WANT THEM TO SEE THIS STORY!
NAH... THEIR DAYS OF GLORY ARE OVER.. THEY'RE ALL OLD + FAT + THEY LOVE TO TALK, LIKE THE REST OF US!
WELL I LET THAT TIP GO FOR AWHILE... BUT!
WELL WAIT A MINIT... AARON + MARILYN, BEFORE YOU GO, I JUST WANTED TO ASK IF ANY OF YOU KNOW ANYTHING ABOUT THE FAMOUS "LUFTHANSA HEIST" IN THE MOVIE "GOODFELLAS"?
IT'S A REAL TRAGEDY..!
OY... DO WE KNOW? SUCH A STORY!
THEN MY MOTHER CAME IN THE ROOM... OBVIOUSLY THIS IS A STORY THAT "TOUCHES" ALL OF THEM... SHE SEEMED EAGER FOR US TO KNOW THE DETAILS OF THIS TALE!
MARILYN, YOU SHOULD TELL THE STORY 'CAUSE YOU KNOW "PERSONALLY" SOME PEOPLE INVOLVED!
YEAH... AWRIGHT IT'S SAD WHAT HAPPENNED TO MY FRIENDS MARTY + FRAN KRUGMAN!
BUT IF YOU WANNA KNOW...

* RELATED TO THE LEONES THRU MARRIAGE + ALSO FRIENDS OF MY AUNT.

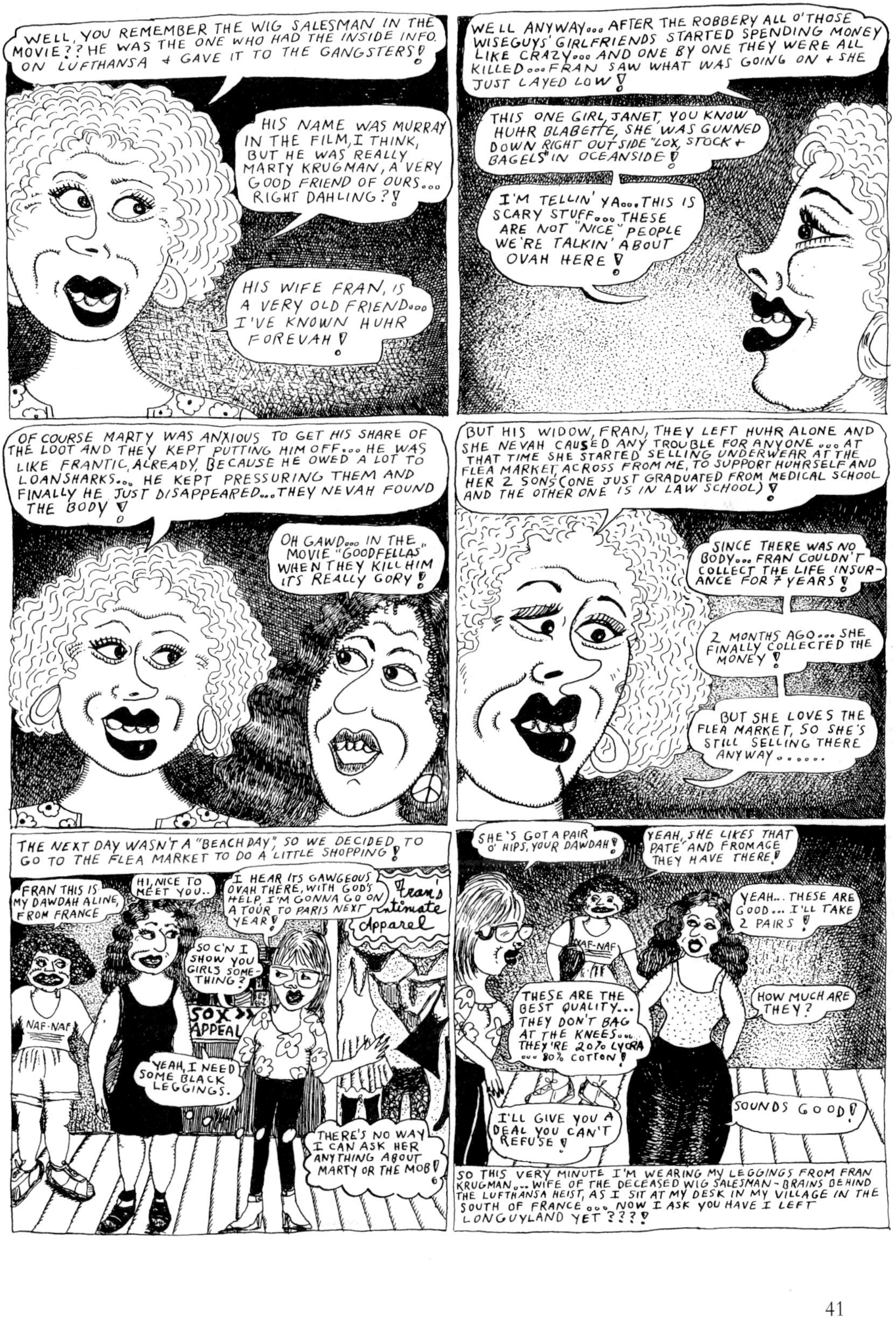
WELL, YOU REMEMBER THE WIG SALESMAN IN THE MOVIE?? HE WAS THE ONE WHO HAD THE INSIDE INFO. ON LUFTHANSA + GAVE IT TO THE GANGSTERS!
HIS NAME WAS MURRAY IN THE FILM, I THINK, BUT HE WAS REALLY MARTY KRUGMAN, A VERY GOOD FRIEND OF OURS... RIGHT DAHLING?!
HIS WIFE FRAN, IS A VERY OLD FRIEND... I'VE KNOWN HUHR FOREVAH!
WELL ANYWAY... AFTER THE ROBBERY ALL O'THOSE WISEGUYS' GIRLFRIENDS STARTED SPENDING MONEY LIKE CRAZY... AND ONE BY ONE THEY WERE ALL KILLED... FRAN SAW WHAT WAS GOING ON + SHE JUST LAYED LOW!
THIS ONE GIRL, JANET, YOU KNOW HUHR BLABETTE, SHE WAS GUNNED DOWN RIGHT OUT-SIDE "LOX, STOCK + BAGELS" IN OCEANSIDE!
I'M TELLIN' YA... THIS IS SCARY STUFF... THESE ARE NOT "NICE" PEOPLE WE'RE TALKIN' ABOUT OVAH HERE!
OF COURSE MARTY WAS ANXIOUS TO GET HIS SHARE OF THE LOOT AND THEY KEPT PUTTING HIM OFF... HE WAS LIKE FRANTIC, ALREADY, BECAUSE HE OWED A LOT TO LOANSHARKS... HE KEPT PRESSURING THEM AND FINALLY HE JUST DISAPPEARED... THEY NEVAH FOUND THE BODY!
OH GAWD... IN THE MOVIE "GOODFELLAS" WHEN THEY KILL HIM ITS REALLY GORY!
BUT HIS WIDOW, FRAN, THEY LEFT HUHR ALONE AND SHE NEVAH CAUSED ANY TROUBLE FOR ANYONE... AT THAT TIME SHE STARTED SELLING UNDERWEAR AT THE FLEA MARKET, ACROSS FROM ME, TO SUPPORT HUHRSELF AND HER 2 SONS (ONE JUST GRADUATED FROM MEDICAL SCHOOL AND THE OTHER ONE IS IN LAW SCHOOL)!
SINCE THERE WAS NO BODY... FRAN COULDN'T COLLECT THE LIFE INSUR-ANCE FOR 7 YEARS!
2 MONTHS AGO... SHE FINALLY COLLECTED THE MONEY!
BUT SHE LOVES THE FLEA MARKET, SO SHE'S STILL SELLING THERE ANYWAY......
THE NEXT DAY WASN'T A "BEACH DAY", SO WE DECIDED TO GO TO THE FLEA MARKET TO DO A LITTLE SHOPPING!
FRAN THIS IS MY DAWDAH ALINE, FROM FRANCE
HI, NICE TO MEET YOU..
I HEAR ITS GAWGEOUS OVAH THERE, WITH GOD'S HELP, I'M GONNA GO ON A TOUR TO PARIS NEXT YEAR!
Fran's Intimate Apparel
SO C'N I SHOW YOU GIRLS SOME-THING?
SOX APPEAL
NAF-NAF
YEAH, I NEED SOME BLACK LEGGINGS.
THERE'S NO WAY I CAN ASK HER ANYTHING ABOUT MARTY OR THE MOB!
SHE'S GOT A PAIR O' HIPS, YOUR DAWDAH!
YEAH, SHE LIKES THAT PATE AND FROMAGE THEY HAVE THERE!
YEAH... THESE ARE GOOD... I'LL TAKE 2 PAIRS!
NAF-NAF
THESE ARE THE BEST QUALITY... THEY DON'T BAG AT THE KNEES... THEY'RE 20% LYCRA ... 80% COTTON!
HOW MUCH ARE THEY?
I'LL GIVE YOU A DEAL YOU CAN'T REFUSE!
SOUNDS GOOD!
SO THIS VERY MINUTE I'M WEARING MY LEGGINGS FROM FRAN KRUGMAN... WIFE OF THE DECEASED WIG SALESMAN-BRAINS BEHIND THE LUFTHANSA HEIST, AS I SIT AT MY DESK IN MY VILLAGE IN THE SOUTH OF FRANCE... NOW I ASK YOU HAVE I LEFT LONGUYLAND YET???!

Home sweet home!

Images from my childhood inspired me to create a range of ironically idyllic paintings. These represent my parents' ideal of what made a perfect home. There I am on my father's lap in the painting below—all the objects I've depicted were in the house, but not necessarily in this room. On the opposite page (top) is "The Dream House," promising the perfect 1950s lifestyle. In reality it was "Our Lovely Tract House Development" and was built on a derelict golf course which was an oppressively claustrophobic environment (opposite below.)

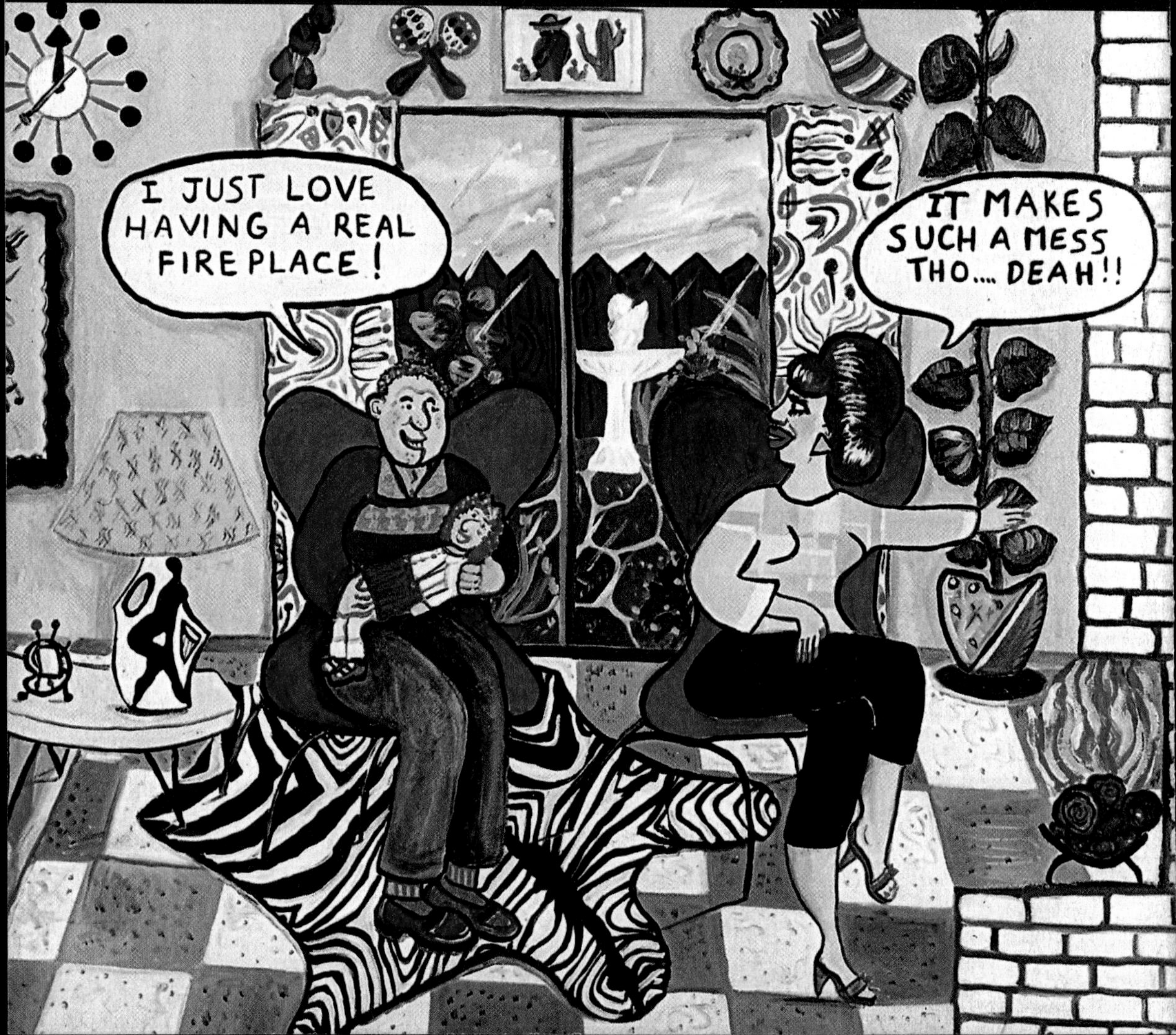

I JUST LOVE HAVING A REAL FIREPLACE!
IT MAKES SUCH A MESS THO.... DEAH!!

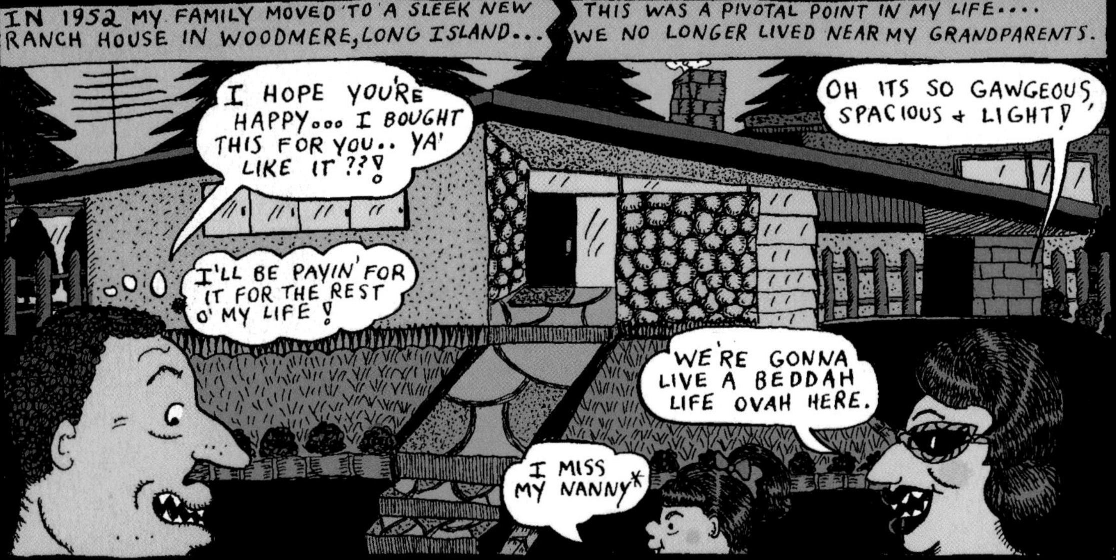
IN 1952 MY FAMILY MOVED TO A SLEEK NEW RANCH HOUSE IN WOODMERE, LONG ISLAND...
THIS WAS A PIVOTAL POINT IN MY LIFE.... WE NO LONGER LIVED NEAR MY GRANDPARENTS.
I HOPE YOU'RE HAPPY... I BOUGHT THIS FOR YOU.. YA' LIKE IT ??!
I'LL BE PAYIN' FOR IT FOR THE REST O' MY LIFE!
OH ITS SO GAWGEOUS, SPACIOUS + LIGHT!
WE'RE GONNA LIVE A BEDDAH LIFE OVAH HERE.
I MISS MY NANNY*

* MY MATERNAL GRANDMOTHER

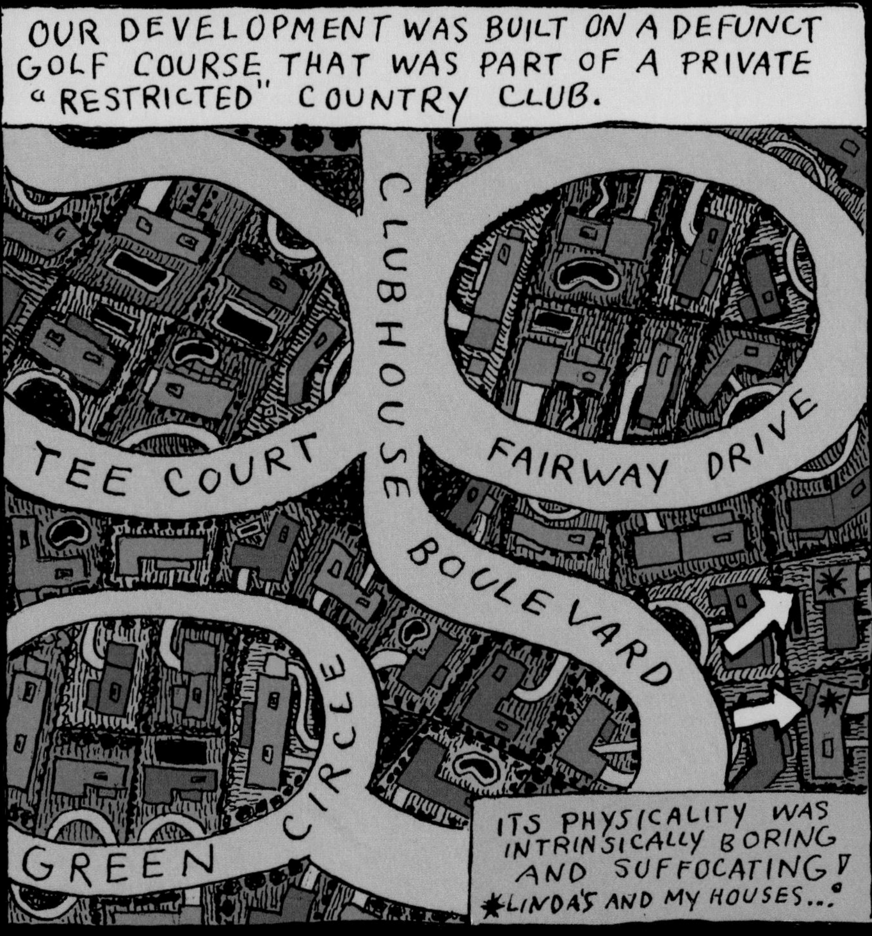
OUR DEVELOPMENT WAS BUILT ON A DEFUNCT GOLF COURSE THAT WAS PART OF A PRIVATE "RESTRICTED" COUNTRY CLUB.
CLUBHOUSE
TEE COURT
FAIRWAY DRIVE
BOULEVARD
GREEN
CIRCLE
ITS PHYSICALITY WAS INTRINSICALLY BORING AND SUFFOCATING!
*LINDA'S AND MY HOUSES...!

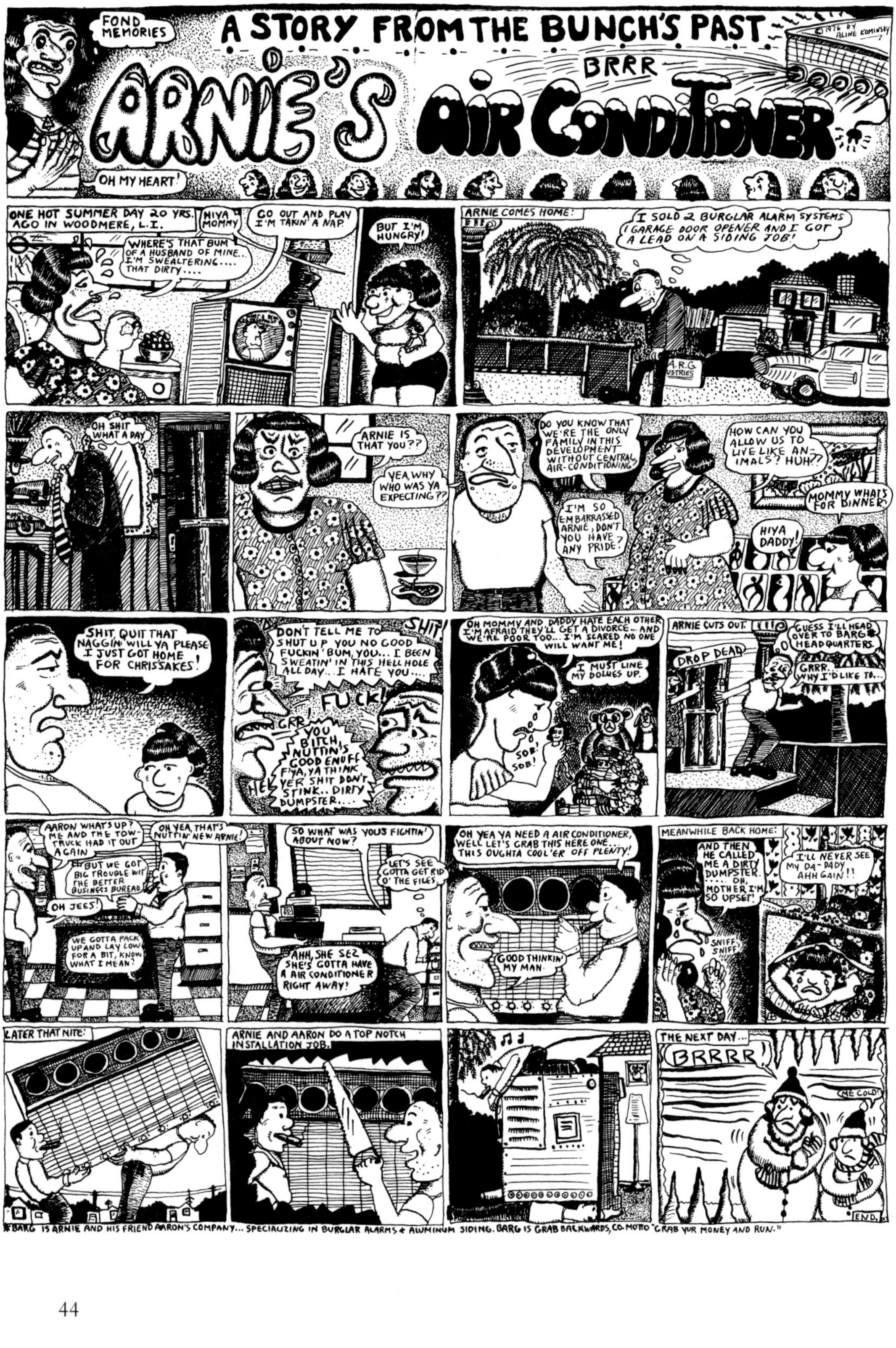
FOND MEMORIES
A STORY FROM THE BUNCH'S PAST
© 1976 BY ALINE KOMINSKY
BRRR
ARNIE'S AIR CONDITIONER
OH MY HEART!
ONE HOT SUMMER DAY 20 YRS. AGO IN WOODMERE, L.I.
HIYA MOMMY
GO OUT AND PLAY I'M TAKIN' A NAP.
BUT I'M HUNGRY!
WHERE'S THAT BUM OF A HUSBAND OF MINE.. I'M SWEALTERING.... THAT DIRTY....
ARNIE COMES HOME:
I SOLD 2 BURGLAR ALARM SYSTEMS 1 GARAGE DOOR OPENER AND I GOT A LEAD ON A SIDING JOB!
OH SHIT WHAT A DAY
ARNIE IS THAT YOU??
YEA, WHY WHO WAS YA EXPECTING??
DO YOU KNOW THAT WE'RE THE ONLY FAMILY IN THIS DEVELOPMENT WITHOUT CENTRAL AIR-CONDITIONING
I'M SO EMBARRASSED ARNIE, DON'T YOU HAVE ANY PRIDE?
HOW CAN YOU ALLOW US TO LIVE LIKE ANIMALS? HUH??
MOMMY WHAT'S FOR DINNER
HIYA DADDY!
SHIT, QUIT THAT NAGGIN' WILL YA PLEASE I JUST GOT HOME FOR CHRISSAKES!
DON'T TELL ME TO SHUT UP YOU NO GOOD FUCKIN' BUM, YOU... I BEEN SWEATIN' IN THIS HELL HOLE ALL DAY... I HATE YOU....
SHIT!
FUCK!
GRR
YOU BITCH, NUTTIN'S GOOD ENUFF F'YA, YA THINK YER SHIT DON'T STINK.. DIRTY DUMPSTER....
HEH
OH MOMMY AND DADDY HATE EACH OTHER I'M AFRAID THEY'LL GET A DIVORCE... AND WE'RE POOR TOO... I'M SCARED NO ONE WILL WANT ME!
I MUST LINE MY DOLLIES UP.
SOB! SOB!
ARNIE CUTS OUT.
DROP DEAD
GUESS I'LL HEAD OVER TO BARG* HEADQUARTERS.
GRRR. WHY I'D LIKE TO...
AARON WHAT'S UP? ME AND THE TOW-TRUCK HAD IT OUT AGAIN
OH YEA, THAT'S NUTTIN' NEW ARNIE!
BUT WE GOT BIG TROUBLE WIT THE BETTER BUSINESS BUREAU
OH JEES!
WE GOTTA PACK UP AND LAY LOW FOR A BIT, KNOW WHAT I MEAN?
SO WHAT WAS YOUS FIGHTIN' ABOUT NOW?
LET'S SEE GOTTA GET RID O' THE FILES
AHH, SHE SEZ SHE'S GOTTA HAVE A AIR CONDITIONER RIGHT AWAY!
OH YEA YA NEED A AIR CONDITIONER, WELL LET'S GRAB THIS HERE ONE... THIS OUGHTA COOL 'ER OFF PLENTY!
GOOD THINKIN' MY MAN.
MEANWHILE BACK HOME:
AND THEN HE CALLED ME A DIRTY DUMPSTER. .... OH, MOTHER I'M SO UPSET!
SNIFF, SNIFF
I'LL NEVER SEE MY DA-DADY AHH GAIN!!
LATER THAT NITE:
ARNIE AND AARON DO A TOP NOTCH INSTALLATION JOB.
THE NEXT DAY...
BRRRR
ME COLD!
END.

*BARG IS ARNIE AND HIS FRIEND AARON'S COMPANY... SPECIALIZING IN BURGLAR ALARMS & ALUMINUM SIDING. BARG IS GRAB BACKWARDS, CO. MOTTO "GRAB YUR MONEY AND RUN."

Nervous wrecks!

When I was a kid, clubs were openly restricted (i.e. 'no Jews allowed'), so the Jews had their own prestigious versions of these hideous institutions, complete with their own set of pretentious rules and unspoken codes.

My parents were totally out of their league in this environment. Arnie never managed to earn a decent living once his business with my grandfather went belly up, and as a result my spoiled mother became a nervous wreck. She started to get enormously fat and resorted to taking powerful diet pills, combined with downers to help her sleep.

These were easily had through Dr. Gordon L. Green, a local quack. My brother and I would find drawers full of pills and we helped ourselves to them. I would take the speed and my brother the downers. Thus began a lifetime of substance abuse for both of us.

I learned very early on how to please the adults around me—as my daughter now says, I learned to "throw 'em a bone." I was the first child, grandchild and great-grandchild, adored by all my relatives and doted on by aunts, uncles, great-aunts and uncles, cousins and neighbors. I craved praise and quickly learned how to get it, playing the model little girl with ease. Life at home with my parents was something else! There, everything was scary and unpredictable.

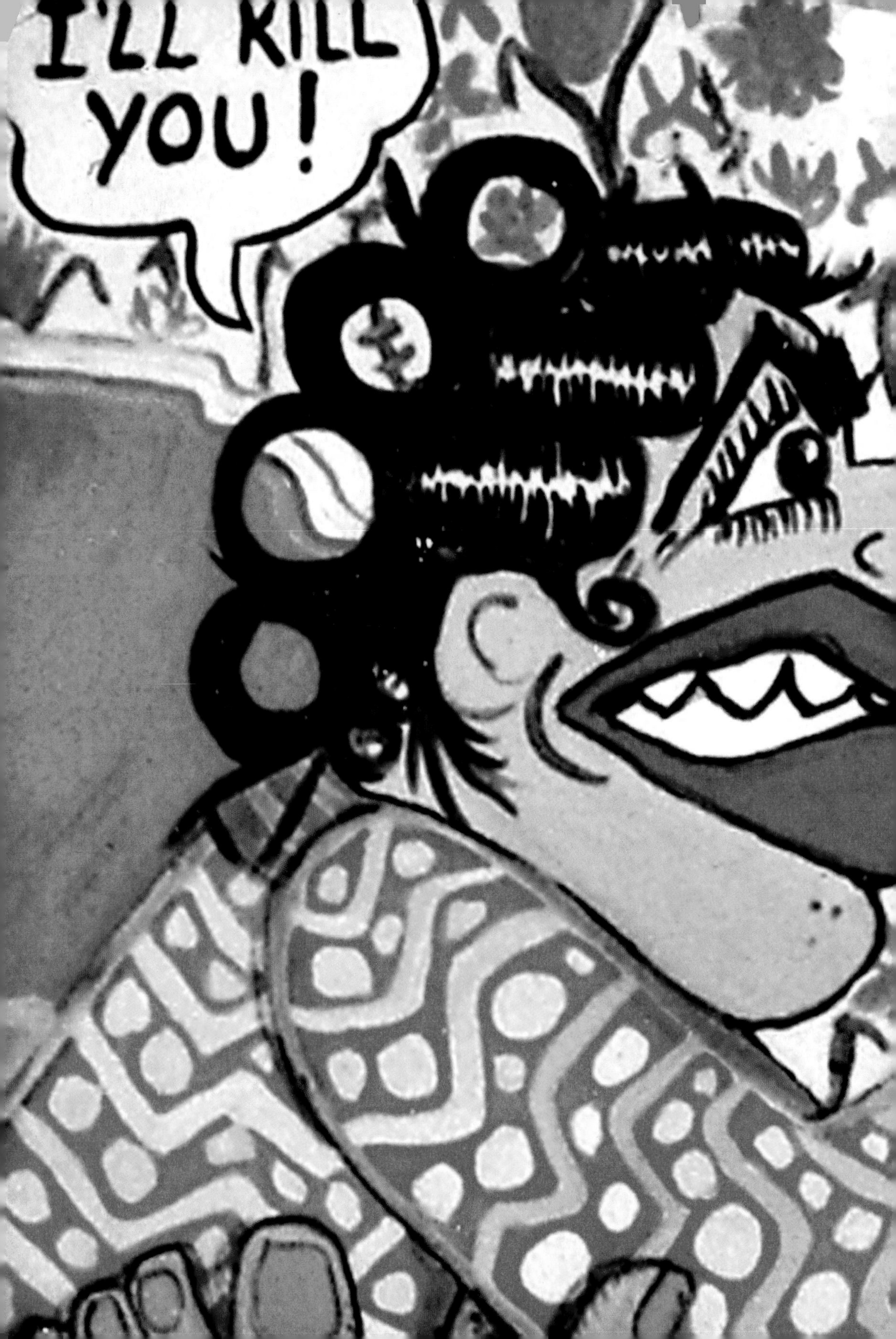
I'LL KILL YOU!

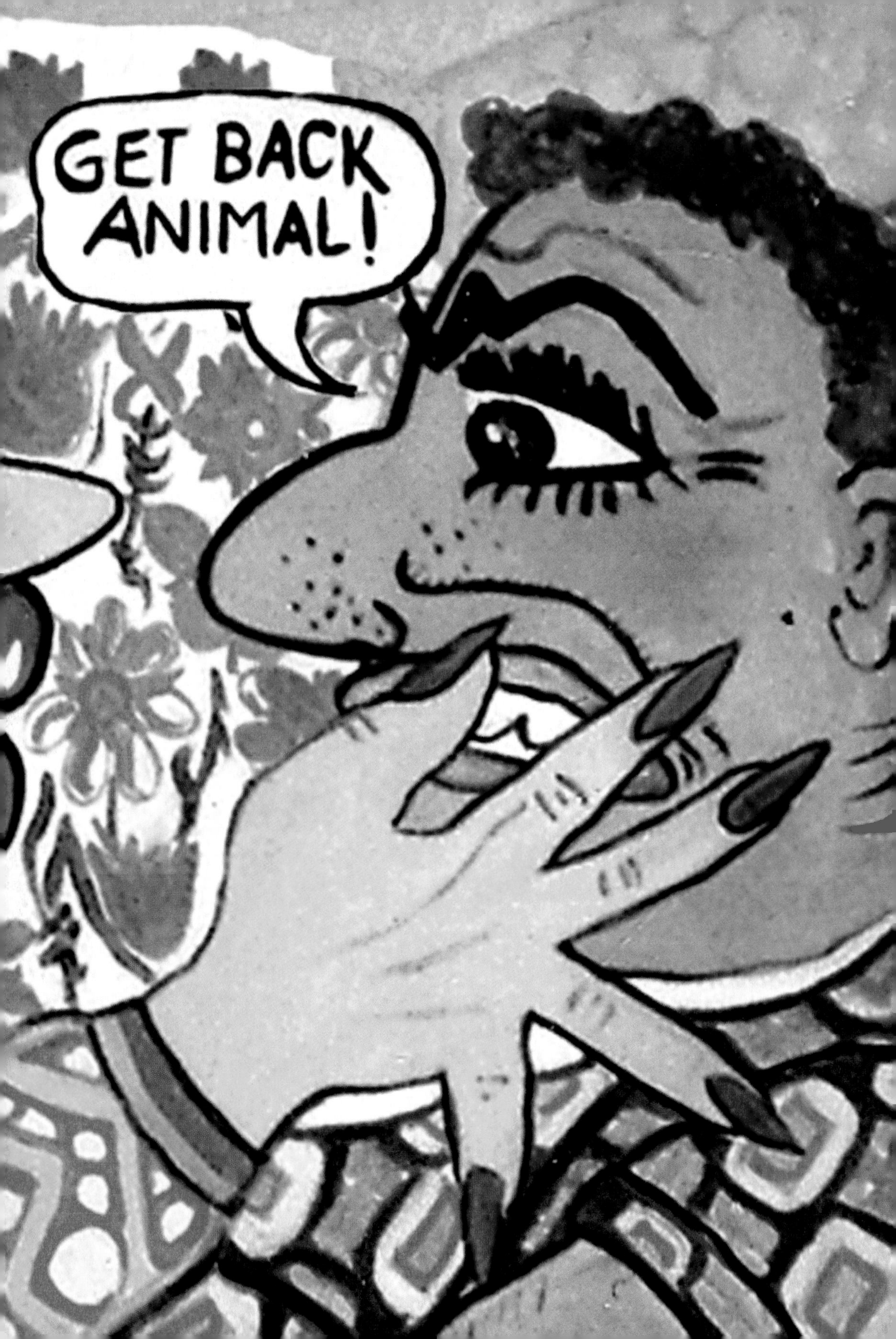
GET BACK ANIMAL!

Deep into the valley of the dolls

During this same period of awakening higher consciousness I became obsessed with dolls. I was especially obsessed with Madame Alexander dolls. I could always manipulate my grandma into buying me the latest model. These dolls were very expensive and beautifully dressed, with fabulous shoes and accessories. They came in various sizes with different color hair, but they all had the same face. I still have many of them. I saved them for my daughter, Sophie, but they weren't her favorites at all. I still look at them now, and experience a certain thrill from gazing into their empty, wide-eyed, fat, rosy-cheeked perfect little prim faces!

I vividly remember the excitement and love I felt for each new acquisition. I created rooms for them on shelves in my bedroom with store-bought furniture and furniture I made out of painted cardboard and fabric. I developed elaborate daily rituals with my dolls. In the morning I would get them out of bed and put them in various rooms to perform their daily activities. I would make fake food for them and talk for them.

They had names and distinctly different personalities. There were all sorts of intrigues, crises, and shifting alliances among them. At night I had to put them all to bed before I could go to bed myself, and could not possibly sleep if my dolls were not in their appropriate beds (slightly obsessive/compulsive, eh?). I also had to line up all my stuffed animals in certain precise positions every night so that I could relax enough to sleep. I was an anxious little neurotic … not so different from the "adult" me.

I still possess a rich imaginary world that enables me to enjoy being alone. I don't exactly talk for my dolls any longer, but I am comforted by their presence and derive an inordinate amount of satisfaction from rearranging my knick-knacks. I continue to have escapist fantasies that involve magic worlds, particularly an underwater world where I am a mermaid and I can breathe and swim freely. Perhaps this is because I was born near the ocean and spent a lot of time diving off my grandfather's boat. I won't spend too much time trying to figure this out, but I have done a lot of paintings with myself as the femme fatale sirène.

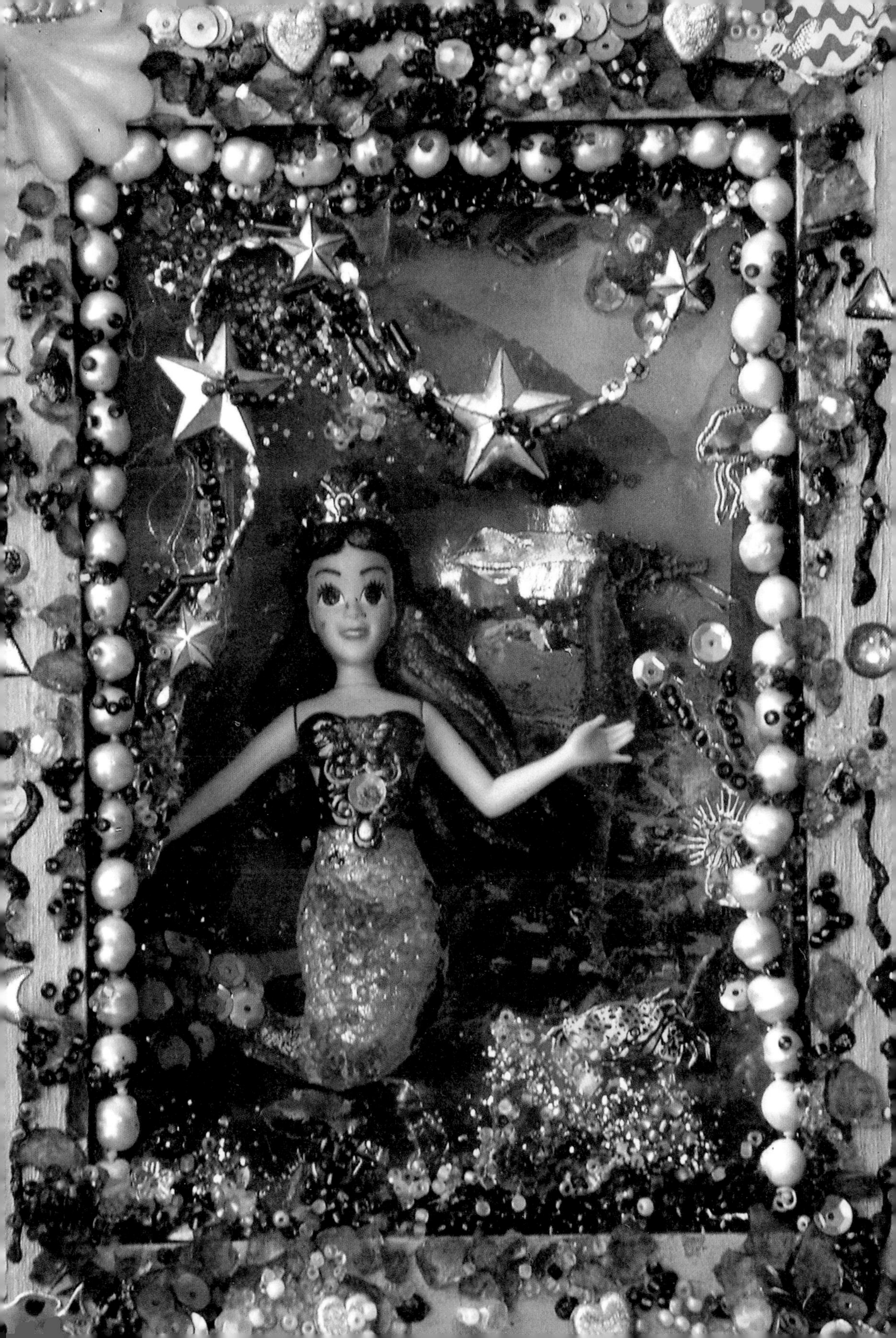

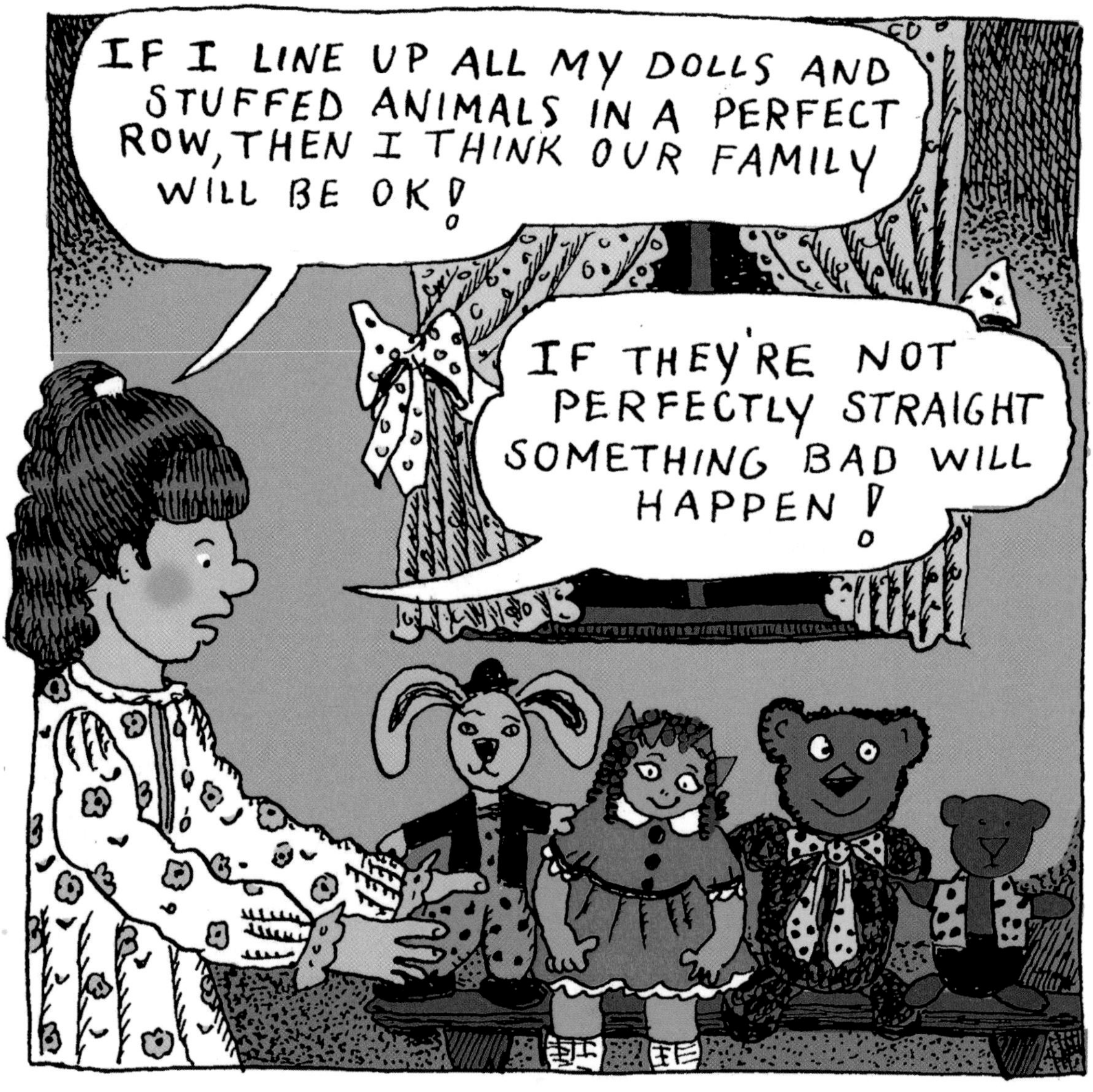
IF I LINE UP ALL MY DOLLS AND STUFFED ANIMALS IN A PERFECT ROW, THEN I THINK OUR FAMILY WILL BE OK!
IF THEY'RE NOT PERFECTLY STRAIGHT SOMETHING BAD WILL HAPPEN!

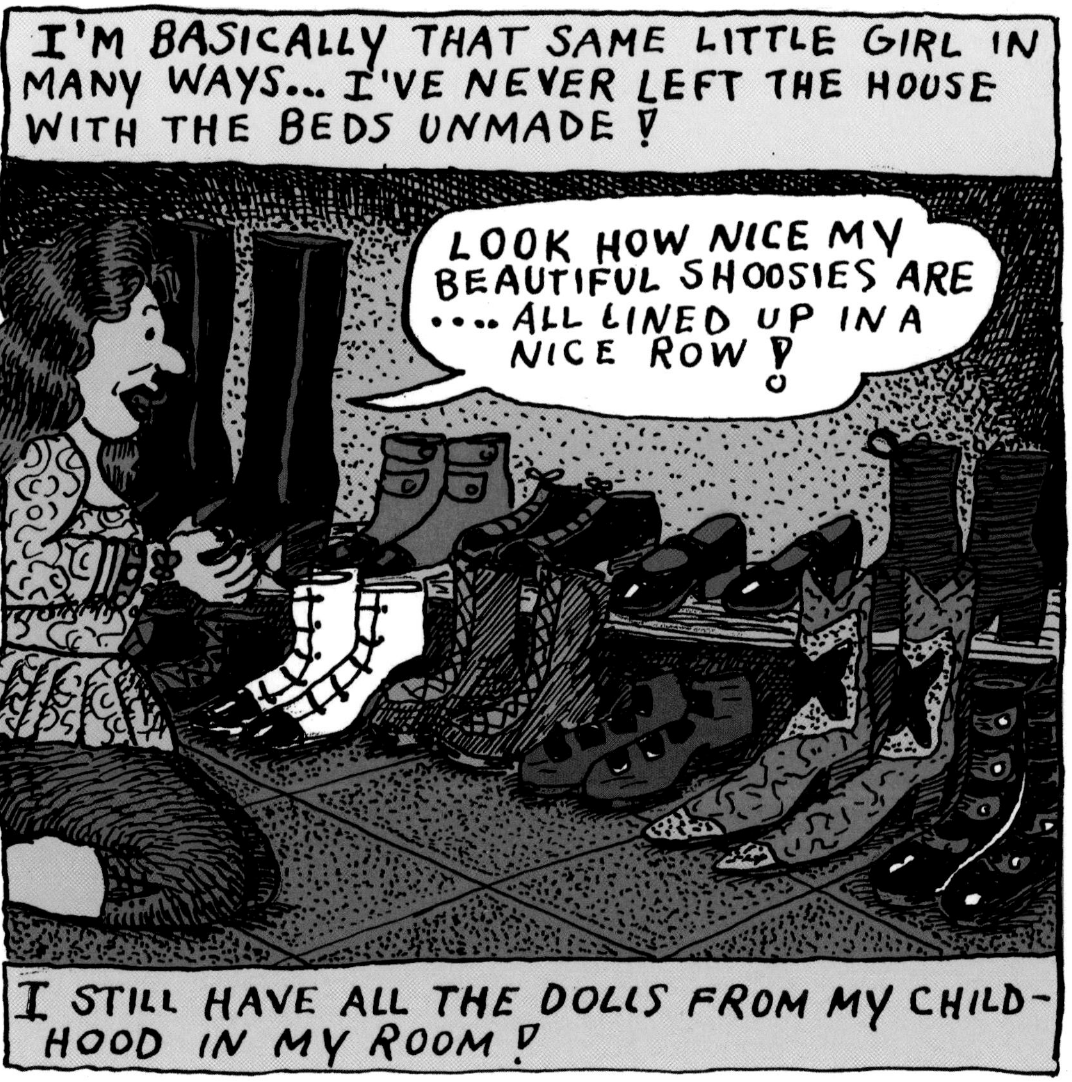

I'M BASICALLY THAT SAME LITTLE GIRL IN MANY WAYS... I'VE NEVER LEFT THE HOUSE WITH THE BEDS UNMADE!
LOOK HOW NICE MY BEAUTIFUL SHOOSIES ARE .... ALL LINED UP IN A NICE ROW!
I STILL HAVE ALL THE DOLLS FROM MY CHILD-HOOD IN MY ROOM!

My brother was in worse shape ...

At school, I was the perfect "straight-A" student, eliciting tearfully admiring accounts of what a smart, well-behaved pupil I was from my young, idealistic female teachers. My parents were all too happy to take credit for my achievements as proof of their excellent parenting and superior intelligence. They grew smug and began to expect absolute perfection from me, with no effort or input on their part. At the time, my father was selling *Encyclopedia Americana* door-to-door—can you imagine a more low-grade, humiliating job? Anyway, he used to pay me for every "A" on my report cards. He would then use them as a sales pitch to bamboozle poor people into buying his encyclopedias—what better way to offer their children a chance to succeed like his brilliant daughter had, thanks to his encyclopedias.

Unfortunately for my brother Alex (we called him Akkie) things were entirely different for him. Akkie had some kind of neurological problem, probably dyslexia or something of that nature, but he was very intelligent and hyper-sensitive. He was born with a strange-looking, potentially dangerous birthmark in the middle of his back that had to be removed through a series of painful treatments using dry ice. I'm convinced that these repeated torture-sessions so early in his life made Alex fearful and distrusting. Who can blame him, what a welcome into this hell life, jeezis!

Akkie was a very beautiful child (he still is very handsome) but he was extremely shy and secretive. There was something dark about him. He was also a miserable student, no doubt due to his undiagnosed dyslexia. He had a lot of trouble reading and writing, and this was especially disastrous on Long Island in a school filled with hyper-aggressive, upward-striving, competitive little Jews, just dying to get their hands up there and be the first with the right answer!

Alex "went under" very early in life. Our parents, spoiled by my scholastic success, resorted to every form of verbal abuse, humiliation and threats to try to make him succeed. He endured endless hours of my mother's horrific screaming and cursing. It was a true horror show that I also had to listen to, but felt helpless to do anything about. To this day, I still feel bad that I couldn't intervene to help him, but I'm doing a pretty good job of making up for it now!

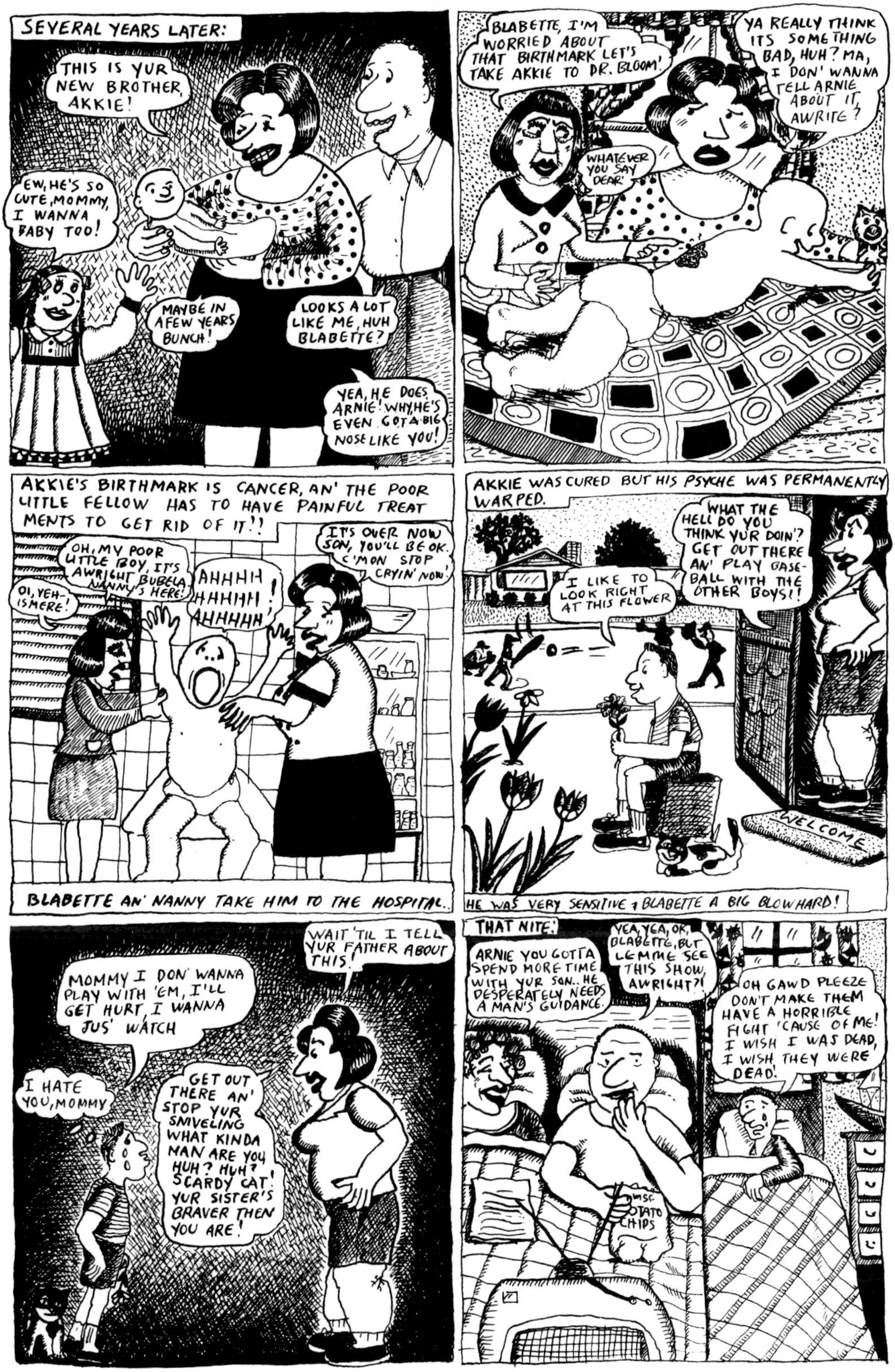
SEVERAL YEARS LATER:
THIS IS YUR NEW BROTHER, AKKIE!
EW, HE'S SO CUTE, MOMMY, I WANNA BABY TOO!
MAYBE IN A FEW YEARS BUNCH!
LOOKS A LOT LIKE ME, HUH BLABETTE?
YEA, HE DOES, ARNIE! WHY, HE'S EVEN GOT A BIG NOSE LIKE YOU!
BLABETTE, I'M WORRIED ABOUT THAT BIRTHMARK LET'S TAKE AKKIE TO DR. BLOOM!
YA REALLY THINK ITS SOMETHING BAD, HUH? MA, I DON' WANNA TELL ARNIE ABOUT IT, AWRITE?
WHATEVER YOU SAY DEAR
AKKIE'S BIRTHMARK IS CANCER, AN' THE POOR LITTLE FELLOW HAS TO HAVE PAINFUL TREATMENTS TO GET RID OF IT!!
OH, MY POOR LITTLE BOY, IT'S AWRIGHT BUBELA NANNY'S HERE!
OI, YEH-ISMERE!
AHHHHH HHHHH! AHHHHH!
IT'S OVER NOW SON, YOU'LL BE OK. C'MON STOP CRYIN' NOW!
BLABETTE AN' NANNY TAKE HIM TO THE HOSPITAL.
AKKIE WAS CURED BUT HIS PSYCHE WAS PERMANENTLY WARPED.
I LIKE TO LOOK RIGHT AT THIS FLOWER
WHAT THE HELL DO YOU THINK YUR DOIN'? GET OUT THERE AN' PLAY BASEBALL WITH THE OTHER BOYS!!
WELCOME
HE WAS VERY SENSITIVE & BLABETTE A BIG BLOWHARD!
MOMMY I DON' WANNA PLAY WITH 'EM, I'LL GET HURT, I WANNA JUS' WATCH
WAIT 'TIL I TELL YUR FATHER ABOUT THIS!
I HATE YOU, MOMMY
GET OUT THERE AN' STOP YUR SNIVELING WHAT KINDA MAN ARE YOU HUH? HUH? SCARDY CAT! YUR SISTER'S BRAVER THEN YOU ARE!
THAT NITE:
ARNIE YOU GOTTA SPEND MORE TIME WITH YUR SON.. HE DESPERATELY NEEDS A MAN'S GUIDANCE.
YEA, YEA, OK, BLABETTE, BUT LEMME SEE THIS SHOW, AWRIGHT?!
OH GAWD PLEEZE DON'T MAKE THEM HAVE A HORRIBLE FIGHT 'CAUSE OF ME! I WISH I WAS DEAD, I WISH THEY WERE DEAD!
POTATO CHIPS

THIS WAS A GLORIOUS STATE OF GRACE FOR ME WHEN I WAS STILL THE ONLY GRANDCHILD AND I REIGNED SUPREME IN MY GRANDMOTHER'S DOMAINE..

YOU'LL ALWAYS BE MY PRINCESS, BUBELLA!

MY LIFE DETERIORATED STEADILY... BUT I ATTRIBUTE MY HEALTHY EGO TO THIS GREAT START!

IN WOODMERE MY PARENTS GOT HEAVILY INTO "MAMBO PATIO LIFE" MY DAD ARNIE WAS BIG ON BAR-B-QUES.

THIS'LL BE READY IN A SECOND... REAL CHARCOAL GRILLED FLAVOR!

LIGHTER FLUID

MY PARENTS BECAME FRIENDS WITH THE DIAMOND FAMILY. THEY HAD TWO SONS; GEORGIE AND STEVIE.

LET'S MAKE A FORT, AFTER..

YEAH. OK

HEY LENNY, HAVE ANOTHAH MAI-TAI!

WE ATE CHARRED BURGERS WHILE THE GROWN UPS DRANK EXOTIC COCTAILS..

HOWSE ABOUT SOME MUSIC?

YEAH.. PUT ON MAMBO ITALIANO!

THERE WAS KAY, LEONARD, ARNIE + BLABETTE...

HEY MAMBO... MAMBO ITALIANO...

THIS WAS MY FIRST POSITIVE VIEW OF OCCASIONAL SUBSTANCE ABUSE!

HEY THIS IS A NEAT FORT..

YEAH BUT MY MOMMY'LL MAKE ME TAKE IT DOWN WHEN SHE'S SOBER.

WHAT'S SOBER?

OH!

THEIR NORMAL MEAN SELVES.

WISE POTATO CHIPS

CHOCO CHIP

More psychotic behavior

My mother vented all her feelings of failure and frustration in the screaming bouts she directed towards my brother. She had the meanest, scariest voice. I remember her screaming, almost like in an opera. There would be a gradual buildup of energy and passion which would reach a crescendo with an angry, hideous burst of emotion. This was especially hurtful and ego-destroying. Then came a lull with quieter, softer insulting and a litany of crimes committed, followed by a gradual rebuilding of force, more explosions, and eventually (it took a while because she was probably peaking on amphetamines) exhaustion.

Sometimes she would be interrupted by a phone call or a neighbor stopping by; she would instantly and miraculously change into a chatty, charming and totally normal person, as though everything was just beautiful! This ability to turn her emotions on and off fascinated and horrified me at the same time, and made me distrust and always question other people's motives.

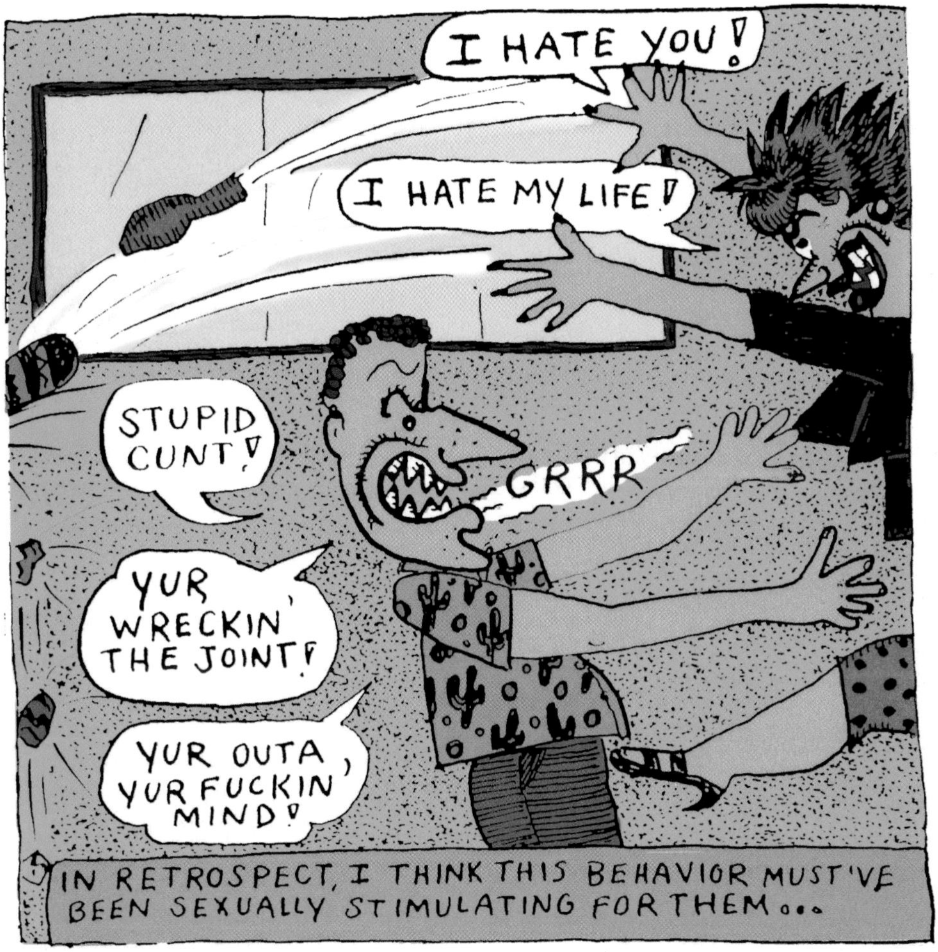
I HATE YOU!
I HATE MY LIFE!
STUPID CUNT!
GRRR
YUR WRECKIN' THE JOINT!
YUR OUTA YUR FUCKIN' MIND!
IN RETROSPECT, I THINK THIS BEHAVIOR MUST'VE BEEN SEXUALLY STIMULATING FOR THEM...

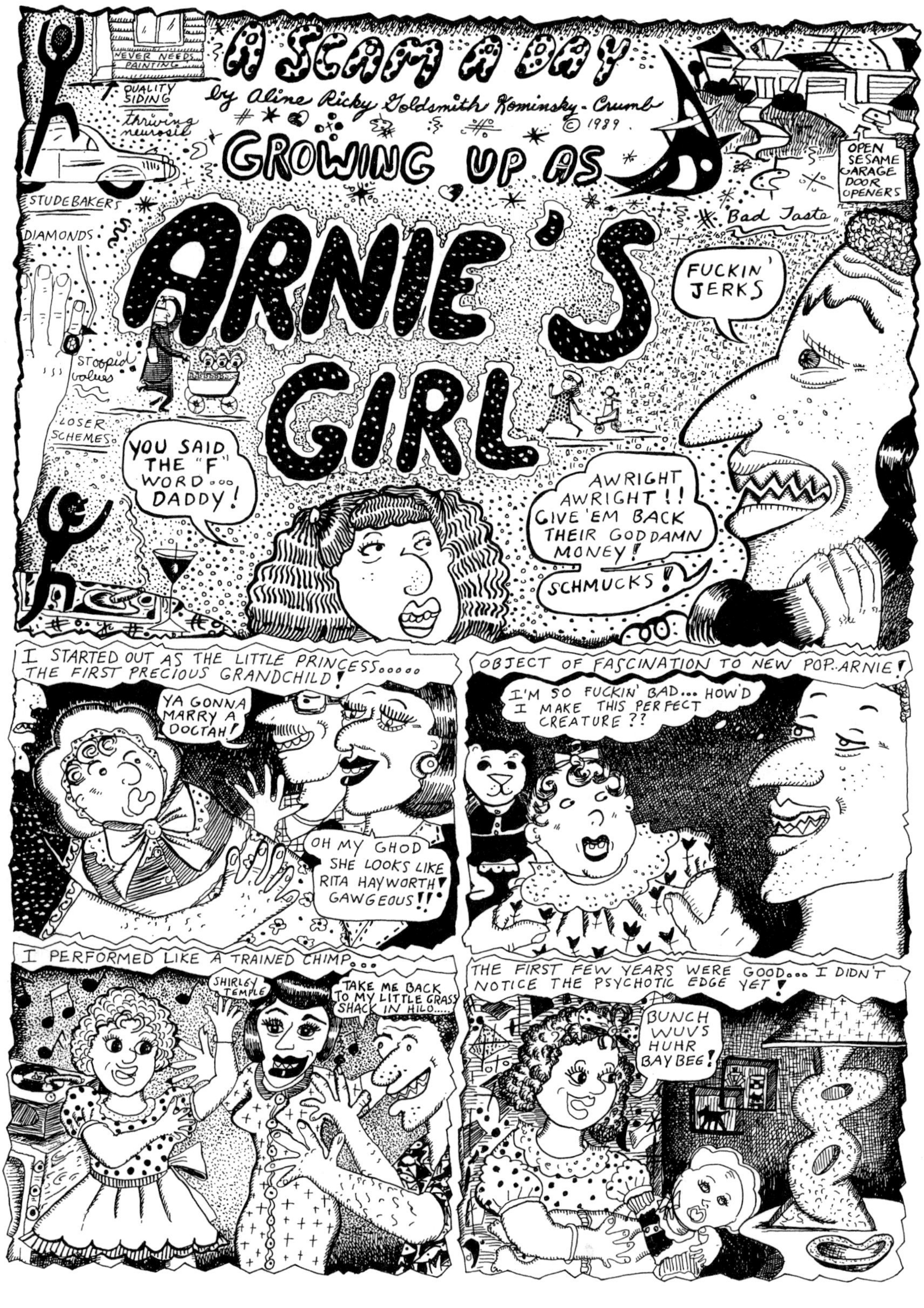
A SCAM A DAY
by Aline Ricky Goldsmith Kominsky-Crumb
© 1989
NEVER NEEDS PAINTING
QUALITY SIDING
thriving neurosis
GROWING UP AS
ARNIE'S GIRL
OPEN SESAME GARAGE DOOR OPENERS
STUDEBAKERS
DIAMONDS
Bad Taste
Stoopid values
LOSER SCHEMES
FUCKIN' JERKS
YOU SAID THE "F" WORD... DADDY!
AWRIGHT AWRIGHT!! GIVE 'EM BACK THEIR GODDAMN MONEY!
SCHMUCKS!
I STARTED OUT AS THE LITTLE PRINCESS..... THE FIRST PRECIOUS GRANDCHILD!
YA GONNA MARRY A DOCTAH!
OH MY GHOD SHE LOOKS LIKE RITA HAYWORTH! GAWGEOUS!!
OBJECT OF FASCINATION TO NEW POP ARNIE!
I'M SO FUCKIN' BAD... HOW'D I MAKE THIS PERFECT CREATURE??
I PERFORMED LIKE A TRAINED CHIMP...
SHIRLEY TEMPLE
TAKE ME BACK TO MY LITTLE GRASS SHACK IN HILO...
THE FIRST FEW YEARS WERE GOOD... I DIDN'T NOTICE THE PSYCHOTIC EDGE YET!
BUNCH WUVS HUHR BAYBEE!

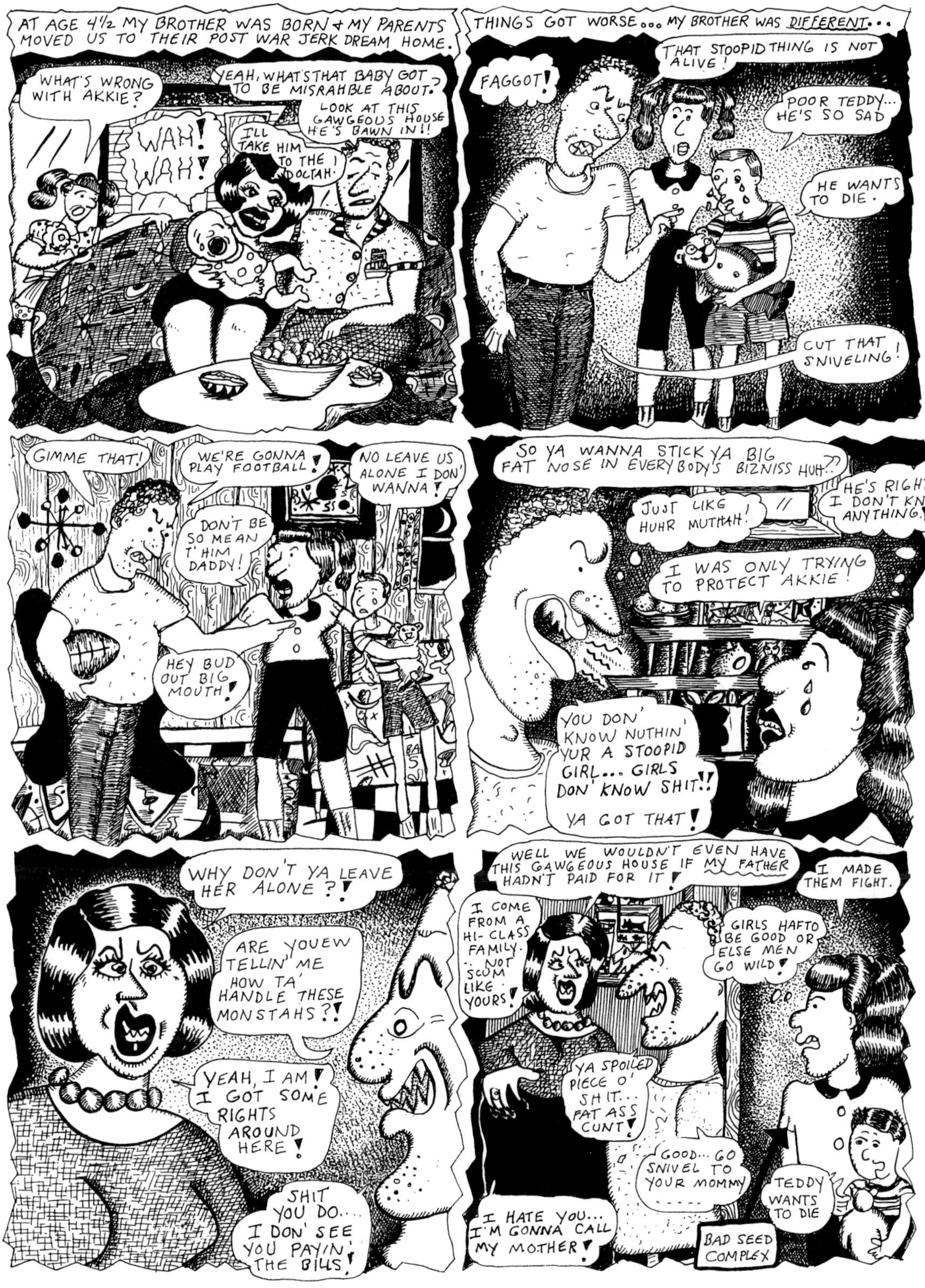
AT AGE 4½ MY BROTHER WAS BORN & MY PARENTS MOVED US TO THEIR POST WAR JERK DREAM HOME.
WHAT'S WRONG WITH AKKIE?
YEAH, WHAT'S THAT BABY GOT TO BE MISRAHBLE ABOUT?
LOOK AT THIS GAWGEOUS HOUSE HE'S BAWN IN!!
WAH! WAH!
I'LL TAKE HIM TO THE DOCTAH.
THINGS GOT WORSE... MY BROTHER WAS DIFFERENT...
FAGGOT!
THAT STOOPID THING IS NOT ALIVE!
POOR TEDDY... HE'S SO SAD
HE WANTS TO DIE.
CUT THAT SNIVELING!
GIMME THAT!
WE'RE GONNA PLAY FOOTBALL!
NO LEAVE US ALONE I DON' WANNA!
DON'T BE SO MEAN T'HIM DADDY!
HEY BUD OUT BIG MOUTH!
SO YA WANNA STICK YA BIG FAT NOSE IN EVERYBODY'S BIZNISS HUH??
JUST LIKE HUHR MUTHAH!
HE'S RIGHT I DON'T KNOW ANYTHING!
I WAS ONLY TRYING TO PROTECT AKKIE!
YOU DON' KNOW NUTHIN' YUR A STOOPID GIRL... GIRLS DON' KNOW SHIT!!
YA GOT THAT!
WHY DON'T YA LEAVE HER ALONE?!
ARE YOUEW TELLIN' ME HOW TA' HANDLE THESE MONSTAHS?!
YEAH, I AM! I GOT SOME RIGHTS AROUND HERE!
SHIT YOU DO... I DON' SEE YOU PAYIN' THE BILLS!
WELL WE WOULDN'T EVEN HAVE THIS GAWGEOUS HOUSE IF MY FATHER HADN'T PAID FOR IT!
I MADE THEM FIGHT.
I COME FROM A HI-CLASS FAMILY... NOT SCUM LIKE YOURS!
GIRLS HAFTO BE GOOD OR ELSE MEN GO WILD!
YA SPOILED PIECE O' SHIT... FAT ASS CUNT!
GOOD... GO SNIVEL TO YOUR MOMMY
I HATE YOU... I'M GONNA CALL MY MOTHER!
BAD SEED COMPLEX
TEDDY WANTS TO DIE

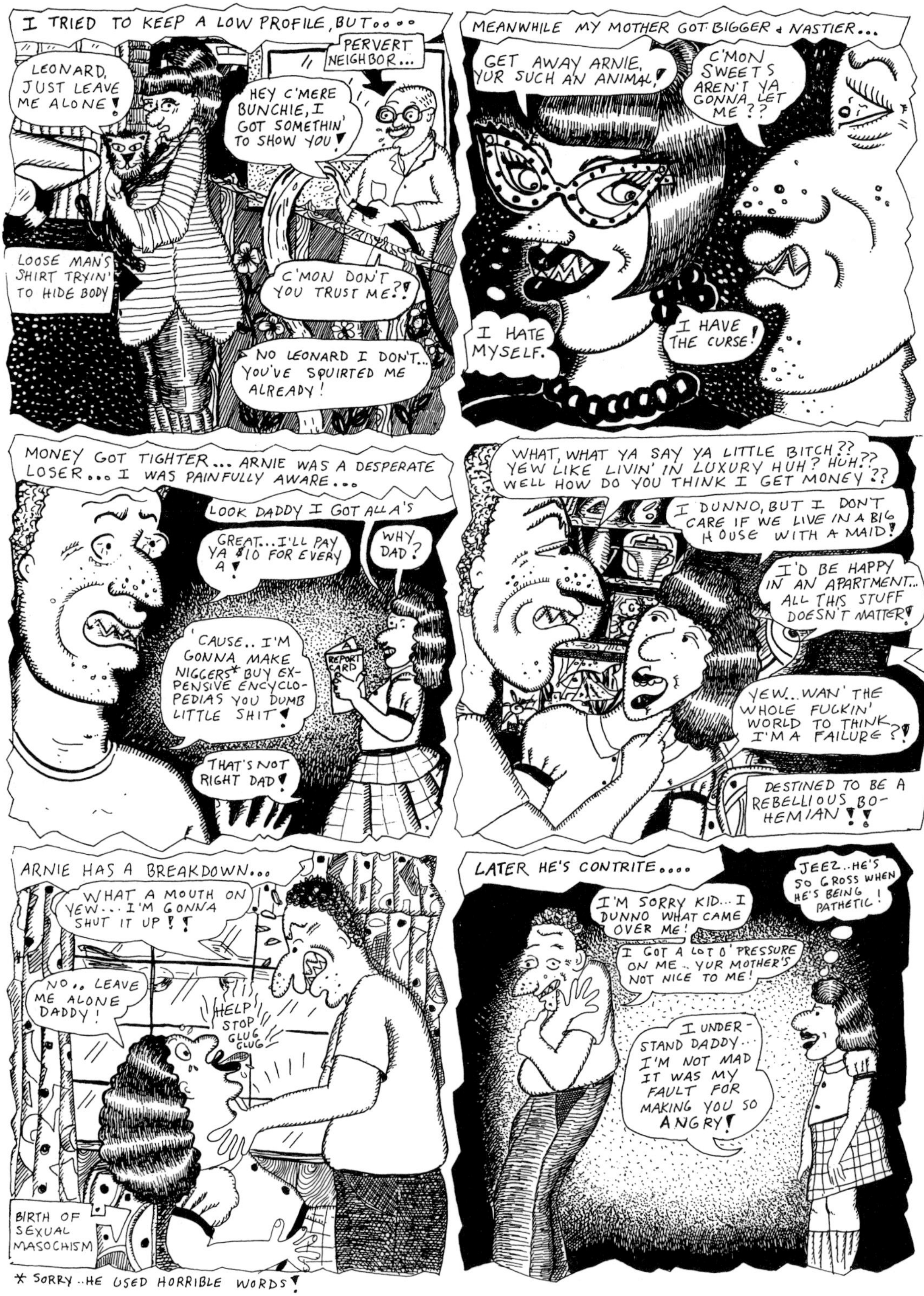
I TRIED TO KEEP A LOW PROFILE, BUT....
LEONARD, JUST LEAVE ME ALONE!
PERVERT NEIGHBOR...
HEY C'MERE BUNCHIE, I GOT SOMETHIN' TO SHOW YOU!
LOOSE MAN'S SHIRT TRYIN' TO HIDE BODY
C'MON DON'T YOU TRUST ME?!
NO LEONARD I DON'T... YOU'VE SQUIRTED ME ALREADY!
MEANWHILE MY MOTHER GOT BIGGER & NASTIER...
GET AWAY ARNIE, YUR SUCH AN ANIMAL!
C'MON SWEETS AREN'T YA GONNA LET ME??
I HATE MYSELF.
I HAVE THE CURSE!
MONEY GOT TIGHTER... ARNIE WAS A DESPERATE LOSER... I WAS PAINFULLY AWARE...
LOOK DADDY I GOT ALL A'S
GREAT...I'LL PAY YA $10 FOR EVERY A!
WHY DAD?
REPORT CARD
'CAUSE.. I'M GONNA MAKE NIGGERS* BUY EXPENSIVE ENCYCLOPEDIAS YOU DUMB LITTLE SHIT!
THAT'S NOT RIGHT DAD!
WHAT, WHAT YA SAY YA LITTLE BITCH?? YEW LIKE LIVIN' IN LUXURY HUH? HUH?? WELL HOW DO YOU THINK I GET MONEY??
I DUNNO, BUT I DON'T CARE IF WE LIVE IN A BIG HOUSE WITH A MAID!
I'D BE HAPPY IN AN APARTMENT... ALL THIS STUFF DOESN'T MATTER!
YEW.. WAN' THE WHOLE FUCKIN' WORLD TO THINK I'M A FAILURE?!
DESTINED TO BE A REBELLIOUS BOHEMIAN!!
ARNIE HAS A BREAKDOWN...
WHAT A MOUTH ON YEW... I'M GONNA SHUT IT UP!!
NO.. LEAVE ME ALONE DADDY!
HELP STOP GLUG GLUG
BIRTH OF SEXUAL MASOCHISM
LATER HE'S CONTRITE....
JEEZ..HE'S SO GROSS WHEN HE'S BEING PATHETIC!
I'M SORRY KID... I DUNNO WHAT CAME OVER ME!
I GOT A LOT O' PRESSURE ON ME.. YUR MOTHER'S NOT NICE TO ME!
I UNDERSTAND DADDY.. I'M NOT MAD IT WAS MY FAULT FOR MAKING YOU SO ANGRY!

* SORRY..HE USED HORRIBLE WORDS!

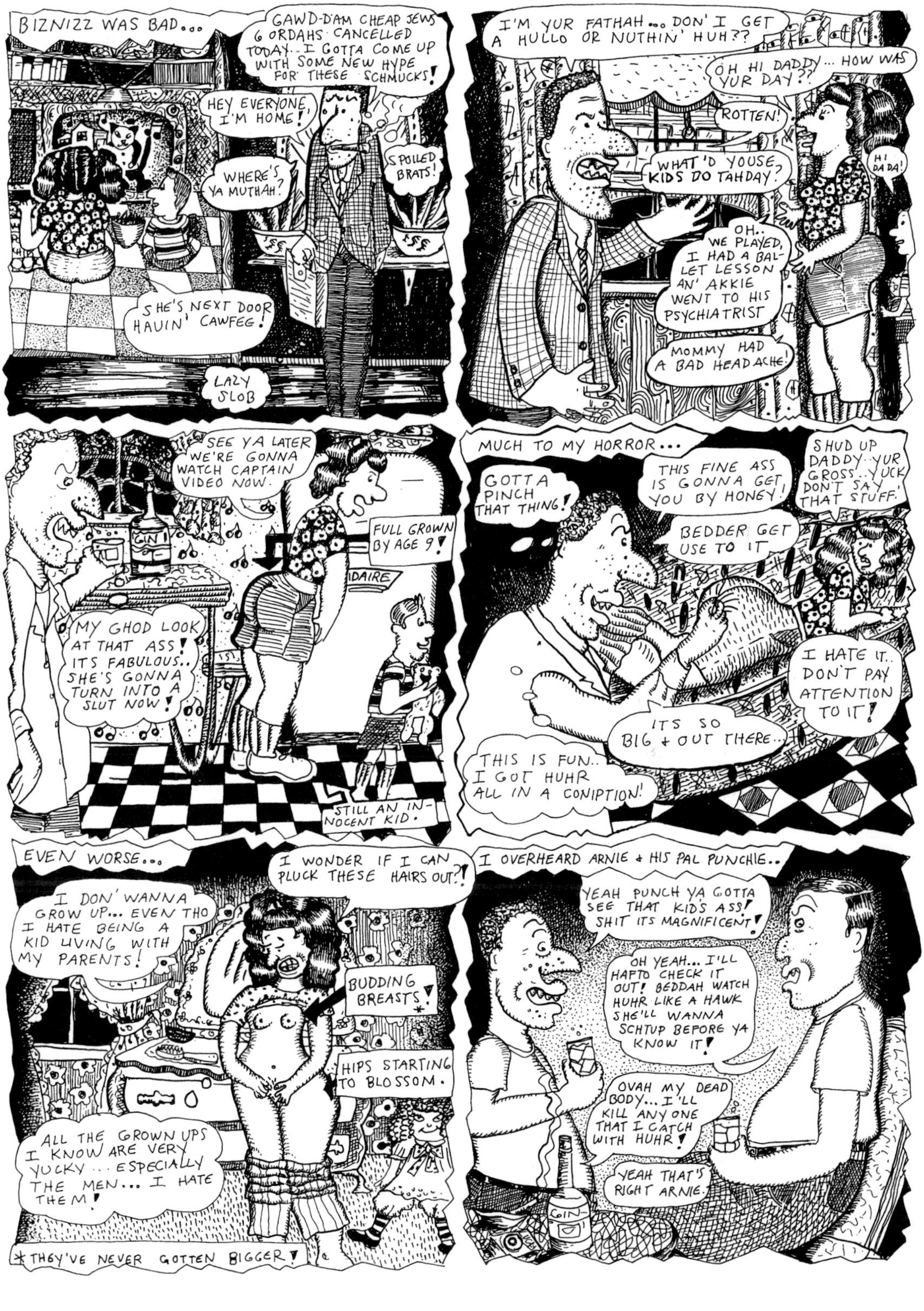
BIZNIZZ WAS BAD...
GAWD-DAM CHEAP JEWS 6 ORDAHS CANCELLED TODAY.. I GOTTA COME UP WITH SOME NEW HYPE FOR THESE SCHMUCKS!
HEY EVERYONE, I'M HOME!
WHERE'S YA MUTHAH?
SPOILED BRATS!
SHE'S NEXT DOOR HAVIN' CAWFEE!
LAZY SLOB
I'M YUR FATHAH... DON' I GET A HULLO OR NUTHIN' HUH??
OH HI DADDY... HOW WAS YUR DAY??
ROTTEN!
WHAT'D YOUSE KIDS DO TAHDAY?
HI DA DA!
OH.. WE PLAYED, I HAD A BAL-LET LESSON AN' AKKIE WENT TO HIS PSYCHIATRIST
MOMMY HAD A BAD HEADACHE!
SEE YA LATER WE'RE GONNA WATCH CAPTAIN VIDEO NOW.
GIN
FULL GROWN BY AGE 9!
MY GHOD LOOK AT THAT ASS! ITS FABULOUS.. SHE'S GONNA TURN INTO A SLUT NOW!
STILL AN IN-NOCENT KID.
MUCH TO MY HORROR...
GOTTA PINCH THAT THING!
THIS FINE ASS IS GONNA GET YOU BY HONEY!
SHUD UP DADDY YUR GROSS.. YUCK DON'T SAY THAT STUFF.
BEDDER GET USE TO IT
I HATE IT.. DON'T PAY ATTENTION TO IT!
ITS SO BIG + OUT THERE..
THIS IS FUN.. I GOT HUHR ALL IN A CONIPTION!
EVEN WORSE...
I WONDER IF I CAN PLUCK THESE HAIRS OUT?!
I DON' WANNA GROW UP... EVEN THO I HATE BEING A KID LIVING WITH MY PARENTS!
BUDDING BREASTS! *
HIPS STARTING TO BLOSSOM.
ALL THE GROWN UPS I KNOW ARE VERY YUCKY... ESPECIALLY THE MEN... I HATE THEM!
* THEY'VE NEVER GOTTEN BIGGER!
I OVERHEARD ARNIE + HIS PAL PUNCHIE..
YEAH PUNCH YA GOTTA SEE THAT KID'S ASS! SHIT ITS MAGNIFICENT!
OH YEAH... I'LL HAFTO CHECK IT OUT! BEDDAH WATCH HUHR LIKE A HAWK SHE'LL WANNA SCHTUP BEFORE YA KNOW IT!
OVAH MY DEAD BODY... I'LL KILL ANY ONE THAT I CATCH WITH HUHR!
YEAH THAT'S RIGHT ARNIE.
GIN

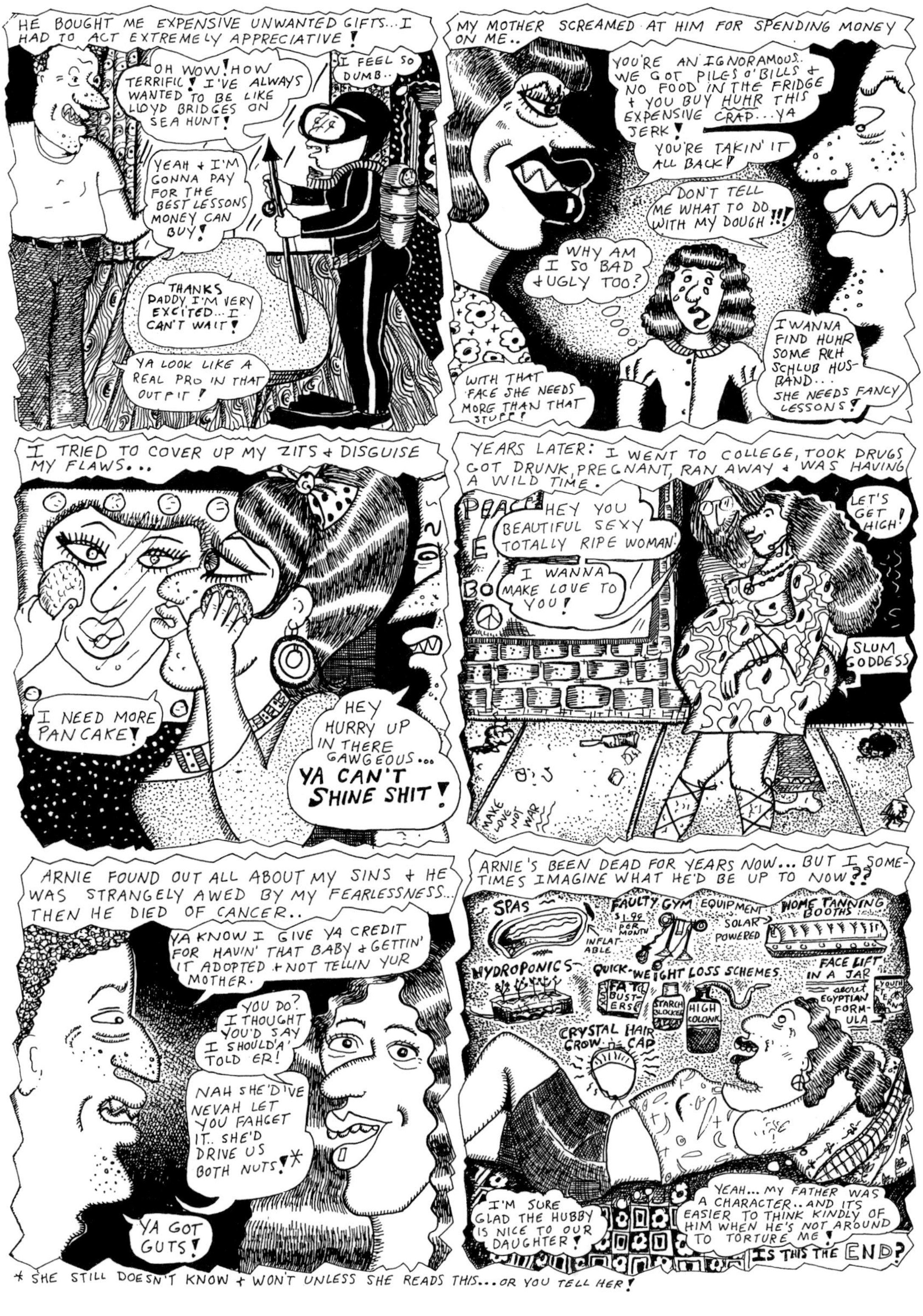
HE BOUGHT ME EXPENSIVE UNWANTED GIFTS... I HAD TO ACT EXTREMELY APPRECIATIVE!
OH WOW! HOW TERRIFIC! I'VE ALWAYS WANTED TO BE LIKE LLOYD BRIDGES ON SEA HUNT!
I FEEL SO DUMB..
YEAH + I'M GONNA PAY FOR THE BEST LESSONS MONEY CAN BUY!
THANKS DADDY, I'M VERY EXCITED... I CAN'T WAIT!
YA LOOK LIKE A REAL PRO IN THAT OUTFIT!
MY MOTHER SCREAMED AT HIM FOR SPENDING MONEY ON ME..
YOU'RE AN IGNORAMOUS. WE GOT PILES O' BILLS + NO FOOD IN THE FRIDGE + YOU BUY HUHR THIS EXPENSIVE CRAP... YA JERK!
YOU'RE TAKIN' IT ALL BACK!
DON'T TELL ME WHAT TO DO WITH MY DOUGH!!!
WHY AM I SO BAD +UGLY TOO?
I WANNA FIND HUHR SOME RICH SCHLUB HUSBAND... SHE NEEDS FANCY LESSONS!
WITH THAT FACE SHE NEEDS MORE THAN THAT STUFF!
I TRIED TO COVER UP MY ZITS + DISGUISE MY FLAWS...
I NEED MORE PANCAKE!
HEY HURRY UP IN THERE GAWGEOUS...
YA CAN'T SHINE SHIT!
YEARS LATER: I WENT TO COLLEGE, TOOK DRUGS GOT DRUNK, PREGNANT, RAN AWAY + WAS HAVING A WILD TIME.
HEY YOU BEAUTIFUL SEXY TOTALLY RIPE WOMAN!
I WANNA MAKE LOVE TO YOU!
LET'S GET HIGH!
SLUM GODDESS
MAKE LOVE NOT WAR
ARNIE FOUND OUT ALL ABOUT MY SINS + HE WAS STRANGELY AWED BY MY FEARLESSNESS... THEN HE DIED OF CANCER..
YA KNOW I GIVE YA CREDIT FOR HAVIN' THAT BABY + GETTIN' IT ADOPTED + NOT TELLIN YUR MOTHER.
YOU DO? I THOUGHT YOU'D SAY I SHOULD'A' TOLD ER!
NAH SHE'D'VE NEVAH LET YOU FAHGET IT.. SHE'D DRIVE US BOTH NUTS!*
YA GOT GUTS!
ARNIE'S BEEN DEAD FOR YEARS NOW... BUT I SOMETIMES IMAGINE WHAT HE'D BE UP TO NOW??
SPAS
INFLATABLE
FAULTY GYM EQUIPMENT
$1.99 PER MONTH
SOLAR POWERED
HOME TANNING BOOTHS
HYDROPONICS
QUICK-WEIGHT LOSS SCHEMES
FAT BUSTERS
STARCH BLOCKER
HIGH COLONIC
FACE LIFT IN A JAR
secret EGYPTIAN FORMULA
CRYSTAL HAIR GROW CAP
I'M SURE GLAD THE HUBBY IS NICE TO OUR DAUGHTER!
YEAH... MY FATHER WAS A CHARACTER.. AND ITS EASIER TO THINK KINDLY OF HIM WHEN HE'S NOT AROUND TO TORTURE ME!
IS THIS THE END?

* SHE STILL DOESN'T KNOW + WON'T UNLESS SHE READS THIS... OR YOU TELL HER!

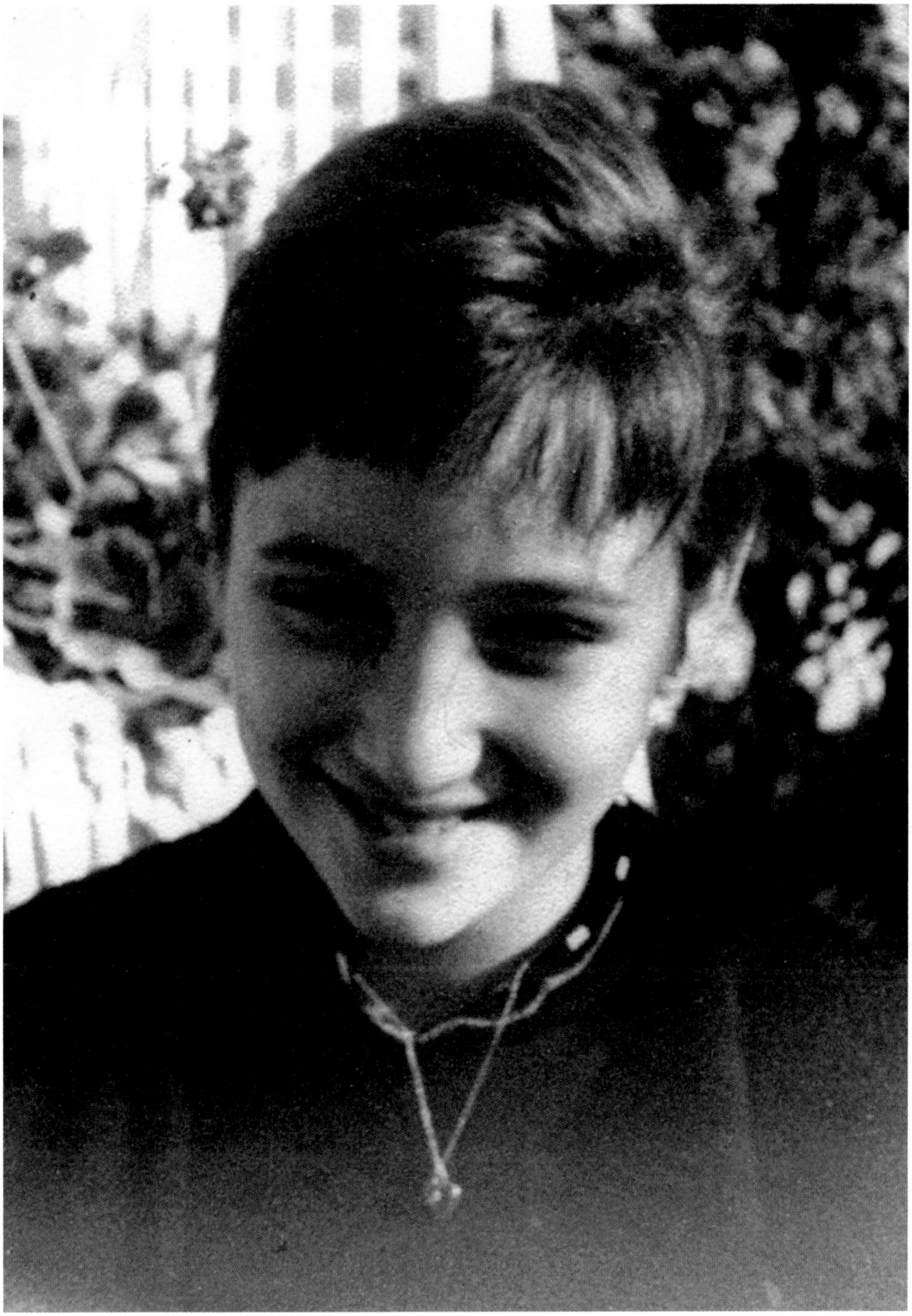

Above: **Me at nine years old, Belle Harbor, New York, 1951**
Still sweet, cute and innocent, this was taken at my grandparents' house.

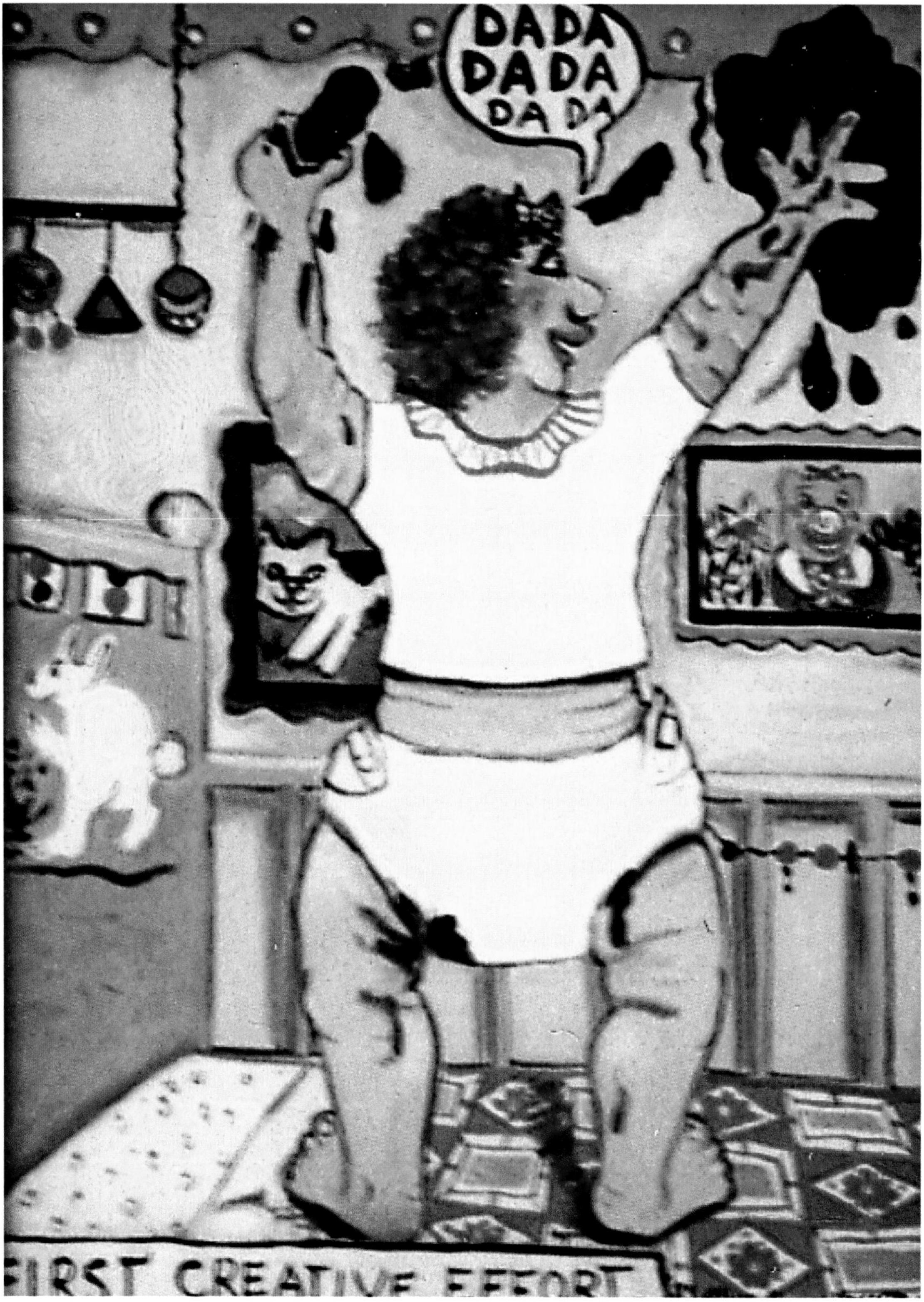
DADA
DADA
DA DA
FIRST CREATIVE EFFORT

The tortured young "Ahtist!"

I more or less became an adult when I was around eight years old. It was then that I discovered that the main adults in my life, my parents, were not in control. This is a scary reality for a kid. I realized that I couldn't rely on anyone for help and that I was in charge of my own destiny. My parents' characters were so extreme that I was forced to confront all this. In some ways, this stress pushed me toward creative expression, perhaps at the expense of emotional health, but what the heck! Nothing years of painful therapy couldn't later resolve!

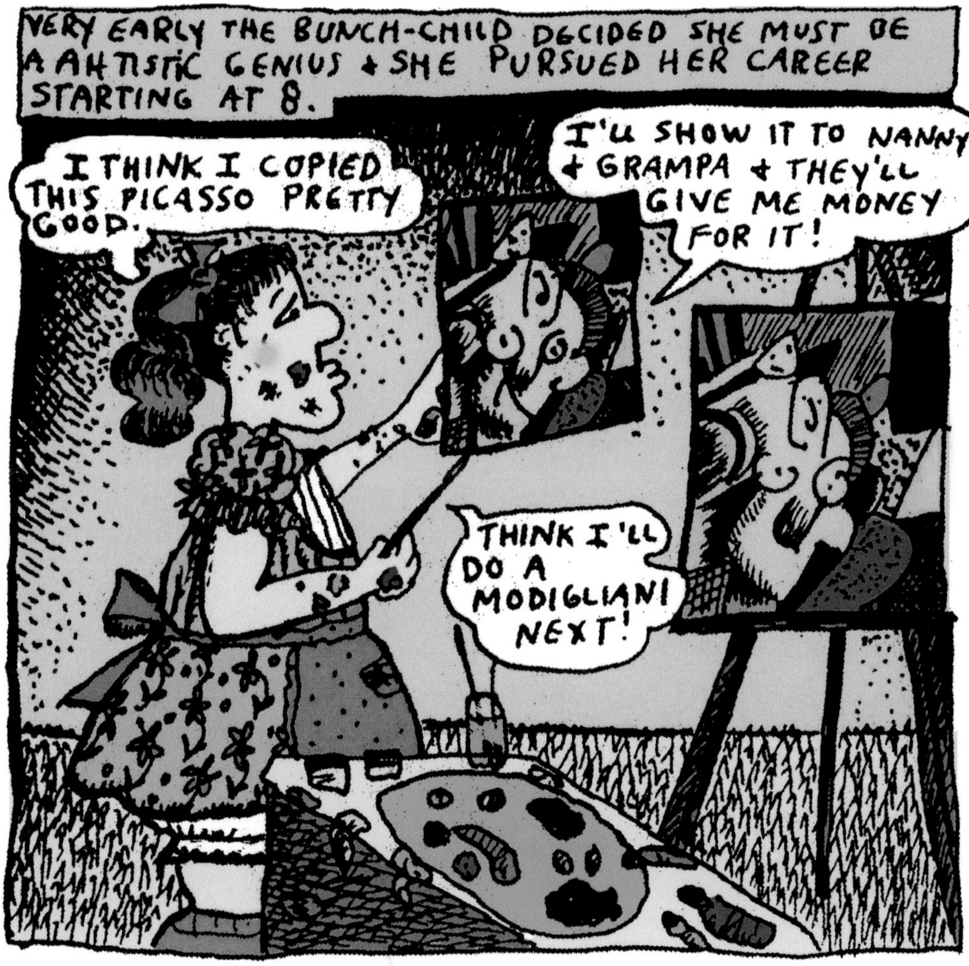
VERY EARLY THE BUNCH-CHILD DECIDED SHE MUST BE A AHTISTIC GENIUS & SHE PURSUED HER CAREER STARTING AT 8.
I THINK I COPIED THIS PICASSO PRETTY GOOD.
I'LL SHOW IT TO NANNY & GRAMPA & THEY'LL GIVE ME MONEY FOR IT!
THINK I'LL DO A MODIGLIANI NEXT!

I become an Expressionist!

When I was about eight, I discovered that one thing I could totally control was the imaginary world. I invented an alternative universe, "Candyland," a place where Alex and I could escape to at night under the covers. It was inspired by the board game, but we made it much more elaborate. Everything in our world was sweet and edible!

I also found that colors affected my emotions. I loved getting a brand-new box of 64 Crayola crayons. I could color perfectly in books and on the mimeographed drawings they gave us in school. I colored so carefully and devotedly that I immediately impressed my art teacher, Miss Luchese, and I received much praise. This, of course, started the imprint for my creative cycle (need for praise, obsessive control and affirmation).

I quickly realized that the school handouts were lame, and started to draw my own stuff. I begged my parents relentlessly to let me take painting classes at the local "Y" (which in this case was the "Young Women's Hebrew Association".) With the added cajoling of my art teacher, who told my parents how talented I was, they finally relented. They signed me up, screaming at me the whole time about the financial strain I was subjecting them to.

My first art class was oil painting. My teacher was a student at the prestigious Pratt Institute in Brooklyn. I was in love from the very start! I loved the smell of oil paint and turpentine, the richness and gooeyness of the paint. I loved the easel, brushes, wooden palette, and the old-fashioned room full of plants and surrounded by windows. I honestly don't remember much about the other students, but I was definitely the youngest and most enthusiastic person in our class. Our assignments consisted of copying paintings, and the first one was a picture of a glass bowl full of roses.

I was good at copying and received much praise from my teacher. My parents weren't sure what to think when I brought my first "masterpiece" home, since they had no knowledge or interest whatsoever in "art." So they showed my painting to our next-door neighbors, the Kimmels, who were both lawyers and were suspected of being intellectuals by my parents and the rest of the neighbors. They said my painting was excellent and that I had artistic talent. This perked up my parents, especially my father, who immediately tried to think of a scheme to profit from my talent, but I don't think he ever managed to crack the fine art market.

My first painting was showcased at the next family gathering. My rich Uncle Ben, Grandma Fanny's brother, was impressed enough to throw a twenty-dollar bill at me, his way of showing affection and approval, and I was hooked! Of course, this monetary acknowledgment helped my parents to accept my artistic ambitions, albeit begrudgingly.

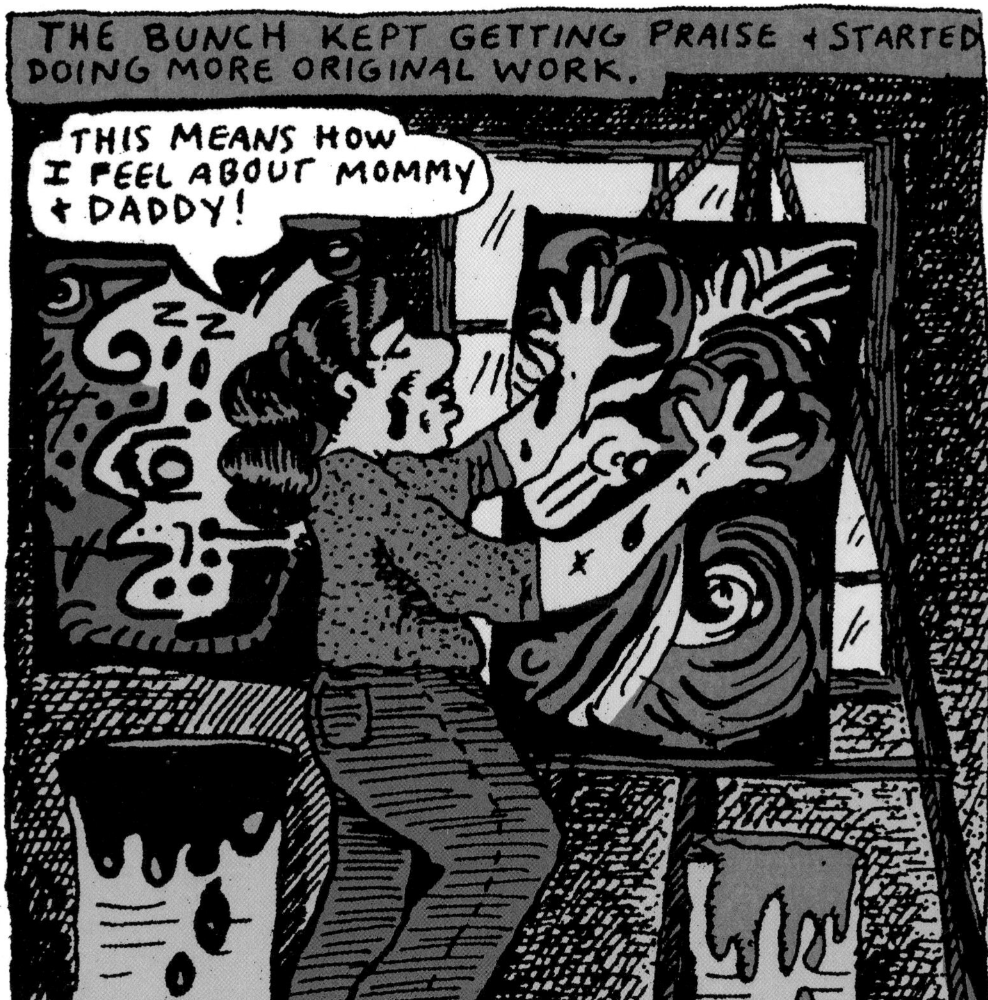
THE BUNCH KEPT GETTING PRAISE + STARTED DOING MORE ORIGINAL WORK.
THIS MEANS HOW I FEEL ABOUT MOMMY + DADDY!
ZZ

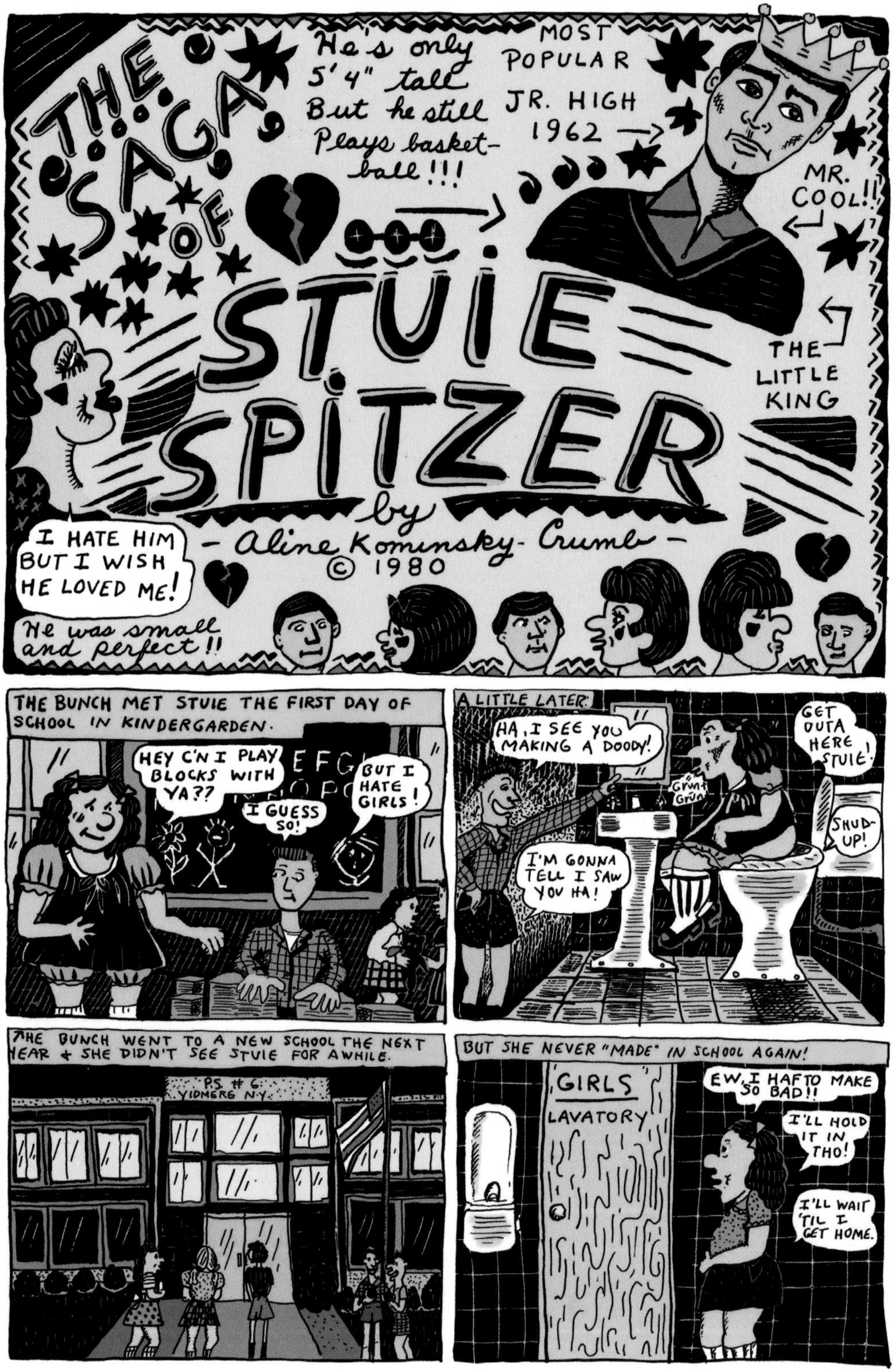
THE SAGA OF
He's only 5'4" tall But he still Plays basket-ball!!!
MOST POPULAR JR. HIGH 1962
MR. COOL!!
STUIE SPITZER
THE LITTLE KING
by
- Aline Kominsky-Crumb -
© 1980
I HATE HIM BUT I WISH HE LOVED ME!
He was small and perfect!!
THE BUNCH MET STUIE THE FIRST DAY OF SCHOOL IN KINDERGARDEN.
HEY C'N I PLAY BLOCKS WITH YA??
I GUESS SO!
BUT I HATE GIRLS!
A LITTLE LATER:
HA, I SEE YOU MAKING A DOODY!
GET OUTA HERE STUIE!
Grunt Grun
SHUD-UP!
I'M GONNA TELL I SAW YOU HA!
THE BUNCH WENT TO A NEW SCHOOL THE NEXT YEAR & SHE DIDN'T SEE STUIE FOR AWHILE.
P.S. # 6 YIDMERG N.Y.
BUT SHE NEVER "MADE" IN SCHOOL AGAIN!
GIRLS LAVATORY
EW, I HAFTO MAKE SO BAD!!
I'LL HOLD IT IN THO!
I'LL WAIT 'TIL I GET HOME.

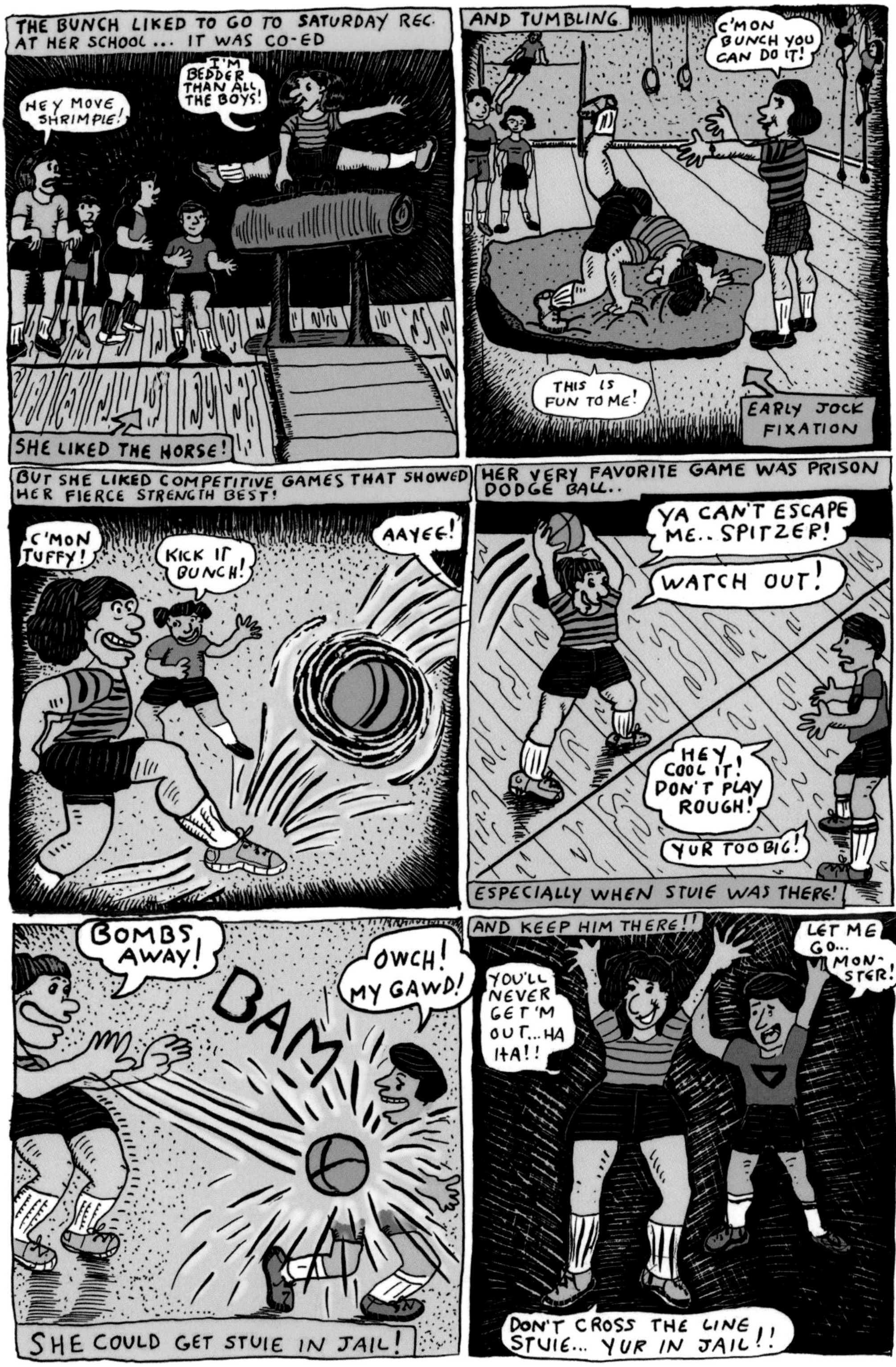
THE BUNCH LIKED TO GO TO SATURDAY REC. AT HER SCHOOL... IT WAS CO-ED
HEY MOVE SHRIMPIE!
I'M BEDDER THAN ALL THE BOYS!
SHE LIKED THE HORSE!
AND TUMBLING.
C'MON BUNCH YOU CAN DO IT!
THIS IS FUN TO ME!
EARLY JOCK FIXATION
BUT SHE LIKED COMPETITIVE GAMES THAT SHOWED HER FIERCE STRENGTH BEST!
C'MON TUFFY!
KICK IT BUNCH!
AAYEE!
HER VERY FAVORITE GAME WAS PRISON DODGE BALL..
YA CAN'T ESCAPE ME.. SPITZER!
WATCH OUT!
HEY COOL IT! DON'T PLAY ROUGH!
YUR TOO BIG!
ESPECIALLY WHEN STUIE WAS THERE!
BOMBS AWAY!
BAM
OWCH! MY GAWD!
SHE COULD GET STUIE IN JAIL!
AND KEEP HIM THERE!!
YOU'LL NEVER GET 'M OUT... HA HA!!
LET ME GO... MON-STER!
DON'T CROSS THE LINE STUIE... YUR IN JAIL!!

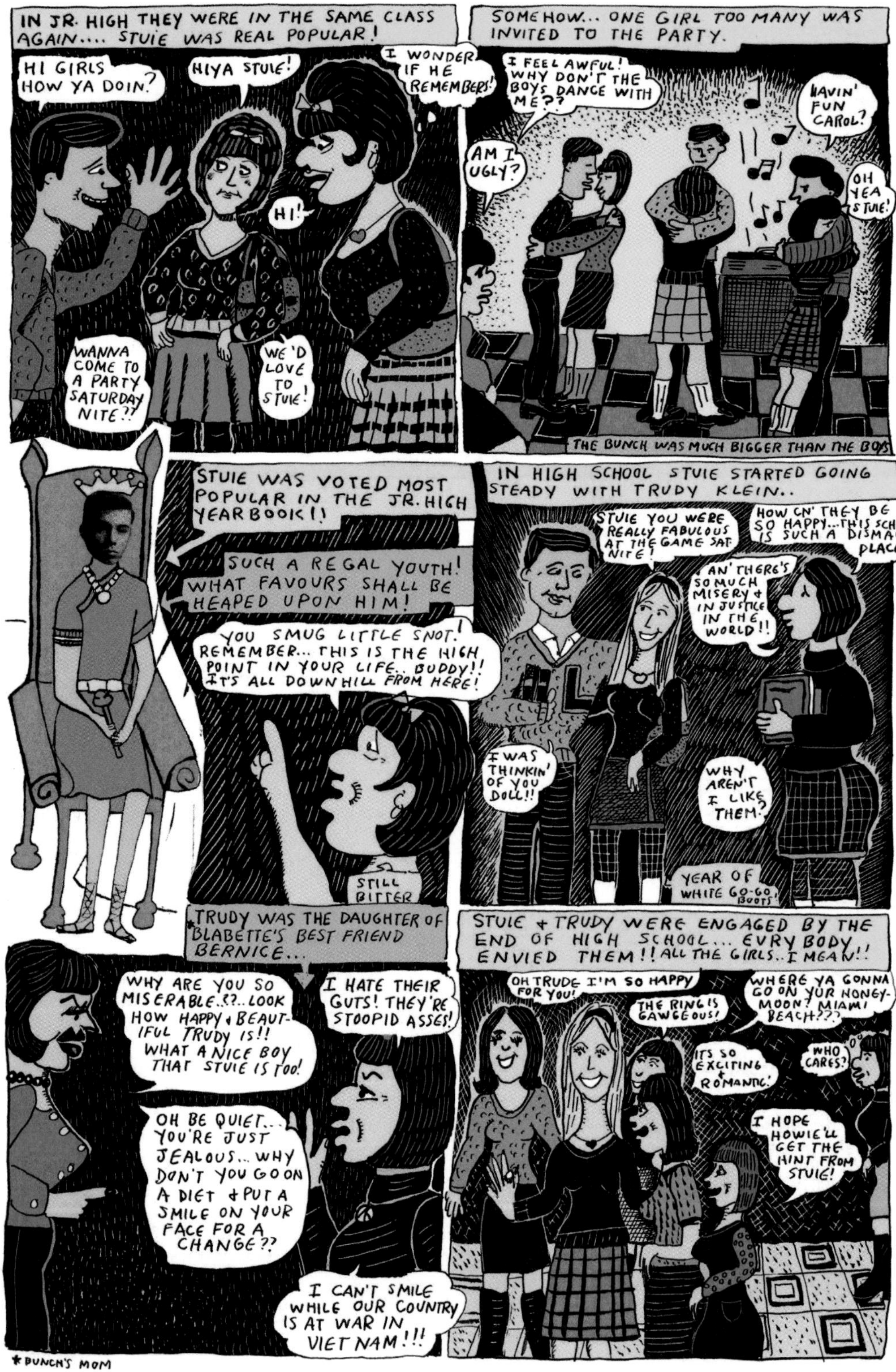
IN JR. HIGH THEY WERE IN THE SAME CLASS AGAIN.... STUIE WAS REAL POPULAR!
HI GIRLS HOW YA DOIN?
HIYA STUIE!
I WONDER IF HE REMEMBERS!
HI!
WANNA COME TO A PARTY SATURDAY NITE?!
WE'D LOVE TO STUIE!
SOMEHOW... ONE GIRL TOO MANY WAS INVITED TO THE PARTY.
I FEEL AWFUL! WHY DON'T THE BOYS DANCE WITH ME??
AM I UGLY?
HAVIN' FUN CAROL?
OH YEA STUIE!
THE BUNCH WAS MUCH BIGGER THAN THE BOYS
STUIE WAS VOTED MOST POPULAR IN THE JR. HIGH YEARBOOK!!
SUCH A REGAL YOUTH! WHAT FAVOURS SHALL BE HEAPED UPON HIM!
YOU SMUG LITTLE SNOT! REMEMBER... THIS IS THE HIGH POINT IN YOUR LIFE.. BUDDY!! IT'S ALL DOWNHILL FROM HERE!
STILL BITTER
IN HIGH SCHOOL STUIE STARTED GOING STEADY WITH TRUDY KLEIN..
STUIE YOU WERE REALLY FABULOUS AT THE GAME SAT NITE!
HOW CN' THEY BE SO HAPPY... THIS SCHOOL IS SUCH A DISMAL PLACE?
AN' THERE'S SO MUCH MISERY & INJUSTICE IN THE WORLD!!
I WAS THINKIN' OF YOU DOLL!!
WHY AREN'T I LIKE THEM?
YEAR OF WHITE GO-GO BOOTS
*TRUDY WAS THE DAUGHTER OF BLABETTE'S BEST FRIEND BERNICE...
WHY ARE YOU SO MISERABLE..?!?.. LOOK HOW HAPPY & BEAUTIFUL TRUDY IS!! WHAT A NICE BOY THAT STUIE IS TOO!
I HATE THEIR GUTS! THEY'RE STOOPID ASSES!
OH BE QUIET... YOU'RE JUST JEALOUS... WHY DON'T YOU GO ON A DIET & PUT A SMILE ON YOUR FACE FOR A CHANGE??
I CAN'T SMILE WHILE OUR COUNTRY IS AT WAR IN VIETNAM!!!
STUIE & TRUDY WERE ENGAGED BY THE END OF HIGH SCHOOL... EVRYBODY ENVIED THEM!! ALL THE GIRLS.. I MEAN!!
OH TRUDE I'M SO HAPPY FOR YOU!
THE RING IS GAWGEOUS!
WHERE YA GONNA GO ON YUR HONEYMOON? MIAMI BEACH???
ITS SO EXCITING & ROMANTIC!
WHO CARES?
I HOPE HOWIE'LL GET THE HINT FROM STUIE!

*BUNCH'S MOM

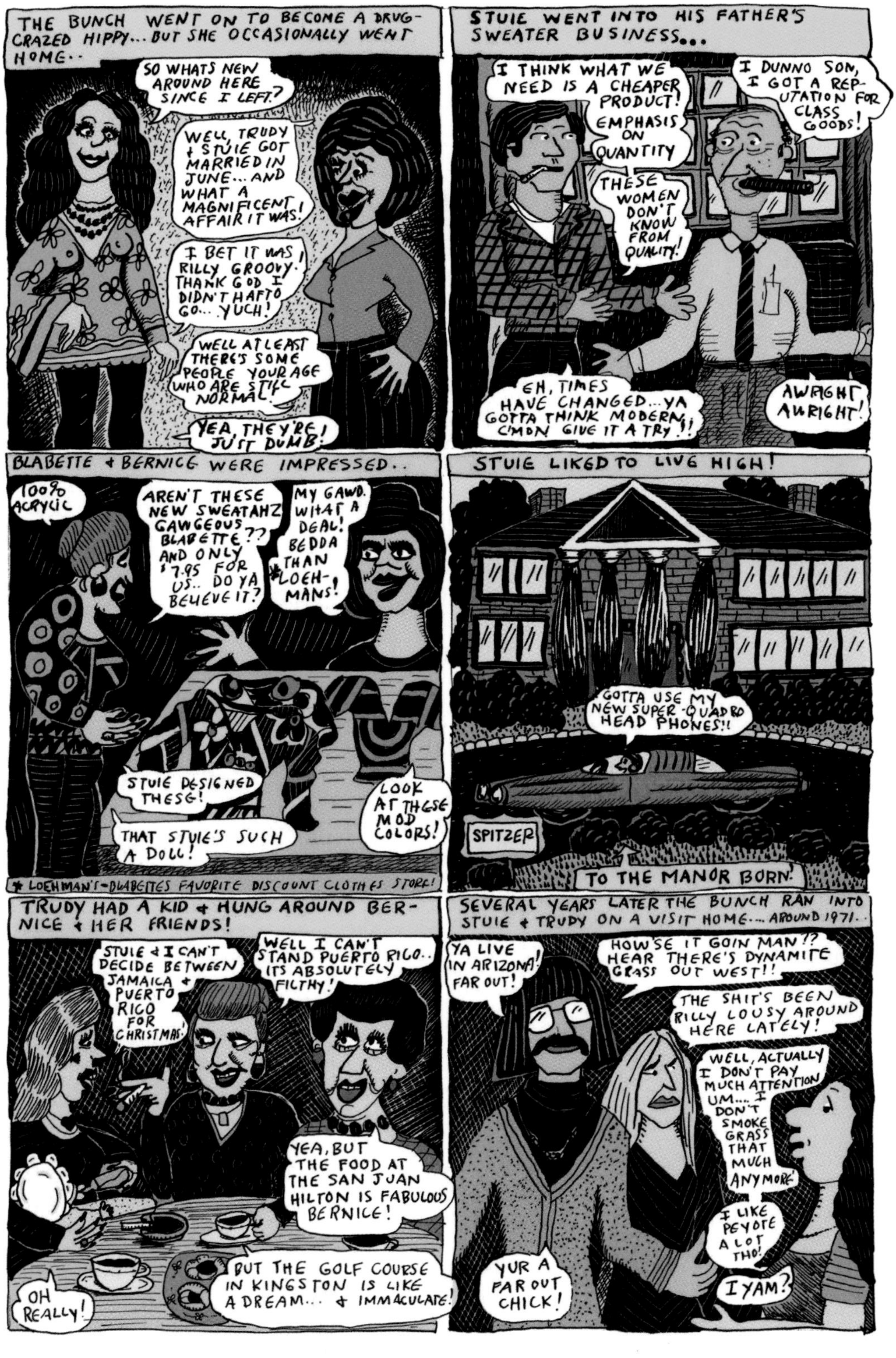
THE BUNCH WENT ON TO BECOME A DRUG-CRAZED HIPPY... BUT SHE OCCASIONALLY WENT HOME..
SO WHATS NEW AROUND HERE SINCE I LEFT?
WELL, TRUDY & STUIE GOT MARRIED IN JUNE... AND WHAT A MAGNIFICENT AFFAIR IT WAS!
I BET IT WAS RILLY GROOVY. THANK GOD I DIDN'T HAFTO GO... YUCH!
WELL AT LEAST THERE'S SOME PEOPLE YOUR AGE WHO ARE STILL NORMAL.
YEA, THEY'RE JUST DUMB!
STUIE WENT INTO HIS FATHER'S SWEATER BUSINESS...
I THINK WHAT WE NEED IS A CHEAPER PRODUCT! EMPHASIS ON QUANTITY
THESE WOMEN DON'T KNOW FROM QUALITY!
I DUNNO SON, I GOT A REPUTATION FOR CLASS GOODS!
EH, TIMES HAVE CHANGED...YA GOTTA THINK MODERN, C'MON GIVE IT A TRY!!
AWRIGHT AWRIGHT!
BLABETTE & BERNICE WERE IMPRESSED..
100% ACRYLIC
AREN'T THESE NEW SWEATAHZ GAWGEOUS BLABETTE?? AND ONLY $7.95 FOR US.. DO YA BELIEVE IT?
MY GAWD. WHAT A DEAL! BEDDA THAN *LOEHMANS!
STUIE DESIGNED THESE!
THAT STUIE'S SUCH A DOLL!
LOOK AT THESE MOD COLORS!
* LOEHMAN'S—BLABETTES FAVORITE DISCOUNT CLOTHES STORE!
STUIE LIKED TO LIVE HIGH!
GOTTA USE MY NEW SUPER-QUADRO HEAD PHONES!!
SPITZER
TO THE MANOR BORN
TRUDY HAD A KID & HUNG AROUND BERNICE & HER FRIENDS!
STUIE & I CAN'T DECIDE BETWEEN JAMAICA & PUERTO RICO FOR CHRISTMAS!
WELL I CAN'T STAND PUERTO RICO.. ITS ABSOLUTELY FILTHY!
YEA, BUT THE FOOD AT THE SAN JUAN HILTON IS FABULOUS BERNICE!
BUT THE GOLF COURSE IN KINGSTON IS LIKE A DREAM... & IMMACULATE!
OH REALLY!
SEVERAL YEARS LATER THE BUNCH RAN INTO STUIE & TRUDY ON A VISIT HOME.... AROUND 1971..
YA LIVE IN ARIZONA! FAR OUT!
HOW'SE IT GOIN MAN!? HEAR THERE'S DYNAMITE GRASS OUT WEST!!
THE SHIT'S BEEN RILLY LOUSY AROUND HERE LATELY!
WELL, ACTUALLY I DON'T PAY MUCH ATTENTION UM.... I DON'T SMOKE GRASS THAT MUCH ANYMORE
I LIKE PEYOTE A LOT THO!
YUR A FAR OUT CHICK!
I YAM?

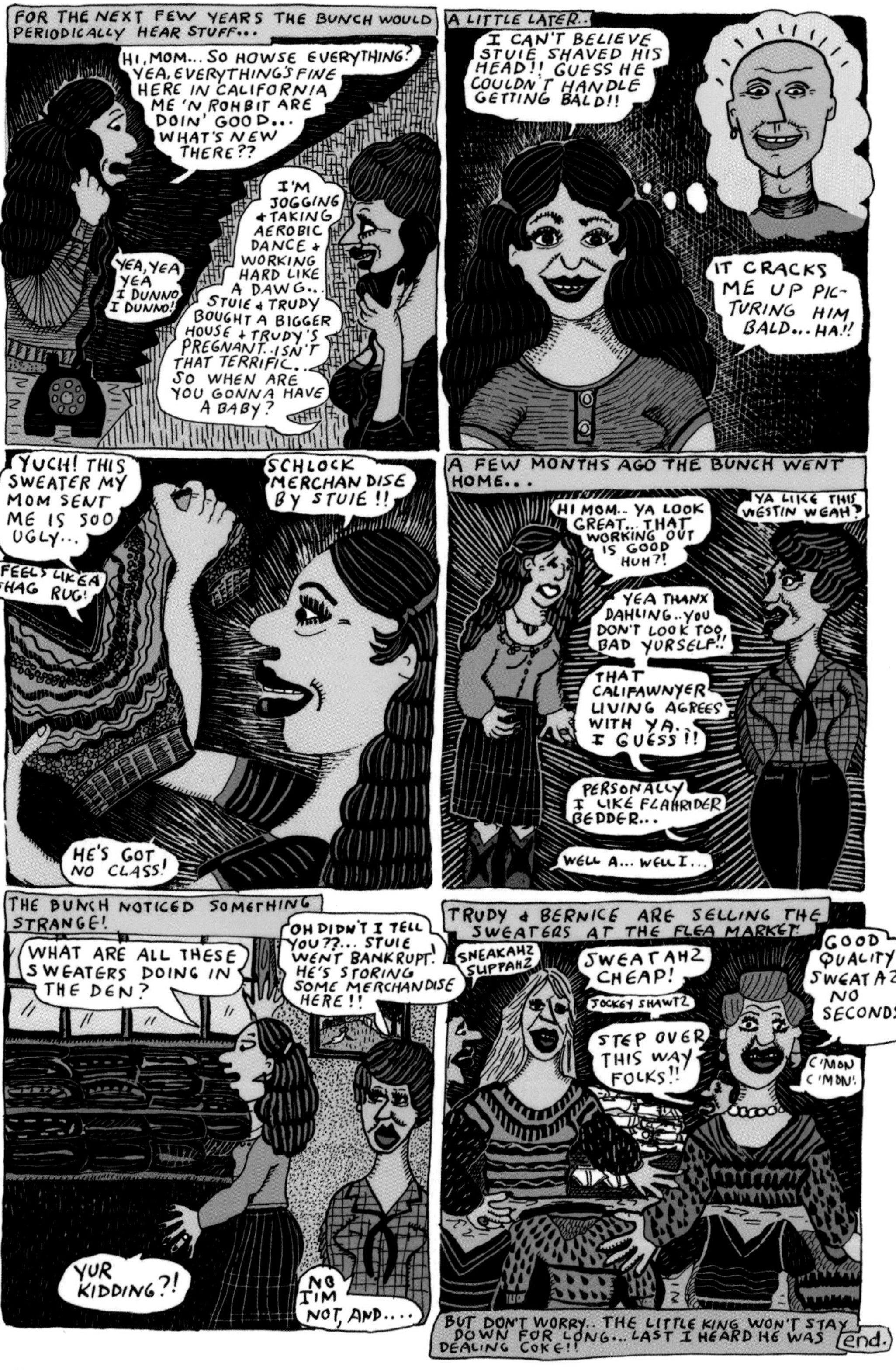

FOR THE NEXT FEW YEARS THE BUNCH WOULD PERIODICALLY HEAR STUFF...
HI, MOM... SO HOWSE EVERYTHING? YEA, EVERYTHING'S FINE HERE IN CALIFORNIA ME 'N ROHBIT ARE DOIN' GOOD... WHAT'S NEW THERE??
I'M JOGGING & TAKING AEROBIC DANCE & WORKING HARD LIKE A DAWG.. STUIE & TRUDY BOUGHT A BIGGER HOUSE & TRUDY'S PREGNANT..ISN'T THAT TERRIFIC.. SO WHEN ARE YOU GONNA HAVE A BABY?
YEA, YEA YEA I DUNNO I DUNNO!
A LITTLE LATER..
I CAN'T BELIEVE STUIE SHAVED HIS HEAD!! GUESS HE COULDN'T HANDLE GETTING BALD!!
IT CRACKS ME UP PICTURING HIM BALD... HA!!
YUCH! THIS SWEATER MY MOM SENT ME IS SOO UGLY...
FEELS LIKE A SHAG RUG!
SCHLOCK MERCHANDISE BY STUIE!!
HE'S GOT NO CLASS!
A FEW MONTHS AGO THE BUNCH WENT HOME...
HI MOM.. YA LOOK GREAT... THAT WORKING OUT IS GOOD HUH?!
YA LIKE THIS WESTIN WEAH?
YEA THANX DAHLING..YOU DON'T LOOK TOO BAD YURSELF!!
THAT CALIFAWNYER LIVING AGREES WITH YA.. I GUESS!!
PERSONALLY I LIKE FLAHRIDER BEDDER...
WELL A... WELL I...
THE BUNCH NOTICED SOMETHING STRANGE!
WHAT ARE ALL THESE SWEATERS DOING IN THE DEN?
OH DIDN'T I TELL YOU??... STUIE WENT BANKRUPT! HE'S STORING SOME MERCHANDISE HERE!!
YUR KIDDING?!
NO I'M NOT, AND....
TRUDY & BERNICE ARE SELLING THE SWEATERS AT THE FLEA MARKET!
SNEAKAHZ SUPPAHZ
SWEATAHZ CHEAP!
JOCKEY SHAWTZ
STEP OVER THIS WAY FOLKS!!
GOOD QUALITY SWEATAZ NO SECONDS!
C'MON C'MON!
BUT DON'T WORRY.. THE LITTLE KING WON'T STAY DOWN FOR LONG... LAST I HEARD HE WAS DEALING COKE!!
end.

Bad hair years!

I was pretty cute as a little girl, but as I approached adolescence, I started to bulk up. This was definitely not desirable in a community that largely descended from squat, eastern European stock. Yes, we came from a long line of 4-by-4's, or "fireplugs," as we affectionately called our not-so-svelte relatives.

Above and left: **Hair modes, Lawrence Junior High**
Below: **Lawrence Junior High Yearbook, 1962**
I'm on the left with the hefty legs, Margie Alpren (with desirable thin legs) is center and Mr. "Most Popular and Likely to Succeed" Ricky Schiffer (also known as my comic character Stuie Spitzer) is sitting on the right.

the YOUNG BUNCH
an unromantic nonadventure story

These are the formative years...fourteen, fifteen, sixteen...

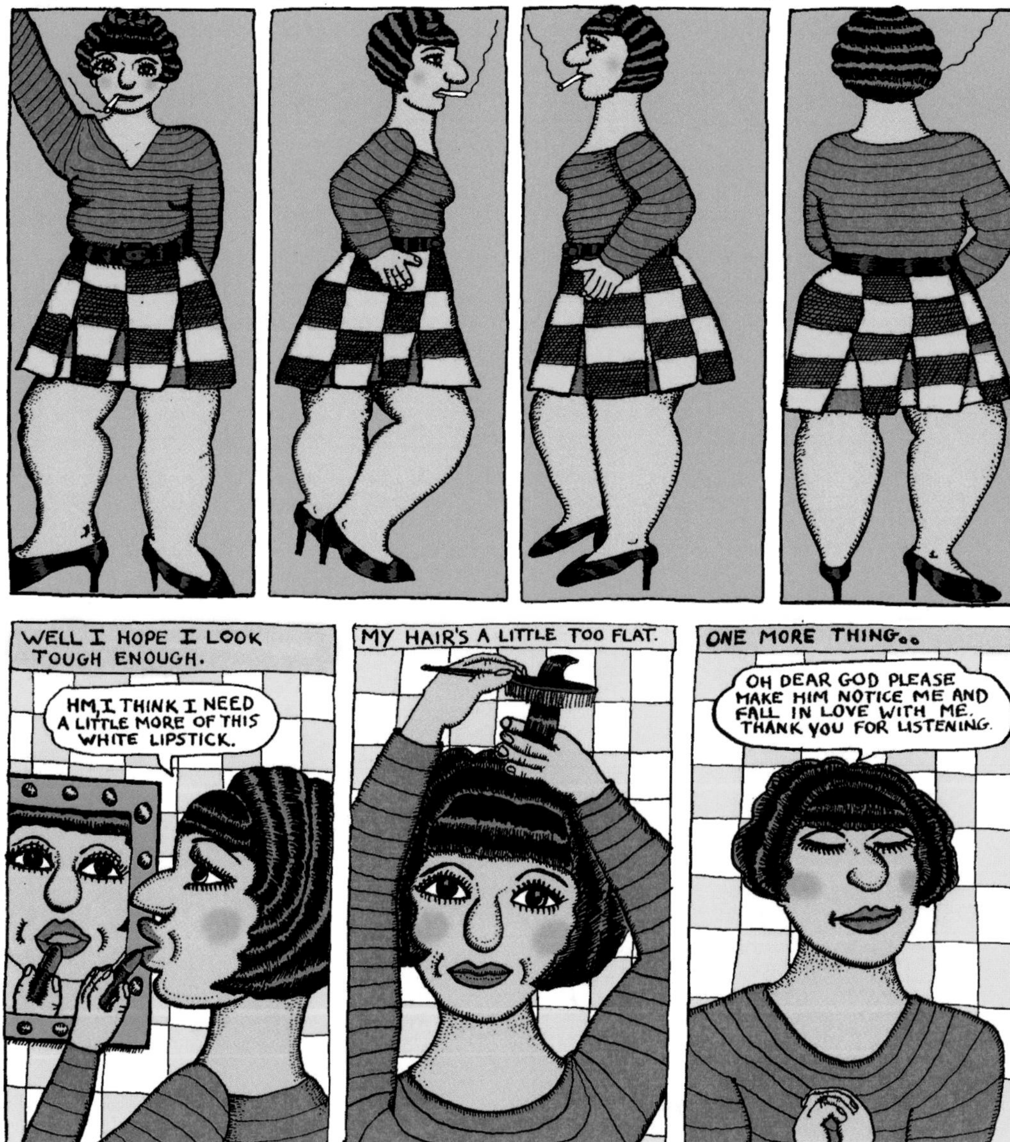
WELL I HOPE I LOOK TOUGH ENOUGH.
HM, I THINK I NEED A LITTLE MORE OF THIS WHITE LIPSTICK.
MY HAIR'S A LITTLE TOO FLAT.
ONE MORE THING..
OH DEAR GOD PLEASE MAKE HIM NOTICE ME AND FALL IN LOVE WITH ME. THANK YOU FOR LISTENING.

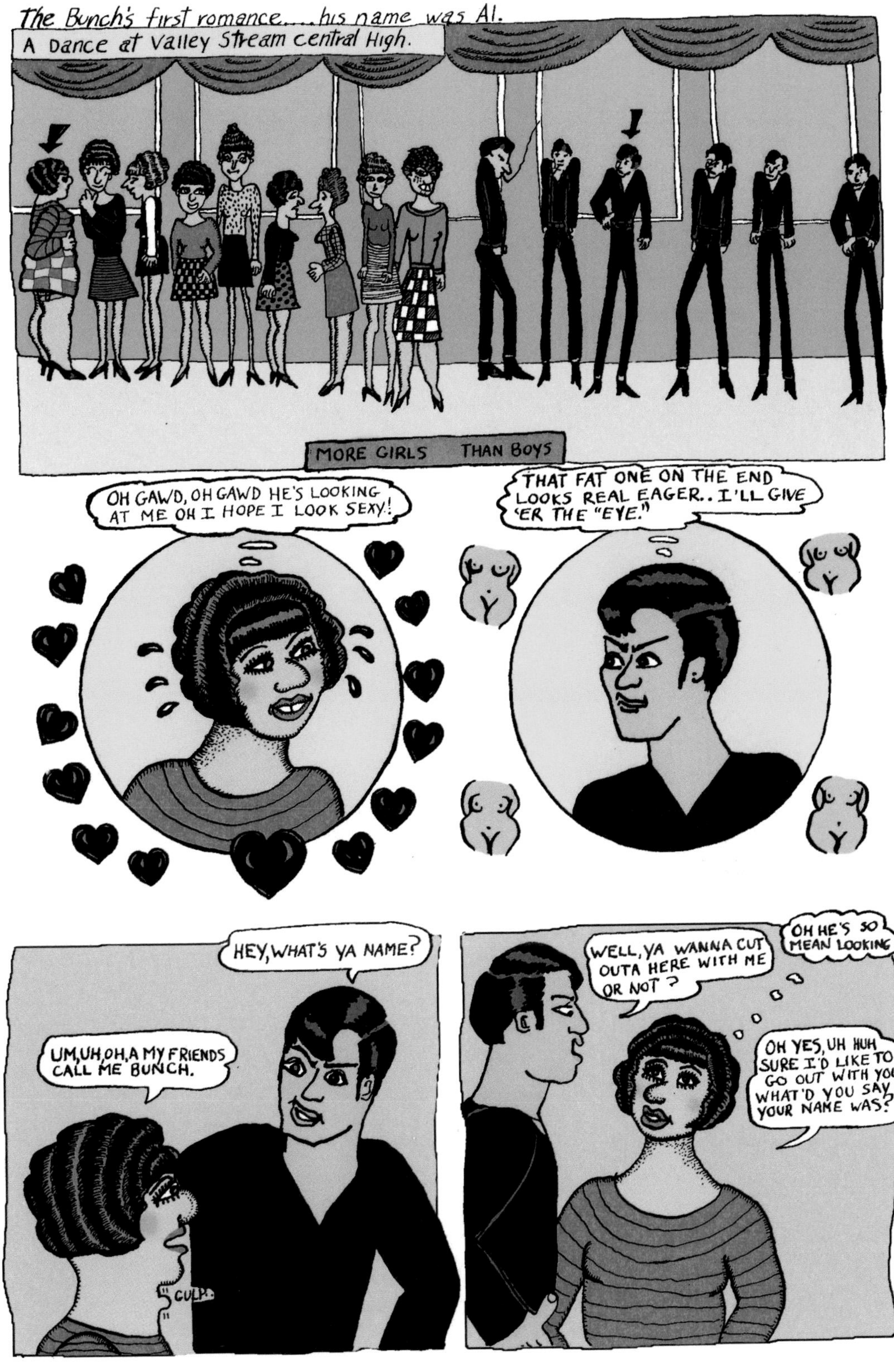

The Bunch's first romance....his name was Al.
A Dance at Valley Stream central High.
MORE GIRLS THAN BOYS
OH GAWD, OH GAWD HE'S LOOKING AT ME OH I HOPE I LOOK SEXY!
THAT FAT ONE ON THE END LOOKS REAL EAGER.. I'LL GIVE 'ER THE "EYE."
HEY, WHAT'S YA NAME?
UM, UH, OH, A MY FRIENDS CALL ME BUNCH.
"GULP."
WELL, YA WANNA CUT OUTA HERE WITH ME OR NOT?
OH HE'S SO MEAN LOOKING
OH YES, UH HUH SURE I'D LIKE TO GO OUT WITH YOU WHAT'D YOU SAY YOUR NAME WAS?

Doing time—the worst years

As I grew bigger, I became overly outgoing, you might even say aggressive. This was not at all alluring to the cute little Jewish princes I desperately sought to attract. My parents' reaction to this difficult passage turned my sensitivities into painful wounds.

The cruelest thing ever said to me was spoken by my father. One day I was looking in the mirror and feeling particularly ugly. I was trying to cover up some unsightly blemishes with makeup when my father barged into the bathroom, took one look at me, and said, "Ya know, ya can't shine shit!" How can I describe the blow I felt? My already fragile psyche was shattered. I know how uncomfortable my own daughter was with her body as an adolescent, and still can't believe that a father could have uttered such hateful words!

In Junior High, my skin started to get really bad. My mother never bothered to take me to a dermatologist or give me any hygiene or grooming advice, so of course I just squeezed and picked at my pimples with dirty hands, creating scabs, oozing sores and scars that I tried to conceal by plastering my puss with even more cheap makeup that I was shoplifting from the cosmetic counter at the local drugstore. My face became a real mess, which infuriated my mother because it lessened my chances of snagging a popular boy from a rich family. She started lashing out at me with a new fury.

Several incidents stand out in my mind. One was the "French fry attack." It was dinner time; my mother had served everyone and had given my brother a big portion of fries and me only three or four (I guess she thought she was saving me from a life of fatness). I started eating his after quickly inhaling my own meager portion. My mother jumped up and strangled me until I choked up the fries. My father put down his newspaper and began calling my mother names like "you fucking animal," "spoiled piece of shit," etc. She lashed back with a stream of vicious insults, calling my father a lazy bum who couldn't even earn a decent living. In the middle of her screaming, my father overturned the table and all the food and plates crashed to the floor. Nothing quite like a dinner from hell to set up some really twisted eating disorders for life!

French fries remain one of my favorite "bad foods." I'm too guilt-ridden to order them myself in a restaurant, so all the people I know and love always order frites so I can have some of theirs. There was another incident a few years later when I had stylistically begun my metamorphosis into a beatnik. That meant no longer setting, teasing and spraying my hair into a grotesque bubble but simply tying it back in a ponytail with a part in the middle and no bangs, and wearing a black turtleneck sweater and Fred Braun sandals. (Fred Braun shoes were famous beatnik shoes that came from a very cool store on 8th Street in the Village.)

I was making breakfast one morning, dressed like that, when my mother came into the kitchen and started glaring at me. Her nostrils were flared, and that meant trouble! (It was probably just a symptom of severe PMS, but we didn't know about that then.) She grabbed my ponytail and pulled it so hard that I thought she would rip it out of my scalp. She screamed that I was making myself as ugly as possible just to torture her. She shrieked that no boy would ever love me, that I was doomed to be a miserable, poor, lonely, childless hag. After all she had sacrificed to make a good life for me! She was in such a frenzy that I almost started to laugh, but stopped myself because I thought she might actually kill me!

The last physically violent exchange I had with my mother happened when I was seventeen. I was setting the table and she smelled cigarette smoke on me. She started pummeling me and really hitting me hard. I finally saw red and hit her back—I was really strong and athletic and the force threw her into the wall. To my surprise, she looked shocked and scared, and she just left the room. She never hit me again, and after that I smoked in front of her.

Junior high school was total hell. No surprise, I was not alone! I started off trying to be a popular kid, but my efforts were doomed: my legs were twice as thick as the cute, desirable girls like Margie Alpren who had beautiful skinny legs, and even though I babysat as much as possible, I never had enough money to keep up with the rich kids. The little princes didn't like me. I mean, they liked me as a friend, but they weren't sexually attracted to me. I was crushed, because I desperately wanted their love.

I became best friends with a shy and sort of popular girl named Carole Milt. I used to crack her up in class by drawing cruel caricatures of other kids and teachers. She could have been really popular because she was cute, small, rich, and not too Jewish-looking, but her family was really screwy and she had low self-esteem.

Oddballs and misfits

Inspired by my feelings of rejection, humiliation and anger, I made a radical proposal to Carole to quit the popular crowd and form our own crowd where we might actually have some fun. I didn't think it was worth the work trying to keep up with the popular kids. What did we really get out of it? I was right, but this was a totally scary idea, especially at Lawrence Junior High in 1962.

Luckily, Carole was sufficiently miserable and mesmerized by me to go along. Later she had some regrets, and maybe even resented me for pressuring her into slinking off into some lower echelon. But from then on until the end of high school, we were inseparable! We never got into lesbian sex or anything (although Carole's mother was suspicious because we took showers together and slept in the same bed). But we had a kind of love, a deeply satisfying all-girl kind of love, and this taught me to appreciate girlfriends my entire life.

Once we freed ourselves from the pressures of striving to be popular, Carole and I attracted a group of misfits and oddballs, all unique and interesting. The way we pulled it off was unheard of, a real coup that got us immediately labeled as weird and suspicious. Every Saturday morning the cool kids would call each other back and forth until they came up with a meeting place for the afternoon. It would be either in Cedarhurst Park or on Central Avenue in Cedarhurst in front of Jildor Shoes or Bea's Tea Room or Sisteen Dress Shop. (Jildor Shoes still exists but I'm not sure about the other places. This whole area, which was a major shopping place for JAPs from all over Long Island, has since become a Hasidic neighborhood and many stores have gone out of business.)

Anyway, all the cool girls would hang out waiting for the cute boys to show up. Then flirting would begin. I was always the clown, loved by everyone, boys and girls both, but never as a real girlfriend. I was not girlfriend material. All we did, and I remember this very clearly, was this: that Saturday morning Carole and I were together as usual. I got on the phone to Margie Alpren and Barbara Kaufman and casually mentioned that Carole and I were going to do something else that day by ourselves. They cried:

- What?
- Oh, maybe we're gonna go into the city.

There was shock and panic on the other end of the phone. They didn't know how to react—this couldn't be happening! We were committing social suicide and we knew it, but we felt exhilarated, scared, and, yes, empowered by our act of rebellion! We continued to boycott the cool crowd, and soon they totally avoided us. At school it was tough, especially at lunchtime in the cafeteria and during recess. All the free time when kids hang out became awkward and we felt our aloneness. But after a while we fell in with some odd, marginal girls whom we had never really noticed before. They turned out to be a group of highly individualistic kids who didn't fit into the standard mold either. These were girls like Stephanie Karasik and Patti Kogen, who were arty and funny and open to all kinds of ideas. We started to go into the city together regularly.

Then in 1963, I had two very significant experiences. I went to the Museum of Modern Art and saw major works of art with my own eyes. I also discovered Washington Square and the Village, and saw real beatniks and folkniks. I realized that there was actually a world I wanted to be a part of! We started to pick up boys from other places. I discovered goys and tough Italian boys, and they seemed to go for me. Carole was very cute and all kinds of boys went for her. I started to enjoy myself with guys and finally awoke to the fact that little Jewish boys and I would never work.

Below: **Lawrence High School Yearbook, 1963**
Legs on parade—the "Go-Go" look!

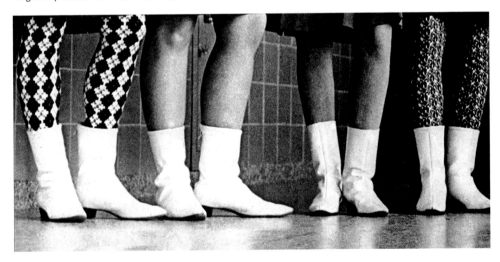

Al—my first love affair

I fell madly in love with Al. He was Italian and four years older than me, which made him dangerously exciting. Carole was going out with his younger half-brother, Douggie. (Yes, these kids' parents had actually divorced and remarried, which was unheard of among our friends' parents, who just suffered and lived together, hating each other and their lives). These boys came from Valley Stream, a slightly more working-class, mixed ethnic neighborhood than the Five Towns where we lived.

All this gave them an attractive edge for us sheltered little things. Al was the sexiest boy I had ever been near. Even thinking about him now, 44 years later, I get a thrill. Oy, can you imagine such a powerful thing? Very dangerous territory! I fell totally in LOVE! At fourteen years old, such emotions aren't taken seriously, but I can tell you that those were probably the most intense feelings I've ever had toward any male in my life.

Unfortunately for me, my whole relationship with Al boiled down to a calculated courtship on his part, which I blindly took for reciprocal love. In fact, he had one idea in his head: to get me to go "all the way" with him. This never once crossed my mind. I was so sincerely in love that I was incapable of finding any fault with him, and was completely trusting. I never have been since.

We had the most passionate make-out sessions imaginable. He'd sneak over to where I was babysitting, and when the kids were asleep we'd get going. Or else we'd double date at Carole's house when her parents were not there.

Al and I would go down to a bed in the basement and he would push me a little further each time. Frankly, this was easy, I was so horny, sexually frustrated, and curious. Plus, I was in love and totally attracted to him. I remember the first time he put my hand on his giant, throbbing dick. This was perhaps the most erotic moment of my life! He showed me how to move my hand up and down on it until it squirted all over the place. Then he started sticking his hand down "there," and drove me wild!

Right: **Me at home aged 14, Woodmere, New York, 1963**
I am wearing Al's ring around my neck.

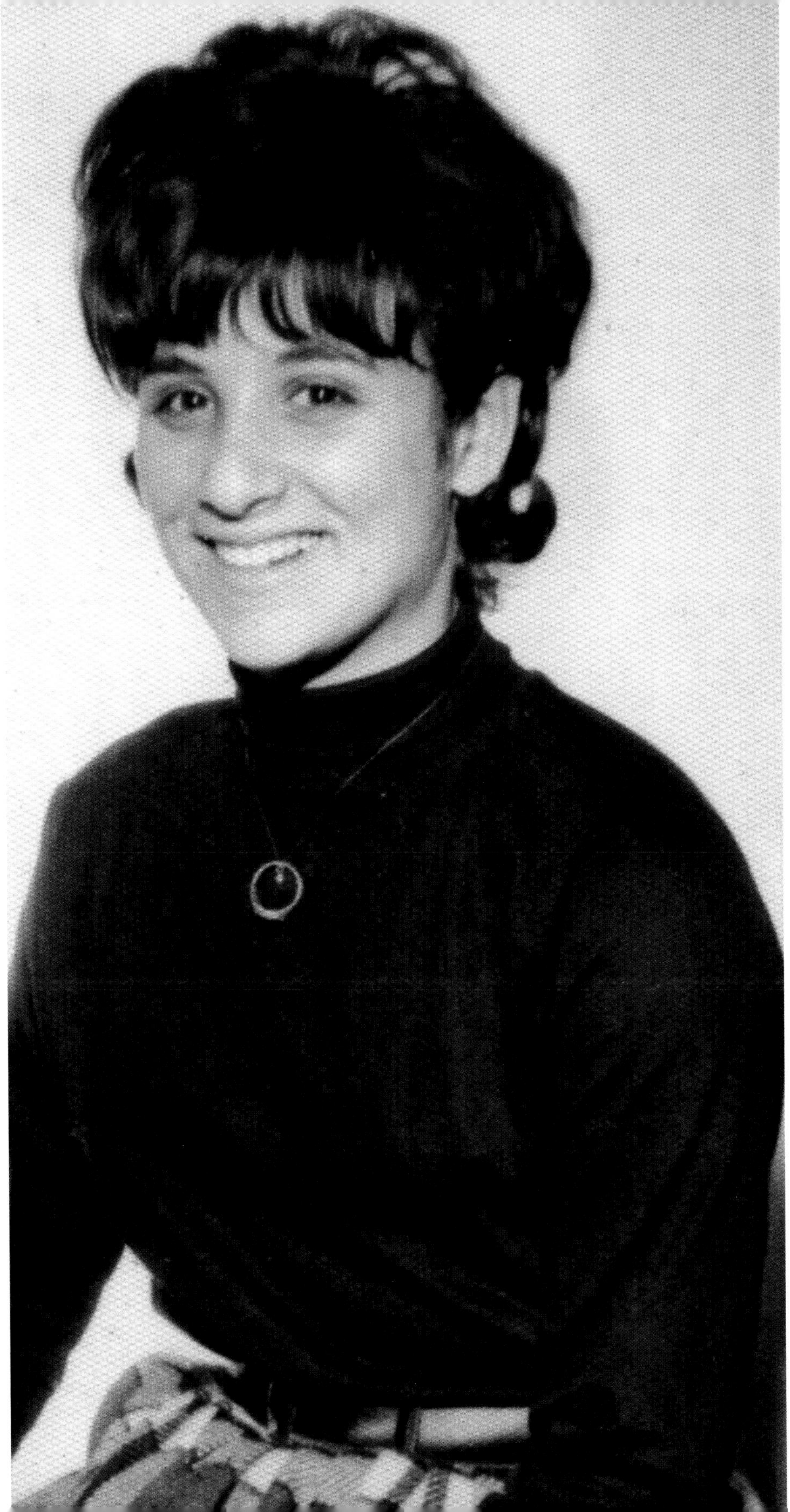

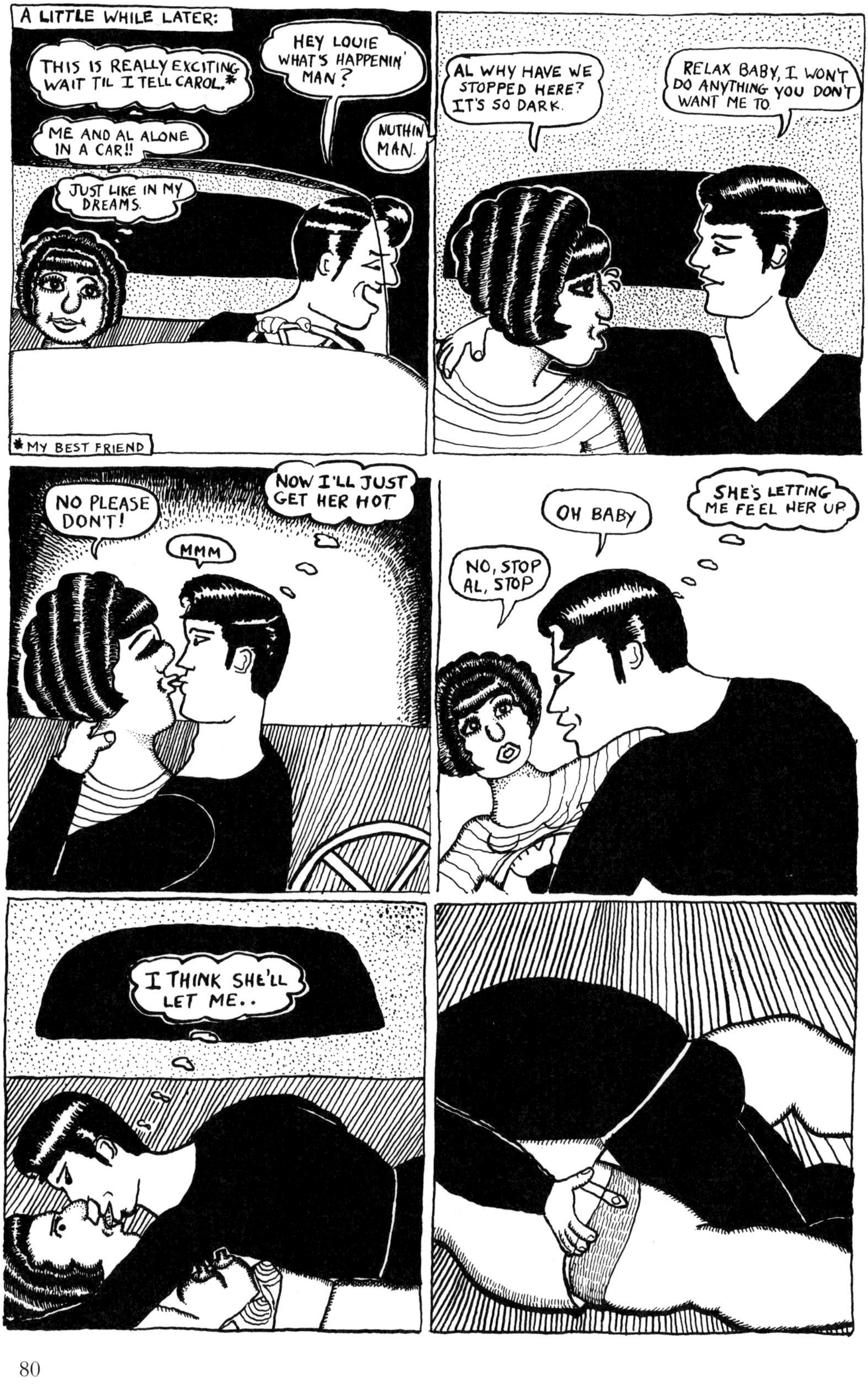
A LITTLE WHILE LATER:
THIS IS REALLY EXCITING WAIT TIL I TELL CAROL.*
HEY LOUIE WHAT'S HAPPENIN' MAN?
ME AND AL ALONE IN A CAR!!
NUTHIN MAN.
JUST LIKE IN MY DREAMS.
*MY BEST FRIEND
AL WHY HAVE WE STOPPED HERE? IT'S SO DARK.
RELAX BABY, I WON'T DO ANYTHING YOU DON'T WANT ME TO.
NO PLEASE DON'T!
NOW I'LL JUST GET HER HOT
MMM
OH BABY
SHE'S LETTING ME FEEL HER UP
NO, STOP AL, STOP
I THINK SHE'LL LET ME..

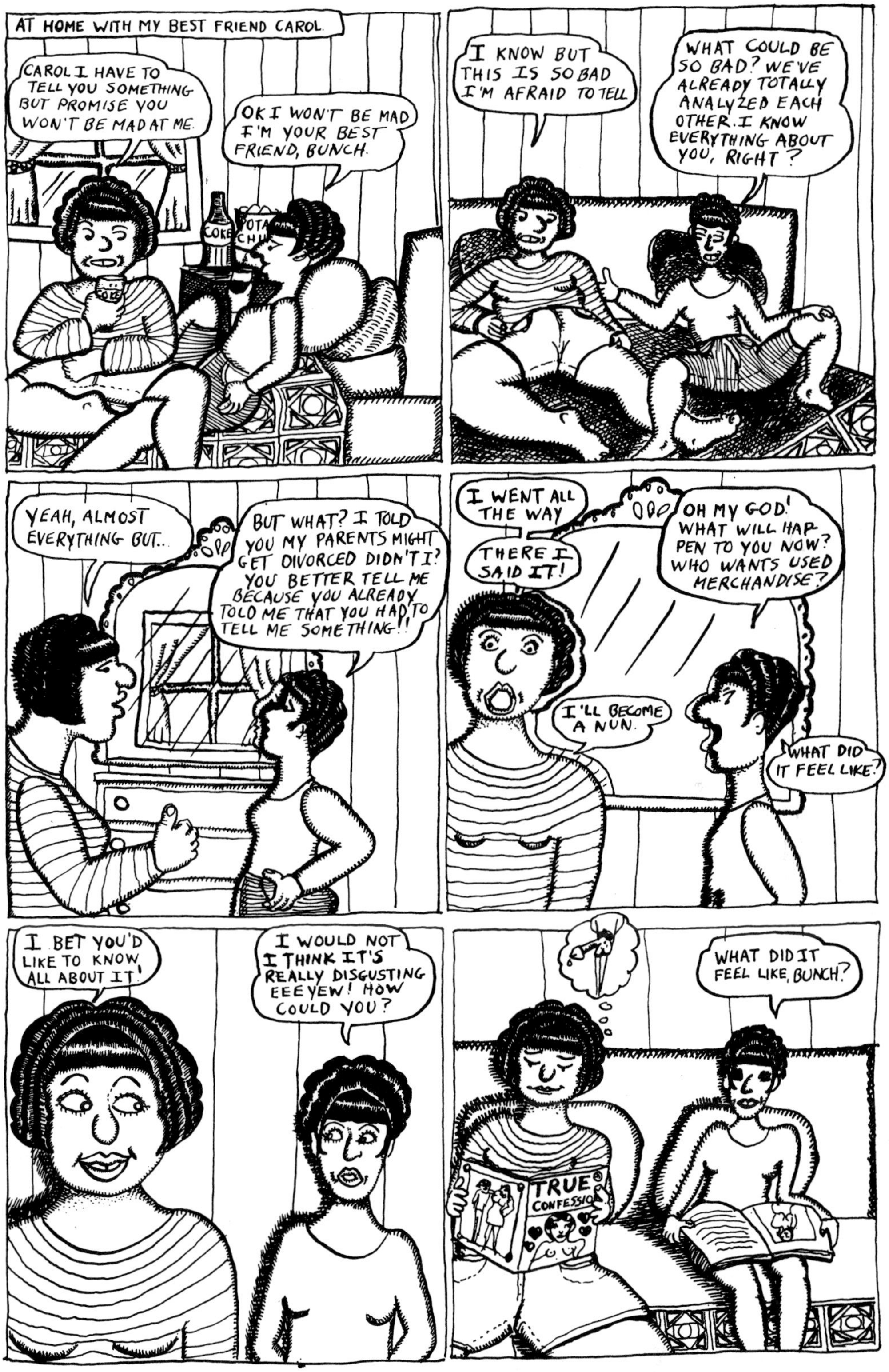
AT HOME WITH MY BEST FRIEND CAROL.
CAROL I HAVE TO TELL YOU SOMETHING BUT PROMISE YOU WON'T BE MAD AT ME.
OK I WON'T BE MAD I'M YOUR BEST FRIEND, BUNCH.
COKE
I KNOW BUT THIS IS SO BAD I'M AFRAID TO TELL
WHAT COULD BE SO BAD? WE'VE ALREADY TOTALLY ANALYZED EACH OTHER. I KNOW EVERYTHING ABOUT YOU, RIGHT?
YEAH, ALMOST EVERYTHING BUT...
BUT WHAT? I TOLD YOU MY PARENTS MIGHT GET DIVORCED DIDN'T I? YOU BETTER TELL ME BECAUSE YOU ALREADY TOLD ME THAT YOU HAD TO TELL ME SOMETHING!!
I WENT ALL THE WAY
THERE I SAID IT!
OH MY GOD! WHAT WILL HAPPEN TO YOU NOW? WHO WANTS USED MERCHANDISE?
I'LL BECOME A NUN.
WHAT DID IT FEEL LIKE?
I BET YOU'D LIKE TO KNOW ALL ABOUT IT!
I WOULD NOT I THINK IT'S REALLY DISGUSTING EEEYEW! HOW COULD YOU?
WHAT DID IT FEEL LIKE, BUNCH?
TRUE CONFESSIO

A disastrous outcome

Meanwhile, Carole and Douggie were making out, but they were not going as far as us. I couldn't admit to Carole what I was doing because I knew it was bad. These sessions went on for months, and we eagerly looked forward to the weekends. Al gave me his high school ring, which I proudly wore on a chain around my neck. I decided that I wanted to give myself to Al because I loved him so much. I was positive that it would make him really happy and that he would love me even more! I was sure we would be together for the rest of our lives, so what did it matter anyway?

We did "It" in my bed one night when my parents were out. It was actually sort of a let down for me after all the months of exciting buildup. I also felt instant guilt and fear for having done something so forbidden. The next day, Al didn't phone. I freaked out and called a friend who lived next door to him. "How could you do what you did?" she said. "Al has lost all respect for you, and he never wants to see you again. It's over, he said you were a whore." I just wanted to die right there. My life was finished.

This is the only time I have actually felt that way—I'm normally the "clinging to life" type and never think about harming myself. But that was more than my little heart could take! He didn't even have the guts to call me myself. What a bastard! For years, I thought about his behavior until I realized that it was his MO. He'd get young girls to go "all the way" with him and then dump them.

I somehow managed to get up the nerve to tell Carole, although I knew she wouldn't approve of what I'd done. She was furious and disgusted and not at all sympathetic. I pretended to her and everyone else that I didn't care any more about Al, but I was in agony!

Over the next six months, I gained about twenty pounds and sank into a period of deep self-hatred. I don't think I have ever allowed myself to be as open and vulnerable to a male again, and I don't think I have ever been as deeply hurt.

One weekend after my breakup with Al, I discovered the thrill of being drunk. This was again at Carole's house when everyone was away. We were bored and started snooping around her parents' bar. We took a little liquor out of every bottle so they wouldn't notice anything, mixed it all together with some Coca-Cola, and gulped down as much as we could. All I can remember after that is crawling around on all fours like a dog on the front lawn, howling like a wolf, while Carole fed me potato chips. In the morning I woke up with my first hangover. I was outside, alone, and covered with leaves and soggy chips. However, the hangover didn't impress me as much as the sheer fun of being drunk! This was the pivotal moment in my subsequent life as a wine lover.

Below: **Lawrence High School Yearbook, 1965**
My evolving hairstyle—now halfway between "the Bubble" and a Hippy hair look.

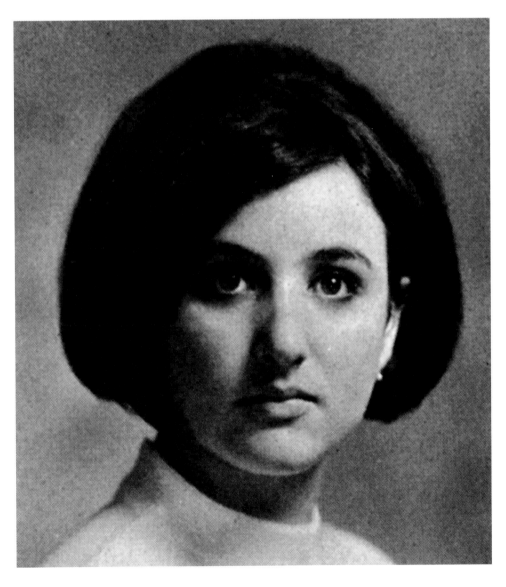

Happy camper

For the rest of junior high and high school, I was basically "doin' time."
Every summer, I would go to sleep-away camp in rural New Jersey, a respite
from my grim suburban life. The place was Camp Lake-Vu, a sorry-assed
little summer camp run by some schoolteachers from Long Island. There
were mostly middle class Jewish kids, but it wasn't any kind of religious or
political camp—I knew some kids who went to lefty socialist camps. No, it
was just a low-grade version of the classier retreats my rich friends went to
in the Adirondacks or the Poconos.

Camp Lake-Vu was small and kind of crowded. We lived in cramped
wooden cabins, eight girls plus two counselors in each one, with only one
toilet. The grounds bordered a very small lake, more like a large mud
puddle, with a patch of scruffy woods behind them. Nevertheless, it was the
country to me, and I loved it. I loved sleeping in a simple cabin with no
windows, open to nature and the sounds of summer nights. I loved all the
outdoor activities like hiking and swimming, all the sports, and even the
dumb arts and crafts projects. I was an all-around happy camper.

I was very content to be in a group with rules to follow, praise for doing
well, and clear punishments for infractions. It was kind of like army life, or a
kibbutz. Whatever, I thrived and developed confidence in my athletic
abilities and social skills. I especially appreciated being away from my
parents' hell-house for eight whole weeks.

During my last year in camp, I was elected General of Color War, a very
important tribal bonding ritual held at the end of every summer to
stimulate camp patriotism and keep the kids coming back each year. This
was a tremendous honor for me. I had been selected by the grown-ups, and
it meant that I possessed leadership qualities. This was great for my
pathetically low self-esteem. Even though my team didn't win, we fought a
noble battle with war-like devotion and discipline, through competing sports
events, art and theater presentations and songs. I discovered my true Amazon
Supergirl self at camp, even though it took me years to figure out what to
do with it.

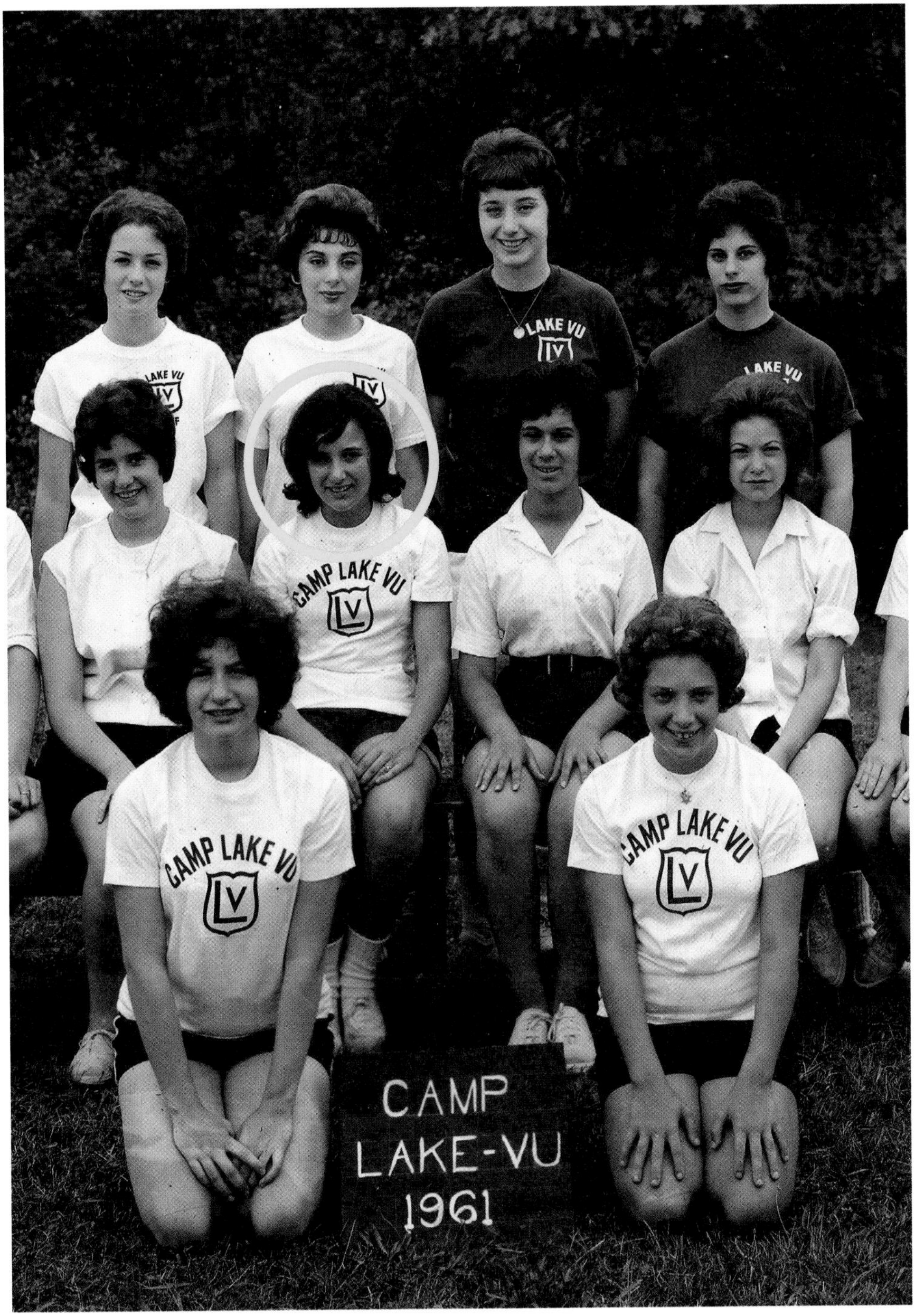
LAKE VU
LAKE VU
CAMP LAKE VU
CAMP LAKE VU
CAMP LAKE VU
CAMP
LAKE-VU
1961

Above: **Camp Lake-Vu, Milford, New Jersey, summer, 1961**
I am in the very center of the picture, seated in the middle row … I may look tortured, but I think I was just squinting in the sun.

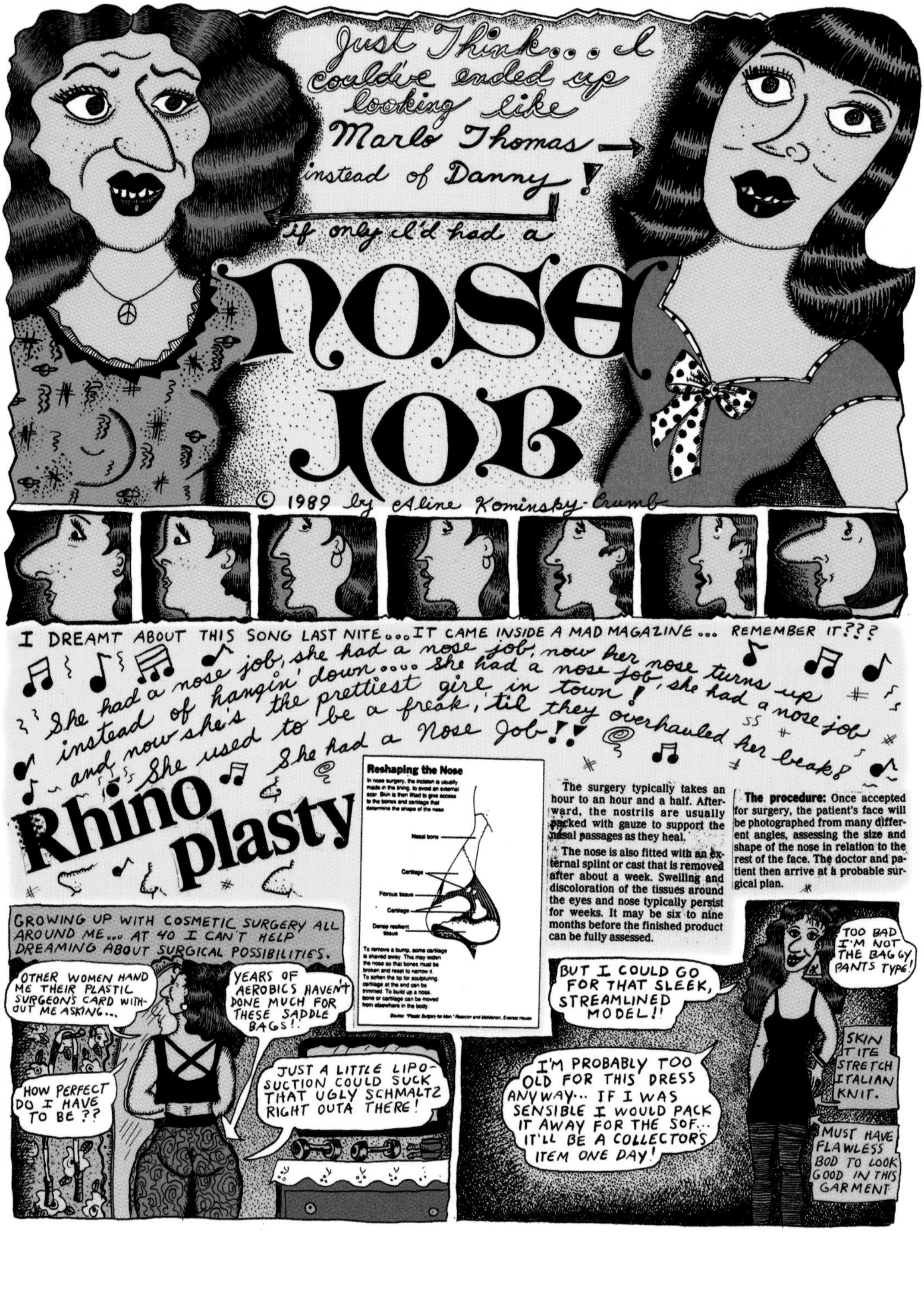
Just Think... I could've ended up looking like Marlo Thomas → instead of Danny!
if only I'd had a
NOSE JOB
© 1989 by Aline Kominsky-Crumb
I DREAMT ABOUT THIS SONG LAST NITE... IT CAME INSIDE A MAD MAGAZINE... REMEMBER IT???
She had a nose job, she had a nose job, now her nose turns up instead of hangin' down.... She had a nose job, she had a nose job and now she's the prettiest girl in town! She used to be a freak, 'til they overhauled her beak! She had a Nose Job!!
Rhino plasty
Reshaping the Nose
In nose surgery, the incision is usually made in the lining, to avoid an external scar. Skin is then lifted to give access to the bones and cartilage that determine the shape of the nose
Nasal bone
Cartilage
Fibrous tissue
Cartilage
Dense resilient tissue
To remove a bump, some cartilage is shaved away. This may widen the nose so that bones must be broken and reset to narrow it. To soften the tip for sculpturing, cartilage at the end can be trimmed. To build up a nose, bone or cartilage can be moved from elsewhere in the body.
The surgery typically takes an hour to an hour and a half. Afterward, the nostrils are usually packed with gauze to support the nasal passages as they heal.
The nose is also fitted with an external splint or cast that is removed after about a week. Swelling and discoloration of the tissues around the eyes and nose typically persist for weeks. It may be six to nine months before the finished product can be fully assessed.
The procedure: Once accepted for surgery, the patient's face will be photographed from many different angles, assessing the size and shape of the nose in relation to the rest of the face. The doctor and patient then arrive at a probable surgical plan.
GROWING UP WITH COSMETIC SURGERY ALL AROUND ME... AT 40 I CAN'T HELP DREAMING ABOUT SURGICAL POSSIBILITIES.
OTHER WOMEN HAND ME THEIR PLASTIC SURGEON'S CARD WITHOUT ME ASKING...
YEARS OF AEROBICS HAVEN'T DONE MUCH FOR THESE SADDLE BAGS!
HOW PERFECT DO I HAVE TO BE??
JUST A LITTLE LIPOSUCTION COULD SUCK THAT UGLY SCHMALTZ RIGHT OUTA THERE!
BUT I COULD GO FOR THAT SLEEK, STREAMLINED MODEL!!
TOO BAD I'M NOT THE BAGGY PANTS TYPE!
I'M PROBABLY TOO OLD FOR THIS DRESS ANYWAY... IF I WAS SENSIBLE I WOULD PACK IT AWAY FOR THE SOF... IT'LL BE A COLLECTORS ITEM ONE DAY!
SKIN TITE STRETCH ITALIAN KNIT.
MUST HAVE FLAWLESS BOD TO LOOK GOOD IN THIS GARMENT

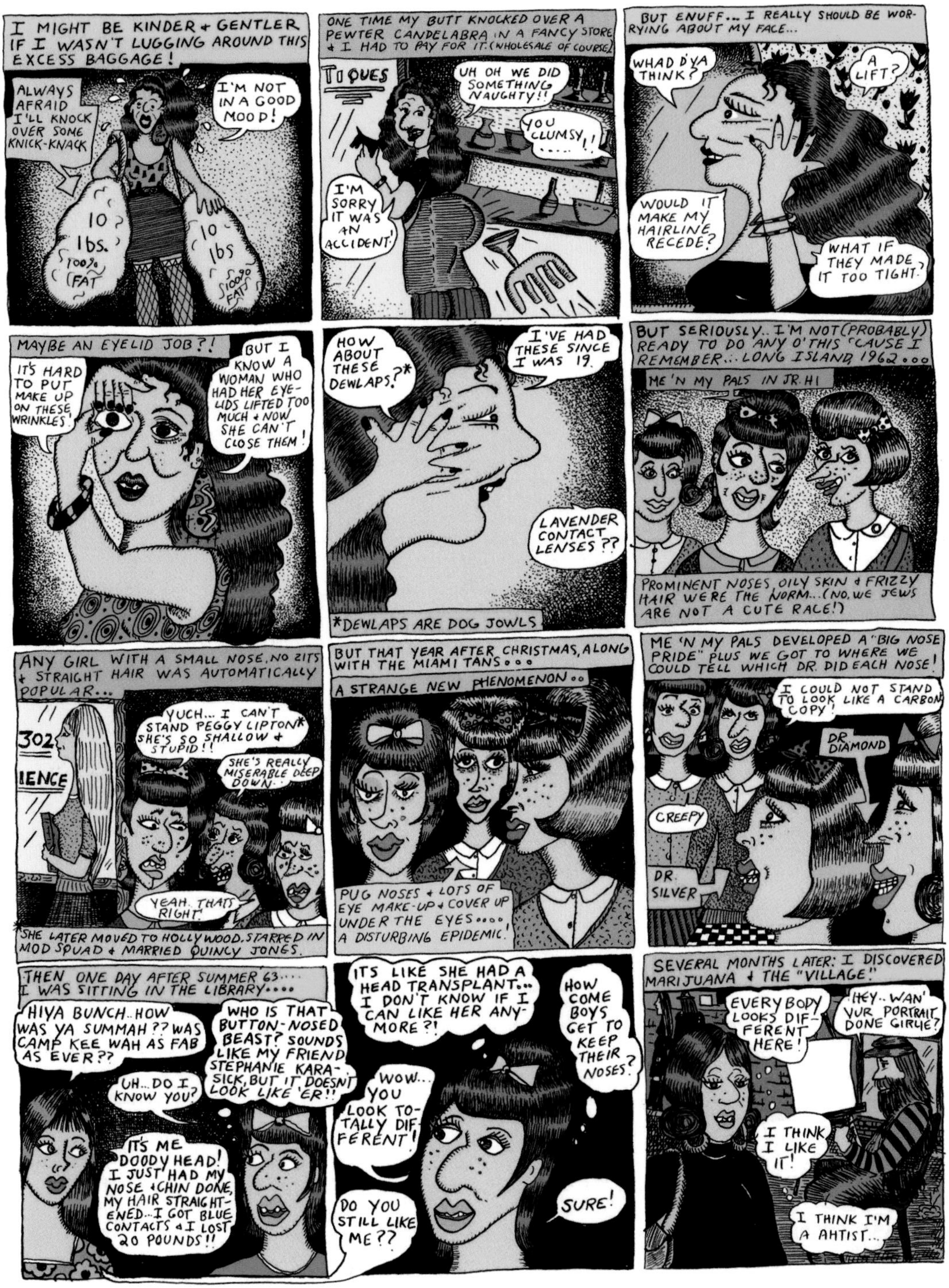
I MIGHT BE KINDER + GENTLER IF I WASN'T LUGGING AROUND THIS EXCESS BAGGAGE!
ALWAYS AFRAID I'LL KNOCK OVER SOME KNICK-KNACK
I'M NOT IN A GOOD MOOD!
10 lbs. 100% FAT
10 lbs 100% FAT
ONE TIME MY BUTT KNOCKED OVER A PEWTER CANDELABRA IN A FANCY STORE + I HAD TO PAY FOR IT. (WHOLESALE OF COURSE)
TIQUES
UH OH WE DID SOMETHING NAUGHTY!!
YOU CLUMSY.....!!
I'M SORRY IT WAS AN ACCIDENT!
BUT ENUFF... I REALLY SHOULD BE WORRYING ABOUT MY FACE...
WHAD D'YA THINK?
A LIFT?
WOULD IT MAKE MY HAIRLINE RECEDE?
WHAT IF THEY MADE IT TOO TIGHT?
MAYBE AN EYELID JOB?!
IT'S HARD TO PUT MAKE UP ON THESE WRINKLES!
BUT I KNOW A WOMAN WHO HAD HER EYELIDS LIFTED TOO MUCH + NOW SHE CAN'T CLOSE THEM!
HOW ABOUT THESE DEWLAPS?*
I'VE HAD THESE SINCE I WAS 19.
LAVENDER CONTACT LENSES??
*DEWLAPS ARE DOG JOWLS
BUT SERIOUSLY.. I'M NOT (PROBABLY) READY TO DO ANY O'THIS 'CAUSE I REMEMBER... LONG ISLAND, 1962...
ME 'N MY PALS IN JR. HI
PROMINENT NOSES, OILY SKIN + FRIZZY HAIR WERE THE NORM... (NO, WE JEWS ARE NOT A CUTE RACE!)
ANY GIRL WITH A SMALL NOSE, NO ZITS + STRAIGHT HAIR WAS AUTOMATICALLY POPULAR...
302
IENCE
YUCH... I CAN'T STAND PEGGY LIPTON* SHE'S SO SHALLOW + STUPID!!
SHE'S REALLY MISERABLE DEEP DOWN.
YEAH. THAT'S RIGHT!
*SHE LATER MOVED TO HOLLYWOOD, STARRED IN MOD SQUAD + MARRIED QUINCY JONES.
BUT THAT YEAR AFTER CHRISTMAS, ALONG WITH THE MIAMI TANS...
A STRANGE NEW PHENOMENON..
PUG NOSES + LOTS OF EYE MAKE-UP + COVER UP UNDER THE EYES.... A DISTURBING EPIDEMIC!
ME 'N MY PALS DEVELOPED A "BIG NOSE PRIDE" PLUS WE GOT TO WHERE WE COULD TELL WHICH DR. DID EACH NOSE!
I COULD NOT STAND TO LOOK LIKE A CARBON COPY!
DR. DIAMOND
CREEPY
DR. SILVER
THEN ONE DAY AFTER SUMMER '63.... I WAS SITTING IN THE LIBRARY....
HIYA BUNCH.. HOW WAS YA SUMMAH?? WAS CAMP KEE WAH AS FAB AS EVER??
WHO IS THAT BUTTON-NOSED BEAST? SOUNDS LIKE MY FRIEND STEPHANIE KARASICK, BUT IT DOESN'T LOOK LIKE 'ER!!
UH... DO I KNOW YOU?
IT'S ME DOODY HEAD! I JUST HAD MY NOSE + CHIN DONE, MY HAIR STRAIGHTENED... I GOT BLUE CONTACTS + I LOST 20 POUNDS!!
ITS LIKE SHE HAD A HEAD TRANSPLANT... I DON'T KNOW IF I CAN LIKE HER ANYMORE?!
HOW COME BOYS GET TO KEEP THEIR NOSES?
WOW... YOU LOOK TOTALLY DIFFERENT!
DO YOU STILL LIKE ME??
SURE!
SEVERAL MONTHS LATER: I DISCOVERED MARIJUANA + THE "VILLAGE."
EVERYBODY LOOKS DIFFERENT HERE!
HEY.. WAN' YUR PORTRAIT DONE GIRLIE?
I THINK I LIKE IT!
I THINK I'M A AHTIST...

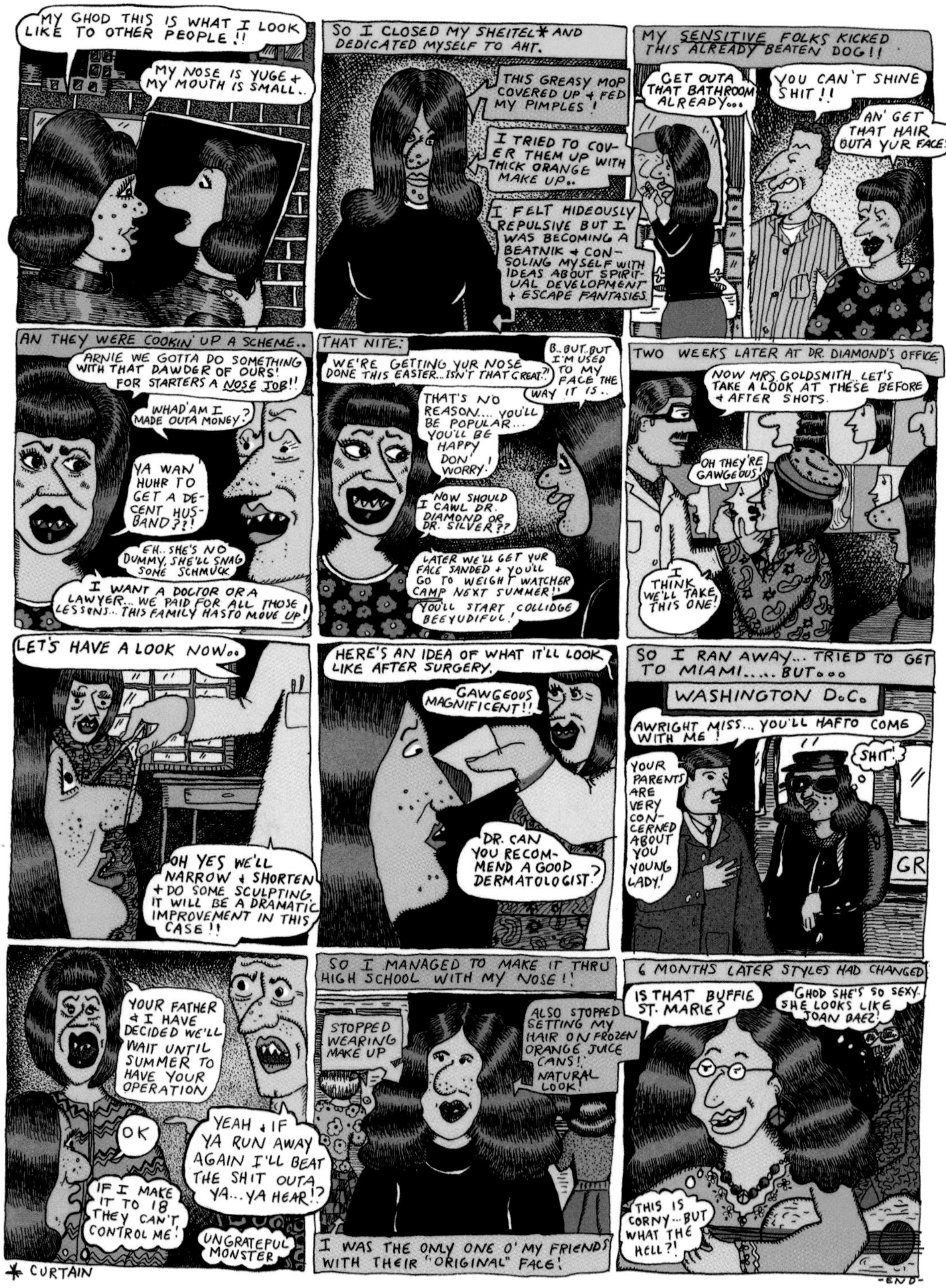

MY GHOD THIS IS WHAT I LOOK LIKE TO OTHER PEOPLE!!
MY NOSE IS YUGE + MY MOUTH IS SMALL..
SO I CLOSED MY SHEITEL* AND DEDICATED MYSELF TO AHT.
THIS GREASY MOP COVERED UP + FED MY PIMPLES!
I TRIED TO COVER THEM UP WITH THICK ORANGE MAKE UP..
I FELT HIDEOUSLY REPULSIVE BUT I WAS BECOMING A BEATNIK + CONSOLING MYSELF WITH IDEAS ABOUT SPIRITUAL DEVELOPMENT + ESCAPE FANTASIES
MY SENSITIVE FOLKS KICKED THIS ALREADY BEATEN DOG!!
GET OUTA THAT BATHROOM ALREADY...
YOU CAN'T SHINE SHIT!!
AN' GET THAT HAIR OUTA YUR FACE!
AN THEY WERE COOKIN' UP A SCHEME..
ARNIE WE GOTTA DO SOMETHING WITH THAT DAWDER OF OURS! FOR STARTERS A NOSE JOB!!
WHAD'AM I MADE OUTA MONEY?
YA WAN' HUHR TO GET A DECENT HUSBAND??!
EH.. SHE'S NO DUMMY, SHE'LL SNAG SOME SCHMUCK
I WANT A DOCTOR OR A LAWYER... WE PAID FOR ALL THOSE LESSONS... THIS FAMILY HASTO MOVE UP!
THAT NITE:
WE'RE GETTING YUR NOSE DONE THIS EASTER... ISN'T THAT GREAT?!
B..BUT..BUT I'M USED TO MY FACE THE WAY IT IS..
THAT'S NO REASON.... YOU'LL BE POPULAR... YOU'LL BE HAPPY DON' WORRY!
NOW SHOULD I CAWL DR. DIAMOND OR DR. SILVER??
LATER WE'LL GET YUR FACE SANDED + YOU'LL GO TO WEIGHT WATCHER CAMP NEXT SUMMER!!
YOU'LL START COLLIDGE BEEYUDIFUL!
TWO WEEKS LATER AT DR. DIAMOND'S OFFICE
NOW MRS. GOLDSMITH.. LET'S TAKE A LOOK AT THESE BEFORE + AFTER SHOTS.
OH THEY'RE GAWGEOUS!
I THINK WE'LL TAKE THIS ONE!
LET'S HAVE A LOOK NOW..
OH YES WE'LL NARROW + SHORTEN + DO SOME SCULPTING. IT WILL BE A DRAMATIC IMPROVEMENT IN THIS CASE!!
HERE'S AN IDEA OF WHAT IT'LL LOOK LIKE AFTER SURGERY.
GAWGEOUS MAGNIFICENT!!
DR. CAN YOU RECOMMEND A GOOD DERMATOLOGIST?
SO I RAN AWAY... TRIED TO GET TO MIAMI..... BUT...
WASHINGTON D.C.
AWRIGHT MISS... YOU'LL HAFTO COME WITH ME!
SHIT!
YOUR PARENTS ARE VERY CONCERNED ABOUT YOU YOUNG LADY!
GR
YOUR FATHER + I HAVE DECIDED WE'LL WAIT UNTIL SUMMER TO HAVE YOUR OPERATION
OK
YEAH + IF YA RUN AWAY AGAIN I'LL BEAT THE SHIT OUTA YA... YA HEAR!?
IF I MAKE IT TO 18 THEY CAN'T CONTROL ME!
UNGRATEFUL MONSTER
SO I MANAGED TO MAKE IT THRU HIGH SCHOOL WITH MY NOSE!
STOPPED WEARING MAKE UP
ALSO STOPPED SETTING MY HAIR ON FROZEN ORANGE JUICE CANS!
NATURAL LOOK!
I WAS THE ONLY ONE O' MY FRIENDS WITH THEIR "ORIGINAL" FACE!
6 MONTHS LATER STYLES HAD CHANGED
IS THAT BUFFIE ST. MARIE?
GHOD SHE'S SO SEXY. SHE LOOKS LIKE JOAN BAEZ!
THIS IS CORNY... BUT WHAT THE HELL?!
* CURTAIN
-END-

Miss perfection—Peggy Lipton

Ah yes! Peggy Lipton. I remember her. She was at school with me, and was tall, thin, blonde, pretty, smart, nice and Jewish. I'm convinced that she must have been placed among us short, fat, curly-haired Jewish girls just to remind us how imperfect we all were.

Above: **Peggy Lipton starring in the TV show *Mod Squad*.**
This further reinforced her "goddess" image and natural superiority, of course.

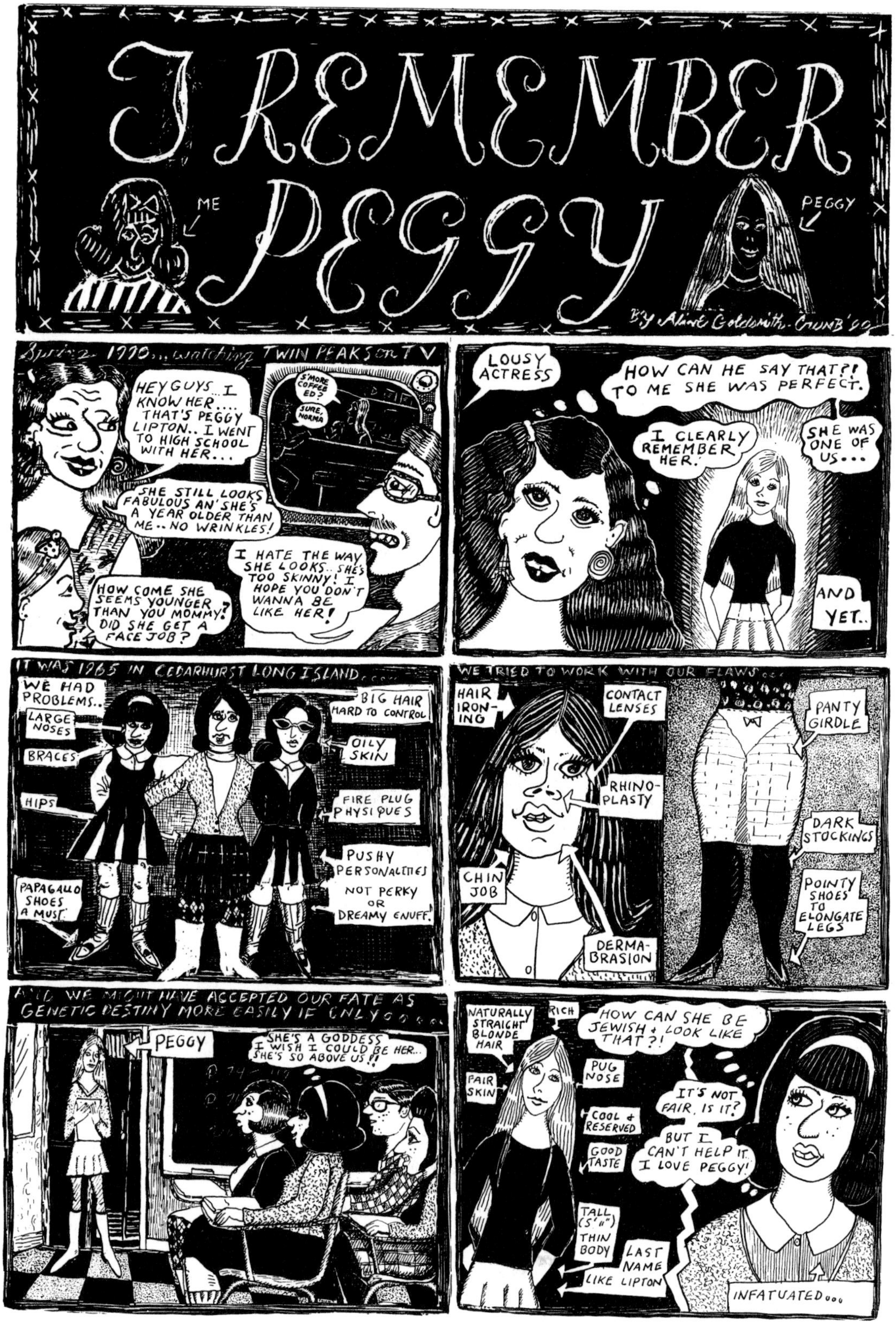

I REMEMBER PEGGY
ME
PEGGY
BY Aline Goldsmith-Crumb '90
Spring 1990... watching TWIN PEAKS on TV
HEY GUYS... I KNOW HER.... THAT'S PEGGY LIPTON.. I WENT TO HIGH SCHOOL WITH HER...
S'MORE COFFEE ED?
SURE, NORMA
SHE STILL LOOKS FABULOUS AN' SHE'S A YEAR OLDER THAN ME.. NO WRINKLES!
I HATE THE WAY SHE LOOKS.. SHE'S TOO SKINNY! I HOPE YOU DON'T WANNA BE LIKE HER!
HOW COME SHE SEEMS YOUNGER THAN YOU MOMMY? DID SHE GET A FACE JOB?
LOUSY ACTRESS
HOW CAN HE SAY THAT?! TO ME SHE WAS PERFECT.
I CLEARLY REMEMBER HER.
SHE WAS ONE OF US...
AND YET..
IT WAS 1965 IN CEDARHURST LONG ISLAND....
WE HAD PROBLEMS..
LARGE NOSES
BRACES
HIPS
PAPAGALLO SHOES A MUST.
BIG HAIR HARD TO CONTROL
OILY SKIN
FIRE PLUG PHYSIQUES
PUSHY PERSONALITIES
NOT PERKY OR DREAMY ENUFF.
WE TRIED TO WORK WITH OUR FLAWS....
HAIR IRON-ING
CONTACT LENSES
RHINO-PLASTY
CHIN JOB
DERMA-BRASION
PANTY GIRDLE
DARK STOCKINGS
POINTY SHOES TO ELONGATE LEGS
AND WE MIGHT HAVE ACCEPTED OUR FATE AS GENETIC DESTINY MORE EASILY IF ONLY.....
PEGGY
SHE'S A GODDESS I WISH I COULD BE HER... SHE'S SO ABOVE US!!
NATURALLY STRAIGHT BLONDE HAIR
RICH
FAIR SKIN
PUG NOSE
COOL & RESERVED
GOOD TASTE
TALL (5'") THIN BODY
LAST NAME LIKE LIPTON
HOW CAN SHE BE JEWISH & LOOK LIKE THAT?!
IT'S NOT FAIR, IS IT?
BUT I CAN'T HELP IT. I LOVE PEGGY!
INFATUATED...

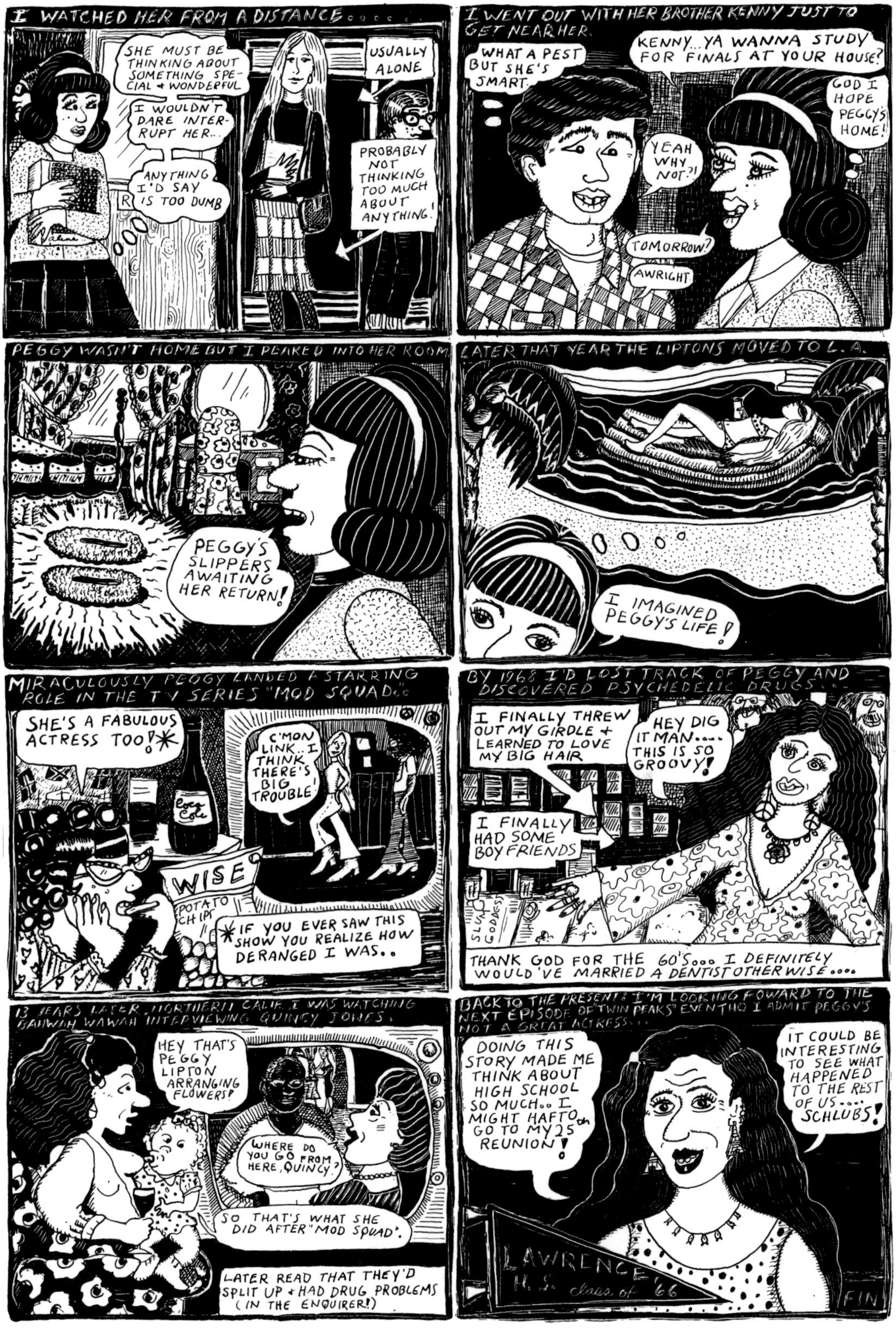
I WATCHED HER FROM A DISTANCE......
SHE MUST BE THINKING ABOUT SOMETHING SPECIAL + WONDERFUL
I WOULDN'T DARE INTERRUPT HER..
ANYTHING I'D SAY IS TOO DUMB
USUALLY ALONE
PROBABLY NOT THINKING TOO MUCH ABOUT ANYTHING!
I WENT OUT WITH HER BROTHER KENNY JUST TO GET NEAR HER.
WHAT A PEST BUT SHE'S SMART
KENNY... YA WANNA STUDY FOR FINALS AT YOUR HOUSE?
GOD I HOPE PEGGY'S HOME!
YEAH WHY NOT?!
TOMORROW?
AWRIGHT
PEGGY WASN'T HOME BUT I PEAKED INTO HER ROOM
PEGGY'S SLIPPERS AWAITING HER RETURN!
LATER THAT YEAR THE LIPTONS MOVED TO L. A.
I IMAGINED PEGGY'S LIFE!
MIRACULOUSLY PEGGY LANDED A STARRING ROLE IN THE TV SERIES "MOD SQUAD"
SHE'S A FABULOUS ACTRESS TOO!*
C'MON LINK.. I THINK THERE'S BIG TROUBLE!
WISE POTATO CHIPS
*IF YOU EVER SAW THIS SHOW YOU REALIZE HOW DERANGED I WAS..
BY 1968 I'D LOST TRACK OF PEGGY AND DISCOVERED PSYCHEDELIC DRUGS...
I FINALLY THREW OUT MY GIRDLE + LEARNED TO LOVE MY BIG HAIR
HEY DIG IT MAN.... THIS IS SO GROOVY!
I FINALLY HAD SOME BOY FRIENDS
SLUM GODDESS
THANK GOD FOR THE 60'S... I DEFINITELY WOULD'VE MARRIED A DENTIST OTHERWISE....
13 YEARS LATER, NORTHERN CALIF. I WAS WATCHING GAHWAH WAWAH INTERVIEWING QUINCY JONES.
HEY THAT'S PEGGY LIPTON ARRANGING FLOWERS!
WHERE DO YOU GO FROM HERE, QUINCY?
SO THAT'S WHAT SHE DID AFTER "MOD SQUAD".
LATER READ THAT THEY'D SPLIT UP + HAD DRUG PROBLEMS (IN THE ENQUIRER!)
BACK TO THE PRESENT: I'M LOOKING FOWARD TO THE NEXT EPISODE OF "TWIN PEAKS" EVEN THO I ADMIT PEGGY'S NOT A GREAT ACTRESS...
DOING THIS STORY MADE ME THINK ABOUT HIGH SCHOOL SO MUCH.. I MIGHT HAFTO GO TO MY 25th REUNION!
IT COULD BE INTERESTING TO SEE WHAT HAPPENED TO THE REST OF US.... SCHLUBS!
LAWRENCE H.S. class of '66
FIN

Sex, drugs and ... The Beatles!

Around this time I started smoking marijuana, which I obtained from my city friends. I did a lot of very stoned-looking, intricate Rapidograph drawings. I filled up lots of notebooks.

I even took one LSD trip, although I didn't find out what it was until later. All I can remember is that while I was high, my parents came home and opened the door to my bedroom. The light was behind them and they both looked like glowing, fire-breathing monsters. Ewwww... Scary! One night my parents found me really stoned. They thought I was drunk and grounded me for a month. I didn't give a damn any more. I just hid a ladder in the bushes outside my bedroom and snuck out and never got caught. My parents were too wrapped up in their financial difficulties and in the ups and downs of their roller-coaster relationship.

I continued to sneak into the Village whenever I could, and desperately tried to meet hip older guys. I accidentally discovered the wacky band The Fugs who were performing at The Players Theater on MacDougal Street. I loved their performances! They were totally outrageous and original. I had never seen or heard anything like them before. I would try to get in backstage after the shows but they would never let me in. I was too young and too un-cool. Betsy Klein, the drummer Ken Weaver's girlfriend, threw me out numerous times (read about Betsy later in this story.) But persistence paid off, and finally one of the guys let me in. I'm sure it was because I was a sexy, young, slutty-looking creature!

During one of the bleakest moments of my adolescence, I succumbed to Beatlemania. I remember hearing *I Wanna Hold Your Hand* and *Please Please Me* and buying the record and listening to it thousands of times. I started buying every piece of Beatle material I could find and afford. I bought all the 'zines with articles and photos and projected all my love, hopes and dreams onto them. I almost passed out while watching them on the Ed Sullivan Show. My mother, who had been a Frank Sinatra fan in her youth, could actually kind of sympathize with my condition.

I re-decorated my room by covering all the furniture with photos of the Beatles, and actually carved their portraits on the back of my bedroom door. I had Beatle dolls with wobbly heads, many of each in different sizes. I had a Beatle suitcase, wallet, lamp, cards, key chains, lunch boxes, and numerous other artifacts. Unfortunately, my priceless collection got thrown out when my aunt Ruth cleaned out her basement, where my stuff was stored, before moving to Florida in the 1970s.

Like millions of pathetic girls with no lives of their own, I was determined to meet the Beatles. In my delusional state, I was convinced that if they could only meet me they would instantly see that I was different and cooler than all their other fans, and they would want me to stay with them forever. I chose George as my favorite because Paul and John were too popular and Ringo just wasn't my type.

George was cute, but not too cute. He was talented but discreet, shy and under-appreciated. With me at his side, all that would change! My uncle Ben owned the drug store at the International Arrivals building at JFK (it was still called Idlewild Airport then). He told me that the Beatles would be secretly arriving on National Airlines at a closed terminal. It had been announced in the media that they would be arriving at Penn Station by train, and thousands of fans were waiting there. This was my chance to get close to them, while everyone else would be waiting miles away! When I got to the terminal there were some police and press and police barricades, but only a few fans. I couldn't believe my luck!

It was a heady feeling to think that the Beatles were going to walk into a room and I would be practically alone with them! I don't know how long I waited, but eventually they arrived amidst a flurry of activity, flashing cameras and cops. All this was not enough to stop me from flinging myself over the barricades and onto George. He did not look at me with instant recognition. No, he had a look of terror on his face! It was not love at first sight, as I had fantasized, it was fear and loathing. I was brusquely escorted to police headquarters and had to call my parents, who arrived in a not so good mood. To add to my humiliation, I could be seen on the news that night, screaming as two annoyed-looking cops dragged me away!

By the way, George Harrison's son now has a copy of the story on the following pages in which I am throwing myself at his horrified father.

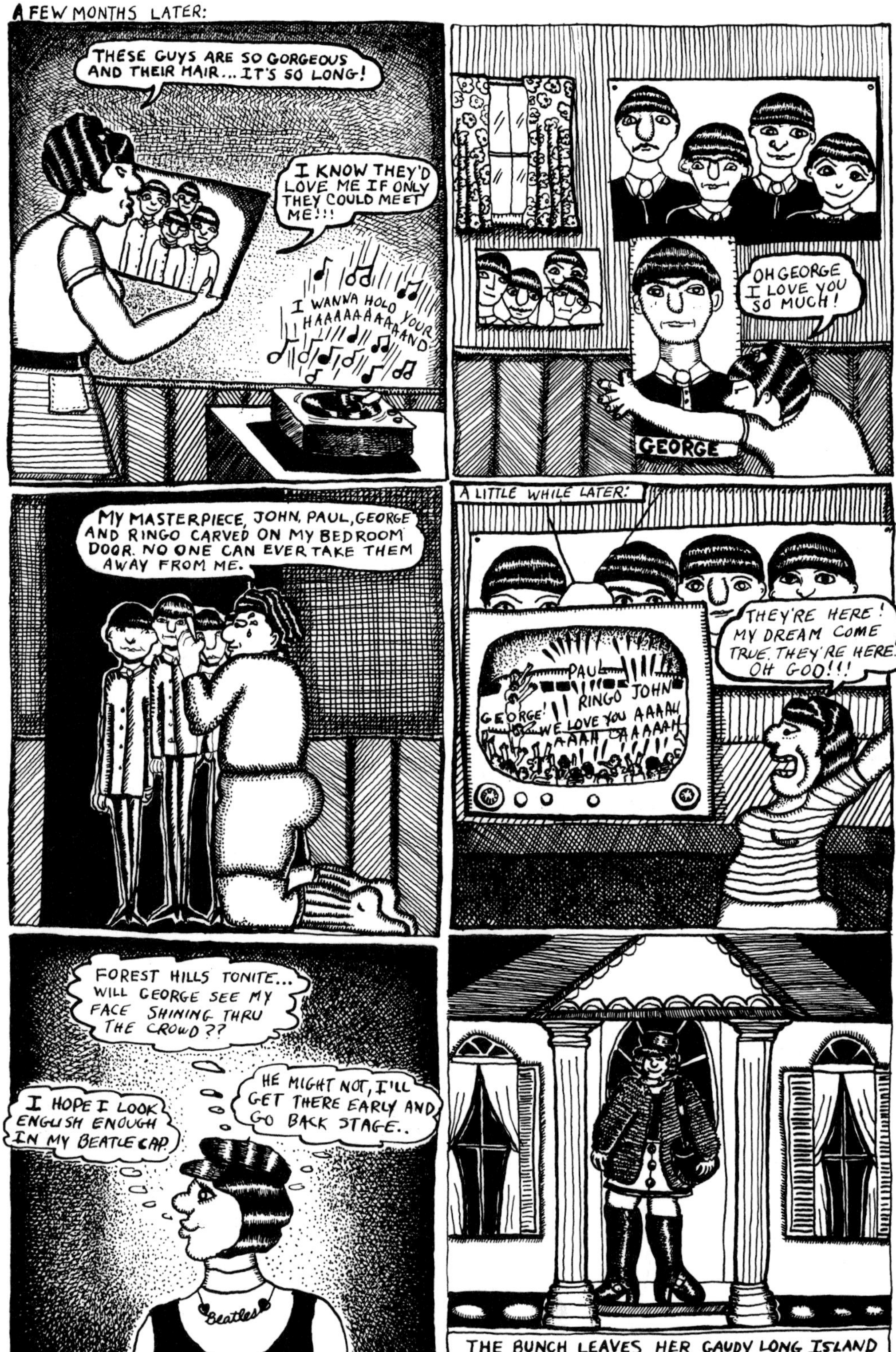

A FEW MONTHS LATER:
THESE GUYS ARE SO GORGEOUS AND THEIR HAIR... IT'S SO LONG!
I KNOW THEY'D LOVE ME IF ONLY THEY COULD MEET ME!!!
I WANNA HOLD YOUR HAAAAAAAAAAAAND
OH GEORGE I LOVE YOU SO MUCH!
GEORGE
MY MASTERPIECE, JOHN, PAUL, GEORGE AND RINGO CARVED ON MY BEDROOM DOOR. NO ONE CAN EVER TAKE THEM AWAY FROM ME.
A LITTLE WHILE LATER:
PAUL
RINGO JOHN
GEORGE
WE LOVE YOU AAAAH AAAH AAAAAH
THEY'RE HERE! MY DREAM COME TRUE. THEY'RE HERE! OH GOD!!!
FOREST HILLS TONITE... WILL GEORGE SEE MY FACE SHINING THRU THE CROWD??
I HOPE I LOOK ENGLISH ENOUGH IN MY BEATLE CAP.
HE MIGHT NOT, I'LL GET THERE EARLY AND GO BACK STAGE..
Beatles
THE BUNCH LEAVES HER GAUDY LONG ISLAND HOME IN HER CARNABY ST OUTFIT, HOPEFUL!!!

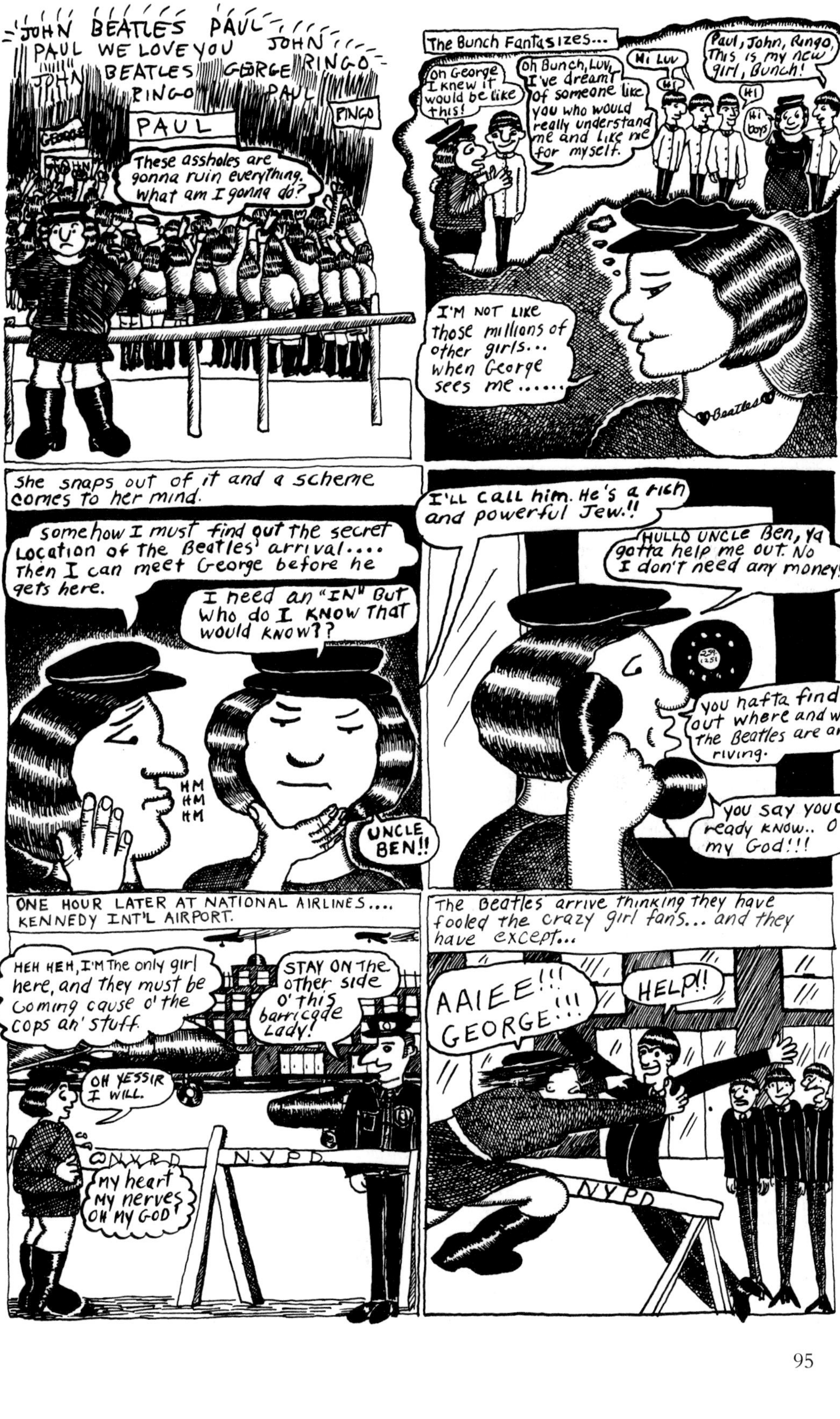

JOHN BEATLES PAUL PAUL WE LOVE YOU JOHN JOHN BEATLES GEORGE RINGO RINGO PAUL
PAUL
PINGO
These assholes are gonna ruin everything. What am I gonna do?
The Bunch Fantasizes...
Oh George I knew it would be like this!
Oh Bunch, Luv, I've dreamt of someone like you who would really understand me and like me for myself.
Hi Luv
Hi
Paul, John, Ringo, This is my new girl, Bunch!
Hi
Hi boys
I'M NOT LIKE those millions of other girls... when George sees me......
Beatles
She snaps out of it and a scheme comes to her mind.
Somehow I must find out the secret location of the Beatles' arrival.... Then I can meet George before he gets here.
I need an "IN" But who do I KNOW THAT would KNOW??
HM HM HM
UNCLE BEN!!
I'LL CALL HIM. HE'S A RICH and powerful Jew.!!
HULLO UNCLE Ben, Ya gotta help me out. No I don't need any money!
You hafta find out where and when the Beatles are arriving.
You say you already KNOW.. Oh my God!!!
ONE HOUR LATER AT NATIONAL AIRLINES.... KENNEDY INT'L AIRPORT.
HEH HEH, I'M The only girl here, and they must be coming cause o' the cops an' stuff.
STAY ON The other side o' this barricade Lady!
OH YESSIR I WILL.
N.Y.P.D.
My heart My nerves OH MY GOD
The Beatles arrive thinking they have fooled the crazy girl fans... and they have except...
AAIEE!!! GEORGE!!!
HELP!!
NYPD

EEEEE EEEE
GULP
EEEEEEEEE
GEEORRRGE
RIGHT THIS WAY GIRLIE
NOW BEAT IT
I WAS SO CLOSE TO TRUE HAPPINESS TODAY. IF ONLY GEORGE HAD REALIZED IT WAS ME.
SOB SOB
THAT NITE AT HOME...
ANOTHER CASE OF BEATLEMANIA STRUCK TODAY.....

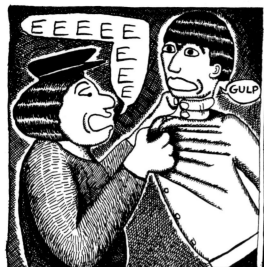

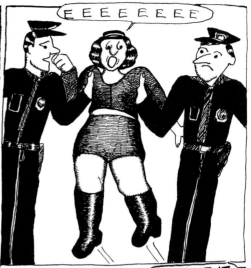

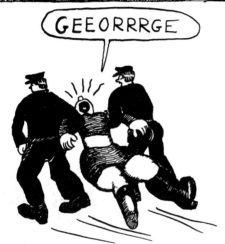

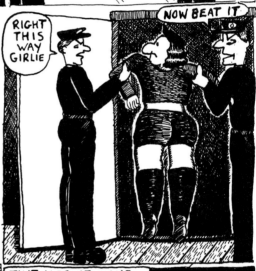

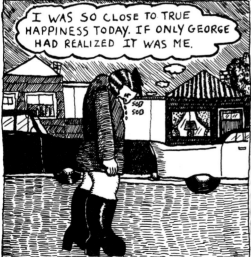

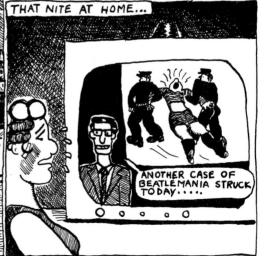

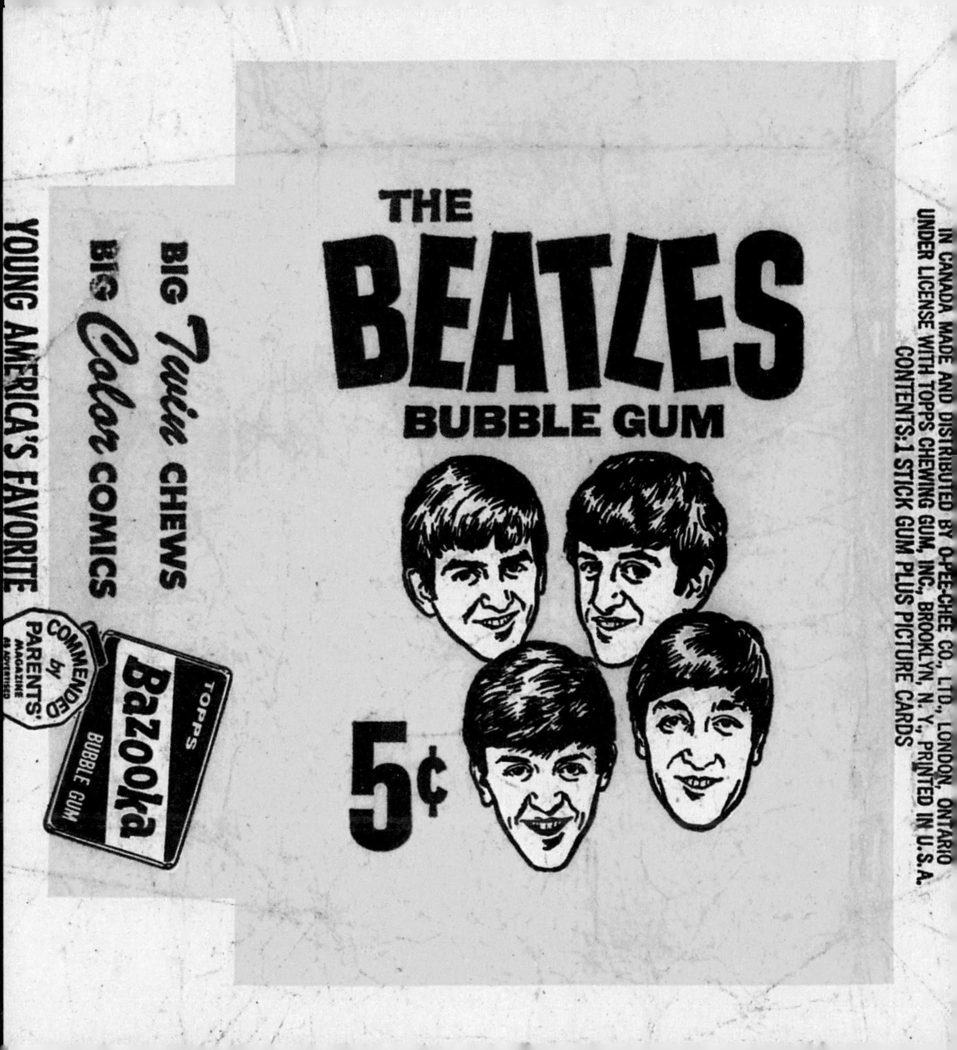

THE
BEATLES
BUBBLE GUM
5¢
BIG Twin CHEWS
BIG Color COMICS
YOUNG AMERICA'S FAVORITE
COMMENDED by PARENTS' MAGAZINE AS ADVERTISED
TOPPS
Bazooka
BUBBLE GUM
IN CANADA MADE AND DISTRIBUTED BY O-PEE-CHEE CO., LTD., LONDON, ONTARIO
UNDER LICENSE WITH TOPPS CHEWING GUM, INC., BROOKLYN, N. Y., PRINTED IN U.S.A.
CONTENTS: 1 STICK GUM PLUS PICTURE CARDS

CHAPTER TWO

Escape ...

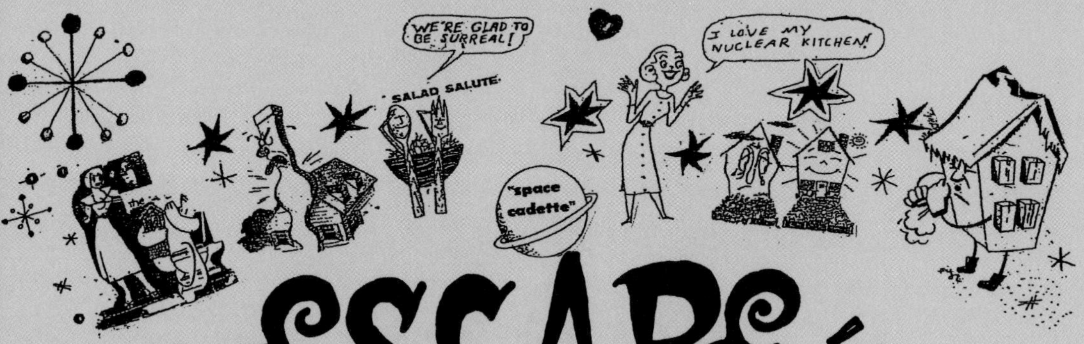
WE'RE GLAD TO BE SURREAL!
SALAD SALUTE
"space cadette"
I LOVE MY NUCLEAR KITCHEN!

ESCAPE...

*Art School
*Flower Power
* Drugs!
* Sex!
*Early Wimmen's Comics
*Twisted Sisters

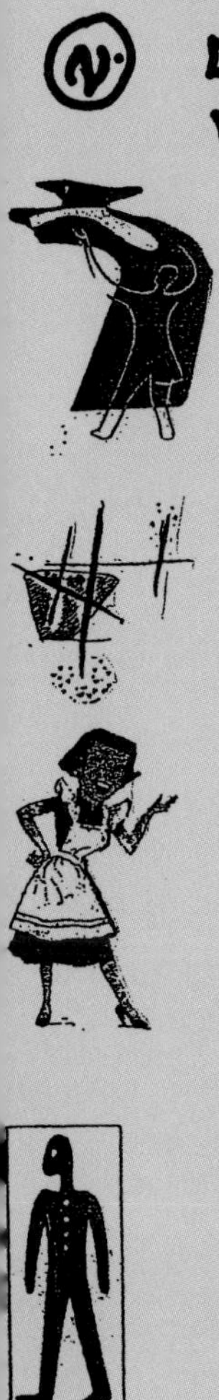

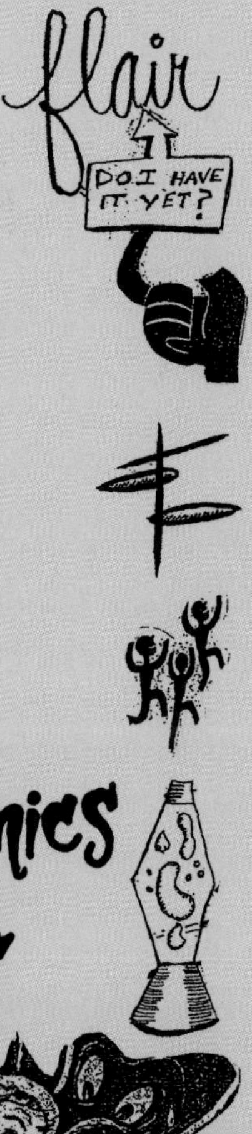
flair
DO I HAVE IT YET?

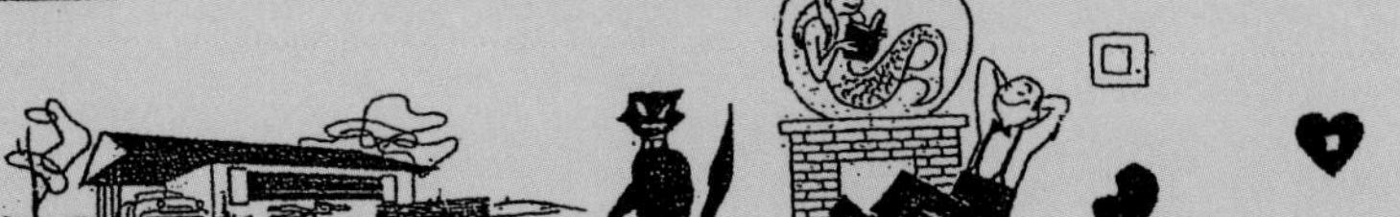

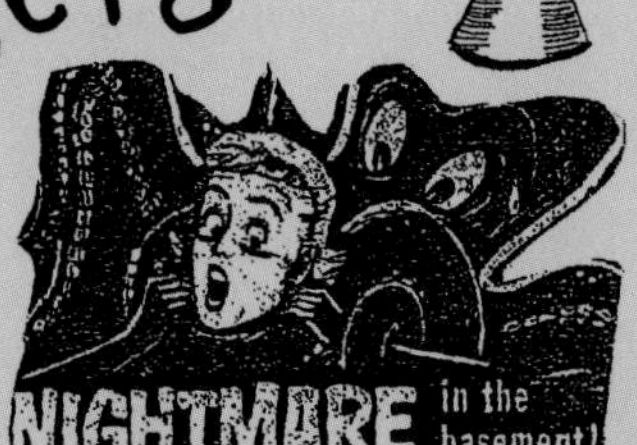
NIGHTMARE in the basement!

Not a promising beginning ...

After high school, I was accepted at a mediocre college, State University Art School. Although tuition cost practically nothing, I still had to take out huge student loans—my parents refused to spend a dime on my education—and I only managed to pay them off much later with Robert's help. I got a summer job through my uncle as a secretary in the duty free shop next to his drug store at JFK, where I worked for a sadistic jerk who tormented me all day long for ten weeks straight.

At night, I would head for the city and drink heavily, smoke pot and take speed so I could stay up all night and party. That summer was so wild and sordid, and I was in such an altered state, that all the details remain a gigantic blur. For example, I can't recall a single name of any of the guys I slept with. I usually made sure they used a condom, but I must have gotten sloppy— not surprising—and by the time I started school in September I was pregnant. This was one year before abortions were legalized, and in any case, I was so out of it I didn't notice anything until several months had passed and it was much too late to intervene.

I shared a bleak dorm room with two girls, neither of whom I could relate to for very different reasons. Barbara Goldman was a sorority girl from Queens who wore her boyfriend Bernie's ring on a chain and was already a married middle aged woman as far as I was concerned. My other roommate was nicknamed "Mike"—she weighed 250 pounds and had a moustache. Mike slept on the bunk bed above me, and I often envisioned her squashing me to death during the night as the flimsy bed gave way to her bulk.

Anyway, by the time I arrived, Leslie Thaler, a snotty majorette from my high school who happened to be living on our floor, had pretty much taken care of my reputation among the interesting girls I might have become friends with. Classes were totally boring. So I spent most of my time drinking beer at the local bars in town, being promiscuous in a desperate attempt to get love and attention. I had really been looking forward to leaving home and starting my "real" life, away from my demented family, but this was not a promising beginning!

Right: **Me with guitar, at my parents' house, Woodmere, New York, 1966**
Heavily identifying with Joan Baez and Judy Collins!

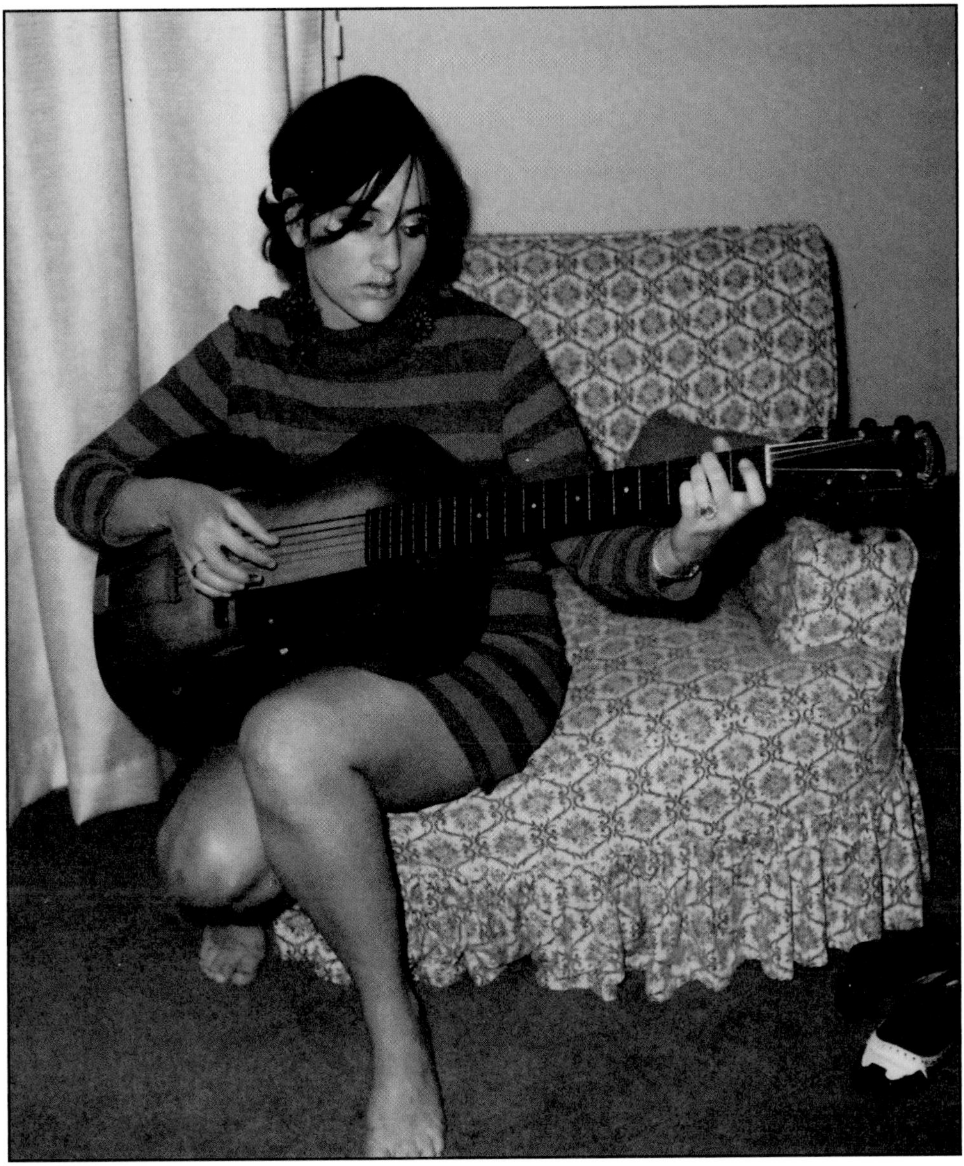

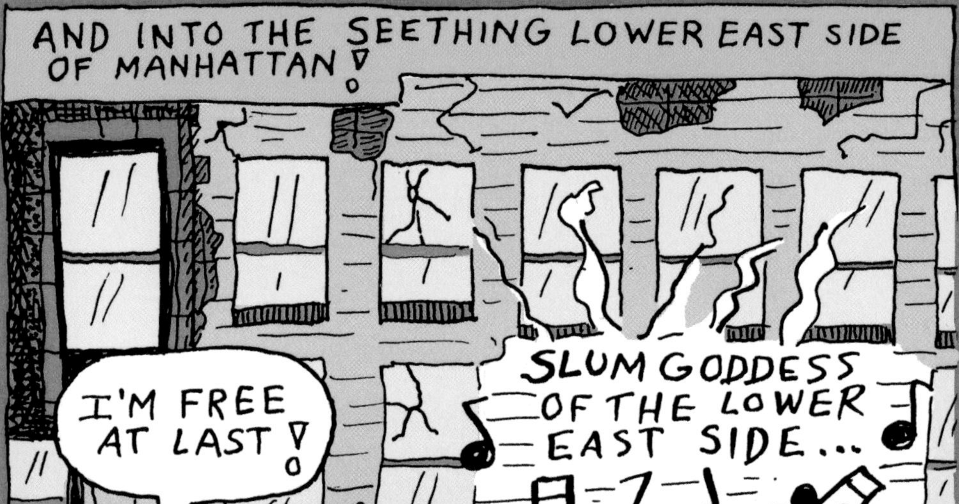
AND INTO THE SEETHING LOWER EAST SIDE OF MANHATTAN!
I'M FREE AT LAST!
SLUM GODDESS OF THE LOWER EAST SIDE...
PEACE EYE BOOKS
PSYCHEDELICATTE
HEAD SHOP
BANANA POWER

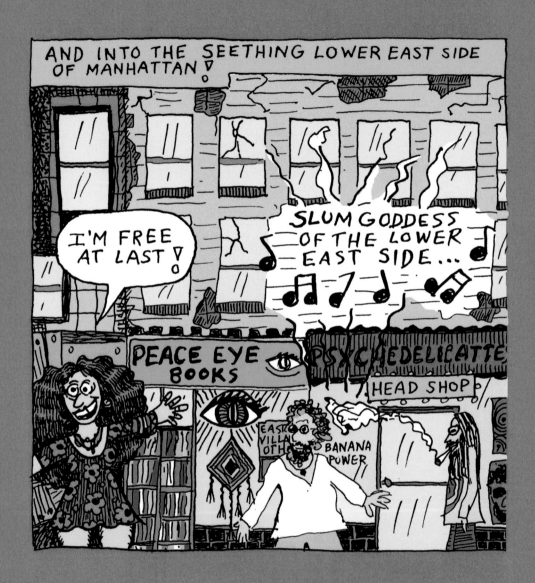

I encounter Flower Power!

Meanwhile, the world was starting to explode around me. This was 1966, the year of flower power, psychedelic drugs and social unrest, and I wanted to be part of the scene. Here was the opportunity to "throw off the shackles of oppression!" I had no political savvy, and was too naïve to understand my plight in any kind of sociological perspective. I was disgusted with everything I'd experienced in my life and eager to connect with kindred spirits. Amazingly, I discovered I was not alone, but at the epicenter of the hippy movement at its height.

I ran away to the Lower East Side of New York. There I discovered a community of young people from all over the country who felt as alienated from their parents and mainstream culture as I did. An alternative culture was rapidly developing—music, art, newspapers—plus a whole new style and different behavior. The wild hippy look suited me perfectly. I let my long curly hair go natural, stopped shaving, gave up wearing a bra, pranced around in flowing mini dresses that barely covered my butt, walked around the city barefoot, and discovered "vintage" and love beads.

For the first time, I had tons of boyfriends—even pregnant I was popular with the hippy guys—it was natural and sensual, right? I had wild sex and took lots of drugs up until the minute I was ready to give birth. I was lucid enough to realize I would not be able to raise a child, and had located a Jewish adoption agency. They were especially nice to me, and happy to have a white Jewish baby to place, which was apparently a rare commodity. They gave me vitamins and had me talk to a psychiatrist.

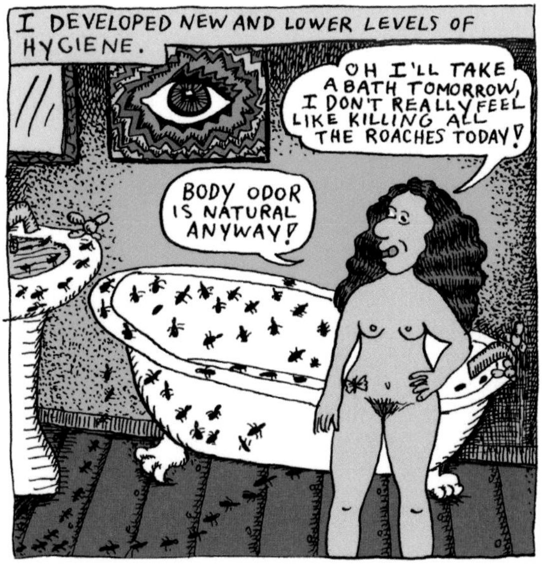
I DEVELOPED NEW AND LOWER LEVELS OF HYGIENE.
OH I'LL TAKE A BATH TOMORROW, I DON'T REALLY FEEL LIKE KILLING ALL THE ROACHES TODAY!
BODY ODOR IS NATURAL ANYWAY!

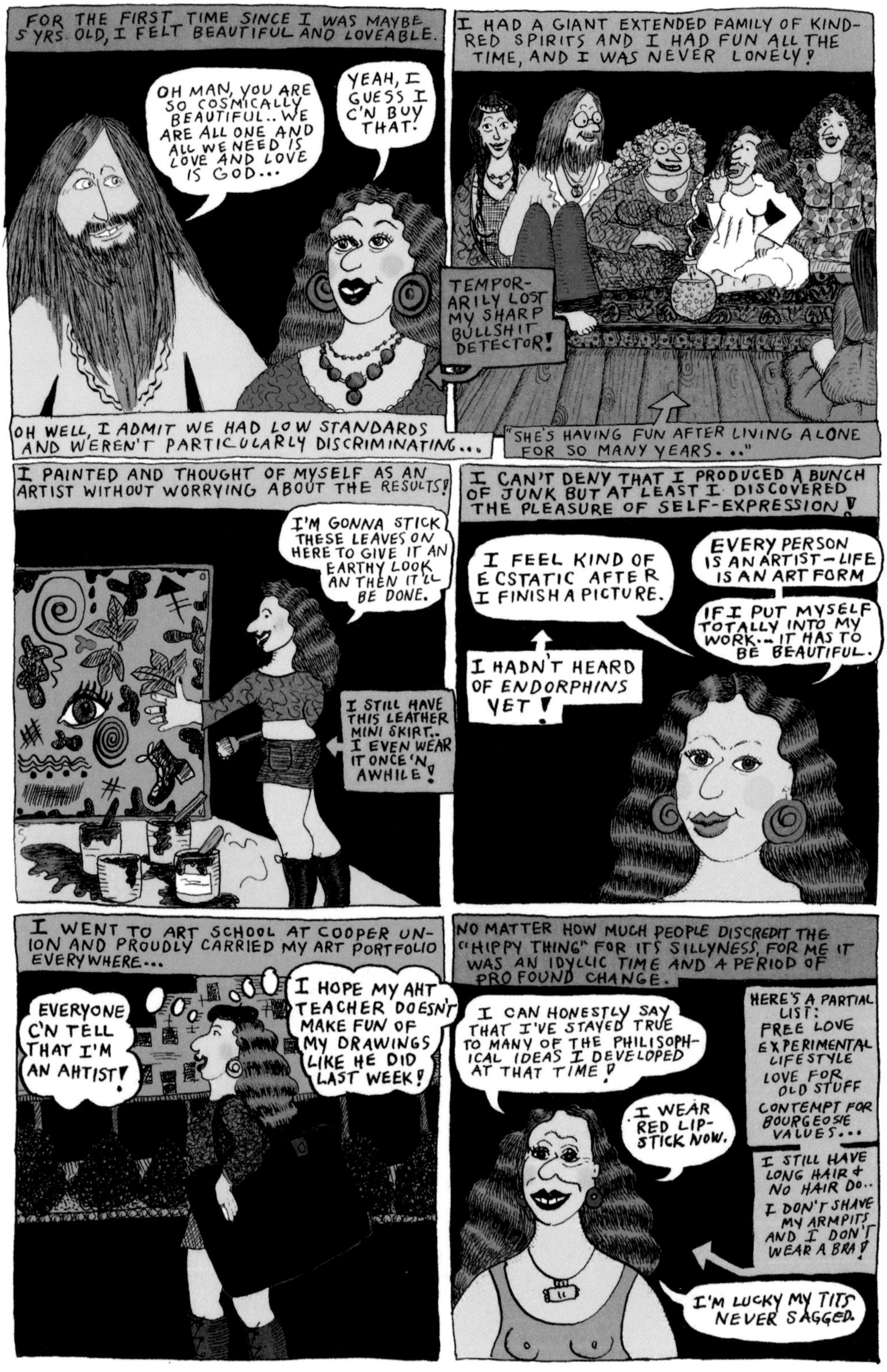
FOR THE FIRST TIME SINCE I WAS MAYBE 5 YRS. OLD, I FELT BEAUTIFUL AND LOVEABLE.
OH MAN, YOU ARE SO COSMICALLY BEAUTIFUL.. WE ARE ALL ONE AND ALL WE NEED IS LOVE AND LOVE IS GOD...
YEAH, I GUESS I C'N BUY THAT.
TEMPOR-ARILY LOST MY SHARP BULLSHIT DETECTOR!
OH WELL, I ADMIT WE HAD LOW STANDARDS AND WEREN'T PARTICULARLY DISCRIMINATING...
I HAD A GIANT EXTENDED FAMILY OF KIND-RED SPIRITS AND I HAD FUN ALL THE TIME, AND I WAS NEVER LONELY!
"SHE'S HAVING FUN AFTER LIVING ALONE FOR SO MANY YEARS..."
I PAINTED AND THOUGHT OF MYSELF AS AN ARTIST WITHOUT WORRYING ABOUT THE RESULTS!
I'M GONNA STICK THESE LEAVES ON HERE TO GIVE IT AN EARTHY LOOK AN THEN IT'LL BE DONE.
I STILL HAVE THIS LEATHER MINI SKIRT.. I EVEN WEAR IT ONCE 'N AWHILE!
I CAN'T DENY THAT I PRODUCED A BUNCH OF JUNK BUT AT LEAST I DISCOVERED THE PLEASURE OF SELF-EXPRESSION!
I FEEL KIND OF ECSTATIC AFTER I FINISH A PICTURE.
I HADN'T HEARD OF ENDORPHINS YET!
EVERY PERSON IS AN ARTIST - LIFE IS AN ART FORM
IF I PUT MYSELF TOTALLY INTO MY WORK.- IT HAS TO BE BEAUTIFUL.
I WENT TO ART SCHOOL AT COOPER UN-ION AND PROUDLY CARRIED MY ART PORTFOLIO EVERYWHERE...
EVERYONE C'N TELL THAT I'M AN AHTIST!
I HOPE MY AHT TEACHER DOESN'T MAKE FUN OF MY DRAWINGS LIKE HE DID LAST WEEK!
NO MATTER HOW MUCH PEOPLE DISCREDIT THE "HIPPY THING" FOR ITS SILLYNESS, FOR ME IT WAS AN IDYLLIC TIME AND A PERIOD OF PROFOUND CHANGE.
I CAN HONESTLY SAY THAT I'VE STAYED TRUE TO MANY OF THE PHILISOPH-ICAL IDEAS I DEVELOPED AT THAT TIME!
HERE'S A PARTIAL LIST: FREE LOVE EXPERIMENTAL LIFESTYLE LOVE FOR OLD STUFF CONTEMPT FOR BOURGEOSIE VALUES...
I WEAR RED LIP-STICK NOW.
I STILL HAVE LONG HAIR + NO HAIR DO.. I DON'T SHAVE MY ARMPITS AND I DON'T WEAR A BRA!
I'M LUCKY MY TITS NEVER SAGGED.

Dad pays a visit ... then dies

Meanwhile, my father had been trying to track me down, and bullied a friend of mine into giving him my address. He showed up at my slum apartment one day and looked through the peephole. I saw him, but didn't open the door. My heart was racing, and I remember looking out the window and watching him walk away. I was terrified, but at the same time touched that he cared enough to look for me. The psychiatrist arranged a meeting with my father on neutral turf; there my father had explained how he respected me for taking care of this "matter" by myself without dragging them, especially my mother, into it.

The psychiatrist assumed that my father would take me home for the rest of my pregnancy to a clean, safe environment, and was shocked when he gave me some money instead and told me I could come home if I wanted to … after the baby was born. I gave birth to a big, healthy baby boy at Beth Israel Hospital in June 1967, and he was immediately put up for adoption. Six months later my father died of pancreatic cancer.

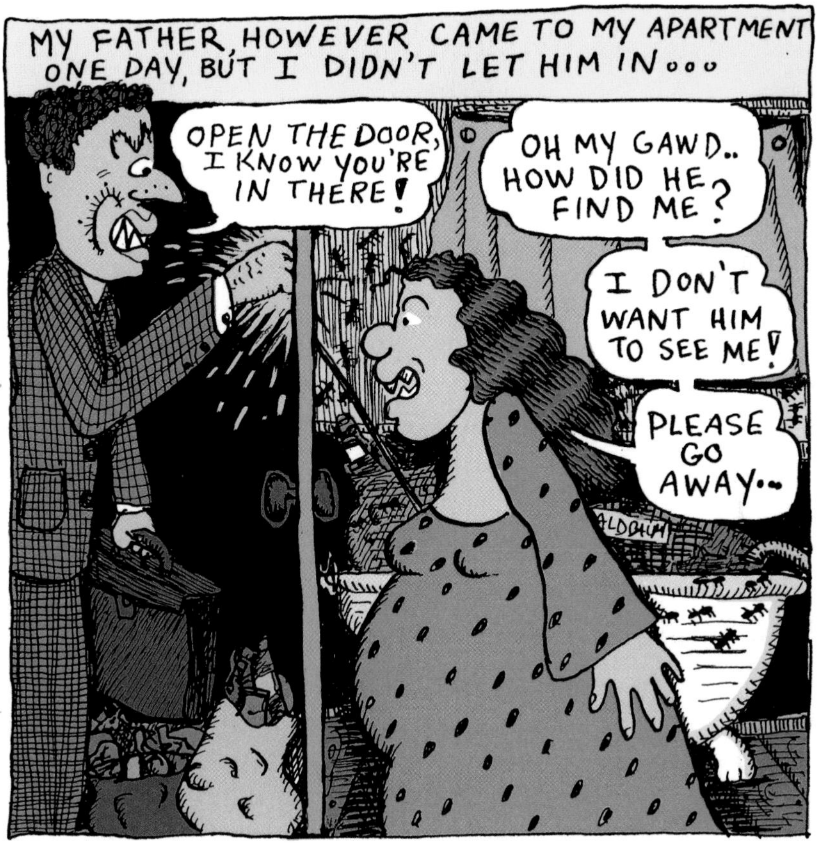
MY FATHER, HOWEVER CAME TO MY APARTMENT ONE DAY, BUT I DIDN'T LET HIM IN...
OPEN THE DOOR, I KNOW YOU'RE IN THERE!
OH MY GAWD.. HOW DID HE FIND ME?
I DON'T WANT HIM TO SEE ME!
PLEASE GO AWAY..

The family regroup

My mother was 38 years old when my father died. She flatly refused to even enter our house again; my grandpa Joe and I went through everything and sold it all. The physical reality of my childhood was thus erased forever. My mother, who had a good job, suggested we share an apartment together on the upper east side of Manhattan so we could be like "swinging singles" roommates—my worst nightmare!

To escape this looming hell, I begged my boyfriend Carl Kominsky to marry me, and he agreed: he was a sweet guy and sort of loved me. He had a plan to move to Arizona already in the works. His family was very generous and really helped us out. So we headed out for Tucson, Arizona.

Luckily, within a year of my father's death, my mother met and married David. They are still happily married and love each other. He's a real sweetheart!

Left: **My father, late 1966**
This was the last photo before he died in February 1967.

Below: **Deauville Hotel, Miami Beach, 1967**
Me and my mother on valium shortly after my father's death—we were supposed to be recovering from our loss.

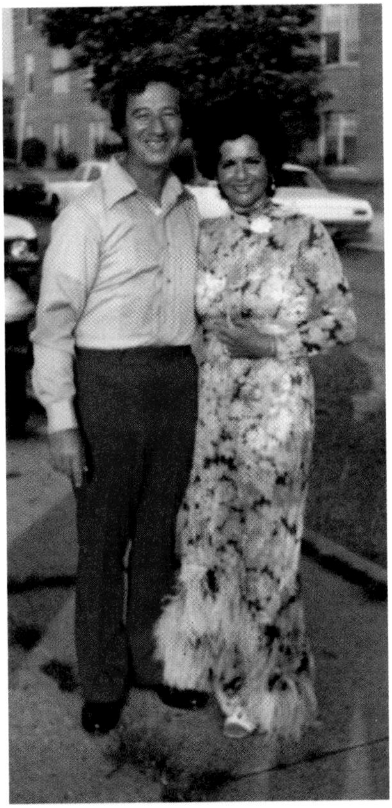

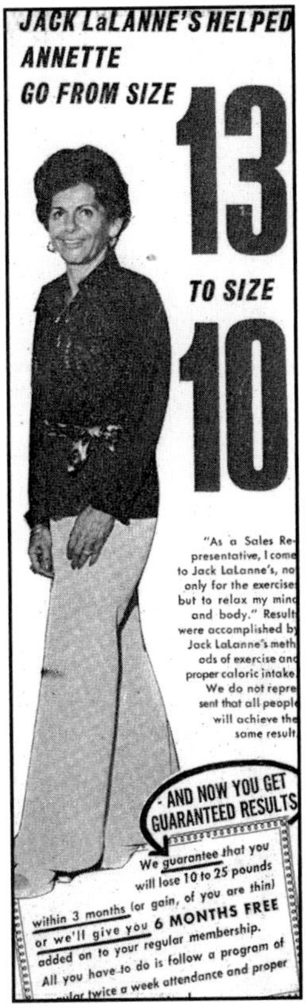
JACK LaLANNE'S HELPED
ANNETTE
GO FROM SIZE
13
TO SIZE
10
"As a Sales Representative, I come to Jack LaLanne's, no only for the exercise but to relax my minc and body." Result were accomplished by Jack LaLanne's methods of exercise anc proper caloric intake. We do not represent that all people will achieve the same result
- AND NOW YOU GET GUARANTEED RESULTS
We guarantee that you will lose 10 to 25 pounds within 3 months (or gain, of you are thin) or we'll give you 6 MONTHS FREE added on to your regular membership.
All you have to do is follow a program of
twice a week attendance and proper

Right: **Brooklyn, New York, 1968**
My mom with her new hubby David, all dolled up, going to a Bar Mitzvah. The ad is for Jack LaLanne's Gym—My mom did a make-over on the gym, and got a year's free membership.

Below: **Long Island, New York,1968**
This is the wedding party photo from my marriage to Carl Kominsky.

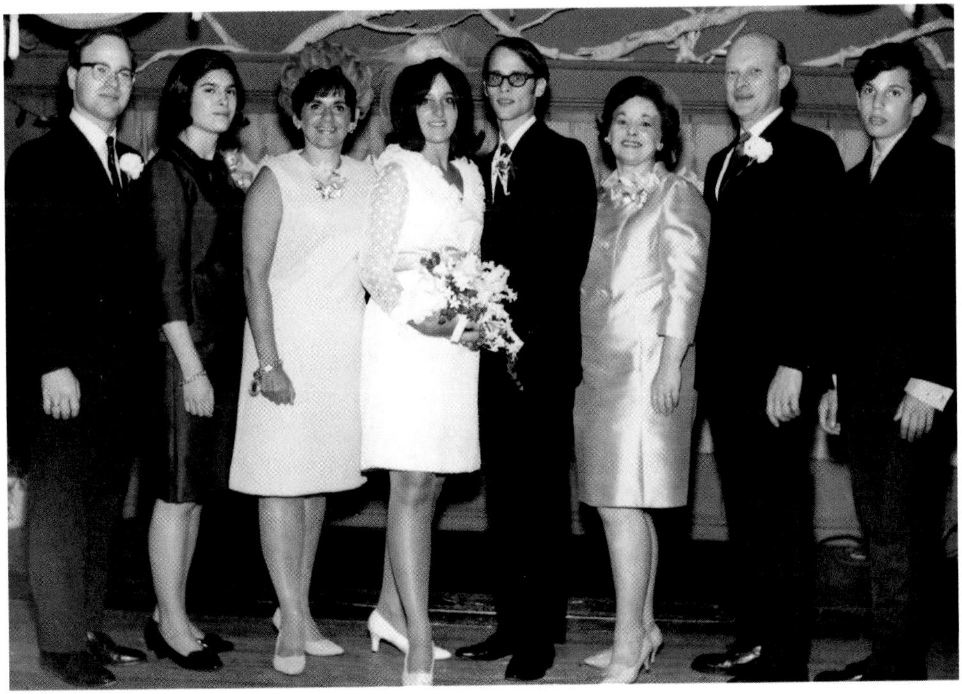

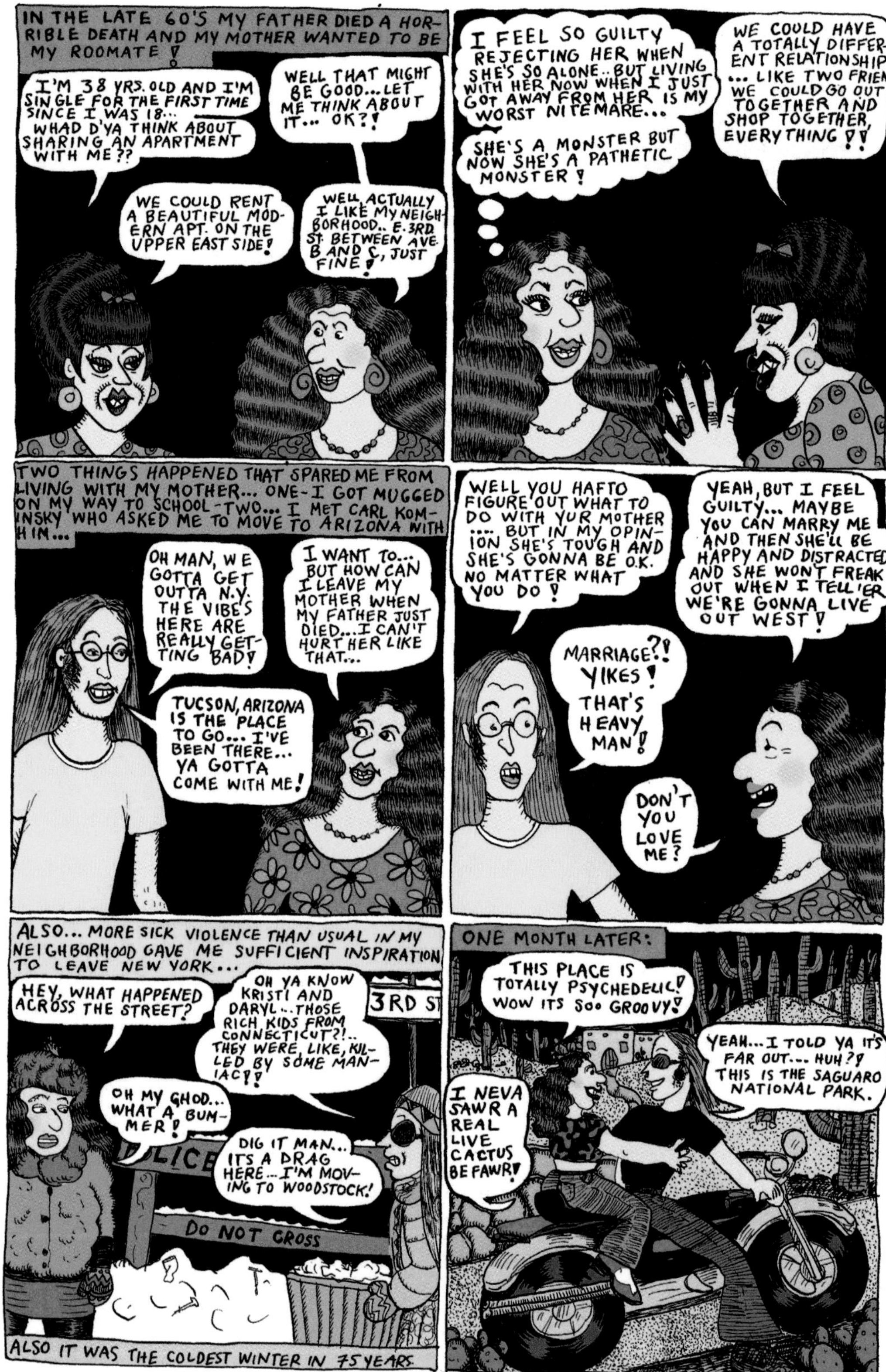

IN THE LATE 60'S MY FATHER DIED A HORRIBLE DEATH AND MY MOTHER WANTED TO BE MY ROOMATE!
I'M 38 YRS. OLD AND I'M SINGLE FOR THE FIRST TIME SINCE I WAS 18... WHAD D'YA THINK ABOUT SHARING AN APARTMENT WITH ME??
WELL THAT MIGHT BE GOOD... LET ME THINK ABOUT IT... OK?!
WE COULD RENT A BEAUTIFUL MODERN APT. ON THE UPPER EAST SIDE!
WELL ACTUALLY I LIKE MY NEIGHBORHOOD.. E. 3RD ST. BETWEEN AVE. B AND C, JUST FINE!
I FEEL SO GUILTY REJECTING HER WHEN SHE'S SO ALONE.. BUT LIVING WITH HER NOW WHEN I JUST GOT AWAY FROM HER IS MY WORST NITEMARE...
SHE'S A MONSTER BUT NOW SHE'S A PATHETIC MONSTER!
WE COULD HAVE A TOTALLY DIFFERENT RELATIONSHIP ... LIKE TWO FRIENDS. WE COULD GO OUT TOGETHER AND SHOP TOGETHER, EVERYTHING!!
TWO THINGS HAPPENED THAT SPARED ME FROM LIVING WITH MY MOTHER... ONE- I GOT MUGGED ON MY WAY TO SCHOOL- TWO... I MET CARL KOMINSKY WHO ASKED ME TO MOVE TO ARIZONA WITH HIM...
OH MAN, WE GOTTA GET OUTTA N.Y. THE VIBE'S HERE ARE REALLY GETTING BAD!
I WANT TO... BUT HOW CAN I LEAVE MY MOTHER WHEN MY FATHER JUST DIED... I CAN'T HURT HER LIKE THAT...
TUCSON, ARIZONA IS THE PLACE TO GO... I'VE BEEN THERE... YA GOTTA COME WITH ME!
WELL YOU HAFTO FIGURE OUT WHAT TO DO WITH YUR MOTHER .... BUT IN MY OPINION SHE'S TOUGH AND SHE'S GONNA BE O.K. NO MATTER WHAT YOU DO!
YEAH, BUT I FEEL GUILTY... MAYBE YOU CAN MARRY ME AND THEN SHE'LL BE HAPPY AND DISTRACTED AND SHE WON'T FREAK OUT WHEN I TELL 'ER WE'RE GONNA LIVE OUT WEST!
MARRIAGE?! YIKES! THAT'S HEAVY MAN!
DON'T YOU LOVE ME?
ALSO... MORE SICK VIOLENCE THAN USUAL IN MY NEIGHBORHOOD GAVE ME SUFFICIENT INSPIRATION TO LEAVE NEW YORK...
HEY, WHAT HAPPENED ACROSS THE STREET?
OH YA KNOW KRISTI AND DARYL.. THOSE RICH KIDS FROM CONNECTICUT?!.. THEY WERE, LIKE, KILLED BY SOME MANIAC!!
3RD ST
OH MY GHOD... WHAT A BUMMER!
DIG IT MAN... ITS A DRAG HERE... I'M MOVING TO WOODSTOCK!
LICE
DO NOT CROSS
ALSO IT WAS THE COLDEST WINTER IN 75 YEARS.
ONE MONTH LATER:
THIS PLACE IS TOTALLY PSYCHEDELIC! WOW ITS SOO GROOVY!
YEAH... I TOLD YA IT'S FAR OUT... HUH?! THIS IS THE SAGUARO NATIONAL PARK.
I NEVA SAWR A REAL LIVE CACTUS BEFAWR!

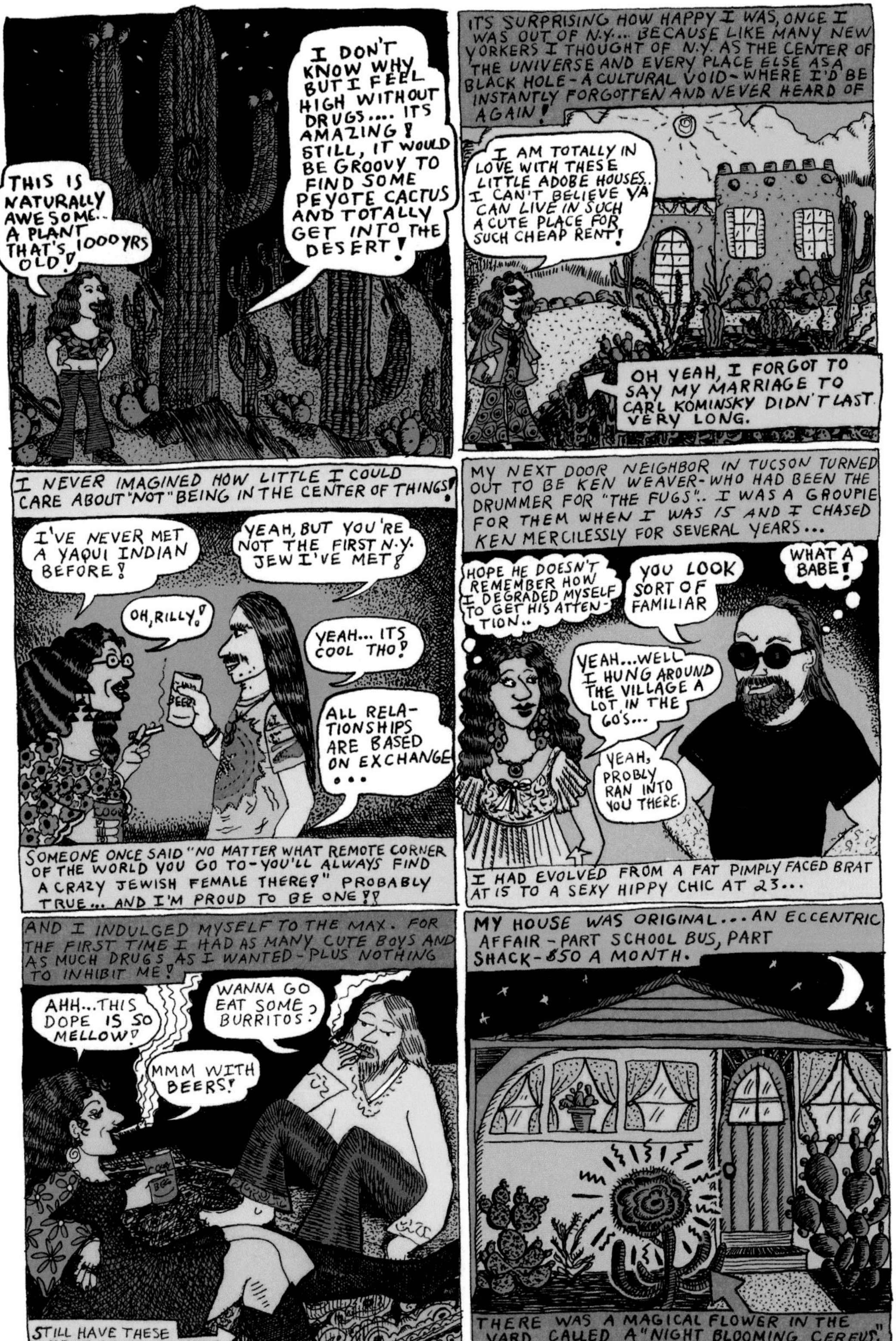
THIS IS NATURALLY AWESOME.. A PLANT THAT'S 1000 YRS OLD!
I DON'T KNOW WHY BUT I FEEL HIGH WITHOUT DRUGS.... ITS AMAZING! STILL, IT WOULD BE GROOVY TO FIND SOME PEYOTE CACTUS AND TOTALLY GET INTO THE DESERT!
ITS SURPRISING HOW HAPPY I WAS, ONCE I WAS OUT OF N.Y... BECAUSE LIKE MANY NEW YORKERS I THOUGHT OF N.Y. AS THE CENTER OF THE UNIVERSE AND EVERY PLACE ELSE AS A BLACK HOLE - A CULTURAL VOID - WHERE I'D BE INSTANTLY FORGOTTEN AND NEVER HEARD OF AGAIN!
I AM TOTALLY IN LOVE WITH THESE LITTLE ADOBE HOUSES.. I CAN'T BELIEVE YA CAN LIVE IN SUCH A CUTE PLACE FOR SUCH CHEAP RENT!
OH YEAH, I FORGOT TO SAY MY MARRIAGE TO CARL KOMINSKY DIDN'T LAST VERY LONG.
I NEVER IMAGINED HOW LITTLE I COULD CARE ABOUT "NOT" BEING IN THE CENTER OF THINGS!
I'VE NEVER MET A YAQUI INDIAN BEFORE!
YEAH, BUT YOU'RE NOT THE FIRST N.Y. JEW I'VE MET!
OH, RILLY?
YEAH... ITS COOL THO!
ALL RELATIONSHIPS ARE BASED ON EXCHANGE...
SOMEONE ONCE SAID "NO MATTER WHAT REMOTE CORNER OF THE WORLD YOU GO TO - YOU'LL ALWAYS FIND A CRAZY JEWISH FEMALE THERE!" PROBABLY TRUE... AND I'M PROUD TO BE ONE!!
MY NEXT DOOR NEIGHBOR IN TUCSON TURNED OUT TO BE KEN WEAVER - WHO HAD BEEN THE DRUMMER FOR "THE FUGS".. I WAS A GROUPIE FOR THEM WHEN I WAS 15 AND I CHASED KEN MERCILESSLY FOR SEVERAL YEARS...
HOPE HE DOESN'T REMEMBER HOW I DEGRADED MYSELF TO GET HIS ATTENTION..
YOU LOOK SORT OF FAMILIAR
WHAT A BABE!
YEAH...WELL I HUNG AROUND THE VILLAGE A LOT IN THE 60'S...
YEAH, PROBLY RAN INTO YOU THERE.
I HAD EVOLVED FROM A FAT PIMPLY FACED BRAT AT 15 TO A SEXY HIPPY CHIC AT 23...
AND I INDULGED MYSELF TO THE MAX. FOR THE FIRST TIME I HAD AS MANY CUTE BOYS AND AS MUCH DRUGS AS I WANTED - PLUS NOTHING TO INHIBIT ME!
AHH...THIS DOPE IS SO MELLOW!
WANNA GO EAT SOME BURRITOS?
MMM WITH BEERS!
STILL HAVE THESE FRYE BOOTS
MY HOUSE WAS ORIGINAL... AN ECCENTRIC AFFAIR - PART SCHOOL BUS, PART SHACK - $50 A MONTH.
THERE WAS A MAGICAL FLOWER IN THE YARD CALLED A "NIGHT BLOOMING CEREUS".

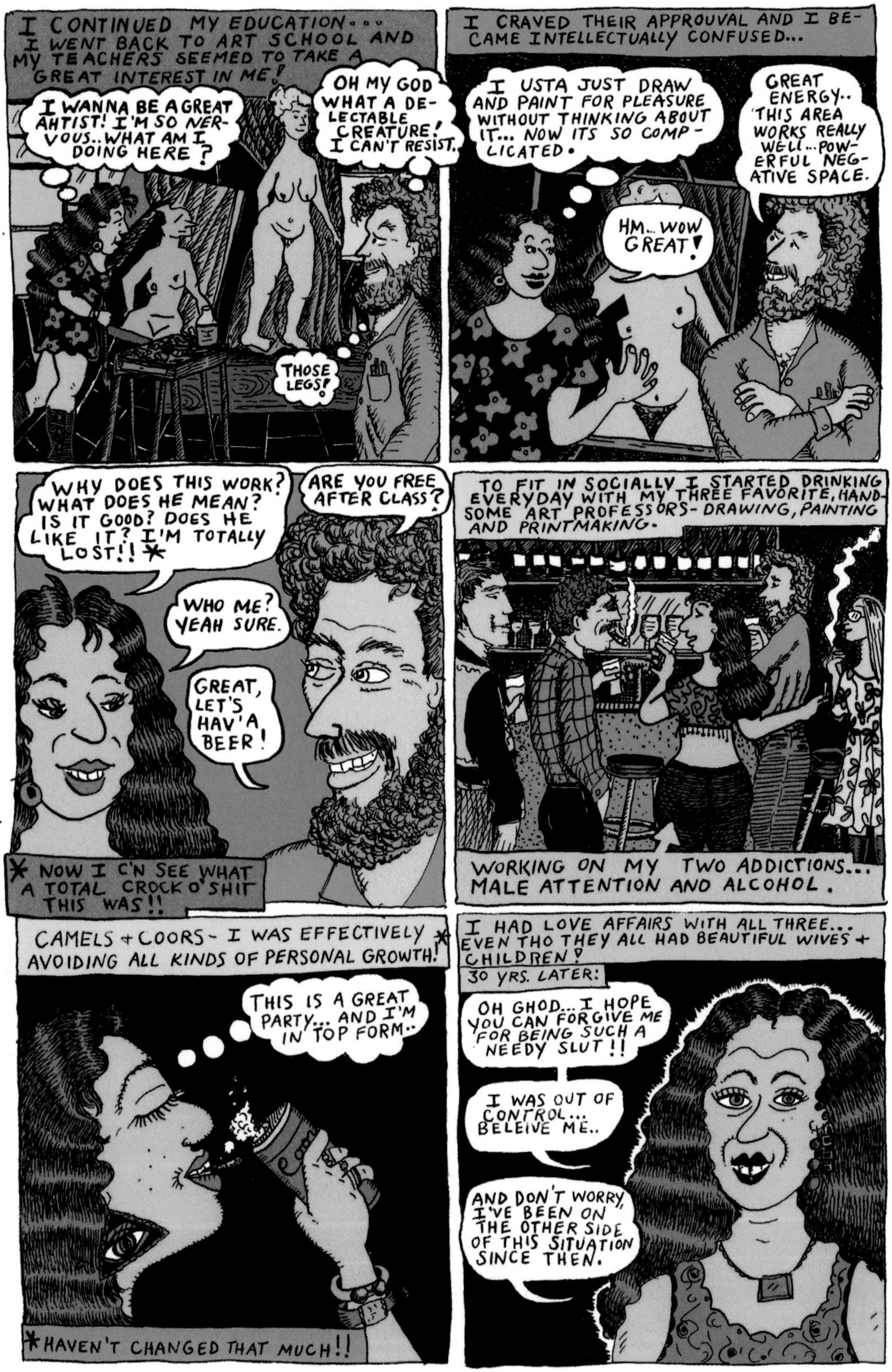
I CONTINUED MY EDUCATION... I WENT BACK TO ART SCHOOL AND MY TEACHERS SEEMED TO TAKE A GREAT INTEREST IN ME!
I WANNA BE A GREAT AHTIST! I'M SO NERVOUS.. WHAT AM I DOING HERE?
OH MY GOD WHAT A DELECTABLE CREATURE! I CAN'T RESIST.
THOSE LEGS!
I CRAVED THEIR APPROUVAL AND I BECAME INTELLECTUALLY CONFUSED...
I USTA JUST DRAW AND PAINT FOR PLEASURE WITHOUT THINKING ABOUT IT... NOW ITS SO COMPLICATED.
GREAT ENERGY.. THIS AREA WORKS REALLY WELL... POWERFUL NEGATIVE SPACE.
HM... WOW GREAT!
WHY DOES THIS WORK? WHAT DOES HE MEAN? IS IT GOOD? DOES HE LIKE IT? I'M TOTALLY LOST!! *
ARE YOU FREE AFTER CLASS?
WHO ME? YEAH SURE.
GREAT, LET'S HAV'A BEER!
* NOW I C'N SEE WHAT A TOTAL CROCK O'SHIT THIS WAS!!
TO FIT IN SOCIALLY I STARTED DRINKING EVERYDAY WITH MY THREE FAVORITE, HANDSOME ART PROFESSORS - DRAWING, PAINTING AND PRINTMAKING.
WORKING ON MY TWO ADDICTIONS... MALE ATTENTION AND ALCOHOL.
CAMELS + COORS - I WAS EFFECTIVELY AVOIDING ALL KINDS OF PERSONAL GROWTH! *
THIS IS A GREAT PARTY... AND I'M IN TOP FORM..
* HAVEN'T CHANGED THAT MUCH!!
I HAD LOVE AFFAIRS WITH ALL THREE... EVEN THO THEY ALL HAD BEAUTIFUL WIVES + CHILDREN!
30 YRS. LATER:
OH GHOD... I HOPE YOU CAN FORGIVE ME FOR BEING SUCH A NEEDY SLUT!!
I WAS OUT OF CONTROL... BELEIVE ME..
AND DON'T WORRY, I'VE BEEN ON THE OTHER SIDE OF THIS SITUATION SINCE THEN.

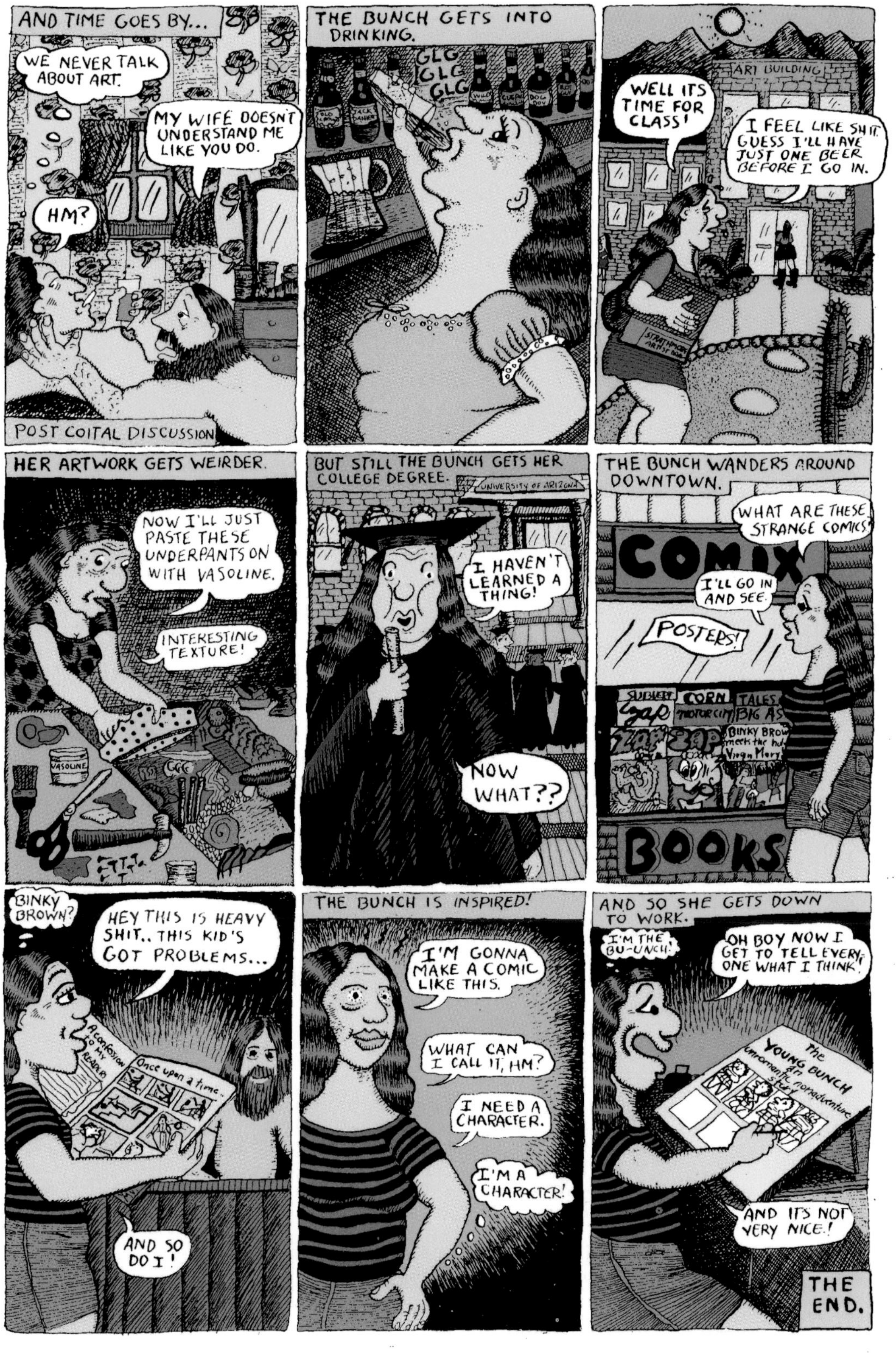
AND TIME GOES BY...
WE NEVER TALK ABOUT ART.
MY WIFE DOESN'T UNDERSTAND ME LIKE YOU DO.
HM?
POST COITAL DISCUSSION
THE BUNCH GETS INTO DRINKING.
GLG GLG GLG
ART BUILDING
WELL ITS TIME FOR CLASS!
I FEEL LIKE SHIT. GUESS I'LL HAVE JUST ONE BEER BEFORE I GO IN.
HER ARTWORK GETS WEIRDER.
NOW I'LL JUST PASTE THESE UNDERPANTS ON WITH VASOLINE.
INTERESTING TEXTURE!
VASOLINE
BUT STILL THE BUNCH GETS HER COLLEGE DEGREE.
UNIVERSITY OF ARIZONA
I HAVEN'T LEARNED A THING!
NOW WHAT??
THE BUNCH WANDERS AROUND DOWNTOWN.
WHAT ARE THESE STRANGE COMICS?
COMIX
I'LL GO IN AND SEE.
POSTERS!
CORN
TALES
ZAP
MOTOR CITY
BIG ASS
BINKY BROWN meets the holy Virgin Mary
BOOKS
BINKY BROWN?
HEY THIS IS HEAVY SHIT.. THIS KID'S GOT PROBLEMS...
A confession to my READERS
Once upon a time...
AND SO DO I!
THE BUNCH IS INSPIRED!
I'M GONNA MAKE A COMIC LIKE THIS.
WHAT CAN I CALL IT, HM?
I NEED A CHARACTER.
I'M A CHARACTER!
AND SO SHE GETS DOWN TO WORK.
I'M THE BU-UNCH!
OH BOY NOW I GET TO TELL EVERYONE WHAT I THINK!
The YOUNG BUNCH an unromantic nonadventure story
AND IT'S NOT VERY NICE!
THE END.

Happiness in Arizona

The desert around Tucson was a miraculous, splendid wonderland to me. I fell in love instantly with the giant saguaro cacti, the creepy crawly creatures and the hot dry weather, and quickly settled into the laid-back pace of southwestern life of the '60s in the "Old Pueblo" (now it looks like just another brand-X L.A.) Carl and I enrolled at the University of Arizona and moved into a tiny adobe house. I was very happy and healthy for about two years, but gradually started drinking beer and hangin' out. I soon discovered peyote, and this very visually stimulating drug permanently imprinted the beauty of the desert on my brain.

Left and Below: **Tucson, Arizona, 1969**
These shots of me were taken by my new husband Carl, with the Nikon camera that had belonged to my father.

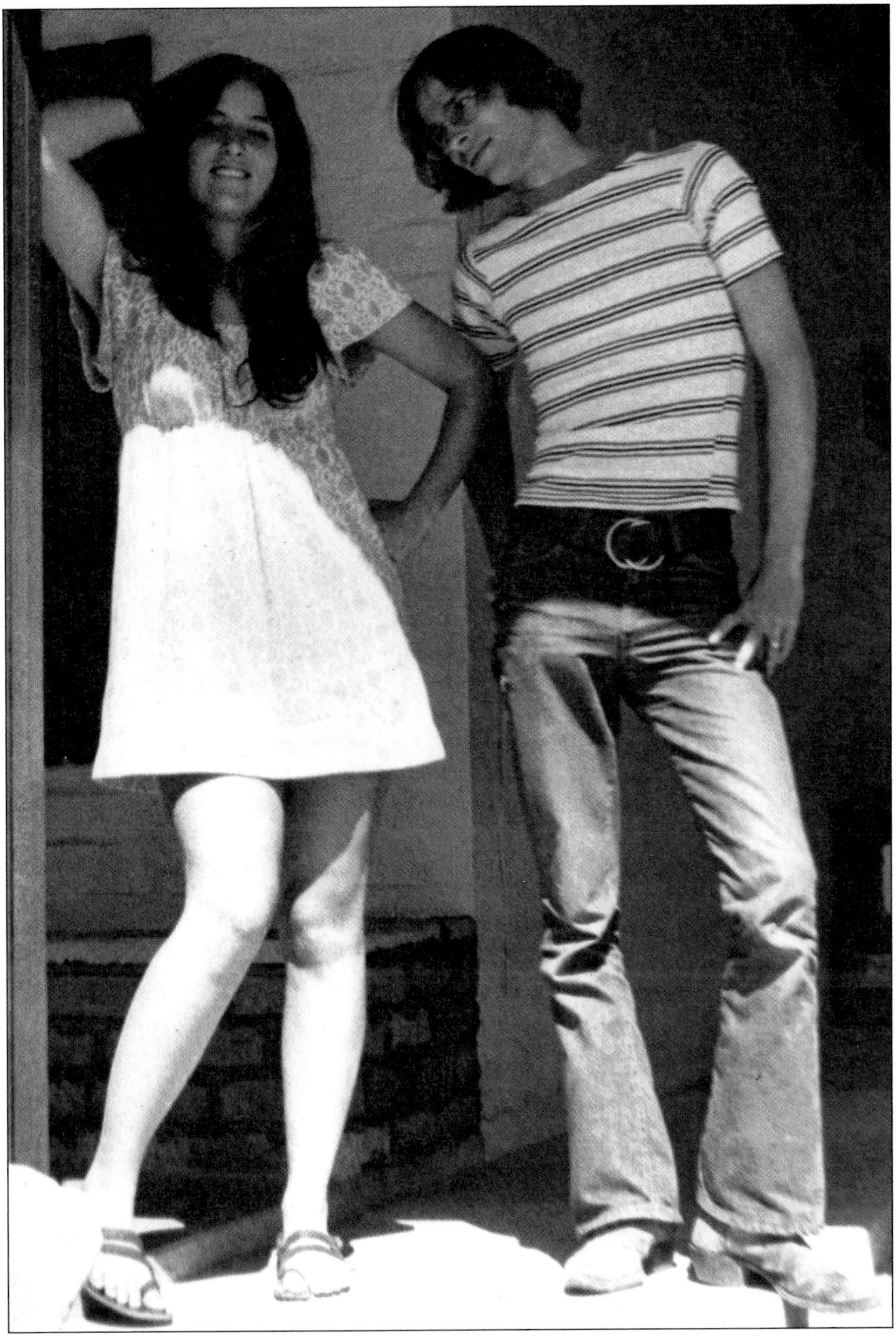

Above: **Tucson, Arizona, 1969**
Me and Carl in front of our house.

Desert beauty

We arrived in Arizona directly from a freezing cold grim winter in New York … the contrast was just incredible. This was a naturally psychedelic environment to me. The desert colors were stark and intense, and I felt like I'd landed on another planet. I still love the giant cacti and that amazing turquoise sky. The landscape was deeply inspiring and became the subject of many of my paintings, watercolors and drawings, some of which are shown on the following pages.

Right top: **The cemetery in Rodeo, New Mexico**

Below and Right below: **Catalina State Park, Tucson, Arizona**

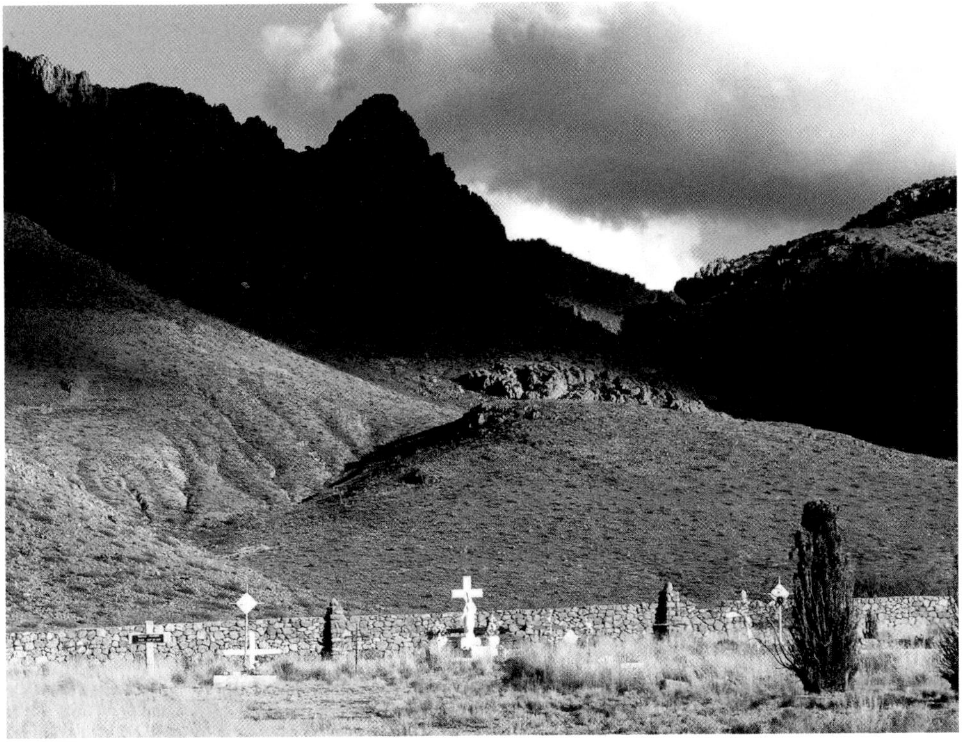

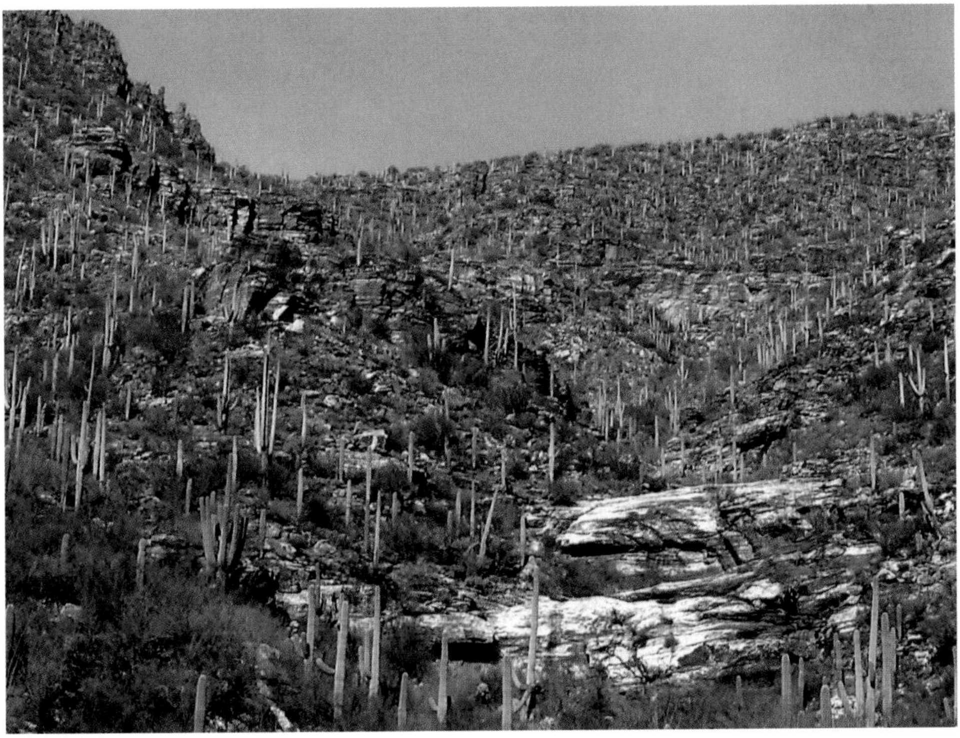

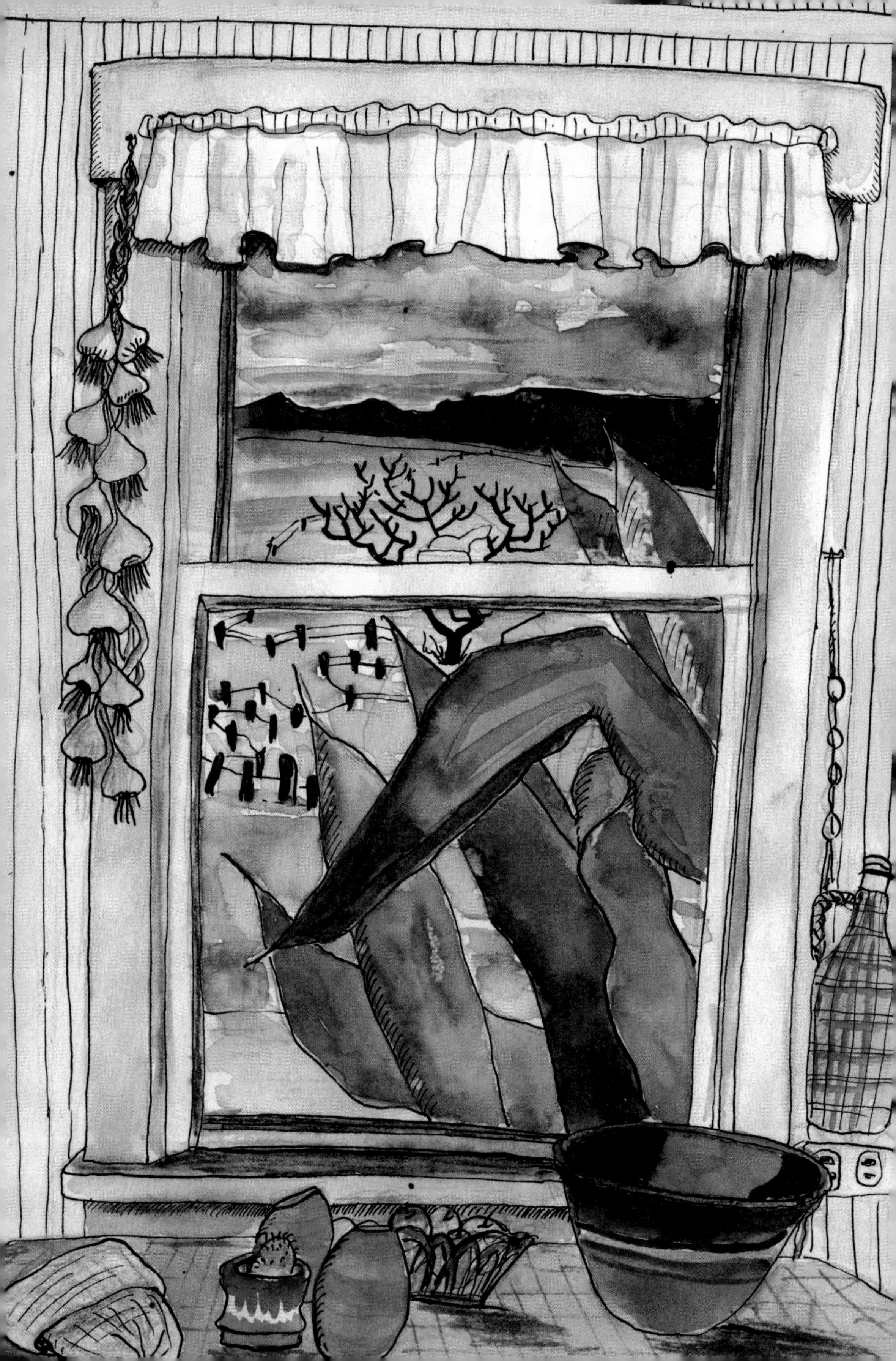

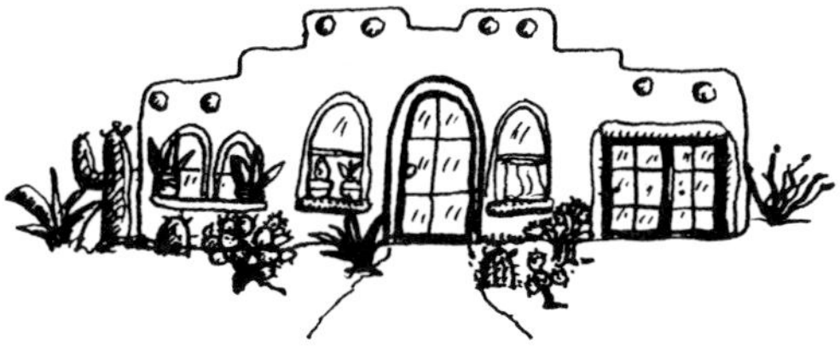

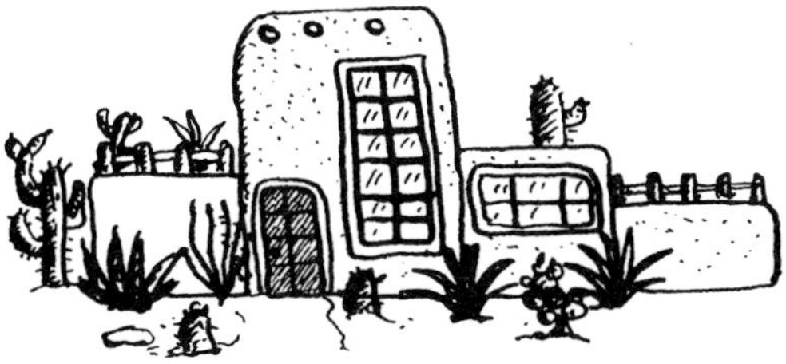

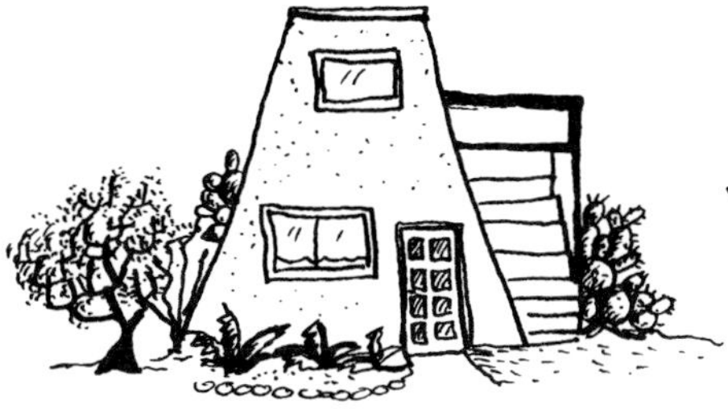

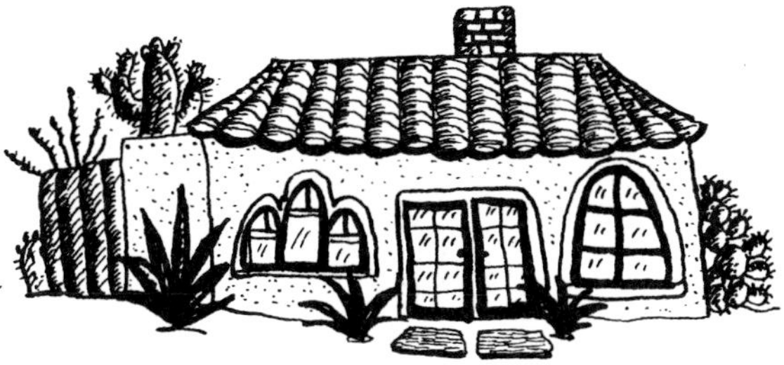

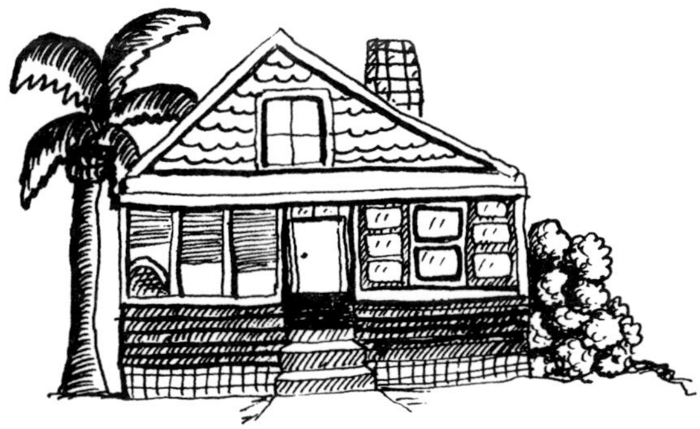

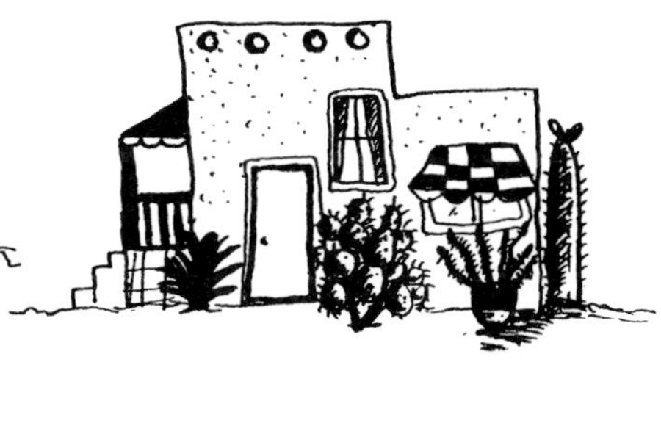

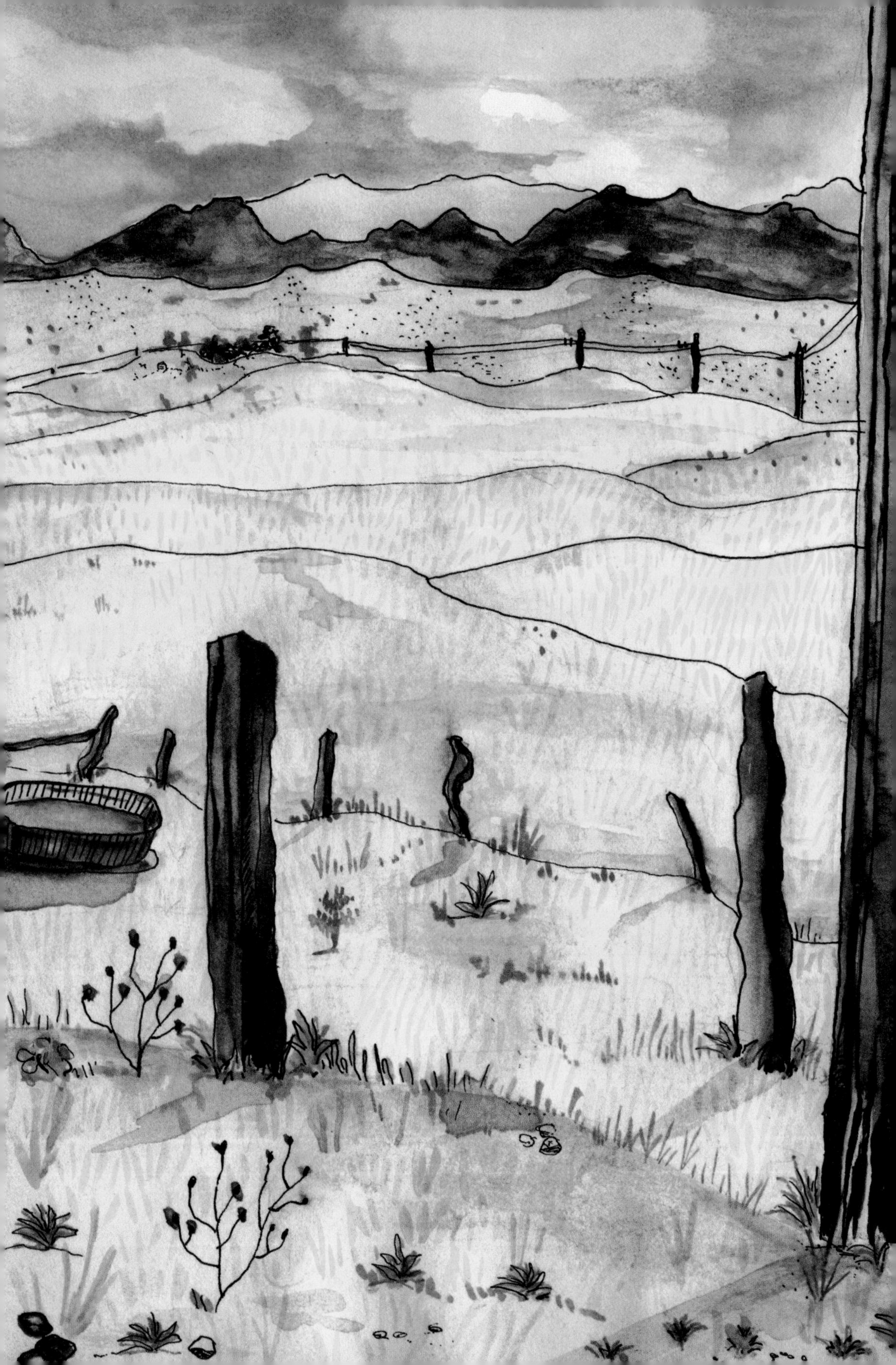

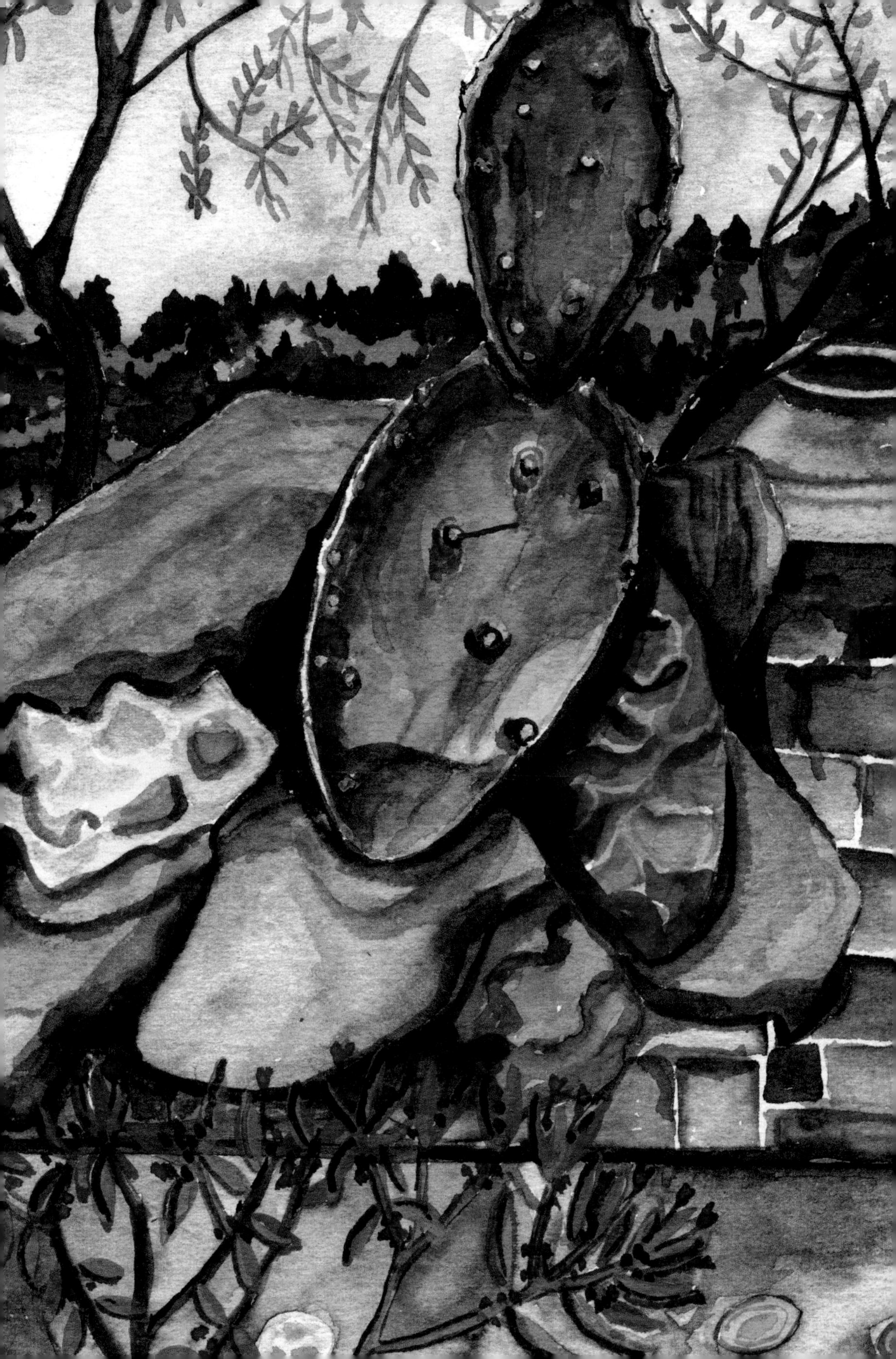

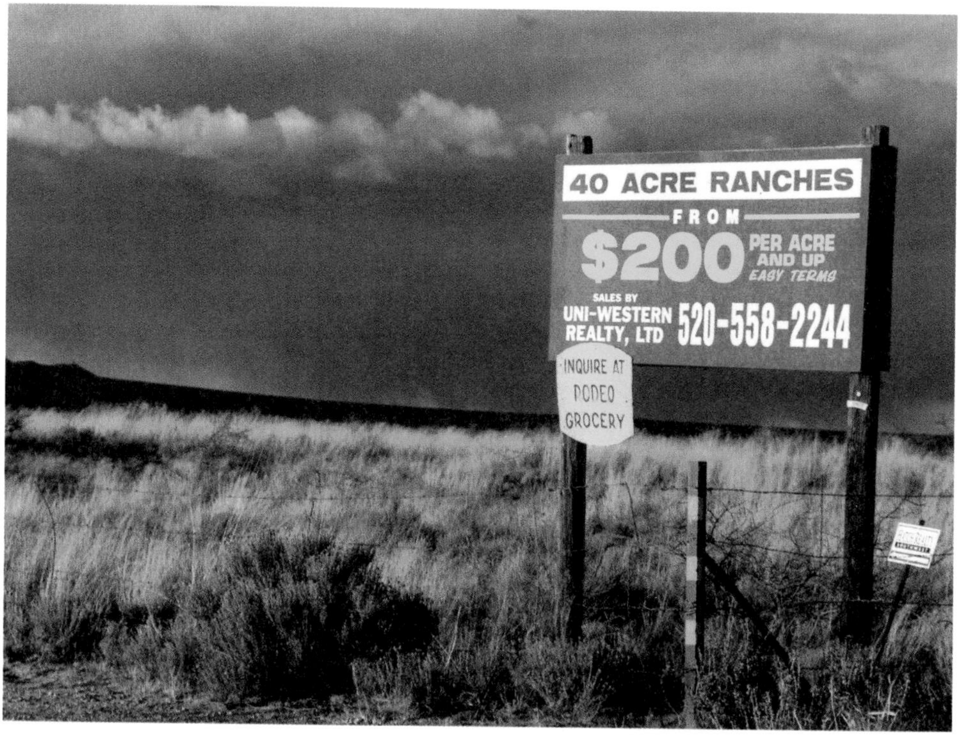
40 ACRE RANCHES
FROM
$200
PER ACRE
AND UP
EASY TERMS
SALES BY
UNI-WESTERN
REALTY, LTD
520-558-2244
INQUIRE AT
RODEO
GROCERY

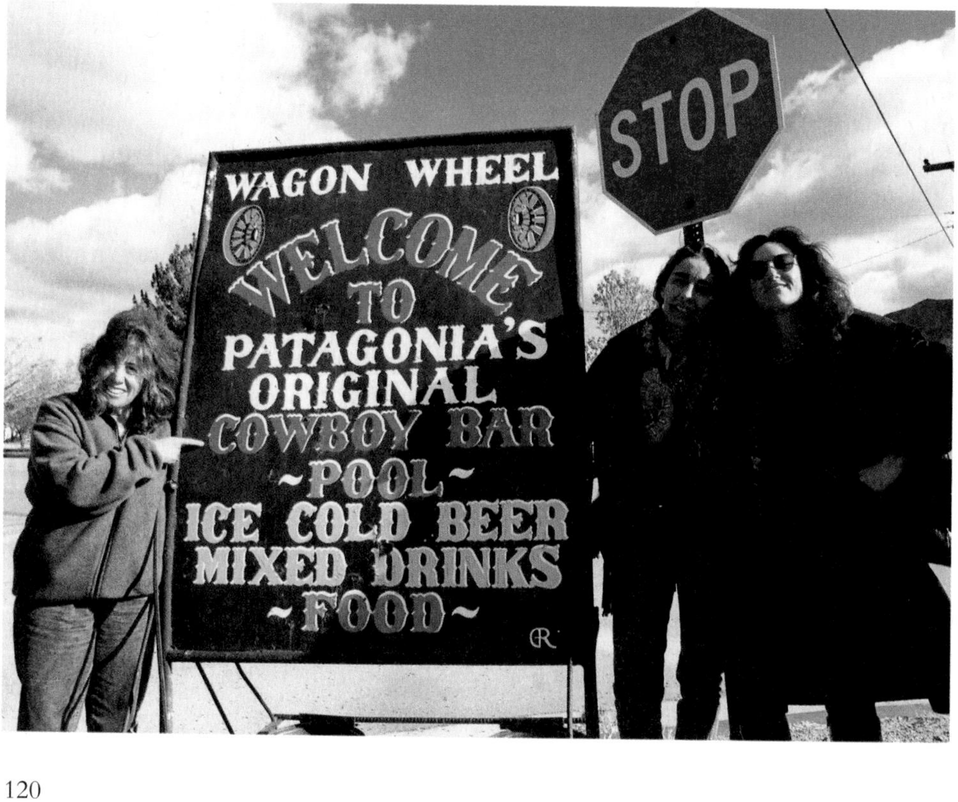
WAGON WHEEL
WELCOME
TO
PATAGONIA'S
ORIGINAL
COWBOY BAR
~POOL~
ICE COLD BEER
MIXED DRINKS
~FOOD~
STOP

Left: **40-acre ranches for sale**

Below left: **Patagonia, Arizona**
Me and my pals in front of a bar.

Below: **Tucson, Arizona**
Cowboy friend Dennis, proud of his pick up truck

Utterly irresistible

Around this time I met a real cowboy named Ray Edington. He was dazzlingly handsome, with light blonde hair, sparkling gold eyes, and a body that looked like it was carved out of ham. OY! He was trouble walkin'. Ray came from Rodeo, a town that is half in Arizona and half in New Mexico. He had run into a bunch of hippies from New York who had started a commune in Paradise, Arizona. Ray and his brothers had not only helped these city folks out with practical matters, but they had become amply acquainted with the wanton hippy chicks, especially the horny, sexy Jewish girls. The commune eventually failed, and most of the people ended up in Tucson.

Ray was making the rounds when he met me. He seduced me, but it actually took awhile, since I was not eager to upset my stable, calm life with Carl. However, he must have triggered off the deep, wild part of me, and my lust for sex and adventure won in the end. I split up with Carl, not without some reservation and sadness, and spent a year and a half living with Ray in the back of various vehicles, drinking Coors beer and smoking Camel non-filters and marijuana. I was barely twenty-one years old.

Whenever our vehicle would break down, Ray could repair it, often by carving a facsimile out of an old fencepost. He earned money fixing other peoples' cars and trucks too, and if there were any parts left over when he was done with a repair, he would toss them away and say, "They were just useless junk anyway!"

Unfortunately Ray was a totally out of control drunk. He would often show up at four in the morning, bruised and bleeding as the result of a fight or because he'd run his car into a ditch. His violent ways quickly lost their charm, and his macho nature inevitably clashed with my independent Jewish monster temperament. We broke up and got back together a couple of times, but I'd had enough.

Ray was killed a few years later, shot in the back by an irate neighbor whom he'd been antagonizing for years. He was only twenty-three years old. He had been armed and drunk at the time. The neighbor pled self-defense and got off. Ray's father died a few months later of a broken heart.

Right: **Handsome Cowboy, Ray Edington, 1969**

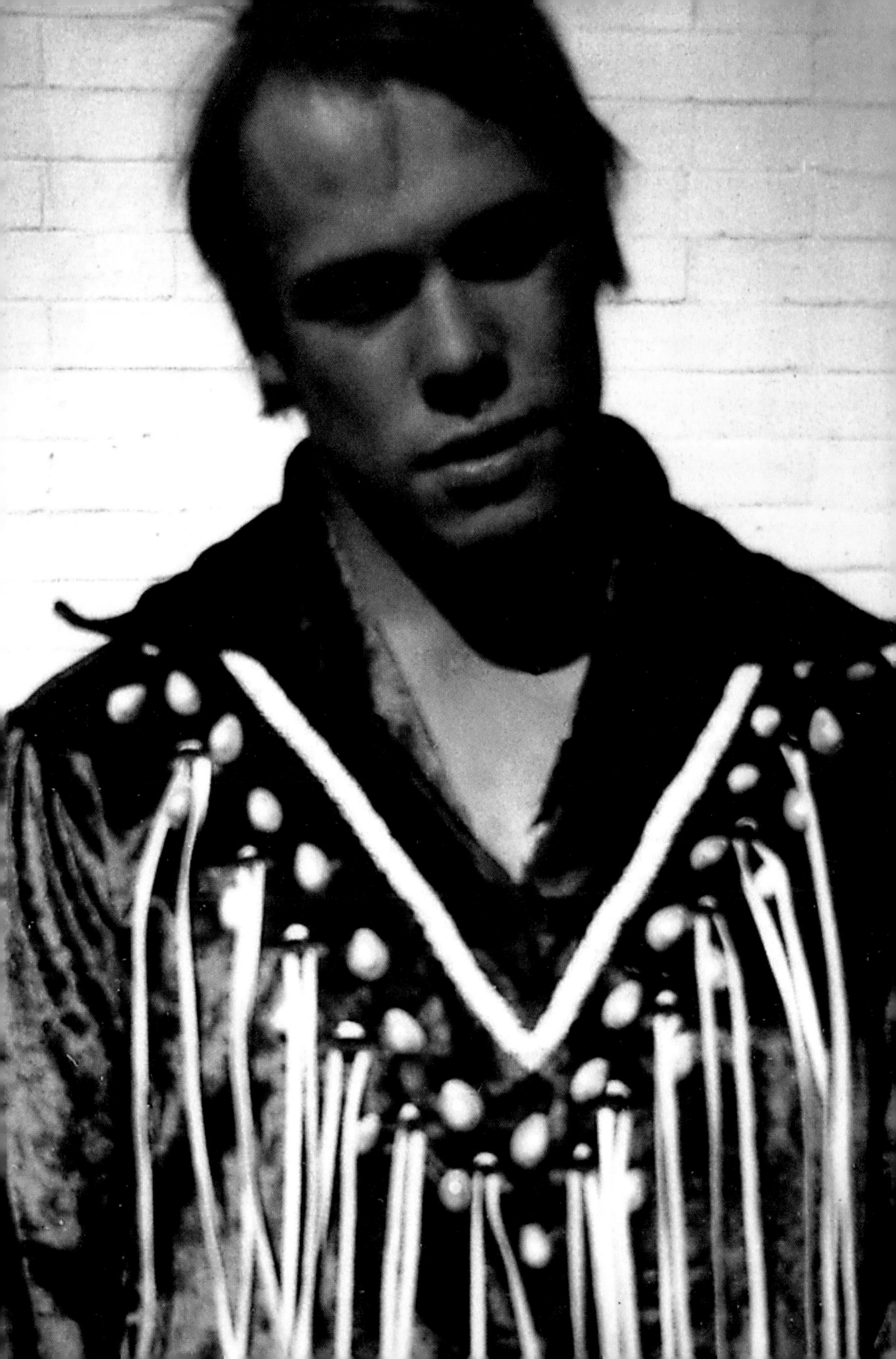

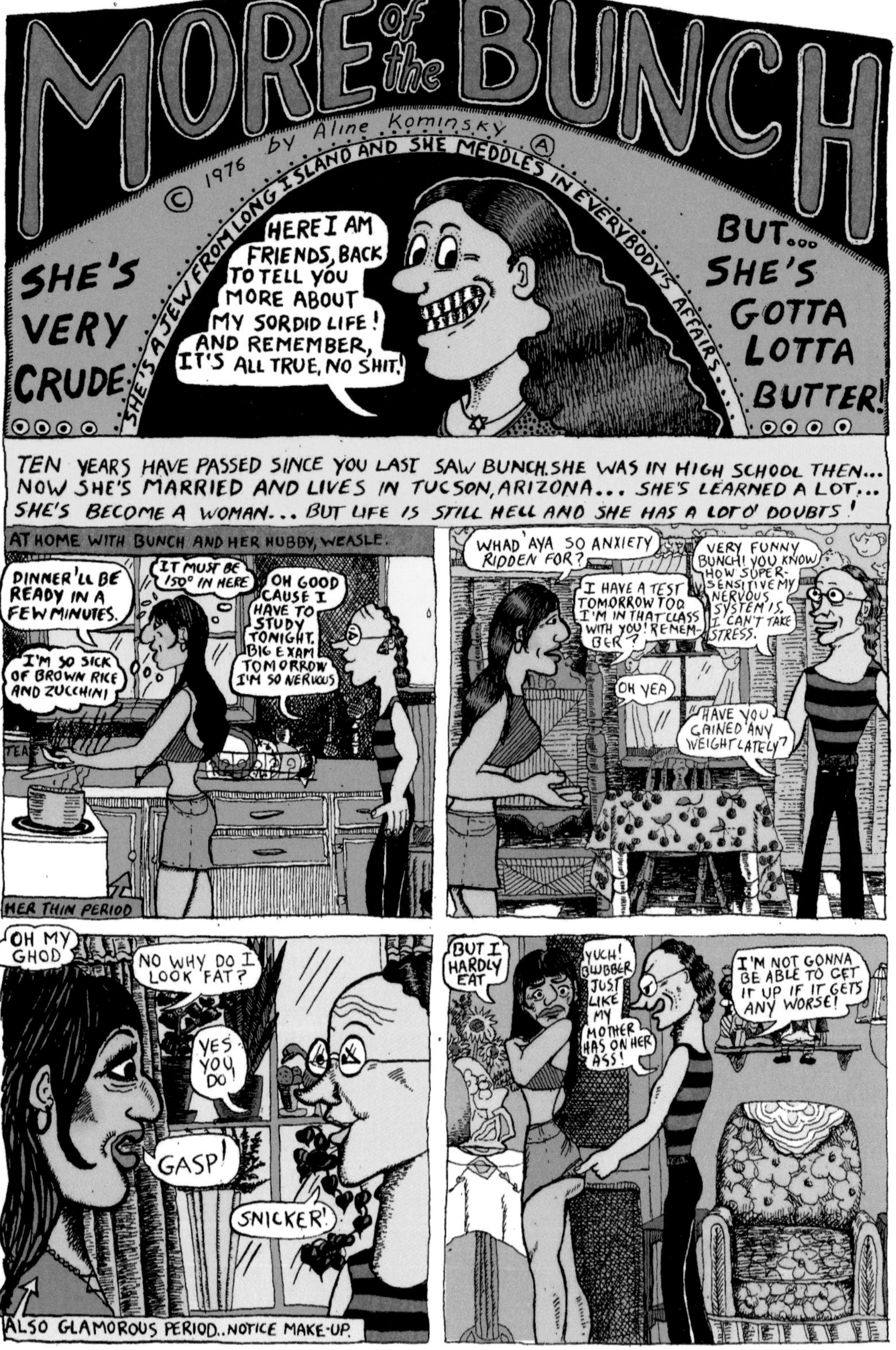
MORE of the BUNCH
by Aline Kominsky
© 1976
SHE'S A JEW FROM LONG ISLAND AND SHE MEDDLES IN EVERYBODY'S AFFAIRS
SHE'S VERY CRUDE
HERE I AM FRIENDS, BACK TO TELL YOU MORE ABOUT MY SORDID LIFE! AND REMEMBER, IT'S ALL TRUE, NO SHIT!
BUT... SHE'S GOTTA LOTTA BUTTER!
TEN YEARS HAVE PASSED SINCE YOU LAST SAW BUNCH. SHE WAS IN HIGH SCHOOL THEN... NOW SHE'S MARRIED AND LIVES IN TUCSON, ARIZONA... SHE'S LEARNED A LOT... SHE'S BECOME A WOMAN... BUT LIFE IS STILL HELL AND SHE HAS A LOT O' DOUBTS!
AT HOME WITH BUNCH AND HER HUBBY, WEASLE.
DINNER'LL BE READY IN A FEW MINUTES.
IT MUST BE 150° IN HERE
I'M SO SICK OF BROWN RICE AND ZUCCHINI
OH GOOD CAUSE I HAVE TO STUDY TONIGHT. BIG EXAM TOMORROW I'M SO NERVOUS
TEA
HER THIN PERIOD
WHAD'AYA SO ANXIETY RIDDEN FOR?
I HAVE A TEST TOMORROW TOO. I'M IN THAT CLASS WITH YOU! REMEMBER?
VERY FUNNY BUNCH! YOU KNOW HOW SUPER-SENSITIVE MY NERVOUS SYSTEM IS. I CAN'T TAKE STRESS.
OH YEA
HAVE YOU GAINED ANY WEIGHT LATELY?
OH MY GHOD
NO WHY DO I LOOK FAT?
YES YOU DO!
GASP!
SNICKER!
ALSO GLAMOROUS PERIOD.. NOTICE MAKE-UP.
BUT I HARDLY EAT
YUCH! BLUBBER JUST LIKE MY MOTHER HAS ON HER ASS!
I'M NOT GONNA BE ABLE TO GET IT UP IF IT GETS ANY WORSE!

Betsy (Klein) Sandlin

MY NEIGHBOR IN TUCSON, ROOM-MATE IN SAN FRANCISCO
AND A DEAR FRIEND

Of course we all need more love. And I'm here to tell you that Aline got it, will always have it, and gives it, too.

She was jailbait at our first encounter. My only recollection of the time is of me hanging round after every Fugs' show to protect those poor overworked entertainers from illicit solicitations from overripe youth. Someone had to do it.

My first genuine memory is of a visit to the home in Tucson she shared with Carl while she attended University of Arizona and got lots of love and her bachelor's degree from the art department. Not too long after that she moved into the schoolbus on the property next door to my rented *casa pequeña* on Halcyon Road in Tucson. It was charming, and although it was difficult to stand up straight inside it, most visitors didn't have to for long.

When there was no longer enough love in Tucson, we decided to hit the road for San Francisco, where there was surely plenty to be had. A drove her orange VW and I drove the red Mercedes with the Ford engine as far as it would go. With good karma and some fancy footwork, we got a great apartment together on Northpoint. Because I was older and because Aline was scared of me (this came out later), I got the secluded aerie on the top floor and A got the front room on the first floor. None of the walls (including the bathroom's) on her floor went to the ceiling—they ended about two feet or so below it—so privacy was not an option.

Before I left Aline to this apartment and its aerie, seeking more love myself, there was one noteworthy moment of needing more love, which I, obliviously, almost sabotaged for A. I came down to rummage in the fridge late at night and heard a ruckus in her room—moaning and shouts and I knew not what incoherent sobbings above the loud music. I knocked on her door several times, shouted, knocked again, to no avail. As I was about to burst in, ready to rescue, ready to do battle, I realized sheepishly that it was truly a moment of getting the most out of love, which I am sure she did that night from the sound of it.

Today we each live in homes with brick or stone walls that go all the way from floor to ceiling, with heavy oaken doors, and we are still friends, ever seeking and always needing more love. After all, that's all you need.

Tucson, April 2006

New directions, inspirations

By the time Ray and I broke up, my marriage was of course a shambles, so I started spending time at the Tally Ho bar and having love affairs with my art professors. I graduated from the University of Arizona in 1971 with a BFA in Fine Art. One day, I went into the Tally Ho Bar and realized I'd "done it" with everyone in there and decided it was time to move on.

In Tucson, I had run into Ken Weaver, who had been the drummer with the Fugs, and Betsy Klein, his ex-girlfriend. We all became neighbors on a little street called Halcyon Road, and eventually good friends. I spent time with Ken, drinking, eating beef jerky and watching TV. Ken introduced me to Spain Rodriguez and Kim Deitch, who were drawing and publishing underground comics in San Francisco.

They showed me tons of comic books that had just come out, and I was really turned on by this new, daring, outrageous art form. I read the works of R. Crumb and Justin Green for the first time, and it changed the course of my life. Crumb had invented HoneyBunch Kaminski, a character who not only resembled me, but even had my last name; then there was also Dale Steinberger, the Jewish Cowgirl, who was living out her Wild West fantasy, exactly like me. We'd never even set eyes on one another! Everyone thought this was really bizarre and that Crumb had to meet me; by the time I arrived in San Francisco, he'd already heard about me.

Justin Green's comic *Binky Brown Meets the Holy Virgin Mary* was a masterpiece of autobiographical revelation, a work that inspired me and helped me find my own voice. I started drawing and writing my own stories and invented my first real character, "Goldie." I wanted to try and get my work published, meet all the other cartoonists and see what the whole scene was about. Betsy Klein was also ready for a change, so we decided to leave Tucson for San Francisco and look for an apartment together.

We arrived in San Francisco in the fall of 1971, and found a nice big flat in a Victorian house on North Point Street in North Beach. We had a sweeping view of the bay from our upper floor, and a beautiful but totally neurotic cat called Yusef—you can meet him on the page 128.

Right: **Comic panel from Justin Green's "Binky Brown Meets The Holy Virgin Mary", 1970**

I was anxious to get my work published, but had only written some crude anecdotal stories and done some very rough preliminary sketches so far. I knew nothing about graphic design or comic page layout, and hadn't the slightest idea of what materials to use. Unlike most of the cartoonists I was to meet later, I'd never been particularly attracted to comic books as a kid. I kinda' liked *Little Lulu* and *Betty and Veronica*, but hadn't spent enough time looking at comics to get any feeling for the art form. I'd always thought of myself as a "fine artiste," and only wanted to paint and draw, hoping one day to be in museums with the other great masters!

So now I had to learn a whole new art form and do away with all the sloppy habits that I had picked up in Art School. I didn't even think about making the text legible for example—a rather essential element if you want the audience to be able to read your stories. I can just barely do that now, after 36 years!

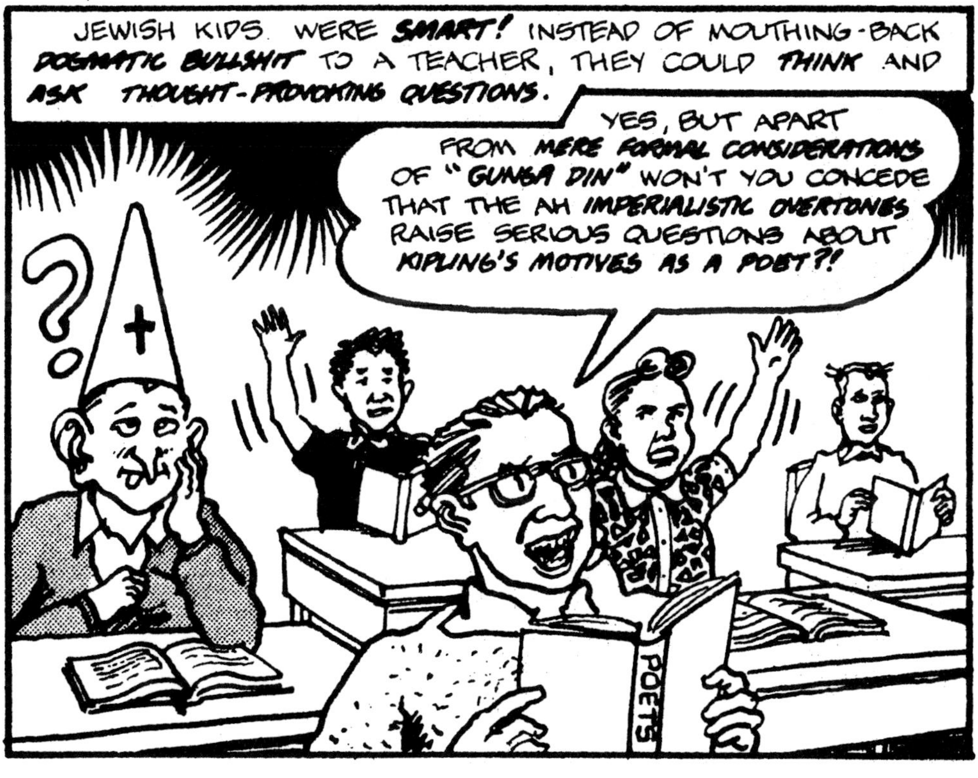

JEWISH KIDS WERE SMART! INSTEAD OF MOUTHING-BACK DOGMATIC BULLSHIT TO A TEACHER, THEY COULD THINK AND ASK THOUGHT-PROVOKING QUESTIONS.
YES, BUT APART FROM MERE FORMAL CONSIDERATIONS OF "GUNGA DIN" WON'T YOU CONCEDE THAT THE AH IMPERIALISTIC OVERTONES RAISE SERIOUS QUESTIONS ABOUT KIPLING'S MOTIVES AS A POET?!
POETS

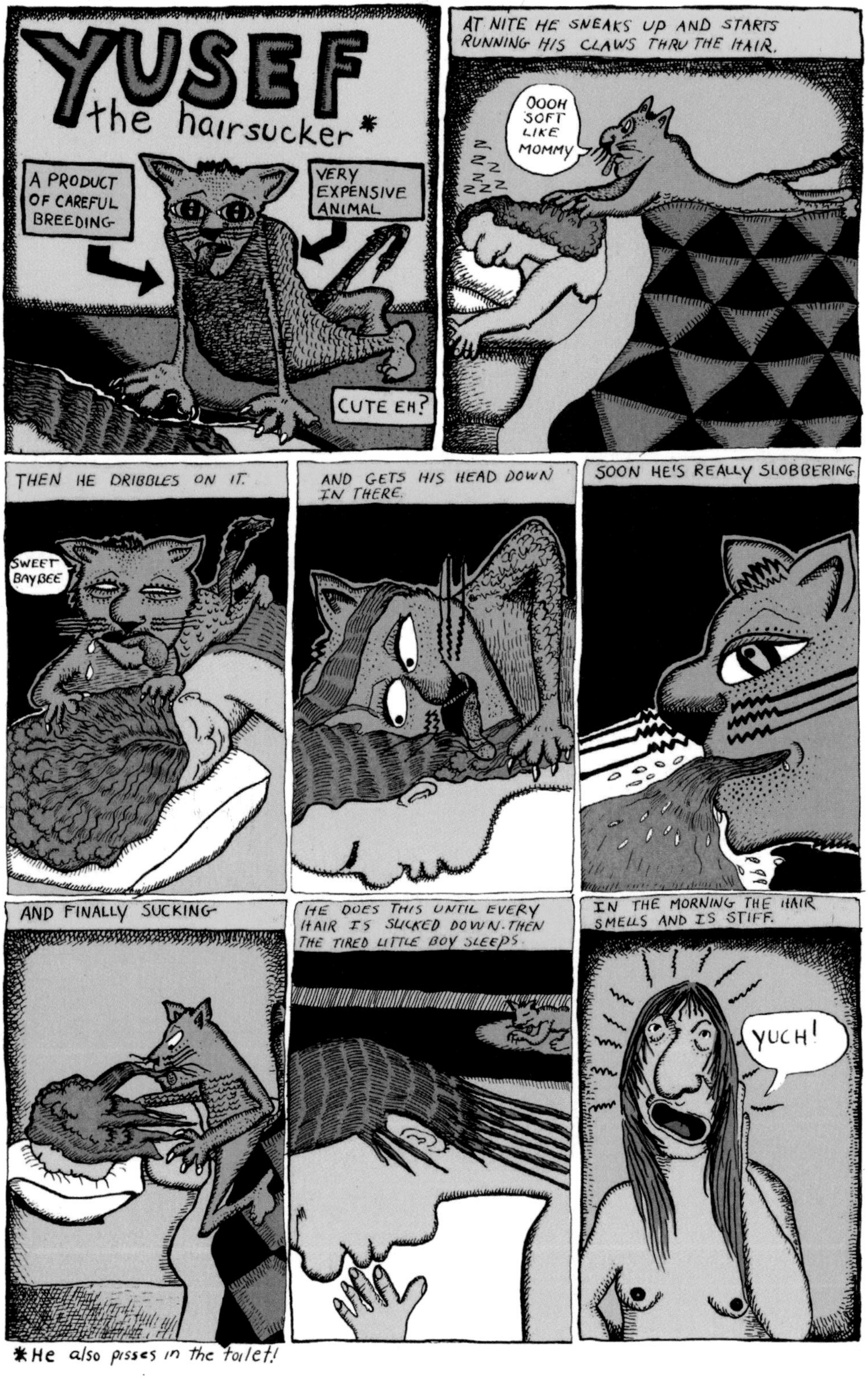
YUSEF
the hairsucker*
A PRODUCT OF CAREFUL BREEDING
VERY EXPENSIVE ANIMAL
CUTE EH?
AT NITE HE SNEAKS UP AND STARTS RUNNING HIS CLAWS THRU THE HAIR.
OOOH SOFT LIKE MOMMY
ZZZZZ
THEN HE DRIBBLES ON IT.
SWEET BAYBEE
AND GETS HIS HEAD DOWN IN THERE.
SOON HE'S REALLY SLOBBERING
AND FINALLY SUCKING
HE DOES THIS UNTIL EVERY HAIR IS SUCKED DOWN. THEN THE TIRED LITTLE BOY SLEEPS.
IN THE MORNING THE HAIR SMELLS AND IS STIFF.
YUCH!
*He also pisses in the toilet!

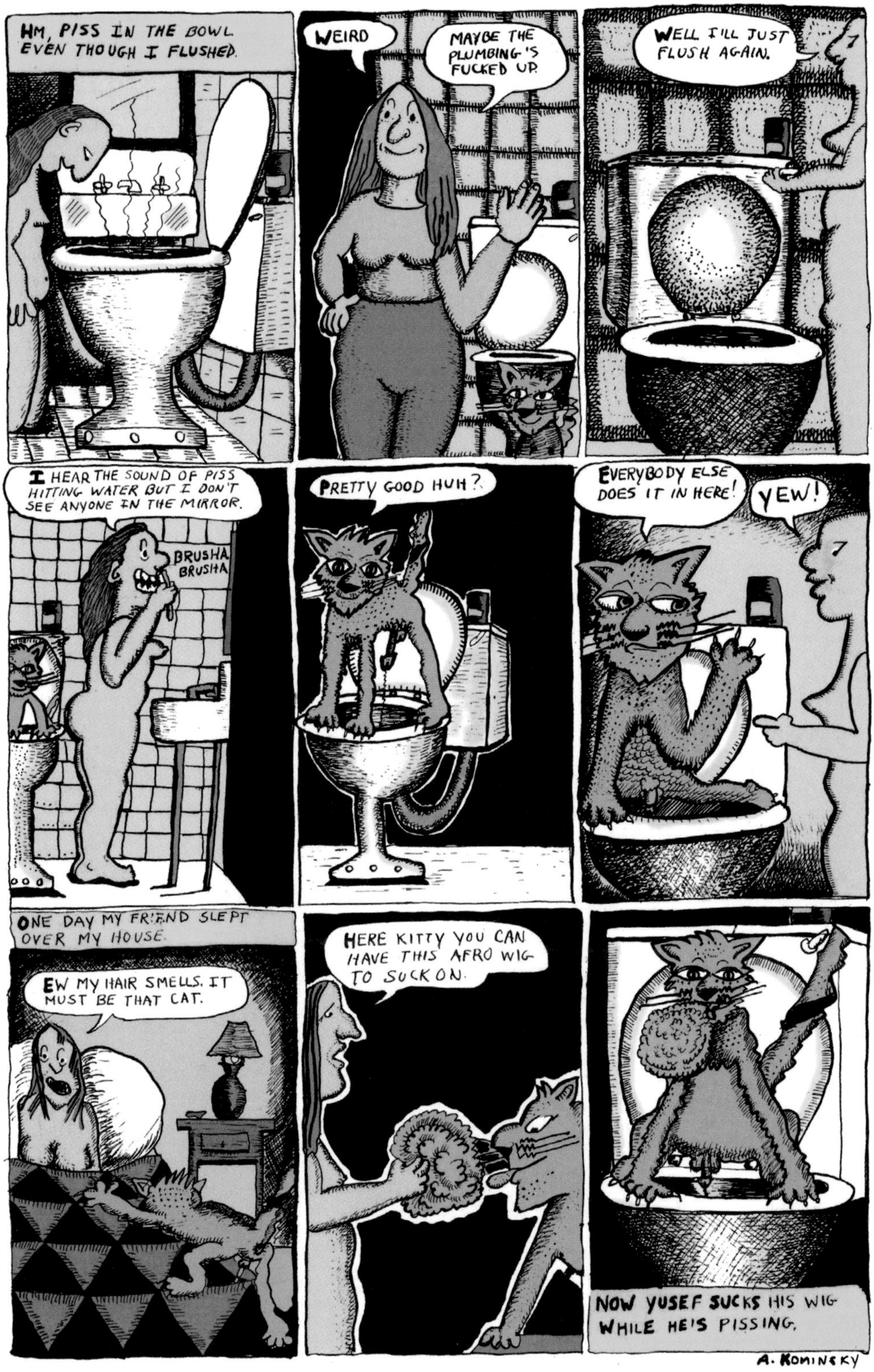
HM, PISS IN THE BOWL EVEN THOUGH I FLUSHED.
WEIRD
MAYBE THE PLUMBING'S FUCKED UP.
WELL I'LL JUST FLUSH AGAIN.
I HEAR THE SOUND OF PISS HITTING WATER BUT I DON'T SEE ANYONE IN THE MIRROR.
BRUSHA BRUSHA
PRETTY GOOD HUH?
EVERYBODY ELSE DOES IT IN HERE!
YEW!
ONE DAY MY FRIEND SLEPT OVER MY HOUSE.
EW MY HAIR SMELLS. IT MUST BE THAT CAT.
HERE KITTY YOU CAN HAVE THIS AFRO WIG TO SUCK ON.
NOW YUSEF SUCKS HIS WIG WHILE HE'S PISSING.
A. KOMINSKY

Meeting R. Crumb

Betsy and I were the new girls in town, and we were invited to all the parties. One of these parties was at Kathy Goodell and Terry Zwigoff's house on Brazil Street. Kathy was then Robert's girlfriend and Terry his best pal, and Robert stayed there when he was in San Francisco. Robert had heard that HoneyBunch Kaminski was coming to this party and he was very curious. I saw Robert the moment I walked in. I had heard from Spain's girlfriend Janet that Robert was really ugly and creepy looking. I didn't think so at all. He was surprisingly cute in an awkward kind of way. I was wearing a red micromini skirt and brown and white high boots. The first thing Robert said to me was, "You have really cute knees!" Funny, I'd never before thought of my knees as an asset.

I remember meeting Kathy Goodell, who was an art student and was busy gluing lima beans on big pieces of canvas to make a work of "aht." She was cute and tough-looking with a fierce but whiny voice. Terry Zwigoff was out of town, so I didn't meet him until a few weeks later, but that very important night I met Lora Fountain and Gilbert Shelton, Bill Griffith, Rick Griffin, Victor Moscoso, and S. Clay Wilson, among others.

The main event of the evening for me was an intense physical encounter between Robert and me. He had offered to show me around the house and we arrived upstairs. There, he started to grope me and play with my face in a most unusual and exciting manner. I became totally absorbed in his strangeness and wanted to continue, but just as he was climbing up on my butt to take his first of thousands of "horsey rides," his girlfriend Kathy showed up hands on hips ready to kick Robert in the shins (can't blame her: we were in her bedroom.)

I apologized and quickly left the room, but Robert and I secretly made a date before I went home. I was thrilled and excited by our brief encounter, and of course dazzled by Robert's talent and fame! I also felt it was not OK to steal someone else's boyfriend, so I wasn't sure what to do, and didn't make any decision about it right away.

A week later Robert came to see me on Northpoint Street. He later told me that he had been surprised and impressed by the neat and cozy atmosphere in our apartment, which he found unusual and incongruous given my brash and wild personality. We spent the night together, and I think we were both touched by how intense and yet tender our sexual connection was. He was much sweeter than I had expected, and he said the same thing about me.

The energy and mental connection between us was always very clear, but everything else around us was a chaotic mess. Robert's celebrity, his passive nature and the conflicting desires of everyone in his life created a special kind of craziness. We were all very young, drinking and taking a lot of drugs—we were constantly stoned on marijuana. We were open to almost any new experience, and there was the excitement of being part of a cultural and social revolution. But at times it was very disorienting. All the codes had been swept away, and no one was sure of how to behave anymore. And there were always plenty of opportunists and 'hangers on' around to take advantage of the confusion and the talent, looking for a free ride on the fun train.

As the months went by, I knew I was falling in love with Robert, but sensed that it was a hopeless situation. Even though he assured me that he wanted to end his twisted relationship with Kathy Goodell and that his relationship with his ex-wife Dana was over for him—she was living with Paul Seidman and pregnant with Paul's child—I could see that he was not emotionally separated from either of them. So I told him I didn't want to see him anymore until he figured out what he was doing. It broke my heart to do this, but I guess I was beginning to show a sense of pride for the first time in my life.

Fame made Robert attractive to hordes of beautiful women who wouldn't have looked at him if he were just an ordinary *schlub*. This was great for him, except he couldn't handle it. I remember one night in particular. Robert was playing with his band, The Cheap Suit Serenaders, at the Magic Cellar in San Francisco. At least five different "Crumb girls" showed up, all in the same white knee socks, jean skirts and big shoes. I was one of them. Time to move on …. Robert has told me many times that it was my ability to detach myself from this absurd situation that ultimately attracted him to me. I did not have the biggest butt or the most magnificent calves. I just had some control of my emotions. I guess this is actually a rare quality. I never thought much about it before!

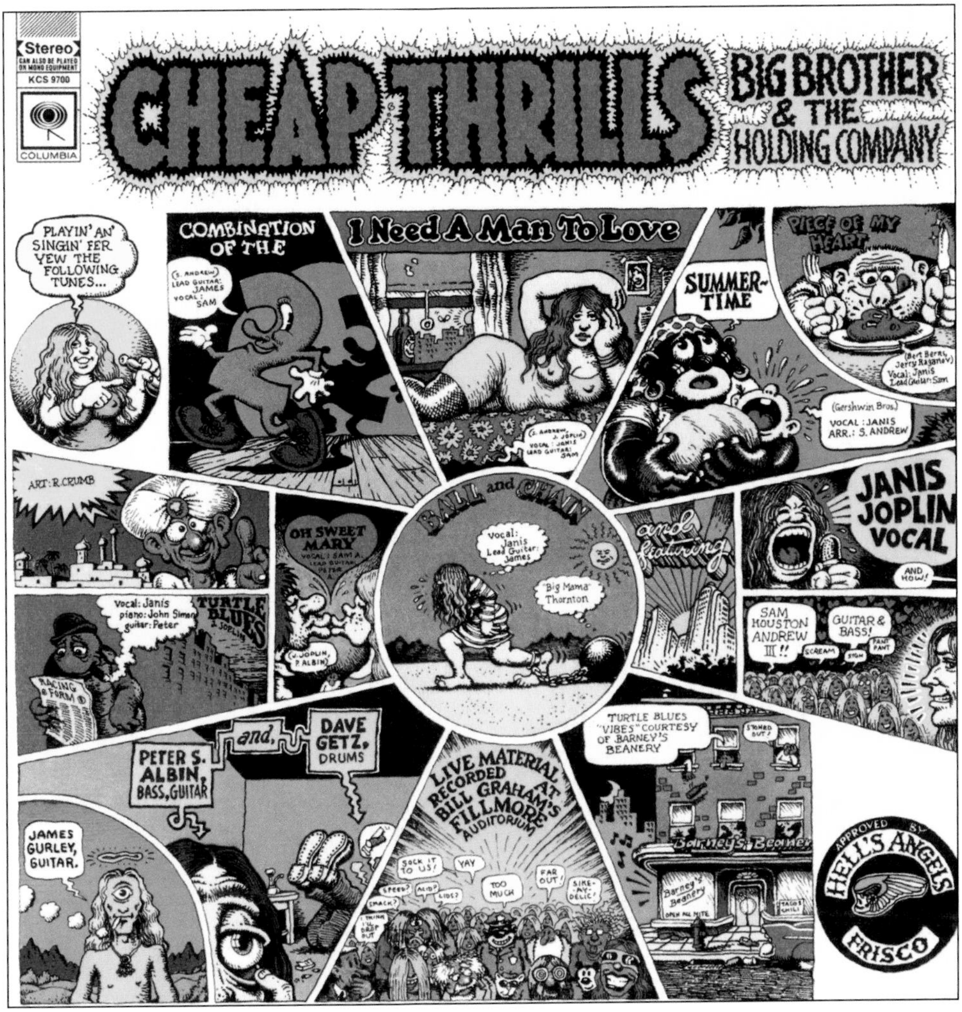
Stereo
KCS 9700
COLUMBIA
CHEAP THRILLS
BIG BROTHER & THE HOLDING COMPANY
PLAYIN' AN' SINGIN' FER YEW THE FOLLOWING TUNES...
COMBINATION OF THE
I Need A Man To Love
SUMMER-TIME
PIECE OF MY HEART
(Gershwin Bros.) VOCAL: JANIS ARR.: S. ANDREW
ART: R. CRUMB
OH SWEET MARY
BALL and CHAIN
Vocal: Janis Lead Guitar: James
"Big Mama" Thornton
and featuring
JANIS JOPLIN VOCAL
AND HOW!
Vocal: Janis piano: John Simon guitar: Peter
TURTLE BLUES
SAM HOUSTON ANDREW III!!
GUITAR & BASS!
TURTLE BLUES "VIBES" COURTESY OF BARNEY'S BEANERY
PETER S. ALBIN, BASS, GUITAR
and
DAVE GETZ, DRUMS
LIVE MATERIAL RECORDED AT BILL GRAHAM'S FILLMORE AUDITORIUM
JAMES GURLEY, GUITAR.
SOCK IT TO US!
YAY
FAR OUT!
TOO MUCH
Barney's Beanery
APPROVED BY HELL'S ANGELS FRISCO

Opposite, above left: **Robert when I first met him**
Opposite, above right: **Robert playing piano, 1971**
Opposite, below: **Me giving Robert a little ride**

Above: **Cover by Robert for Janis Joplin's *Cheap Thrills* Album**
This was originally supposed to be the back cover, but Janis liked it better than the other image.

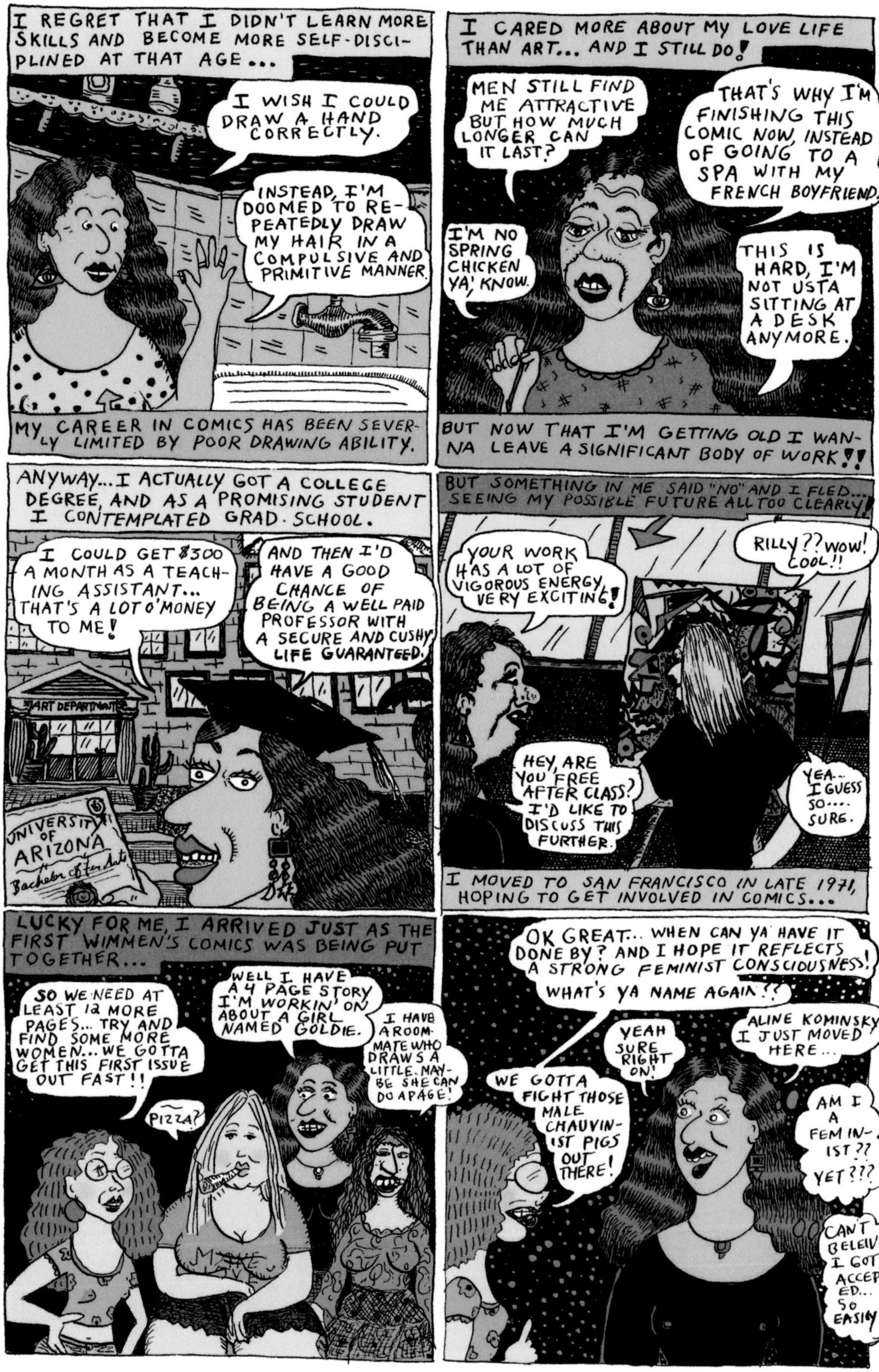

I REGRET THAT I DIDN'T LEARN MORE SKILLS AND BECOME MORE SELF-DISCIPLINED AT THAT AGE...
I WISH I COULD DRAW A HAND CORRECTLY.
INSTEAD, I'M DOOMED TO REPEATEDLY DRAW MY HAIR IN A COMPULSIVE AND PRIMITIVE MANNER.
MY CAREER IN COMICS HAS BEEN SEVERLY LIMITED BY POOR DRAWING ABILITY.
I CARED MORE ABOUT MY LOVE LIFE THAN ART... AND I STILL DO!
MEN STILL FIND ME ATTRACTIVE BUT HOW MUCH LONGER CAN IT LAST?
THAT'S WHY I'M FINISHING THIS COMIC NOW, INSTEAD OF GOING TO A SPA WITH MY FRENCH BOYFRIEND.
I'M NO SPRING CHICKEN YA' KNOW.
THIS IS HARD, I'M NOT USTA SITTING AT A DESK ANYMORE.
BUT NOW THAT I'M GETTING OLD I WANNA LEAVE A SIGNIFICANT BODY OF WORK!!
ANYWAY... I ACTUALLY GOT A COLLEGE DEGREE, AND AS A PROMISING STUDENT I CONTEMPLATED GRAD. SCHOOL.
I COULD GET $300 A MONTH AS A TEACHING ASSISTANT... THAT'S A LOT O'MONEY TO ME!
AND THEN I'D HAVE A GOOD CHANCE OF BEING A WELL PAID PROFESSOR WITH A SECURE AND CUSHY LIFE GUARANTEED.
ART DEPARTMENT
UNIVERSITY OF ARIZONA
Bachelor of Fine Arts
BUT SOMETHING IN ME SAID "NO" AND I FLED... SEEING MY POSSIBLE FUTURE ALL TOO CLEARLY!
YOUR WORK HAS A LOT OF VIGOROUS ENERGY, VERY EXCITING!
RILLY?? WOW! COOL!!
HEY, ARE YOU FREE AFTER CLASS? I'D LIKE TO DISCUSS THIS FURTHER.
YEA.. I GUESS SO.... SURE.
I MOVED TO SAN FRANCISCO IN LATE 1971, HOPING TO GET INVOLVED IN COMICS...
LUCKY FOR ME, I ARRIVED JUST AS THE FIRST WIMMEN'S COMICS WAS BEING PUT TOGETHER...
SO WE NEED AT LEAST 12 MORE PAGES... TRY AND FIND SOME MORE WOMEN... WE GOTTA GET THIS FIRST ISSUE OUT FAST!!
WELL I HAVE A 4 PAGE STORY I'M WORKIN' ON ABOUT A GIRL NAMED GOLDIE.
I HAVE A ROOMMATE WHO DRAWS A LITTLE. MAYBE SHE CAN DO A PAGE!
PIZZA?
OK GREAT... WHEN CAN YA HAVE IT DONE BY? AND I HOPE IT REFLECTS A STRONG FEMINIST CONSCIOUSNESS!
WHAT'S YA NAME AGAIN??
ALINE KOMINSKY I JUST MOVED HERE...
YEAH SURE RIGHT ON!
WE GOTTA FIGHT THOSE MALE CHAUVINIST PIGS OUT THERE!
AM I A FEMINIST?? YET???
CAN'T BELEIVE I GOT ACCEPTED... SO EASILY

Discovering Wimmen's Comix

While all this was going on, I was pursuing my cartooning career. I was too ashamed to show my amateurish comics to Robert, well, because he really was, and is, a genius. I had never seen anyone draw like him before. In fact the only other person who draws the same way is our daughter Sophie. They draw as though there is a complete pencil sketch already there and they are merely copying it in ink. In fact, the drawing is complete only in their heads.

I, on the other hand, draw, erase and scratch out some tortured looking image that clearly shows how much I am struggling with the medium. I honestly don't think this makes my work less interesting, just very expressionistic and often very ugly. Robert can make something quite disgusting look kind o' cute and juicy like an old carton from the 1920s. My work is more in the George Grosz-James Ensor tradition.

I heard there was a group of women putting together a comic book of women's work and they were looking for women artists, and a few of the male cartoonists, including Willy Murphy, Dan O'Neil and Spain, encouraged me to submit my work. This was to be *Wimmen's Comix* No. 1.

Trina Robbins was the editor, organizer and the real energy behind the project. She had been involved in the Underground Comics scene for a while, and had published a book with another group of women called *It Ain't Me Babe*. It was pretty silly, hippy, romantic stuff with Women's Lib overtones. Now she was becoming more political and an angry feminist.

Below: **Trina Robbins and other artists**
A group of artists contributing to *It Ain't Me Babe*—a very Hippy, Earth Mother, Feminist anthology of comix that preceded *Wimmen's Comix*.

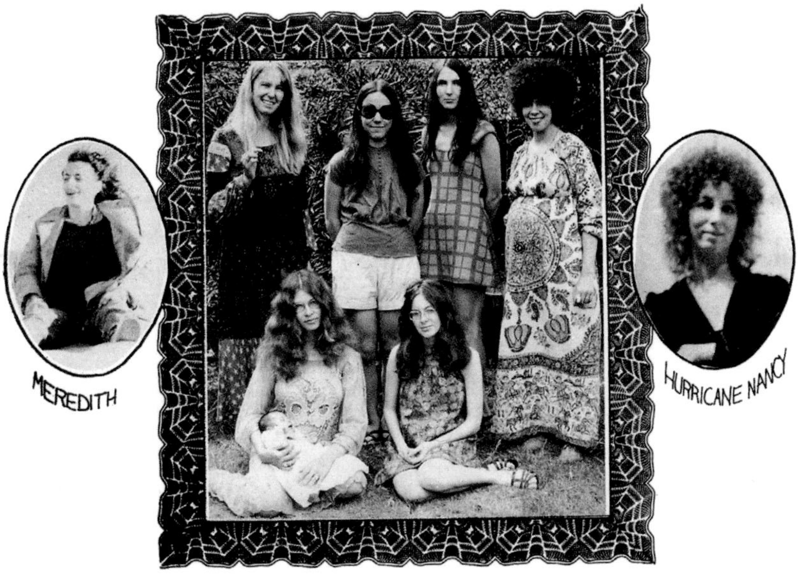
MEREDITH
HURRICANE NANCY

The pioneering sisterhood

In 1971 there were very few women interested in drawing comics, and very few skilled women cartoonists. The work was very crude. Some women cartoonists like Dale Messick, who did Brenda Starr, were accomplished, but in the '60s and '70s, cartooning was not an obvious career choice for a woman. It's hard to imagine now, because there have been so many great women cartoonists since then—Diane Noomin, Phoebe Gloeckner, Julie Doucet, Carol Tyler, Lauren Weinstein, Dori Seda, Debbie Dreschler, Penny Moran, and Sophie Crumb, to name a few.

Now graphic novels and reality-based comics are all the rage, but in the 1970s Justin Green and I were pioneers in autobiographical "let it all hang out" genre comics. I didn't know we were evolving a new art form: I did what came naturally, writing and drawing what I knew and felt deeply from personal experience. At one point, some of the cartoonists in the "Air Pirates," like Bobby London and Sherry Flenikan, encouraged me to choose an old-style comic artist to emulate as they had done, to make my work more palatable. But like George Grosz and Alice Neal, I was unable to see life as anything but grotesque and absurd.

I showed up at one of the first *Wimmen's Comix* meetings in late 1971 at Pat Moodian's house. There was a filthy mattress surrounded by empty beer bottles and cigarette butts. Pat was a kind of white trash biker hippy chick. She was good natured and welcomed me warmly. Michelle Brand, Lora Fountain and Sharon Rudall were also there.

This first meeting was very exciting—there was strong sisterly support and plenty of tales of "male chauvinist pig" behavior. I was happy to be so easily accepted, and thrilled at the idea of having my work published. But in all honesty, I didn't feel the sort of overwhelming feminist anger toward men that, for example, Trina Robbins did.

I was grateful that men found me attractive, and after the death of my father, I hadn't really had any terrible experiences with men. Maybe my male art professors had exploited me a little, but then I was having a pretty good time too. And in San Francisco, all the male cartoonists had been friendly and encouraging. I didn't feel exploited or discriminated against, and had never felt like a victim—more like an Amazon ready to conquer the world! I also loved the company of other women and cherished my bonds with female friends as I always have and still do now.

Right: **Inside front cover of *Wimmen's Comix*, Number 1, 1972**
The artists are all drawing themselves .

WIMMEN'S COMIX ARE DONE BY WOMEN FOR EVERYONE! WHETHER YEA OR NAY — WRITE US!

HEH HEH HEH

SURPRISE! **ABSOLUTELY FREE!** AN ORIGINAL *FU MANCHU TOENAIL* (ca.1923) TO THE FIRST 43 ESKIMOS WHO SEND IN THIS PAGE PLUS ONE RECENTLY USED KUMQUAT BEFORE THE DRUID EQUINOX OR AFTER ROBERT E. LEE'S BIRTHDAY. VOID WHERE PROHIBITED BY OUTLAW OR FROWNED UPON BY RAMPANT GREMLINS. OFFER EXPIRES AFTER WE DO ★

WIMMEN'S COMIX #1 COPYRIGHT 1972 BY (ABOVE, LEFT TO RIGHT): MICHELLE BRAND, LEE MARRS, LORA FOUNTAIN, PATRICIA MOODIAN (EDITOR), SHARON RUDALL, SHELBY, ALINE KOMINSKY, TRINA, KAREN MARIE HASKELL, & JANET WOLFE STANLEY ★ WORLD RIGHTS RESERVED • *ANY SIMILARITY TO PERSONS LIVING, DEAD, OR IN TRANSIT IS COMPLETELY COINKIDINKAL* • ☆ THIS BOOK MAY NOT BE REPRODUCED IN WHOLE OR PART WITHOUT PUBLISHER'S PERMISSION • *DEALERS ARE INSTRUCTED TO SELL ONLY TO ADULTS* & FOR NOT MORE THAN 50¢ • SEND **XEROXES** OF ARTWORK OR MANUSCRIPTS WITH A SUFFICIENTLY-POSTAGED, LARGE-ENUFF ENVELOPE (WE CANNOT BE RESPONSIBLE FOR UNSOLICITED ORIGINALS.) TO **WIMMEN'S COMIX EDITOR** (WE ROTATE) %o OUR PUBLISHER: **LAST GASP-ECO FUNNIES INC. BOX 212 • BERKELEY, CA. 94701•**

137

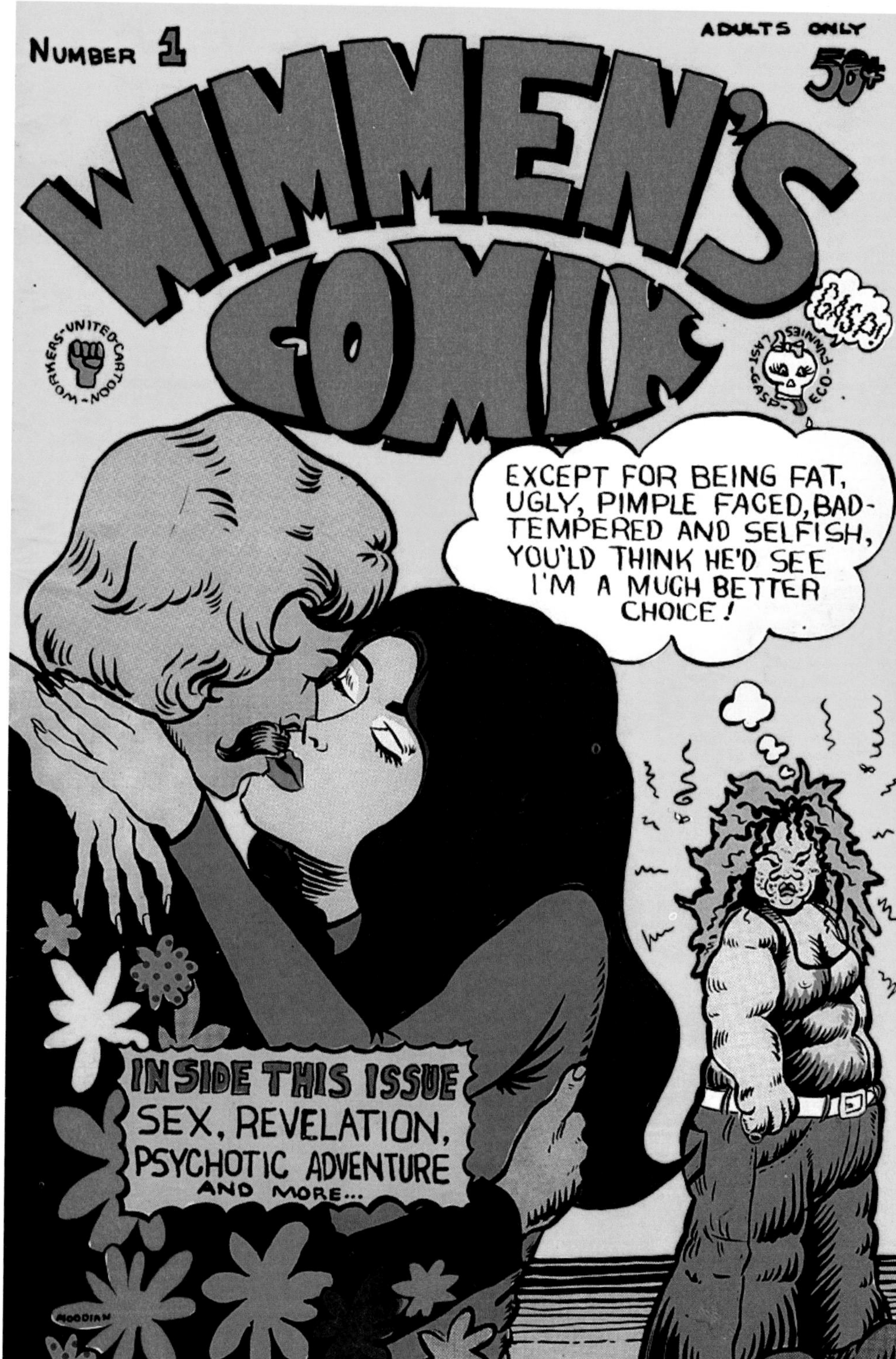
NUMBER 1
ADULTS ONLY
50¢
WIMMEN'S COMIX
GASP!!
WORKERS-UNITED-CARTOON-
LAST-GASP-ECO-FUNNIES
EXCEPT FOR BEING FAT, UGLY, PIMPLE FACED, BAD-TEMPERED AND SELFISH, YOU'LD THINK HE'D SEE I'M A MUCH BETTER CHOICE!
INSIDE THIS ISSUE
SEX, REVELATION, PSYCHOTIC ADVENTURE AND MORE...

Men—the love-hate debate

Trina Robbins seemed to have suffered countless indignities at the hands of male chauvinist pigs. At the time I felt she was very sincere and I admired her; she seemed very "together" to me. She lived in a little house filled with plants, lace and old furniture; it was cozy and appealing. She was a single mother with an adorable little girl, and appeared to support herself through her art. Trina was eight years older than me, and had been on the scene a lot longer. She was tiny, cute, with a big head of curly blonde hair and big blue eyes. She was real feisty, but she had a high-pitched voice that made it hard to take her seriously.

Because she was so petite and cute, men probably treated her like a little baby doll. I later found out that she had posed nude for men's magazines in the early '60s and had later become a rock star groupie. I understand how that had totally turned her off, and why she felt exploited by men. I know some other petite women who became bodybuilders to defend themselves against big men. My experience was the exact opposite: I had always felt like a big ox, and little Jewish men were scared of me!

I do not mean to downplay the importance of the Feminist Movement that was gathering steam. There were, and are very crucial issues: women deserve to have access to qualified jobs and receive equal pay, girls need to benefit from the same opportunities as boys, and sexist attitudes persist in the most advanced societies. But in those days, I saw a lot of hysteria and hypocrisy. Women claimed they wanted sensitive men who treated them as equals, and then ended up with bad boy pirates and cowboys. And women who supposedly have it all seemed stressed and miserable. If there has been any progress in male–female relations, it is not obvious to me.

Back to the early years of *Wimmen's Comix*. Trina was charismatic and attracted various women acolytes, many of whom were in awe of her. I liked her a lot, but balked at being controlled by anyone. She tried to get me to dress differently. Once she told me I should wear long flowing dresses to distract from my big unattractive legs. I was deeply insulted by that and continued to wear hot pants and micro minis! Still do! Anyway, my first story entitled "Goldie A Neurotic Woman", got published in *Wimmen's Comix* No.1, and this inspired me to continue drawing comics. Interestingly, Trina's story in this issue was about Robert's sister Sandra coming out as a lesbian. I didn't know at the time that Sandy and Trina were building a real case against Robert, allegedly because of his sexist comics. But people's motivations, as always, were more complex.

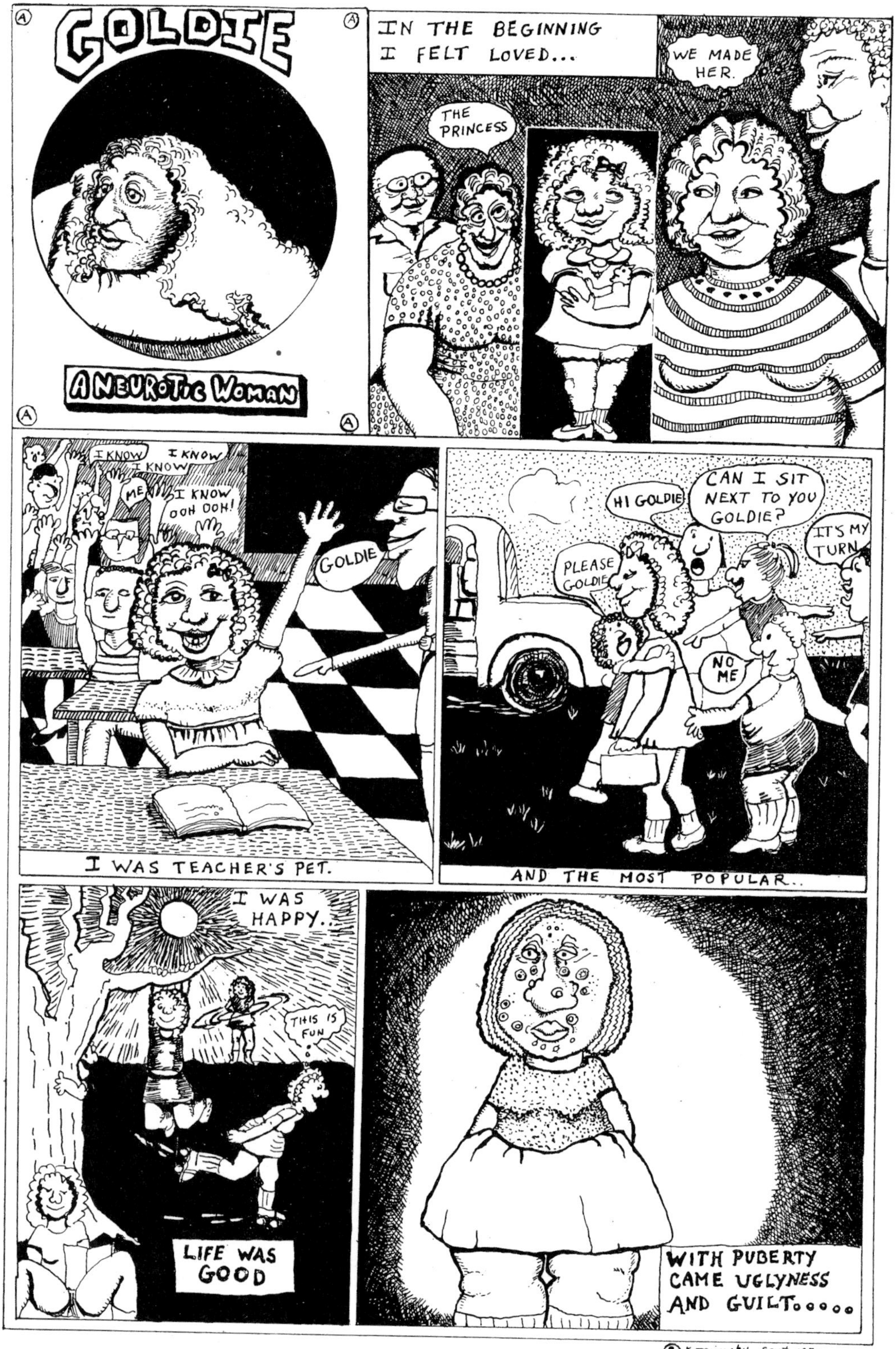
GOLDIE
A NEUROTIC WOMAN
IN THE BEGINNING I FELT LOVED...
THE PRINCESS
WE MADE HER.
I KNOW
I KNOW
I KNOW
ME
I KNOW OOH OOH!
GOLDIE
I WAS TEACHER'S PET.
HI GOLDIE
CAN I SIT NEXT TO YOU GOLDIE?
IT'S MY TURN
PLEASE GOLDIE
NO ME
AND THE MOST POPULAR..
I WAS HAPPY..
THIS IS FUN
LIFE WAS GOOD
WITH PUBERTY CAME UGLYNESS AND GUILT.....

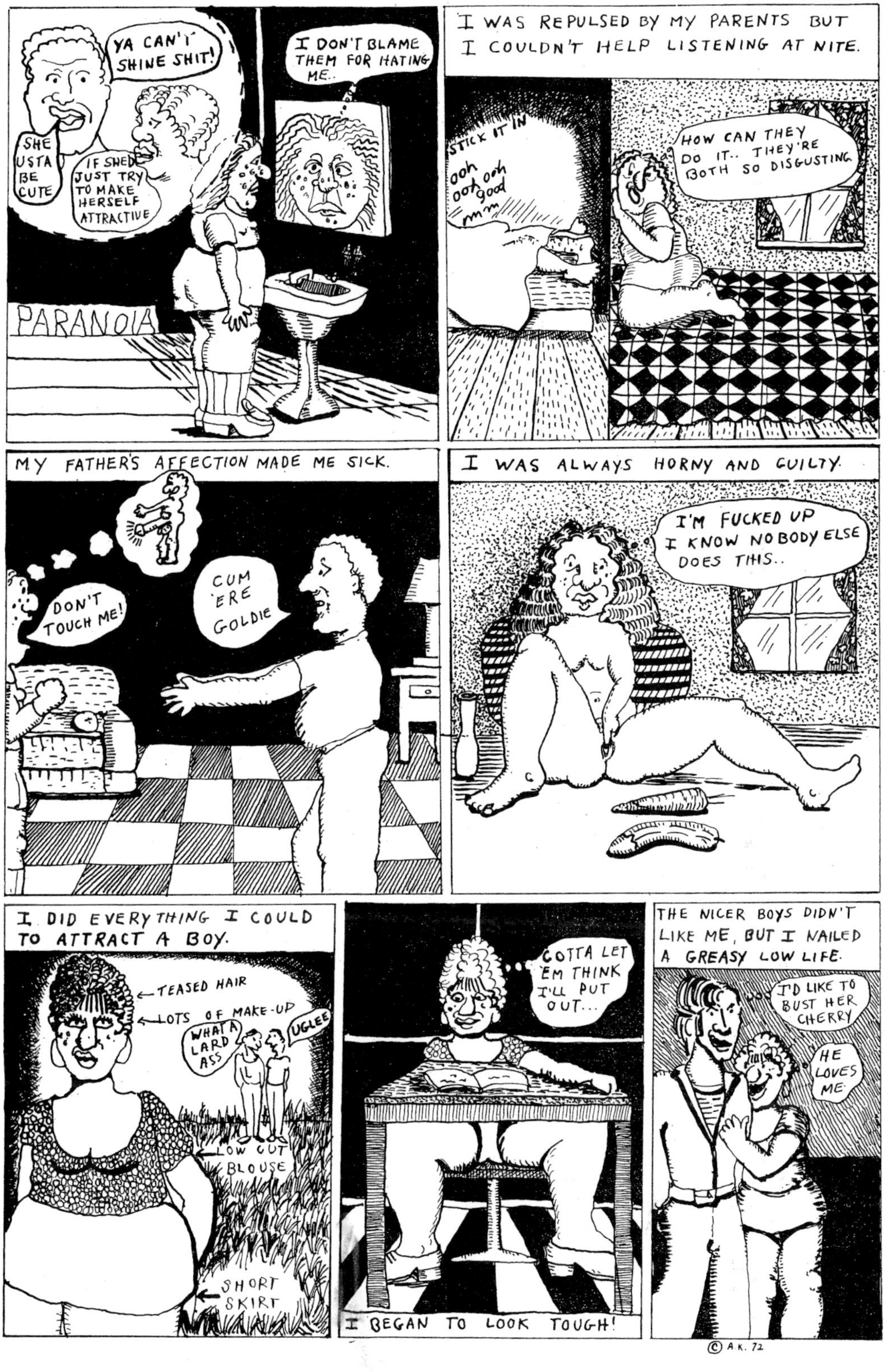
YA CAN'T SHINE SHIT!
SHE USTA BE CUTE
IF SHED JUST TRY TO MAKE HERSELF ATTRACTIVE
I DON'T BLAME THEM FOR HATING ME..
PARANOIA
I WAS REPULSED BY MY PARENTS BUT I COULDN'T HELP LISTENING AT NITE.
STICK IT IN
ooh ooh ooh good
mmm
HOW CAN THEY DO IT.. THEY'RE BOTH SO DISGUSTING.
MY FATHER'S AFFECTION MADE ME SICK.
DON'T TOUCH ME!
CUM 'ERE GOLDIE
I WAS ALWAYS HORNY AND GUILTY.
I'M FUCKED UP I KNOW NO BODY ELSE DOES THIS..
I DID EVERYTHING I COULD TO ATTRACT A BOY.
TEASED HAIR
LOTS OF MAKE-UP
WHAT A LARD ASS
UGLEE
LOW CUT BLOUSE
SHORT SKIRT
GOTTA LET 'EM THINK I'LL PUT OUT...
I BEGAN TO LOOK TOUGH!
THE NICER BOYS DIDN'T LIKE ME, BUT I NAILED A GREASY LOW LIFE.
I'D LIKE TO BUST HER CHERRY
HE LOVES ME.
© A.K. 72

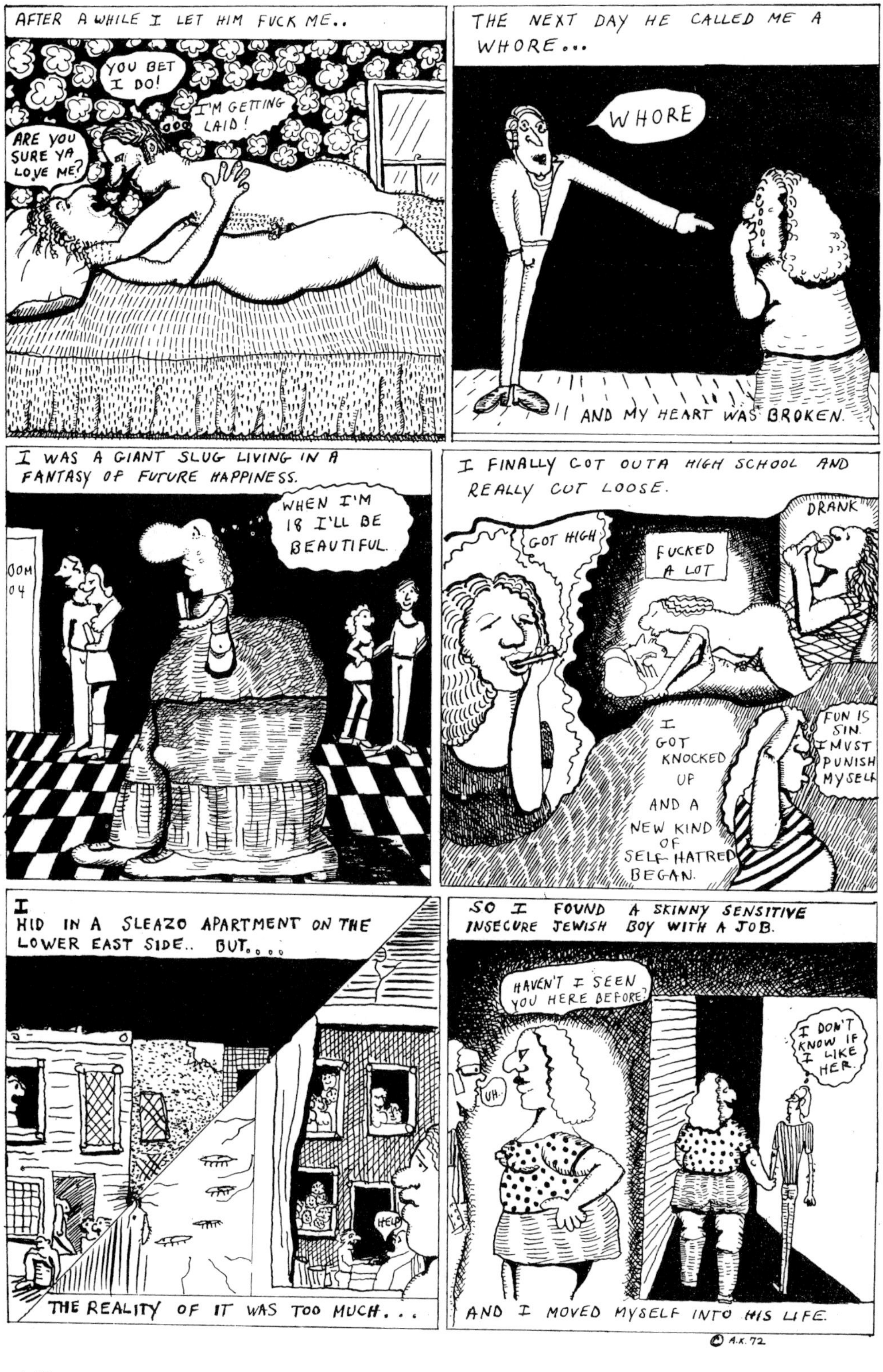
AFTER A WHILE I LET HIM FUCK ME..
ARE YOU SURE YA LOVE ME?
YOU BET I DO!
I'M GETTING LAID!
THE NEXT DAY HE CALLED ME A WHORE...
WHORE
AND MY HEART WAS BROKEN.
I WAS A GIANT SLUG LIVING IN A FANTASY OF FUTURE HAPPINESS.
WHEN I'M 18 I'LL BE BEAUTIFUL.
I FINALLY GOT OUTA HIGH SCHOOL AND REALLY CUT LOOSE.
GOT HIGH
FUCKED A LOT
DRANK
I GOT KNOCKED UP AND A NEW KIND OF SELF-HATRED BEGAN.
FUN IS SIN. I MUST PUNISH MYSELF
I HID IN A SLEAZO APARTMENT ON THE LOWER EAST SIDE.. BUT....
HELP
THE REALITY OF IT WAS TOO MUCH...
SO I FOUND A SKINNY SENSITIVE INSECURE JEWISH BOY WITH A JOB.
HAVEN'T I SEEN YOU HERE BEFORE?
UH.
I DON'T KNOW IF I LIKE HER.
AND I MOVED MYSELF INTO HIS LIFE.
© A.K. 72

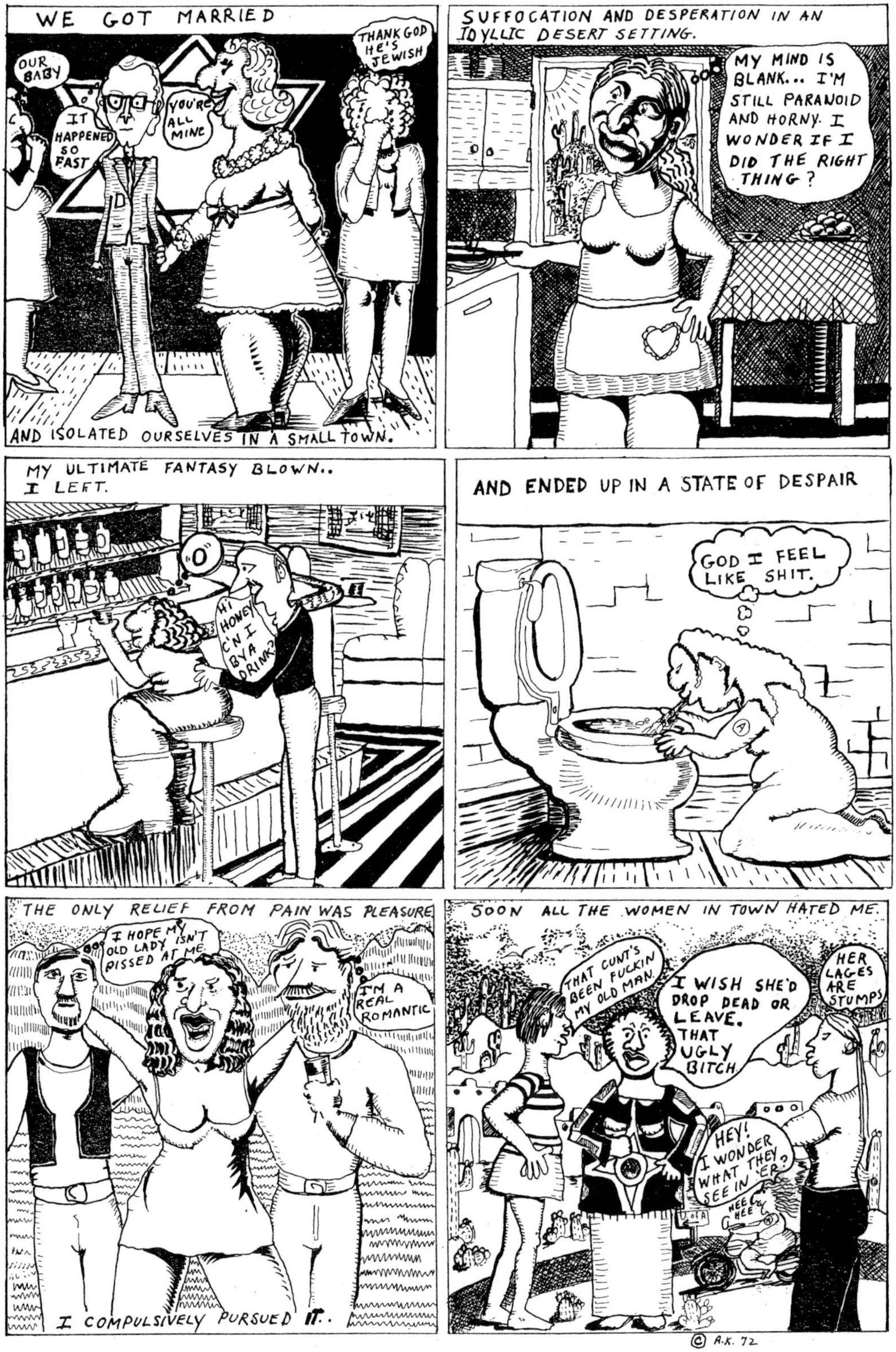
WE GOT MARRIED
OUR BABY
IT HAPPENED SO FAST
YOU'RE ALL MINE
THANK GOD HE'S JEWISH
AND ISOLATED OURSELVES IN A SMALL TOWN.
SUFFOCATION AND DESPERATION IN AN IDYLLIC DESERT SETTING.
MY MIND IS BLANK... I'M STILL PARANOID AND HORNY. I WONDER IF I DID THE RIGHT THING?
MY ULTIMATE FANTASY BLOWN.. I LEFT.
HI HONEY C'N I BY A DRINK?
AND ENDED UP IN A STATE OF DESPAIR
GOD I FEEL LIKE SHIT.
THE ONLY RELIEF FROM PAIN WAS PLEASURE
I HOPE MY OLD LADY ISN'T PISSED AT ME.
I'M A REAL ROMANTIC
I COMPULSIVELY PURSUED IT..
SOON ALL THE WOMEN IN TOWN HATED ME.
THAT CUNT'S BEEN FUCKIN MY OLD MAN.
I WISH SHE'D DROP DEAD OR LEAVE. THAT UGLY BITCH
HER LAGES ARE STUMPS
HEY! I WONDER WHAT THEY SEE IN 'ER?
HEE HEE
© A.K. 72

THE MORE I WAS OSTRACIZED THE MORE I DEGENERATED

COME IN

THERE WAS A CONSTANT STREAM IN AND OUT MY DOOR.

EVEN MY OWN BROTHER TURNED AGAINST ME.

SLUT

WATSA MATTA YA ASHAMED O' ME? YA PUNK

HM.. I'VE ALREADY MADE IT WITH EVERYONE IN THERE

IT SEEMED LIKE I HAD EXHAUSTED THE SUPPLY OF MEN.

SO I HUNG OUT ALONE.

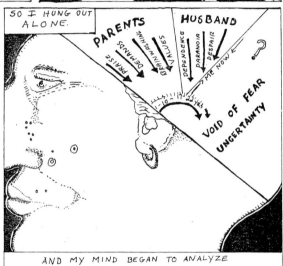

PARENTS   HUSBAND

PRAISE   DEMANDS   BRAINWASHING   VALUES   DEPENDENCE   PARANOIA   DESPAIR   ME NOW?

VOID OF FEAR UNCERTAINTY

AND MY MIND BEGAN TO ANALYZE THE PAST EVENTS OF MY LIFE.

INSTEAD OF HATING MYSELF, I WAS INDIGNANT AT EVERYONE ELSE.

I HAVE A LOTTA PUTENCIAL

SOME LONG-LOST SENSE OF PRIDE CAME TO THE SURFACE.

FINALLY AFTER 22 YEARS OF TRYING TO PLEASE OTHER PEOPLE.

N CISCO

I SET OUT TO LIVE IN MY OWN STYLE!

© A.K.72   erd

144

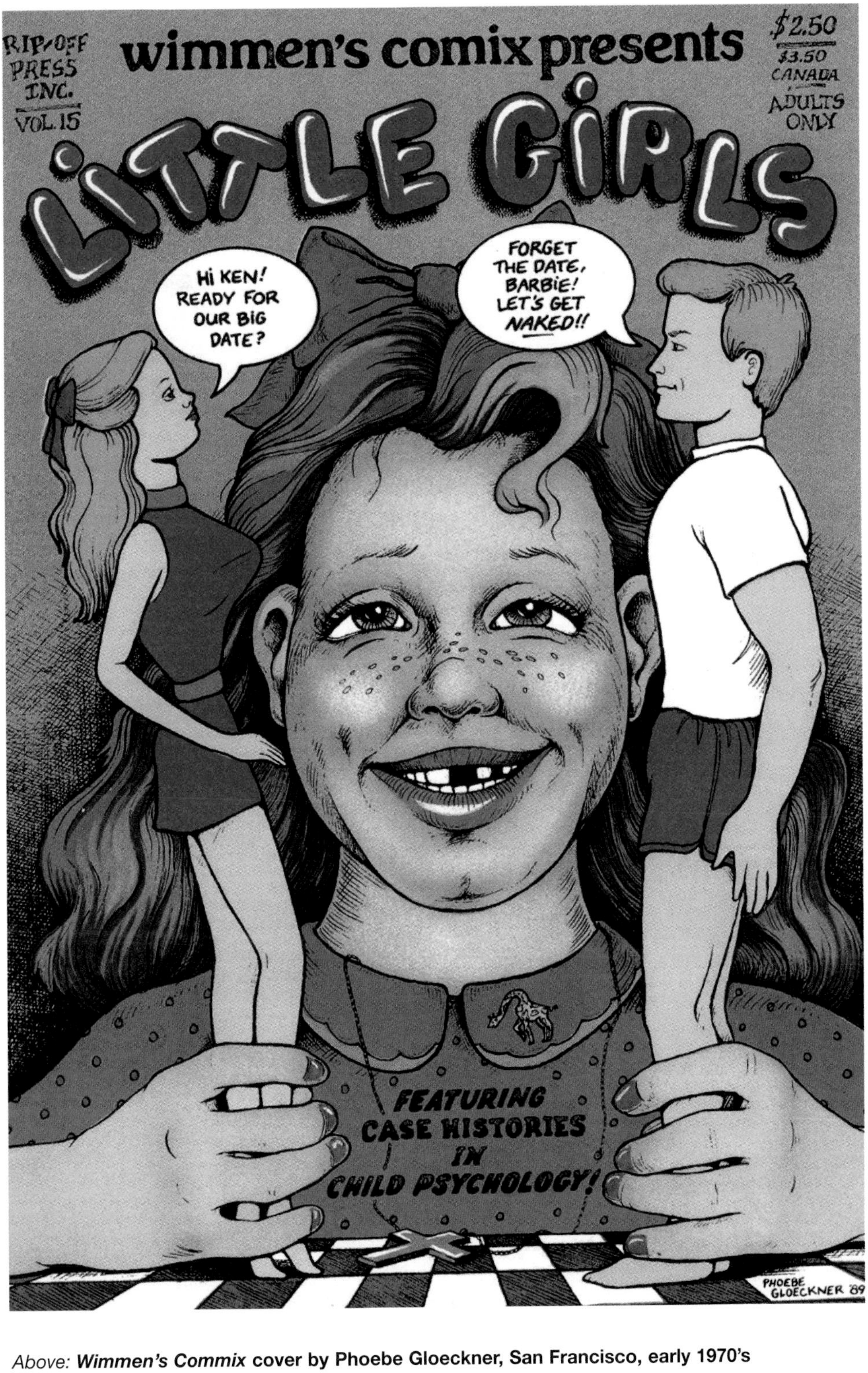
RIP/OFF PRESS INC.
VOL. 15
wimmen's comix presents
$2.50
$3.50 CANADA
ADULTS ONLY
LITTLE GIRLS
HI KEN! READY FOR OUR BIG DATE?
FORGET THE DATE, BARBIE! LET'S GET NAKED!!
FEATURING CASE HISTORIES IN CHILD PSYCHOLOGY!
PHOEBE GLOECKNER '89

Above: ***Wimmen's Commix*** **cover by Phoebe Gloeckner, San Francisco, early 1970's**

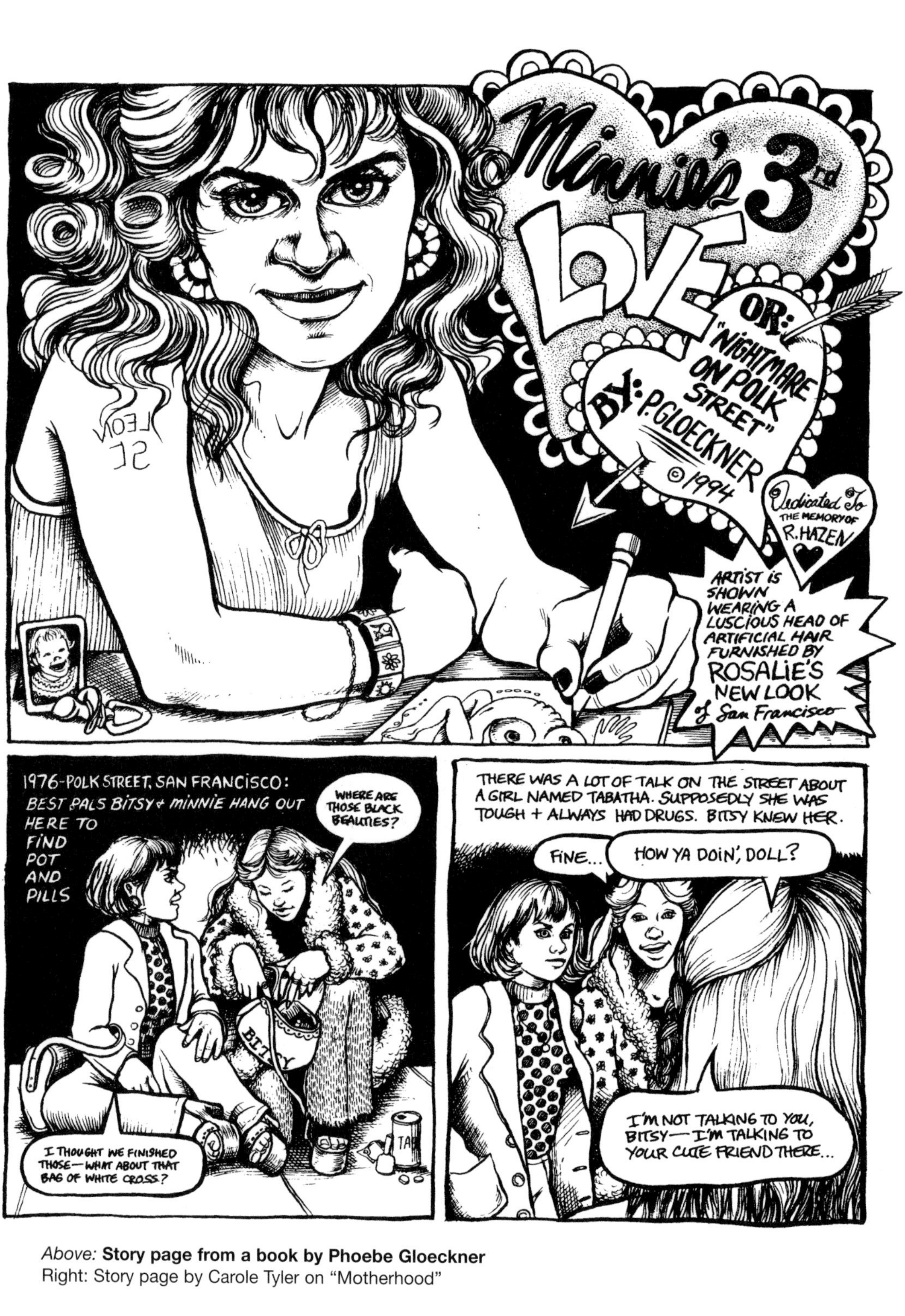
Minnie's 3rd LOVE
OR: "NIGHTMARE ON POLK STREET"
BY: P. GLOECKNER ©1994
Dedicated To THE MEMORY OF R. HAZEN
ARTIST IS SHOWN WEARING A LUSCIOUS HEAD OF ARTIFICIAL HAIR FURNISHED BY ROSALIE'S NEW LOOK of San Francisco
1976-POLK STREET, SAN FRANCISCO: BEST PALS BITSY + MINNIE HANG OUT HERE TO FIND POT AND PILLS
WHERE ARE THOSE BLACK BEAUTIES?
I THOUGHT WE FINISHED THOSE—WHAT ABOUT THAT BAG OF WHITE CROSS?
BITSY
THERE WAS A LOT OF TALK ON THE STREET ABOUT A GIRL NAMED TABATHA. SUPPOSEDLY SHE WAS TOUGH + ALWAYS HAD DRUGS. BITSY KNEW HER.
HOW YA DOIN', DOLL?
FINE...
I'M NOT TALKING TO YOU, BITSY—I'M TALKING TO YOUR CUTE FRIEND THERE...

Above: **Story page from a book by Phoebe Gloeckner**
Right: Story page by Carole Tyler on "Motherhood"

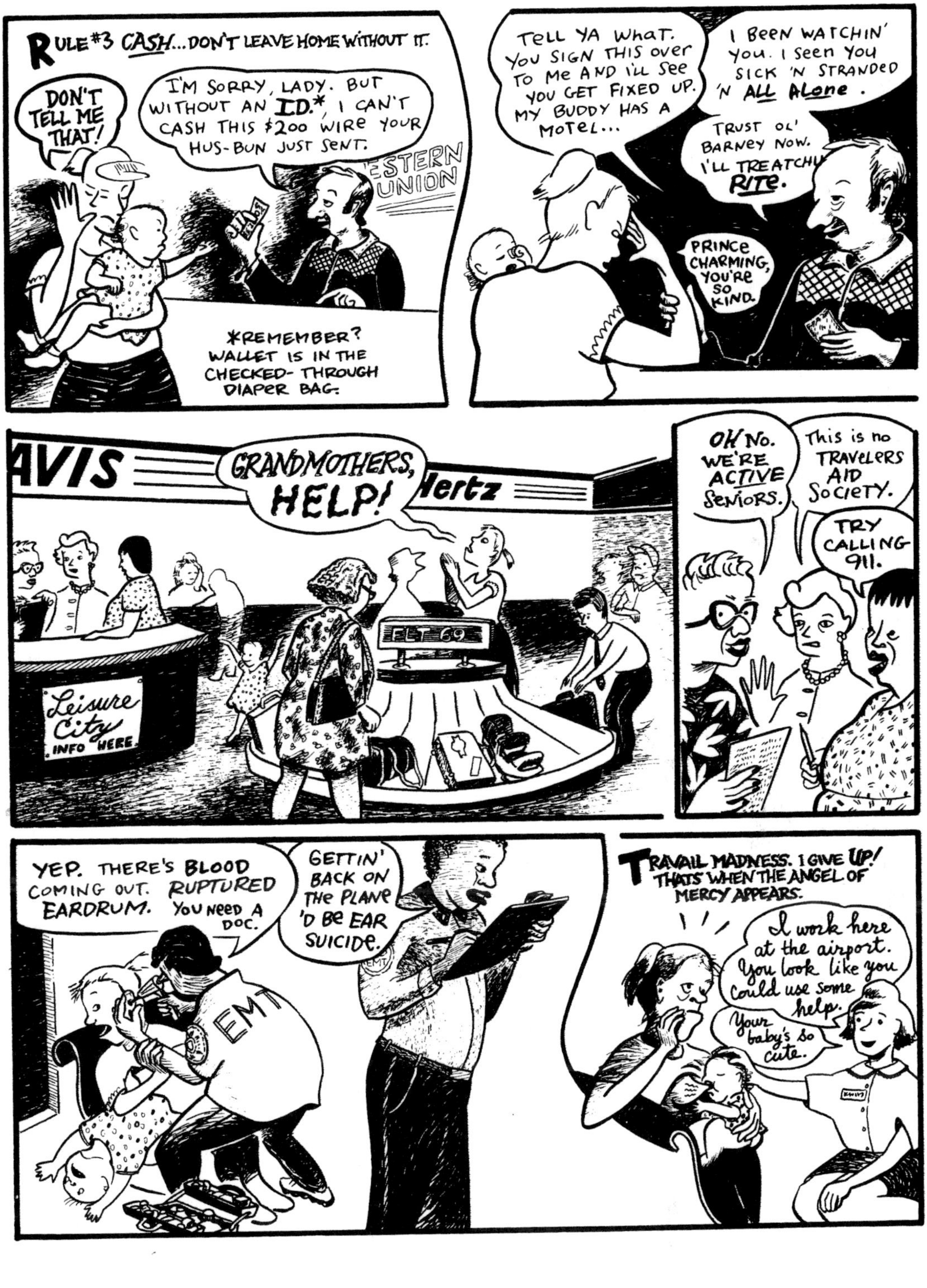

RULE #3 CASH...DON'T LEAVE HOME WITHOUT IT.
DON'T TELL ME THAT!
I'M SORRY, LADY. BUT WITHOUT AN I.D.*, I CAN'T CASH THIS $200 WIRE YOUR HUS-BUN JUST SENT.
ESTERN UNION
*REMEMBER? WALLET IS IN THE CHECKED-THROUGH DIAPER BAG.
TELL YA WHAT. YOU SIGN THIS OVER TO ME AND I'LL SEE YOU GET FIXED UP. MY BUDDY HAS A MOTEL...
I BEEN WATCHIN' YOU. I SEEN YOU SICK 'N STRANDED 'N ALL ALONE.
TRUST OL' BARNEY NOW. I'LL TREATCHU RITE.
PRINCE CHARMING, YOU'RE SO KIND.
AVIS
GRANDMOTHERS, HELP!
Hertz
FLT 69
Leisure City INFO HERE
OH NO. WE'RE ACTIVE SENIORS.
THIS IS NO TRAVELERS AID SOCIETY.
TRY CALLING 911.
YEP. THERE'S BLOOD COMING OUT. RUPTURED EARDRUM. YOU NEED A DOC.
GETTIN' BACK ON THE PLANE 'D BE EAR SUICIDE.
EMT
TRAVAIL MADNESS. I GIVE UP! THATS WHEN THE ANGEL OF MERCY APPEARS.
I work here at the airport. You look like you could use some help.
Your baby's so cute.

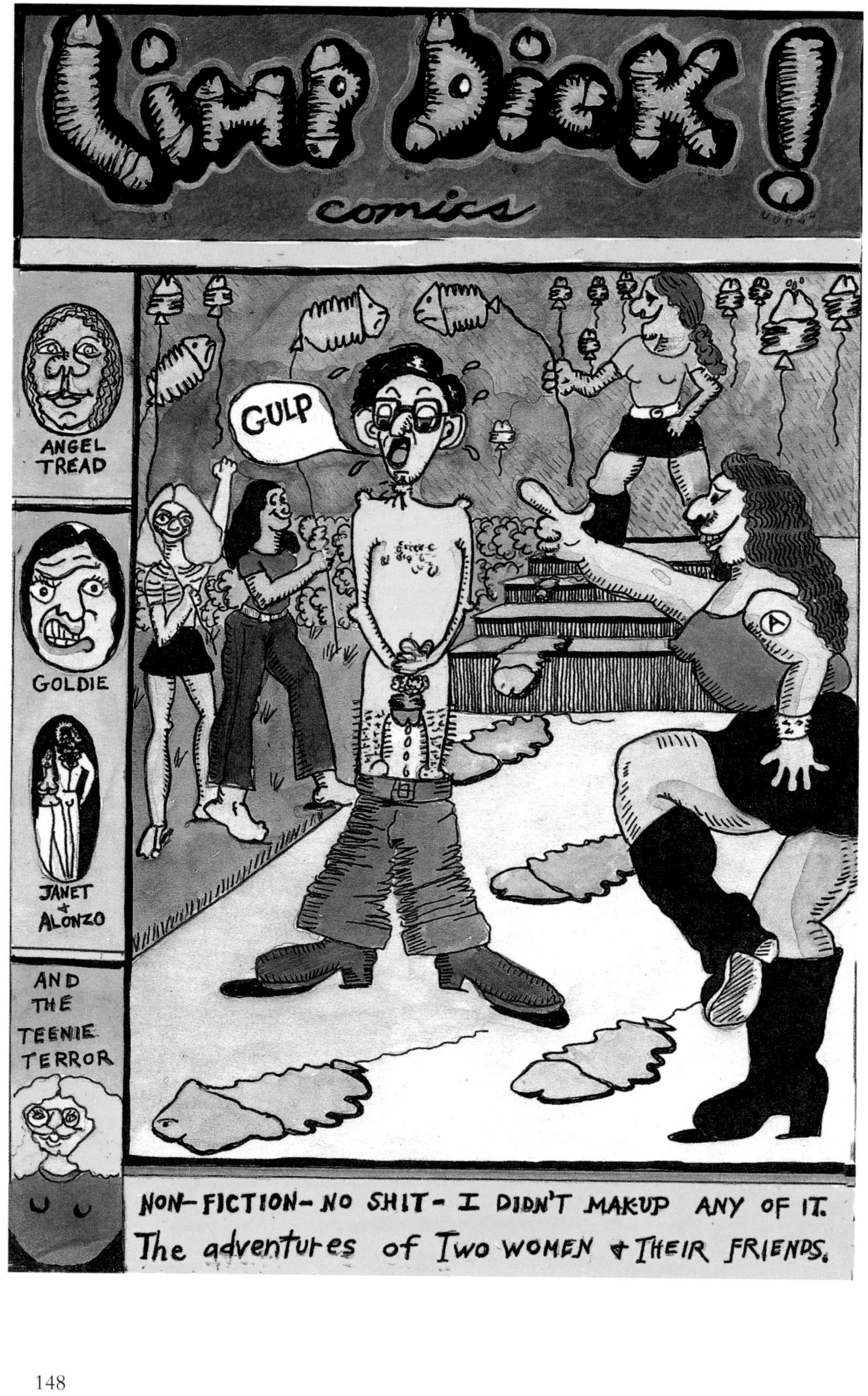
Limp Dick!
comics
ANGEL TREAD
GOLDIE
JANET + ALONZO
AND THE TEENIE TERROR
GULP
NON-FICTION- NO SHIT- I DIDN'T MAKUP ANY OF IT.
The adventures of Two WOMEN + THEIR FRIENDS.

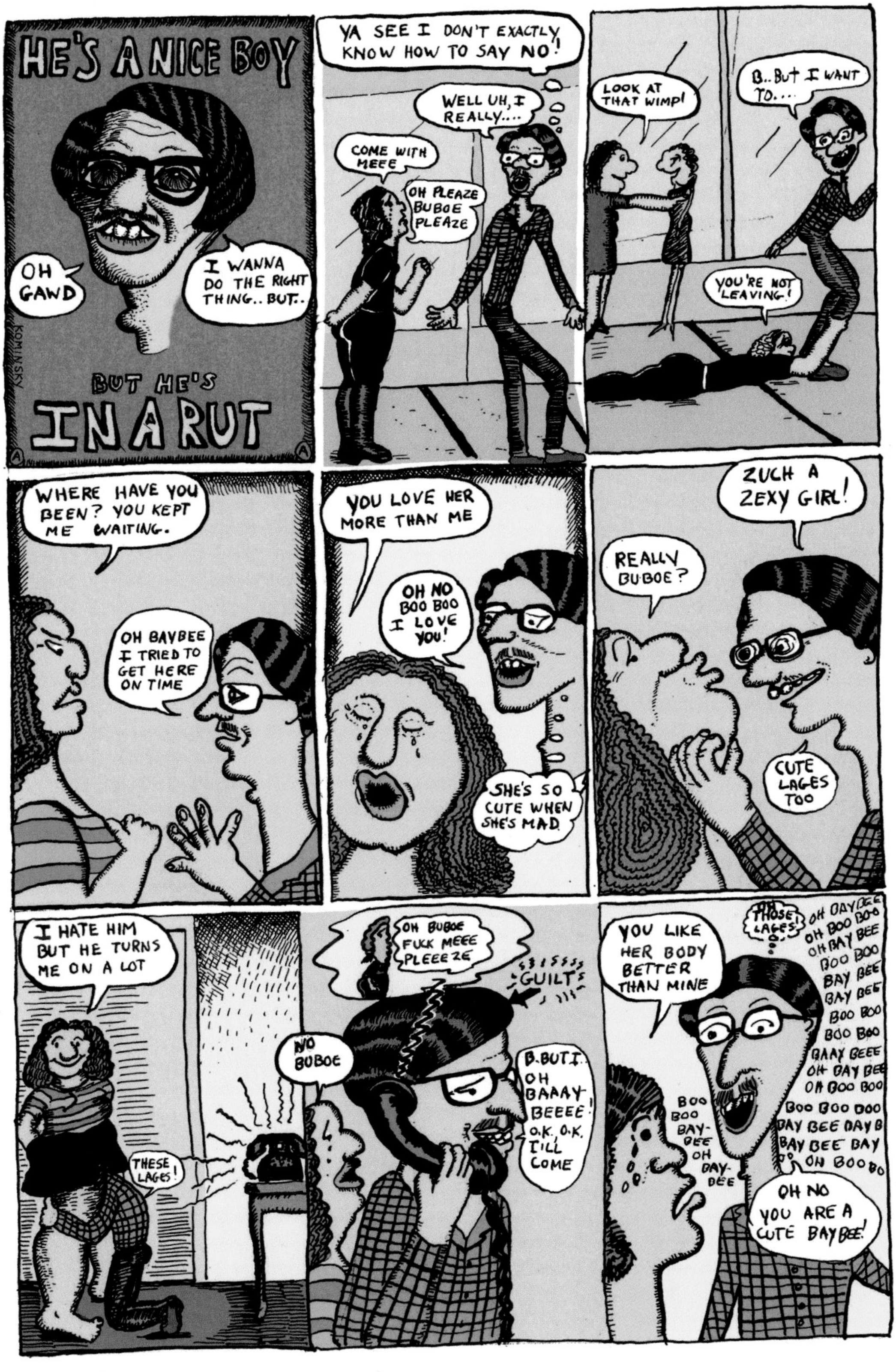
HE'S A NICE BOY
OH GAWD
I WANNA DO THE RIGHT THING.. BUT..
KOMINSKY
BUT HE'S IN A RUT
YA SEE I DON'T EXACTLY KNOW HOW TO SAY NO!
WELL UH, I REALLY....
COME WITH MEEE
OH PLEAZE BUBOE PLEAZE
LOOK AT THAT WIMP!
B.. BUT I WANT TO....
YOU'RE NOT LEAVING!
WHERE HAVE YOU BEEN? YOU KEPT ME WAITING.
OH BAYBEE I TRIED TO GET HERE ON TIME
YOU LOVE HER MORE THAN ME
OH NO BOO BOO I LOVE YOU!
SHE'S SO CUTE WHEN SHE'S MAD
ZUCH A ZEXY GIRL!
REALLY BUBOE?
CUTE LAGES TOO
I HATE HIM BUT HE TURNS ME ON A LOT
THESE LAGES!
OH BUBOE FUCK MEEE PLEEEZE
GUILT
NO BUBOE
B. BUT I. OH BAAAY BEEEE! O.K. O.K. I'LL COME
YOU LIKE HER BODY BETTER THAN MINE
THOSE LAGES!
OH BAYBEE OH BOO BOO OH BAY BEE BOO BOO BAY BEE BAY BEE BOO BOO BOO BOO BAAY BEEE OH BAY BEE OH BOO BOO BOO BOO BOO BAY BEE BAY B BAY BEE BAY OH BOO BO
BOO BOO BAY-BEE OH BAY-BEE
OH NO YOU ARE A CUTE BAYBEE!

The ultimate male chauvinist pig!

One day shortly after my first story came out I came home and found Robert sitting on my front steps. I was so happy to see him! It had been six months since I'd last seen him. I had been dating other people, like Willy Murphy, who was really a sweet guy, but I still had a lot of feelings toward Robert.

We had a strange and passionate reunion. Part of me wanted to resist the magnetic attraction I felt toward him, but I was too turned on, and the mutual passion was intoxicating and had nothing to do with good sense! After we "did it," I showed Robert my comic. He really cracked up and from that moment on he has always been my best audience. He always "gets it" and finds my drawings intrinsically funny. Our relationship could never have worked if we didn't share this admiration for each other's work.

Trina Robbins and the tight group of women around her, including Sharon Rudall, judged me harshly when they found out I was seeing "the ultimate male chauvinist pig R. Crumb." I still went to meetings, and participated in *Wimmen's Comix* No. 2, but I felt Trina's disapproval.

During this time I met Diane Noomin. I noticed she had a sketchbook and asked to see it. Based on what I saw, and because I really liked her—she was smart, funny in a self-deprecating sort of way, and beautiful—I asked her if she'd be interested in participating in the next *Wimmen's Comix*. She was really appreciative, because she was just emerging from a bad relationship in New York and looking for a reason to move to San Francisco. We went to the next *Wimmen's Comix* meeting together, and I also invited her to a party where she met Bill Griffith … and they're still happily married, one of my most satisfying *yenta* interventions!

Diane's story, *The Agony and the Ecstasy of a Shayna Madela,* appeared in *Wimmen's Comix* No. 3. My submission, however, was rejected by the editor, Sharon Rudall. She wrote me a letter explaining that my "feminist consciousness had not significantly evolved since my last story," and that she felt obliged to reject my submission on that basis. Ironically, I found out later that Sharon had had a little fling with Robert, but he had dumped her and she was really bitter. So the bad propaganda Sharon was feeding Trina against me was at least partially due to jealousy.

Wait—the plot thickens: Sharon was quite homely, but she drew herself as

*Right: **Wimmen's Comix** cover by Diane Noomin, featuring her alter ego Didi Glitz, 1987*

a beautiful heroic female, riding stallions in flowing diaphanous robes. I was actually pretty cute at that time, but I portrayed myself as a hideous monster. When our Women's Art Collective was being photographed for an article about the New Women Cartoonists, they mistook me for Sharon and vice versa based on our comics. This was painfully embarrassing.

Shortly after I received Sharon's rejection letter, I realized I had crabs. I confronted Robert and he admitted to having slept with Sharon, and said he had caught them from her. I thought a lot about the backbiting hypocrisy of these "Sisters" while I dabbed my crabs with poison!

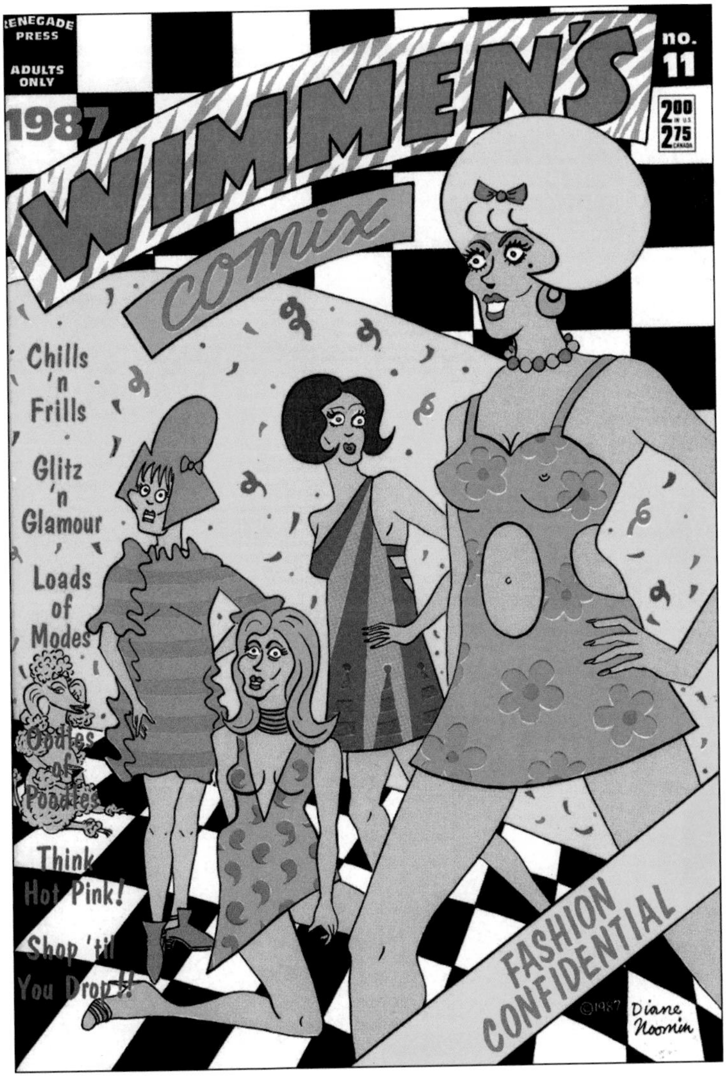
RENEGADE PRESS
ADULTS ONLY
1987
WIMMEN'S
comix
no. 11
2.00 IN U.S.
2.75 CANADA
Chills 'n Frills
Glitz 'n Glamour
Loads of Modes
Oodles of Poodles
Think Hot Pink!
Shop 'til You Drop!!
FASHION CONFIDENTIAL
©1987 Diane Noomin

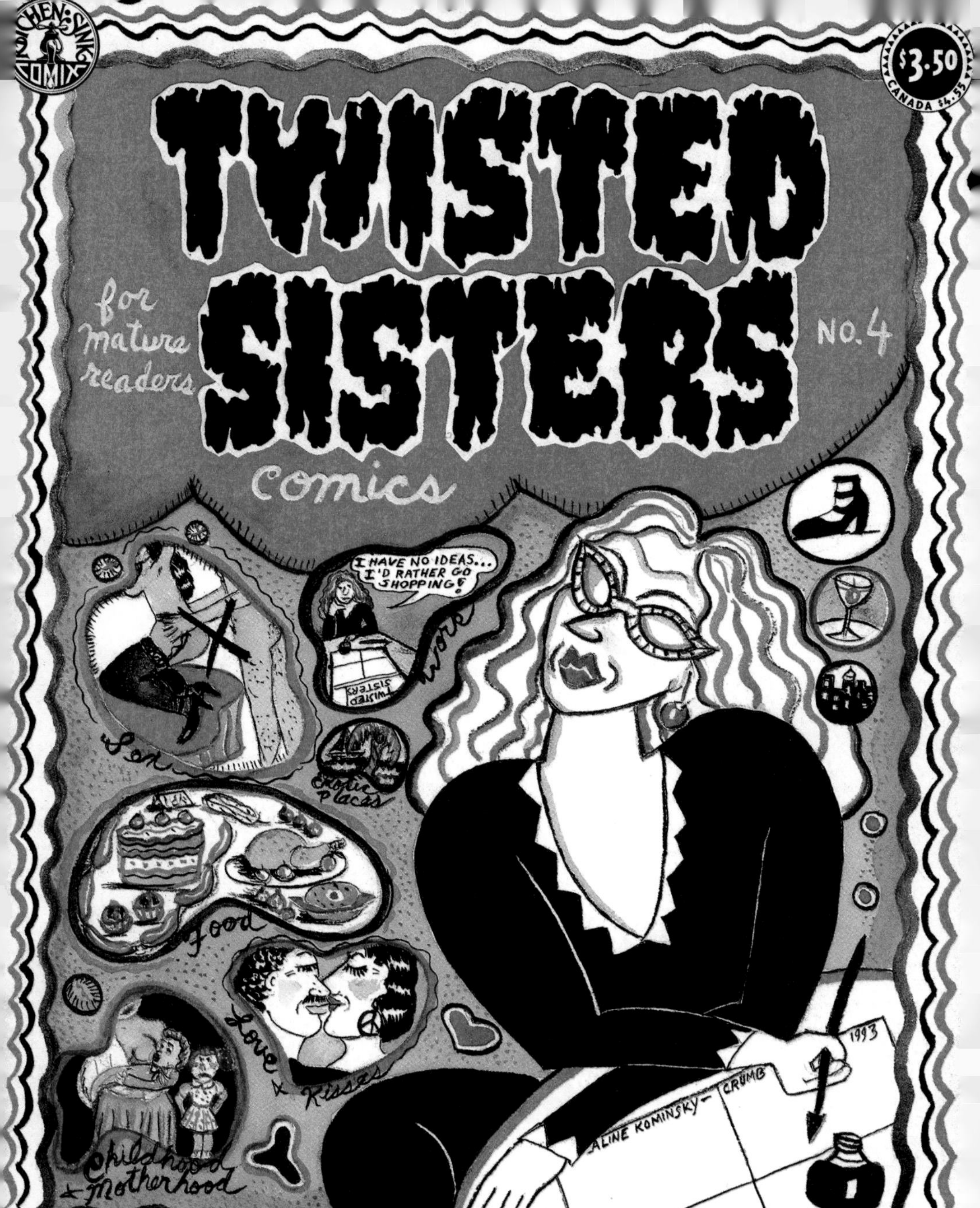
KITCHEN SINK COMIX
$3.50
CANADA $4.55
TWISTED SISTERS
for mature readers
No. 4
comics
I HAVE NO IDEAS... I'D RATHER GO SHOPPING!
work
Sex
exotic places
Food
Love & Kisses
Childhood & Motherhood
1993
ALINE KOMINSKY-CRUMB

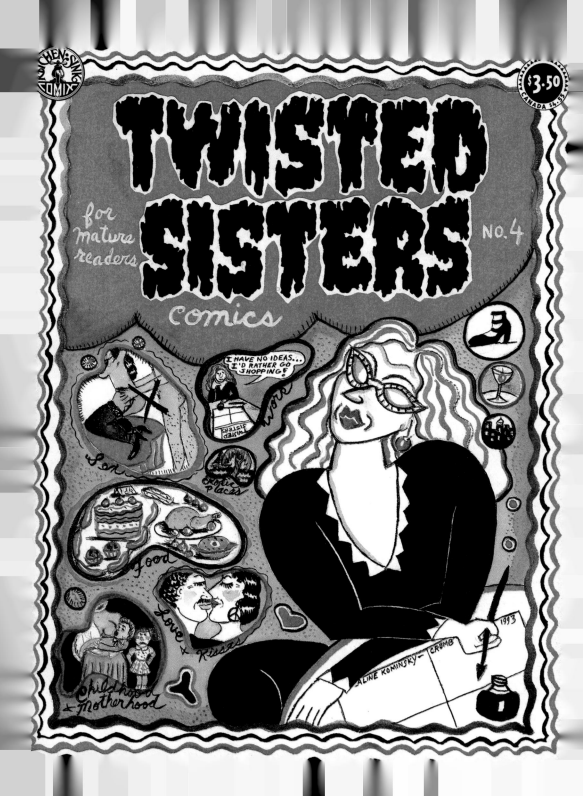

Twisted Sisters comic is born

Diane Noomin and I became good friends, and allies in the shark-infested waters of the *Wimmen's Comix* Art Collective. I have never been involved in such a backbiting nasty group of women since those good old feminist days! Diane and I were both found guilty of going out with male cartoonists. Even though Bill Griffith was considered a lesser evil than Robert, he was still a male chauvinist pig cartoonist. Diane and I were sellouts for being sex objects to men artists. At one point, Trina and a writer named Sally Harms referred to Diane and me as "camp followers" in an article in the *Berkeley Barb*—like the whores who follow soldiers around from camp to camp.

Although Diane and I continued to work for some issues of subsequent *Wimmen's Comix*, we were feeling increasingly annoyed and alienated from the group, especially from Trina Robbins and her minions. We unabashedly liked men. We liked being sexy, and felt our Female Power to be a positive force. We felt excited about our comic work, and didn't see any conflict since both of our boyfriends were encouraging and supportive of our efforts.

We also started looking at Trina's and Sharon Rudall's work more critically, and concluded that it was shallow, childish, simplistic and humorless. We were more comfortable seeing ourselves as "Bad Girls," sluts, anarchist artists doing whatever we pleased. We decided to do our own book, and so *Twisted Sisters* was born. (Later there was a band that took this name from our comic.) Diane developed her alter-ego "Didi Glitz," and I created "The Bunch."

Left: **One of my *Twisted Sisters* covers, inspired by old *New Yorker* covers, 1993**

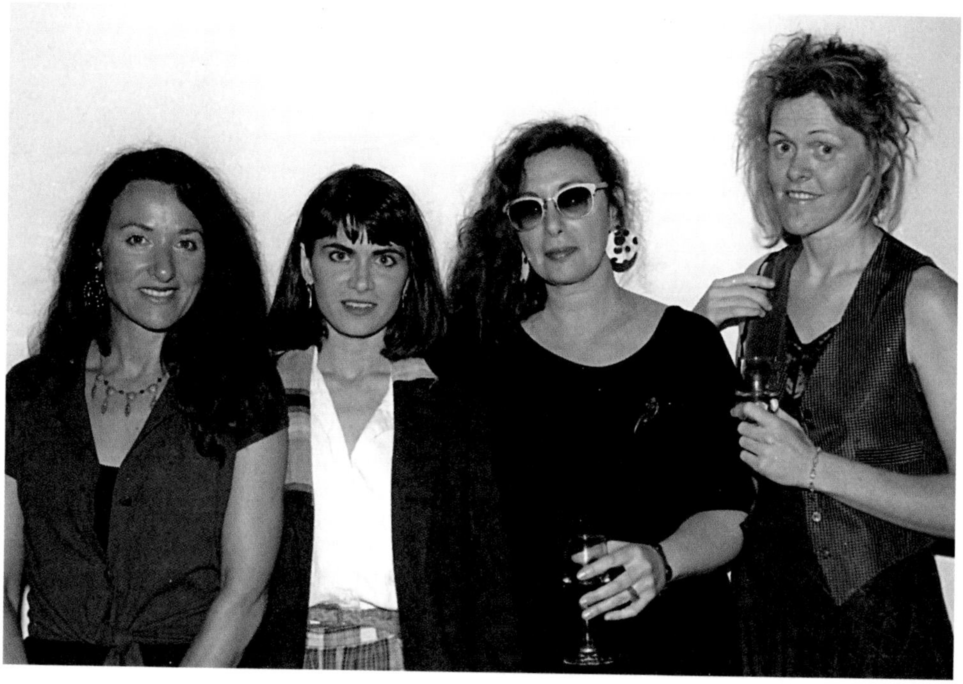

Above: **Me, Phoebe Gloeckner, Diane Noomin, and Carol Tyler**

Right: **Diane Noomin as her character Didi Glitz, San Francisco, 1973**

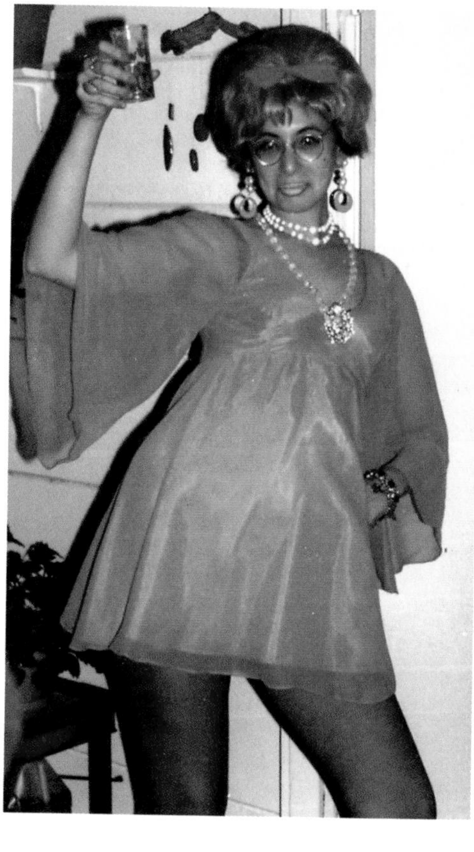

Above: **Diane Noomin and me, San Francisco, 1974**

Diane Noomin

MY CREATIVE "TWISTED SISTER"—INVENTOR OF "DIDI
GLITZ"—AND A LIFE-LONG FRIEND

It's funny how you can look back at a fairly typical event in your life and
suddenly see how pivotal it has been. For instance, if you missed a
certain party or drove down a certain street everything important in
your life would be different.

The night I met Aline Kominsky was like that. And naturally, at the
time (1972) I had no idea.

It was a party on Clipper Street in San Francisco. Judy Green, a friend
who had gone to high school with my ex-husband, lived there with a
group of left-wing radicals. Aline's connection was a Jewish dentist from
the upper West Side. I recognized him as the friendly friend of a friend
who was pretty free with the Quaaludes.

Aline and I clicked—two Jewish Art girls from "the Guyland"—(Long
Island, N.Y.) She told me she was a cartoonist and invited me to the next
meeting of the *Wimmen's Comix* Collective.

I was already an avid reader of underground comics and was
constantly "doodling" in the sketchbook I schlepped around with me,
embellishing my drawings with my captions—even the occasional
thought-balloon. It hadn't occurred to me until that exact moment that I
might become a cartoonist.

I showed up at the next meeting of the *Wimmen's Comix* Collective
and met Michele Brand, Pat Moodian, Shelby, Lee Mars, Trina Robbins,
Lora Fountain and some others that I can't recall. They were getting the
first issue ready to go—trying to decide on the title, and planning the
next issue.

I was overwhelmed with ideas for stories and very eager to get
started on my own comic for issue number two. It was 1973 and I was
suddenly looking at life as "material." It felt " right" to me that I had left
my old East Coast life behind and was now living in San Francisco—a
hotbed of underground comics publishers and cartoonists.

Most of the woman I met were open and friendly. Michele Brand,
married to *Real Pulp* cartoonist, Roger Brand, brought me over to Art
Spiegelman's place on Abbey Street to meet Art, his girlfriend Michelle
Gross, Roger and Bill Griffith.

Through Aline, I met my roommate-to-be Lela Janushkowsky. Lela had been Kathy Goodell's best friend in high school. Kathy, a conceptual artist, was the girlfriend of Robert Crumb, and was sharing a place on Brazil Street with Terry Zwigoff, a good friend of Robert's who ran a comic bookstore.

Aline was seeing Robert at the same time—soon more and more often. As Lela's roommate and Aline's close friend I heard lots of drama from two sides of the triangle.

Aline was very serious about drawing comics and extremely productive and disciplined. She was a tremendous influence—the life she portrayed in her stories evoked strong emotional response. Her drawing style seemed the perfect counterpoint. She used herself as a character, which seemed very brave to me.

I created Didi Glitz in 1973 (for a Halloween party at Lora Fountain and Gilbert Shelton's house on Saturn Street) and soon discovered that I preferred to hide behind Didi when I was doing comics. I did keep a blonde wig in the closet for emergencies.

By now, Aline was seriously involved with Robert Crumb and I was living with Bill Griffith. Meanwhile, the *Wimmen's Comix* Collective was lurching forward and I was thrilled to see my work in print for the first time. I had no idea how lucky I was to be in the right place at the right time—to be able to get my work in print so easily and learn while I earned my $25.00 a page.

The *Wimmen's Comix* Collective turned out to be the zealously guarded realm of Trina Robbins as Guardian of Feminist Comics with a serious Queen Bee complex. Trina was hard to take. She was very competitive and easily threatened if you refused to kowtow. Often, she would have awed protégés bobbing in her wake.

When one of them became editor of an issue of *Wimmen's Comix*, Trina, of course, would be the de facto editor. Many of the women resented her presumption of power but were too intimidated by her shrilly vehement persona to protest.

By the third or fourth issue Aline and I found her hostility, coupled with her predilection for blandly idealized stories, increasingly difficult to stomach. Perhaps the final straw was an article on women cartoonists in the *Berkeley Barb* written by Sally Harms (girlfriend of "Inner City Romance" cartoonist Guy Colwell) and a Trina protégé. In it she praised many of the women in the so-called collective but called Aline and me "Camp Followers."

Finally, in 1976, Aline and I, beyond bored with the psuedo-feminist perfect paragons that the "collective" deemed acceptable, decided to put out our own comic, *Twisted Sisters*.

Ron Turner of the *Last Gasp* agreed to publish it. Aline did the front cover and I did the back. We did a jam on the inside front cover and each did whatever we wanted on the inside pages. We were free to do anything and made the most of it. I was inspired and energized by our twisted sisters partnership. And Didi was let loose at last.

It was 8 years before I again got involved with *Wimmen's Comix* at the behest of the editor, Dori Seda. Dori was part of a new wave of younger, talented cartoonists who gave *Wimmen's Comix* an injection of sorely needed energy.

Decades later, Aline and I would start to collaborate on a new *Twisted Sisters* anthology, inspired by the gifted women cartoonists that Aline, as editor of *Weirdo*, had "discovered" and published.

Before we could get very far, Aline moved to France. I decided to keep going and wound up editing *Twisted Sisters: A Collection of Bad Girl Art* and *Twisted Sisters: Drawing the Line*.

In retrospect, I can draw a direct line from that party, that night in 1972 when I first met Aline, to one of my most important contributions to cartooning, bringing a wide range of talented cartoonists, who happen to be women, up from the underground and into the shopping malls.

New York, April 2006

Right: **Diane Noomin and Bill Griffith as cartoon characters, Halloween Party, San Francisco, 1973**

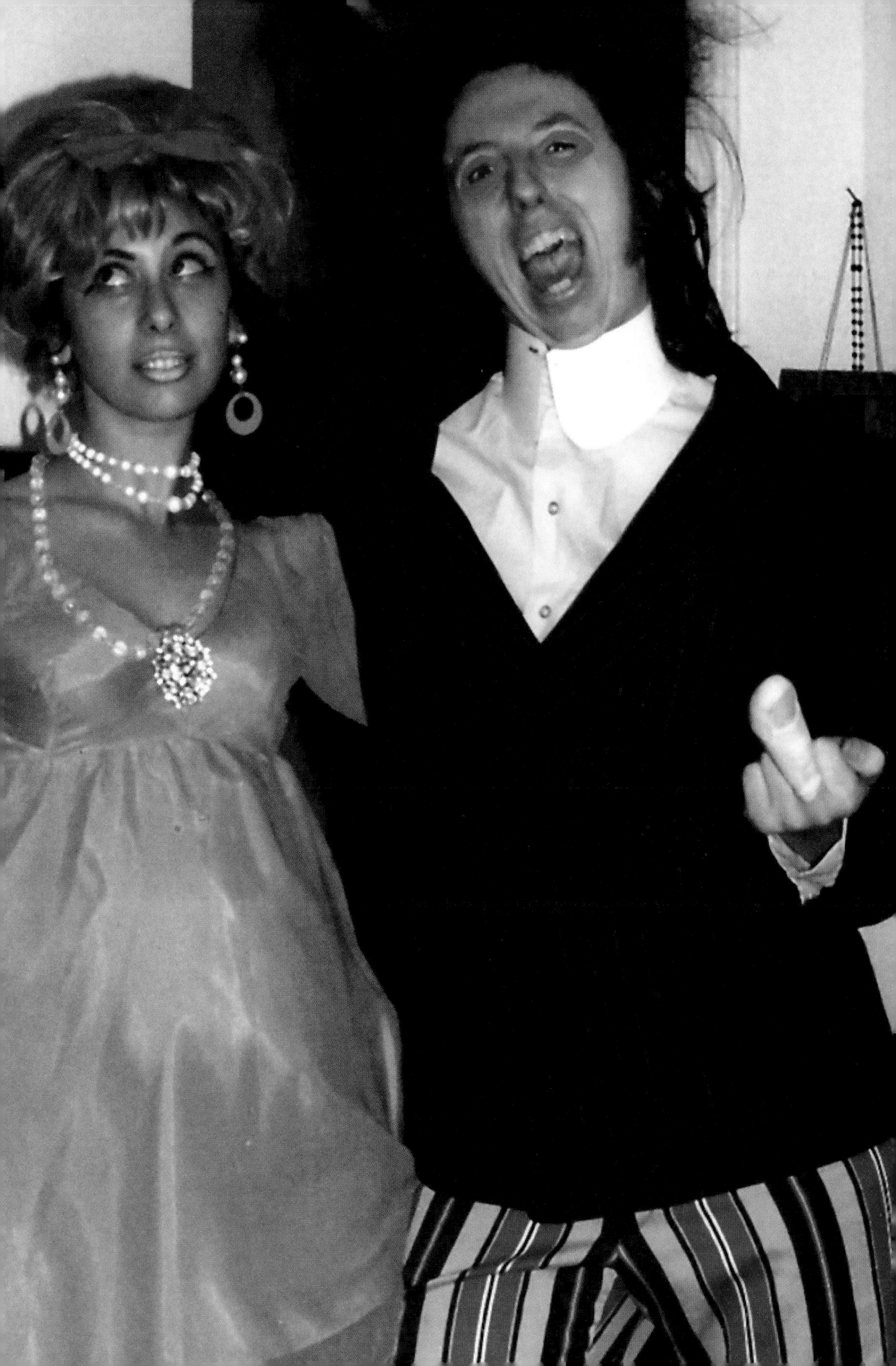

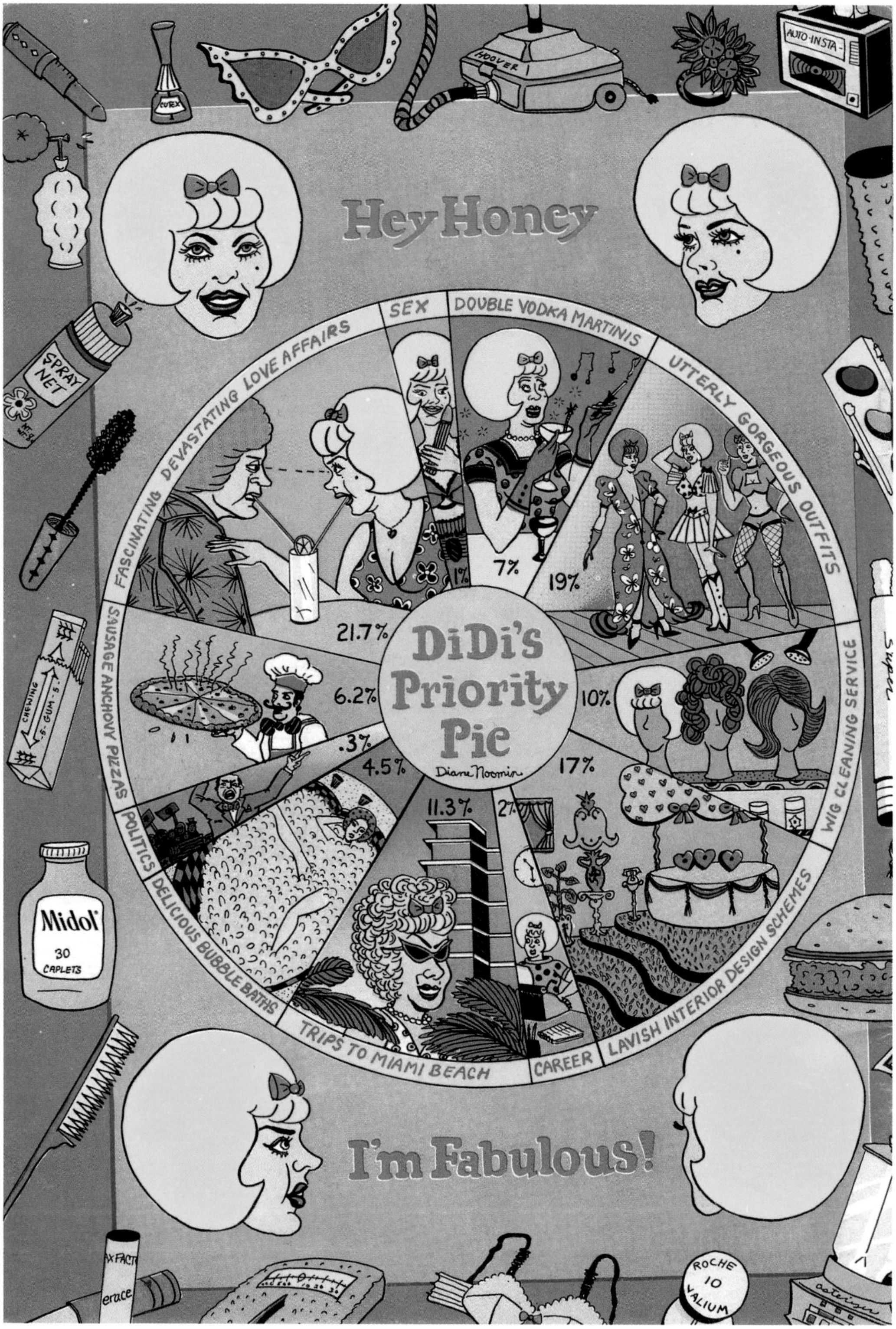
Hey Honey
DiDi's Priority Pie
Diane Noomin
I'm Fabulous!
SEX
DOUBLE VODKA MARTINIS
UTTERLY GORGEOUS OUTFITS
WIG CLEANING SERVICE
LAVISH INTERIOR DESIGN SCHEMES
CAREER
TRIPS TO MIAMI BEACH
DELICIOUS BUBBLE BATHS
POLITICS
SAUSAGE ANCHOVY PIZZAS
FASCINATING DEVASTATING LOVE AFFAIRS
21.7%
1%
7%
19%
10%
17%
2%
11.3%
4.5%
.3%
6.2%
CUTEX
HOOVER
AUTO-INSTA
SPRAY NET
CHEWING GUM
Midol
30 CAPLETS
ROCHE 10 VALIUM
erace

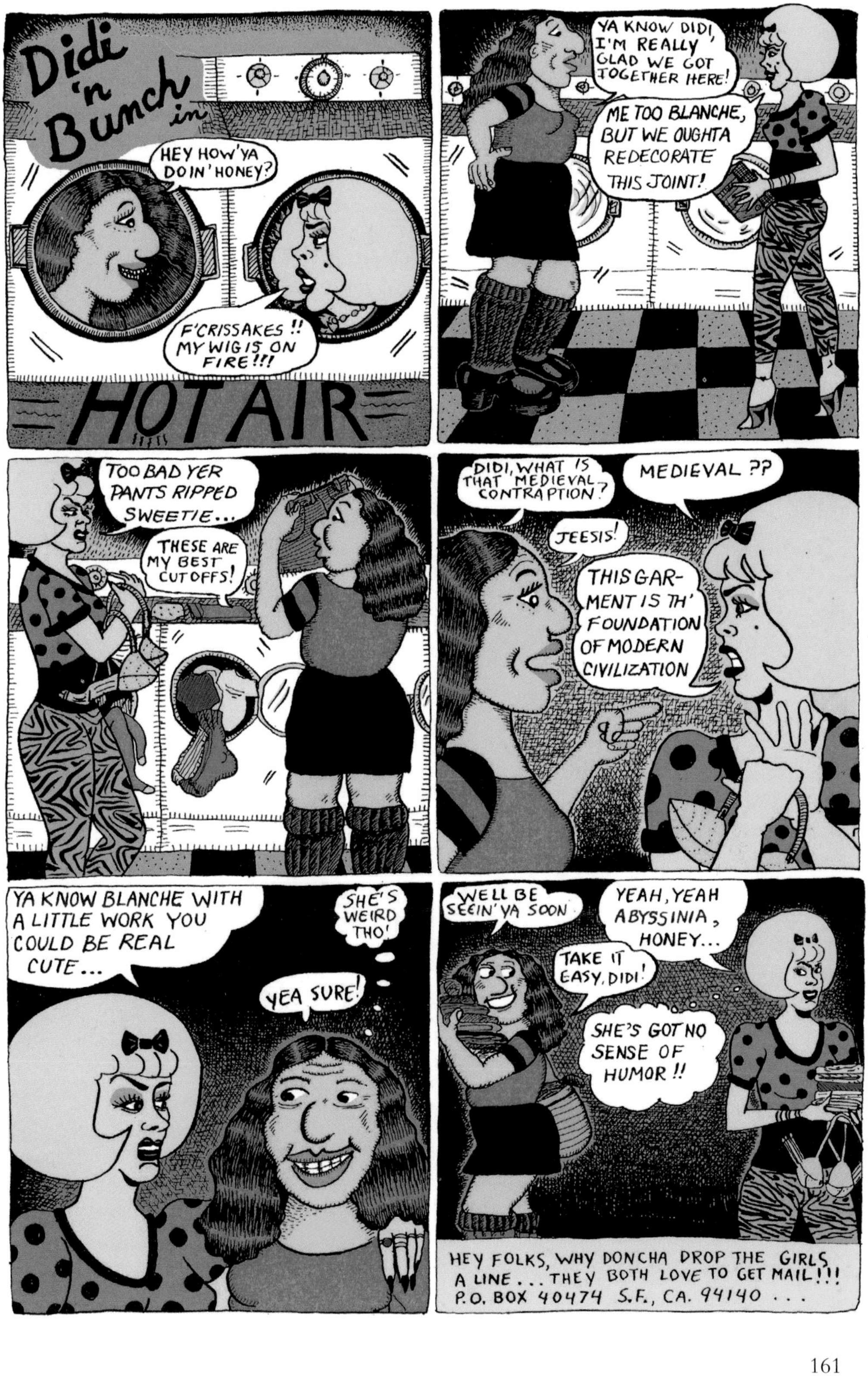
Didi 'n Bunch in
HEY HOW'YA DOIN' HONEY?
F'CRISSAKES !! MY WIG IS ON FIRE!!!
HOT AIR
YA KNOW DIDI, I'M REALLY GLAD WE GOT TOGETHER HERE!
ME TOO BLANCHE, BUT WE OUGHTA REDECORATE THIS JOINT!
TOO BAD YER PANTS RIPPED SWEETIE...
THESE ARE MY BEST CUT OFFS!
DIDI, WHAT IS THAT MEDIEVAL CONTRAPTION?
MEDIEVAL ??
JEESIS!
THIS GARMENT IS TH' FOUNDATION OF MODERN CIVILIZATION
YA KNOW BLANCHE WITH A LITTLE WORK YOU COULD BE REAL CUTE...
SHE'S WEIRD THO'
YEA SURE!
WELL BE SEEIN' YA SOON
YEAH, YEAH ABYSSINIA, HONEY...
TAKE IT EASY, DIDI!
SHE'S GOT NO SENSE OF HUMOR !!
HEY FOLKS, WHY DONCHA DROP THE GIRLS A LINE... THEY BOTH LOVE TO GET MAIL!!! P.O. BOX 40474 S.F., CA. 94140 . . .

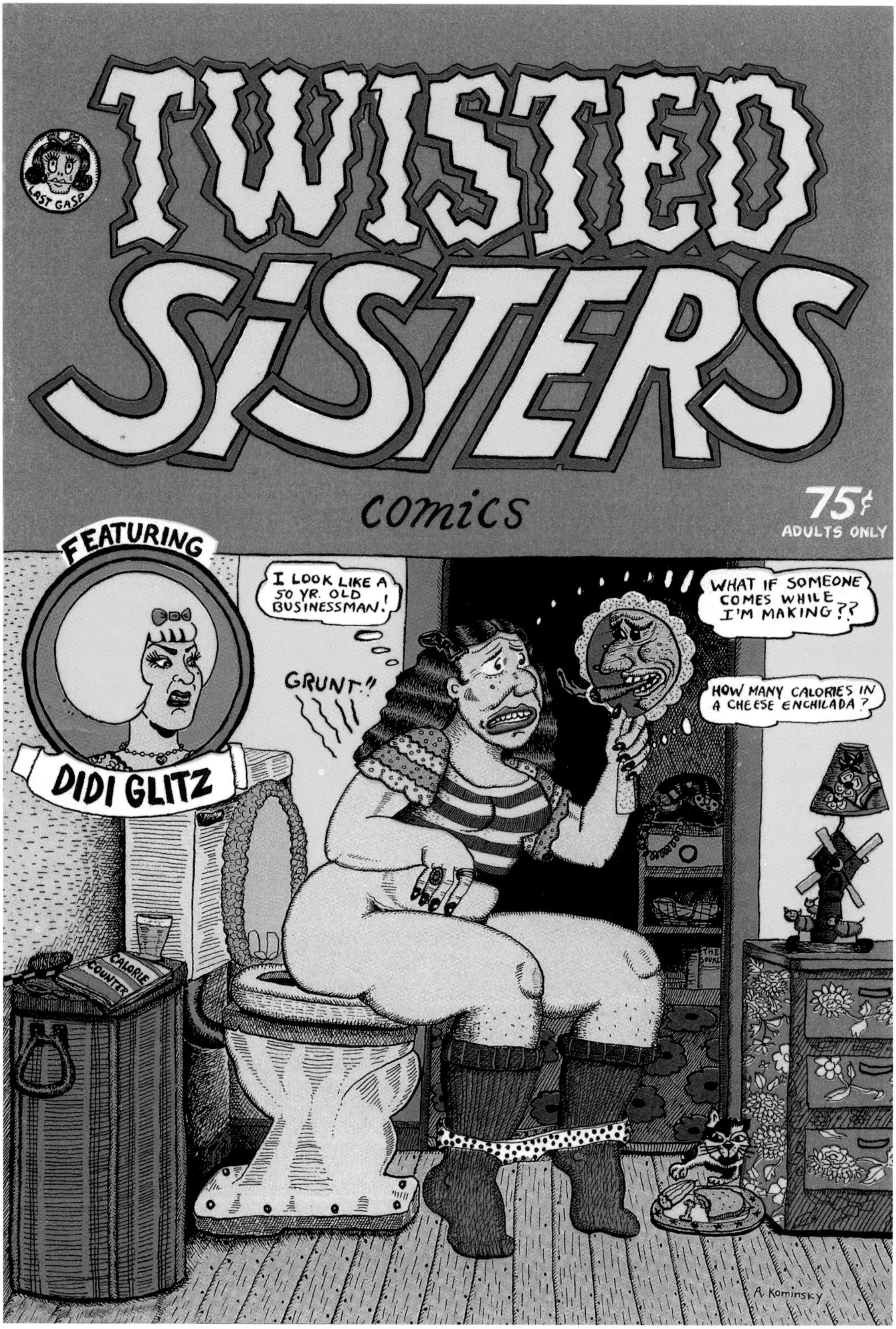
LAST GASP
TWISTED SISTERS
comics
75¢
ADULTS ONLY
FEATURING
DIDI GLITZ
I LOOK LIKE A 50 YR. OLD BUSINESSMAN!
GRUNT!!
WHAT IF SOMEONE COMES WHILE I'M MAKING??
HOW MANY CALORIES IN A CHEESE ENCHILADA?
CALORIE COUNTER
A. Kominsky

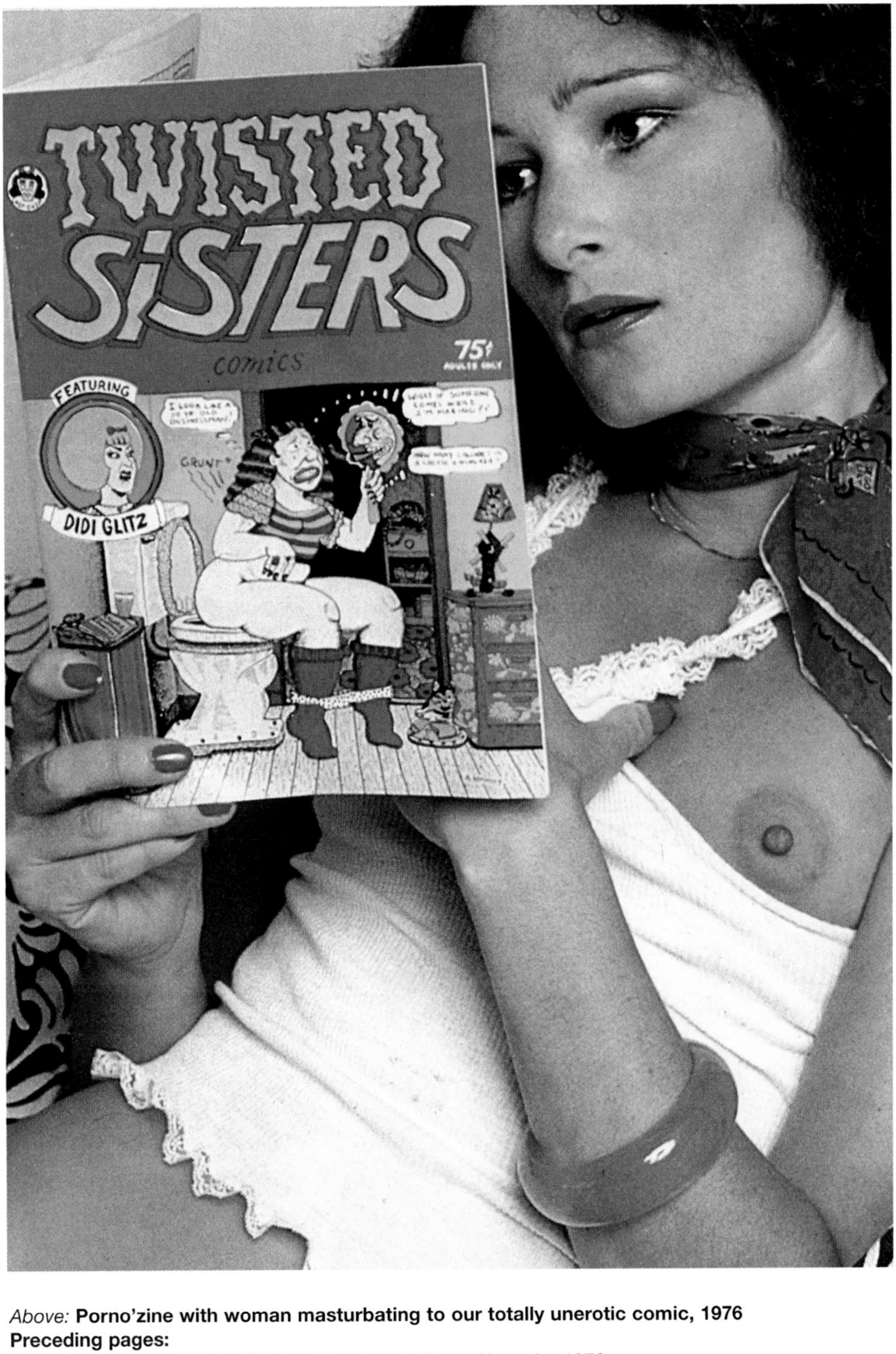
TWISTED SiSTERS
comics
75¢
FEATURING
DIDI GLITZ
GRUNT*

Above: **Porno'zine with woman masturbating to our totally unerotic comic, 1976**
Preceding pages:
p160 **Back cover, *Twisted Sisters* Number 1, Diane Noomin, 1976**
p161 **Inside front cover, *Twisted Sisters* Number 1, by me and Diane Noomin**
p162 **Front cover, *Twisted Sisters* Number 1, by me**

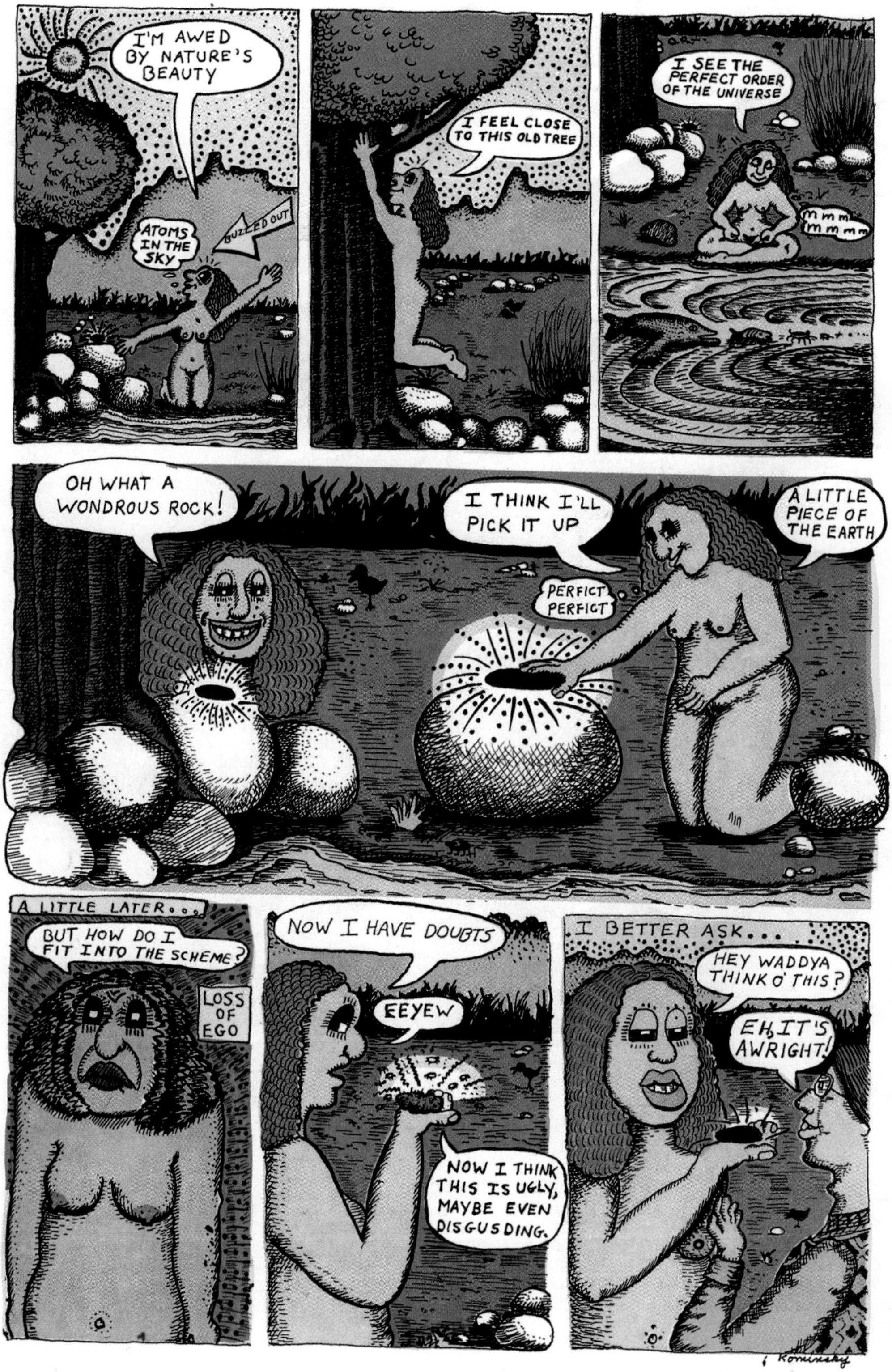
I'M AWED BY NATURE'S BEAUTY
ATOMS IN THE SKY
BUZZED OUT
I FEEL CLOSE TO THIS OLD TREE
I SEE THE PERFECT ORDER OF THE UNIVERSE
mmm mmmm
OH WHAT A WONDROUS ROCK!
I THINK I'LL PICK IT UP
PERFICT PERFICT
A LITTLE PIECE OF THE EARTH
A LITTLE LATER...
BUT HOW DO I FIT INTO THE SCHEME?
LOSS OF EGO
NOW I HAVE DOUBTS
EEYEW
NOW I THINK THIS IS UGLY, MAYBE EVEN DISGUSDING.
I BETTER ASK...
HEY WADDYA THINK O' THIS?
EH, IT'S AWRIGHT!
Kominsky

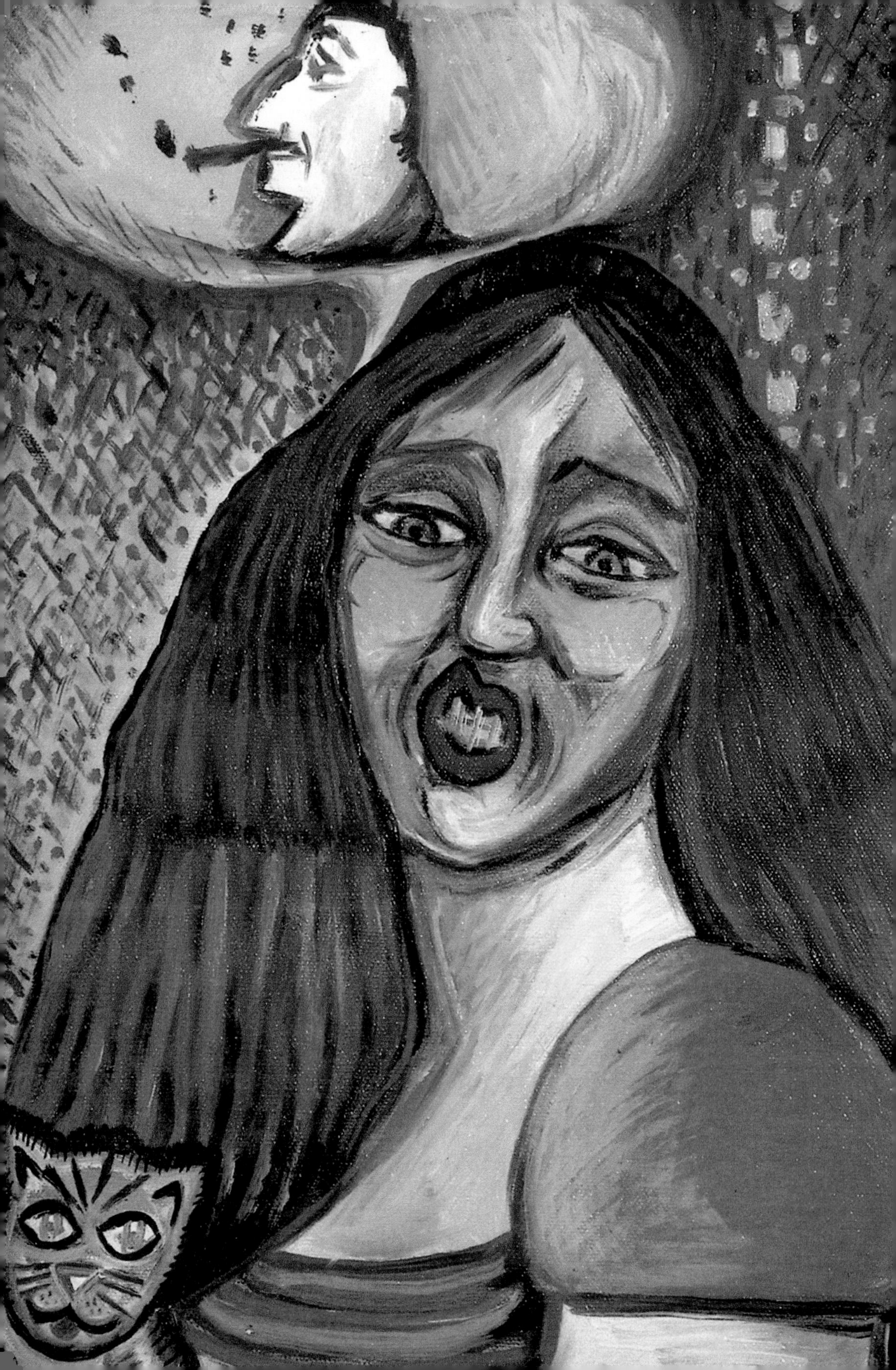

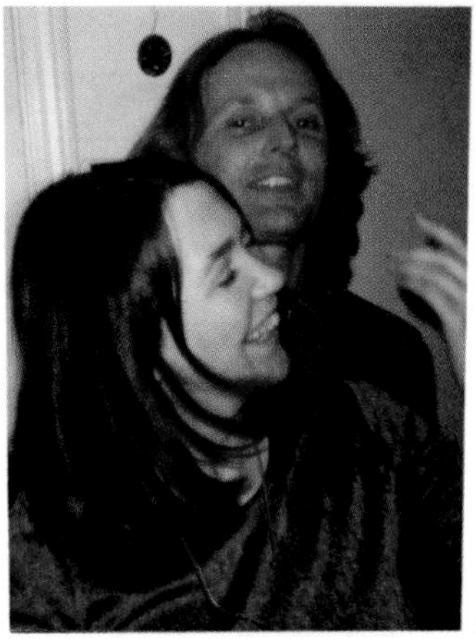
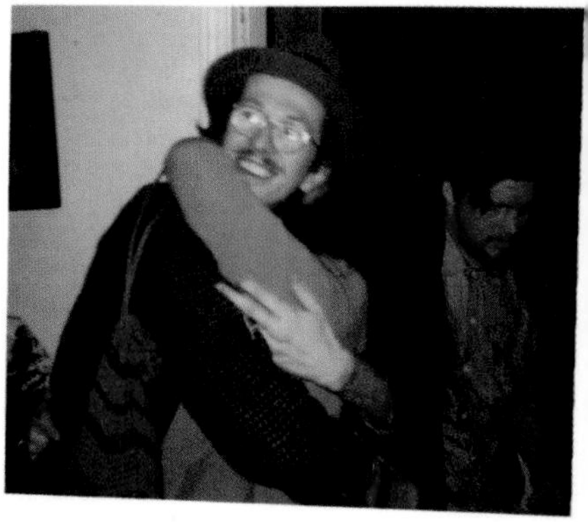
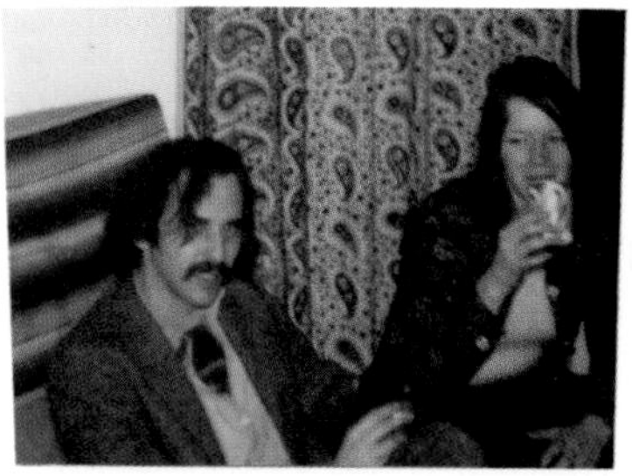
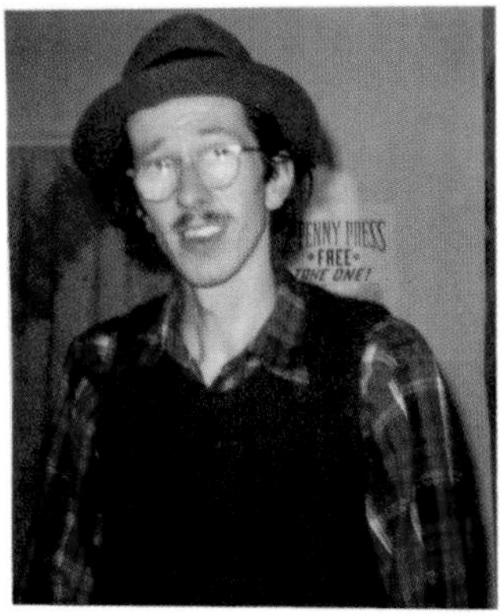
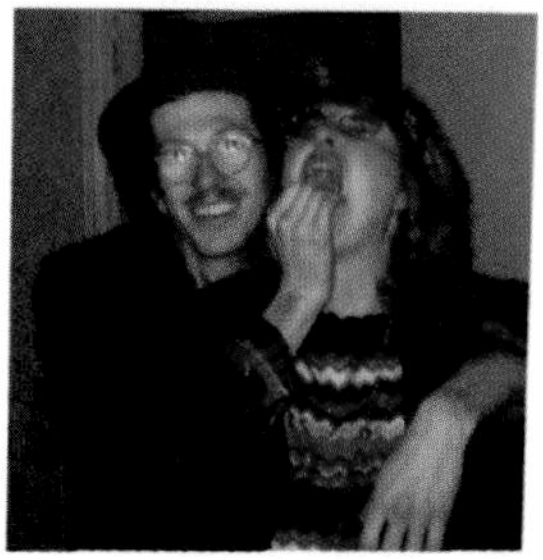
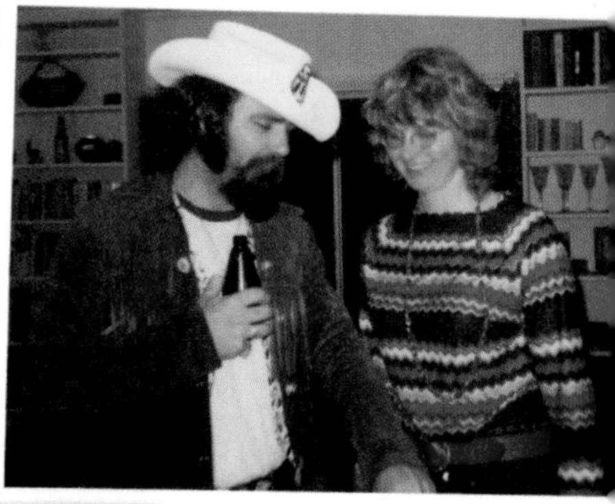
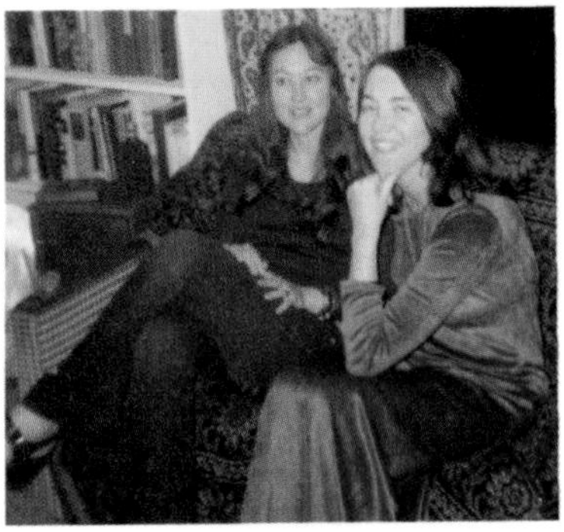
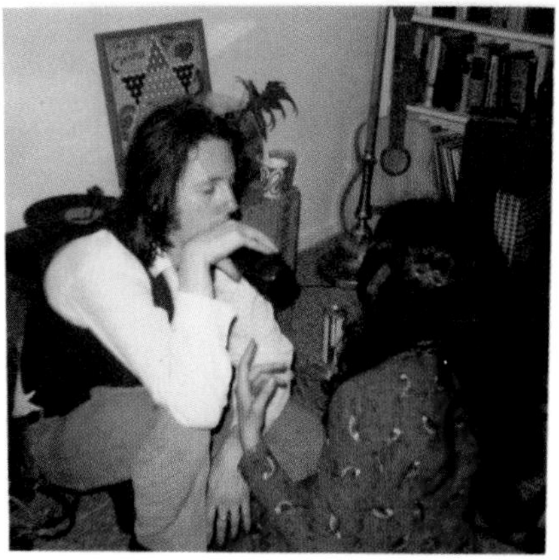
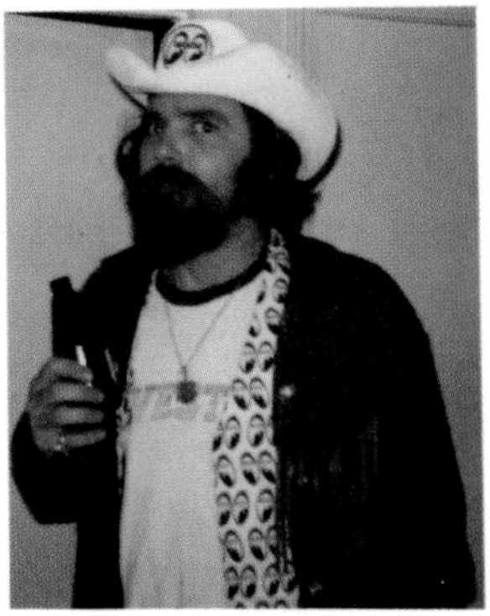
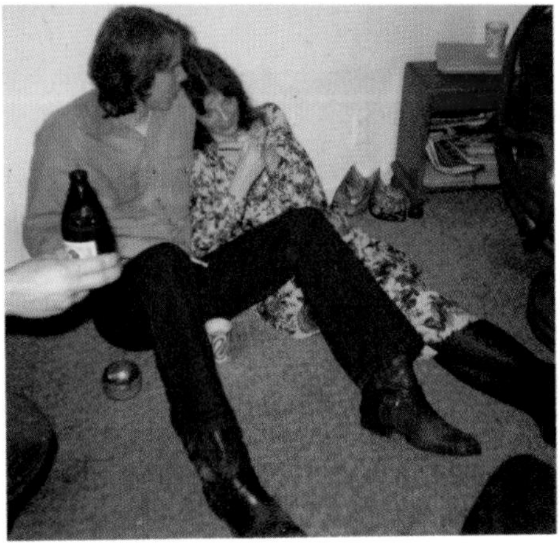
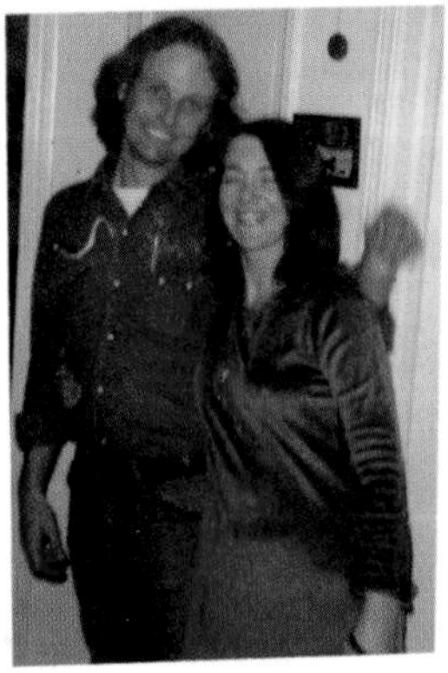
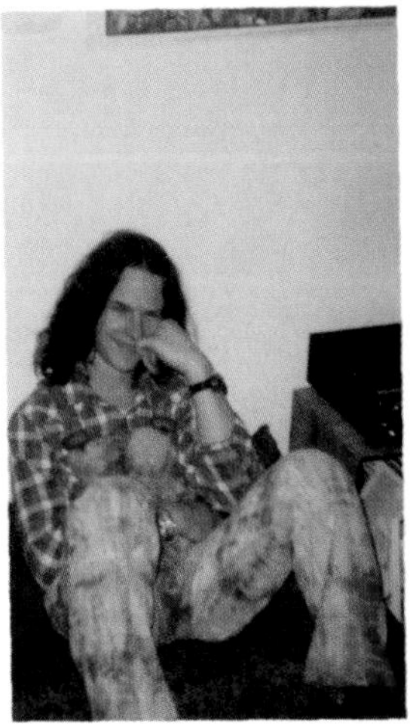

Those wild California nights ...

Preceding page 164: **My back cover for *El Perfecto* comic.**
This was edited by me and featured one-page strips by cartoonists about taking LSD. The proceeds were donated to the fund to free Timothy Leary from prison but unfortunately his girlfriend spent it on a stereo system!

Preceding page 165: **Self portrait in oil**
Me with my male alter-ego Mr. Bunch

Left: **Party photo album from Lora Fountain**
Top row, left to right: Art Spiegelman and girlfriend Michelle Gross; Lora Fountain and Gilbert Shelton; Robert and me.
Second row, left to right: Robert; Robert with girl; Ken Weaver
Third row, left to right: Lora Fountain and friend; Diane Noomin and Bill Griffith; Ken Weaver
Bottom row, left to right: Ted and Terry Richards; Lora Fountain and Gilbert Shelton

Below: **Image of my comic character, 1972**
Depicting "the morning after a wild night" just before I left San Francisco to live in the country with Robert.

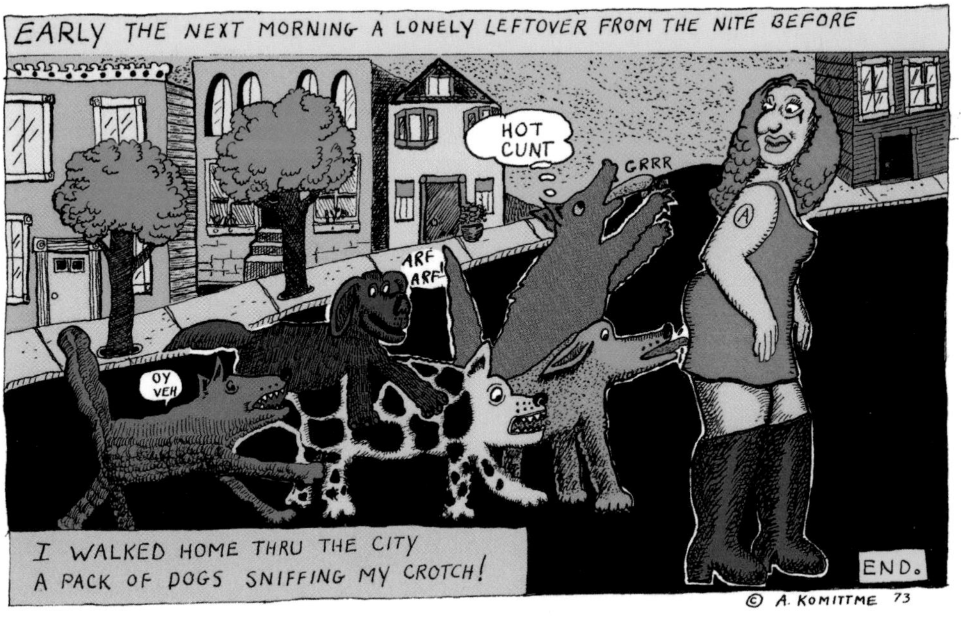

EARLY THE NEXT MORNING A LONELY LEFTOVER FROM THE NITE BEFORE
HOT CUNT
GRRR
ARF ARF!
OY VEH
I WALKED HOME THRU THE CITY
A PACK OF DOGS SNIFFING MY CROTCH!
END.
© A. KOMITTME 73

CHAPTER THREE
Love, marriage and motherhood

WE'RE GLAD TO BE SURREAL!
SALAD SALUTE
"space cadette"
I LOVE MY NUCLEAR KITCHEN!

3. The CALIFORNIA Years

flair
DO I HAVE IT YET?

- *Love
- *Marriage
- *Motherhood
- *Weirdo Mag.
- *European Adventures

NIGHTMARE in the basement!

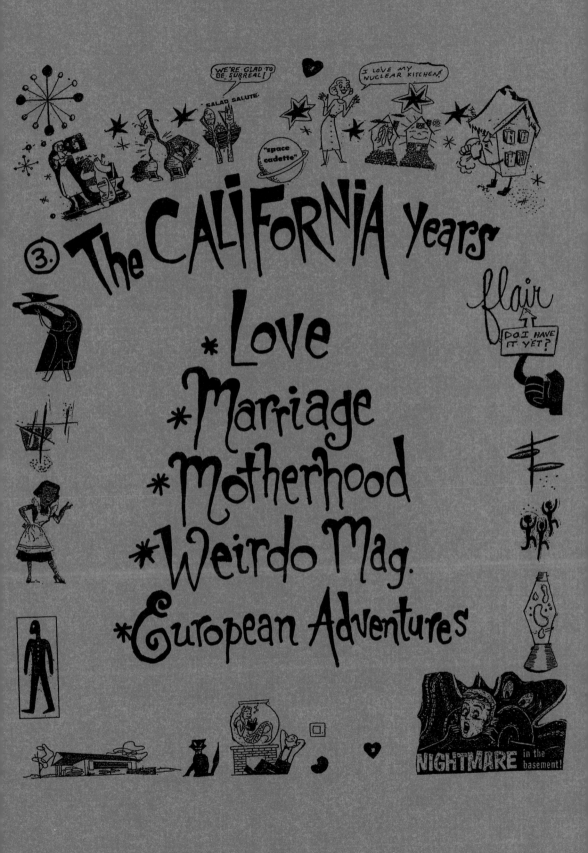

Rural sophisticates

In 1973, I moved up north to Potter Valley, California, to live next door to Robert. We created our own crazy version of communal living: Robert lived in a dilapidated old cabin, and his ex-wife, Dana, lived in the "big house" next door with Paul Seidman, their son Adam, and Robert's son Jesse, and I lived in a 1950s trailer on the other side of Robert's cabin. If that's not complicated enough for you, Ken Weaver moved into another 1950s trailer below Dana's house. Dana had met Ken while he was staying in my apartment in San Francisco and Betsy Klein was off trying to free Timothy Leary from prison. Whew! I'm really trying to get this all down correctly before Alzheimer's sets in …

Things quickly turned into chaos. Resentment over perceived injustices, our different energy levels and standards of honesty, drug consumption, and the stress of having two wild little boys to look after soon took their toll and we were all fuming at one another. Dana had big expansion plans and numerous schemes to spend Robert's money, but suffered from migraine headaches, a Demerol habit and severe obesity, so she would get Paul to execute her projects. Paul was a serious pill popper and a big mess maker. He would buy all sorts of elaborate equipment, begin working on some scheme, and then abandon the idea for something else and just leave everything lying around.

These big messes were left to rot, and all the parts would end up smashed by kids or crushed by our vehicles. Robert and I would end up cleaning everything up and hauling it to the dump. No one showed any appreciation for our efforts or even acknowledged that they had created a nightmare and left it for somebody else to clean up. I'm not whining, just stating the facts. The first casualty was Paul Seidman. Actually, Dana had the "hots" for Ken, so she got rid of Paul. None of us complained.

Right: **Me and Robert in the garden, Winters, California**

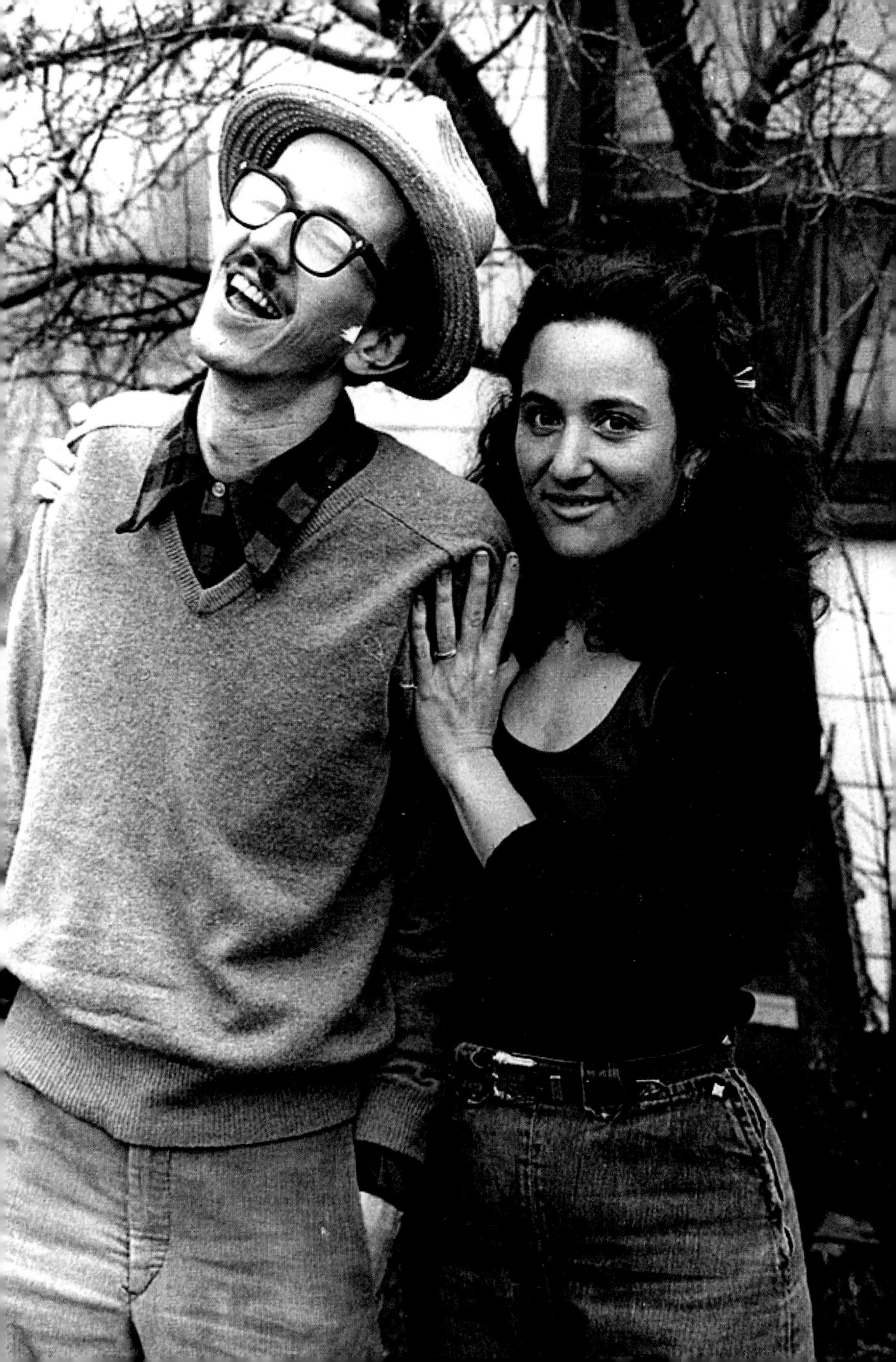

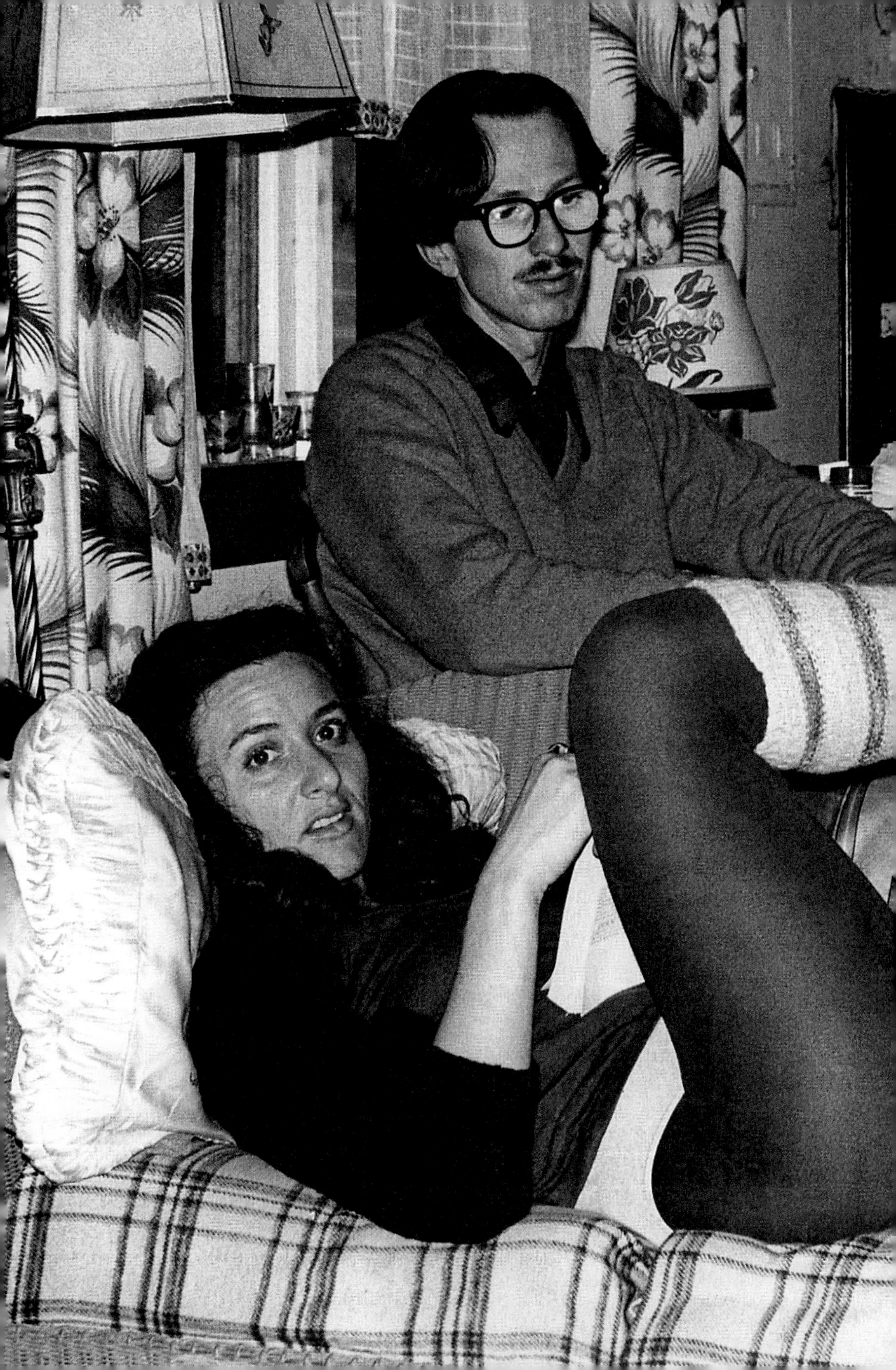

Peace and quiet

Robert and I learned during this period that we both needed order in our lives to feel comfortable. We deepened our relationship, hangin' around in front of the fireplace in his cabin, talking, listening to old records (a great new pleasure for me), and enjoying our lustful play sessions. Plus we discovered that our collections went very well together. His records and old cars were a perfect complement to my dolls, dishes and old quilts and curtains. We spent a lot of time looking for old junk together. There were some beautiful moments.

Left: **Relaxing at home with our "stuff," Winters, California**

Next page (left): **My doll collection**

Next page (right): **Robert with our cat Weanie**
We have never lived without at least a few cats (coincidentally my astrological sign is Leo and my moon is in Leo!).

173

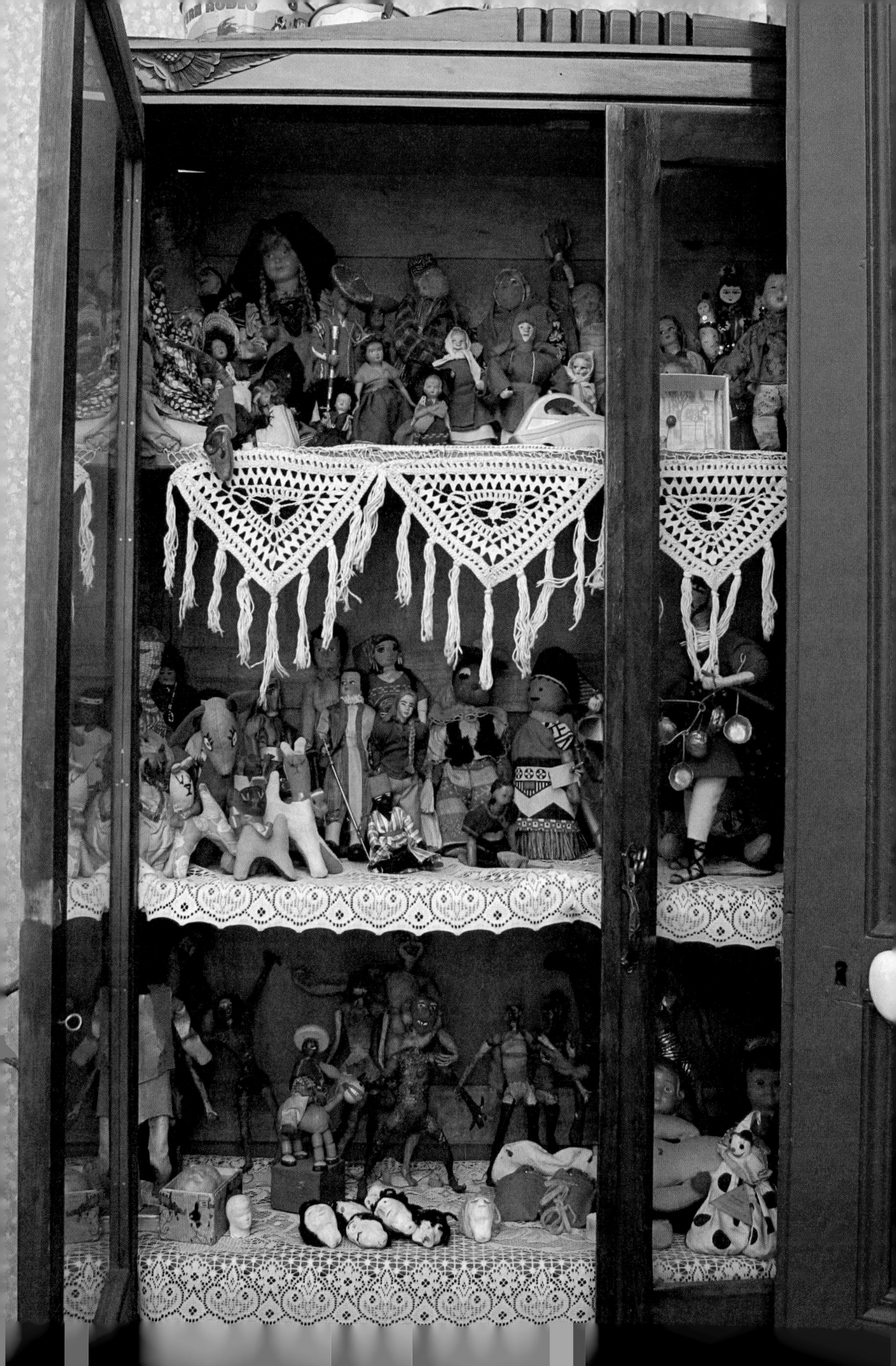

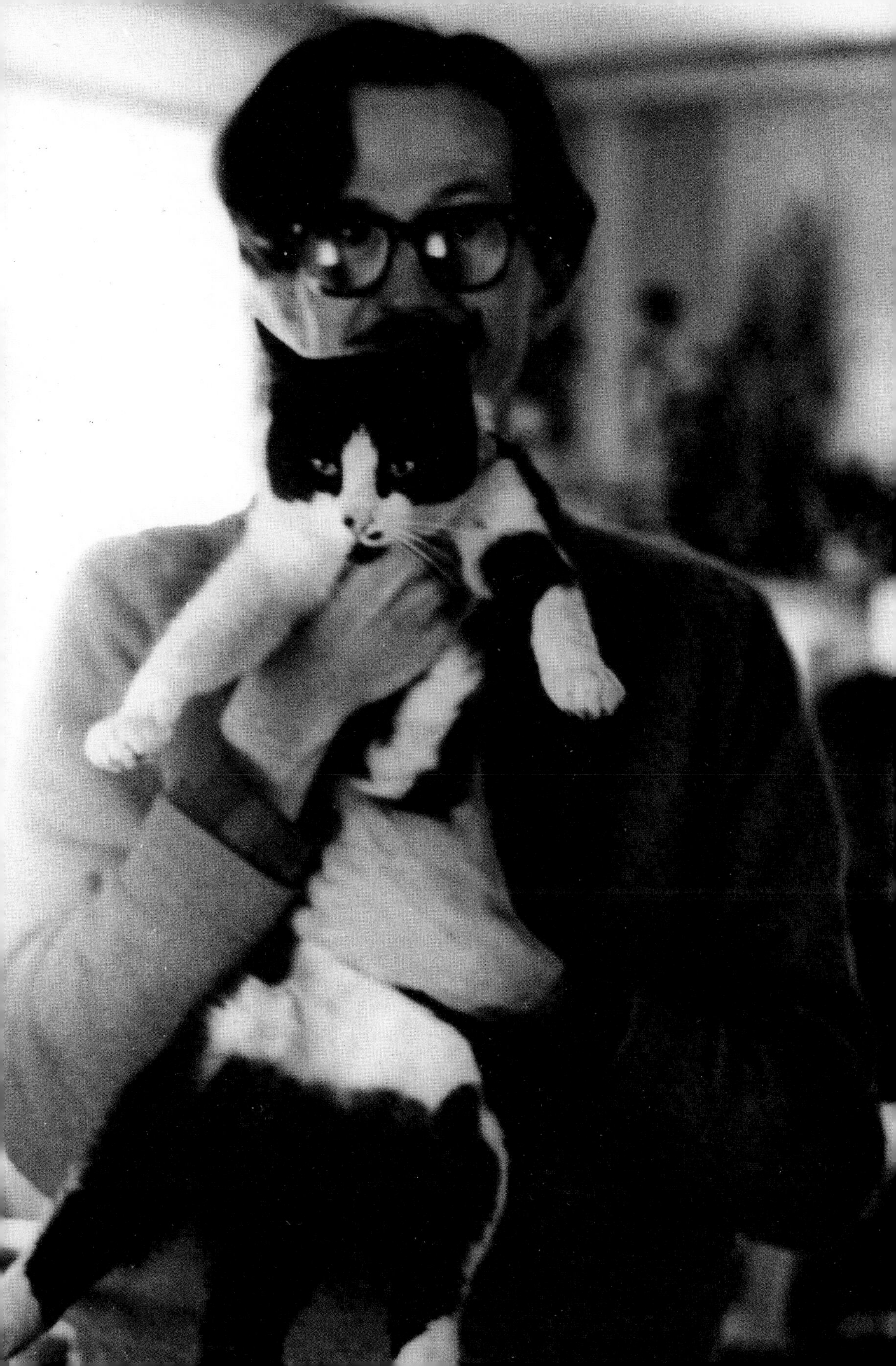

Trouble in paradise

One rainy day, a girl named Frankie whom Robert had met while traveling with his band showed up with all her worldly possessions to live happily ever after … with Robert. I had a fit! There was definitely not enough room in our little commune for yet another intensity case, and Frankie was a demanding, obnoxious brat.

Robert and I got into a huge argument, and I insisted that Frankie leave immediately. At one point, I ran out of his cabin in my platform shoes and fell down hard on the slippery cement porch. I was so furious that I ran back to my trailer—I didn't know it, but my foot was broken in six places. I woke up the next day in excruciating pain. Ken Weaver had to drive me to the hospital, and I came home with a big cast on my right leg.

Robert had miraculously gotten rid of Frankie in the meanwhile. My brother Alex was hanging around our commune at the time, and he drove the spurned Frankie to the bus station. I guess she wasn't too traumatized, 'cause Alex sez that she tried to get it on with him on the way to the bus …

Robert and I quickly made up and settled in for the long rainy winter. I was in a cast for six weeks.

To keep me from getting too bored, we started to work on a two-man comic story, something Robert had done with his brother Charles when they were kids. We just rambled on without any particular aim, plunging into crazy fantasies about invading aliens and Tim Leary, mixed with real details about the floods we were living through, and for the first time drawing our mutual "sexploitation." We just let ourselves go and had fun with it. We had no intention of publishing this work, so we were totally unselfconscious about how dumb and personal it was.

One day Keith Green, Justin Green's brother and a publisher, came to visit us and saw our work, and said that he'd like to publish it. We said okay, but didn't really think about it too much and didn't have a title. Later, we showed Terry Zwigoff our comic to see what he thought, and he said, "God this is so embarrassing, it's like hangin' out your dirty laundry for everyone to see!"

So that's how our collaborative comics got the name *Dirty Laundry Comics*. We eventually did two volumes of *Dirty Laundry Comics*, plus numerous strips for a local left wing newspaper called *Winds of Change,* stories for *Weirdo* magazine, *Self Loathing* comics, and our collaborative work for the *New Yorker*. A lot of Crumb fans resent me for putting my scratchy, ugly drawing on the same page as the great master Crumb, and quite frankly

I understand their point. We once got a letter from an irate reader who said, "Maybe she's a great lay, but keep her off the fucking page!" Recently, some people who have seen our strips in the *New Yorker* have said to me, "Why does your husband draw you so ugly? You're so good looking in person!" I always patiently explain that I draw myself and write my own dialogues, and that Robert does himself—but I'm sure they still don't get it. It certainly makes you wonder if people really look closely at anything!

In the summer of 1974, Robert and I went on separate trips. I went to Tucson, and to Truchas, New Mexico, and Robert went to Chicago and New York. We had a romantic reunion at the Boulderado Hotel in Boulder, Colorado. There we made a coupla' giant wooden cartoon cutouts of some of Robert's well known characters for a local comic book store, in exchange for a 1937 dark green Chevy sedan, which we drove back to California (I actually drove and Robert was the passenger since he had failed driver's ed and didn't have a license.)

We were gone for three months. When we arrived back in Potter Valley, we found my trailer shot full of bullet holes. The whole place was a wreck. Robert asked Dana what had happened. She blamed it on some cowboy friends of hers, and told Robert she didn't want me around and that he had to get rid of me. Robert said, "But Aline is my friend. Don't I have a right to have someone here if I want? Didn't my money pay for this place? If she goes, I go!" Dana said, "Then you get outta here too!"

We left, but were devastated about leaving Robert's son Jesse behind. We tried to buy a little house in a nearby town so we could continue to help raise Jesse. We were both very attached to him and wanted to be involved in his life, but Dana didn't want us anywhere near her. With the help of her lawyer, she managed to make it impossible for Robert to access his money, and therefore impossible for us to find a place to live nearby. This was a very painful experience for Robert. He knew he was leaving Jesse in a totally chaotic slob pit, in the care of an emotional wreck of a mother who was whacked out on Demerol most of the time.

Above: **Our home in Winters, California**
This is our humble little cottage. Right after I met Robert, years before
moving here, I had a dream that we lived in this exact house and that
we had a curly blonde haired child…

Our little house in the valley

Robert and I ended up in the hot, un-hip Central Valley of California, where friends and fellow musicians Al Dodge and Robert Armstrong had rented a cheap ramshackle old farmhouse, located in an almond orchard near a small farm town called Dixon. This was definitely not the romantic northern California of magical redwood forests and coastal beauty, but the California of *The Grapes Of Wrath,* populated by rednecks and Mexican migrant workers.

Although we were only eighty miles from San Francisco, we might as well have been in Oklahoma. And yet, after the craziness of the past few years, Robert and I found something comforting about the dull ordinariness of the Big Valley. We explored the area around Dixon and ended up finding a little shack along the banks of Putah Creek, in a nearby town called Winters. As random as this choice was, we ended up staying there for the next seventeen years. We eventually bought a little house five miles outside of Winters, and made a cozy scene for ourselves.

But the early years in Central Valley were difficult for us. In addition to the ongoing pain of having left Jesse behind, and our frustrated attempts to see him, we had to deal with a big tax debt in Robert's name that had been engineered by Dana and her lawyer. We worked incredibly hard, sold most of our possessions and eventually paid the IRS. But in many other ways, it was a positive and romantic time for us, and we stimulated each other intellectually to the point that we were pretty content to spend a lot of time alone, just the two of us.

We were both very horny, and our sex life was intense and became more and more satisfying as we lost our inhibitions. I would probably have been happy if things remained like that for the rest of our lives, but Robert still had a lot of sexual exploring to do. (More about our extracurricular love affairs later!)

I became totally passionate about collecting and decorating my house with 1920s and '30s dishes, curtains, furniture, knick-knacks, lamps, paintings, and anything else I could lay my hands on. There was great cheap stuff to be found at the Salvation Army and junk stores around Sacramento. The yard sales were rich, and sometimes Robert and I would even come across brand new "old stock" in out-of-the way shops. I still have many top-notch items in my house in France that I found during that period.

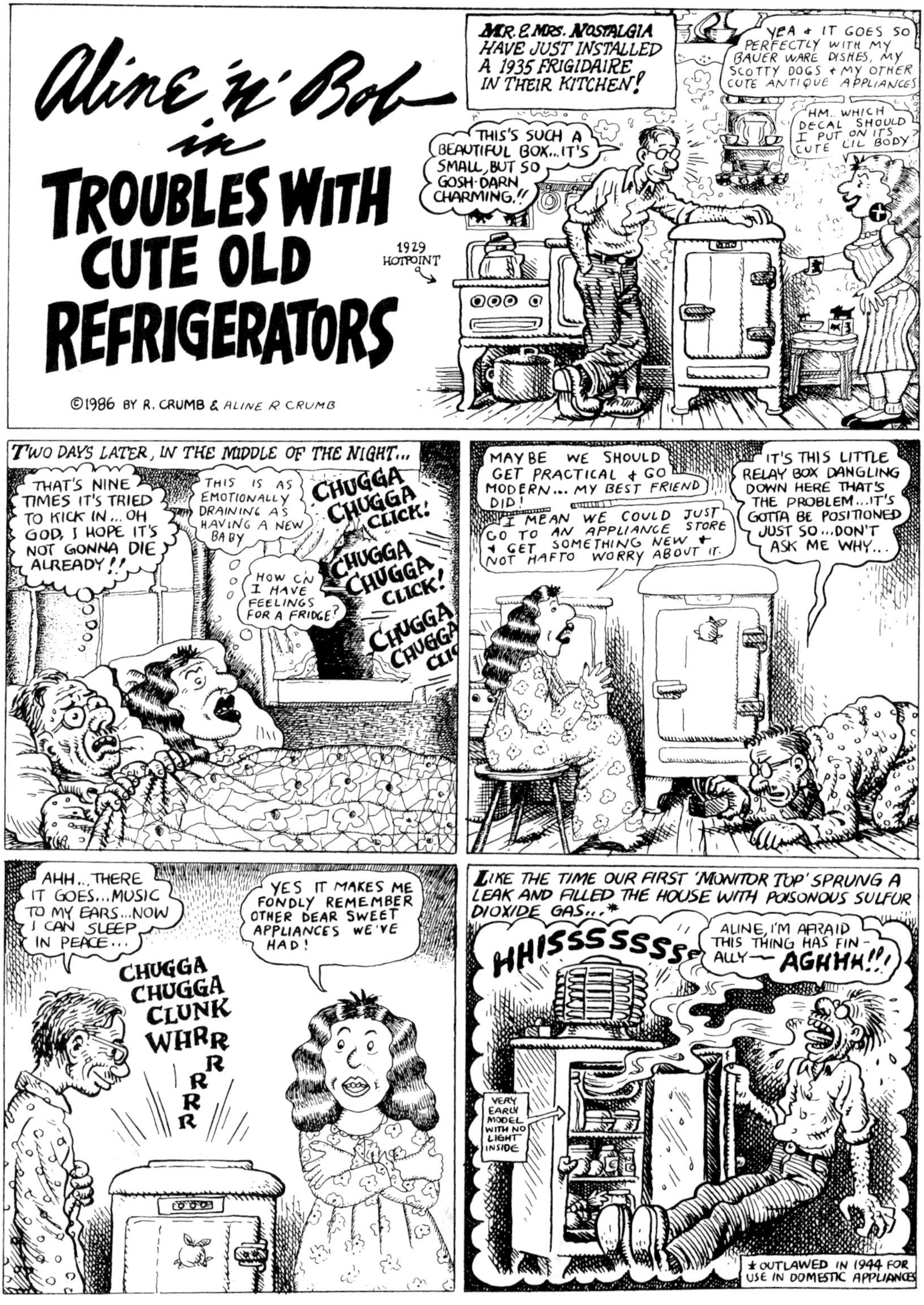

Aline 'n' Bob in
TROUBLES WITH CUTE OLD REFRIGERATORS
©1986 BY R. CRUMB & ALINE R. CRUMB
1929 HOTPOINT
MR. & MRS. NOSTALGIA HAVE JUST INSTALLED A 1935 FRIGIDAIRE IN THEIR KITCHEN!
YEA & IT GOES SO PERFECTLY WITH MY BAUER WARE DISHES, MY SCOTTY DOGS & MY OTHER CUTE ANTIQUE APPLIANCES
THIS'S SUCH A BEAUTIFUL BOX...IT'S SMALL, BUT SO GOSH-DARN CHARMING.!!
HM.. WHICH DECAL SHOULD I PUT ON ITS CUTE LIL BODY
TWO DAYS LATER, IN THE MIDDLE OF THE NIGHT...
THAT'S NINE TIMES IT'S TRIED TO KICK IN... OH GOD, I HOPE IT'S NOT GONNA DIE ALREADY!!
THIS IS AS EMOTIONALLY DRAINING AS HAVING A NEW BABY
HOW C'N I HAVE FEELINGS FOR A FRIDGE?
CHUGGA CHUGGA CLICK!
CHUGGA CHUGGA CLICK!
CHUGGA CHUGGA
MAYBE WE SHOULD GET PRACTICAL & GO MODERN... MY BEST FRIEND DID!
I MEAN WE COULD JUST GO TO AN APPLIANCE STORE & GET SOMETHING NEW & NOT HAFTO WORRY ABOUT IT.
IT'S THIS LITTLE RELAY BOX DANGLING DOWN HERE THAT'S THE PROBLEM...IT'S GOTTA BE POSITIONED JUST SO...DON'T ASK ME WHY...
AHH.. THERE IT GOES... MUSIC TO MY EARS...NOW I CAN SLEEP IN PEACE...
YES IT MAKES ME FONDLY REMEMBER OTHER DEAR SWEET APPLIANCES WE'VE HAD!
CHUGGA CHUGGA CLUNK WHRRRRR
LIKE THE TIME OUR FIRST 'MONITOR TOP' SPRUNG A LEAK AND FILLED THE HOUSE WITH POISONOUS SULFUR DIOXIDE GAS...*
HHISSSSSSS
ALINE, I'M AFRAID THIS THING HAS FIN-ALLY— AGHHH!!!
VERY EARLY MODEL WITH NO LIGHT INSIDE
*OUTLAWED IN 1944 FOR USE IN DOMESTIC APPLIANCES

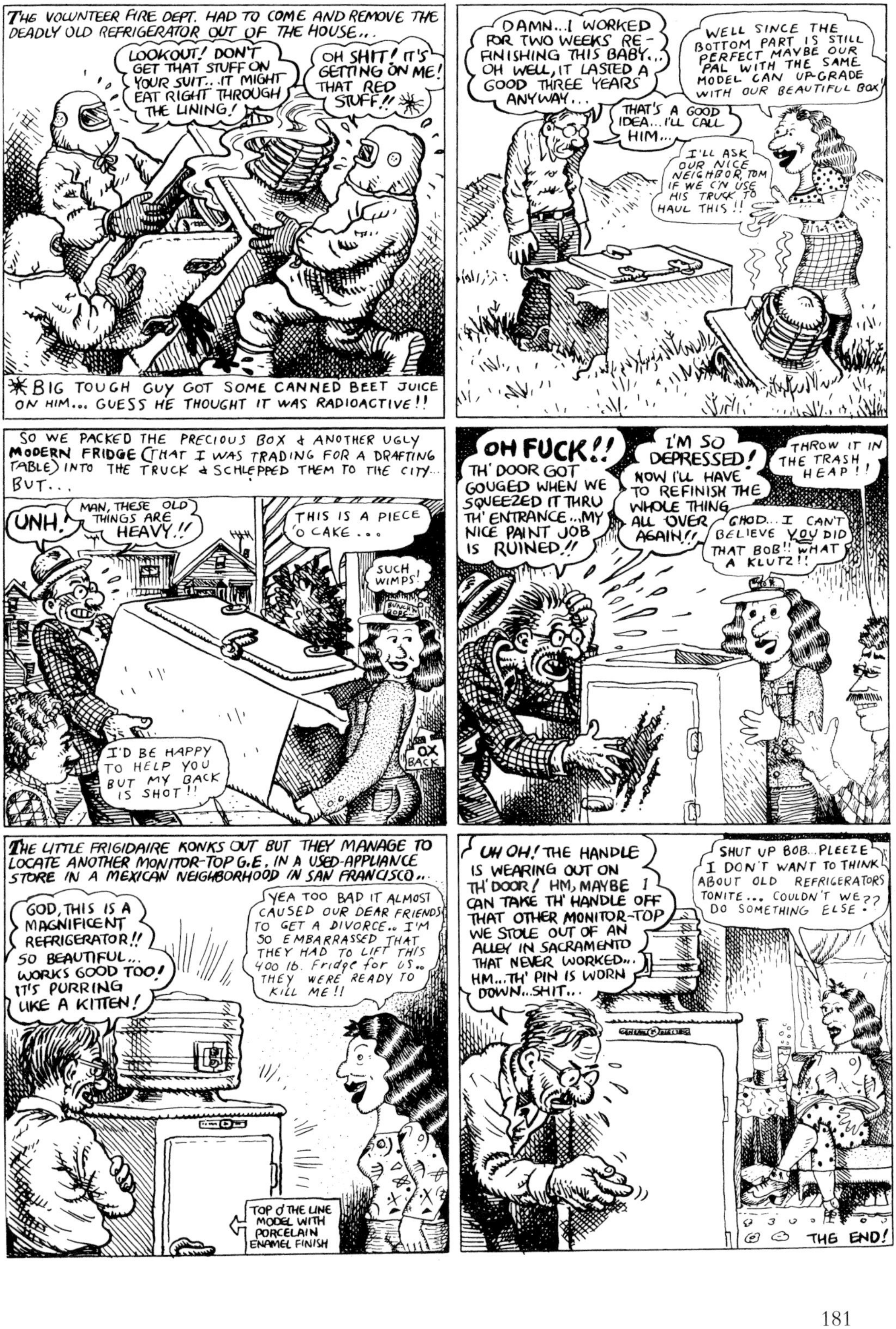
THE VOLUNTEER FIRE DEPT. HAD TO COME AND REMOVE THE DEADLY OLD REFRIGERATOR OUT OF THE HOUSE...
LOOKOUT! DON'T GET THAT STUFF ON YOUR SUIT... IT MIGHT EAT RIGHT THROUGH THE LINING!
OH SHIT! IT'S GETTING ON ME! THAT RED STUFF!! *
* BIG TOUGH GUY GOT SOME CANNED BEET JUICE ON HIM... GUESS HE THOUGHT IT WAS RADIOACTIVE!!
DAMN... I WORKED FOR TWO WEEKS RE-FINISHING THIS BABY... OH WELL, IT LASTED A GOOD THREE YEARS ANYWAY...
WELL SINCE THE BOTTOM PART IS STILL PERFECT MAYBE OUR PAL WITH THE SAME MODEL CAN UP-GRADE WITH OUR BEAUTIFUL BOX!
THAT'S A GOOD IDEA... I'LL CALL HIM...
I'LL ASK OUR NICE NEIGHBOR TOM IF WE C'N USE HIS TRUCK TO HAUL THIS!!
SO WE PACKED THE PRECIOUS BOX & ANOTHER UGLY MODERN FRIDGE (THAT I WAS TRADING FOR A DRAFTING TABLE) INTO THE TRUCK & SCHLEPPED THEM TO THE CITY... BUT...
UNH!
MAN, THESE OLD THINGS ARE HEAVY!!
THIS IS A PIECE 'O CAKE...
SUCH WIMPS!
I'D BE HAPPY TO HELP YOU BUT MY BACK IS SHOT!!
OX BACK
OH FUCK!!
TH' DOOR GOT GOUGED WHEN WE SQUEEZED IT THRU TH' ENTRANCE... MY NICE PAINT JOB IS RUINED!!
I'M SO DEPRESSED! NOW I'LL HAVE TO REFINISH THE WHOLE THING ALL OVER AGAIN!!
THROW IT IN THE TRASH HEAP!!
GHOD... I CAN'T BELIEVE YOU DID THAT BOB!! WHAT A KLUTZ!!
THE LITTLE FRIGIDAIRE KONKS OUT BUT THEY MANAGE TO LOCATE ANOTHER MONITOR-TOP G.E. IN A USED-APPLIANCE STORE IN A MEXICAN NEIGHBORHOOD IN SAN FRANCISCO...
GOD, THIS IS A MAGNIFICENT REFRIGERATOR!! SO BEAUTIFUL... WORKS GOOD TOO! IT'S PURRING LIKE A KITTEN!
YEA TOO BAD IT ALMOST CAUSED OUR DEAR FRIENDS TO GET A DIVORCE.. I'M SO EMBARRASSED THAT THEY HAD TO LIFT THIS 400 lb. Fridge for us.. THEY WERE READY TO KILL ME!!
TOP O' THE LINE MODEL WITH PORCELAIN ENAMEL FINISH
UH OH! THE HANDLE IS WEARING OUT ON TH' DOOR! HM, MAYBE I CAN TAKE TH' HANDLE OFF THAT OTHER MONITOR-TOP WE STOLE OUT OF AN ALLEY IN SACRAMENTO THAT NEVER WORKED... HM... TH' PIN IS WORN DOWN... SHIT...
SHUT UP BOB... PLEEZE I DON'T WANT TO THINK ABOUT OLD REFRIGERATORS TONITE... COULDN'T WE?? DO SOMETHING ELSE.
THE END!

Simple pleasures

We became very interested in the history of the area. Winters had remained a sleepy farm town in the mid-1970s, and there were still many old timers living there. I began taking violin lessons from a guy named Claude Wild, who was part of a family orchestra that had played for country dances before World War Two.

I would go to the Wilds' house every week and got to know them well. Eventually I even played music with them. This was a deeply moving experience that had a profound effect on a middle class brat like me—it was like stepping back into an old 78 rpm record. It deepened my love for pre-war America, an America I could only dream about, and heightened my disgust for post-war jerk modern America.

Robert spent a lot of time on the road with his band, The Cheap Suit Serenaders. I was very productive during this period—my life was quite simple and I spent long periods of time alone. I exercised a lot, riding my bike on the flat valley roads and taking dance classes, and also worked on comics. I did *Power Pak* 1 and *Power Pak* 2 in the late 1970s, and worked with Bill Griffith, Diane Noomin and Art Spiegelman on *Arcade Magazine*. Robert and I continued working on our collaborative *Dirty Laundry Comics,* and we contributed to goody-goody left-wing magazines like *Co-Evolution Quarterly* and to the local paper, *Winds of Change*.

Right above: **The Wild Family Orchestra, Zamora, California, 1978**
Fred, Harold, Eva, Margaret, and Claude (my violin teacher.)

Right below: **The Palms Playhouse, Davis, California, 1978**
Robert and me playing country music.

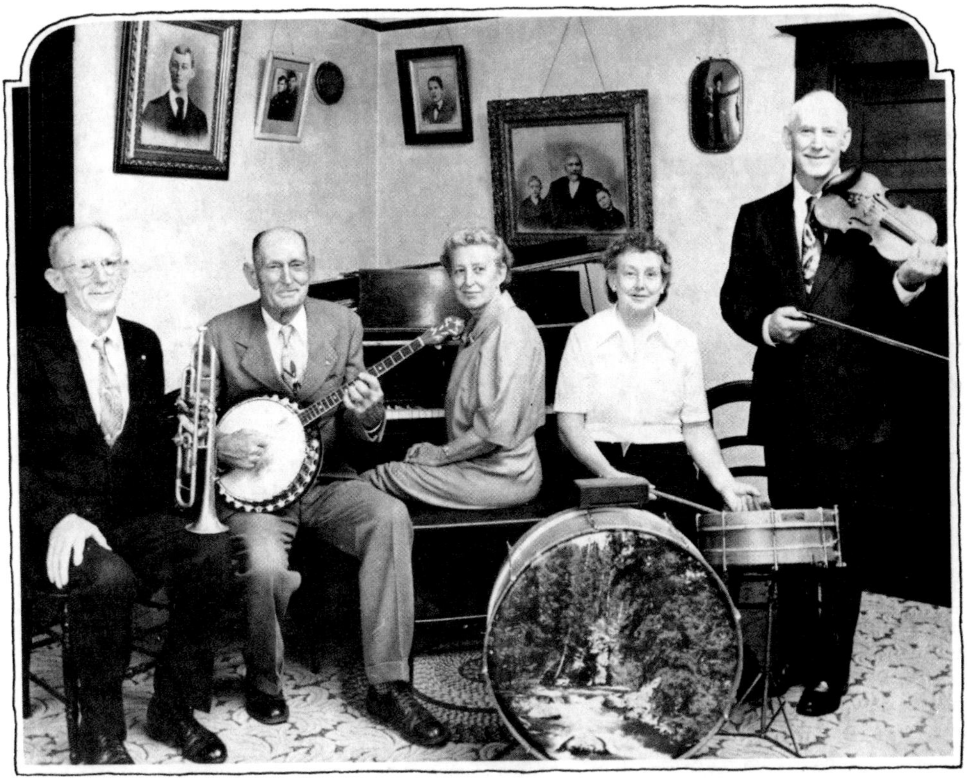

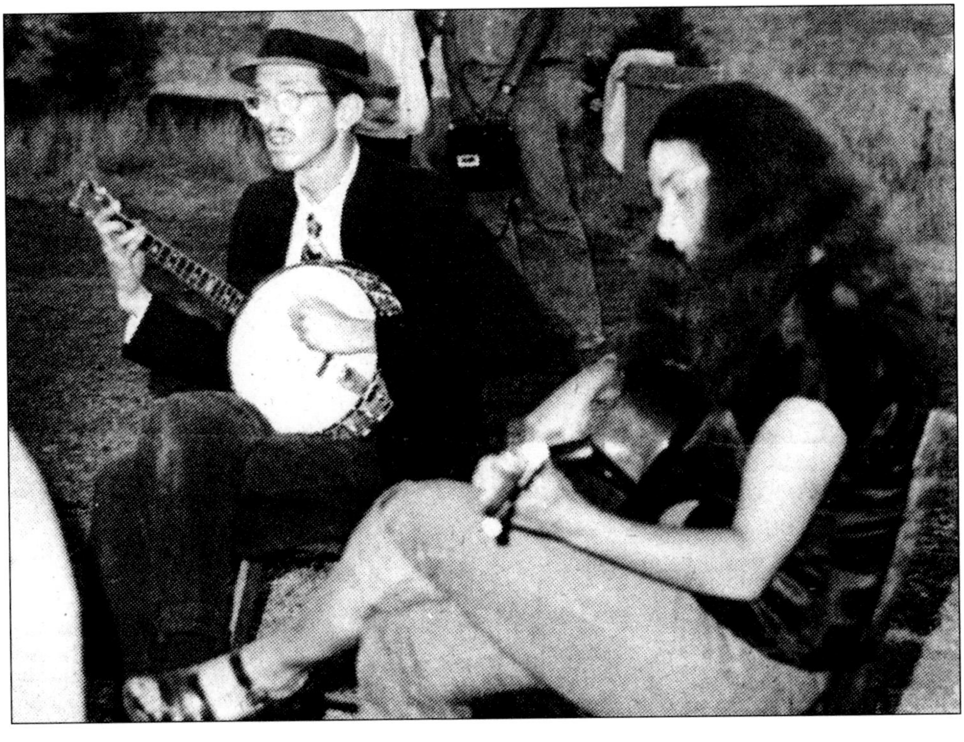

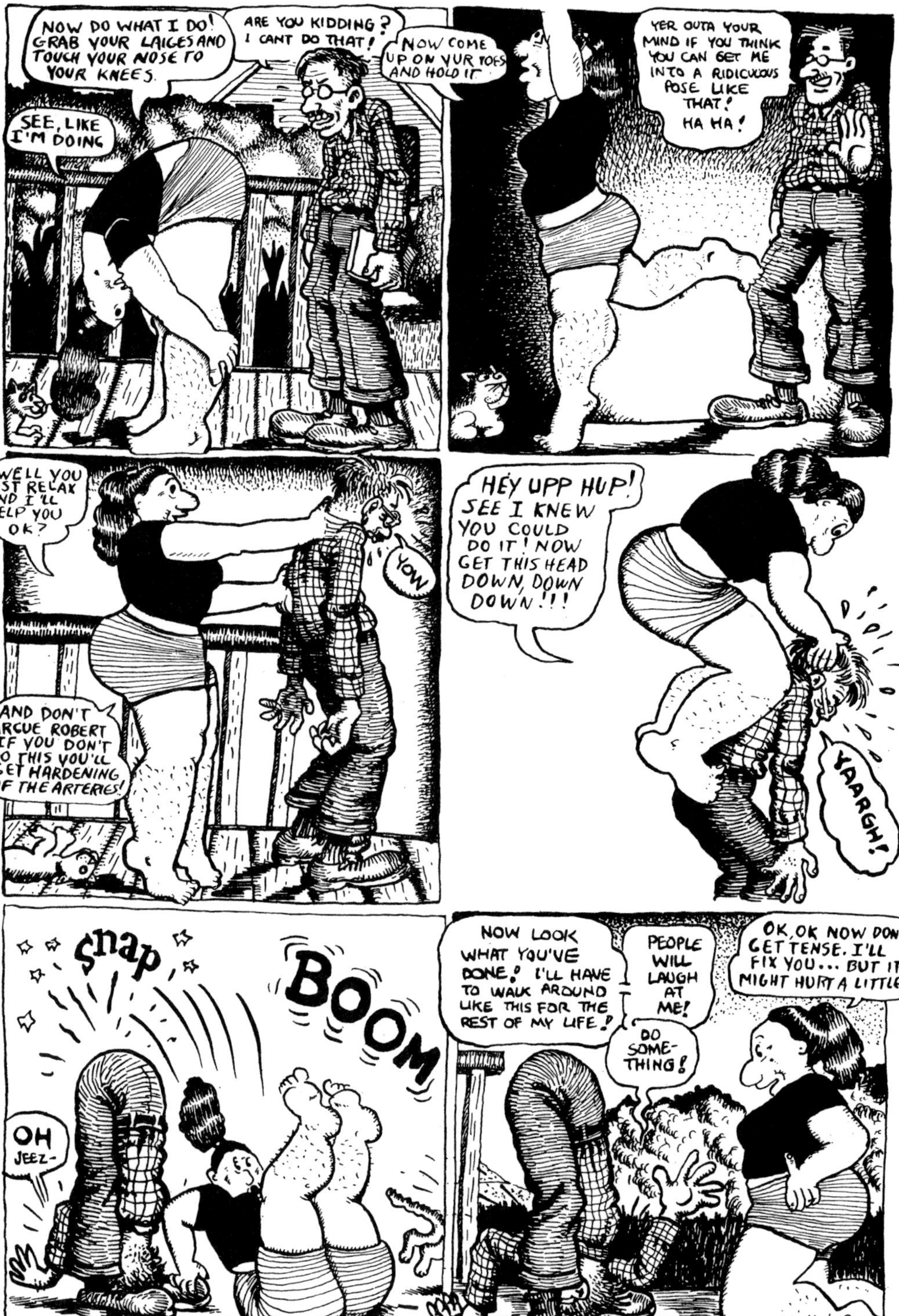
NOW DO WHAT I DO! GRAB YOUR LAIGES AND TOUCH YOUR NOSE TO YOUR KNEES.
ARE YOU KIDDING? I CANT DO THAT!
SEE, LIKE I'M DOING
NOW COME UP ON YUR TOES AND HOLD IT.
YER OUTA YOUR MIND IF YOU THINK YOU CAN GET ME INTO A RIDICULOUS POSE LIKE THAT! HA HA!
WELL YOU JUST RELAX AND I'LL HELP YOU OK?
YOW
AND DON'T ARGUE ROBERT IF YOU DON'T DO THIS YOU'LL GET HARDENING OF THE ARTERIES!
HEY UPP HUP! SEE I KNEW YOU COULD DO IT! NOW GET THIS HEAD DOWN, DOWN DOWN!!!
YAARGH!
SNAP
BOOM
OH JEEZ-
NOW LOOK WHAT YOU'VE DONE! I'LL HAVE TO WALK AROUND LIKE THIS FOR THE REST OF MY LIFE!
PEOPLE WILL LAUGH AT ME!
DO SOME-THING!
OK, OK NOW DON'T GET TENSE. I'LL FIX YOU... BUT IT MIGHT HURT A LITTLE!

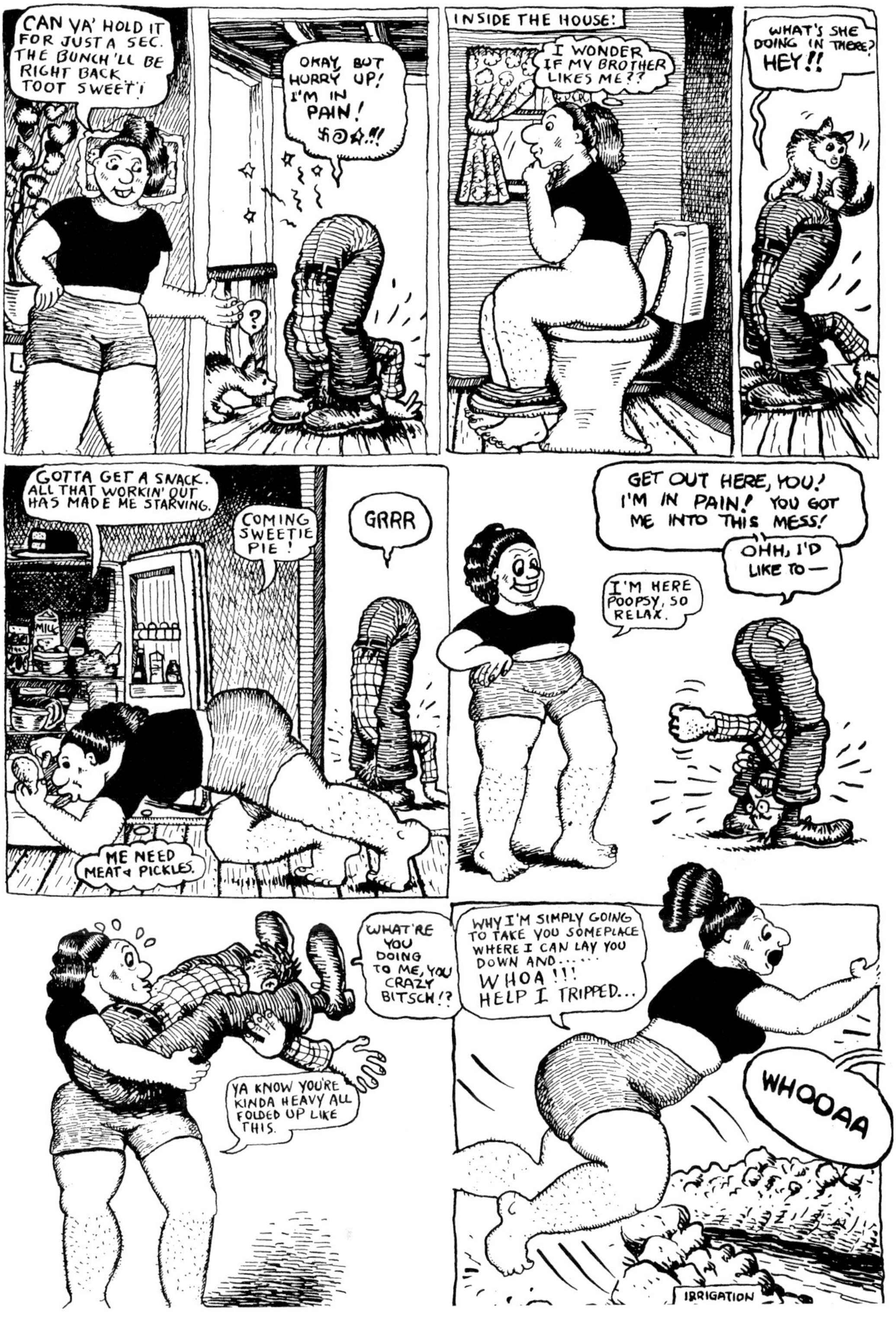

CAN YA' HOLD IT FOR JUST A SEC. THE BUNCH'LL BE RIGHT BACK TOOT SWEET'!
OKAY, BUT HURRY UP! I'M IN PAIN!
INSIDE THE HOUSE:
I WONDER IF MY BROTHER LIKES ME??
WHAT'S SHE DOING IN THERE? HEY!!
GOTTA GET A SNACK. ALL THAT WORKIN' OUT HAS MADE ME STARVING.
COMING SWEETIE PIE!
ME NEED MEAT & PICKLES.
GRRR
GET OUT HERE, YOU! I'M IN PAIN! YOU GOT ME INTO THIS MESS!
OHH, I'D LIKE TO—
I'M HERE POOPSY, SO RELAX.
WHAT'RE YOU DOING TO ME, YOU CRAZY BITSCH!?
YA KNOW YOU'RE KINDA HEAVY ALL FOLDED UP LIKE THIS.
WHY I'M SIMPLY GOING TO TAKE YOU SOMEPLACE WHERE I CAN LAY YOU DOWN AND...... WHOA!!! HELP I TRIPPED...
WHOOAA
IRRIGATION

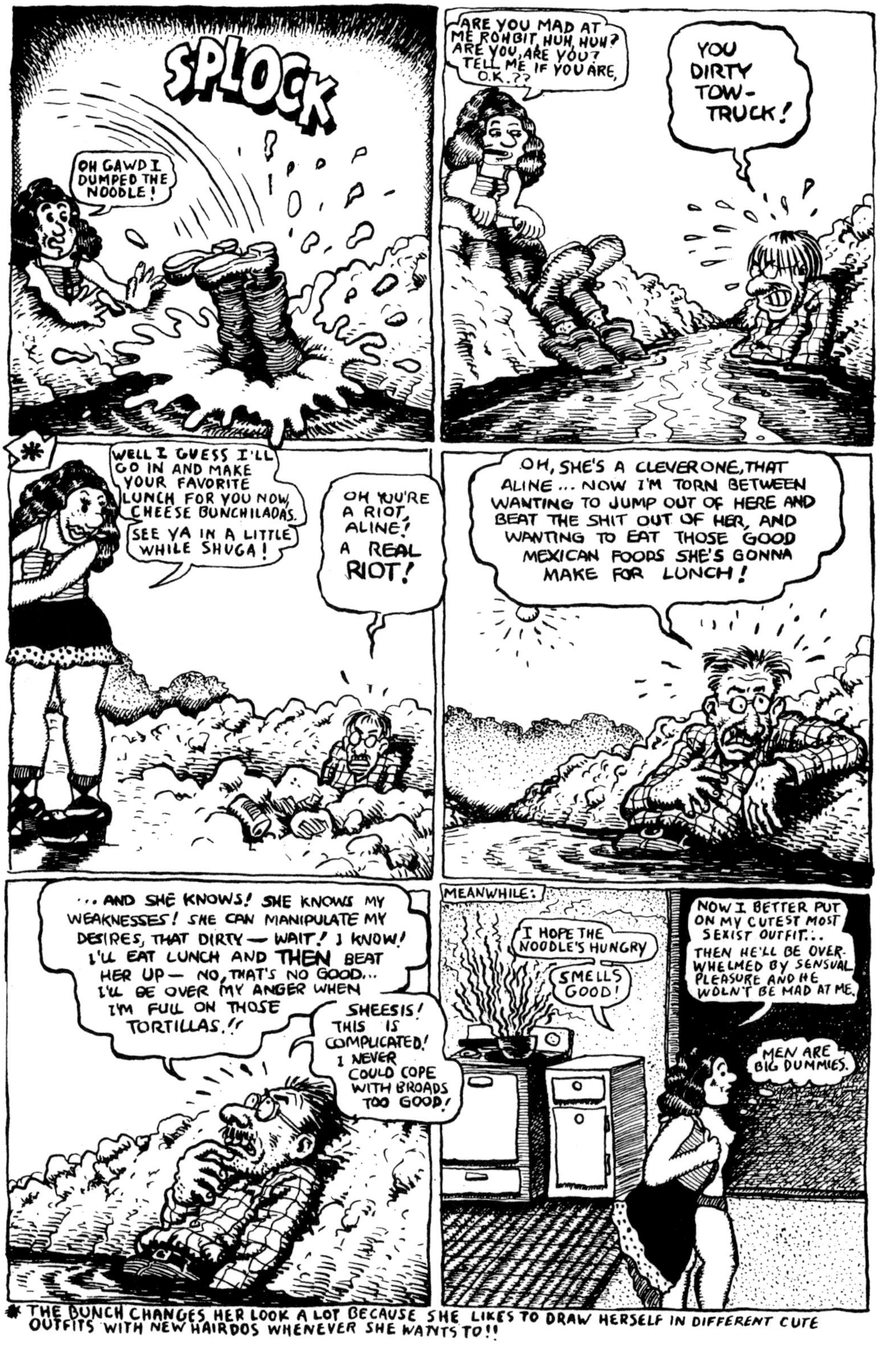
SPLOCK
OH GAWD I DUMPED THE NOODLE!
ARE YOU MAD AT ME ROHBIT HUH HUH? ARE YOU, ARE YOU? TELL ME IF YOU ARE, O.K.??
YOU DIRTY TOW-TRUCK!
*
WELL I GUESS I'LL GO IN AND MAKE YOUR FAVORITE LUNCH FOR YOU NOW, CHEESE BUNCHILADAS.
SEE YA IN A LITTLE WHILE SHUGA!
OH YOU'RE A RIOT, ALINE! A REAL RIOT!
OH, SHE'S A CLEVER ONE, THAT ALINE... NOW I'M TORN BETWEEN WANTING TO JUMP OUT OF HERE AND BEAT THE SHIT OUT OF HER, AND WANTING TO EAT THOSE GOOD MEXICAN FOODS SHE'S GONNA MAKE FOR LUNCH!
...AND SHE KNOWS! SHE KNOWS MY WEAKNESSES! SHE CAN MANIPULATE MY DESIRES, THAT DIRTY — WAIT! I KNOW! I'LL EAT LUNCH AND THEN BEAT HER UP — NO, THAT'S NO GOOD... I'LL BE OVER MY ANGER WHEN I'M FULL ON THOSE TORTILLAS!!
SHEESIS! THIS IS COMPLICATED! I NEVER COULD COPE WITH BROADS TOO GOOD!
MEANWHILE:
I HOPE THE NOODLE'S HUNGRY
SMELLS GOOD!
NOW I BETTER PUT ON MY CUTEST MOST SEXIST OUTFIT... THEN HE'LL BE OVERWHELMED BY SENSUAL PLEASURE AND HE WON'T BE MAD AT ME.
MEN ARE BIG DUMMIES.
* THE BUNCH CHANGES HER LOOK A LOT BECAUSE SHE LIKES TO DRAW HERSELF IN DIFFERENT CUTE OUTFITS WITH NEW HAIRDOS WHENEVER SHE WANTS TO!!

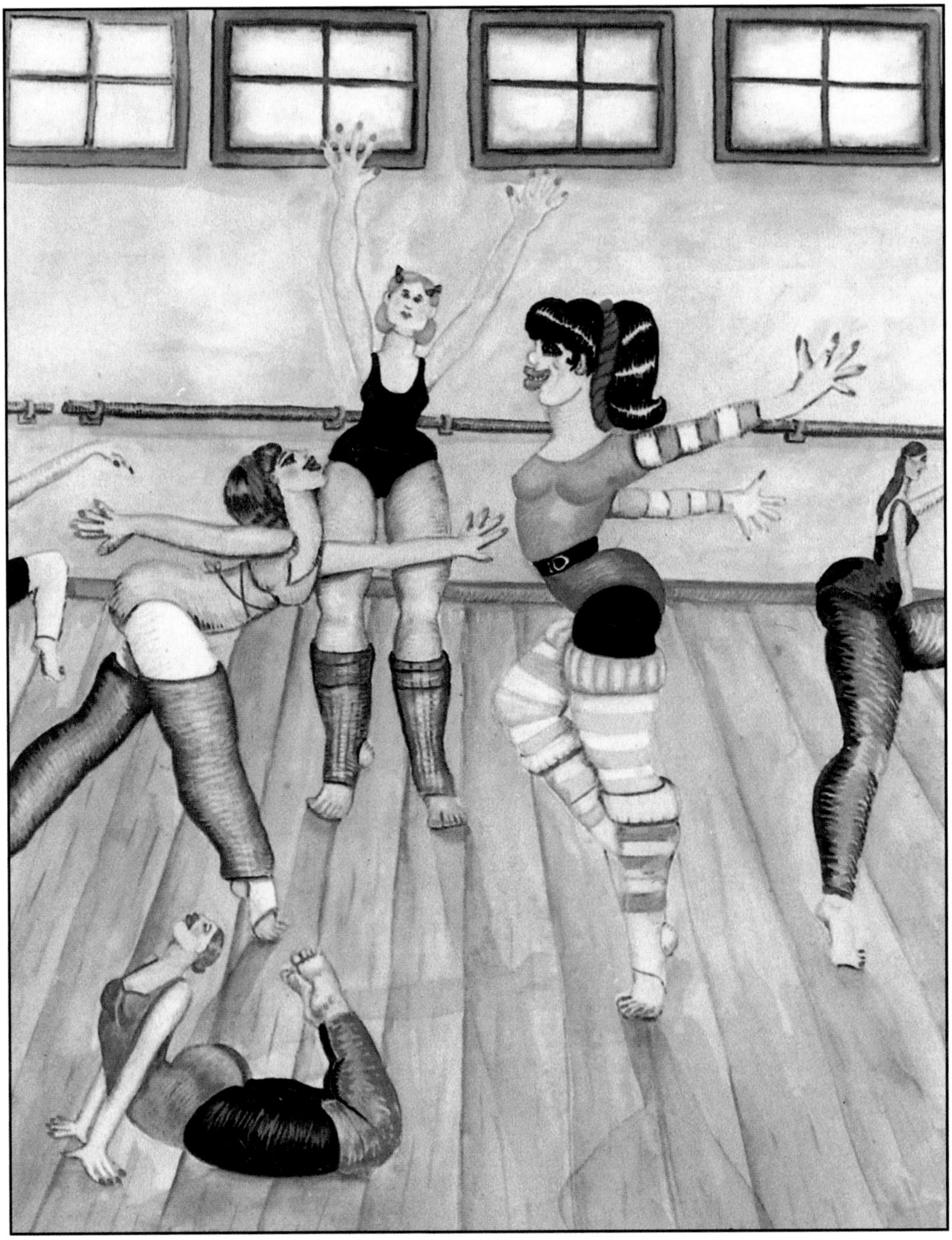

Above: **A water color I did about my dance class**
I had a fantasy that my head got smaller as my muscles got bigger.

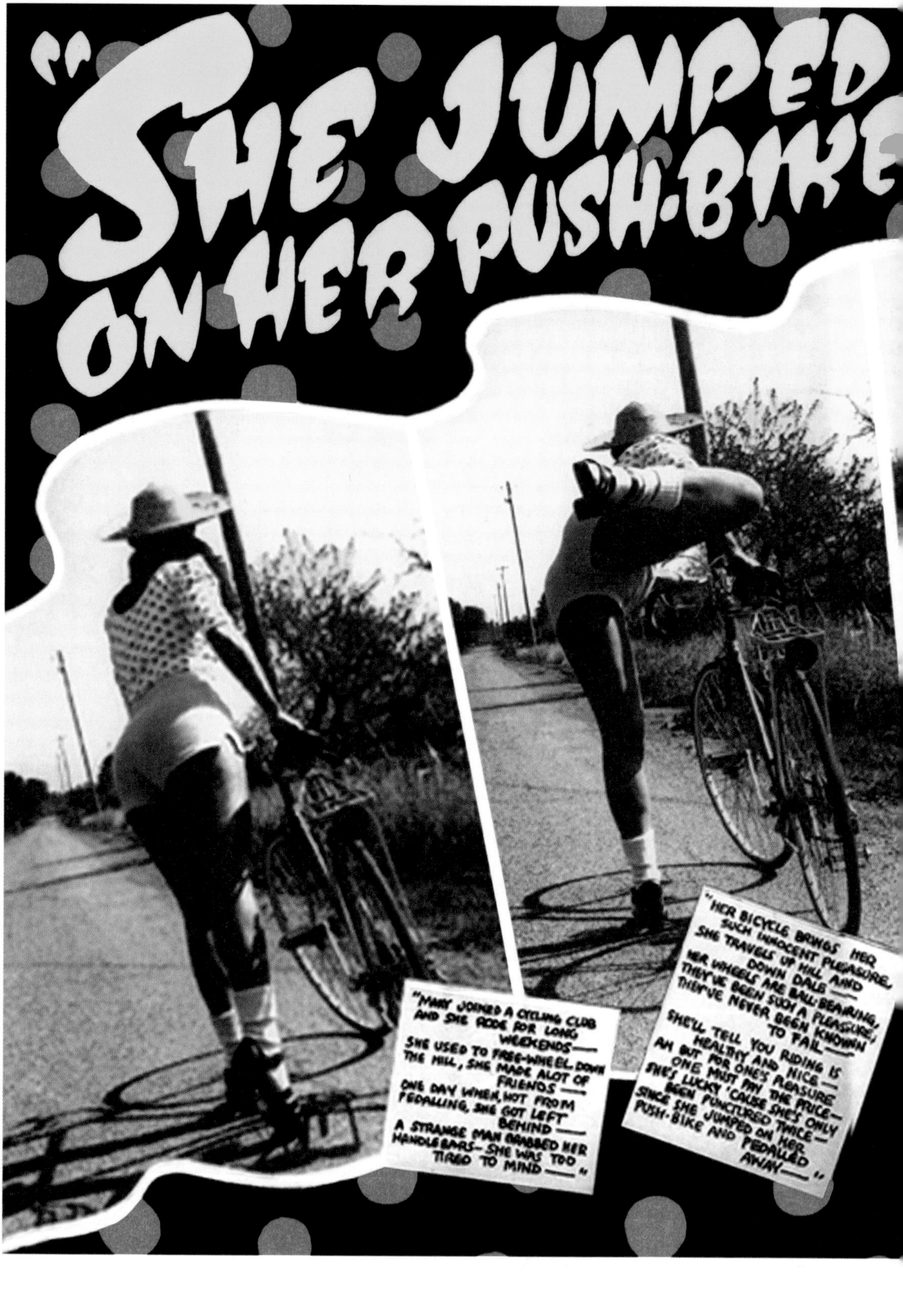
"SHE JUMPED ON HER PUSH-BIKE
"MARY JOINED A CYCLING CLUB AND SHE RODE FOR LONG WEEKENDS—— SHE USED TO FREE-WHEEL DOWN THE HILL, SHE MADE ALOT OF FRIENDS —— ONE DAY WHEN, HOT FROM PEDALLING, SHE GOT LEFT BEHIND —— A STRANGE MAN GRABBED HER HANDLEBARS– SHE WAS TOO TIRED TO MIND ——"
"HER BICYCLE BRINGS HER SUCH INNOCENT PLEASURE, SHE TRAVELS UP HILL AND DOWN DALE —— HER WHEELS ARE BALL-BEARING, THEY'VE BEEN SUCH A PLEASURE, THEY'VE NEVER BEEN KNOWN TO FAIL—— SHE'LL TELL YOU RIDING IS HEALTHY AND NICE— AH BUT FOR ONE'S PLEASURE ONE MUST PAY THE PRICE– SHE'S LUCKY 'CAUSE SHE'S ONLY BEEN PUNCTURED TWICE— SINCE SHE JUMPED ON HER PUSH-BIKE AND PEDALLED AWAY——"

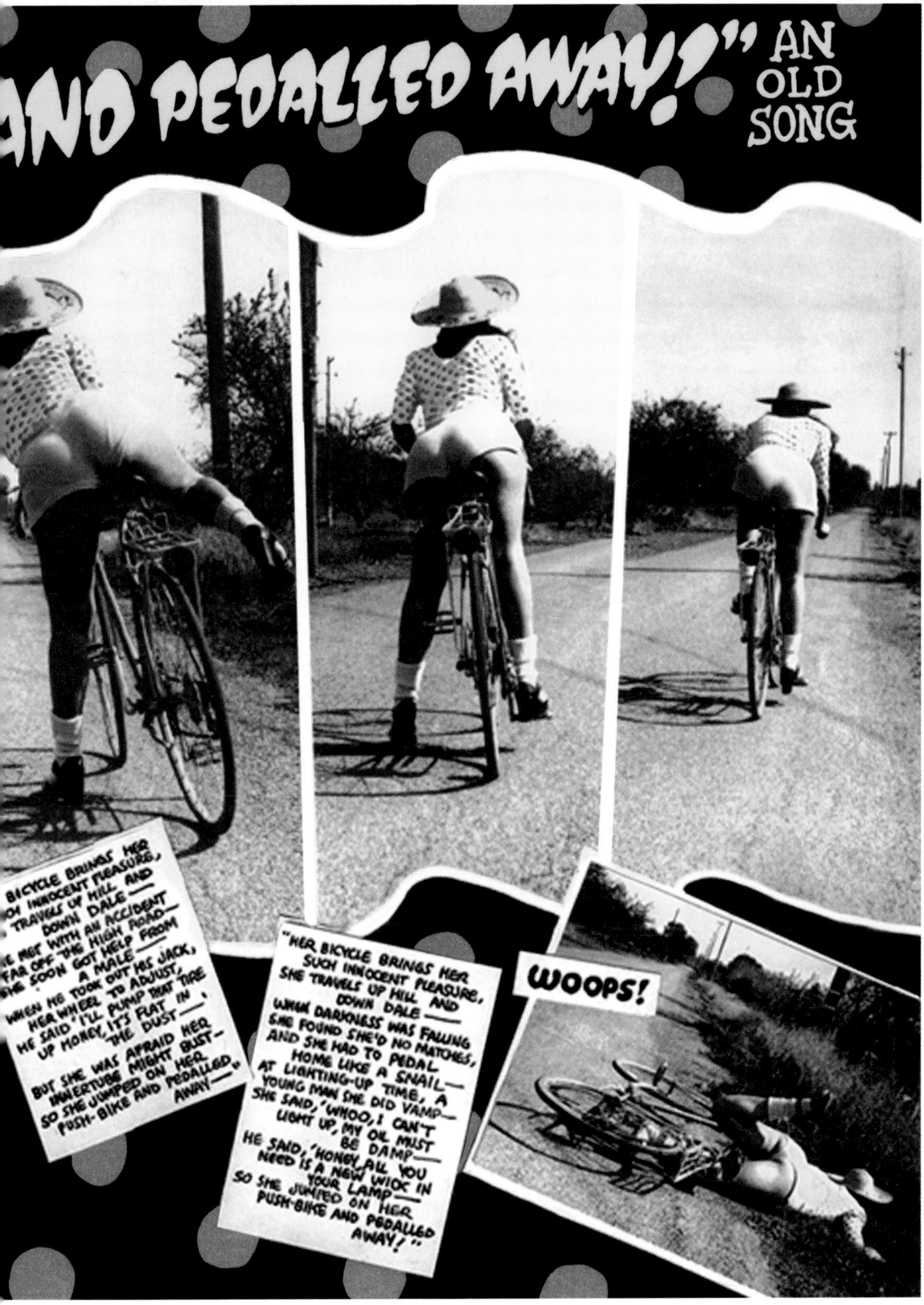

AND PEDALLED AWAY!" AN OLD SONG
BICYCLE BRINGS HER
INNOCENT PLEASURE,
TRAVELS UP HILL AND
DOWN DALE—
MET WITH AN ACCIDENT
FAR OFF THE HIGH ROAD—
SOON GOT HELP FROM
A MALE—
WHEN HE TOOK OUT HIS JACK,
HER WHEEL TO ADJUST,
HE SAID 'I'LL PUMP THAT TIRE
UP HONEY, IT'S FLAT IN
THE DUST—',
BUT SHE WAS AFRAID HER
INNERTUBE MIGHT BUST—
SO SHE JUMPED ON HER
PUSH-BIKE AND PEDALLED
AWAY—"
"HER BICYCLE BRINGS HER
SUCH INNOCENT PLEASURE,
SHE TRAVELS UP HILL AND
DOWN DALE—
WHEN DARKNESS WAS FALLING
SHE FOUND SHE'D NO MATCHES,
AND SHE HAD TO PEDAL
HOME LIKE A SNAIL—
AT LIGHTING-UP TIME, A
YOUNG MAN SHE DID VAMP—
SHE SAID, 'WHOO, I CAN'T
LIGHT UP, MY OIL MUST
BE DAMP—
HE SAID, 'HONEY, ALL YOU
NEED IS A NEW WICK IN
YOUR LAMP—
SO SHE JUMPED ON HER
PUSH-BIKE AND PEDALLED
AWAY!"
WOOPS!

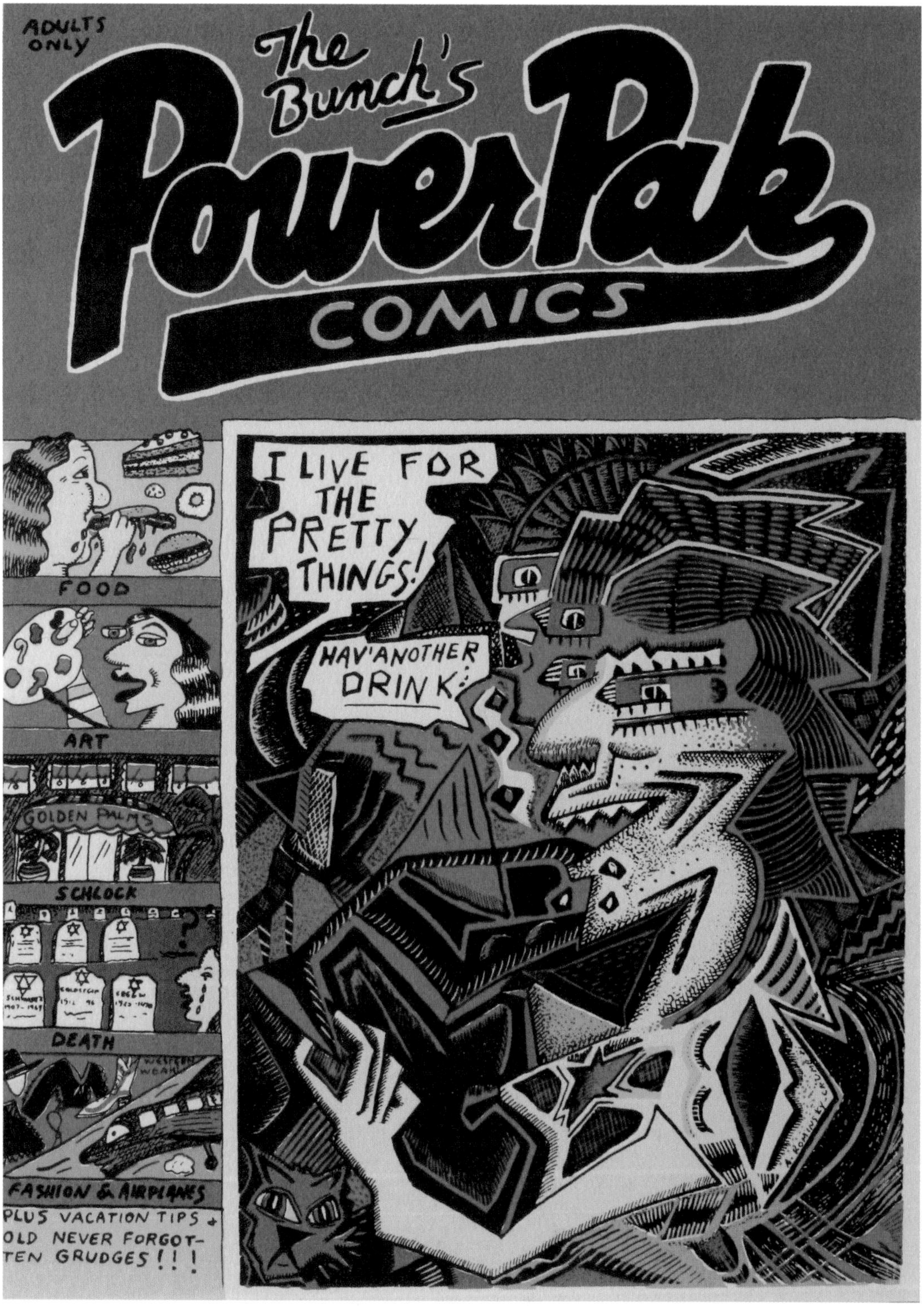
ADULTS ONLY
The Bunch's
Power Pak
COMICS
FOOD
ART
GOLDEN PALMS
SCHLOCK
DEATH
FASHION & AIRPLANES
PLUS VACATION TIPS & OLD NEVER FORGOTTEN GRUDGES!!!
I LIVE FOR THE PRETTY THINGS!
HAV'ANOTHER DRINK

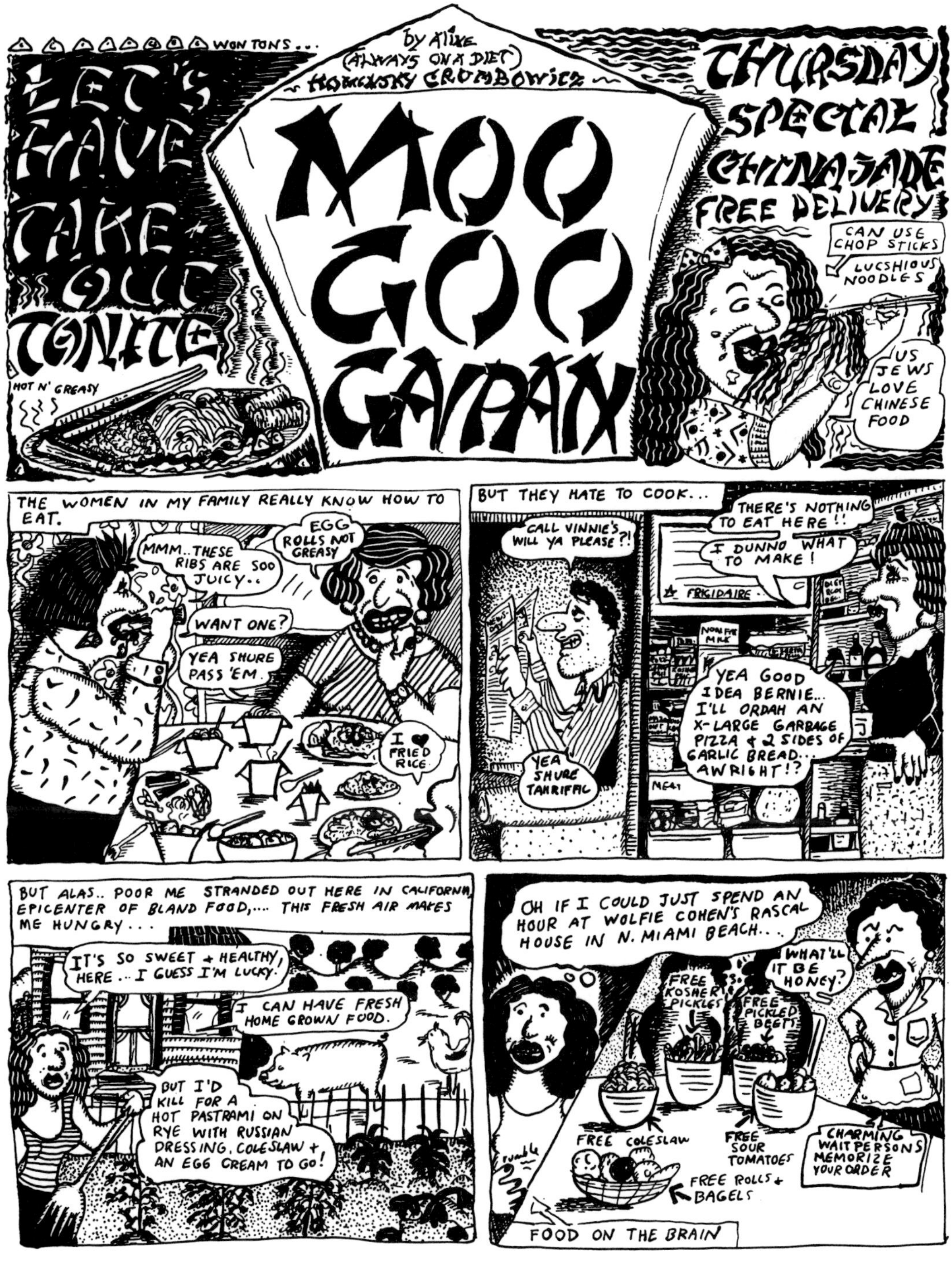
WON TONS...
BY ALINE
(ALWAYS ON A DIET)
~ KOMINSKY CRUMBOWICZ ~
LET'S HAVE TAKE-OUT TONITE
MOO GOO GAI PAN
THURSDAY SPECIAL
CHINA JADE
FREE DELIVERY
CAN USE CHOP STICKS
LUCSHIOUS NOODLES
US JEWS LOVE CHINESE FOOD
HOT N' GREASY
THE WOMEN IN MY FAMILY REALLY KNOW HOW TO EAT.
MMM.. THESE RIBS ARE SOO JUICY..
EGG ROLLS NOT GREASY
WANT ONE?
YEA SHURE PASS 'EM.
I ♥ FRIED RICE
BUT THEY HATE TO COOK...
CALL VINNIE'S.. WILL YA PLEASE?!
THERE'S NOTHING TO EAT HERE!!
I DUNNO WHAT TO MAKE!
FRIGIDAIRE
YEA GOOD IDEA BERNIE.. I'LL ORDAH AN X-LARGE GARBAGE PIZZA & 2 SIDES OF GARLIC BREAD... AWRIGHT!?
YEA SHURE TAHRIFFIC
MEAT
BUT ALAS.. POOR ME STRANDED OUT HERE IN CALIFORNIA EPICENTER OF BLAND FOOD,.... THIS FRESH AIR MAKES ME HUNGRY...
IT'S SO SWEET & HEALTHY, HERE.. I GUESS I'M LUCKY.
I CAN HAVE FRESH HOME GROWN FOOD.
BUT I'D KILL FOR A HOT PASTRAMI ON RYE WITH RUSSIAN DRESSING, COLESLAW & AN EGG CREAM TO GO!
OH IF I COULD JUST SPEND AN HOUR AT WOLFIE COHEN'S RASCAL HOUSE IN N. MIAMI BEACH...
WHAT'LL IT BE HONEY?
FREE KOSHER PICKLES
FREE PICKLED BEETS
FREE COLESLAW
FREE SOUR TOMATOES
CHARMING WAITPERSONS MEMORIZE YOUR ORDER
FREE ROLLS & BAGELS
FOOD ON THE BRAIN

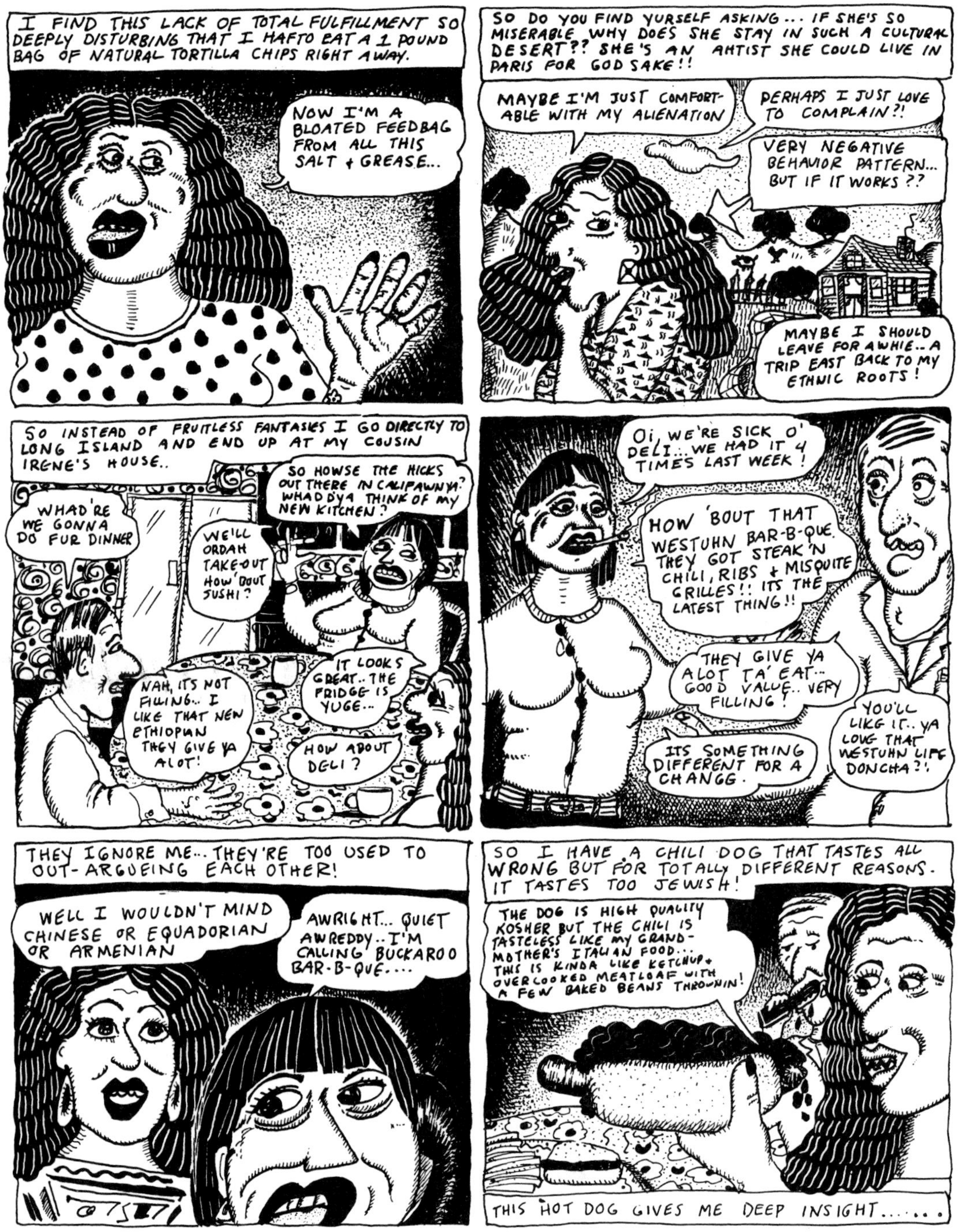

I FIND THIS LACK OF TOTAL FULFILLMENT SO DEEPLY DISTURBING THAT I HAFTO EAT A 1 POUND BAG OF NATURAL TORTILLA CHIPS RIGHT AWAY.
NOW I'M A BLOATED FEEDBAG FROM ALL THIS SALT + GREASE...
SO DO YOU FIND YURSELF ASKING... IF SHE'S SO MISERABLE WHY DOES SHE STAY IN SUCH A CULTURAL DESERT?? SHE'S AN AHTIST SHE COULD LIVE IN PARIS FOR GOD SAKE!!
MAYBE I'M JUST COMFORTABLE WITH MY ALIENATION
PERHAPS I JUST LOVE TO COMPLAIN?!
VERY NEGATIVE BEHAVIOR PATTERN... BUT IF IT WORKS??
MAYBE I SHOULD LEAVE FOR AWHIE.. A TRIP EAST BACK TO MY ETHNIC ROOTS!
SO INSTEAD OF FRUITLESS FANTASIES I GO DIRECTLY TO LONG ISLAND AND END UP AT MY COUSIN IRENE'S HOUSE..
SO HOWSE THE HICKS OUT THERE IN CALIFAWNYA? WHAD'DYA THINK OF MY NEW KITCHEN?
WHAD'RE WE GONNA DO FUR DINNER
WE'LL ORDAH TAKE-OUT HOW'BOUT SUSHI?
NAH, ITS NOT FILLING.. I LIKE THAT NEW ETHIOPIAN THEY GIVE YA ALOT!
IT LOOKS GREAT.. THE FRIDGE IS YUGE...
HOW ABOUT DELI?
Oi, WE'RE SICK O' DELI... WE HAD IT 4 TIMES LAST WEEK!
HOW 'BOUT THAT WESTUHN BAR-B-QUE. THEY GOT STEAK 'N CHILI, RIBS + MISQUITE GRILLES!! ITS THE LATEST THING!!
THEY GIVE YA ALOT TA' EAT... GOOD VALUE.. VERY FILLING!
ITS SOMETHING DIFFERENT FOR A CHANGE.
YOU'LL LIKE IT.. YA LOVE THAT WESTUHN LIFE DONCHA?!
THEY IGNORE ME... THEY'RE TOO USED TO OUT-ARGUEING EACH OTHER!
WELL I WOULDN'T MIND CHINESE OR EQUADORIAN OR ARMENIAN
AWRIGHT... QUIET AWREDDY.. I'M CALLING BUCKAROO BAR-B-QUE....
SO I HAVE A CHILI DOG THAT TASTES ALL WRONG BUT FOR TOTALLY DIFFERENT REASONS. IT TASTES TOO JEWISH!
THE DOG IS HIGH QUALITY KOSHER BUT THE CHILI IS TASTELESS LIKE MY GRAND-MOTHER'S ITALIAN FOOD... THIS IS KINDA LIKE KETCHUP + OVERCOOKED MEATLOAF WITH A FEW BAKED BEANS THROWNIN!
THIS HOT DOG GIVES ME DEEP INSIGHT.......

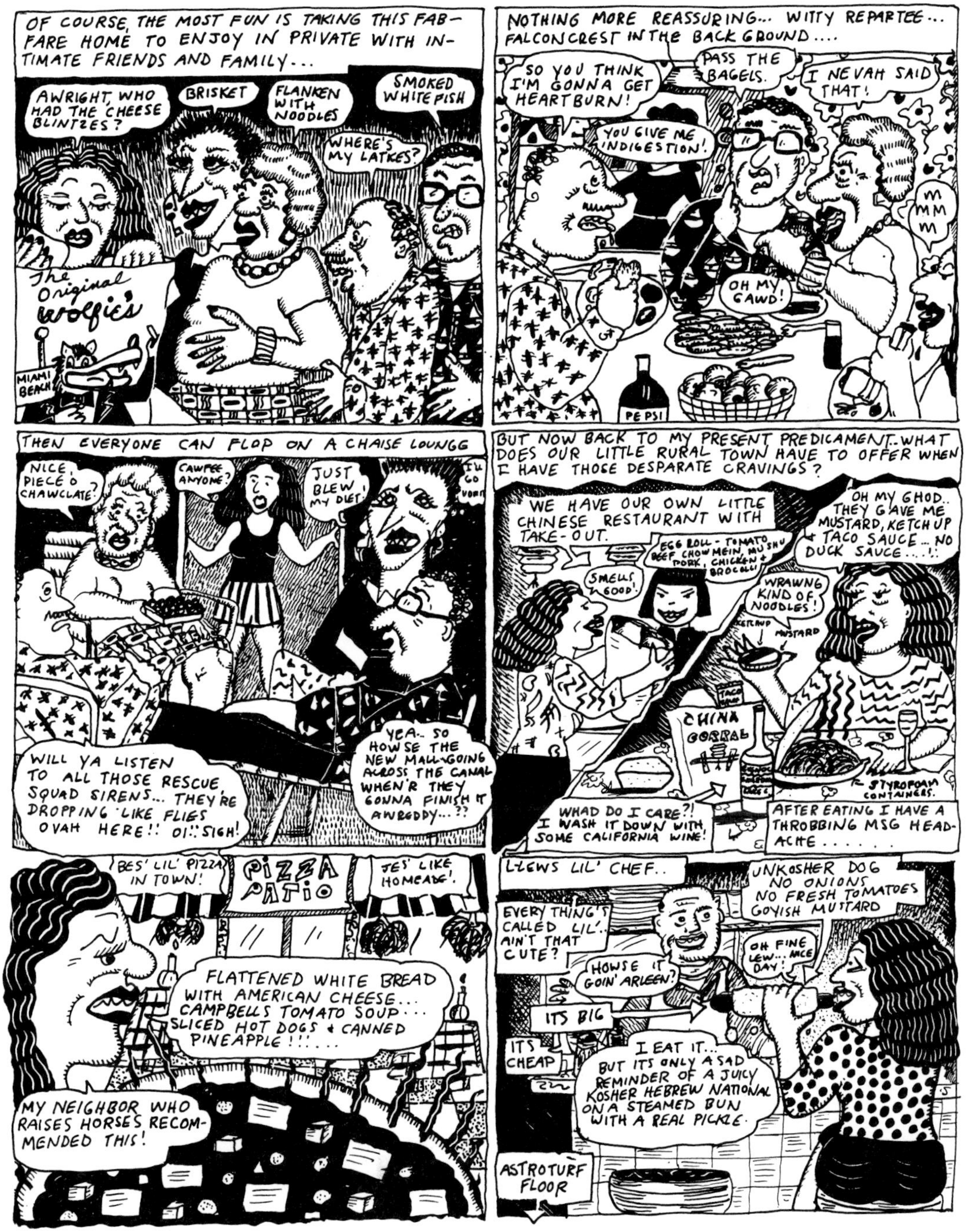

OF COURSE, THE MOST FUN IS TAKING THIS FAB-FARE HOME TO ENJOY IN PRIVATE WITH IN-TIMATE FRIENDS AND FAMILY...
AWRIGHT, WHO HAD THE CHEESE BLINTZES?
BRISKET
FLANKEN WITH NOODLES
SMOKED WHITEFISH
WHERE'S MY LATKES?
The Original Wolfie's
MIAMI BEACH
NOTHING MORE REASSURING... WITTY REPARTEE... FALCONCREST IN THE BACKGROUND....
SO YOU THINK I'M GONNA GET HEARTBURN!
PASS THE BAGELS.
I NEVAH SAID THAT!
YOU GIVE ME INDIGESTION!
M MM M
OH MY GAWD!
PEPSI
THEN EVERYONE CAN FLOP ON A CHAISE LOUNGG
NICE, PIECE O CHAWCLATE?
CAWFEE ANYONE?
JUST BLEW MY DIET!
WILL YA LISTEN TO ALL THOSE RESCUE SQUAD SIRENS... THEY'RE DROPPING LIKE FLIES OVAH HERE!! OI!! SIGH!
YEA.. SO HOWSE THE NEW MALL GOING ACROSS THE CANAL WHEN'R THEY GONNA FINISH IT AWREDDY...??
BUT NOW BACK TO MY PRESENT PREDICAMENT..WHAT DOES OUR LITTLE RURAL TOWN HAVE TO OFFER WHEN I HAVE THOSE DESPARATE CRAVINGS?
WE HAVE OUR OWN LITTLE CHINESE RESTAURANT WITH TAKE-OUT.
EGG ROLL - TOMATO BEEF CHOW MEIN, MUSHU PORK, CHICKEN & BROCOLLI
SMELLS GOOD!
OH MY GHOD.. THEY GAVE ME MUSTARD, KETCHUP + TACO SAUCE... NO DUCK SAUCE...!!
WRAWNG KIND OF NOODLES!
KETCHUP
MUSTARD
CHINA CORRAL
STYROFOAM CONTAINERS.
WHAD DO I CARE?! I WASH IT DOWN WITH SOME CALIFORNIA WINE!
AFTER EATING I HAVE A THROBBING MSG HEAD-ACHE......
BES' LIL' PIZZA IN TOWN!
PIZZA PATIO
JES' LIKE HOMEADE!
FLATTENED WHITE BREAD WITH AMERICAN CHEESE... CAMPBELLS TOMATO SOUP... SLICED HOT DOGS & CANNED PINEAPPLE!!!...
MY NEIGHBOR WHO RAISES HORSES RECOM-MENDED THIS!
LEWS LIL' CHEF..
UNKOSHER DOG NO ONIONS NO FRESH TOMATOES GOYISH MUSTARD
EVERYTHING'S CALLED LIL'.. AIN'T THAT CUTE?
HOWSE IT GOIN' ARLEEN?
OH FINE LEW... NICE DAY!
ITS BIG
ITS CHEAP
I EAT IT... BUT ITS ONLY A SAD REMINDER OF A JUICY KOSHER HEBREW NATIONAL ON A STEAMED BUN WITH A REAL PICKLE.
ASTROTURF FLOOR

Our first taste of Europe

We took our first trip to Europe together in 1978. We went to Germany to meet with Lutz Reinecke, who had a publishing house called *Zweithousandeins* that was putting out Robert's first sketchbook. We talked with the printers and all the artisans who would be working on his book, and were immediately struck by the difference between the Europeans and the Americans. In our American books, we were lucky if they got the pages in the right order, whereas in Germany they were asking if we wanted gilt-edged pages and what color we preferred for the silk bookmark. It was an eye opening experience. We were treated as serious artists in Europe, and this too was quite a surprise.

My exuberant personality soon proved too much for our sensitive German publisher, so he dropped us off in Hamburg to stay with Harry and Ulla Rowohlt, who were his wildest friends. We all hit it off instantly, and

Left: **Ulla Rowohlt, me and Dorla Reinecke, Hamburg, Germany 1978** We are all still friends. Ulla and I have had many adventures together in Europe, America, and India.

for Ulla and me it was the beginning of a major lifelong friendship. We have since traveled all over the world together. Ulla is one of the few women who has profoundly influenced my style.

The day after we arrived was Harry's brother Ledig's 70th birthday party, and we were invited along. We had nothing decent to wear—I was in jeans and a tee shirt, and Robert in worn corduroy pants and a threadbare flannel shirt—so the Rowohlts borrowed some clothes from friends. Robert got a white shirt, tie and jacket, and I got a silk dress and shoes and make-up and hairdo, and I really felt like Cinderella. It was the most elegant party I'd ever been to, and I loved it! I found out that German men really liked me too. I flirted with a very handsome German politician who said, "Next time you come to Europe, call me and we can have our love affair." I did, eight years later!

After Germany, Robert and I traveled separately for a while, and I went to Paris alone. When I stepped out of the Metro for the first time and began to wander around, I somehow felt I had come home—I have never felt so instantly comfortable before or since in an unfamiliar city. I couldn't speak a word of French, but this didn't bother me. Neurologically, I fit in; my physical and spiritual being felt totally at ease.

I can't really explain why—perhaps I was to fulfill my father's dream, or maybe he had planted the seed of his Paris fantasy in me when I was a little girl. Who knows? Anyway it's nice to think that he may have left me with something positive. I stayed in a cheap, quaint hotel on the Left Bank, and walked around the city for days, reveling in the sights, smells and tastes … I was enchanted!

Robert arrived, and we were wined and dined by his French publishers and even taken to the flea markets where we found old French records. These turned out to be fabulous Musette recordings which inspired a whole new area of collecting. (I think we now have the best collection of old French 78s in the world.) Robert liked Paris too, but it certainly did not affect him as much as it affected me.

The next major event to happen at home was the the death of my Grandfather Joe, and the following comic story is all about that and the sadness and sleaziness surrounding the event.

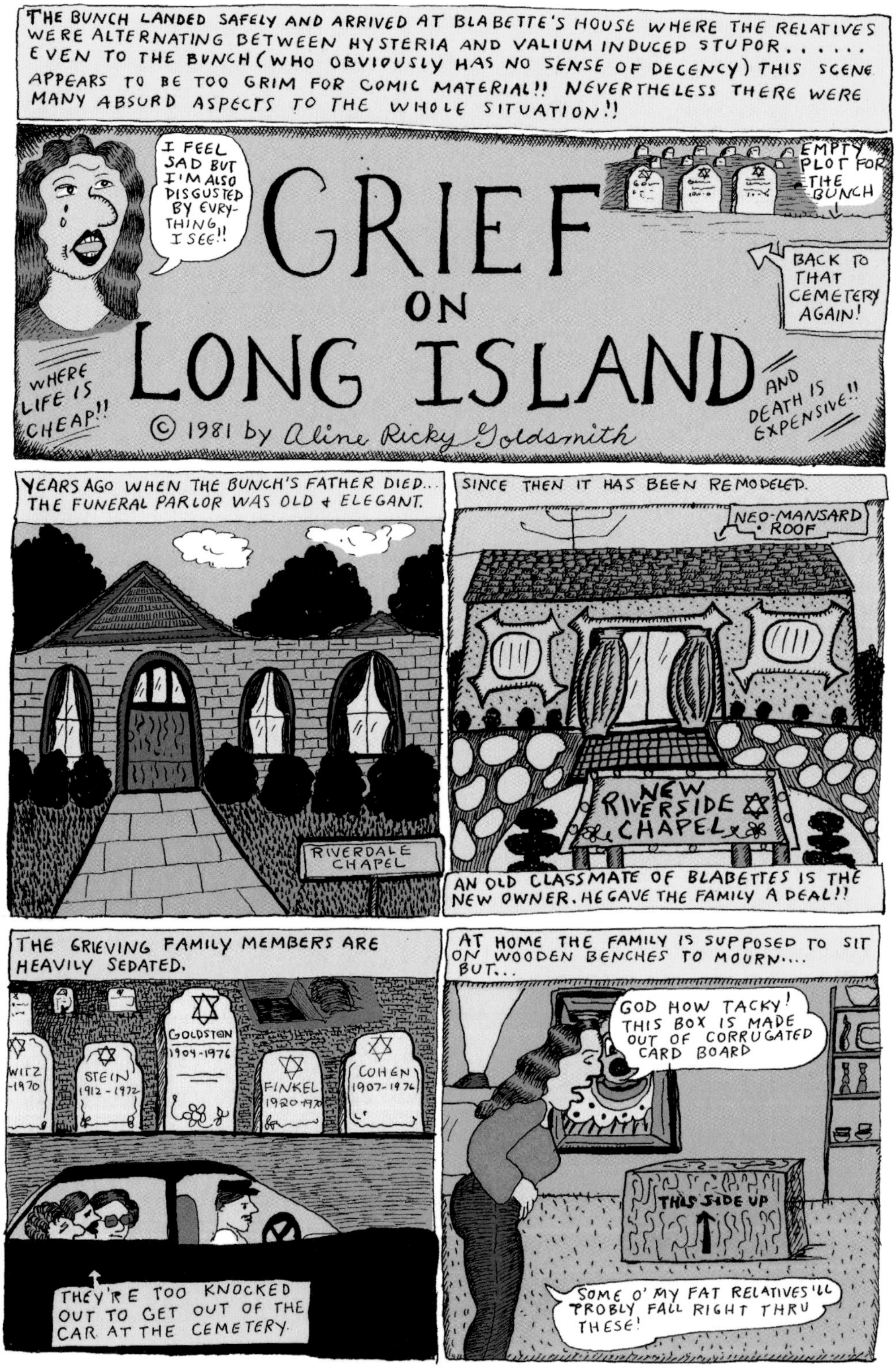
THE BUNCH LANDED SAFELY AND ARRIVED AT BLABETTE'S HOUSE WHERE THE RELATIVES WERE ALTERNATING BETWEEN HYSTERIA AND VALIUM INDUCED STUPOR..... EVEN TO THE BUNCH (WHO OBVIOUSLY HAS NO SENSE OF DECENCY) THIS SCENE APPEARS TO BE TOO GRIM FOR COMIC MATERIAL!! NEVERTHELESS THERE WERE MANY ABSURD ASPECTS TO THE WHOLE SITUATION!!
I FEEL SAD BUT I'M ALSO DISGUSTED BY EVRYTHING I SEE!!
GRIEF ON LONG ISLAND
EMPTY PLOT FOR THE BUNCH
BACK TO THAT CEMETERY AGAIN!
WHERE LIFE IS CHEAP!!
AND DEATH IS EXPENSIVE!!
© 1981 by Aline Ricky Goldsmith
YEARS AGO WHEN THE BUNCH'S FATHER DIED... THE FUNERAL PARLOR WAS OLD & ELEGANT.
RIVERDALE CHAPEL
SINCE THEN IT HAS BEEN REMODELED.
NEO-MANSARD ROOF
NEW RIVERSIDE CHAPEL
AN OLD CLASSMATE OF BLABETTES IS THE NEW OWNER. HE GAVE THE FAMILY A DEAL!!
THE GRIEVING FAMILY MEMBERS ARE HEAVILY SEDATED.
GOLDSTEN 1904-1976
STEIN 1912-1972
FINKEL 1920-1970
COHEN 1907-1976
THEY'RE TOO KNOCKED OUT TO GET OUT OF THE CAR AT THE CEMETERY.
AT HOME THE FAMILY IS SUPPOSED TO SIT ON WOODEN BENCHES TO MOURN.... BUT...
GOD HOW TACKY! THIS BOX IS MADE OUT OF CORRUGATED CARD BOARD
THIS SIDE UP
SOME O' MY FAT RELATIVES'LL PROBLY FALL RIGHT THRU THESE!

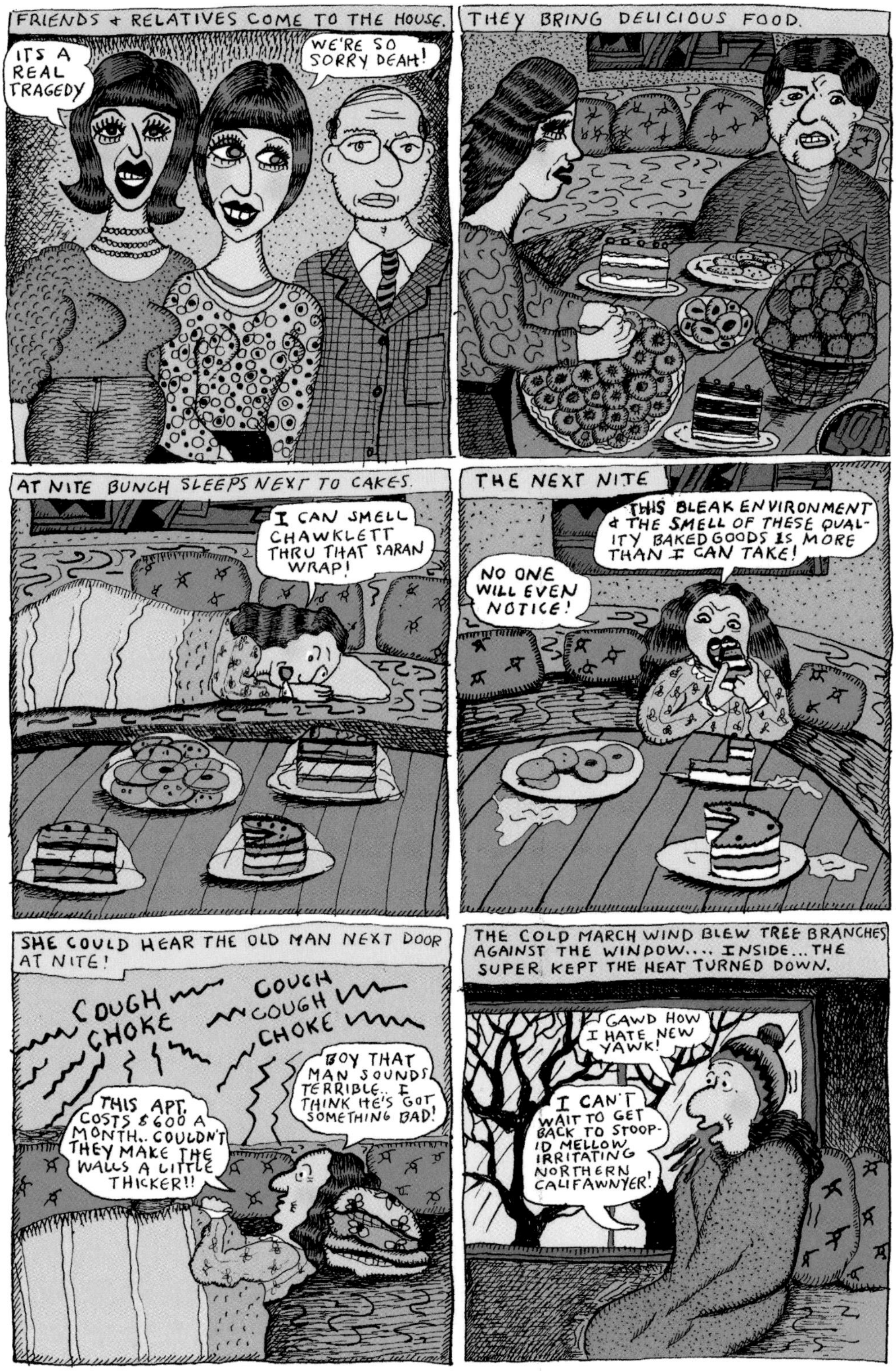
FRIENDS + RELATIVES COME TO THE HOUSE.
IT'S A REAL TRAGEDY
WE'RE SO SORRY DEAH!
THEY BRING DELICIOUS FOOD.
AT NITE BUNCH SLEEPS NEXT TO CAKES.
I CAN SMELL CHAWKLETT THRU THAT SARAN WRAP!
THE NEXT NITE
THIS BLEAK ENVIRONMENT & THE SMELL OF THESE QUALITY BAKED GOODS IS MORE THAN I CAN TAKE!
NO ONE WILL EVEN NOTICE!
SHE COULD HEAR THE OLD MAN NEXT DOOR AT NITE!
COUGH CHOKE
COUGH COUGH CHOKE
BOY THAT MAN SOUNDS TERRIBLE.. I THINK HE'S GOT SOMETHING BAD!
THIS APT. COSTS $600 A MONTH.. COULDN'T THEY MAKE THE WALLS A LITTLE THICKER!!
THE COLD MARCH WIND BLEW TREE BRANCHES AGAINST THE WINDOW.... INSIDE... THE SUPER KEPT THE HEAT TURNED DOWN.
GAWD HOW I HATE NEW YAWK!
I CAN'T WAIT TO GET BACK TO STOOPID MELLOW IRRITATING NORTHERN CALIFAWNYER!

And then came Sophia ...

On September 27th, 1981, Sophia Violet Crumb was born, and our life was forever changed. I was thirty-four years old and Robert thirty-eight, and it was the most intense psychedelic trip we had experienced thus far. It was a natural birth—Robert caught Sophie as she came flying out and it was love at first sight. He's never gotten over that. Sophie was a very fussy and demanding baby. She completely dominated our lives. We were overwhelmed, ill-prepared and totally head-over-heels in love with this little bundle of trouble.

Around this time, Robert started *Weirdo* magazine, which lasted for 27 issues, with me and Peter Bagge as alternative editors when Robert got burned out. Artists like Julie Doucet, Carol Tyler, Joe Matt and Dori Seda got their early work published in *Weirdo*. There were columns by Terry Zwigoff and Harvey Pekar, and we introduced our *Photo Funnies*, which were inspired by Mexican photo novellas that I had found at the local market. No one really liked them: they wanted more comics for their money, especially Crumb comics.

In order to make sure the artists got paid, I delivered the artwork to Ron Turner at *Last Gasp Comics* publishing house, and just waited there all day while Ron Turner ate burritos, talked on the phone and wrote a few checks now and then. I would stay until I had all the checks for the artists, and then I mailed them out immediately. There wasn't much pay to speak of, but sometimes it was a great magazine.

Right: **Robert and a heavily pregnant me**
This photograph was taken shortly before I gave birth to Sophie. I remember vividly the day I went into labor—I had no pain, just a restless kind of energy. I took a shower to relax, went outside and looked up at the sky. It was intensely blue, and I saw rainbow grid patterns and swirling bands of color exactly the same as the hallucinations I'd had on LSD. My daughter was born about 2 hours later—so fast that I barely made it to the hospital ... it's funny, but I've never heard anyone describe a similar experience about childbirth.

Next page: **Sophie one day old, September 28, 1981**

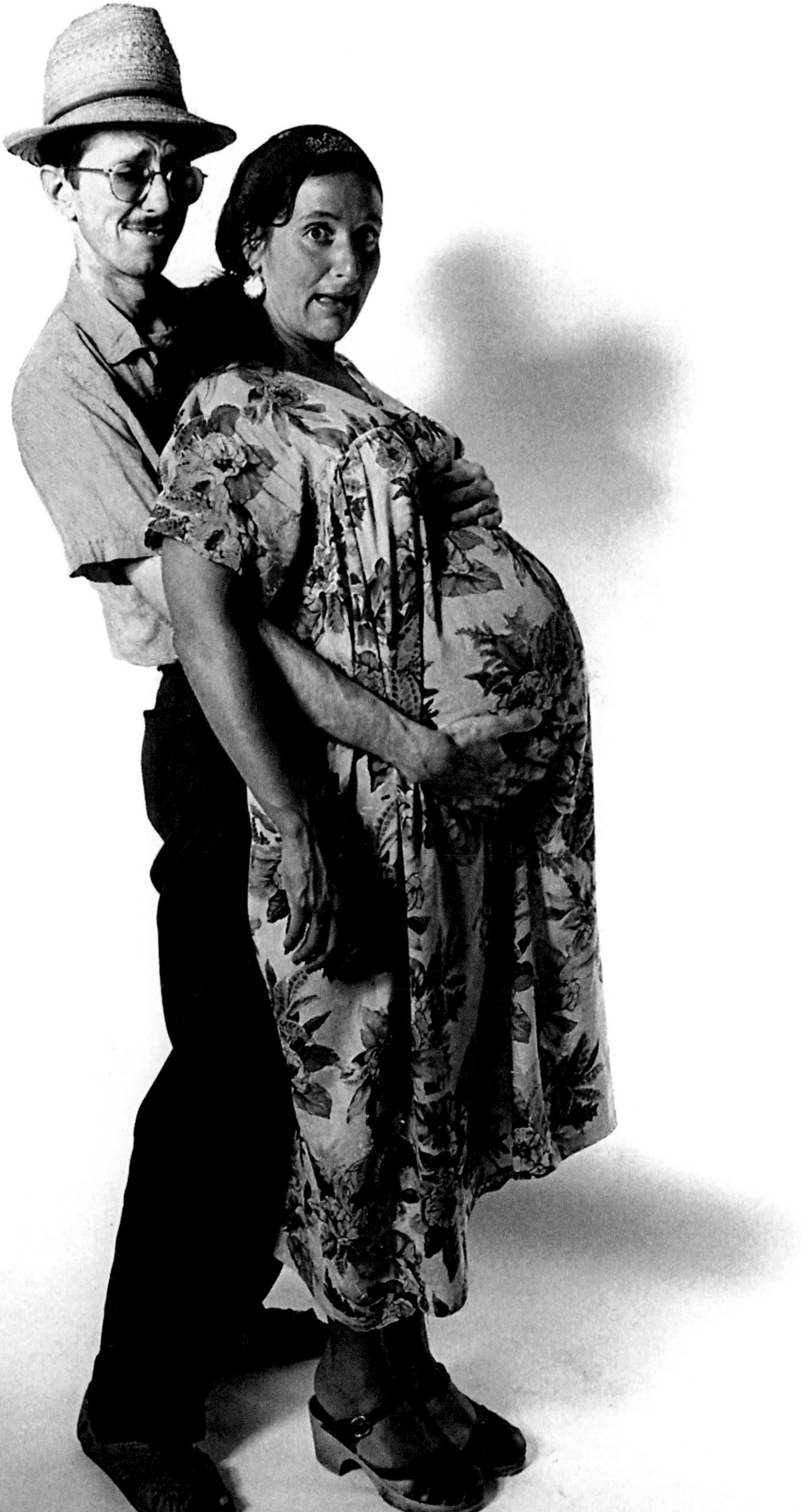

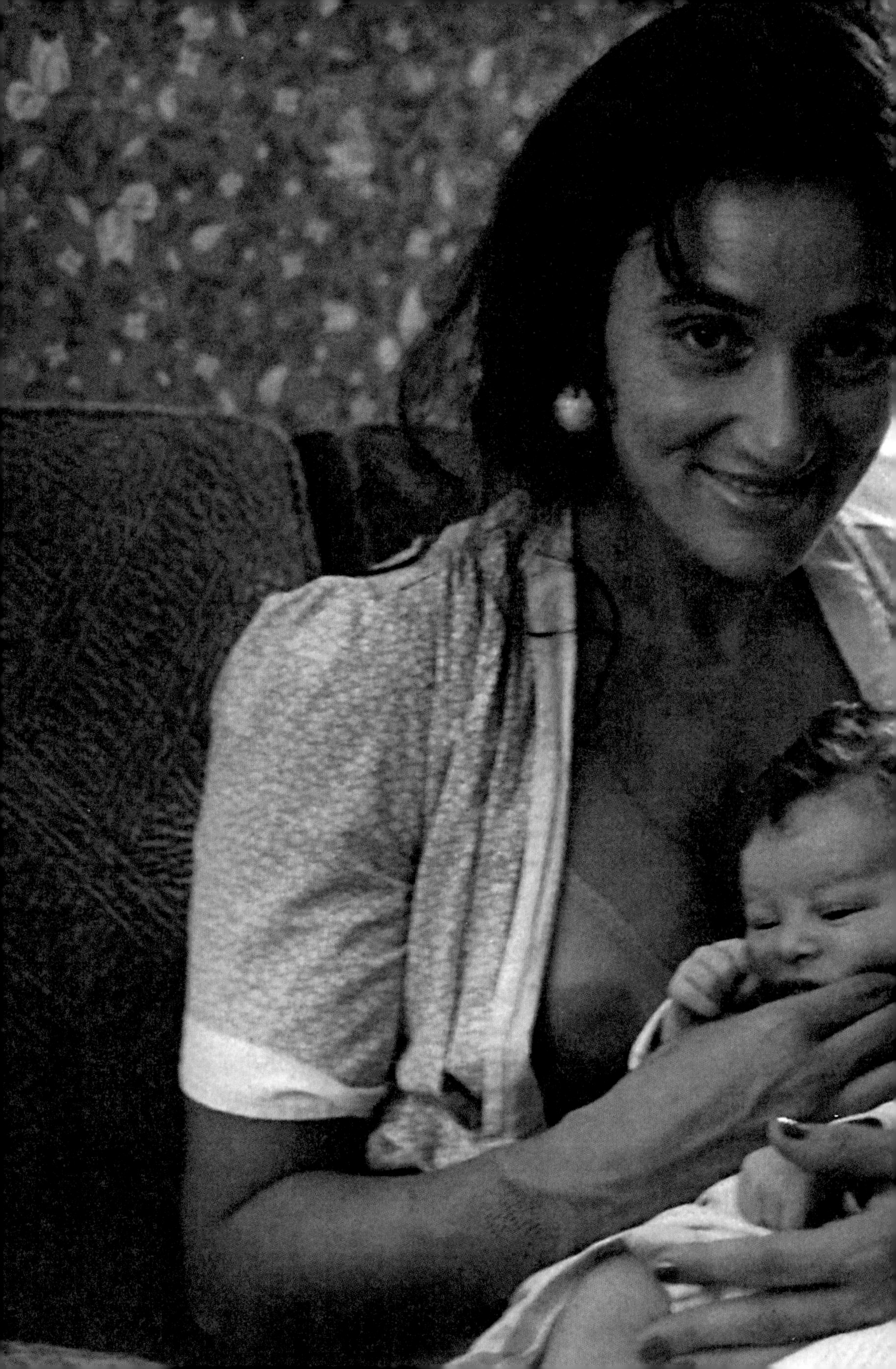

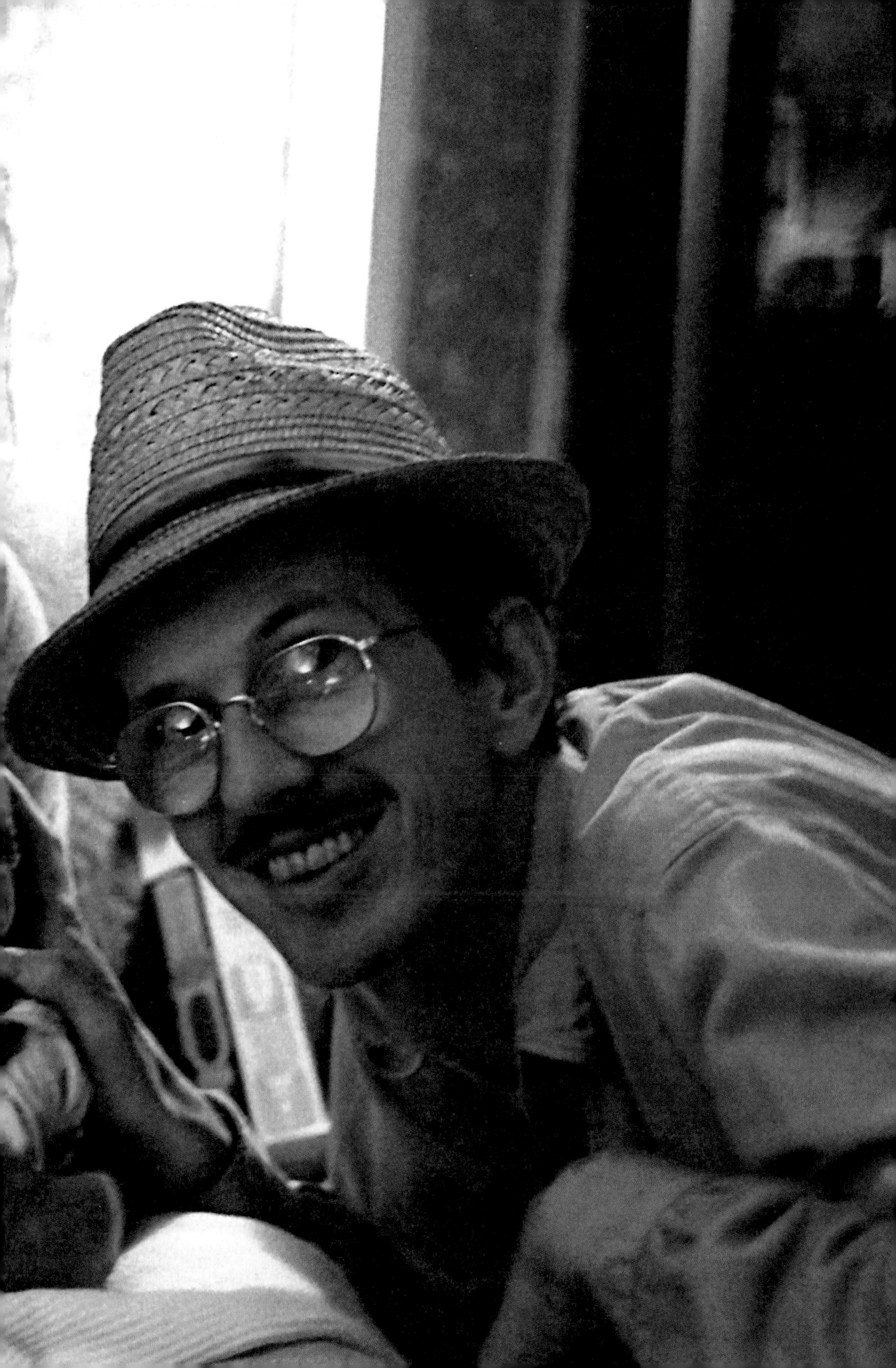

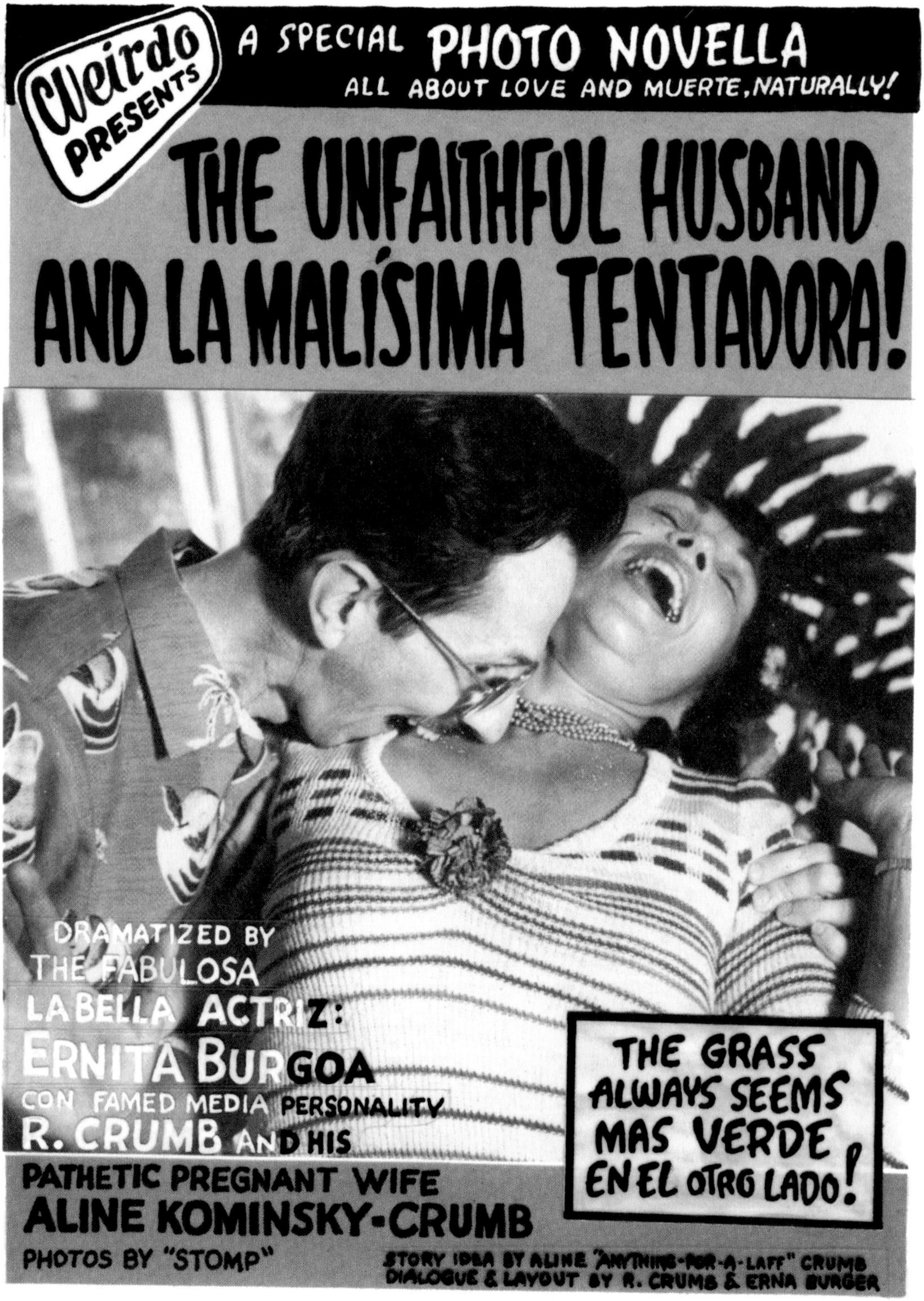
Weirdo PRESENTS
A SPECIAL PHOTO NOVELLA
ALL ABOUT LOVE AND MUERTE, NATURALLY!
THE UNFAITHFUL HUSBAND AND LA MALÍSIMA TENTADORA!
DRAMATIZED BY
THE FABULOSA
LA BELLA ACTRIZ:
ERNITA BURGOA
CON FAMED MEDIA PERSONALITY
R. CRUMB AND HIS
PATHETIC PREGNANT WIFE
ALINE KOMINSKY-CRUMB
THE GRASS ALWAYS SEEMS MAS VERDE EN EL OTRO LADO!
PHOTOS BY "STOMP"
STORY IDEA BY ALINE "ANYTHING-FOR-A-LAFF" CRUMB
DIALOGUE & LAYOUT BY R. CRUMB & ERNA BURGER

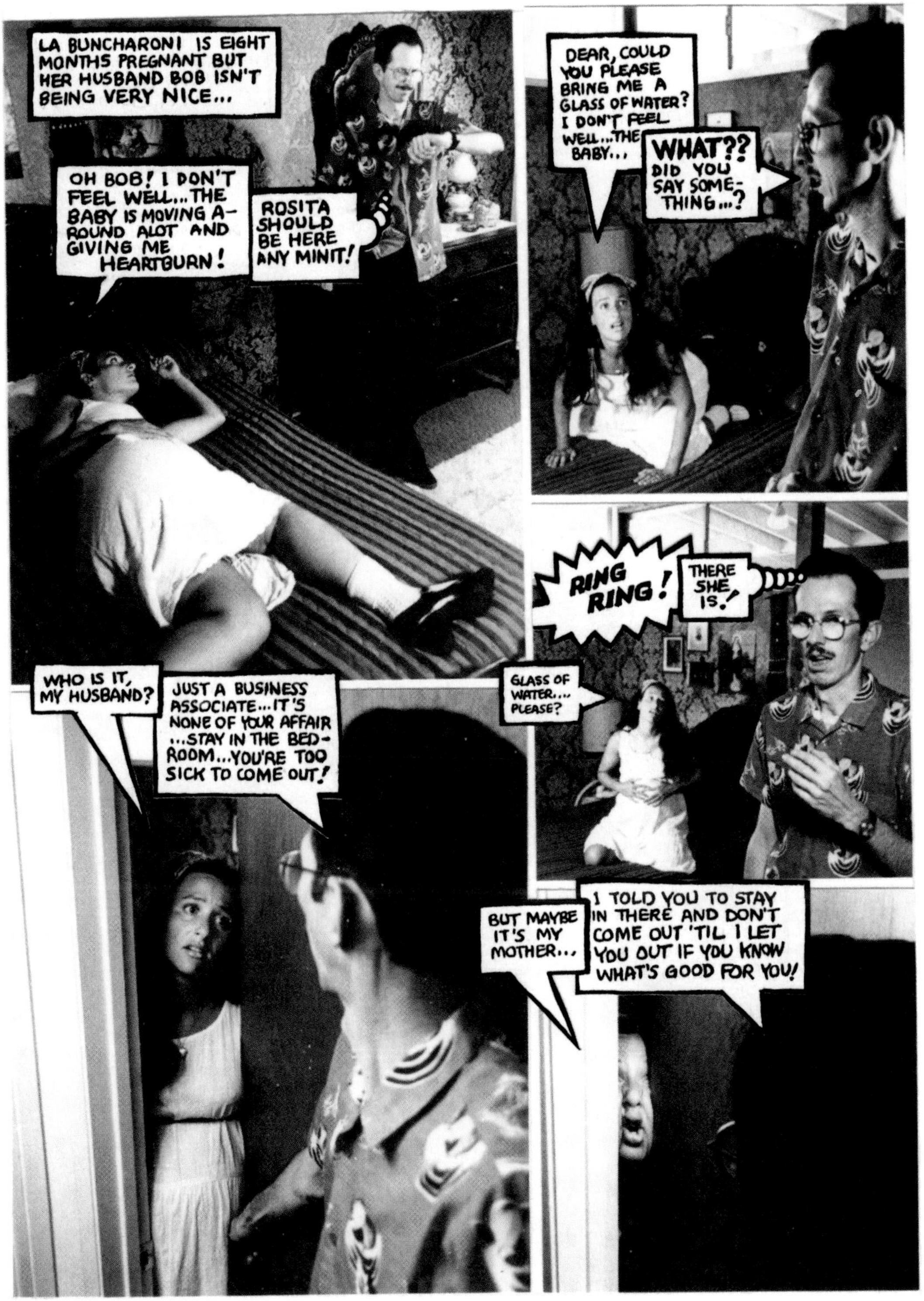

LA BUNCHARONI IS EIGHT MONTHS PREGNANT BUT HER HUSBAND BOB ISN'T BEING VERY NICE...
OH BOB! I DON'T FEEL WELL...THE BABY IS MOVING A-ROUND ALOT AND GIVING ME HEARTBURN!
ROSITA SHOULD BE HERE ANY MINIT!
DEAR, COULD YOU PLEASE BRING ME A GLASS OF WATER? I DON'T FEEL WELL...THE BABY...
WHAT?? DID YOU SAY SOME-THING...?
RING RING!
THERE SHE IS!
GLASS OF WATER... PLEASE?
WHO IS IT, MY HUSBAND?
JUST A BUSINESS ASSOCIATE...IT'S NONE OF YOUR AFFAIR ...STAY IN THE BED-ROOM...YOU'RE TOO SICK TO COME OUT!
BUT MAYBE IT'S MY MOTHER...
I TOLD YOU TO STAY IN THERE AND DON'T COME OUT 'TIL I LET YOU OUT IF YOU KNOW WHAT'S GOOD FOR YOU!

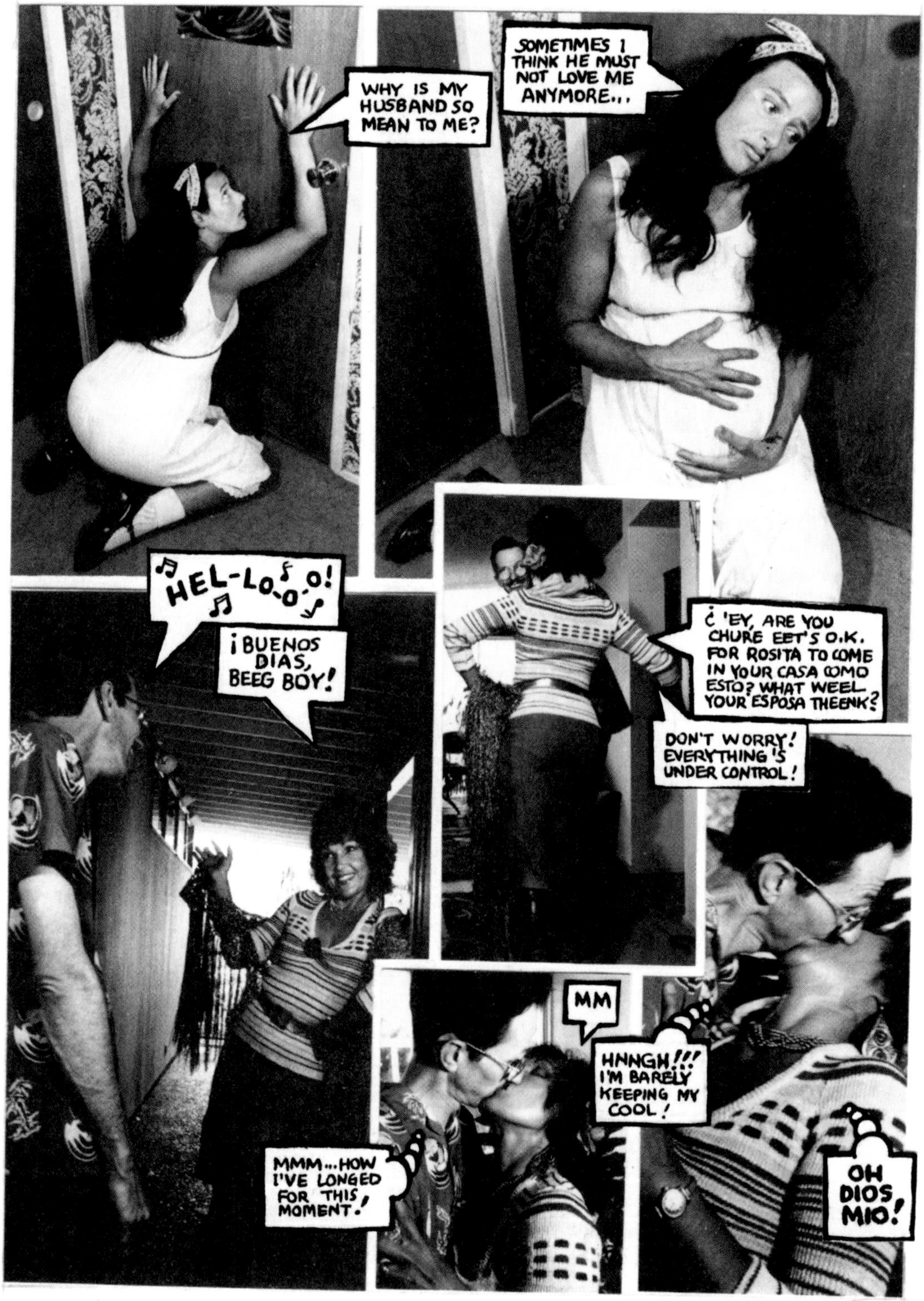
WHY IS MY HUSBAND SO MEAN TO ME?
SOMETIMES I THINK HE MUST NOT LOVE ME ANYMORE...
HEL-LO-O-O!
¡BUENOS DIAS, BEEG BOY!
¿'EY, ARE YOU CHURE EET'S O.K. FOR ROSITA TO COME IN YOUR CASA COMO ESTO? WHAT WEEL YOUR ESPOSA THEENK?
DON'T WORRY! EVERYTHING'S UNDER CONTROL!
MM
HNNGH!!! I'M BARELY KEEPING MY COOL!
MMM... HOW I'VE LONGED FOR THIS MOMENT!
OH DIOS MIO!

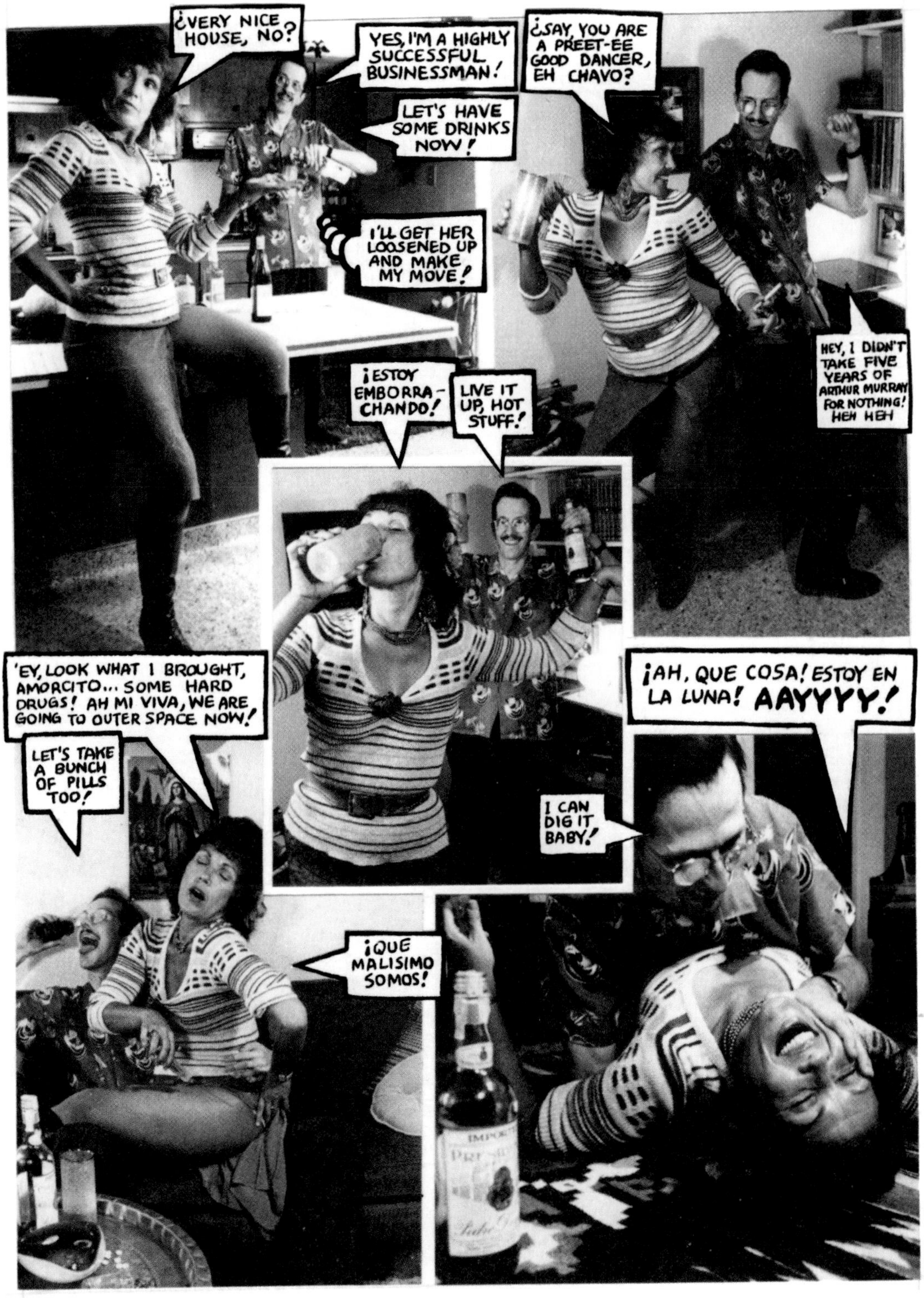
¿VERY NICE HOUSE, NO?
YES, I'M A HIGHLY SUCCESSFUL BUSINESSMAN!
LET'S HAVE SOME DRINKS NOW!
I'LL GET HER LOOSENED UP AND MAKE MY MOVE!
¿SAY, YOU ARE A PREET-EE GOOD DANCER, EH CHAVO?
HEY, I DIDN'T TAKE FIVE YEARS OF ARTHUR MURRAY FOR NOTHING! HEH HEH
¡ESTOY EMBORRA-CHANDO!
LIVE IT UP, HOT STUFF!
'EY, LOOK WHAT I BROUGHT, AMORCITO... SOME HARD DRUGS! AH MI VIVA, WE ARE GOING TO OUTER SPACE NOW!
LET'S TAKE A BUNCH OF PILLS TOO!
¡QUE MALISIMO SOMOS!
¡AH, QUE COSA! ESTOY EN LA LUNA! AAYYYY!
I CAN DIG IT BABY!

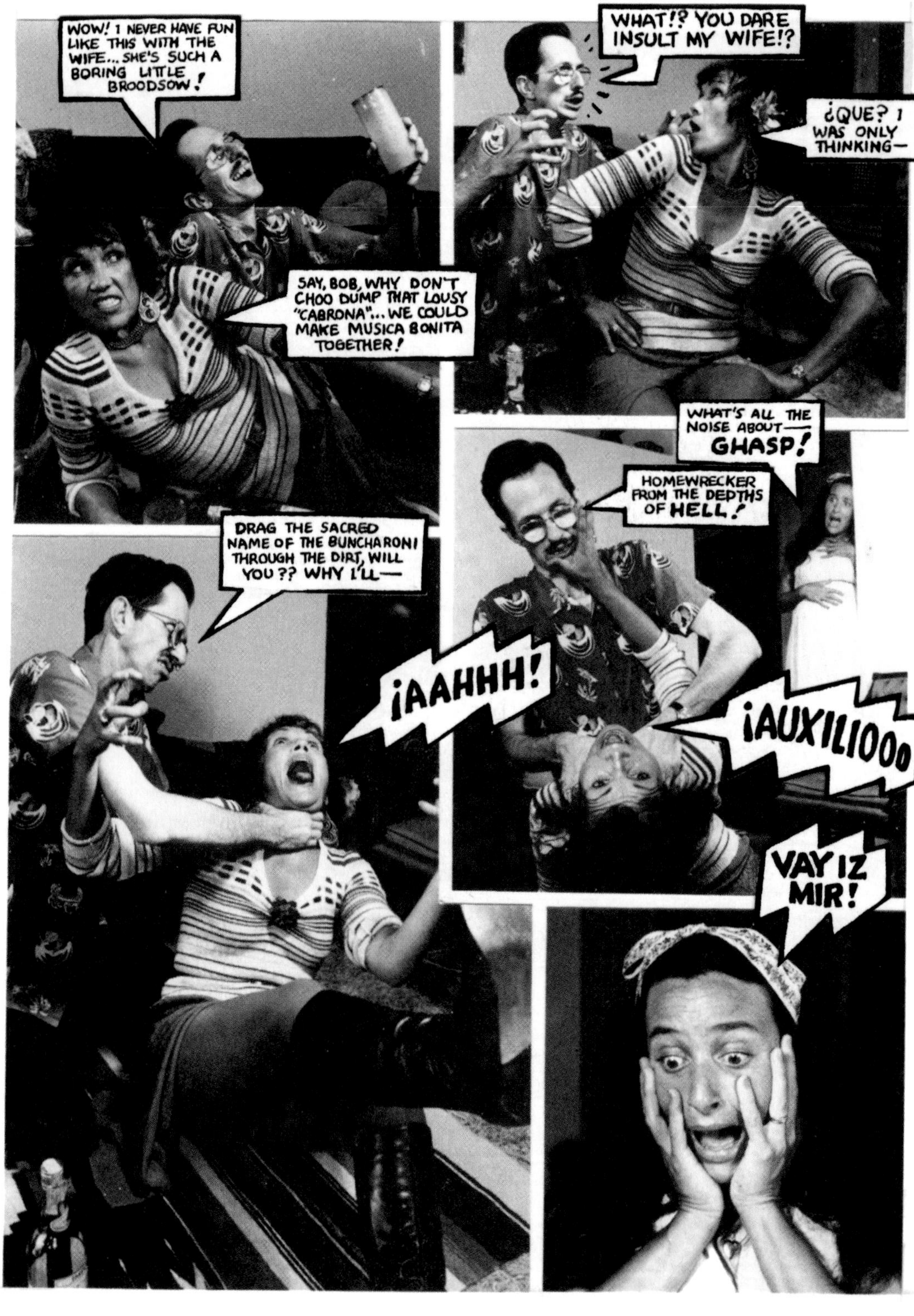
WOW! I NEVER HAVE FUN LIKE THIS WITH THE WIFE... SHE'S SUCH A BORING LITTLE BROODSOW!
SAY, BOB, WHY DON'T CHOO DUMP THAT LOUSY "CABRONA"... WE COULD MAKE MUSICA BONITA TOGETHER!
WHAT!? YOU DARE INSULT MY WIFE!?
¿QUE? I WAS ONLY THINKING—
DRAG THE SACRED NAME OF THE BUNCHARONI THROUGH THE DIRT, WILL YOU?? WHY I'LL—
¡AAHHH!
WHAT'S ALL THE NOISE ABOUT— GHASP!
HOMEWRECKER FROM THE DEPTHS OF HELL!
¡AUXILIOOO
VAY IZ MIR!

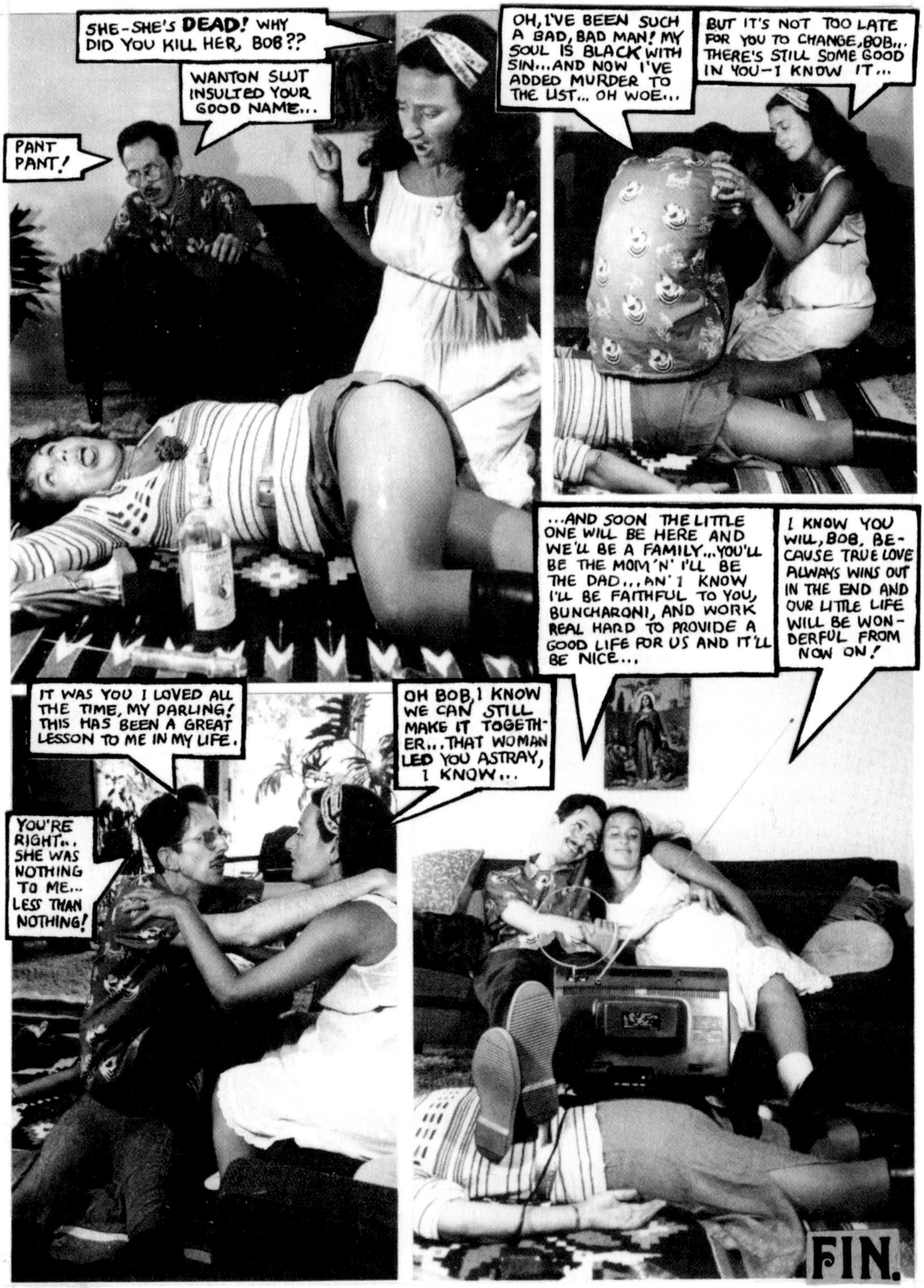
SHE-SHE'S **DEAD!** WHY DID YOU KILL HER, BOB??
WANTON SLUT INSULTED YOUR GOOD NAME...
PANT PANT!
OH, I'VE BEEN SUCH A BAD, BAD MAN! MY SOUL IS **BLACK** WITH SIN... AND NOW I'VE ADDED MURDER TO THE LIST... OH WOE...
BUT IT'S NOT TOO LATE FOR YOU TO CHANGE, BOB... THERE'S STILL SOME GOOD IN YOU—I KNOW IT...
IT WAS YOU I LOVED ALL THE TIME, MY DARLING! THIS HAS BEEN A GREAT LESSON TO ME IN MY LIFE.
OH BOB, I KNOW WE CAN STILL MAKE IT TOGETH-ER... THAT WOMAN LED YOU ASTRAY, I KNOW...
YOU'RE RIGHT... SHE WAS NOTHING TO ME... LESS THAN NOTHING!
...AND SOON THE LITTLE ONE WILL BE HERE AND WE'LL BE A FAMILY... YOU'LL BE THE MOM 'N' I'LL BE THE DAD... AN' I KNOW I'LL BE FAITHFUL TO YOU, BUNCHARONI, AND WORK REAL HARD TO PROVIDE A GOOD LIFE FOR US AND IT'LL BE NICE...
I KNOW YOU WILL, BOB, BE-CAUSE TRUE LOVE ALWAYS WINS OUT IN THE END AND OUR LITTLE LIFE WILL BE WON-DERFUL FROM NOW ON!
FIN.

Left: **Four generations, 1981**
Me, my mother and Grandma Fanny holding
Sophie, who is two weeks old.

Below: **Terry Zwigoff holding Sophie**
He looks horrified! He had told me not to have
a kid!

Right: **Sophie and Robert with** *Weirdo*
Magazine, 1982
This picture was taken for *People Magazine.*

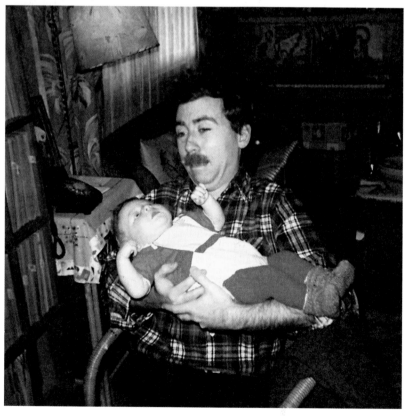

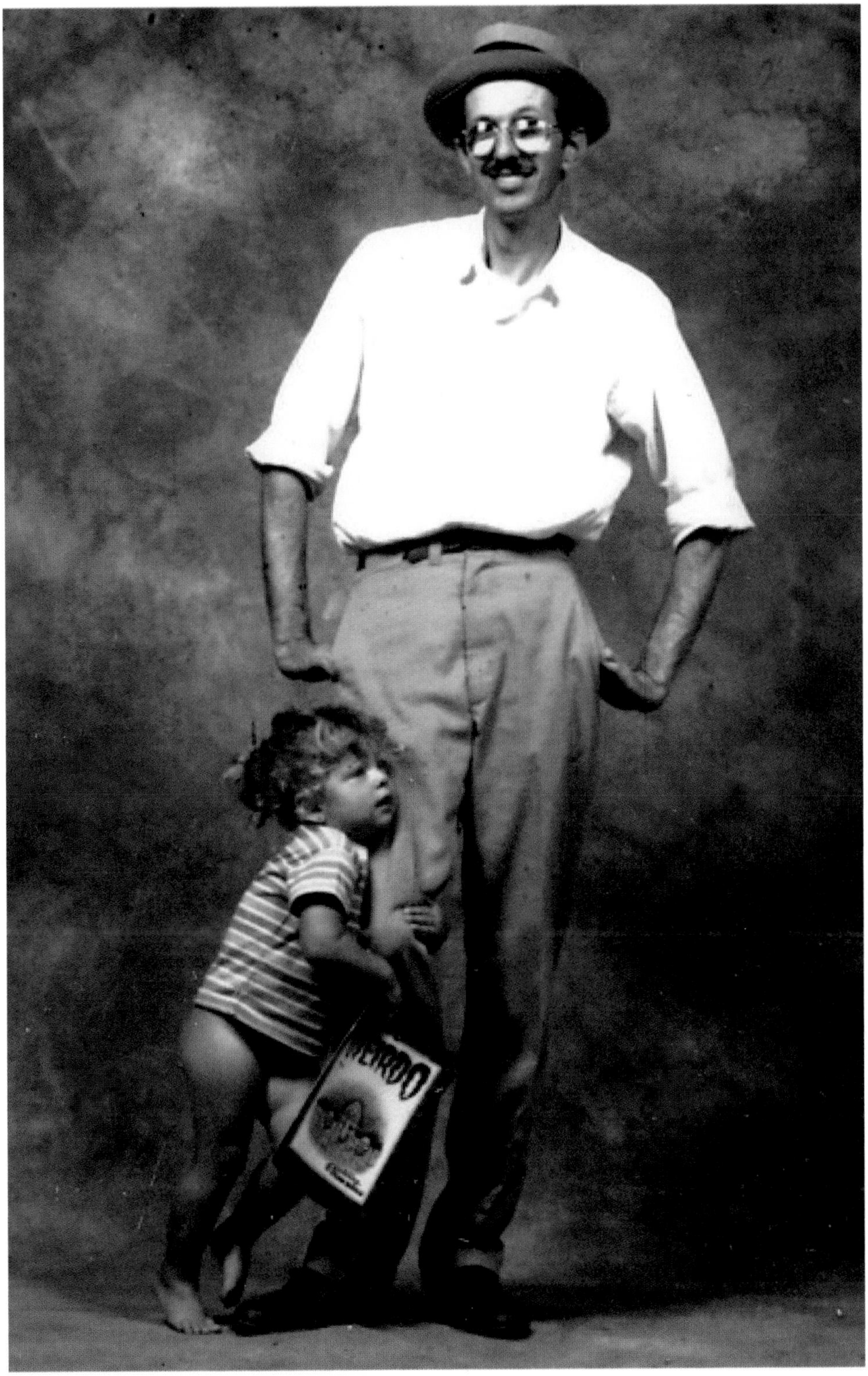

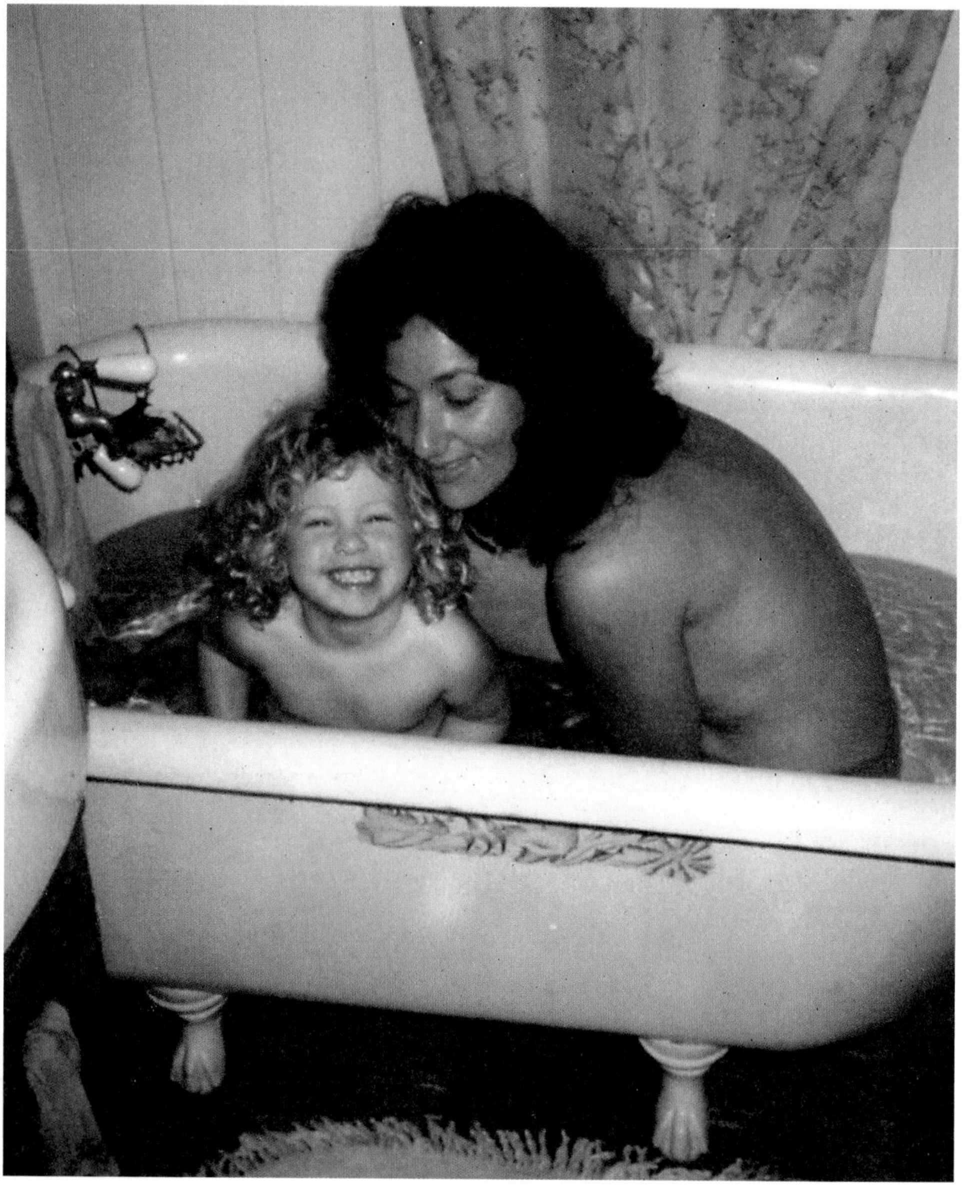

Above: **Bathing Beauties, 1983**
Right: Me and Sophie in our house in Winters, California

Next pages: **Portraits in oil paint of Sophie and Robert**

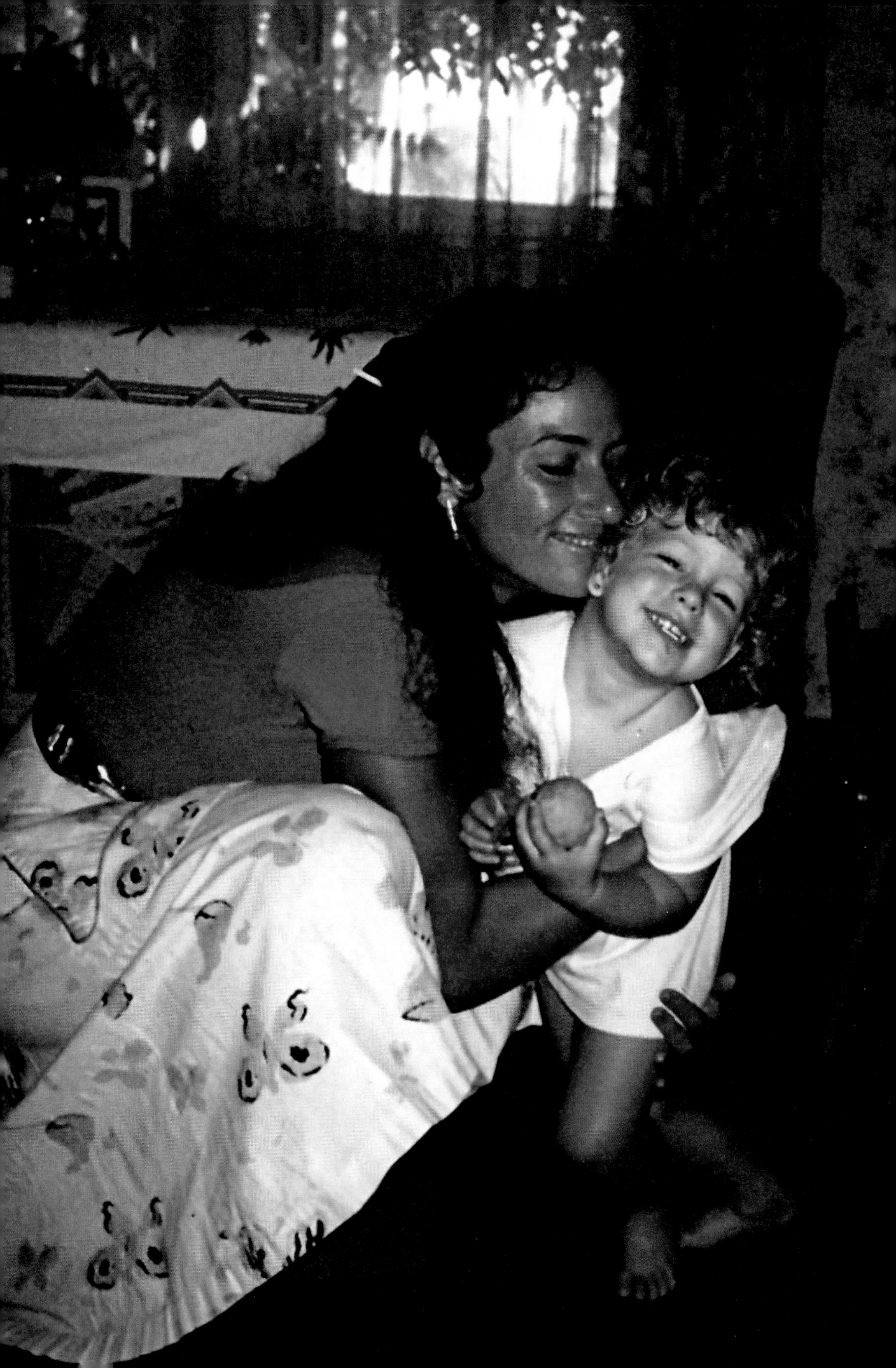

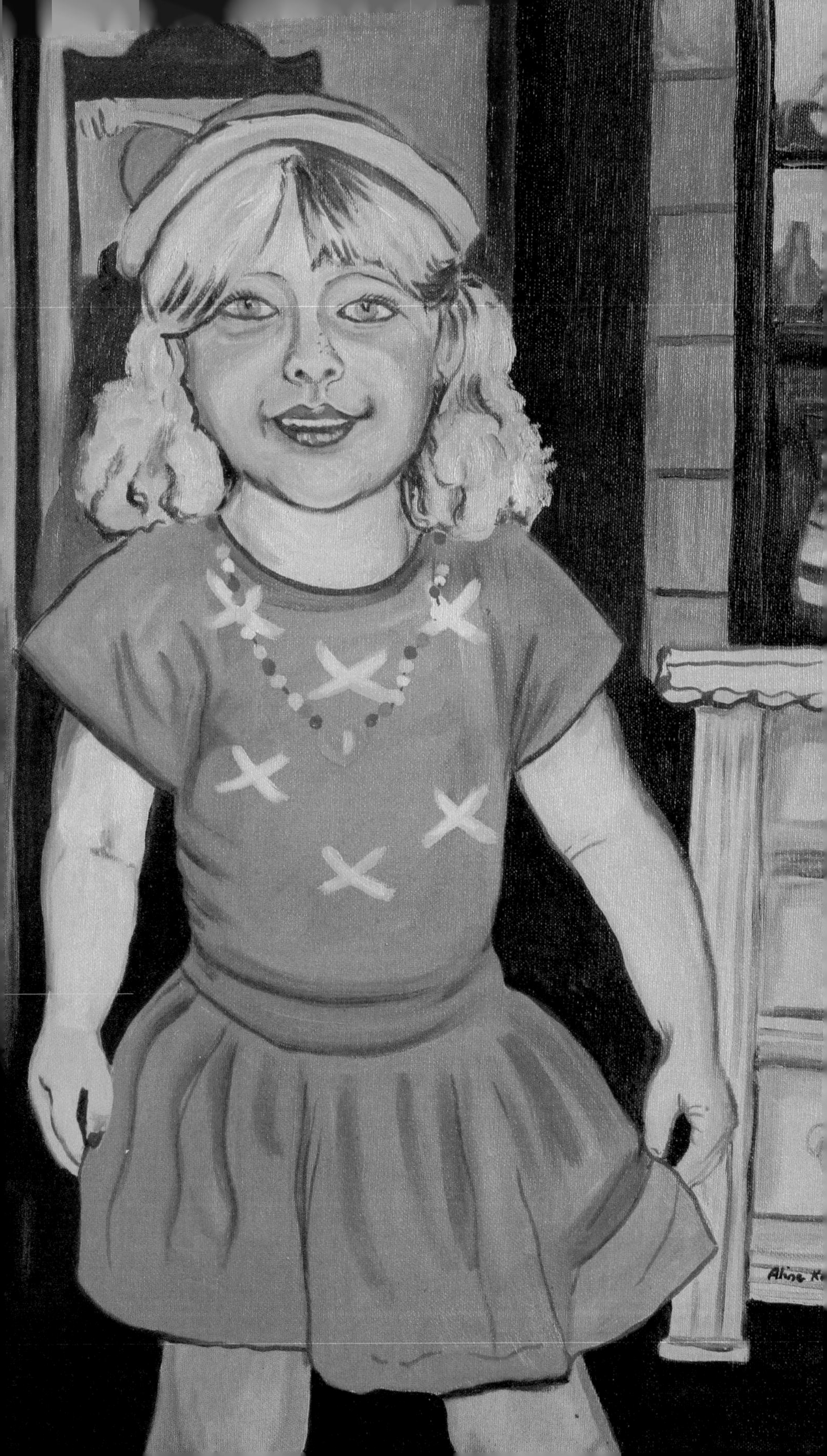

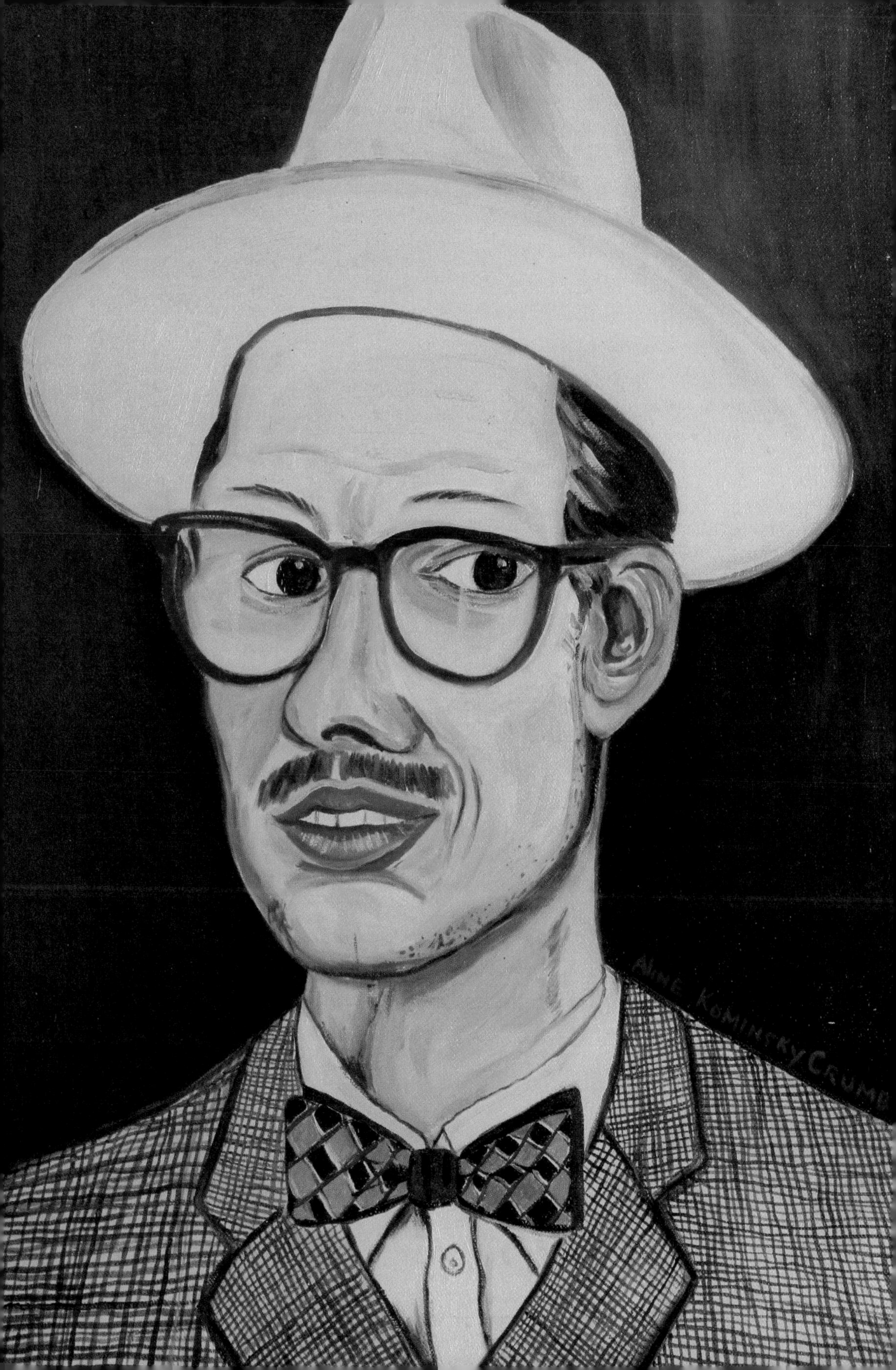
ALINE KOMINSKY CRUMB

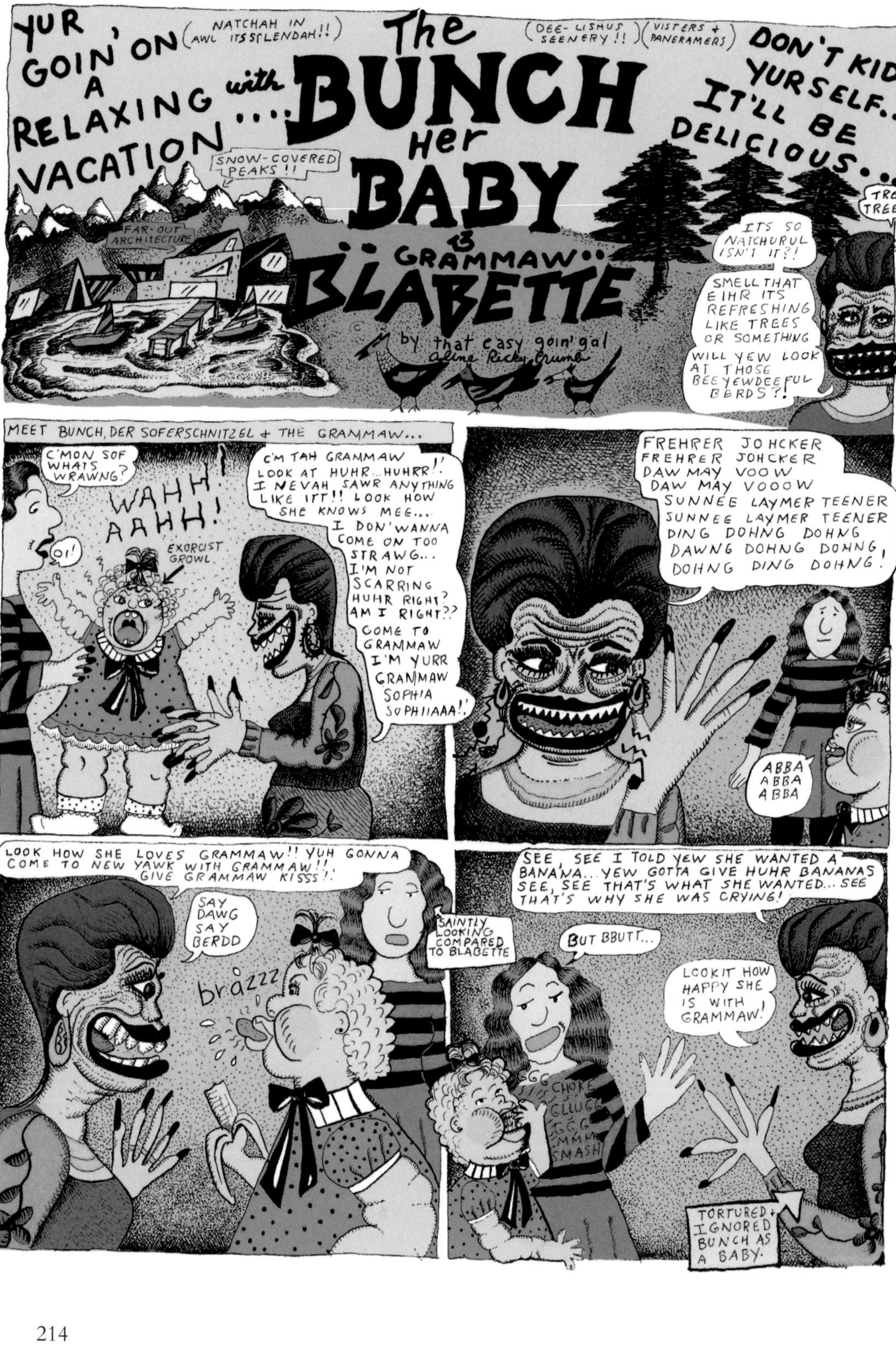

YUR GOIN' ON A RELAXING VACATION....
(NATCHAH IN AWL ITS SPLENDAH!!)
The BUNCH with Her BABY & GRAMMAW.. BLABETTE
(DEE-LISHUS SEENERY!!)
(VISTERS + PANERAMERS)
DON'T KID YURSELF.. IT'LL BE DELICIOUS...
SNOW-COVERED PEAKS!!
FAR-OUT ARCHITECTURE
TREES TREES
ITS SO NATCHURUL ISN'T IT?!
SMELL THAT EIHR ITS REFRESHING LIKE TREES OR SOMETHING
WILL YEW LOOK AT THOSE BEEYEWDEEFUL BERDS?!
by that easy goin' gal Aline Ricky Crumb
MEET BUNCH, DER SOFERSCHNITZEL + THE GRAMMAW...
C'MON SOF WHATS WRAWNG?
WAHH! AAHH!
OI!
EXORCIST GROWL
C'M TAH GRAMMAW!! LOOK AT HUHR.. HUHRR!! I NEVAH SAWR ANYTHING LIKE ITT!! LOOK HOW SHE KNOWS MEE... I DON'WANNA COME ON TOO STRAWG... I'M NOT SCARRING HUHR RIGHT? AM I RIGHT?? COME TO GRAMMAW I'M YURR GRAMMAW SOPHIA SOPHIAAA!!
FREHRER JOHCKER FREHRER JOHCKER DAW MAY VOOW DAW MAY VOOOW SUNNEE LAYMER TEENER SUNNEE LAYMER TEENER DING DOHNG DOHNG DAWNG DOHNG DOHNG, DOHNG DING DOHNG!
ABBA ABBA ABBA
LOOK HOW SHE LOVES GRAMMAW!! YUH GONNA COME TO NEW YAWK WITH GRAMMAW!! GIVE GRAMMAW KISSS!!
SAY DAWG SAY BERDD
SAINTLY LOOKING COMPARED TO BLABETTE
brazzz
SEE, SEE I TOLD YEW SHE WANTED A BANANA... YEW GOTTA GIVE HUHR BANANAS SEE, SEE THAT'S WHAT SHE WANTED... SEE THAT'S WHY SHE WAS CRYING!
BUT BBUTT...
LOOKIT HOW HAPPY SHE IS WITH GRAMMAW!
CHOKE GLLUGG GGG MMM SMASH
TORTURED + IGNORED BUNCH AS A BABY.

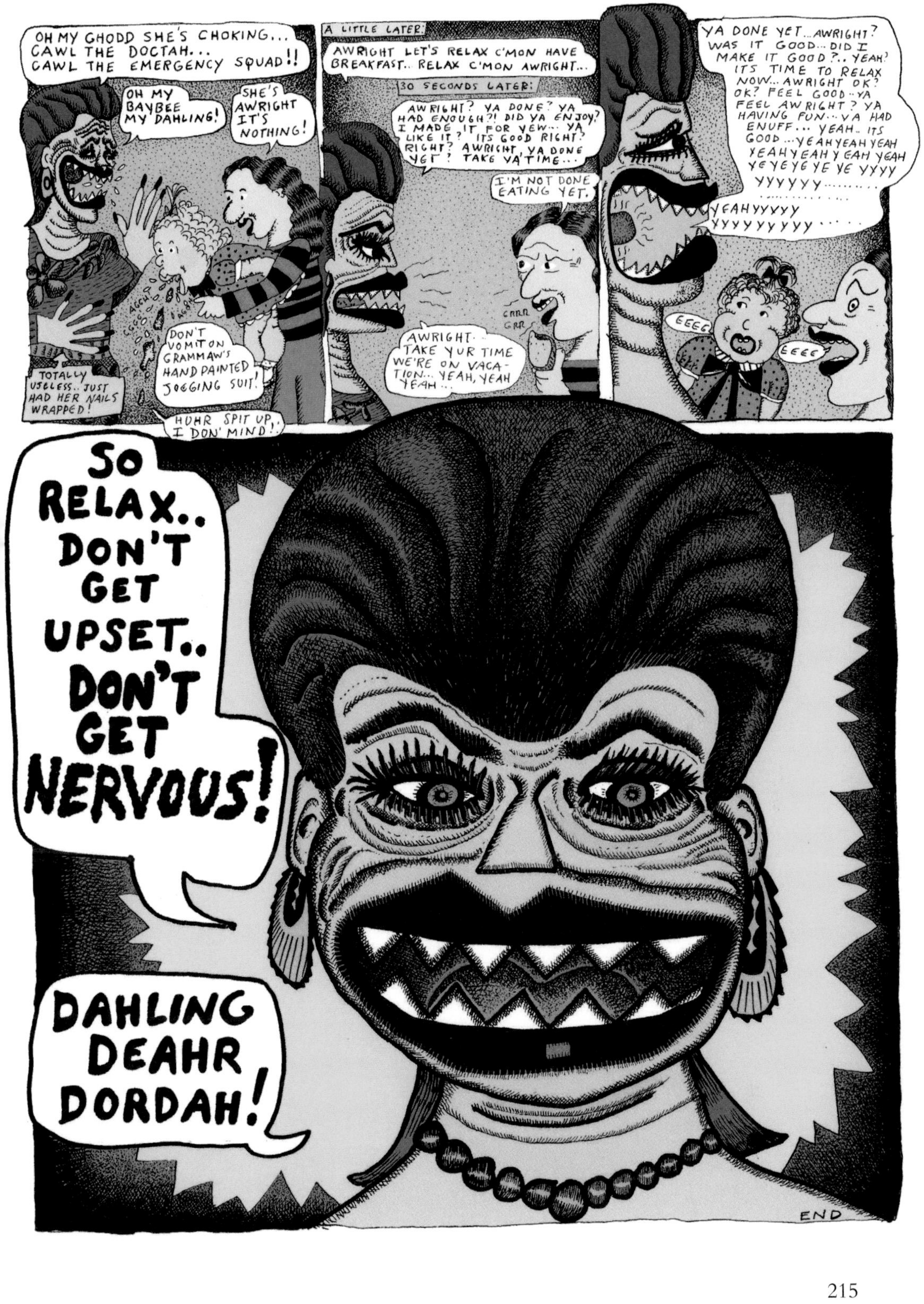

OH MY GHODD SHE'S CHOKING... CAWL THE DOCTAH... CAWL THE EMERGENCY SQUAD!!
OH MY BAYBEE MY DAHLING!
SHE'S AWRIGHT IT'S NOTHING!
AGCH
CGCG
AGGH
DON'T VOMIT ON GRAMMAW'S HAND PAINTED JOGGING SUIT!
TOTALLY USELESS.. JUST HAD HER NAILS WRAPPED!
HUHR SPIT UP, I DON' MIND!
A LITTLE LATER:
AWRIGHT LET'S RELAX C'MON HAVE BREAKFAST.. RELAX C'MON AWRIGHT...
30 SECONDS LATER:
AWRIGHT? YA DONE? YA HAD ENOUGH?! DID YA ENJOY? I MADE IT FOR YEW... YA LIKE IT? ITS GOOD RIGHT? RIGHT? AWRIGHT, YA DONE YET? TAKE YA'TIME...
I'M NOT DONE EATING YET.
GRRR GRR
AWRIGHT.. TAKE YUR TIME WE'RE ON VACA-TION... YEAH, YEAH YEAH...
YA DONE YET...AWRIGHT? WAS IT GOOD...DID I MAKE IT GOOD?.. YEAH? ITS TIME TO RELAX NOW... AWRIGHT OK? OK? FEEL GOOD..YA FEEL AWRIGHT? YA HAVING FUN...YA HAD ENUFF... YEAH.. ITS GOOD ...YEAH YEAH YEAH YEAH YEAH YEAH YEAH YE YE YE YE YE YYYY YYYYYY........ YEAHYYYYY YYYYYYYYY.....
EEEG
EEEG
SO RELAX.. DON'T GET UPSET.. DON'T GET NERVOUS!
DAHLING DEAHR DORDAH!
END

Desperate housewife!

When Sophie was four, I went to Paris for the second time to take care of some business for Robert while he stayed home and looked after her. It was my first trip alone since Sophie was born, and it was to catapult me out of the "Desperate Housewife" syndrome into which I had been slowly sinking: I had become a station wagon driving, racquet ball club member mom, hanging around with other mothers with whom I had little in common beyond the fact that our kids were the same age and got along. I couldn't concentrate on art too much, so I was teaching exercise classes and drinking a lot of white wine.

In Paris, I collapsed on the street and wept at the sudden realization of what I was becoming. The beauty of the city somehow brought me out of my creative limbo. I made certain promises to myself and I kept most of them. I also began the first of several important extramarital love affairs: I called the German politician I had met eight years earlier in Hamburg and said "I'm here, so we can have our love affair now." I think he was surprised but not displeased. I only saw this man a few times afterwards, but it made good fantasy material. I bought some sexy shoes and black silk Dior underwear. I lost my appetite for food, except for alcohol and chocolate.

I met and charmed Robert's publishers, and miraculously collected $8,000 owed to him. I returned home much happier with my improved inner self; however, I was never quite as satisfied again with my little life in the Big Valley. When I unpacked, I realized that someone had been in my closet and tried on my clothes. I confronted Robert, and he confessed that he had had an affair with my ex-best friend Mary. I forgave him, but not her. I forgave her for sleeping with my husband, but not for snooping in my closet!

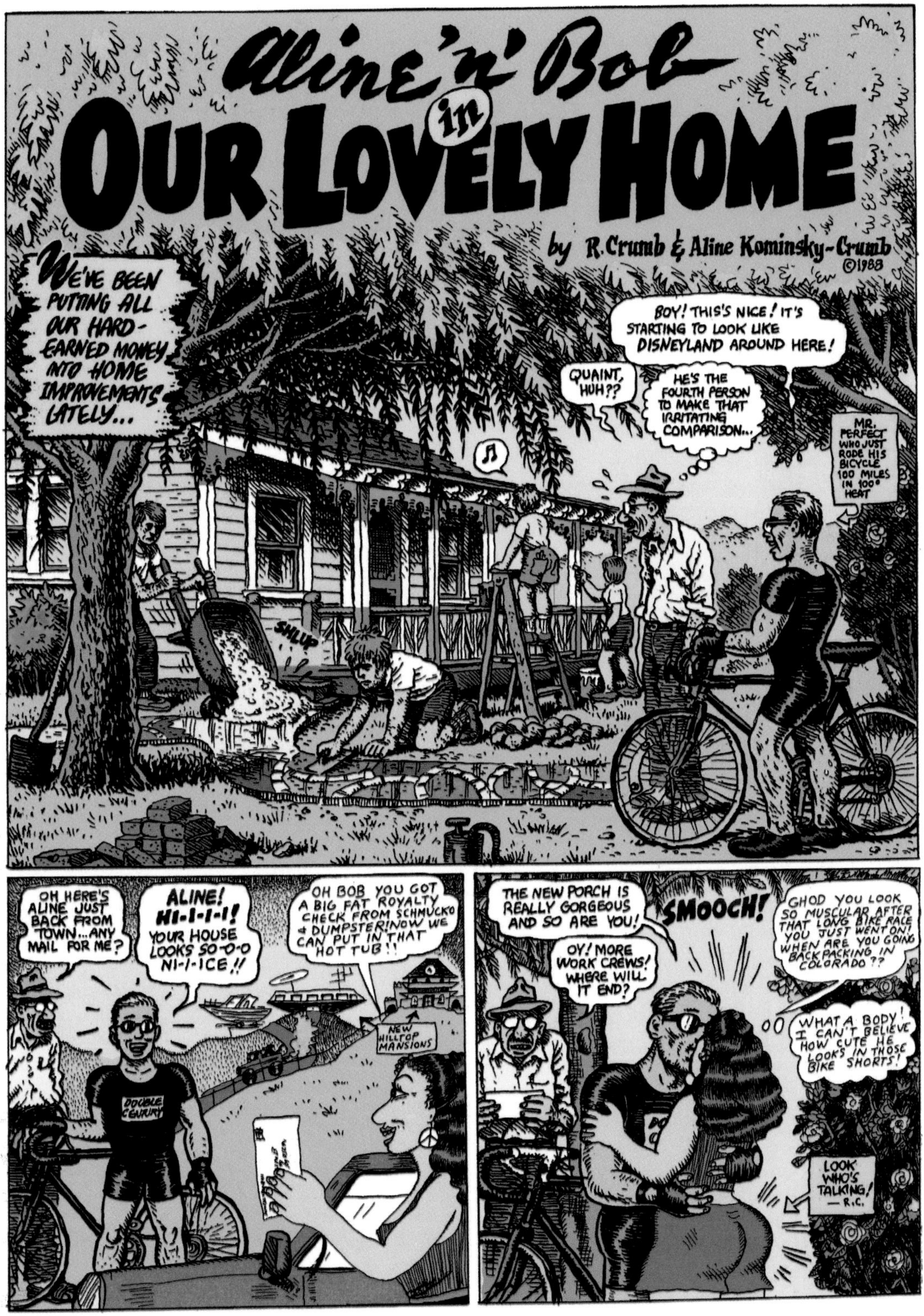
Aline 'n' Bob
in
OUR LOVELY HOME
by R. Crumb & Aline Kominsky-Crumb ©1988
WE'VE BEEN PUTTING ALL OUR HARD-EARNED MONEY INTO HOME IMPROVEMENTS LATELY...
BOY! THIS'S NICE! IT'S STARTING TO LOOK LIKE DISNEYLAND AROUND HERE!
QUAINT, HUH??
HE'S THE FOURTH PERSON TO MAKE THAT IRRITATING COMPARISON...
MR. PERFECT WHO JUST RODE HIS BICYCLE 100 MILES IN 100° HEAT
SHLUP
OH HERE'S ALINE JUST BACK FROM TOWN... ANY MAIL FOR ME?
ALINE! HI-I-I-I! YOUR HOUSE LOOKS SO-O-O NI-I-ICE!!
OH BOB YOU GOT A BIG FAT ROYALTY CHECK FROM SCHMUCKO & DUMPSTER! NOW WE CAN PUT IN THAT HOT TUB!!
NEW HILLTOP MANSIONS
DOUBLE CENTURY
THE NEW PORCH IS REALLY GORGEOUS AND SO ARE YOU!
SMOOCH!
OY! MORE WORK CREWS! WHERE WILL IT END?
GHOD YOU LOOK SO MUSCULAR AFTER THAT LONG BIKE RACE YOU JUST WENT ON! WHEN ARE YOU GOING BACKPACKING IN COLORADO??
WHAT A BODY! I CAN'T BELIEVE HOW CUTE HE LOOKS IN THOSE BIKE SHORTS!
LOOK WHO'S TALKING! —R.C.

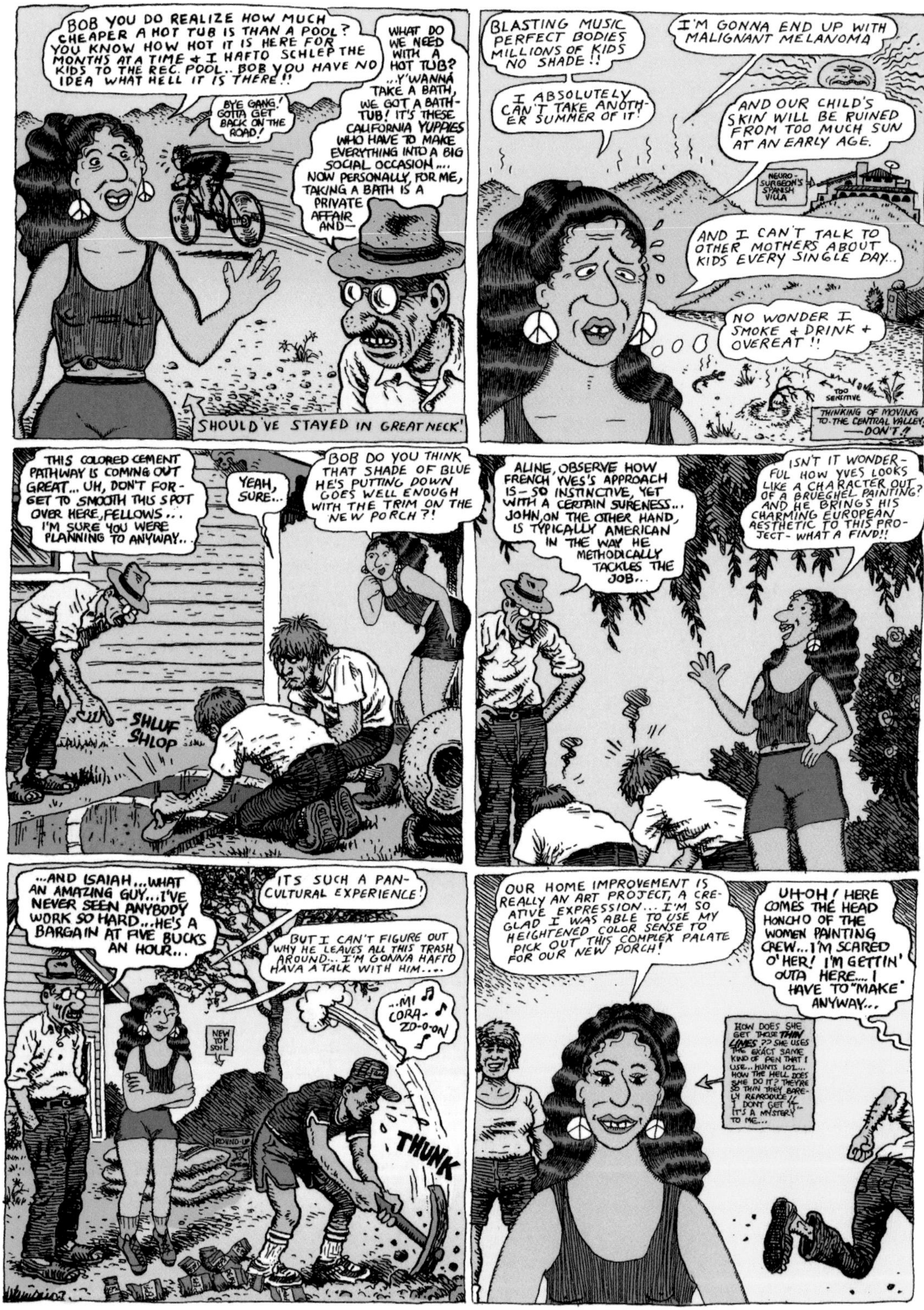
BOB YOU DO REALIZE HOW MUCH CHEAPER A HOT TUB IS THAN A POOL? YOU KNOW HOW HOT IT IS HERE FOR MONTHS AT A TIME & I HAFTO SCHLEP THE KIDS TO THE REC. POOL.. BOB YOU HAVE NO IDEA WHAT HELL IT IS THERE!!
BYE GANG! GOTTA GET BACK ON THE ROAD!
WHAT DO WE NEED WITH A HOT TUB? ..Y'WANNA TAKE A BATH, WE GOT A BATH-TUB! IT'S THESE CALIFORNIA YUPPIES WHO HAVE TO MAKE EVERYTHING INTO A BIG SOCIAL OCCASION.... NOW PERSONALLY, FOR ME, TAKING A BATH IS A PRIVATE AFFAIR AND—
SHOULD'VE STAYED IN GREAT NECK!
BLASTING MUSIC PERFECT BODIES MILLIONS OF KIDS NO SHADE!!
I ABSOLUTELY CAN'T TAKE ANOTHER SUMMER OF IT!
I'M GONNA END UP WITH MALIGNANT MELANOMA
AND OUR CHILD'S SKIN WILL BE RUINED FROM TOO MUCH SUN AT AN EARLY AGE.
NEURO-SURGEON'S SPANISH VILLA
AND I CAN'T TALK TO OTHER MOTHERS ABOUT KIDS EVERY SINGLE DAY...
NO WONDER I SMOKE & DRINK + OVEREAT!!
TOO SENSITIVE
THINKING OF MOVING TO THE CENTRAL VALLEY? —DON'T!!
THIS COLORED CEMENT PATHWAY IS COMING OUT GREAT... UH, DON'T FORGET TO SMOOTH THIS SPOT OVER HERE, FELLOWS.. I'M SURE YOU WERE PLANNING TO ANYWAY..
YEAH, SURE...
BOB DO YOU THINK THAT SHADE OF BLUE HE'S PUTTING DOWN GOES WELL ENOUGH WITH THE TRIM ON THE NEW PORCH?!
SHLUF SHLOP
ALINE, OBSERVE HOW FRENCH YVES'S APPROACH IS—SO INSTINCTIVE, YET WITH A CERTAIN SURENESS... JOHN, ON THE OTHER HAND, IS TYPICALLY AMERICAN IN THE WAY HE METHODICALLY TACKLES THE JOB...
ISN'T IT WONDERFUL HOW YVES LOOKS LIKE A CHARACTER OUT OF A BRUEGHEL PAINTING? AND HE BRINGS HIS CHARMING EUROPEAN AESTHETIC TO THIS PROJECT- WHAT A FIND!!
...AND ISAIAH... WHAT AN AMAZING GUY... I'VE NEVER SEEN ANYBODY WORK SO HARD... HE'S A BARGAIN AT FIVE BUCKS AN HOUR...
ITS SUCH A PAN-CULTURAL EXPERIENCE!
BUT I CAN'T FIGURE OUT WHY HE LEAVES ALL THIS TRASH AROUND... I'M GONNA HAFTO HAVA A TALK WITH HIM....
NEW TOP SOIL
..MI CORA-ZO-O-ON
ROUND-UP
THUNK
OUR HOME IMPROVEMENT IS REALLY AN ART PROJECT, A CREATIVE EXPRESSION... I'M SO GLAD I WAS ABLE TO USE MY HEIGHTENED COLOR SENSE TO PICK OUT THIS COMPLEX PALATE FOR OUR NEW PORCH!
UH-OH! HERE COMES THE HEAD HONCHO OF THE WOMEN PAINTING CREW... I'M SCARED O' HER! I'M GETTIN' OUTA HERE... I HAVE TO "MAKE" ANYWAY...
HOW DOES SHE GET THOSE THIN LINES?? SHE USES THE EXACT SAME KIND OF PEN THAT I USE... HUNTS 102... HOW THE HELL DOES SHE DO IT? THEY'RE SO THIN THEY BARELY REPRODUCE!! I DONT GET IT.. IT'S A MYSTERY TO ME...

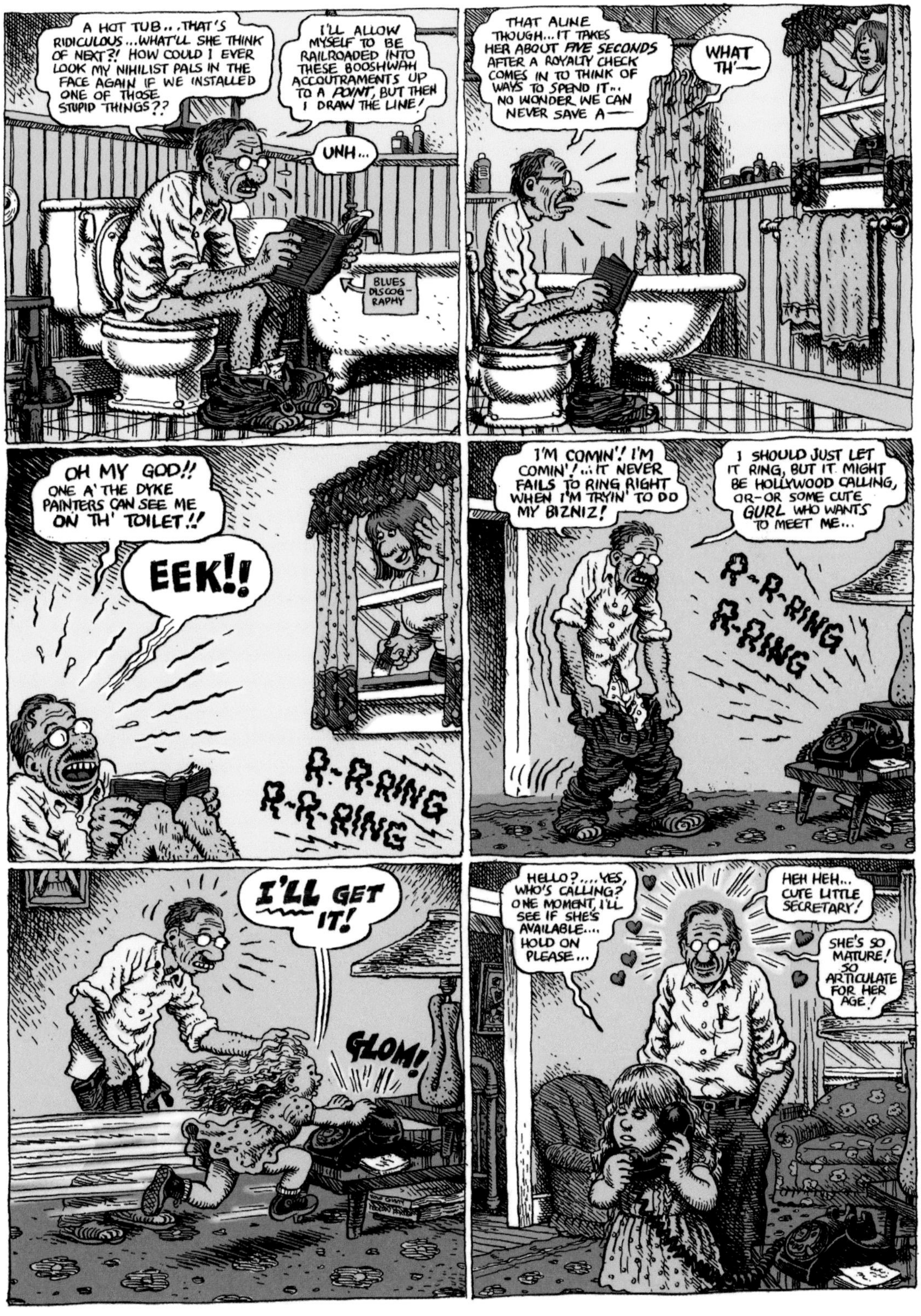
A HOT TUB...THAT'S RIDICULOUS...WHAT'LL SHE THINK OF NEXT?! HOW COULD I EVER LOOK MY NIHILIST PALS IN THE FACE AGAIN IF WE INSTALLED ONE OF THOSE STUPID THINGS??
I'LL ALLOW MYSELF TO BE RAILROADED INTO THESE BOOSHWAH ACCOUTRAMENTS UP TO A POINT, BUT THEN I DRAW THE LINE!
UNH...
BLUES DISCOGRAPHY
THAT ALINE THOUGH... IT TAKES HER ABOUT FIVE SECONDS AFTER A ROYALTY CHECK COMES IN TO THINK OF WAYS TO SPEND IT... NO WONDER WE CAN NEVER SAVE A—
WHAT TH'—
OH MY GOD!! ONE A' THE DYKE PAINTERS CAN SEE ME ON TH' TOILET!!
EEK!!
R-R-RING R-R-RING
I'M COMIN'! I'M COMIN'!...IT NEVER FAILS TO RING RIGHT WHEN I'M TRYIN' TO DO MY BIZNIZ!
I SHOULD JUST LET IT RING, BUT IT MIGHT BE HOLLYWOOD CALLING, OR-OR SOME CUTE GURL WHO WANTS TO MEET ME...
R-R-RING R-RING
I'LL GET IT!
GLOM!
HELLO?....YES, WHO'S CALLING? ONE MOMENT, I'LL SEE IF SHE'S AVAILABLE.... HOLD ON PLEASE...
HEH HEH... CUTE LITTLE SECRETARY!
SHE'S SO MATURE! SO ARTICULATE FOR HER AGE!

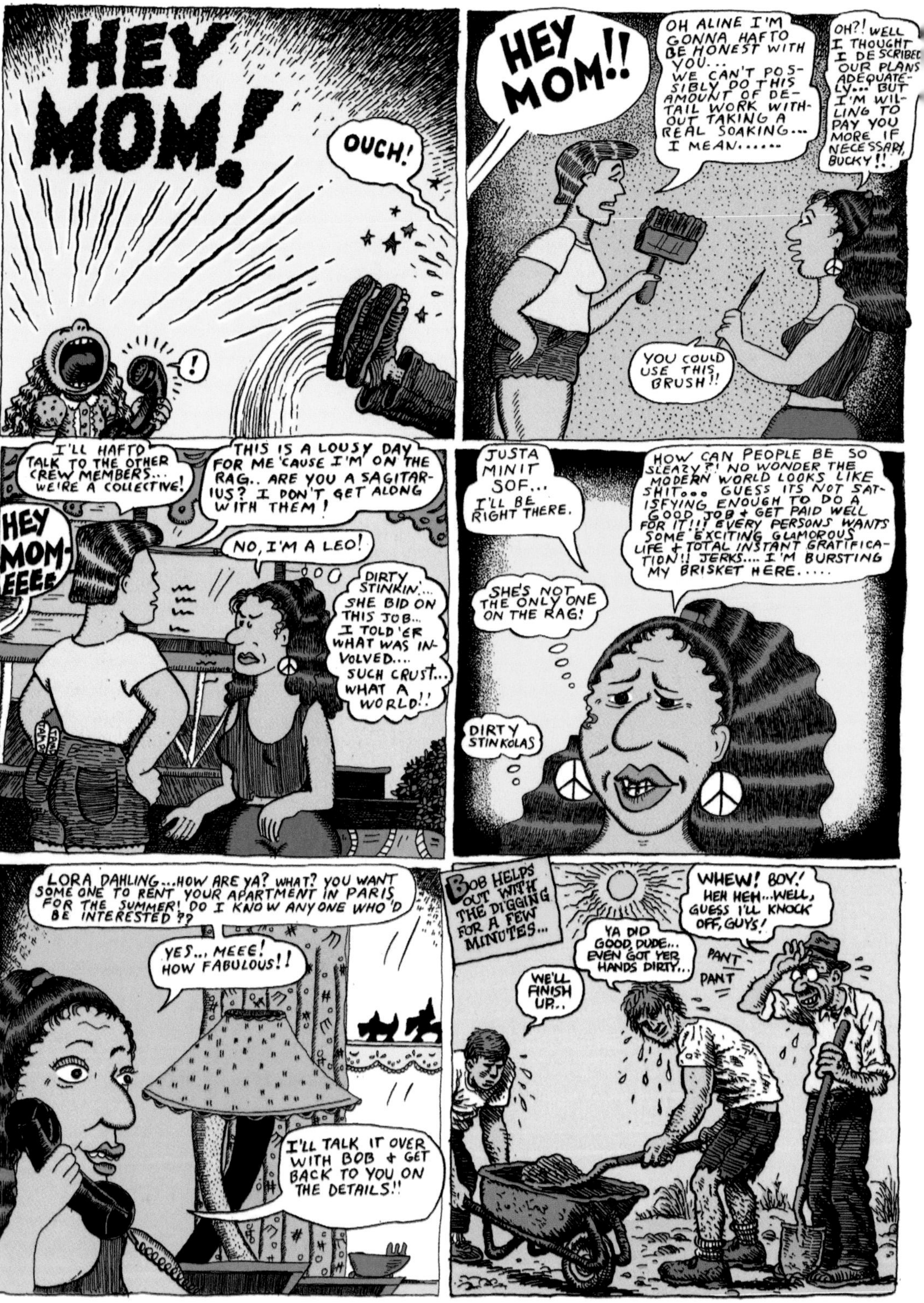

HEY MOM!
OUCH!
!
HEY MOM!!
OH ALINE I'M GONNA HAFTO BE HONEST WITH YOU... WE CAN'T POS-SIBLY DO THIS AMOUNT OF DE-TAIL WORK WITH-OUT TAKING A REAL SOAKING... I MEAN......
OH?! WELL I THOUGHT I DESCRIBED OUR PLANS ADEQUATE-LY... BUT I'M WIL-LING TO PAY YOU MORE IF NECESSARY, BUCKY!!
YOU COULD USE THIS BRUSH!!
I'LL HAFTO TALK TO THE OTHER CREW MEMBERS... WE'RE A COLLECTIVE!
THIS IS A LOUSY DAY FOR ME 'CAUSE I'M ON THE RAG.. ARE YOU A SAGITAR-IUS? I DON'T GET ALONG WITH THEM!
HEY MOM-EEEE
NO, I'M A LEO!
DIRTY STINKIN'... SHE BID ON THIS JOB... I TOLD 'ER WHAT WAS IN-VOLVED.... SUCH CRUST... WHAT A WORLD!!
JUSTA MINIT SOF... I'LL BE RIGHT THERE.
HOW CAN PEOPLE BE SO SLEAZY?! NO WONDER THE MODERN WORLD LOOKS LIKE SHIT... GUESS ITS NOT SAT-ISFYING ENOUGH TO DO A GOOD JOB + GET PAID WELL FOR IT!!! EVERY PERSONS WANTS SOME EXCITING GLAMOROUS LIFE + TOTAL INSTANT GRATIFICA-TION!! JERKS.... I'M BURSTING MY BRISKET HERE.....
SHE'S NOT THE ONLY ONE ON THE RAG!
DIRTY STINKOLAS
LORA DAHLING...HOW ARE YA? WHAT? YOU WANT SOME ONE TO RENT YOUR APARTMENT IN PARIS FOR THE SUMMER! DO I KNOW ANYONE WHO'D BE INTERESTED??
YES.., MEEE! HOW FABULOUS!!
I'LL TALK IT OVER WITH BOB + GET BACK TO YOU ON THE DETAILS!!
BOB HELPS OUT WITH THE DIGGING FOR A FEW MINUTES...
WHEW! BOY! HEH HEH...WELL, GUESS I'LL KNOCK OFF, GUYS!
YA DID GOOD, DUDE... EVEN GOT YER HANDS DIRTY...
PANT PANT
WE'LL FINISH UP..

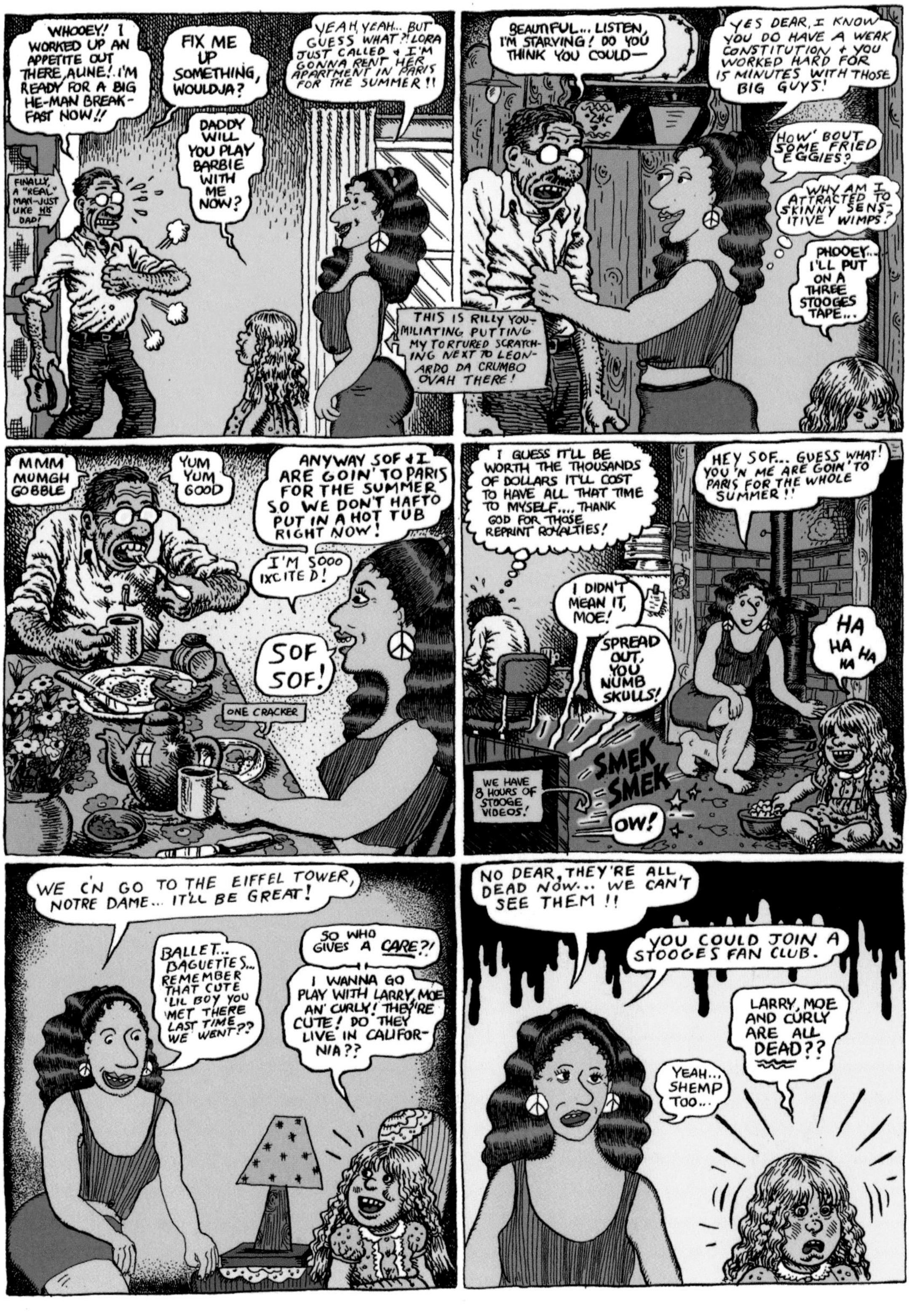
WHOOEY! I WORKED UP AN APPETITE OUT THERE, ALINE! I'M READY FOR A BIG HE-MAN BREAK-FAST NOW!!
FIX ME UP SOMETHING, WOULDJA?
FINALLY, A "REAL" MAN-JUST LIKE HIS DAD!
DADDY WILL YOU PLAY BARBIE WITH ME NOW?
YEAH, YEAH... BUT GUESS WHAT?! LORA JUST CALLED & I'M GONNA RENT HER APARTMENT IN PARIS FOR THE SUMMER!!
THIS IS RILLY YOU-MILIATING PUTTING MY TORTURED SCRATCH-ING NEXT TO LEON-ARDO DA CRUMBO OVAH THERE!
BEAUTIFUL... LISTEN, I'M STARVING! DO YOU THINK YOU COULD—
YES DEAR, I KNOW YOU DO HAVE A WEAK CONSTITUTION & YOU WORKED HARD FOR 15 MINUTES WITH THOSE BIG GUYS!
HOW' BOUT SOME FRIED EGGIES?
WHY AM I ATTRACTED TO SKINNY SENS-ITIVE WIMPS?
PHOOEY... I'LL PUT ON A THREE STOOGES TAPE...
MMM MUMGH GOBBLE
YUM YUM GOOD
ANYWAY SOF & I ARE GOIN' TO PARIS FOR THE SUMMER SO WE DON'T HAFTO PUT IN A HOT TUB RIGHT NOW!
I'M SOOO IXCITED!
SOF SOF!
ONE CRACKER
I GUESS IT'LL BE WORTH THE THOUSANDS OF DOLLARS IT'LL COST TO HAVE ALL THAT TIME TO MYSELF.... THANK GOD FOR THOSE REPRINT ROYALTIES!
HEY SOF... GUESS WHAT! YOU 'N ME ARE GOIN' TO PARIS FOR THE WHOLE SUMMER!!
I DIDN'T MEAN IT, MOE!
SPREAD OUT, YOU NUMB SKULLS!
HA HA HA HA
SMEK SMEK
OW!
WE HAVE 8 HOURS OF STOOGE VIDEOS!
WE C'N GO TO THE EIFFEL TOWER, NOTRE DAME... IT'LL BE GREAT!
BALLET... BAGUETTES... REMEMBER THAT CUTE 'LIL BOY YOU MET THERE LAST TIME WE WENT??
SO WHO GIVES A CARE?!
I WANNA GO PLAY WITH LARRY, MOE AN' CURLY! THEY'RE CUTE! DO THEY LIVE IN CALIFOR-NIA??
NO DEAR, THEY'RE ALL DEAD NOW... WE CAN'T SEE THEM!!
YOU COULD JOIN A STOOGES FAN CLUB.
LARRY, MOE AND CURLY ARE ALL DEAD??
YEAH... SHEMP TOO...

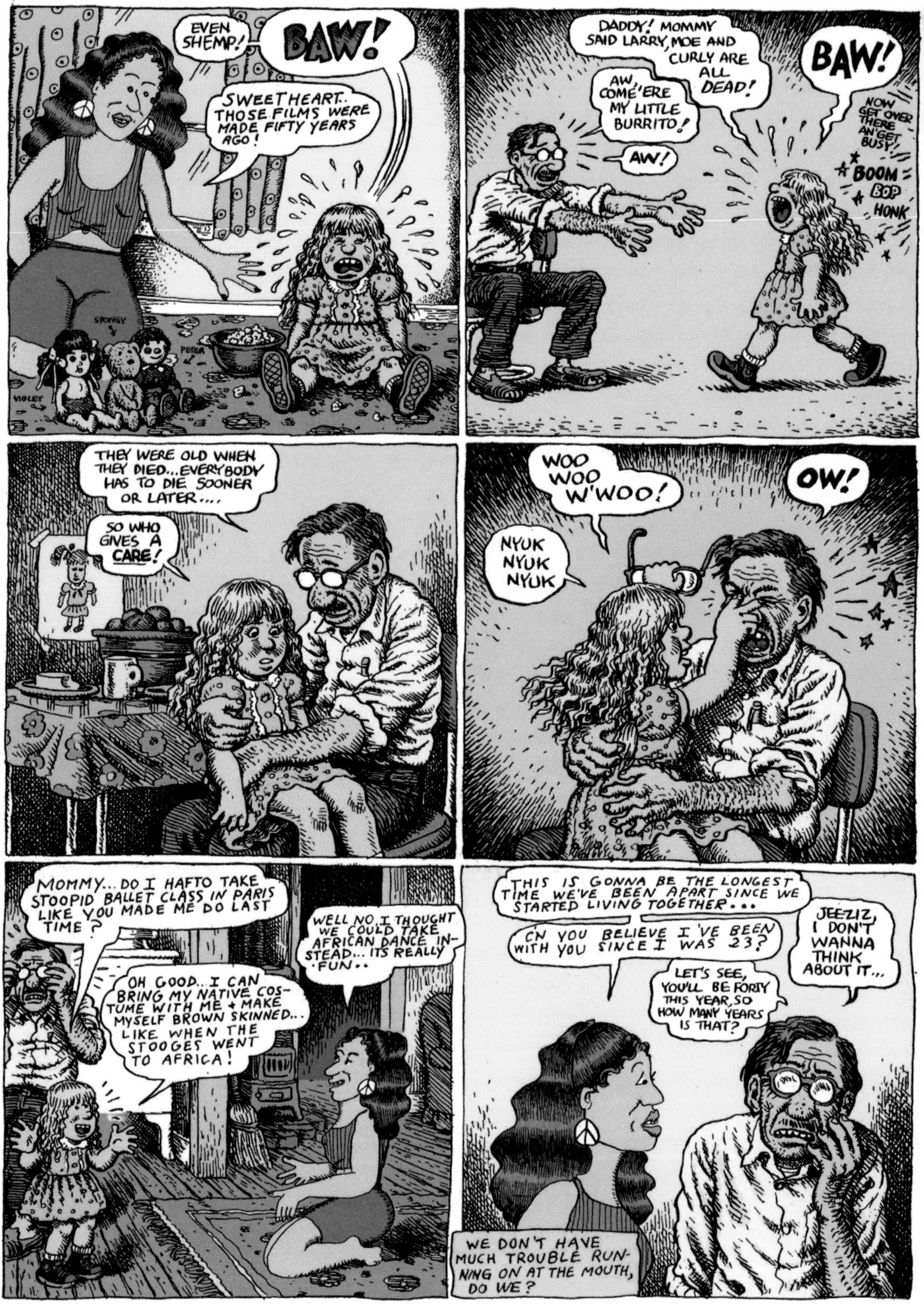
EVEN SHEMP!
BAW!
SWEETHEART.. THOSE FILMS WERE MADE FIFTY YEARS AGO!
SPONGY
PETER
VIOLET
DADDY! MOMMY SAID LARRY, MOE AND CURLY ARE ALL DEAD!
BAW!
AW, COME'ERE MY LITTLE BURRITO!
AW!
NOW GET OVER THERE AN'GET BUSY!
BOOM
BOP
HONK
THEY WERE OLD WHEN THEY DIED... EVERYBODY HAS TO DIE SOONER OR LATER....
SO WHO GIVES A CARE!
WOO WOO W'WOO!
OW!
NYUK NYUK NYUK
MOMMY... DO I HAFTO TAKE STOOPID BALLET CLASS IN PARIS LIKE YOU MADE ME DO LAST TIME?
WELL NO, I THOUGHT WE COULD TAKE AFRICAN DANCE INSTEAD... ITS REALLY FUN..
OH GOOD... I CAN BRING MY NATIVE COSTUME WITH ME + MAKE MYSELF BROWN SKINNED... LIKE WHEN THE STOOGES WENT TO AFRICA!
THIS IS GONNA BE THE LONGEST TIME WE'VE BEEN APART SINCE WE STARTED LIVING TOGETHER...
C'N YOU BELIEVE I'VE BEEN WITH YOU SINCE I WAS 23?
JEEZIZ, I DON'T WANNA THINK ABOUT IT...
LET'S SEE, YOU'LL BE FORTY THIS YEAR, SO HOW MANY YEARS IS THAT?
WE DON'T HAVE MUCH TROUBLE RUNNING ON AT THE MOUTH, DO WE?

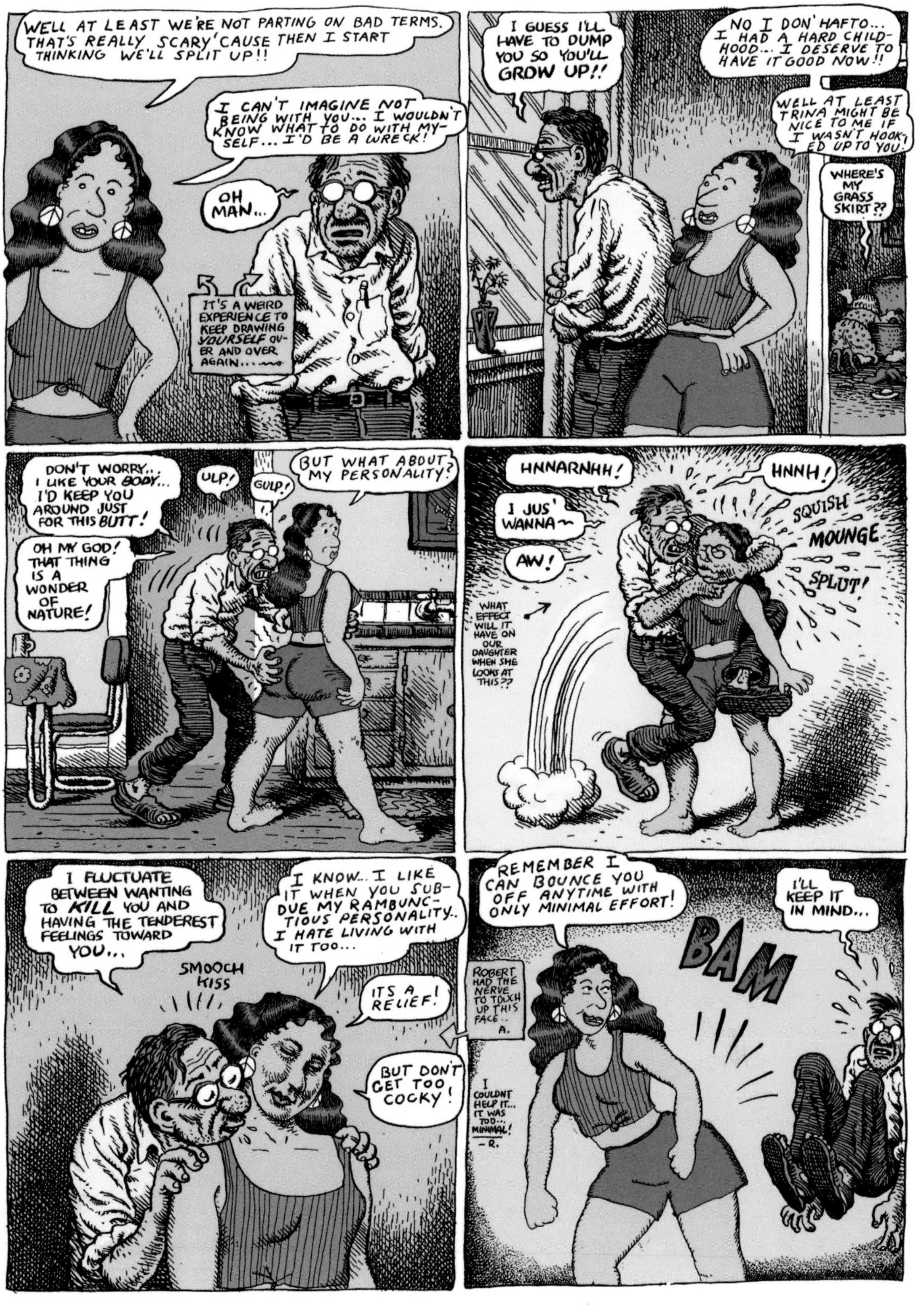

WELL AT LEAST WE'RE NOT PARTING ON BAD TERMS. THAT'S REALLY SCARY 'CAUSE THEN I START THINKING WE'LL SPLIT UP!!
I CAN'T IMAGINE NOT BEING WITH YOU... I WOULDN'T KNOW WHAT TO DO WITH MYSELF... I'D BE A WRECK!
OH MAN...
IT'S A WEIRD EXPERIENCE TO KEEP DRAWING YOURSELF OVER AND OVER AGAIN.......
I GUESS I'LL HAVE TO DUMP YOU SO YOU'LL GROW UP!!
NO I DON' HAFTO... I HAD A HARD CHILDHOOD... I DESERVE TO HAVE IT GOOD NOW!!
WELL AT LEAST TRINA MIGHT BE NICE TO ME IF I WASN'T HOOKED UP TO YOU!
WHERE'S MY GRASS SKIRT??
DON'T WORRY.. I LIKE YOUR BODY... I'D KEEP YOU AROUND JUST FOR THIS BUTT!
ULP!
GULP!
BUT WHAT ABOUT MY PERSONALITY?
OH MY GOD! THAT THING IS A WONDER OF NATURE!
HNNARNHH!
HNNH!
I JUS' WANNA~
AW!
SQUISH
MOUNGE
SPLUT!
WHAT EFFECT WILL IT HAVE ON OUR DAUGHTER WHEN SHE LOOKS AT THIS??
I FLUCTUATE BETWEEN WANTING TO KILL YOU AND HAVING THE TENDEREST FEELINGS TOWARD YOU...
I KNOW.. I LIKE IT WHEN YOU SUBDUE MY RAMBUNCTIOUS PERSONALITY.. I HATE LIVING WITH IT TOO...
SMOOCH KISS
ITS A RELIEF!
BUT DON'T GET TOO COCKY!
ROBERT HAD THE NERVE TO TOUCH UP THIS FACE.. A.
I COULDNT HELP IT... IT WAS TOO... MINIMAL! —R.
REMEMBER I CAN BOUNCE YOU OFF ANYTIME WITH ONLY MINIMAL EFFORT!
I'LL KEEP IT IN MIND...
BAM

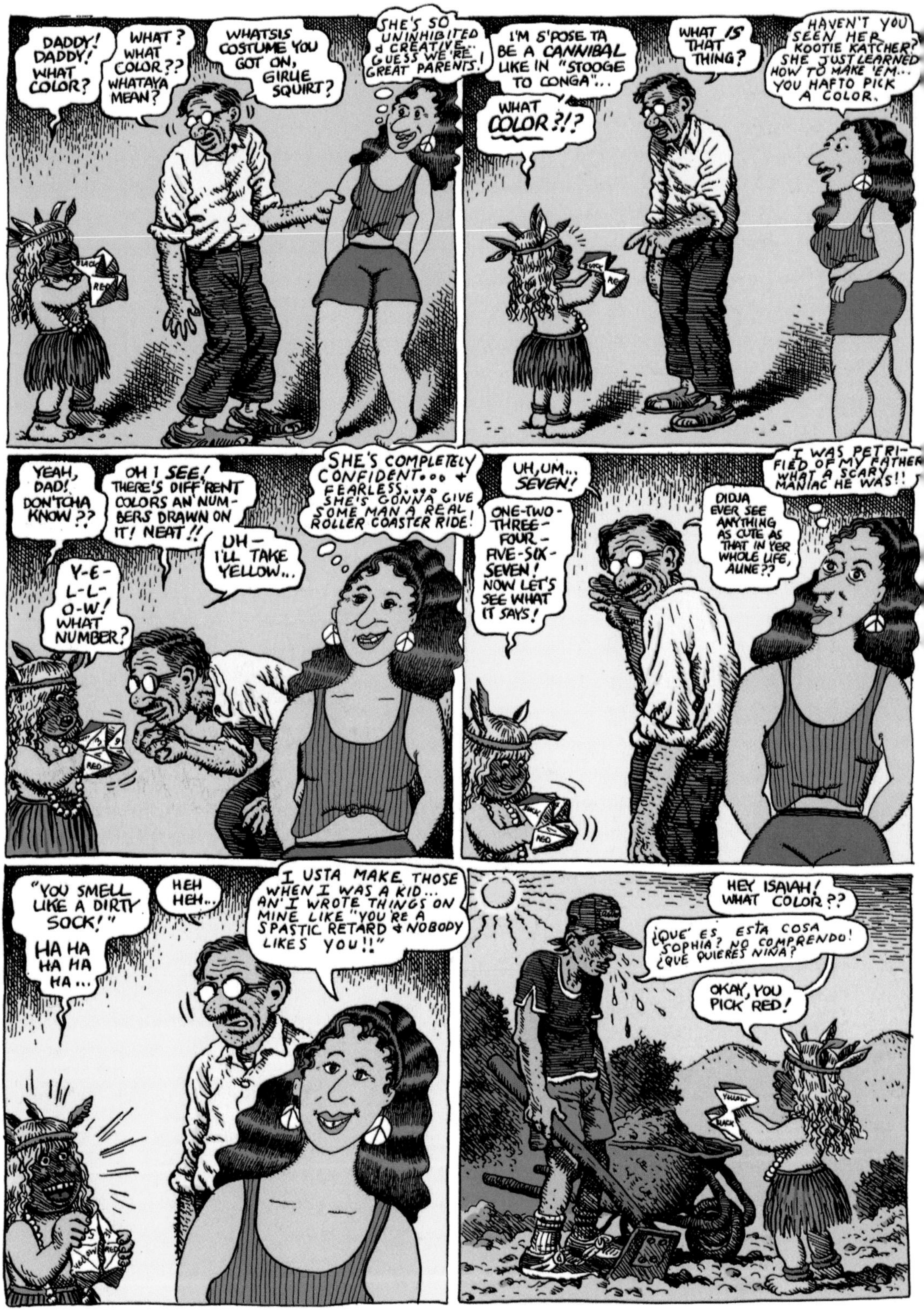
DADDY! DADDY! WHAT COLOR?
WHAT? WHAT COLOR?? WHATAYA MEAN?
WHATSIS COSTUME YOU GOT ON, GIRLIE SQUIRT?
SHE'S SO UNINHIBITED & CREATIVE. GUESS WE'RE GREAT PARENTS!
I'M S'POSE TA BE A CANNIBAL LIKE IN "STOOGE TO CONGA"...
WHAT COLOR?!?
WHAT IS THAT THING?
HAVEN'T YOU SEEN HER KOOTIE KATCHER? SHE JUST LEARNED HOW TO MAKE 'EM... YOU HAFTO PICK A COLOR.
YEAH, DAD! DON'TCHA KNOW??
OH I SEE! THERE'S DIFF'RENT COLORS AN' NUMBERS DRAWN ON IT! NEAT!!
SHE'S COMPLETELY CONFIDENT... & FEARLESS... SHE'S GONNA GIVE SOME MAN A REAL ROLLER COASTER RIDE!
UH– I'LL TAKE YELLOW...
Y-E-L-L-O-W! WHAT NUMBER?
UH, UM... SEVEN!
ONE-TWO-THREE-FOUR-FIVE-SIX-SEVEN! NOW LET'S SEE WHAT IT SAYS!
DIDJA EVER SEE ANYTHING AS CUTE AS THAT IN YER WHOLE LIFE, AUNE??
I WAS PETRIFIED OF MY FATHER WHAT A SCARY MANIAC HE WAS!!
"YOU SMELL LIKE A DIRTY SOCK!" HA HA HA HA HA...
HEH HEH...
I USTA MAKE THOSE WHEN I WAS A KID... AN' I WROTE THINGS ON MINE LIKE "YOU'RE A SPASTIC RETARD & NOBODY LIKES YOU!!"
HEY ISAIAH! WHAT COLOR??
¿QUÉ ES ESTA COSA SOPHIA? NO COMPRENDO! ¿QUÉ QUIERES NIÑA?
OKAY, YOU PICK RED!

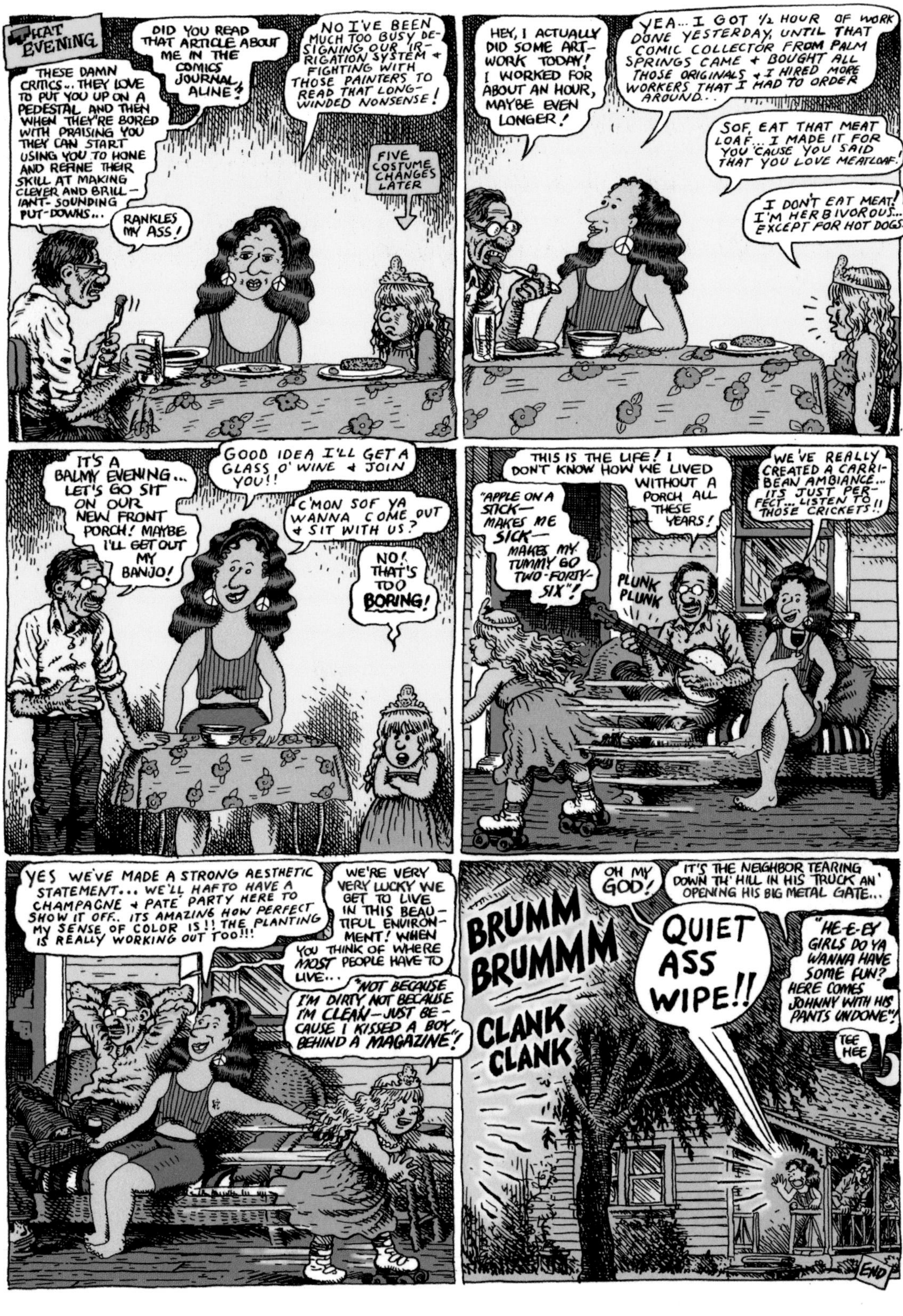
THAT EVENING
DID YOU READ THAT ARTICLE ABOUT ME IN THE COMICS JOURNAL, ALINE?
THESE DAMN CRITICS.. THEY LOVE TO PUT YOU UP ON A PEDESTAL AND THEN WHEN THEY'RE BORED WITH PRAISING YOU THEY CAN START USING YOU TO HONE AND REFINE THEIR SKILL AT MAKING CLEVER AND BRILL-IANT-SOUNDING PUT-DOWNS...
NO I'VE BEEN MUCH TOO BUSY DE-SIGNING OUR IR-RIGATION SYSTEM + FIGHTING WITH THOSE PAINTERS TO READ THAT LONG-WINDED NONSENSE!
RANKLES MY ASS!
FIVE COSTUME CHANGES LATER
HEY, I ACTUALLY DID SOME ART-WORK TODAY! I WORKED FOR ABOUT AN HOUR, MAYBE EVEN LONGER!
YEA... I GOT 1/2 HOUR OF WORK DONE YESTERDAY, UNTIL THAT COMIC COLLECTOR FROM PALM SPRINGS CAME + BOUGHT ALL THOSE ORIGINALS + I HIRED MORE WORKERS THAT I HAD TO ORDER AROUND...
SOF, EAT THAT MEAT LOAF... I MADE IT FOR YOU 'CAUSE YOU SAID THAT YOU LOVE MEATLOAF!
I DON'T EAT MEAT! I'M HERBIVOROUS... EXCEPT FOR HOT DOGS!
IT'S A BALMY EVENING... LET'S GO SIT ON OUR NEW FRONT PORCH! MAYBE I'LL GET OUT MY BANJO!
GOOD IDEA I'LL GET A GLASS O' WINE + JOIN YOU!!
C'MON SOF YA WANNA COME OUT + SIT WITH US?
NO! THAT'S TOO BORING!
THIS IS THE LIFE! I DON'T KNOW HOW WE LIVED WITHOUT A PORCH ALL THESE YEARS!
"APPLE ON A STICK— MAKES ME SICK— MAKES MY TUMMY GO TWO-FORTY-SIX"!
WE'VE REALLY CREATED A CARRI-BEAN AMBIANCE... ITS JUST PER-FECT... LISTEN TO THOSE CRICKETS!!
PLUNK PLUNK
YES WE'VE MADE A STRONG AESTHETIC STATEMENT... WE'LL HAFTO HAVE A CHAMPAGNE + PATE' PARTY HERE TO SHOW IT OFF.. ITS AMAZING HOW PERFECT MY SENSE OF COLOR IS!! THE PLANTING IS REALLY WORKING OUT TOO!!!
WE'RE VERY VERY LUCKY WE GET TO LIVE IN THIS BEAU-TIFUL ENVIRON-MENT! WHEN YOU THINK OF WHERE MOST PEOPLE HAVE TO LIVE...
"NOT BECAUSE I'M DIRTY NOT BECAUSE I'M CLEAN—JUST BE-CAUSE I KISSED A BOY BEHIND A MAGAZINE"!
OH MY GOD!
IT'S THE NEIGHBOR TEARING DOWN TH' HILL IN HIS TRUCK AN' OPENING HIS BIG METAL GATE...
BRUMM BRUMMM
CLANK CLANK
QUIET ASS WIPE!!
"HE-E-EY GIRLS DO YA WANNA HAVE SOME FUN? HERE COMES JOHNNY WITH HIS PANTS UNDONE"!
TEE HEE
END

Oy! the redneck neighbors ...

Life went on. We built studios in our barn. I started working again (I wrote a lot of stories about motherhood and frustrated housewives), and Sophie started kindergarten in the local public school. We had some wonderful friends, like neighbors Yves Boisrame and Karen Klonsky, and the McNamara clan—Robert McNamara's son's family.

But little by little our world had been transformed by the wealthy "rednecks" who had built giant McMansions on the hilltops all around us. Each pretentious "castle" had a different style: there was the Ponderosa Ranch, the Swiss Chalet, the fake stone Medieval Fort, the Mediterranean Hacienda, Addams Family Victorian, and the post-modern Police Station look, complete with a yard laid out like a helicopter pad. The ugliness and the noisy dust-producing vehicles that these new neighbors drove made us increasingly cranky. Many people had their own bulldozers and tractors.

On weekends, they would lapse into "vehicular behavior syndrome," a kind of motorized mania where they would bulldoze, dig and scrape the land, and then race down the hills in pick ups, 4x4s and dirt bikes, finishing off with a little chain sawing, roto-tilling, and weed eating before dinner. They were all armed to the hilt, and would spend countless hours doing target practice. Our nerves were continually jangled by the sound of gunshots.

Randy, our Viet Nam Vet neighbor, lived on the highest hilltop across the road. He skydived for relaxation when he wasn't motorcycle racing. One year, he had a big party for his birthday, and he and his Vet skydiving pals got real high and then went for a jump. We all watched as the pretty chutes opened, but Randy was so stoned, he forgot to open his and he landed, or actually exploded, in the middle of his partying wife and friends. An ambulance came and took his body away, but everyone kept on partying as he would have wanted them too.

I asked myself if these were really "my kind o' people," and more importantly, did I want my daughter going to school and hanging around with them? Up until then, we had been able to control the kinds of things she was exposed to, but once she started school it became more complicated. We had raised Sophie on old cartoons like Betty Boop, Popeye, old Disney stuff, Laurel and Hardy, The Little Rascals, The Three Stooges and the Marx Brothers. Robert would play old records for her, and she started drawing cartoons and playing the piano very young. We fed her organic high quality foods and dressed her in natural fiber clothing (I have already confessed to being a hopeless 1960s case in many respects). Once she began venturing out into the world, we had to relax our standards and allow her to be a normal kid, but we were increasingly worried about the kind of people and ideas that she would encounter.

Even in the late 1980s, the rising tide of Christian Fundamentalism was evident in Winters, California. We may have been only two hours away from the hip, laid back California coast, but the inland valley was decidedly Middle America. When we first moved to Winters, there were three churches, one Catholic, one Methodist and one Mormon; by the time we left in 1990, there were thirteen! All the newer ones were Evangelical, Fundamentalist congregations that emphasized being born again, and hundreds of local folks were.

We also ran into problems at Sophie's school. Both Robert and I had volunteered to give art classes for free, since there was no money in the California school budget for music, art, and other cultural activities, thanks to Governor Ronald Reagan who had slashed school funding by severely lowering property taxes. I worked once a week in Sophie's class from the time she started kindergarten up until 3rd grade. One day, I noticed that about half the kids were absent when I arrived. When I asked the teacher why, she explained that the minister of the New Foursquare Church had told his congregation that I was an agent of the Devil, and that their children should not be allowed near me! (Well, I am a Jewish anarchist pornographer, so maybe he had a point…) I never went back to the school after that.

Then one day, I went for some coffee in the local café with a friend who was a teacher in Winters. When she returned to school, one of her colleagues asked her what she was doing having coffee with the wife of "the child pornographer." At that point I started seeing images of lynch mobs and burning crosses and I knew we had to get our daughter out of there!

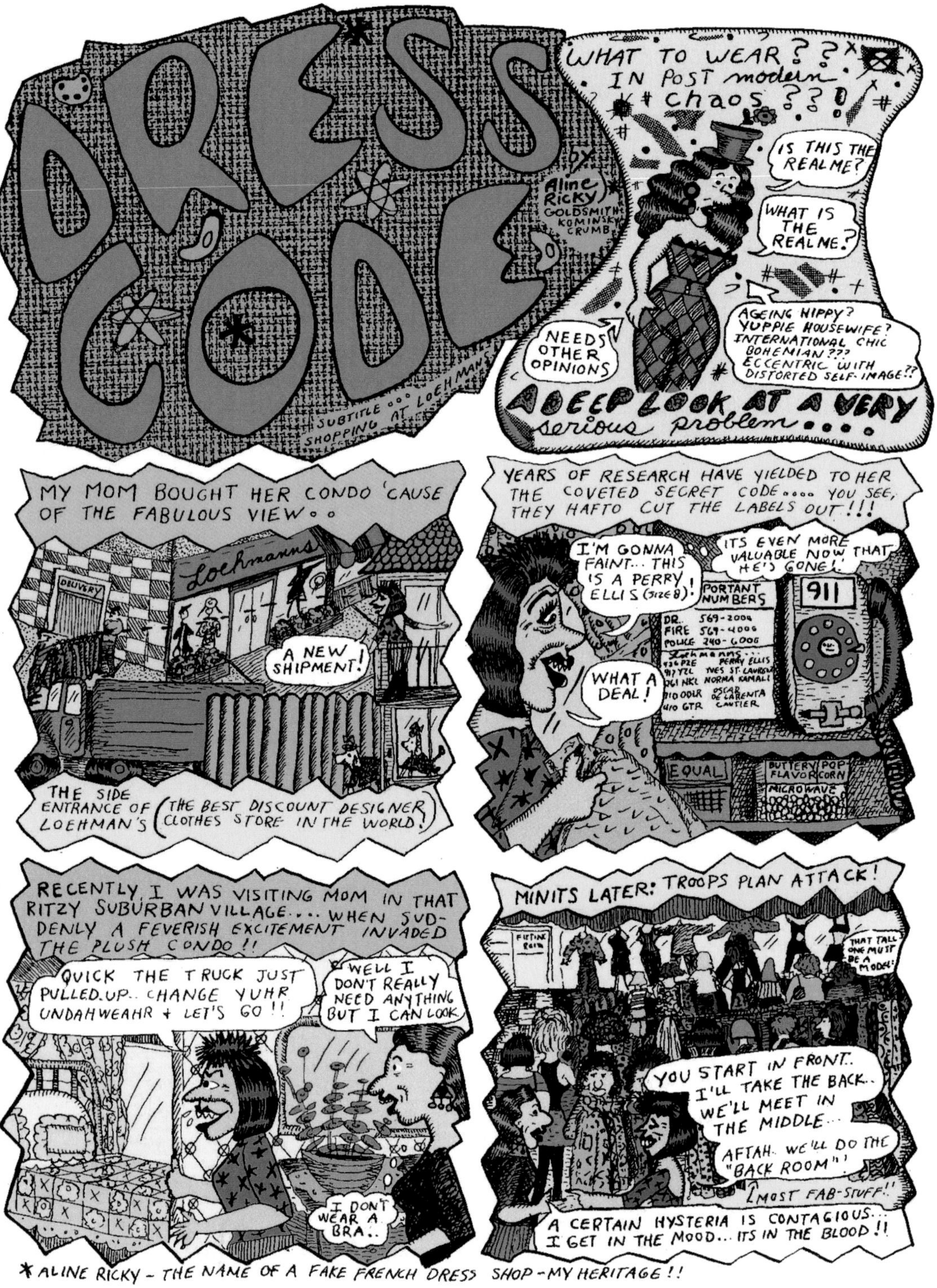
DRESS CODE
by Aline Ricky* GOLDSMITH KOMINSKY CRUMB
SUBTITLE ... SHOPPING AT LOEHMANS
WHAT TO WEAR??? IN POST modern chaos???!
IS THIS THE REALME?
WHAT IS THE REALME?
NEEDS OTHER OPINIONS
AGEING HIPPY? YUPPIE HOUSEWIFE? INTERNATIONAL CHIC BOHEMIAN??? ECCENTRIC WITH DISTORTED SELF-IMAGE??
A DEEP LOOK AT A VERY serious problem....
MY MOM BOUGHT HER CONDO 'CAUSE OF THE FABULOUS VIEW..
DELIVERY
Loehmanns
A NEW SHIPMENT!
THE SIDE ENTRANCE OF LOEHMAN'S (THE BEST DISCOUNT DESIGNER CLOTHES STORE IN THE WORLD!)
YEARS OF RESEARCH HAVE YIELDED TO HER THE COVETED SECRET CODE.... YOU SEE, THEY HAFTO CUT THE LABELS OUT!!!
I'M GONNA FAINT... THIS IS A PERRY ELLIS (SIZE 8)!
ITS EVEN MORE VALUABLE NOW THAT HE'S GONE!
PORTANT NUMBERS
DR. 569-2000
FIRE 569-4000
POLICE 240-6000
Loehmanns...
PERRY ELLIS
YVES ST. LAURENT
NORMA KAMALI
OSCAR DE LARENTA
CARTIER
911
WHAT A DEAL!
EQUAL
BUTTERY FLAVOR POP CORN
MICROWAVE
RECENTLY I WAS VISITING MOM IN THAT RITZY SUBURBAN VILLAGE... WHEN SUDDENLY A FEVERISH EXCITEMENT INVADED THE PLUSH CONDO!!
QUICK THE TRUCK JUST PULLED UP.. CHANGE YUHR UNDAHWEAHR + LET'S GO!!
WELL I DON'T REALLY NEED ANYTHING BUT I CAN LOOK.
I DON'T WEAR A BRA..
MINITS LATER: TROOPS PLAN ATTACK!
THAT TALL ONE MUST BE A MODEL!
YOU START IN FRONT.. I'LL TAKE THE BACK.. WE'LL MEET IN THE MIDDLE...
AFTAH.. WE'LL DO THE "BACK ROOM"!
(MOST FAB-STUFF!)
A CERTAIN HYSTERIA IS CONTAGIOUS... I GET IN THE MOOD... ITS IN THE BLOOD!!

*ALINE RICKY - THE NAME OF A FAKE FRENCH DRESS SHOP - MY HERITAGE!!

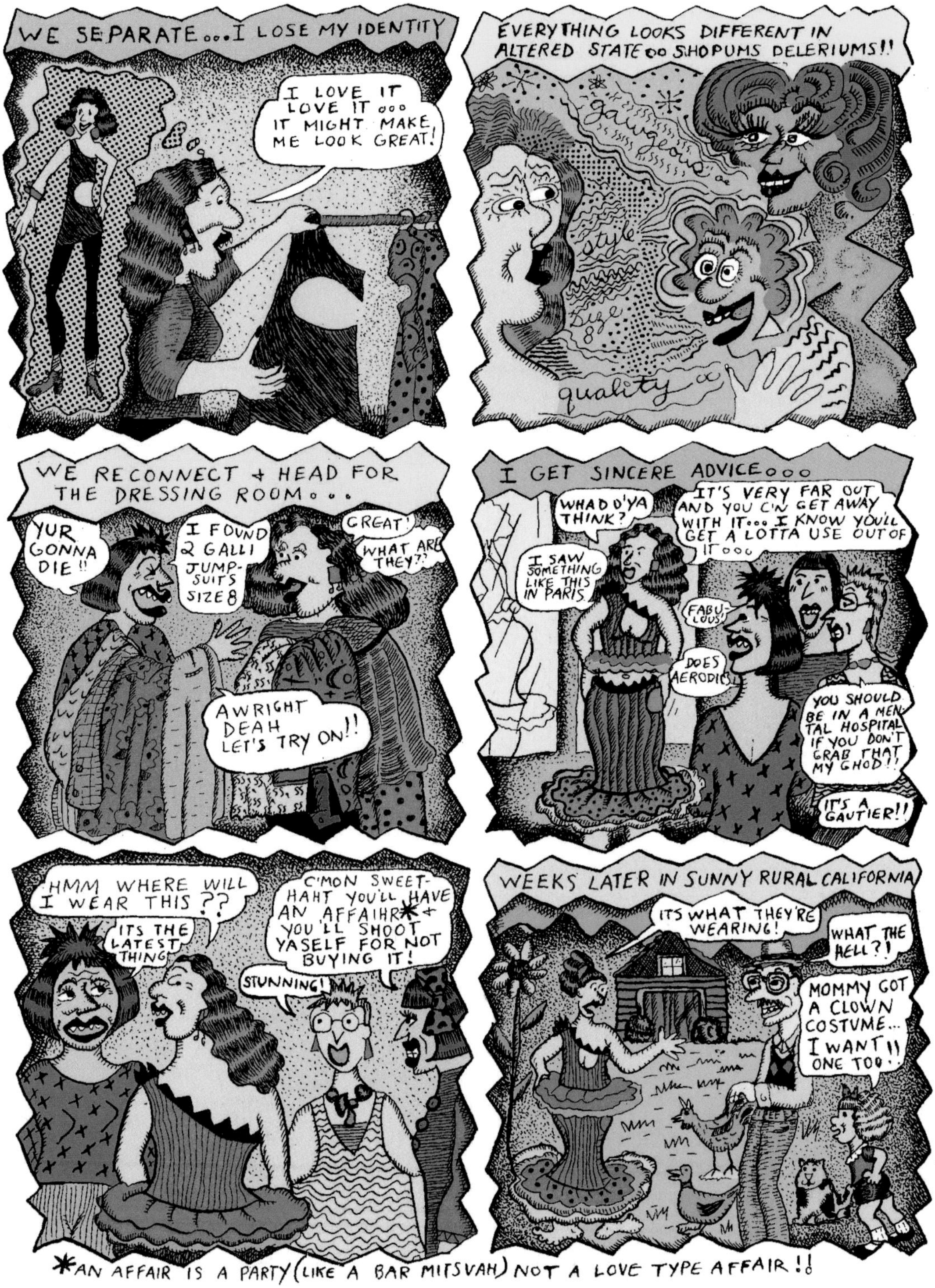
WE SEPARATE... I LOSE MY IDENTITY
I LOVE IT LOVE IT... IT MIGHT MAKE ME LOOK GREAT!
EVERYTHING LOOKS DIFFERENT IN ALTERED STATE.. SHOPUMS DELERIUMS!!
gawgeous
style
size 8
quality
WE RECONNECT + HEAD FOR THE DRESSING ROOM...
YUR GONNA DIE!!
I FOUND 2 GALLI JUMP-SUITS SIZE 8
GREAT!
WHAT ARE THEY??
AWRIGHT DEAH LET'S TRY ON!!
I GET SINCERE ADVICE...
WHAD D'YA THINK?
IT'S VERY FAR OUT AND YOU C'N GET AWAY WITH IT... I KNOW YOU'LL GET A LOTTA USE OUT OF IT...
I SAW SOMETHING LIKE THIS IN PARIS
FABU-LOUS!
DOES AERODIC
YOU SHOULD BE IN A MEN-TAL HOSPITAL IF YOU DON'T GRAB THAT MY GHOD!!
IT'S A GAUTIER!!
HMM WHERE WILL I WEAR THIS??
ITS THE LATEST THING
C'MON SWEET-HAHT YOU'LL HAVE AN AFFAIHR* + YOU'LL SHOOT YASELF FOR NOT BUYING IT!
STUNNING!
WEEKS LATER IN SUNNY RURAL CALIFORNIA
ITS WHAT THEY'RE WEARING!
WHAT THE HELL?!
MOMMY GOT A CLOWN COSTUME... I WANT ONE TOO!!
*AN AFFAIR IS A PARTY (LIKE A BAR MITSVAH) NOT A LOVE TYPE AFFAIR!!

A summer escape ...

During the summer of 1987, I had the chance to house-sit Gilbert Shelton and Lora Fountain's apartment in Paris. I went with Sophie, who was then nearly seven years old, and Oceana Callum, the fourteen year-old daughter of a good friend. We spent six great weeks in Paris. The three of us explored the whole city by foot and metro. We went swimming in the floating Victorian "Piscine Deligny," sat in cafés, went shopping, ate chocolate, and I turned 40. We celebrated my birthday in a decaying villa with the family of French-Corsican friends in a mountain village near Ajaccio, Corsica. The villagers killed a pig for my birthday, and the party lasted three days. Back in Paris, Diane Noomin came to visit and joined our all-girl summer adventure. By the time our vacation was over, I had my mind made up to somehow move my family to France. I wasn't sure how, when, or in what part of the country we would live, but I was determined to figure it out.

Above left: **Photo of me in the window of a typical Paris apartment, 1984**

Above right: **Me and my baguette, Paris, 1984**

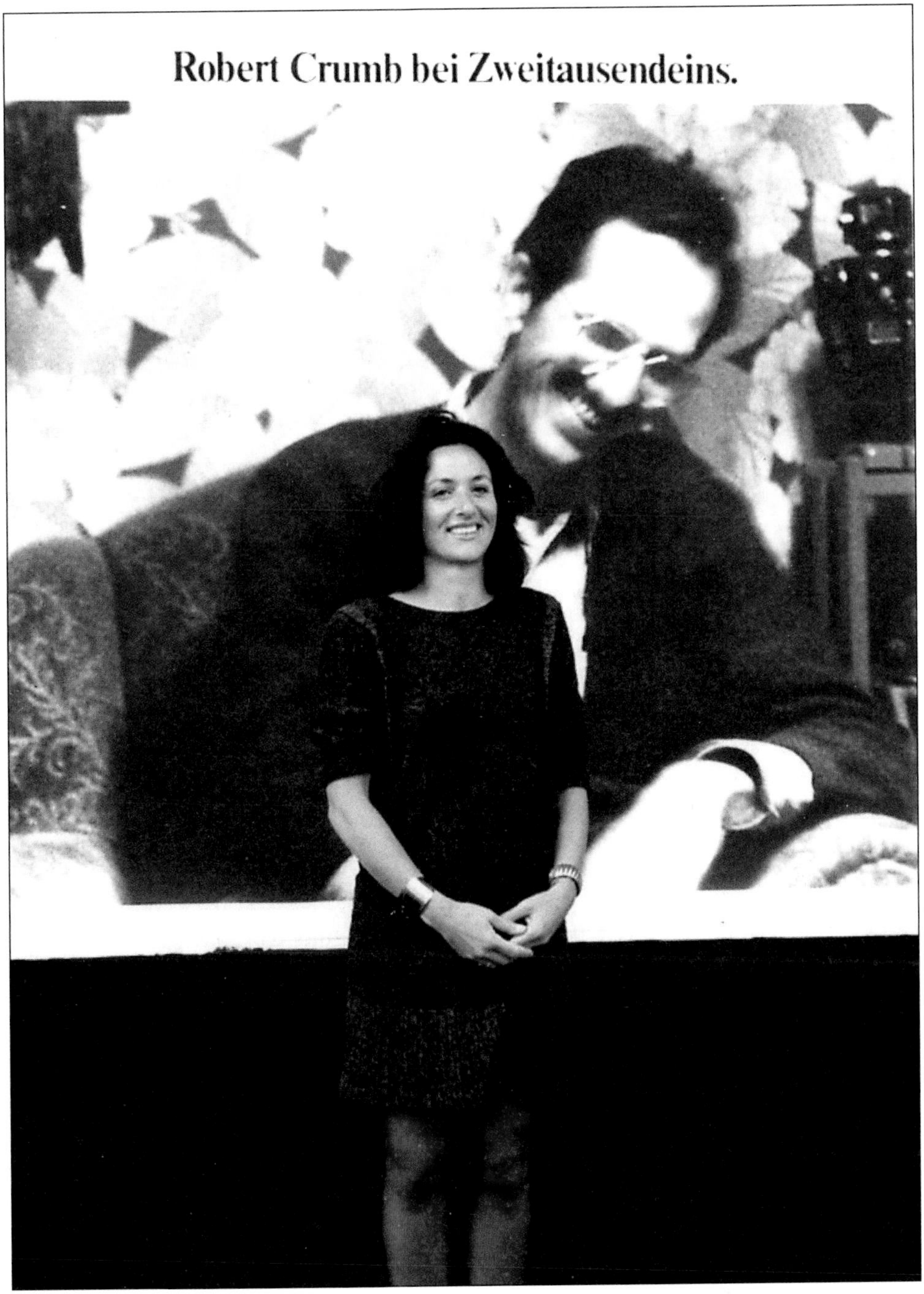
Robert Crumb bei Zweitausendeins.

Above: **Me in front of publicity photo of Robert for his German Publisher in Hamburg, 1984**

Back home and totally alienated!

When we arrived back home, my dear friends had organized a belated 40th birthday party for me, and I was very touched. However, my pal Julie McNamara had written and directed a skit based on my life, in which she played the lead role, and she gave it at the party. Julie, who was blonde and big busted, wore a wig and workout clothes, and even acted out the telephone voice of my mother. I had just been through two years of therapy to learn how to deal with my feelings toward my family, and her well-meaning gesture turned out to be a painfully embarrassing, nightmarish parody of my life. It deepened my alienation and my passionate desire to escape from the "Big Valley." Although I was very attached to our little wooden house and our scruffy piece of land, I started fantasizing more and more about other possibilities.

Robert had been complaining bitterly about life in America for years, often making it difficult for me to function. He lived in "Crumbland," his self-created womb of old records, toys, pictures and books, in a 1920s décor with heavy drapes to shut out the ugliness of the modern world. He would rant and rave about the hideousness of it all, while I had to deal with the outside world and take Sophie to dance classes and Chuck E. Cheese birthdays and ski vacations and zoos and amusement parks and malls, because I knew she had to learn to cope and not to feel completely alienated. (At twenty-four, she is in fact totally alienated.)

Finally, my frustrations came to a head, and I was determined to move somewhere that would provide us with some peace and harmony. Or call it a run o' the mill mid-life crisis exacerbated by a few years of intense therapy and my restless Jewish Gypsy genes mixed with what in retrospect I believe was a premonition of what was lurking on the horizon.

Several years after we left the States, Terry Zwigoff's film *Crumb* became an unimaginable box office success, and we were even hounded by the media in France. Luckily Sophie was totally spared and had really no idea until much later that we were well-known.

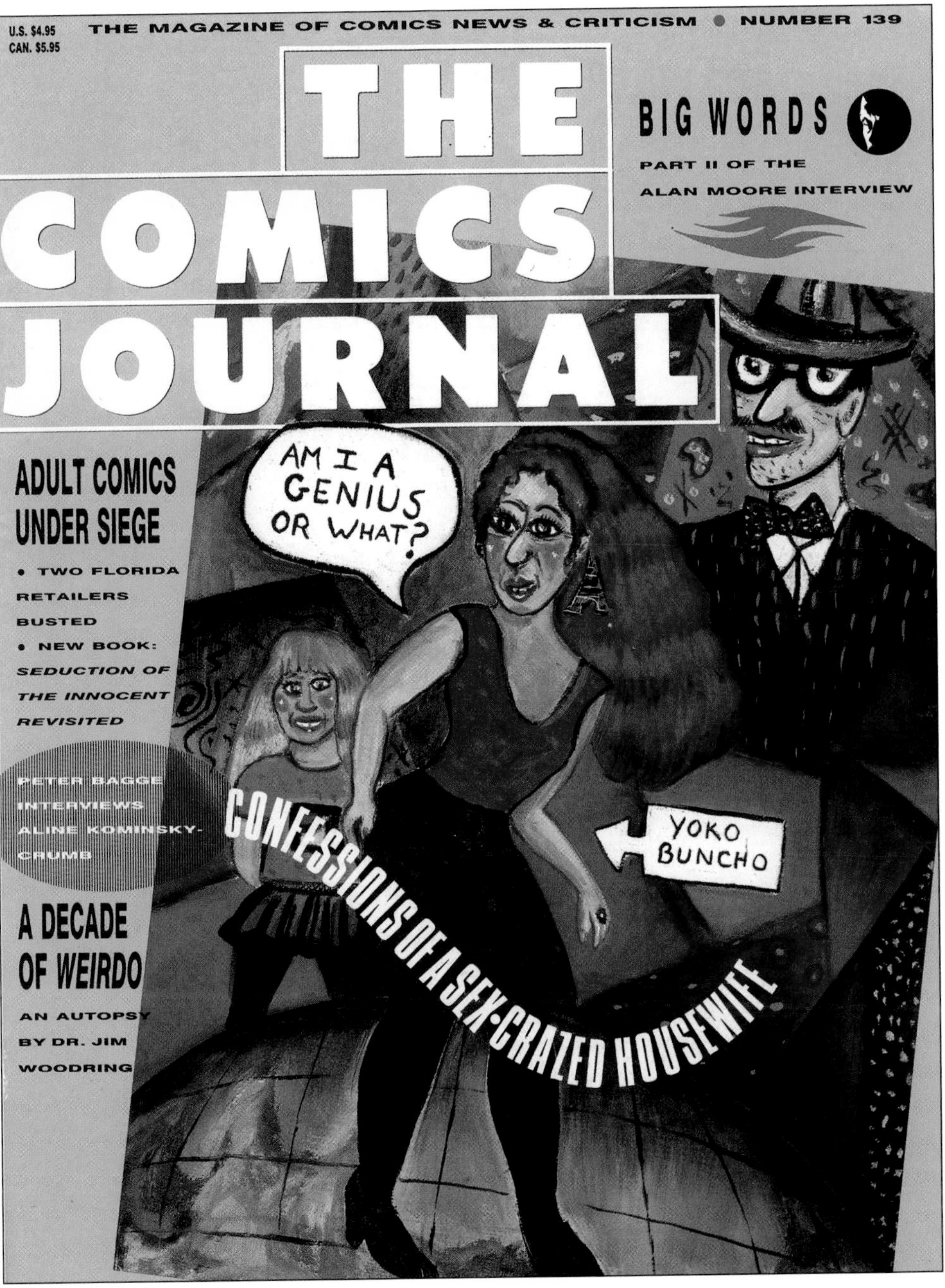

U.S. $4.95
CAN. $5.95
THE MAGAZINE OF COMICS NEWS & CRITICISM • NUMBER 139
THE COMICS JOURNAL
BIG WORDS
PART II OF THE ALAN MOORE INTERVIEW
ADULT COMICS UNDER SIEGE
• TWO FLORIDA RETAILERS BUSTED
• NEW BOOK: SEDUCTION OF THE INNOCENT REVISITED
PETER BAGGE INTERVIEWS ALINE KOMINSKY-CRUMB
A DECADE OF WEIRDO
AN AUTOPSY BY DR. JIM WOODRING
AM I A GENIUS OR WHAT?
YOKO BUNCHO
CONFESSIONS OF A SEX-CRAZED HOUSEWIFE

Above: **Cover for The Comics Journal that featured a long interview with me by the editor Gary Groth**

MY CHILDREN EXPOSE & HUMILIATE ME...
MORE CHAMPAGNE DEAR?
JUST A TOUCH PLEZE!
MOMMEE SHUT UP
DON'T TALK TO HER!
I HATE YOU!
PLAY BARBI NOW!
I HAVE MEAN & JEALOUS THOUGHTS..
BAGUET
BOULANGERIE
PATISSERIE
ESPRESSO
GELATO
COOKIES
Cafe Roma
I DESPISE YOUTH...
I HATE THEIR MUSIC...
THEY DON'T KNOW A DAM THING!
LOOK AT THOSE CARE-FREE JERKS... DUMMIES..
CONFORM-IST ROBOTS!
AT LEAST I HAVE SOME WISDOM!
I THINK I NEED TO GET AWAY....
BECAUSE.... MY ....
1 WRINKLES ARE DEEPENING
MY
2 SEXUAL DESIRE DIMINISHING
HAVE
3 IRRATIONAL ANGER ON THE RISE
AND
4 CREATIVITY LIMITED TO REARRANGING KNICK-KNACKS
I'M
5 OBSESSED BY CANCER & OTHER DEADLY DISEASES
HAVE
6 UNCONTROL-LABLE NEED TO SHOP
7 DRINKING IS MY GREATEST PLEASURE
8 THE FUTURE SEEMS GRIM
MY FAMILY IS CONVINCED & SOON...
DRUGSTORE PUBLICIS
WHAT A FABULOUS PLACE!
I CAN'T BELIEVE I'M HERE
SO.. I CAN'T SPEAK FRENCH!

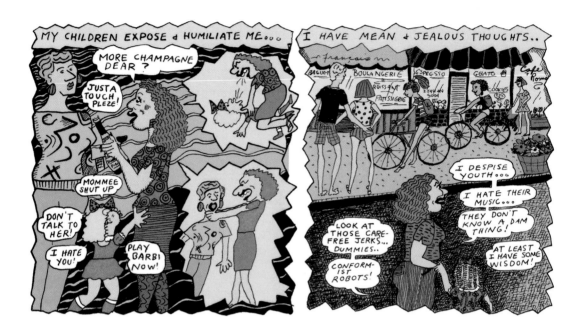

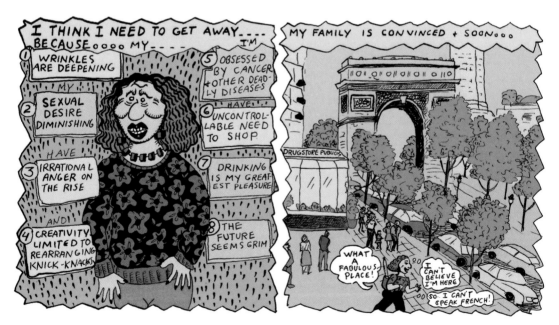

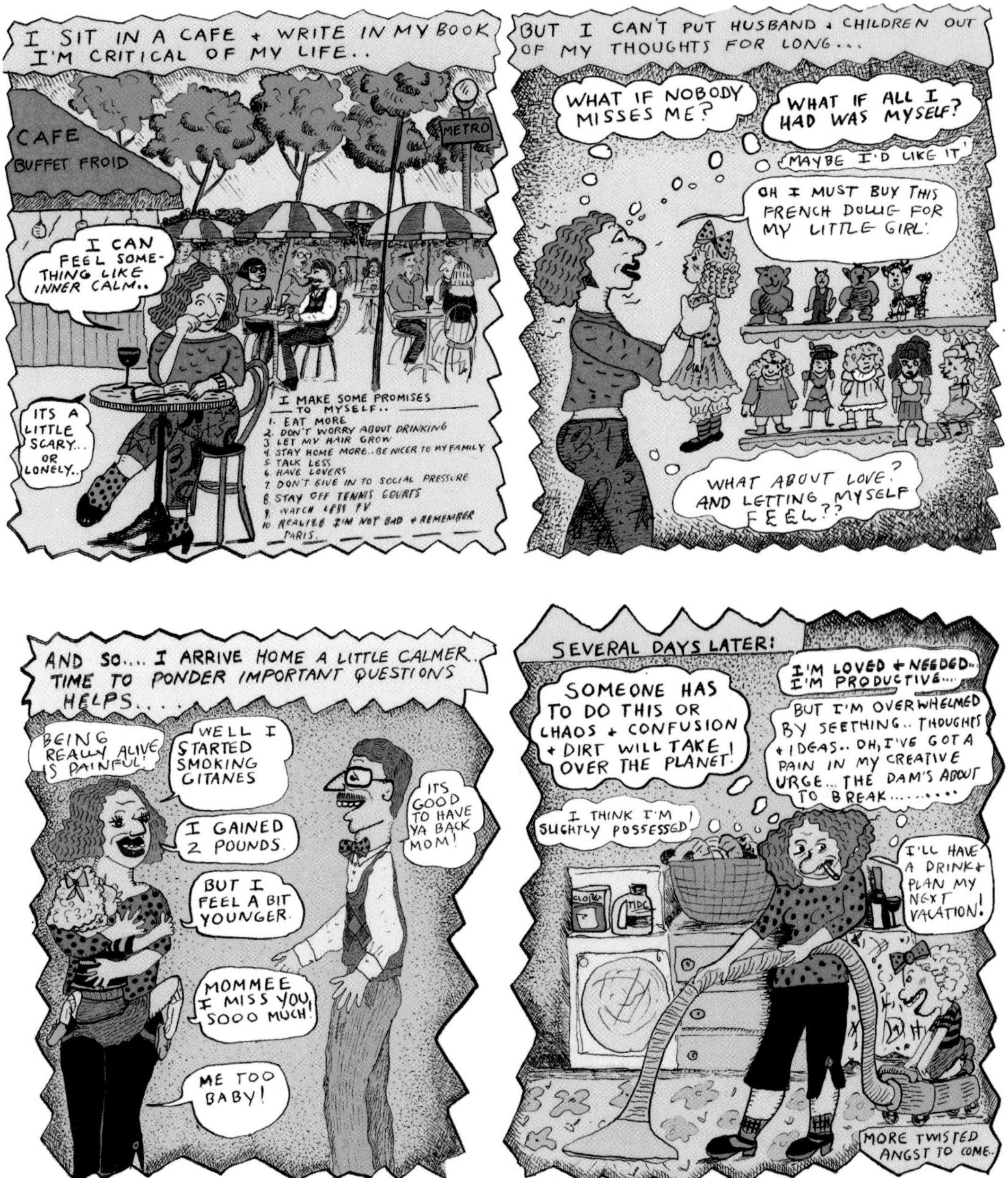
I SIT IN A CAFE + WRITE IN MY BOOK I'M CRITICAL OF MY LIFE..
CAFE
BUFFET FROID
METRO
I CAN FEEL SOMETHING LIKE INNER CALM..
ITS A LITTLE SCARY... OR LONELY..
I MAKE SOME PROMISES TO MYSELF..
1. EAT MORE
2. DON'T WORRY ABOUT DRINKING
3. LET MY HAIR GROW
4. STAY HOME MORE.. BE NICER TO MY FAMILY
5. TALK LESS
6. HAVE LOVERS
7. DON'T GIVE IN TO SOCIAL PRESSURE
8. STAY OFF TENNIS COURTS
9. WATCH LESS TV
10. REALIZE I'M NOT BAD + REMEMBER PARIS.
BUT I CAN'T PUT HUSBAND + CHILDREN OUT OF MY THOUGHTS FOR LONG...
WHAT IF NOBODY MISSES ME?
WHAT IF ALL I HAD WAS MYSELF?
MAYBE I'D LIKE IT
OH I MUST BUY THIS FRENCH DOLLIE FOR MY LITTLE GIRL!
WHAT ABOUT LOVE? AND LETTING MYSELF FEEL??
AND SO.... I ARRIVE HOME A LITTLE CALMER. TIME TO PONDER IMPORTANT QUESTIONS HELPS....
BEING REALLY ALIVE IS PAINFUL!
WELL I STARTED SMOKING GITANES
I GAINED 2 POUNDS.
BUT I FEEL A BIT YOUNGER.
ITS GOOD TO HAVE YA BACK MOM!
MOMMEE I MISS YOU SOOO MUCH!
ME TOO BABY!
SEVERAL DAYS LATER!
SOMEONE HAS TO DO THIS OR CHAOS + CONFUSION + DIRT WILL TAKE OVER THE PLANET!
I'M LOVED + NEEDED.. I'M PRODUCTIVE....
BUT I'M OVERWHELMED BY SEETHING.. THOUGHTS + IDEAS.. OH, I'VE GOT A PAIN IN MY CREATIVE URGE... THE DAM'S ABOUT TO BREAK.........
I THINK I'M SLIGHTLY POSSESSED!
I'LL HAVE A DRINK + PLAN MY NEXT VACATION!
MORE TWISTED ANGST TO COME..

Looking for a new life

I knew that Robert would recreate his insular world wherever we landed, and thought it would be a good challenge for Sophie to learn a new culture and language and to be shaken up a bit—she was very intelligent and had effortlessly mastered everything I'd thrown at her so far. What I had underestimated was Robert's attachment to his pals like Terry Zwigoff and Robert Armstrong and to his son Jesse. I never considered how difficult it would be for Sophie to fit in or to feel comfortable with French kids.

I knew we were rural sophisticates and that I couldn't realistically move us to a big city, so I had eliminated Paris as a choice. In my ever energetic, optimistic and headstrong manner, I dragged my family to a small medieval village in the south of France. We arrived for a summer of exploration, but immediately got sucked into looking at houses because as it turned out, half the village was empty and almost everything was potentially for sale. Houses were very cheap, a shock after California, where even a run-down shack cost a fortune.

Gail Wagman and her husband Alain Schons—she's American and he's French—owned a great restaurant in the village, and helped us from the start with everything. We could never have pulled off this complicated move without their support. Their daughter Emily was the same age as Sophie and luckily was fluent in English as well as French. As it turned out, the girls didn't get along at first but they eventually became great friends. We looked at lots of amazing and strange old stone houses: some had been modernized during the post-war years in bizarre and hideous ways, but each one was unique and fascinating.

One day in mid-July, Gail made an appointment for us to look at a house that was in ruins but was cheap and big and in a great location right on the river. She couldn't go with us, so we went by ourselves to the Rue du Pont Vieux, where we saw an old lady standing outside the front door of a house. We asked if she was Madame Rigal and she said yes, so we asked if we could see the house. She took us inside, and I instantly got the goose bumps. It was the most beautiful house I could have imagined. It went on and on, and the rooms just got better and better. It was full of furniture, drapes, rugs—everything from the 1920s or earlier. We had heard that the house we were to visit was practically a ruin, but this house seemed to be in really good shape, so we were surprised and a little confused.

I thought we'd better go back and talk to Gail about this, so I thanked Madame Rigal and I told her I thought her house was beautiful, but that we couldn't afford it. She said "Make me an offer." I replied that I didn't want to insult her, and that we really didn't have enough money for such a house. She was insistent, so I offered her honestly every penny we had. She started screaming at me—my French was so bad I could hardly understand her—but I gathered the sum was half of what she wanted. So I apologized and said we had to go and look at another house. She planted herself in front of me, and literally ordered us to go back to Gail's house for lunch while she discussed the matter with "Maman" (Maman was ninety-eight years old). She said she would call us at 2 p.m. The Rigals accepted our offer and the next day we signed a promesse de vente, or pre-sale agreement.

As it turned out, we had gone to the wrong house! The house we were supposed to look at was two doors down and belonged to Madame Rigal, while our house was owned by Mademoiselle Rigal (she was 78 and had never married). Out of curiosity, we visited the other house and hated it. Later we learned that Mademoiselle Rigal and Maman had moved to a new house across the river nine years ago, and that they had meant to put their old house up for sale, but just hadn't gotten around to it. When a family of rich extraterrestrials suddenly showed up at the front door as Mademoiselle was emptying a bucket of dirty water, she took it as a sign from God that it was time to sell. Welcome to the sunny south of France!

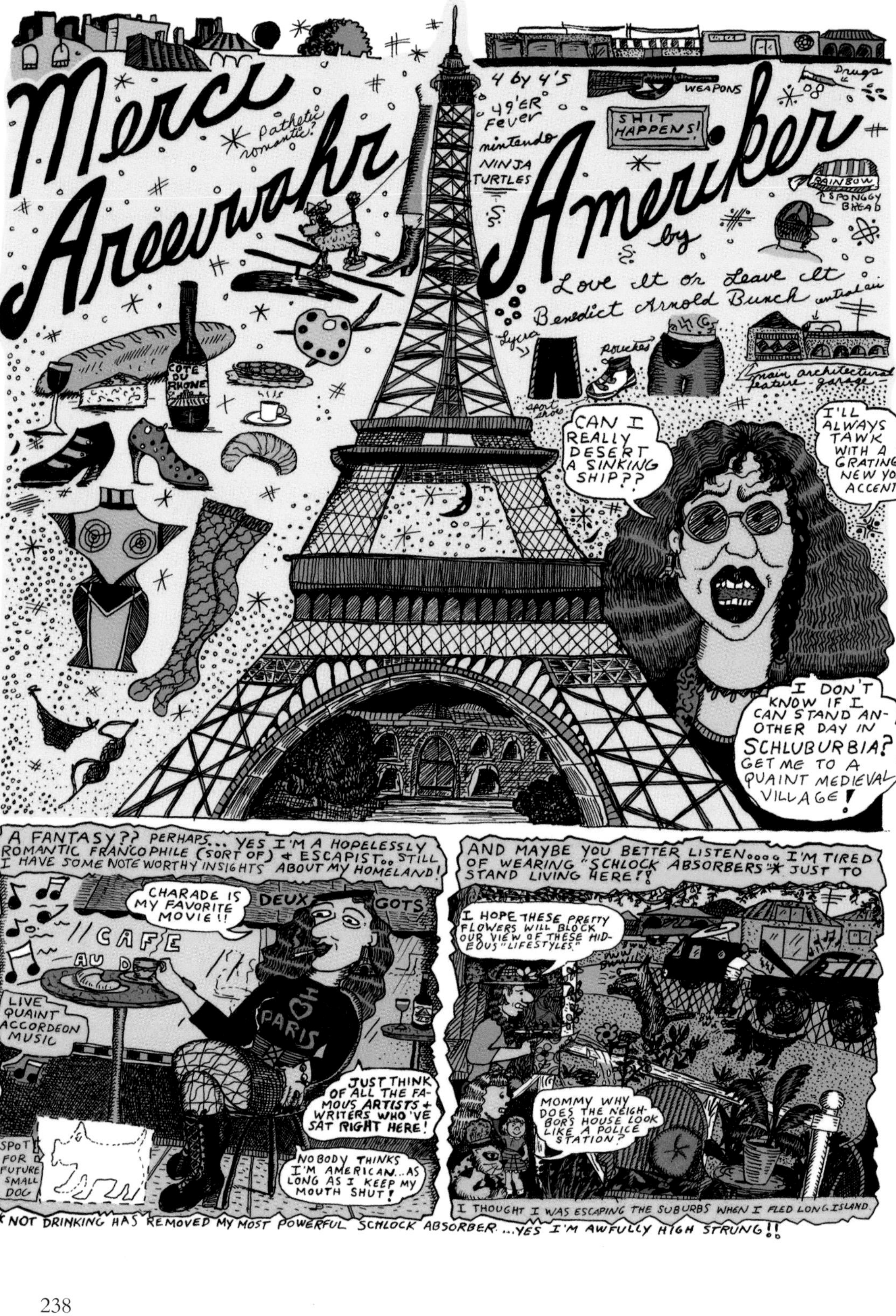
Merci Areevwahr Ameriker
by
Love It or Leave It
Benedict Arnold Bunch
pathetic romantic?
4 by 4's
49'ER Fever
nintendo
NINJA TURTLES
SHIT HAPPENS!
WEAPONS
Drugs
RAINBOW
SPONGGY BREAD
COTE DU RHONE
Lycra
Rouches
sport shoe
main architectural feature garage
CAN I REALLY DESERT A SINKING SHIP??
I'LL ALWAYS TAWK WITH A GRATING NEW YORK ACCENT!
I DON'T KNOW IF I CAN STAND ANOTHER DAY IN SCHLUBURBIA? GET ME TO A QUAINT MEDIEVAL VILLAGE!
A FANTASY?? PERHAPS... YES I'M A HOPELESSLY ROMANTIC FRANCOPHILE (SORT OF) + ESCAPIST.. STILL I HAVE SOME NOTEWORTHY INSIGHTS ABOUT MY HOMELAND!
CHARADE IS MY FAVORITE MOVIE!!
DEUX GOTS
CAFE AU D
LIVE QUAINT ACCORDEON MUSIC
I ♥ PARIS
JUST THINK OF ALL THE FAMOUS ARTISTS + WRITERS WHO'VE SAT RIGHT HERE!
NOBODY THINKS I'M AMERICAN... AS LONG AS I KEEP MY MOUTH SHUT!
SPOT FOR FUTURE SMALL DOG
AND MAYBE YOU BETTER LISTEN.... I'M TIRED OF WEARING "SCHLOCK ABSORBERS"* JUST TO STAND LIVING HERE!!
I HOPE THESE PRETTY FLOWERS WILL BLOCK OUR VIEW OF THESE HIDEOUS "LIFESTYLES."
MOMMY WHY DOES THE NEIGHBOR'S HOUSE LOOK LIKE A POLICE STATION?
I THOUGHT I WAS ESCAPING THE SUBURBS WHEN I FLED LONG ISLAND.
* NOT DRINKING HAS REMOVED MY MOST POWERFUL SCHLOCK ABSORBER... YES I'M AWFULLY HIGH STRUNG!!

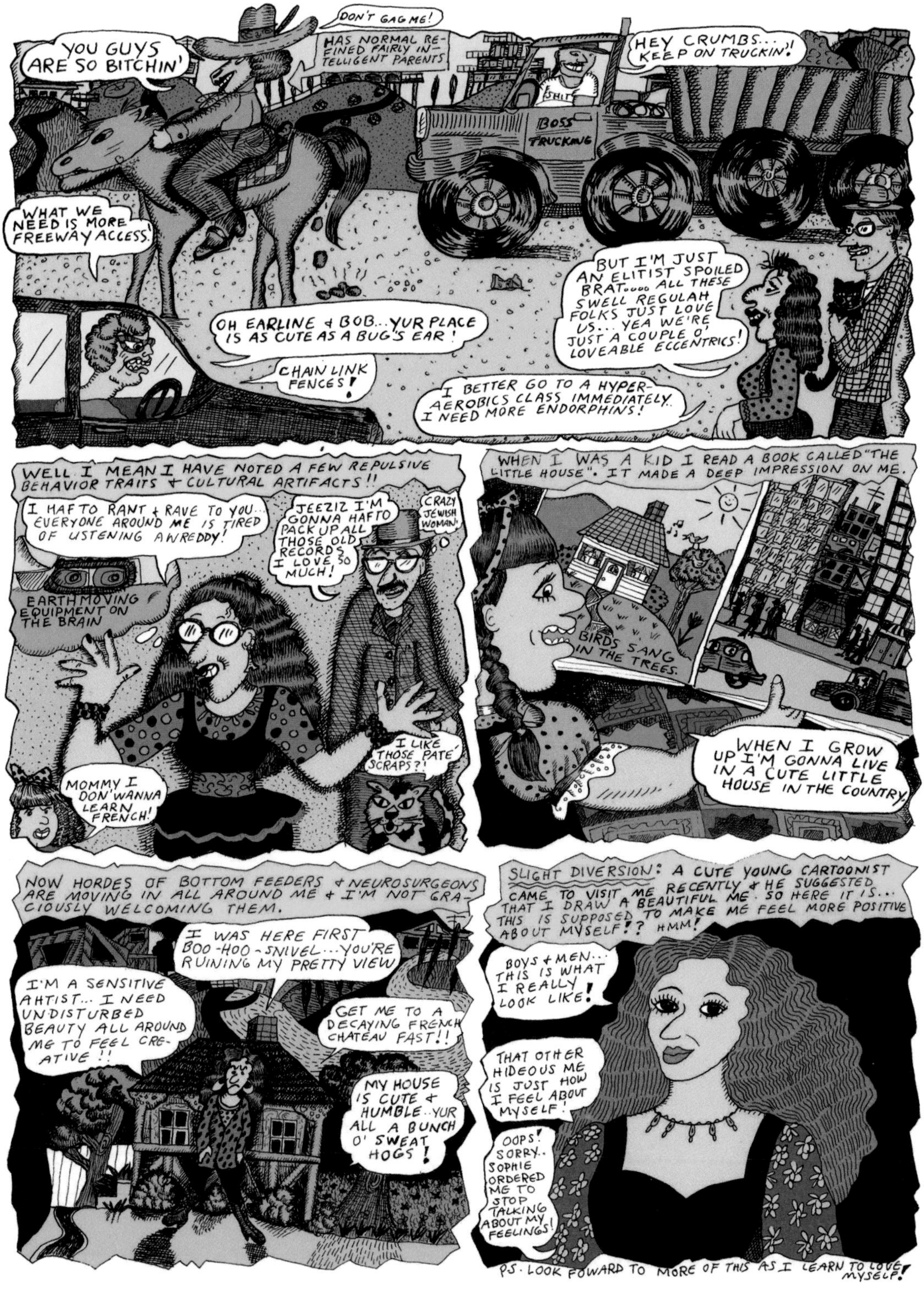
YOU GUYS ARE SO BITCHIN'
DON'T GAG ME!
HAS NORMAL REFINED FAIRLY INTELLIGENT PARENTS
HEY CRUMBS... KEEP ON TRUCKIN'!
SHIT
BOSS TRUCKING
WHAT WE NEED IS MORE FREEWAY ACCESS!
BUT I'M JUST AN ELITIST SPOILED BRAT..... ALL THESE SWELL REGULAH FOLKS JUST LOVE US... YEA WE'RE JUST A COUPLE O' LOVEABLE ECCENTRICS!
OH EARLINE & BOB... YUR PLACE IS AS CUTE AS A BUG'S EAR!
CHAIN LINK FENCES!
I BETTER GO TO A HYPER-AEROBICS CLASS IMMEDIATELY.. I NEED MORE ENDORPHINS!
WELL I MEAN I HAVE NOTED A FEW REPULSIVE BEHAVIOR TRAITS & CULTURAL ARTIFACTS!!
I HAFTO RANT & RAVE TO YOU... EVERYONE AROUND ME IS TIRED OF LISTENING AWREDDY!
JEEZIZ I'M GONNA HAFTO PACK UP ALL THOSE OLD RECORDS. I LOVE SO MUCH!
CRAZY JEWISH WOMAN.
EARTHMOVING EQUIPMENT ON THE BRAIN
I LIKE THOSE PATE' SCRAPS?!
MOMMY I DON'WANNA LEARN FRENCH!
WHEN I WAS A KID I READ A BOOK CALLED "THE LITTLE HOUSE". IT MADE A DEEP IMPRESSION ON ME.
BIRDS SANG IN THE TREES.
WHEN I GROW UP I'M GONNA LIVE IN A CUTE LITTLE HOUSE IN THE COUNTRY.
NOW HORDES OF BOTTOM FEEDERS & NEUROSURGEONS ARE MOVING IN ALL AROUND ME & I'M NOT GRACIOUSLY WELCOMING THEM.
I WAS HERE FIRST BOO-HOO-SNIVEL... YOU'RE RUINING MY PRETTY VIEW
I'M A SENSITIVE AHTIST... I NEED UNDISTURBED BEAUTY ALL AROUND ME TO FEEL CREATIVE!!
GET ME TO A DECAYING FRENCH CHATEAU FAST!!
MY HOUSE IS CUTE & HUMBLE.. YUR ALL A BUNCH O' SWEAT HOGS!
SLIGHT DIVERSION: A CUTE YOUNG CARTOONIST CAME TO VISIT ME RECENTLY & HE SUGGESTED THAT I DRAW A BEAUTIFUL ME. SO HERE IT IS... THIS IS SUPPOSED TO MAKE ME FEEL MORE POSITIVE ABOUT MYSELF!? HMM!
BOYS & MEN... THIS IS WHAT I REALLY LOOK LIKE!
THAT OTHER HIDEOUS ME IS JUST HOW I FEEL ABOUT MYSELF!
OOPS! SORRY.. SOPHIE ORDERED ME TO STOP TALKING ABOUT MY FEELINGS!
P.S. LOOK FOWARD TO MORE OF THIS AS I LEARN TO LOVE MYSELF!

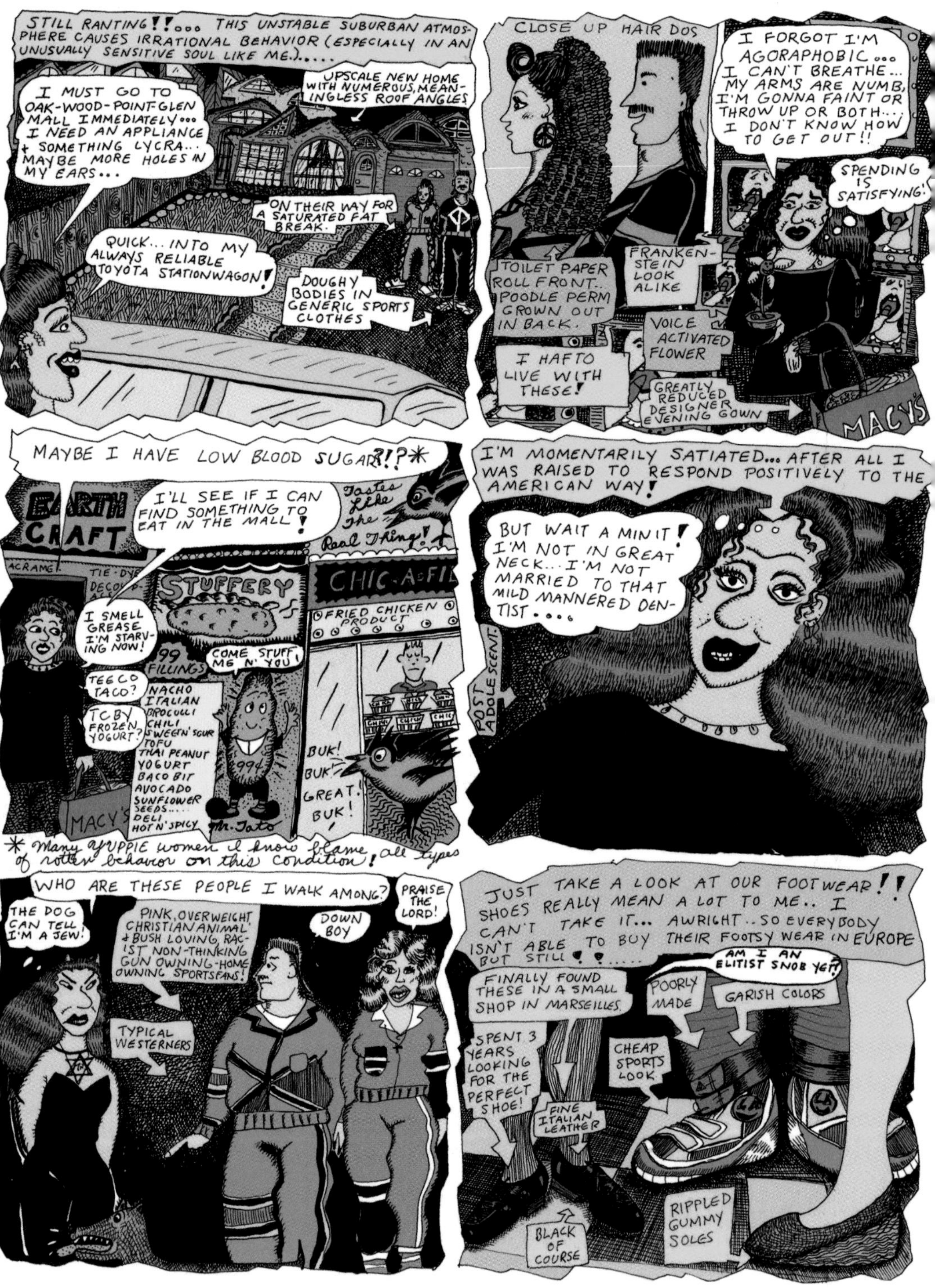

STILL RANTING!!... THIS UNSTABLE SUBURBAN ATMOSPHERE CAUSES IRRATIONAL BEHAVIOR (ESPECIALLY IN AN UNUSUALLY SENSITIVE SOUL LIKE ME.)....
I MUST GO TO OAK-WOOD-POINT-GLEN MALL IMMEDIATELY... I NEED AN APPLIANCE + SOMETHING LYCRA... MAYBE MORE HOLES IN MY EARS...
UPSCALE NEW HOME WITH NUMEROUS, MEANINGLESS ROOF ANGLES
ON THEIR WAY FOR A SATURATED FAT BREAK.
QUICK... INTO MY ALWAYS RELIABLE TOYOTA STATIONWAGON!
DOUGHY BODIES IN GENERIC SPORTS CLOTHES
CLOSE UP HAIR DOS
TOILET PAPER ROLL FRONT.. POODLE PERM GROWN OUT IN BACK.
FRANKENSTEIN LOOK ALIKE
I HAFTO LIVE WITH THESE!
I FORGOT I'M AGORAPHOBIC... I CAN'T BREATHE... MY ARMS ARE NUMB, I'M GONNA FAINT OR THROW UP OR BOTH... I DON'T KNOW HOW TO GET OUT!!
SPENDING IS SATISFYING!
VOICE ACTIVATED FLOWER
GREATLY REDUCED DESIGNER EVENING GOWN
MACY'S
MAYBE I HAVE LOW BLOOD SUGAR?!?*
I'LL SEE IF I CAN FIND SOMETHING TO EAT IN THE MALL!
EARTH CRAFT
Tastes like the Real Thing!
STUFFERY
CHIC-A-FIL
FRIED CHICKEN PRODUCT
I SMELL GREASE I'M STARVING NOW!
99 FILLINGS
COME STUFF ME N' YOU!
TEE CO TACO?
TCBY FROZEN YOGURT?
NACHO ITALIAN BROCOLLI CHILI SWEET'N SOUR TOFU THAI PEANUT YOGURT BACO BIT AVOCADO SUNFLOWER SEEDS..... DELI HOT N' SPICY
99¢
Mr. Tato
BUK! BUK! GREAT! BUK!
MACY'S
* Many yuppie women I know blame all types of rotten behavior on this condition!
I'M MOMENTARILY SATIATED... AFTER ALL I WAS RAISED TO RESPOND POSITIVELY TO THE AMERICAN WAY!
BUT WAIT A MINIT! I'M NOT IN GREAT NECK... I'M NOT MARRIED TO THAT MILD MANNERED DENTIST....
POST ADOLESCENT.
WHO ARE THESE PEOPLE I WALK AMONG?
THE DOG CAN TELL I'M A JEW!
PINK, OVERWEIGHT CHRISTIAN ANIMAL & BUSH LOVING, RACIST NON-THINKING GUN OWNING-HOME OWNING SPORTSFANS!
DOWN BOY
PRAISE THE LORD!
TYPICAL WESTERNERS
JUST TAKE A LOOK AT OUR FOOTWEAR!! SHOES REALLY MEAN A LOT TO ME.. I CAN'T TAKE IT... AWRIGHT.. SO EVERYBODY ISN'T ABLE TO BUY THEIR FOOTSY WEAR IN EUROPE BUT STILL!!.....
AM I AN ELITIST SNOB YET?
FINALLY FOUND THESE IN A SMALL SHOP IN MARSEILLES.
POORLY MADE
GARISH COLORS
SPENT 3 YEARS LOOKING FOR THE PERFECT SHOE!
CHEAP SPORTS LOOK
FINE ITALIAN LEATHER
RIPPLED GUMMY SOLES
BLACK OF COURSE

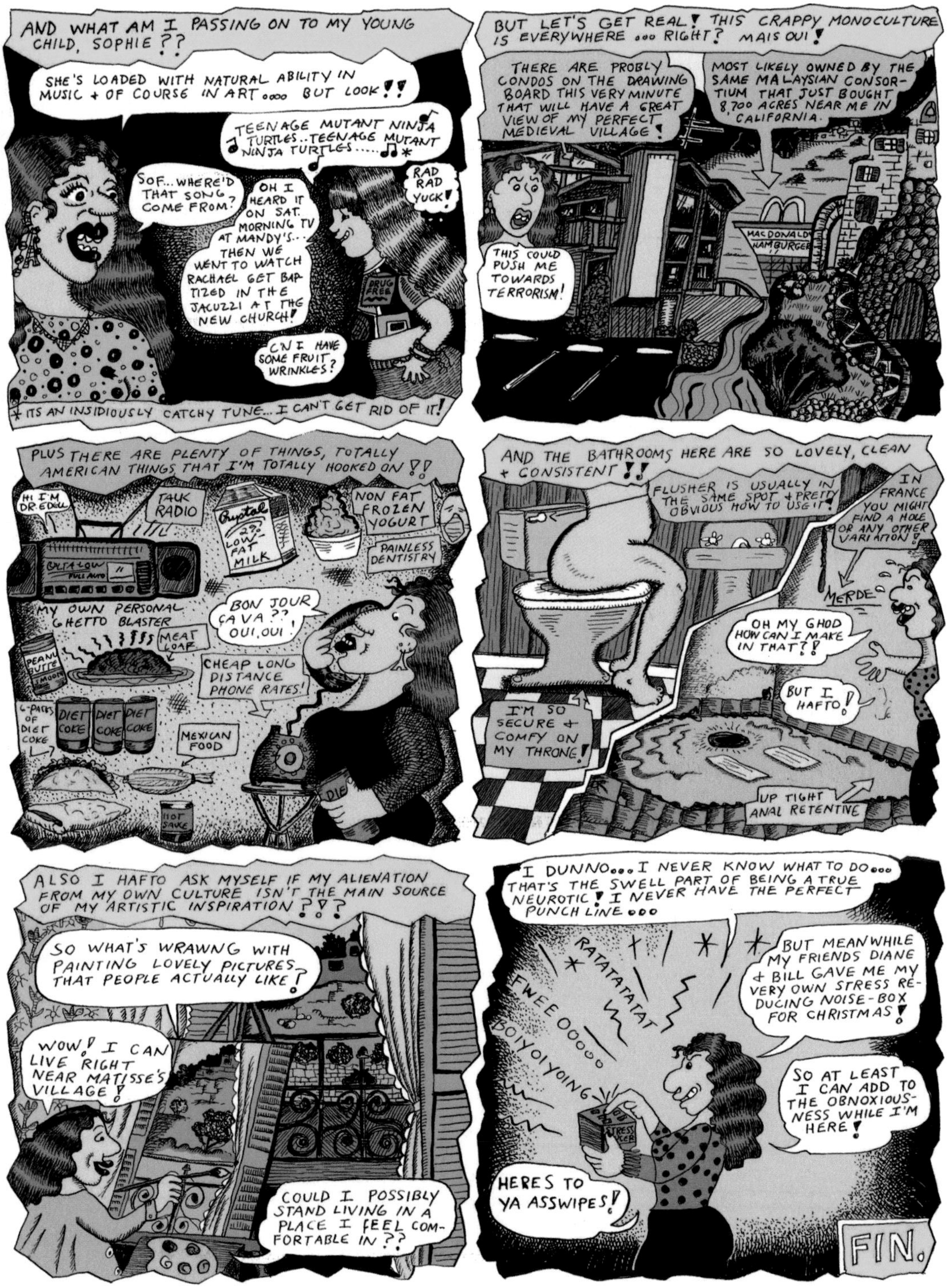

AND WHAT AM I PASSING ON TO MY YOUNG CHILD, SOPHIE ??
SHE'S LOADED WITH NATURAL ABILITY IN MUSIC + OF COURSE IN ART.... BUT LOOK!!
TEENAGE MUTANT NINJA TURTLES.. TEENAGE MUTANT NINJA TURTLES..... *
SOF... WHERE'D THAT SONG COME FROM?
OH I HEARD IT ON SAT. MORNING TV AT MANDY'S.. THEN WE WENT TO WATCH RACHAEL GET BAPTIZED IN THE JACUZZI AT THE NEW CHURCH!
RAD RAD YUCK!
DRUG FREE
C'N I HAVE SOME FRUIT WRINKLES?
* ITS AN INSIDIOUSLY CATCHY TUNE... I CAN'T GET RID OF IT!
BUT LET'S GET REAL! THIS CRAPPY MONOCULTURE IS EVERYWHERE ... RIGHT? MAIS OUI!
THERE ARE PROBLY CONDOS ON THE DRAWING BOARD THIS VERY MINUTE THAT WILL HAVE A GREAT VIEW OF MY PERFECT MEDIEVAL VILLAGE!
MOST LIKELY OWNED BY THE SAME MALAYSIAN CONSORTIUM THAT JUST BOUGHT 8,700 ACRES NEAR ME IN CALIFORNIA.
MACDONALD HAMBURGER
THIS COULD PUSH ME TOWARDS TERRORISM!
PLUS THERE ARE PLENTY OF THINGS, TOTALLY AMERICAN THINGS THAT I'M TOTALLY HOOKED ON !!
HI I'M DR. EDELL
TALK RADIO
Crystal 2% LOW-FAT MILK
NON FAT FROZEN YOGURT
PAINLESS DENTISTRY
MY OWN PERSONAL GHETTO BLASTER
BON JOUR ÇA VA ?? OUI, OUI!
MEAT LOAF
PEANUT BUTTER
CHEAP LONG DISTANCE PHONE RATES!
6-PAKS OF DIET COKE
DIET COKE
MEXICAN FOOD
HOT SAUCE
AND THE BATHROOMS HERE ARE SO LOVELY, CLEAN + CONSISTENT!!
FLUSHER IS USUALLY IN THE SAME SPOT + PRETTY OBVIOUS HOW TO USE IT!
IN FRANCE YOU MIGHT FIND A HOLE OR ANY OTHER VARIATION!
MERDE
OH MY GHOD HOW CAN I MAKE IN THAT?!
BUT I HAFTO!
I'M SO SECURE + COMFY ON MY THRONE!
UP TIGHT ANAL RETENTIVE
ALSO I HAFTO ASK MYSELF IF MY ALIENATION FROM MY OWN CULTURE ISN'T THE MAIN SOURCE OF MY ARTISTIC INSPIRATION ???
SO WHAT'S WRAWNG WITH PAINTING LOVELY PICTURES THAT PEOPLE ACTUALLY LIKE?
WOW! I CAN LIVE RIGHT NEAR MATISSE'S VILLAGE!
COULD I POSSIBLY STAND LIVING IN A PLACE I FEEL COMFORTABLE IN??
I DUNNO... I NEVER KNOW WHAT TO DO... THAT'S THE SWELL PART OF BEING A TRUE NEUROTIC! I NEVER HAVE THE PERFECT PUNCH LINE...
BUT MEANWHILE MY FRIENDS DIANE + BILL GAVE ME MY VERY OWN STRESS REDUCING NOISE-BOX FOR CHRISTMAS!
RATATATATAT
FWEE OOOOOO
BOIYOIYOING
SO AT LEAST I CAN ADD TO THE OBNOXIOUSNESS WHILE I'M HERE!
HERES TO YA ASSWIPES!
FIN.

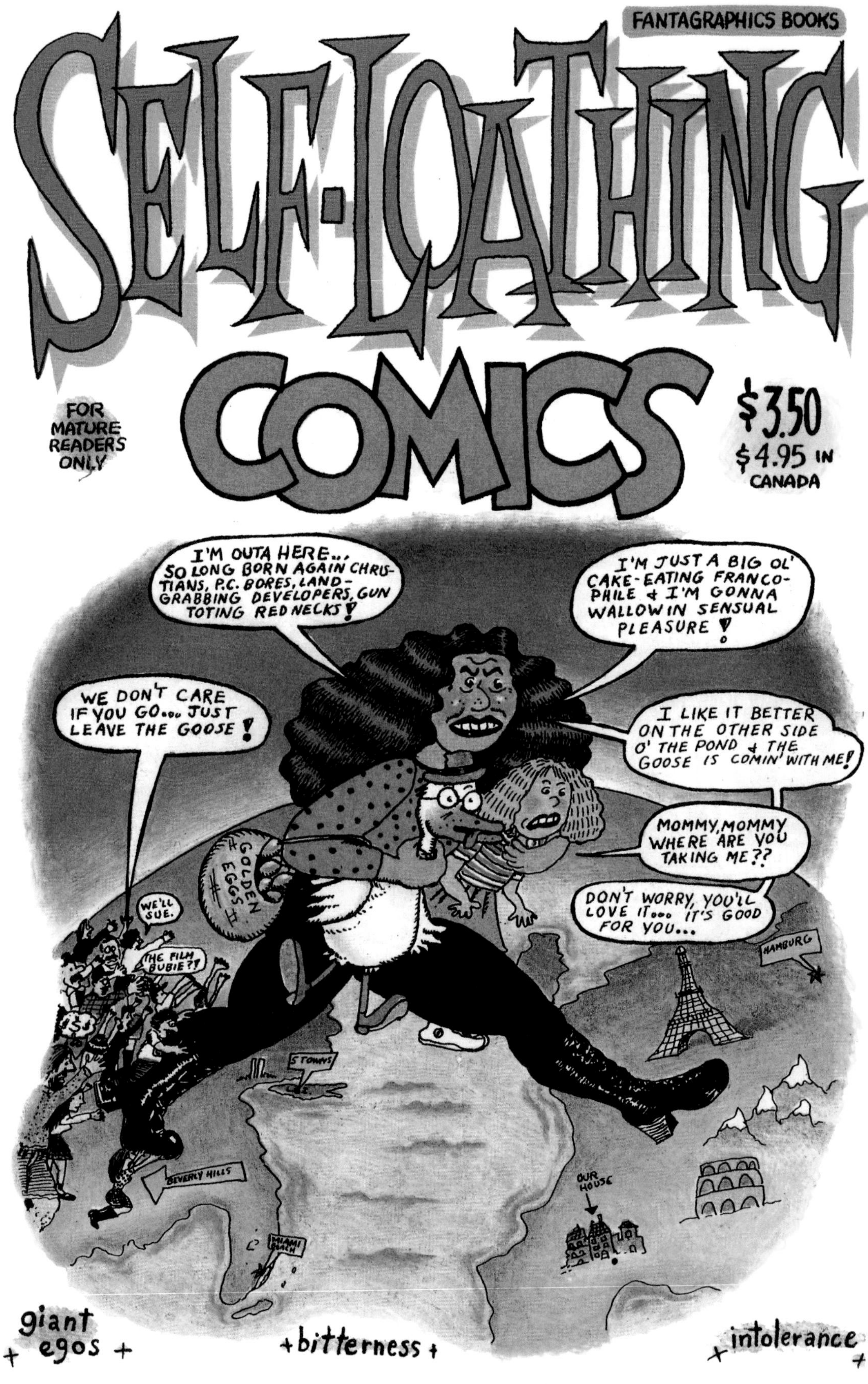
FANTAGRAPHICS BOOKS
SELF-LOATHING COMICS
FOR MATURE READERS ONLY
$3.50
$4.95 IN CANADA
I'M OUTA HERE... SO LONG BORN AGAIN CHRISTIANS, P.C. BORES, LAND-GRABBING DEVELOPERS, GUN TOTING REDNECKS!
I'M JUST A BIG OL' CAKE-EATING FRANCOPHILE & I'M GONNA WALLOW IN SENSUAL PLEASURE!
WE DON'T CARE IF YOU GO... JUST LEAVE THE GOOSE!
I LIKE IT BETTER ON THE OTHER SIDE O' THE POND & THE GOOSE IS COMIN' WITH ME!
MOMMY, MOMMY WHERE ARE YOU TAKING ME??
DON'T WORRY, YOU'LL LOVE IT... IT'S GOOD FOR YOU...
GOLDEN EGGS
WE'LL SUE.
THE FILM BUBIE?!
HAMBURG
5 TOWNS
BEVERLY HILLS
OUR HOUSE
MIAMI BEACH
giant egos +
+ bitterness +
+ intolerance +

Au revoir America!

In the fall of 1989, we returned to California to pack up our stuff and make this monumental change in our lives. If you saw the film *Crumb* by Terry Zwigoff, you might remember the last scene where the United Van Lines truck pulls away with all our possessions, and Robert looks totally bereft and I look old, tired and stressed and Sophie is just doing handstands through it all. We had rented our house to some friends, so I reasoned that we could move back after a few years if it didn't work out, and at least Sophie would have learned another language. I had no idea what I was taking on and the monumental changes that would follow

Above: **Sophie and Grandma taken just after we moved to France**

CHAPTER FOUR
The sunny south
of France

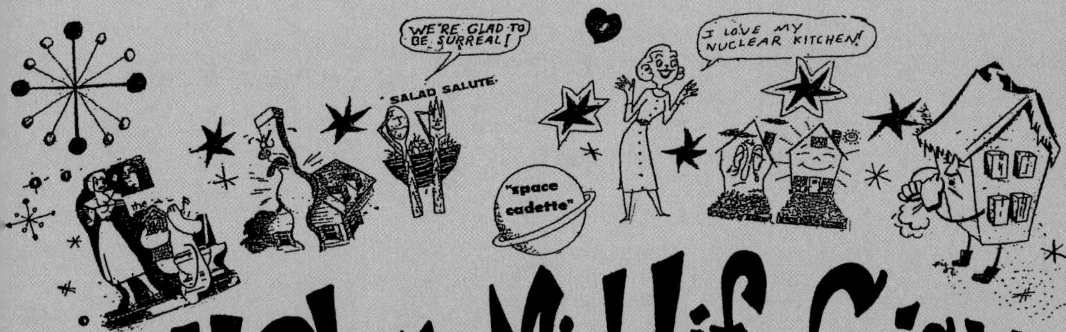
WE'RE GLAD TO BE SURREAL!
SALAD SALUTE
"space cadette"
I LOVE MY NUCLEAR KITCHEN!

4. Full-Blown Mid-Life Crisis

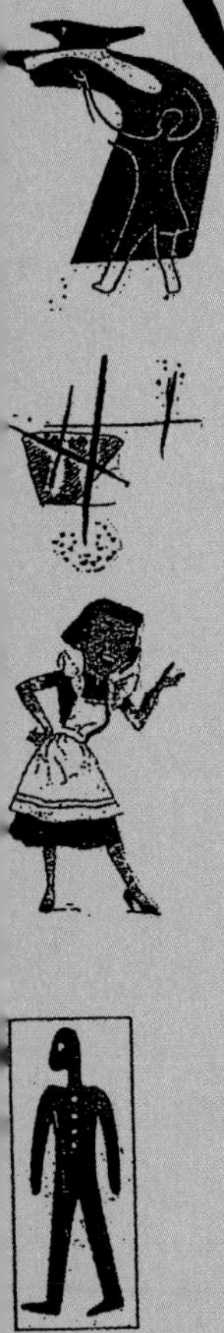

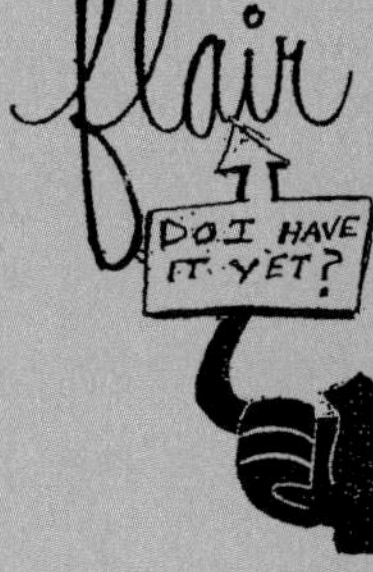
flair
DO I HAVE IT YET?

- The Sunny South of France
- Decadence
- Romance
- Creative Joy

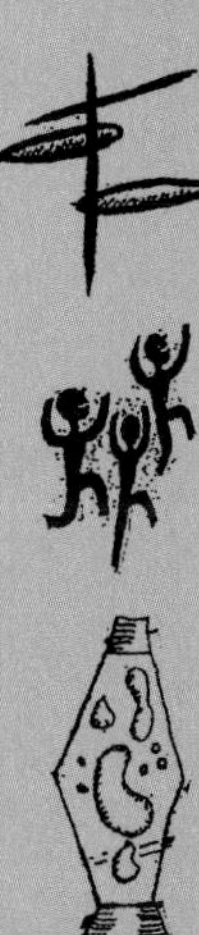

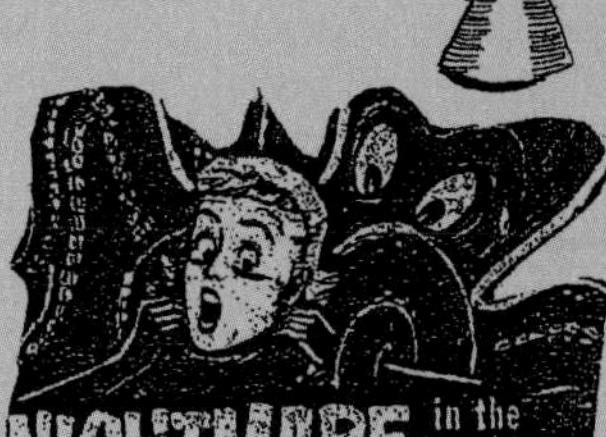
NIGHTMARE in the basement!

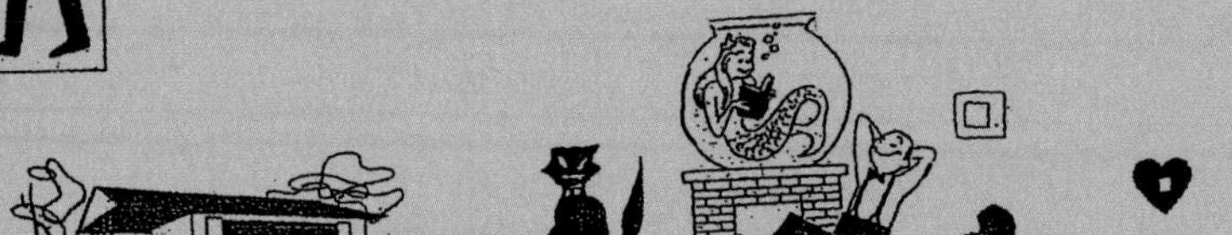

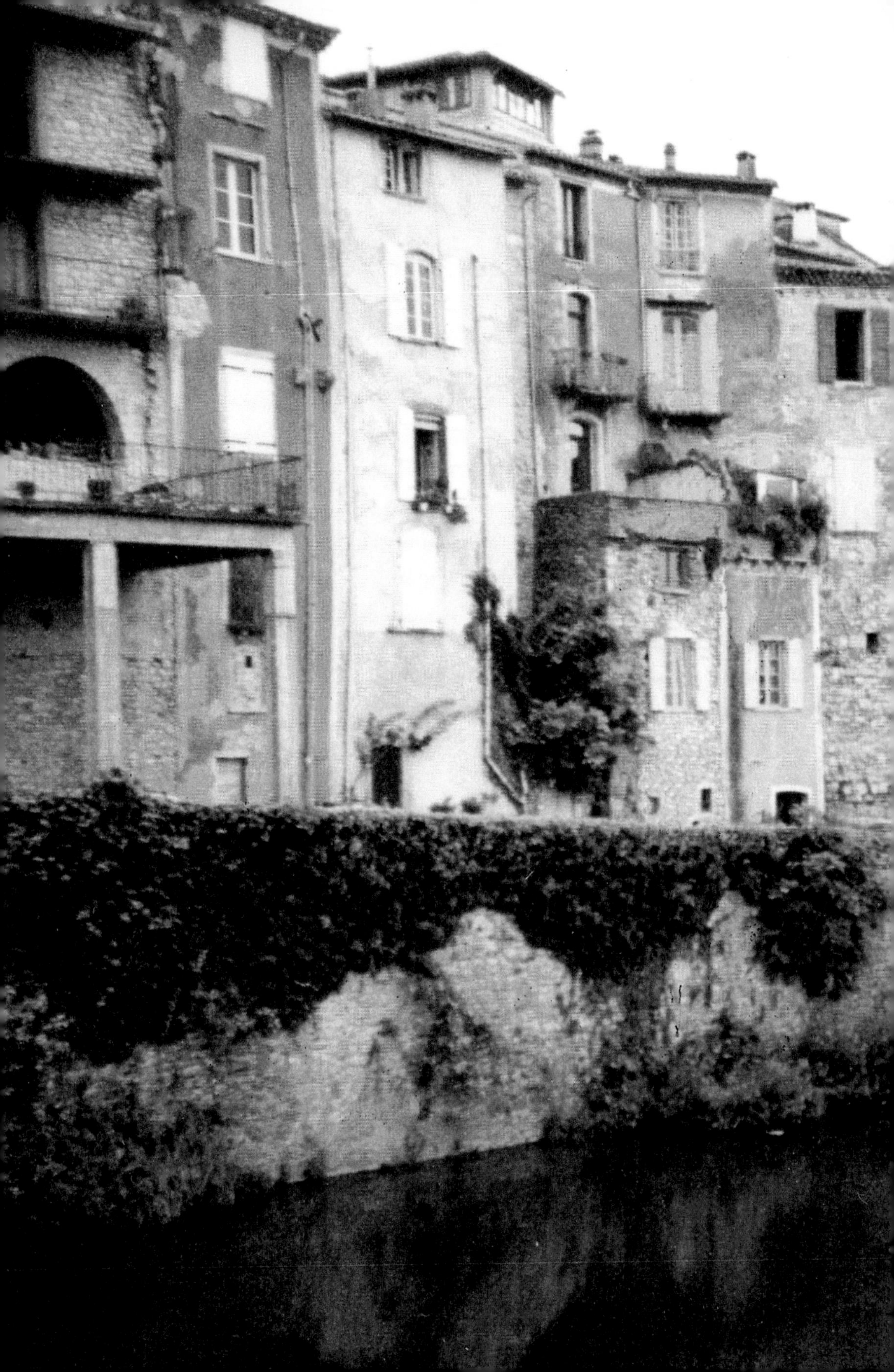

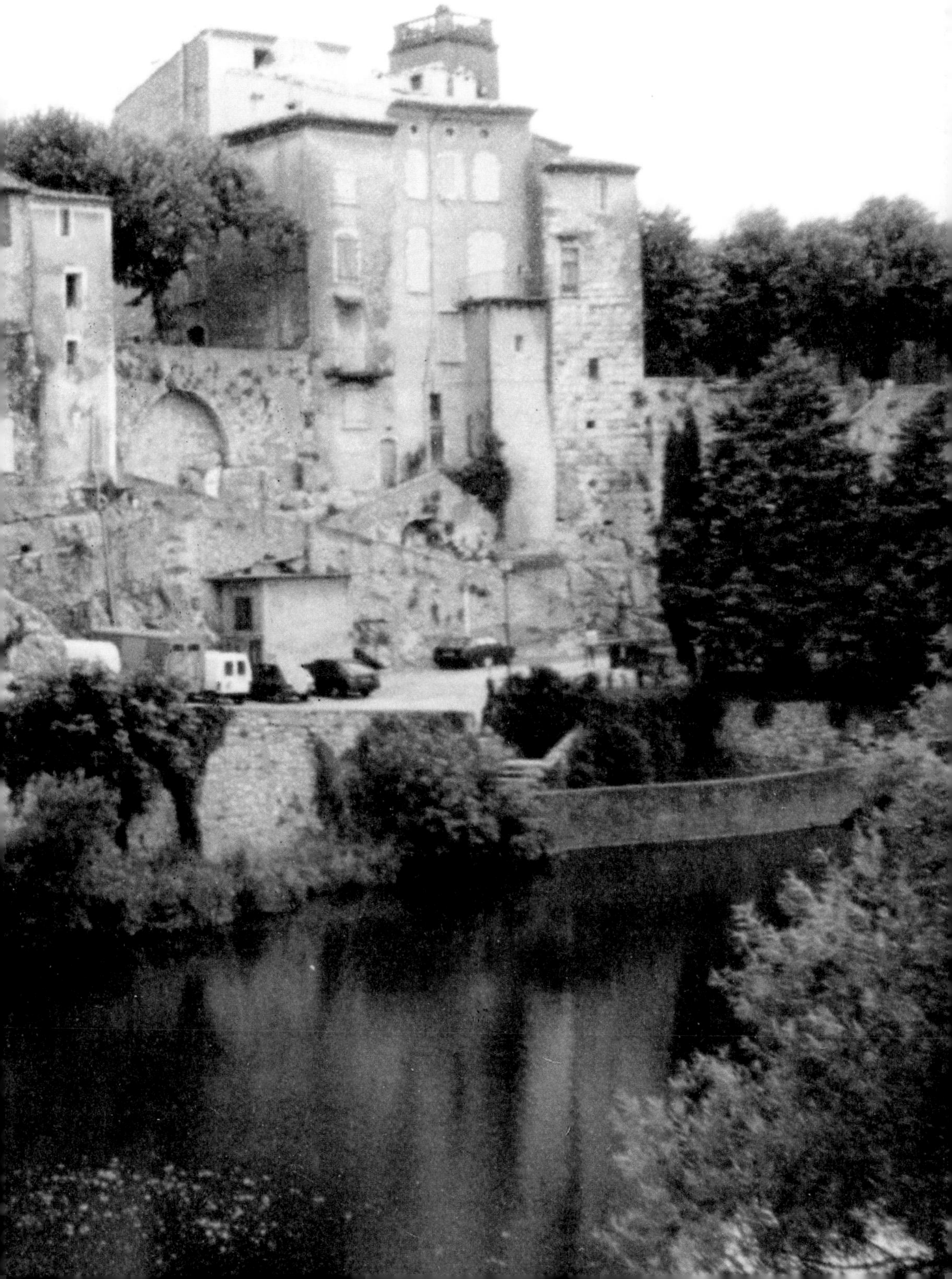

Not a promising beginning ...

We arrived in our medieval village in the south of France in April 1990. It had been a long and complicated saga getting there—not just getting all our stuff packed and shipped, but also the doubts, worries, second thoughts, and endless discussions about what the hell we were doing. The comic story on the following pages describes what all that was like.

When we arrive at the village, the bitter Mistral wind was blowing down the Rhone River Valley. It was freezing cold, and there was no heat in our empty, old, thirteen-room stone house. During our first week there, Robert broke his front teeth bridge biting into a delicious baguette, and a flower pot blew off our terrace and dented the car of an old peasant neighbor—before we'd had time to look into house insurance. We all slept huddled together in Robert's future studio. Fortunately, I had shipped ahead some bedding and familiar toys and a few favorite dishes so we could at least make a homey campsite. We bought mattresses and borrowed a space heater, and at first, before reality sank in, Sophie enjoyed the novelty of roughing it.

Preceding page: **Jolie view of our house and village, circa 1992**
Please note that my terrace has the most flowers.

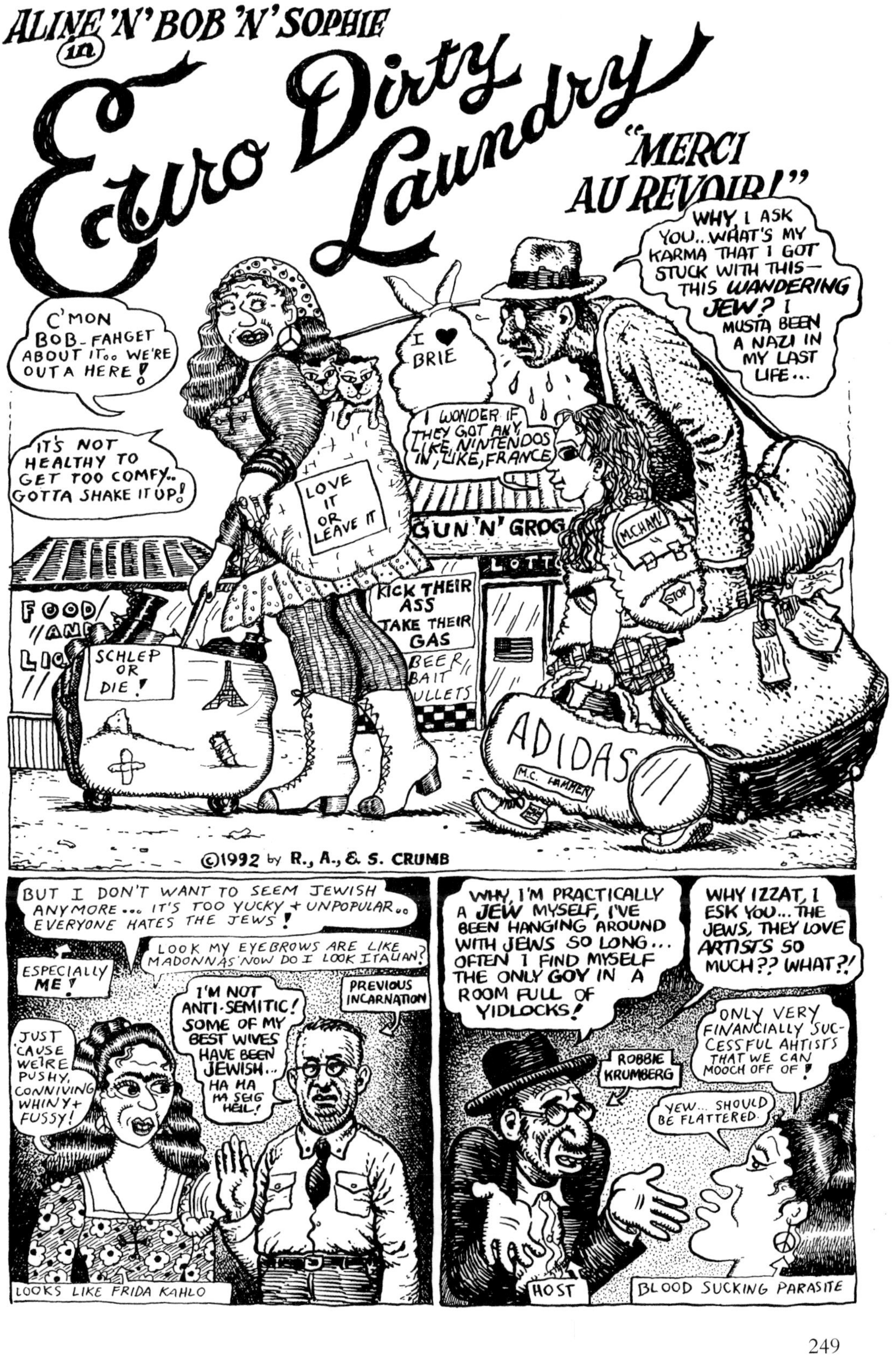

ALINE 'N' BOB 'N' SOPHIE
in
Euro Dirty Laundry
"MERCI AU REVOIR!"
WHY, I ASK YOU... WHAT'S MY KARMA THAT I GOT STUCK WITH THIS— THIS WANDERING JEW? I MUSTA BEEN A NAZI IN MY LAST LIFE...
C'MON BOB– FAHGET ABOUT IT.. WE'RE OUTA HERE!
I ♥ BRIE
I WONDER IF THEY GOT ANY, LIKE, NINTENDOS IN, LIKE, FRANCE
IT'S NOT HEALTHY TO GET TOO COMFY.. GOTTA SHAKE IT UP!
LOVE IT OR LEAVE IT
GUN 'N' GROG
LOTT
KICK THEIR ASS TAKE THEIR GAS
BEER BAIT ULLETS
FOOD AN LIQ
SCHLEP OR DIE!
M.C. HAMMER
STOP
ADIDAS
M.C. HAMMER
©1992 by R., A., & S. CRUMB
BUT I DON'T WANT TO SEEM JEWISH ANYMORE... IT'S TOO YUCKY + UNPOPULAR.. EVERYONE HATES THE JEWS!
LOOK MY EYEBROWS ARE LIKE MADONNAS' NOW DO I LOOK ITALIAN?
ESPECIALLY ME!
I'M NOT ANTI-SEMITIC! SOME OF MY BEST WIVES HAVE BEEN JEWISH... HA HA HA SEIG HEIL!
PREVIOUS INCARNATION
JUST 'CAUSE WE'RE PUSHY, CONNIVING WHINY + FUSSY!
LOOKS LIKE FRIDA KAHLO
WHY, I'M PRACTICALLY A JEW MYSELF, I'VE BEEN HANGING AROUND WITH JEWS SO LONG... OFTEN I FIND MYSELF THE ONLY GOY IN A ROOM FULL OF YIDLOCKS!
WHY IZZAT, I ESK YOU... THE JEWS, THEY LOVE ARTISTS SO MUCH?? WHAT?!
ONLY VERY FINANCIALLY SUCCESSFUL AHTISTS THAT WE CAN MOOCH OFF OF!
ROBBIE KRUMBERG
YEW... SHOULD BE FLATTERED.
HOST
BLOOD SUCKING PARASITE

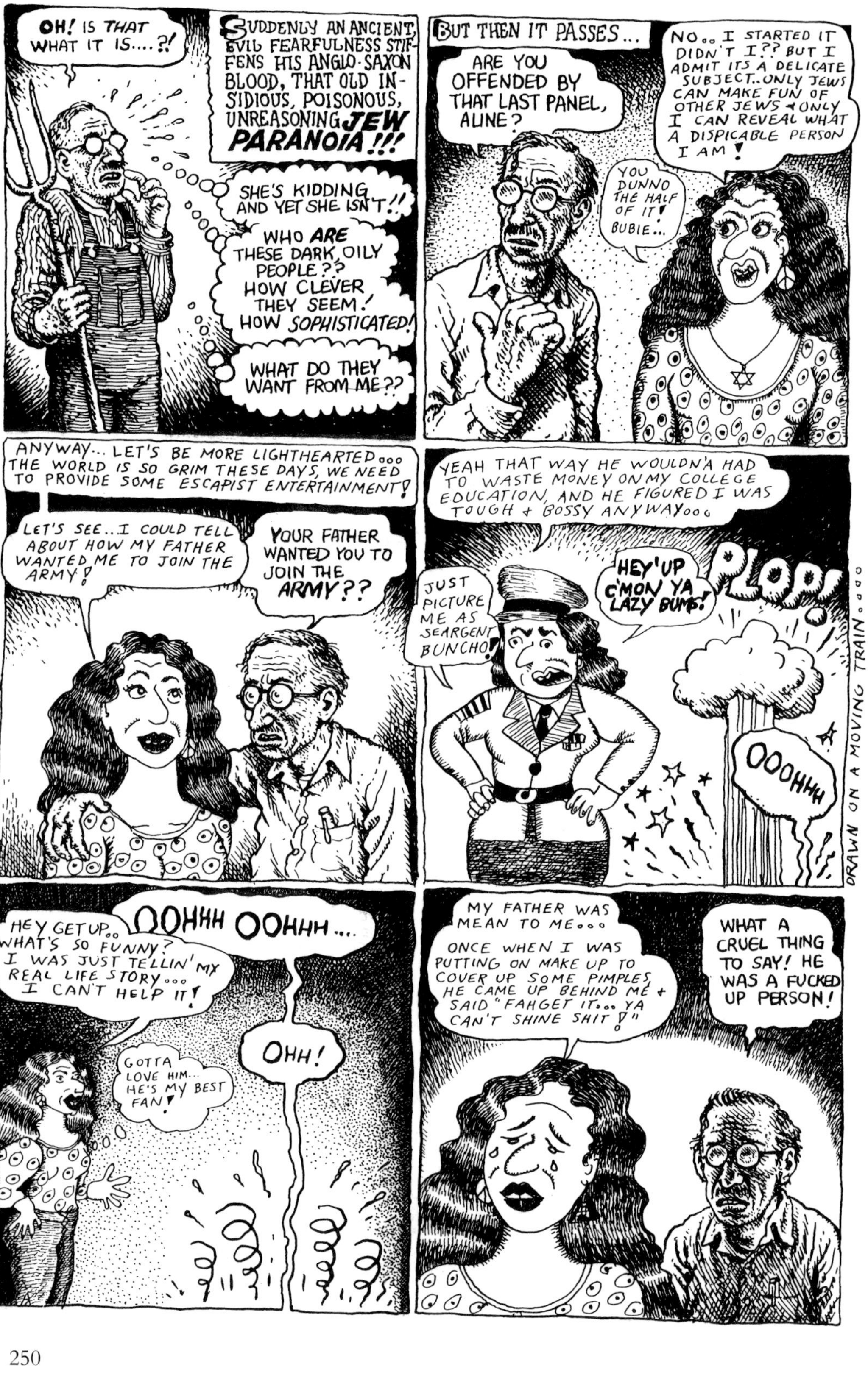

OH! IS THAT WHAT IT IS....?!
SUDDENLY AN ANCIENT, EVIL FEARFULNESS STIFFENS HIS ANGLO-SAXON BLOOD, THAT OLD INSIDIOUS, POISONOUS, UNREASONING JEW PARANOIA!!!
SHE'S KIDDING AND YET SHE ISN'T!!
WHO ARE THESE DARK, OILY PEOPLE?? HOW CLEVER THEY SEEM! HOW SOPHISTICATED!
WHAT DO THEY WANT FROM ME??
BUT THEN IT PASSES...
ARE YOU OFFENDED BY THAT LAST PANEL, ALINE?
NO.. I STARTED IT DIDN'T I?? BUT I ADMIT ITS A DELICATE SUBJECT..ONLY JEWS CAN MAKE FUN OF OTHER JEWS + ONLY I CAN REVEAL WHAT A DISPICABLE PERSON I AM!
YOU DUNNO THE HALF OF IT! BUBIE...
ANYWAY... LET'S BE MORE LIGHTHEARTED... THE WORLD IS SO GRIM THESE DAYS, WE NEED TO PROVIDE SOME ESCAPIST ENTERTAINMENT!
LET'S SEE.. I COULD TELL ABOUT HOW MY FATHER WANTED ME TO JOIN THE ARMY!
YOUR FATHER WANTED YOU TO JOIN THE ARMY??
YEAH THAT WAY HE WOULDN'A HAD TO WASTE MONEY ON MY COLLEGE EDUCATION, AND HE FIGURED I WAS TOUGH + BOSSY ANYWAY...
JUST PICTURE ME AS SEARGENT BUNCHO!
HEY'UP C'MON YA LAZY BUMS!
PLOP!
OOOHHH
DRAWN ON A MOVING TRAIN...
HEY GET UP.. WHAT'S SO FUNNY? I WAS JUST TELLIN' MY REAL LIFE STORY... I CAN'T HELP IT!
OOHHH OOHHH....
GOTTA LOVE HIM... HE'S MY BEST FAN!
OHH!
MY FATHER WAS MEAN TO ME...
ONCE WHEN I WAS PUTTING ON MAKE UP TO COVER UP SOME PIMPLES, HE CAME UP BEHIND ME + SAID "FAHGET IT... YA CAN'T SHINE SHIT!"
WHAT A CRUEL THING TO SAY! HE WAS A FUCKED UP PERSON!

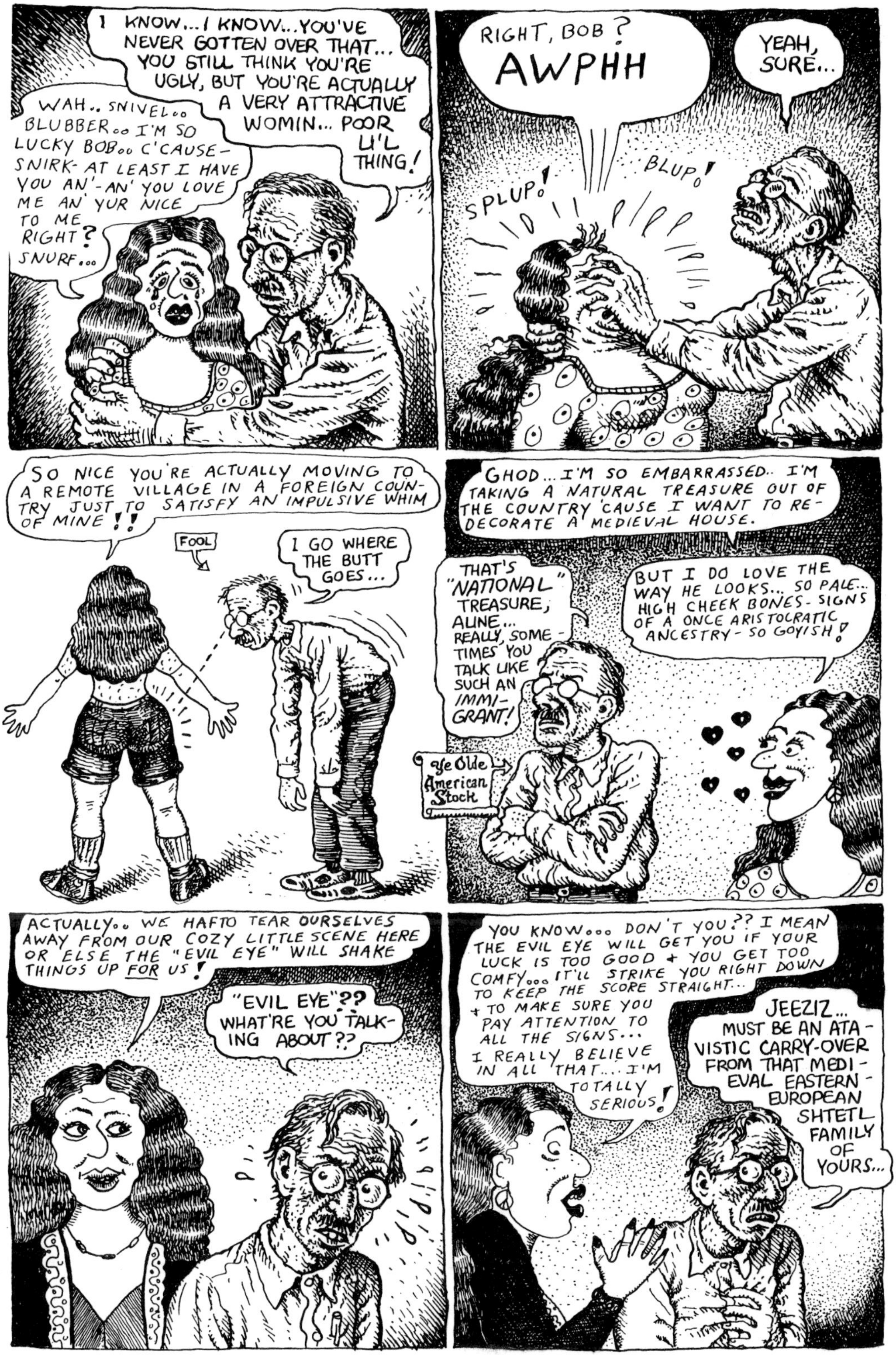
I KNOW...I KNOW...YOU'VE NEVER GOTTEN OVER THAT... YOU STILL THINK YOU'RE UGLY, BUT YOU'RE ACTUALLY A VERY ATTRACTIVE WOMIN... POOR LI'L THING!
WAH.. SNIVEL.. BLUBBER.. I'M SO LUCKY BOB.. C'CAUSE- SNIRK- AT LEAST I HAVE YOU AN'-AN' YOU LOVE ME AN' YUR NICE TO ME RIGHT? SNURF...
RIGHT, BOB? AWPHH
YEAH, SURE...
SPLUP!
BLUP!
SO NICE YOU'RE ACTUALLY MOVING TO A REMOTE VILLAGE IN A FOREIGN COUNTRY JUST TO SATISFY AN IMPULSIVE WHIM OF MINE!!
FOOL
I GO WHERE THE BUTT GOES...
GHOD... I'M SO EMBARRASSED.. I'M TAKING A NATURAL TREASURE OUT OF THE COUNTRY 'CAUSE I WANT TO REDECORATE A MEDIEVAL HOUSE.
THAT'S "NATIONAL" TREASURE, ALINE... REALLY, SOMETIMES YOU TALK LIKE SUCH AN IMMIGRANT!
BUT I DO LOVE THE WAY HE LOOKS... SO PALE... HIGH CHEEK BONES- SIGNS OF A ONCE ARISTOCRATIC ANCESTRY- SO GOYISH!
Ye Olde American Stock
ACTUALLY.. WE HAFTO TEAR OURSELVES AWAY FROM OUR COZY LITTLE SCENE HERE OR ELSE THE "EVIL EYE" WILL SHAKE THINGS UP FOR US!
"EVIL EYE"?? WHAT'RE YOU TALKING ABOUT??
YOU KNOW... DON'T YOU?? I MEAN THE EVIL EYE WILL GET YOU IF YOUR LUCK IS TOO GOOD + YOU GET TOO COMFY... IT'LL STRIKE YOU RIGHT DOWN TO KEEP THE SCORE STRAIGHT... + TO MAKE SURE YOU PAY ATTENTION TO ALL THE SIGNS... I REALLY BELIEVE IN ALL THAT... I'M TOTALLY SERIOUS!
JEEZIZ... MUST BE AN ATAVISTIC CARRY-OVER FROM THAT MEDIEVAL EASTERN-EUROPEAN SHTETL FAMILY OF YOURS...

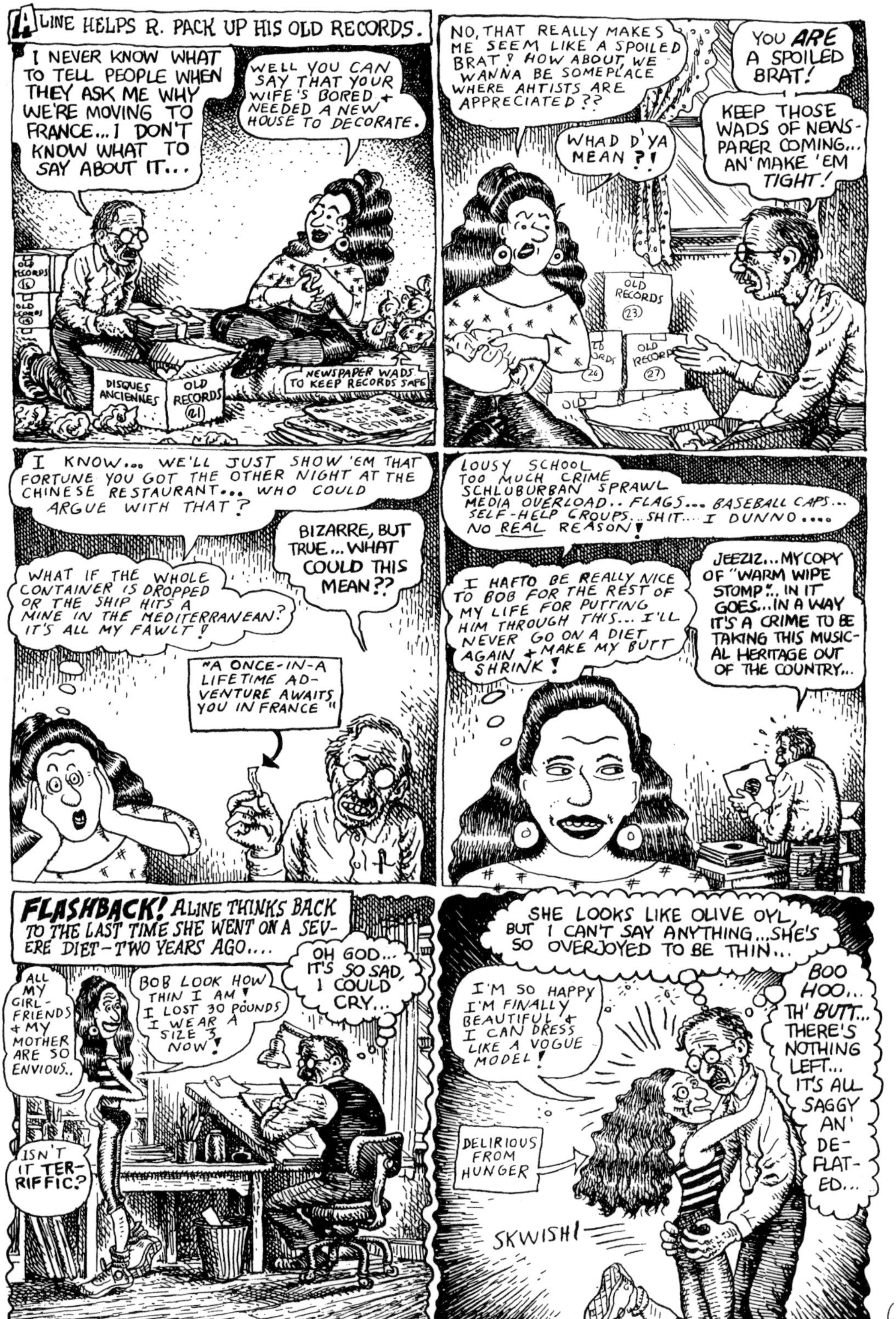
ALINE HELPS R. PACK UP HIS OLD RECORDS.
I NEVER KNOW WHAT TO TELL PEOPLE WHEN THEY ASK ME WHY WE'RE MOVING TO FRANCE... I DON'T KNOW WHAT TO SAY ABOUT IT...
WELL YOU CAN SAY THAT YOUR WIFE'S BORED + NEEDED A NEW HOUSE TO DECORATE.
DISQUES ANCIENNES
OLD RECORDS 21
NEWSPAPER WADS TO KEEP RECORDS SAFE
NO, THAT REALLY MAKES ME SEEM LIKE A SPOILED BRAT! HOW ABOUT, WE WANNA BE SOMEPLACE WHERE AHTISTS ARE APPRECIATED??
WHAD D'YA MEAN ?!
YOU ARE A SPOILED BRAT!
KEEP THOSE WADS OF NEWS-PAPER COMING... AN' MAKE 'EM TIGHT!
OLD RECORDS 23
OLD RECORDS 27
I KNOW... WE'LL JUST SHOW 'EM THAT FORTUNE YOU GOT THE OTHER NIGHT AT THE CHINESE RESTAURANT... WHO COULD ARGUE WITH THAT?
BIZARRE, BUT TRUE... WHAT COULD THIS MEAN??
WHAT IF THE WHOLE CONTAINER IS DROPPED OR THE SHIP HITS A MINE IN THE MEDITERRANEAN? IT'S ALL MY FAWLT!
"A ONCE-IN-A LIFETIME AD-VENTURE AWAITS YOU IN FRANCE"
LOUSY SCHOOL
TOO MUCH CRIME
SCHLUBURBAN SPRAWL
MEDIA OVERLOAD.. FLAGS... BASEBALL CAPS...
SELF-HELP GROUPS... SHIT... I DUNNO....
NO REAL REASON!
I HAFTO BE REALLY NICE TO BOB FOR THE REST OF MY LIFE FOR PUTTING HIM THROUGH THIS... I'LL NEVER GO ON A DIET AGAIN + MAKE MY BUTT SHRINK!
JEEZIZ... MY COPY OF "WARM WIPE STOMP"... IN IT GOES... IN A WAY IT'S A CRIME TO BE TAKING THIS MUSICAL HERITAGE OUT OF THE COUNTRY...
FLASHBACK! ALINE THINKS BACK TO THE LAST TIME SHE WENT ON A SEVERE DIET—TWO YEARS AGO....
ALL MY GIRLFRIENDS + MY MOTHER ARE SO ENVIOUS..
BOB LOOK HOW THIN I AM! I LOST 30 POUNDS I WEAR A SIZE 3 NOW!
OH GOD... IT'S SO SAD, I COULD CRY...
ISN'T IT TERRIFIC?
SHE LOOKS LIKE OLIVE OYL, BUT I CAN'T SAY ANYTHING... SHE'S SO OVERJOYED TO BE THIN...
I'M SO HAPPY I'M FINALLY BEAUTIFUL + I CAN DRESS LIKE A VOGUE MODEL!
BOO HOO... TH' BUTT... THERE'S NOTHING LEFT... IT'S ALL SAGGY AN' DEFLATED...
DELIRIOUS FROM HUNGER
SKWISH!

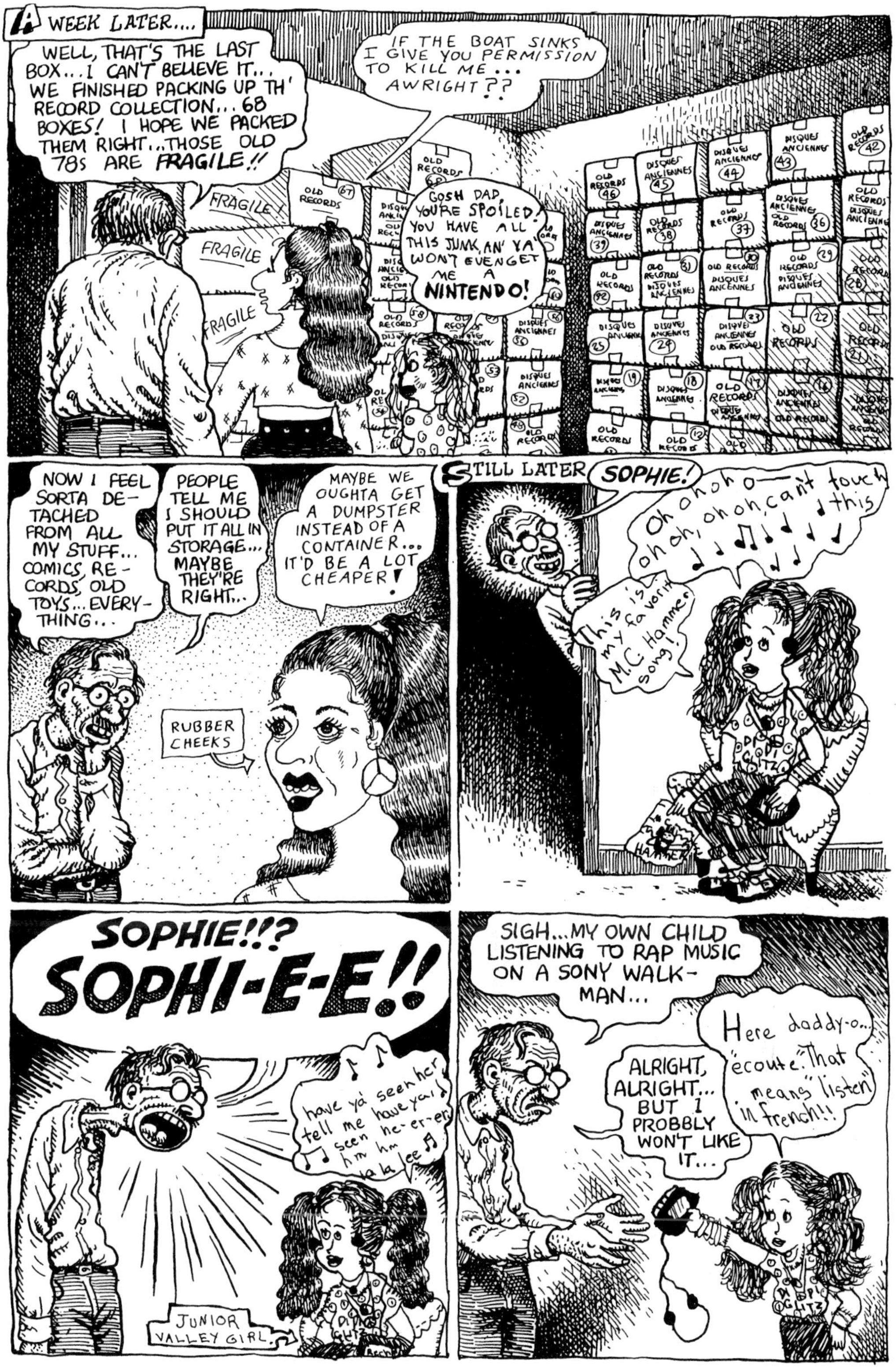
A WEEK LATER....
WELL, THAT'S THE LAST BOX... I CAN'T BELIEVE IT... WE FINISHED PACKING UP TH' RECORD COLLECTION... 68 BOXES! I HOPE WE PACKED THEM RIGHT...THOSE OLD 78s ARE FRAGILE!!
IF THE BOAT SINKS I GIVE YOU PERMISSION TO KILL ME... AWRIGHT??
GOSH DAD, YOU'RE SPOILED! YOU HAVE ALL THIS JUNK AN' YA WON'T EVEN GET ME A NINTENDO!
FRAGILE
FRAGILE
FRAGILE
OLD RECORDS
DISQUES ANCIENNES
NOW I FEEL SORTA DETACHED FROM ALL MY STUFF... COMICS, RECORDS, OLD TOYS... EVERYTHING...
PEOPLE TELL ME I SHOULD PUT IT ALL IN STORAGE... MAYBE THEY'RE RIGHT...
MAYBE WE OUGHTA GET A DUMPSTER INSTEAD OF A CONTAINER... IT'D BE A LOT CHEAPER!
RUBBER CHEEKS
STILL LATER
SOPHIE!
Oh oh oh o— oh oh, oh oh, can't touch this
This is my favorite M.C. Hammer song!
SOPHIE!!? SOPHI-E-E!!
have ya seen her tell me have ya seen he-er-er hm hm la la lee
JUNIOR VALLEY GIRL
SIGH... MY OWN CHILD LISTENING TO RAP MUSIC ON A SONY WALK-MAN...
ALRIGHT, ALRIGHT... BUT I PROBBLY WON'T LIKE IT...
Here daddy-o... "ecoute." That means "listen" in french!!

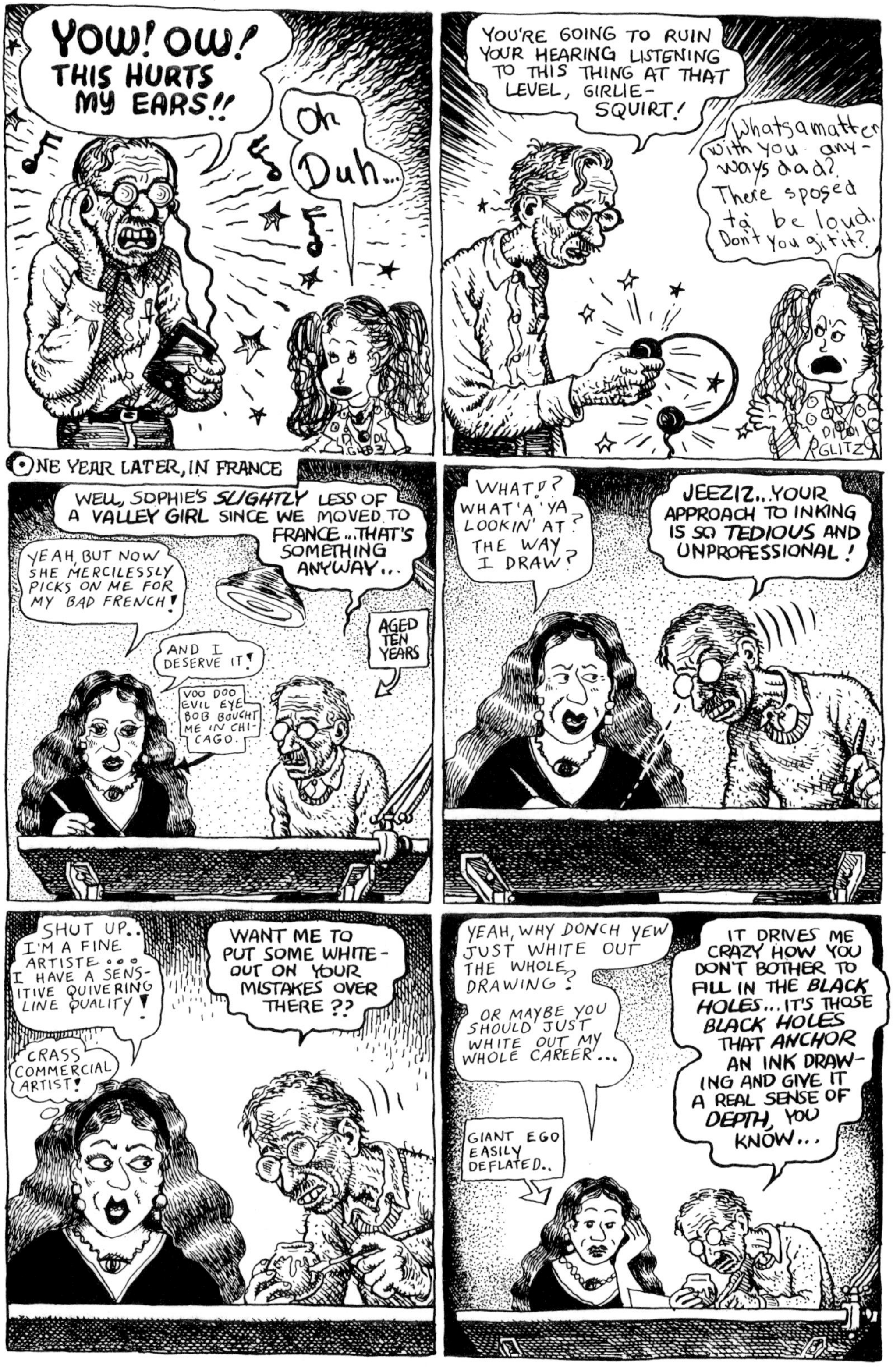
YOW! OW! THIS HURTS MY EARS!!
Oh Duh...
YOU'RE GOING TO RUIN YOUR HEARING LISTENING TO THIS THING AT THAT LEVEL, GIRLIE-SQUIRT!
Whatsamatter with you any-ways dad? There sposed tá be loud. Don't you git it?
ONE YEAR LATER, IN FRANCE
WELL, SOPHIE'S SLIGHTLY LESS OF A VALLEY GIRL SINCE WE MOVED TO FRANCE...THAT'S SOMETHING ANYWAY...
YEAH, BUT NOW SHE MERCILESSLY PICKS ON ME FOR MY BAD FRENCH!
AND I DESERVE IT!
AGED TEN YEARS
VOO DOO EVIL EYE BOB BOUGHT ME IN CHI-CAGO.
WHAT?? WHAT'A 'YA LOOKIN' AT? THE WAY I DRAW?
JEEZIZ...YOUR APPROACH TO INKING IS SO TEDIOUS AND UNPROFESSIONAL!
SHUT UP.. I'M A FINE ARTISTE... I HAVE A SENS-ITIVE QUIVERING LINE QUALITY!
WANT ME TO PUT SOME WHITE-OUT ON YOUR MISTAKES OVER THERE??
CRASS COMMERCIAL ARTIST!
YEAH, WHY DONCH YEW JUST WHITE OUT THE WHOLE DRAWING?
OR MAYBE YOU SHOULD JUST WHITE OUT MY WHOLE CAREER...
IT DRIVES ME CRAZY HOW YOU DON'T BOTHER TO FILL IN THE BLACK HOLES...IT'S THOSE BLACK HOLES THAT ANCHOR AN INK DRAW-ING AND GIVE IT A REAL SENSE OF DEPTH, YOU KNOW...
GIANT EGO EASILY DEFLATED..

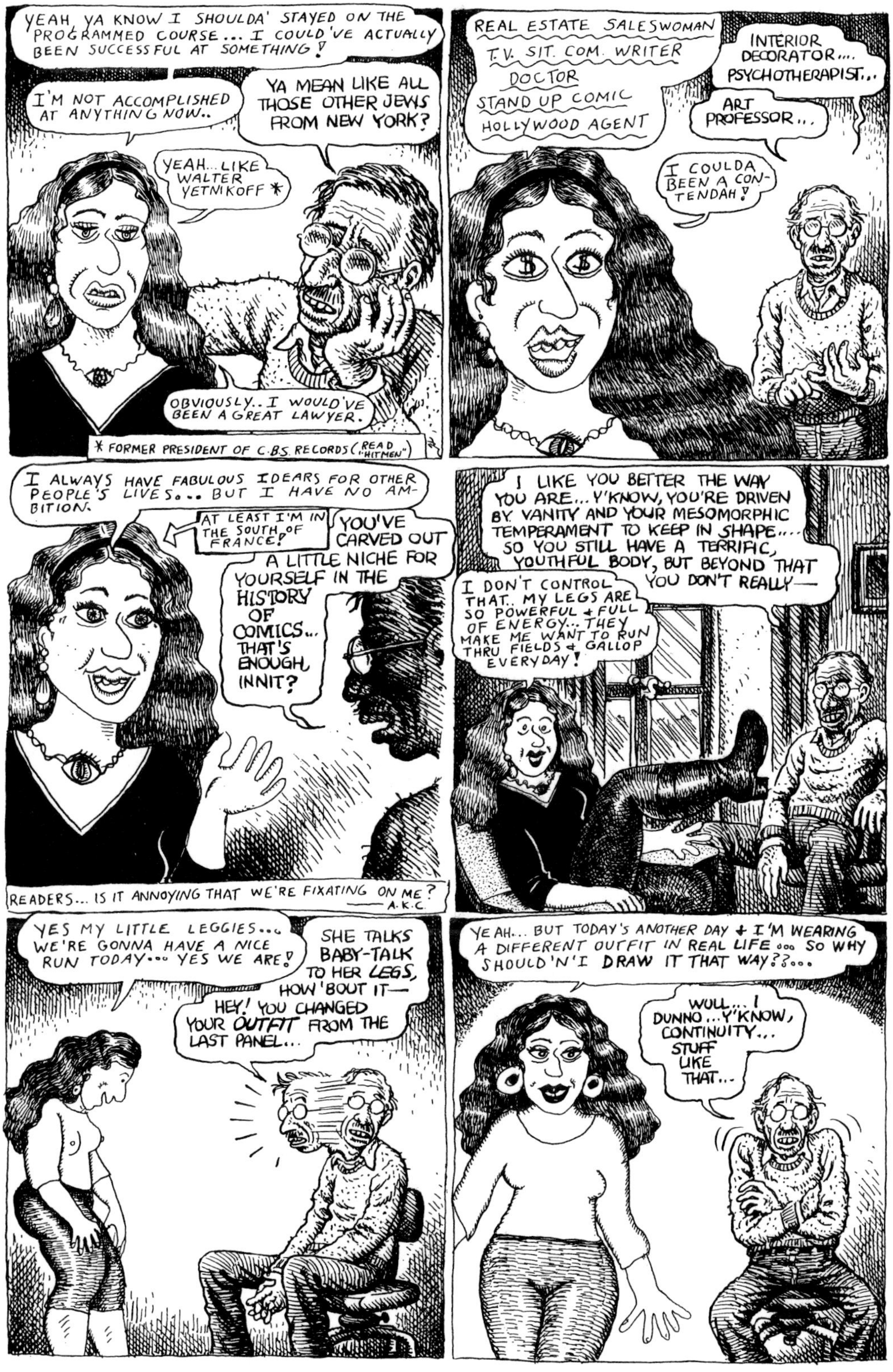
YEAH, YA KNOW I SHOULDA' STAYED ON THE PROGRAMMED COURSE... I COULD'VE ACTUALLY BEEN SUCCESSFUL AT SOMETHING!
I'M NOT ACCOMPLISHED AT ANYTHING NOW..
YA MEAN LIKE ALL THOSE OTHER JEWS FROM NEW YORK?
YEAH...LIKE WALTER YETNIKOFF *
OBVIOUSLY.. I WOULD'VE BEEN A GREAT LAWYER.
* FORMER PRESIDENT OF C.B.S. RECORDS (READ "HITMEN")
REAL ESTATE SALESWOMAN
T.V. SIT. COM. WRITER
DOCTOR
STAND UP COMIC
HOLLYWOOD AGENT
INTERIOR DECORATOR.... PSYCHOTHERAPIST...
ART PROFESSOR...
I COULDA BEEN A CONTENDAH!
I ALWAYS HAVE FABULOUS IDEARS FOR OTHER PEOPLE'S LIVES... BUT I HAVE NO AMBITION.
AT LEAST I'M IN THE SOUTH OF FRANCE!
YOU'VE CARVED OUT A LITTLE NICHE FOR YOURSELF IN THE HISTORY OF COMICS... THAT'S ENOUGH, INNIT?
READERS... IS IT ANNOYING THAT WE'RE FIXATING ON ME? —A.K.C.
I LIKE YOU BETTER THE WAY YOU ARE... Y'KNOW, YOU'RE DRIVEN BY VANITY AND YOUR MESOMORPHIC TEMPERAMENT TO KEEP IN SHAPE.... SO YOU STILL HAVE A TERRIFIC, YOUTHFUL BODY, BUT BEYOND THAT YOU DON'T REALLY—
I DON'T CONTROL THAT.. MY LEGS ARE SO POWERFUL + FULL OF ENERGY.. THEY MAKE ME WANT TO RUN THRU FIELDS + GALLOP EVERYDAY!
YES MY LITTLE LEGGIES... WE'RE GONNA HAVE A NICE RUN TODAY... YES WE ARE!
SHE TALKS BABY-TALK TO HER LEGS, HOW 'BOUT IT—
HEY! YOU CHANGED YOUR OUTFIT FROM THE LAST PANEL...
YEAH... BUT TODAY'S ANOTHER DAY + I'M WEARING A DIFFERENT OUTFIT IN REAL LIFE... SO WHY SHOULD'N'I DRAW IT THAT WAY??...
WULL... I DUNNO... Y'KNOW, CONTINUITY... STUFF LIKE THAT...

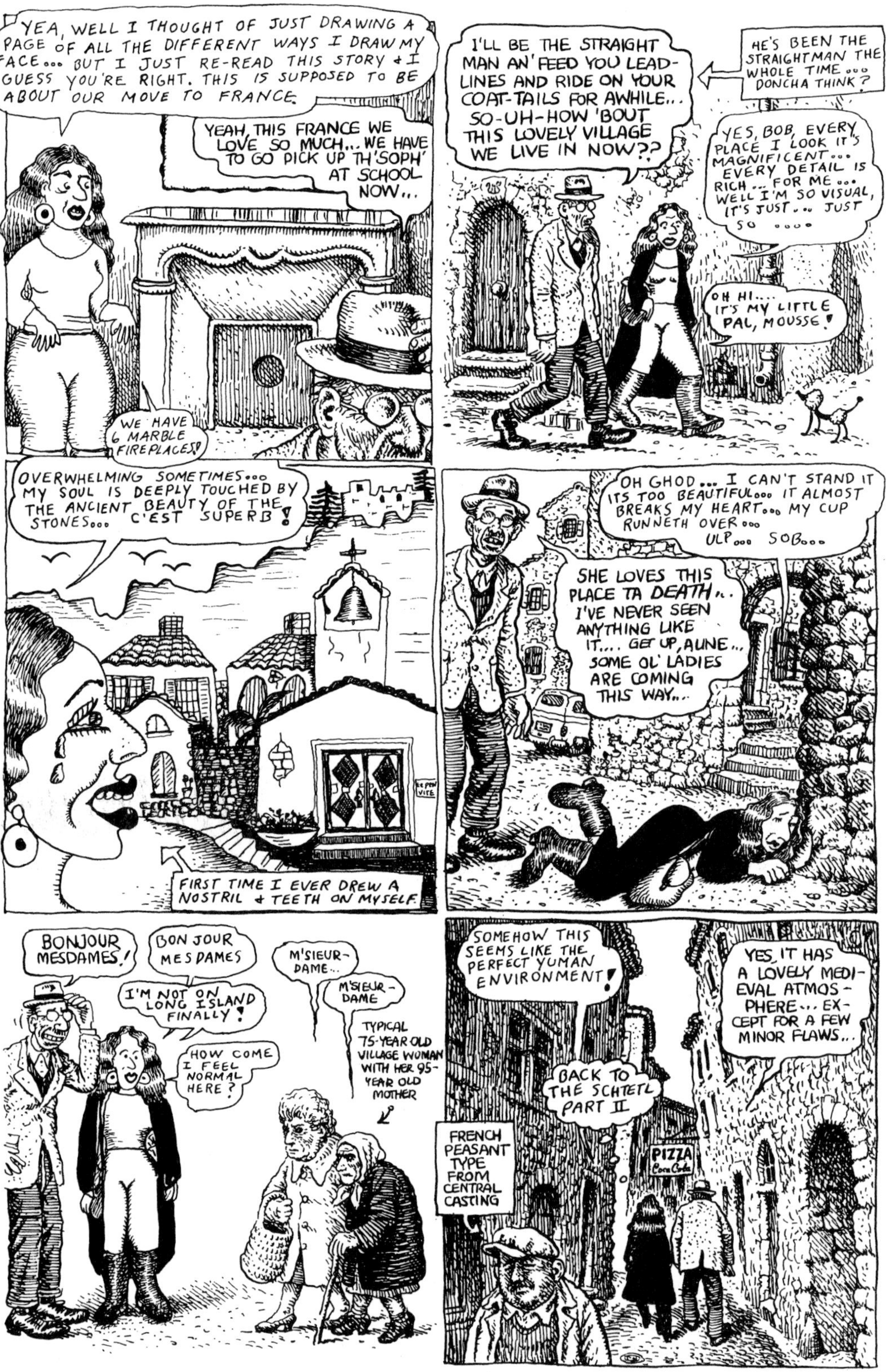

YEA, WELL I THOUGHT OF JUST DRAWING A PAGE OF ALL THE DIFFERENT WAYS I DRAW MY FACE... BUT I JUST RE-READ THIS STORY & I GUESS YOU'RE RIGHT. THIS IS SUPPOSED TO BE ABOUT OUR MOVE TO FRANCE.
YEAH, THIS FRANCE WE LOVE SO MUCH... WE HAVE TO GO PICK UP TH' SOPH' AT SCHOOL NOW..
WE HAVE 6 MARBLE FIREPLACES!
I'LL BE THE STRAIGHT MAN AN' FEED YOU LEAD-LINES AND RIDE ON YOUR COAT-TAILS FOR AWHILE... SO-UH-HOW 'BOUT THIS LOVELY VILLAGE WE LIVE IN NOW??
HE'S BEEN THE STRAIGHTMAN THE WHOLE TIME... DONCHA THINK?
YES, BOB, EVERY PLACE I LOOK IT'S MAGNIFICENT... EVERY DETAIL IS RICH... FOR ME... WELL I'M SO VISUAL, IT'S JUST... JUST SO ....
OH HI.... IT'S MY LITTLE PAL, MOUSSE!
OVERWHELMING SOMETIMES... MY SOUL IS DEEPLY TOUCHED BY THE ANCIENT BEAUTY OF THE STONES... C'EST SUPERB!
FIRST TIME I EVER DREW A NOSTRIL & TEETH ON MYSELF.
OH GHOD... I CAN'T STAND IT ITS TOO BEAUTIFUL... IT ALMOST BREAKS MY HEART... MY CUP RUNNETH OVER... ULP... SOB...
SHE LOVES THIS PLACE TA DEATH.. I'VE NEVER SEEN ANYTHING LIKE IT.... GET UP, ALINE... SOME OL' LADIES ARE COMING THIS WAY...
BONJOUR MESDAMES!
BON JOUR MES DAMES
I'M NOT ON LONG ISLAND FINALLY!
HOW COME I FEEL NORMAL HERE?
M'SIEUR-DAME...
M'SIEUR-DAME
TYPICAL 75-YEAR-OLD VILLAGE WOMAN WITH HER 95-YEAR OLD MOTHER
SOMEHOW THIS SEEMS LIKE THE PERFECT YUMAN ENVIRONMENT!
YES, IT HAS A LOVELY MEDI-EVAL ATMOS-PHERE... EX-CEPT FOR A FEW MINOR FLAWS...
BACK TO THE SCHTETL PART II
FRENCH PEASANT TYPE FROM CENTRAL CASTING
PIZZA
Coca Cola

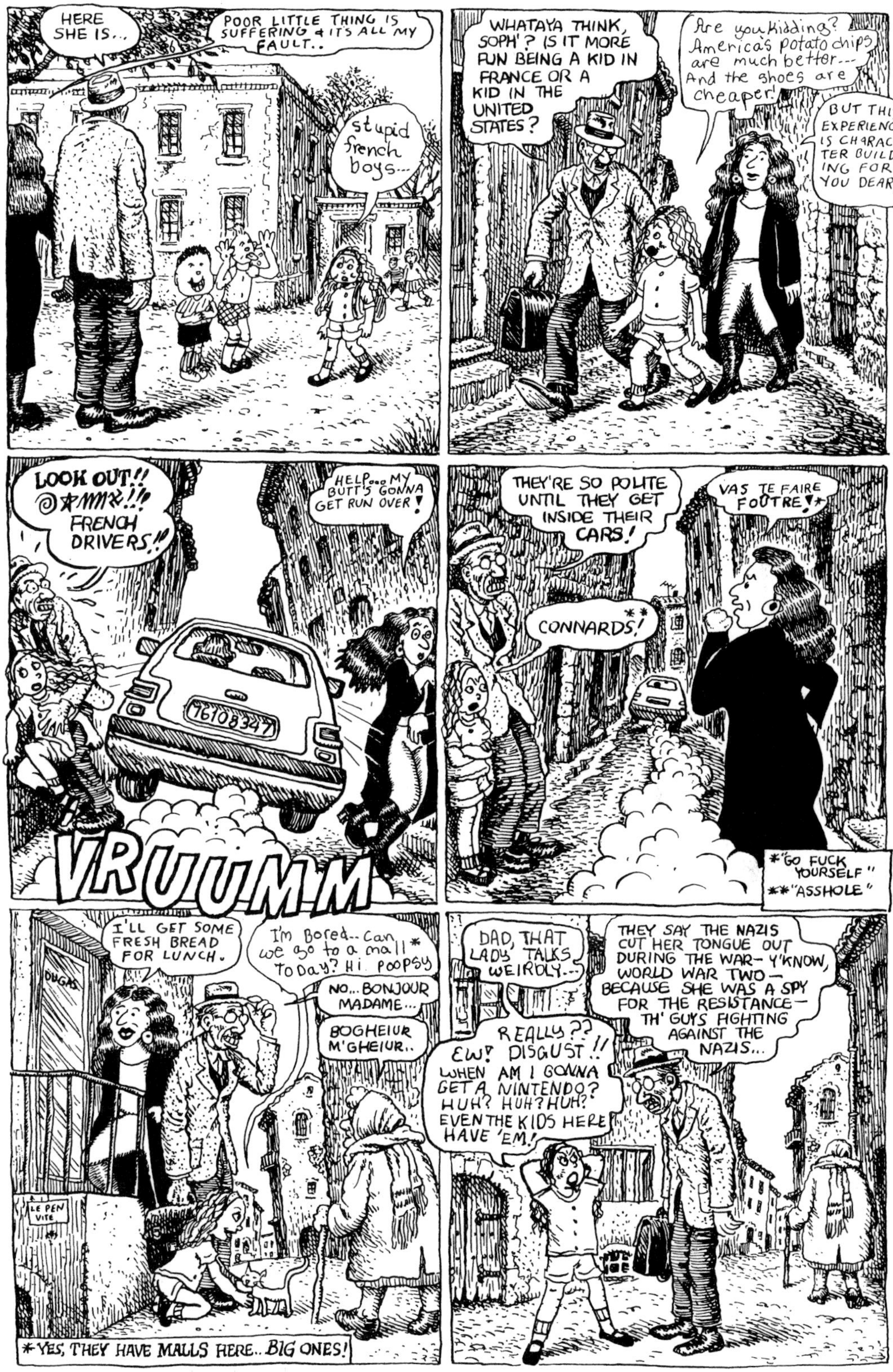
HERE SHE IS...
POOR LITTLE THING IS SUFFERING & IT'S ALL MY FAULT..
stupid french boys...
WHATAYA THINK, SOPH'? IS IT MORE FUN BEING A KID IN FRANCE OR A KID IN THE UNITED STATES?
Are you kidding? America's potato chips are much better--- And the shoes are cheaper!
BUT THIS EXPERIENCE IS CHARACTER BUILDING FOR YOU DEAR!
LOOK OUT!! @*!!! FRENCH DRIVERS!!
HELP... MY BUTT'S GONNA GET RUN OVER!
76108347
VRUUMM
THEY'RE SO POLITE UNTIL THEY GET INSIDE THEIR CARS!
VAS TE FAIRE FOUTRE!*
CONNARDS!**
*"GO FUCK YOURSELF"
**"ASSHOLE"
I'LL GET SOME FRESH BREAD FOR LUNCH.
I'm Bored.. Can we go to a mall* today? Hi Poopsy
NO... BONJOUR MADAME...
BOGHEIUR M'GHEIUR..
DUGAS
LE PEN VITE
*YES, THEY HAVE MALLS HERE.. BIG ONES!
DAD, THAT LADY TALKS WEIRDLY...
THEY SAY THE NAZIS CUT HER TONGUE OUT DURING THE WAR- Y'KNOW, WORLD WAR TWO- BECAUSE SHE WAS A SPY FOR THE RESISTANCE- TH' GUYS FIGHTING AGAINST THE NAZIS..
REALLY?? EW! DISGUST!! WHEN AM I GONNA GET A NINTENDO? HUH? HUH? HUH? EVEN THE KIDS HERE HAVE 'EM!

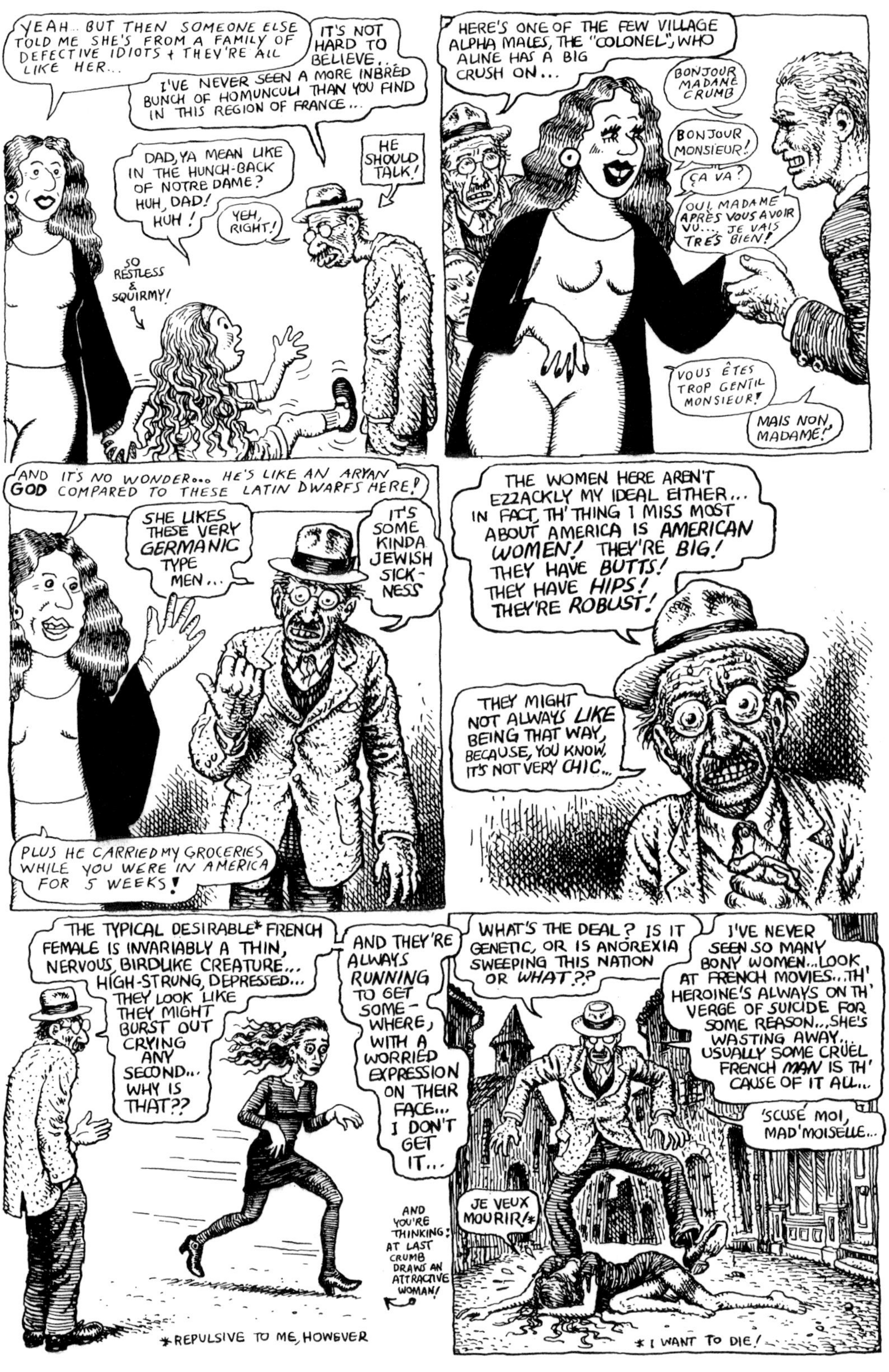
YEAH.. BUT THEN SOMEONE ELSE TOLD ME SHE'S FROM A FAMILY OF DEFECTIVE IDIOTS + THEY'RE ALL LIKE HER...
IT'S NOT HARD TO BELIEVE...
I'VE NEVER SEEN A MORE INBRED BUNCH OF HOMUNCULI THAN YOU FIND IN THIS REGION OF FRANCE...
DAD, YA MEAN LIKE IN THE HUNCH-BACK OF NOTRE DAME? HUH, DAD! HUH!
YEH, RIGHT!
HE SHOULD TALK!
SO RESTLESS & SQUIRMY!
HERE'S ONE OF THE FEW VILLAGE ALPHA MALES, THE "COLONEL", WHO ALINE HAS A BIG CRUSH ON...
BONJOUR MADAME CRUMB
BONJOUR MONSIEUR!
ÇA VA?
OUI, MADAME APRÈS VOUS AVOIR VU... JE VAIS TRÈS BIEN!
VOUS ÊTES TROP GENTIL MONSIEUR!
MAIS NON, MADAME!
AND IT'S NO WONDER... HE'S LIKE AN ARYAN GOD COMPARED TO THESE LATIN DWARFS HERE!
SHE LIKES THESE VERY GERMANIC TYPE MEN...
IT'S SOME KINDA JEWISH SICK-NESS
PLUS HE CARRIED MY GROCERIES WHILE YOU WERE IN AMERICA FOR 5 WEEKS!
THE WOMEN HERE AREN'T EZZACKLY MY IDEAL EITHER... IN FACT, TH' THING I MISS MOST ABOUT AMERICA IS AMERICAN WOMEN! THEY'RE BIG! THEY HAVE BUTTS! THEY HAVE HIPS! THEY'RE ROBUST!
THEY MIGHT NOT ALWAYS LIKE BEING THAT WAY, BECAUSE, YOU KNOW, IT'S NOT VERY CHIC...
THE TYPICAL DESIRABLE* FRENCH FEMALE IS INVARIABLY A THIN, NERVOUS BIRDLIKE CREATURE... HIGH-STRUNG, DEPRESSED... THEY LOOK LIKE THEY MIGHT BURST OUT CRYING ANY SECOND... WHY IS THAT??
AND THEY'RE ALWAYS RUNNING TO GET SOME-WHERE, WITH A WORRIED EXPRESSION ON THEIR FACE... I DON'T GET IT...
AND YOU'RE THINKING: AT LAST CRUMB DRAWS AN ATTRACTIVE WOMAN!
*REPULSIVE TO ME, HOWEVER
WHAT'S THE DEAL? IS IT GENETIC, OR IS ANOREXIA SWEEPING THIS NATION OR WHAT??
I'VE NEVER SEEN SO MANY BONY WOMEN... LOOK AT FRENCH MOVIES... TH' HEROINE'S ALWAYS ON TH' VERGE OF SUICIDE FOR SOME REASON... SHE'S WASTING AWAY... USUALLY SOME CRUEL FRENCH MAN IS TH' CAUSE OF IT ALL...
'SCUSÉ MOI, MAD'MOISELLE...
JE VEUX MOURIR!*
*I WANT TO DIE!

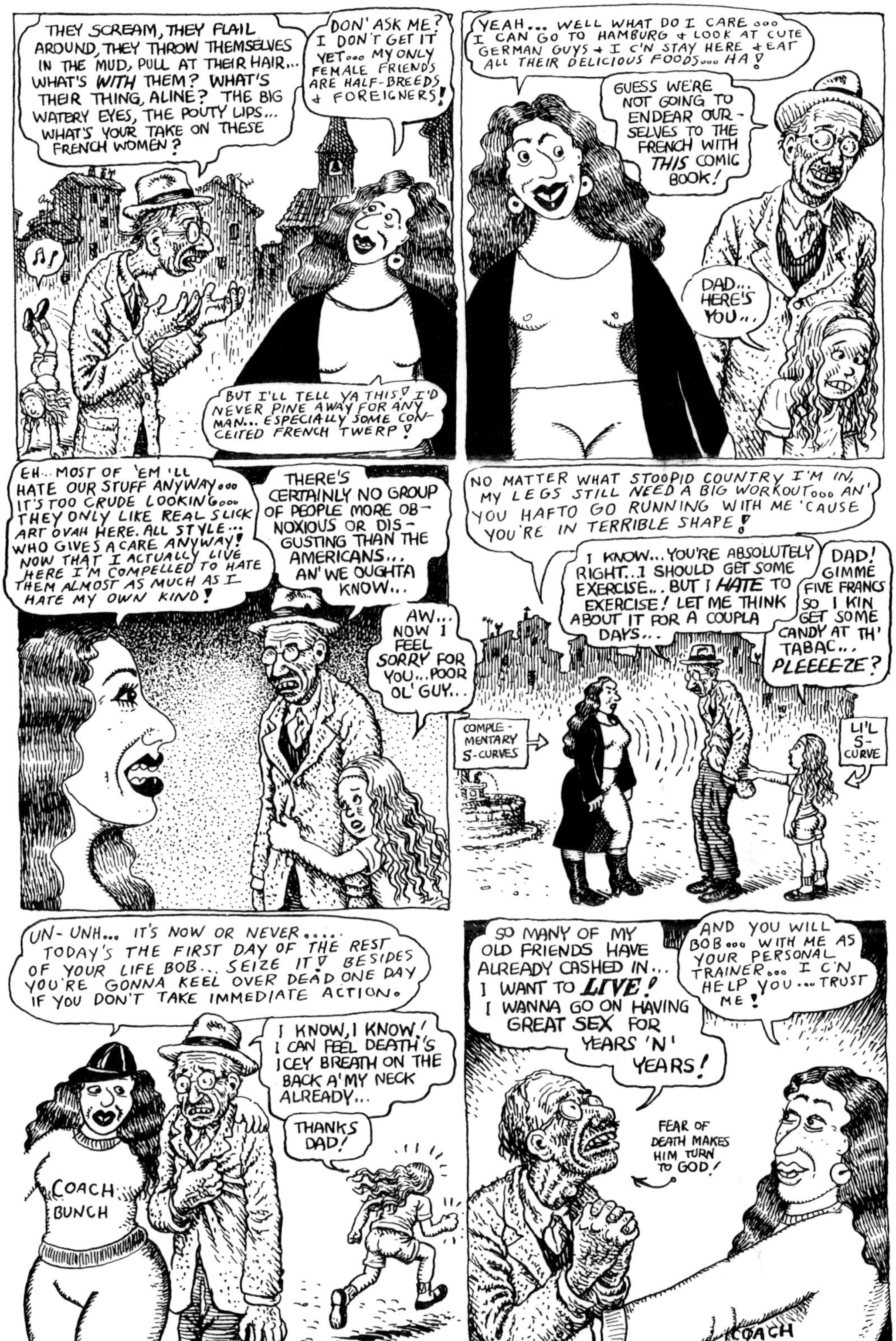

THEY SCREAM, THEY FLAIL AROUND, THEY THROW THEMSELVES IN THE MUD, PULL AT THEIR HAIR... WHAT'S WITH THEM? WHAT'S THEIR THING, ALINE? THE BIG WATERY EYES, THE POUTY LIPS... WHAT'S YOUR TAKE ON THESE FRENCH WOMEN?
DON' ASK ME? I DON'T GET IT YET... MY ONLY FEMALE FRIENDS ARE HALF-BREEDS & FOREIGNERS!
BUT I'LL TELL YA THIS! I'D NEVER PINE AWAY FOR ANY MAN... ESPECIALLY SOME CONCEITED FRENCH TWERP!
YEAH... WELL WHAT DO I CARE... I CAN GO TO HAMBURG & LOOK AT CUTE GERMAN GUYS & I C'N STAY HERE & EAT ALL THEIR DELICIOUS FOODS... HA!
GUESS WE'RE NOT GOING TO ENDEAR OURSELVES TO THE FRENCH WITH THIS COMIC BOOK!
DAD... HERE'S YOU...
EH... MOST OF 'EM 'LL HATE OUR STUFF ANYWAY... IT'S TOO CRUDE LOOKING... THEY ONLY LIKE REAL SLICK ART OVAH HERE. ALL STYLE... WHO GIVES A CARE ANYWAY! NOW THAT I ACTUALLY LIVE HERE I'M COMPELLED TO HATE THEM ALMOST AS MUCH AS I HATE MY OWN KIND!
THERE'S CERTAINLY NO GROUP OF PEOPLE MORE OBNOXIOUS OR DISGUSTING THAN THE AMERICANS... AN' WE OUGHTA KNOW...
AW... NOW I FEEL SORRY FOR YOU... POOR OL' GUY...
NO MATTER WHAT STOOPID COUNTRY I'M IN, MY LEGS STILL NEED A BIG WORKOUT... AN' YOU HAFTO GO RUNNING WITH ME 'CAUSE YOU'RE IN TERRIBLE SHAPE!
I KNOW... YOU'RE ABSOLUTELY RIGHT... I SHOULD GET SOME EXERCISE... BUT I HATE TO EXERCISE! LET ME THINK ABOUT IT FOR A COUPLA DAYS...
DAD! GIMME FIVE FRANCS SO I KIN GET SOME CANDY AT TH' TABAC... PLEEEEZE?
COMPLEMENTARY S-CURVES
LI'L S-CURVE
UN-UNH... IT'S NOW OR NEVER.... TODAY'S THE FIRST DAY OF THE REST OF YOUR LIFE BOB... SEIZE IT! BESIDES YOU'RE GONNA KEEL OVER DEAD ONE DAY IF YOU DON'T TAKE IMMEDIATE ACTION.
I KNOW, I KNOW! I CAN FEEL DEATH'S ICEY BREATH ON THE BACK A' MY NECK ALREADY...
THANKS DAD!
COACH BUNCH
SO MANY OF MY OLD FRIENDS HAVE ALREADY CASHED IN... I WANT TO LIVE! I WANNA GO ON HAVING GREAT SEX FOR YEARS 'N' YEARS!
AND YOU WILL BOB... WITH ME AS YOUR PERSONAL TRAINER... I C'N HELP YOU... TRUST ME!
FEAR OF DEATH MAKES HIM TURN TO GOD!
COACH BUNCH

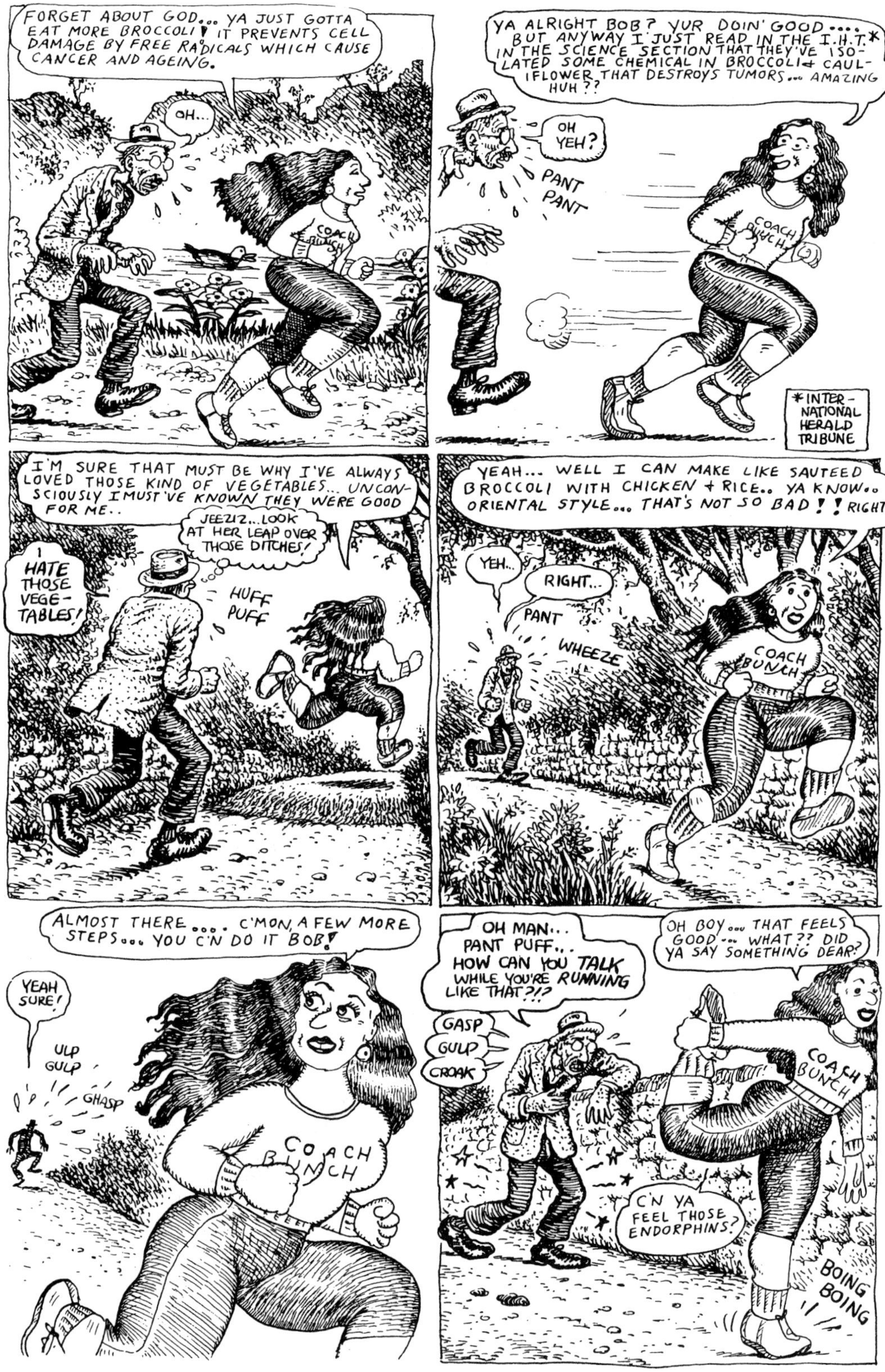

FORGET ABOUT GOD... YA JUST GOTTA EAT MORE BROCCOLI! IT PREVENTS CELL DAMAGE BY FREE RADICALS WHICH CAUSE CANCER AND AGEING.
OH...
COACH BUNCH
YA ALRIGHT BOB? YUR DOIN' GOOD.... BUT ANYWAY I JUST READ IN THE I.H.T.* IN THE SCIENCE SECTION THAT THEY'VE ISOLATED SOME CHEMICAL IN BROCCOLI + CAULIFLOWER THAT DESTROYS TUMORS... AMAZING HUH??
OH YEH?
PANT PANT
COACH BUNCH
*INTERNATIONAL HERALD TRIBUNE
I'M SURE THAT MUST BE WHY I'VE ALWAYS LOVED THOSE KIND OF VEGETABLES... UNCONSCIOUSLY I MUST'VE KNOWN THEY WERE GOOD FOR ME..
JEEZIZ...LOOK AT HER LEAP OVER THOSE DITCHES!
I HATE THOSE VEGETABLES!
HUFF PUFF
YEAH... WELL I CAN MAKE LIKE SAUTEED BROCCOLI WITH CHICKEN + RICE.. YA KNOW.. ORIENTAL STYLE... THAT'S NOT SO BAD!! RIGHT?
YEH...
RIGHT...
PANT
WHEEZE
COACH BUNCH
ALMOST THERE.... C'MON, A FEW MORE STEPS... YOU C'N DO IT BOB!
YEAH SURE!
ULP GULP
GHASP
COACH BUNCH
OH MAN... PANT PUFF... HOW CAN YOU TALK WHILE YOU'RE RUNNING LIKE THAT?!?
OH BOY... THAT FEELS GOOD... WHAT?? DID YA SAY SOMETHING DEAR?
GASP
GULP
CROAK
COACH BUNCH
C'N YA FEEL THOSE ENDORPHINS?
BOING BOING

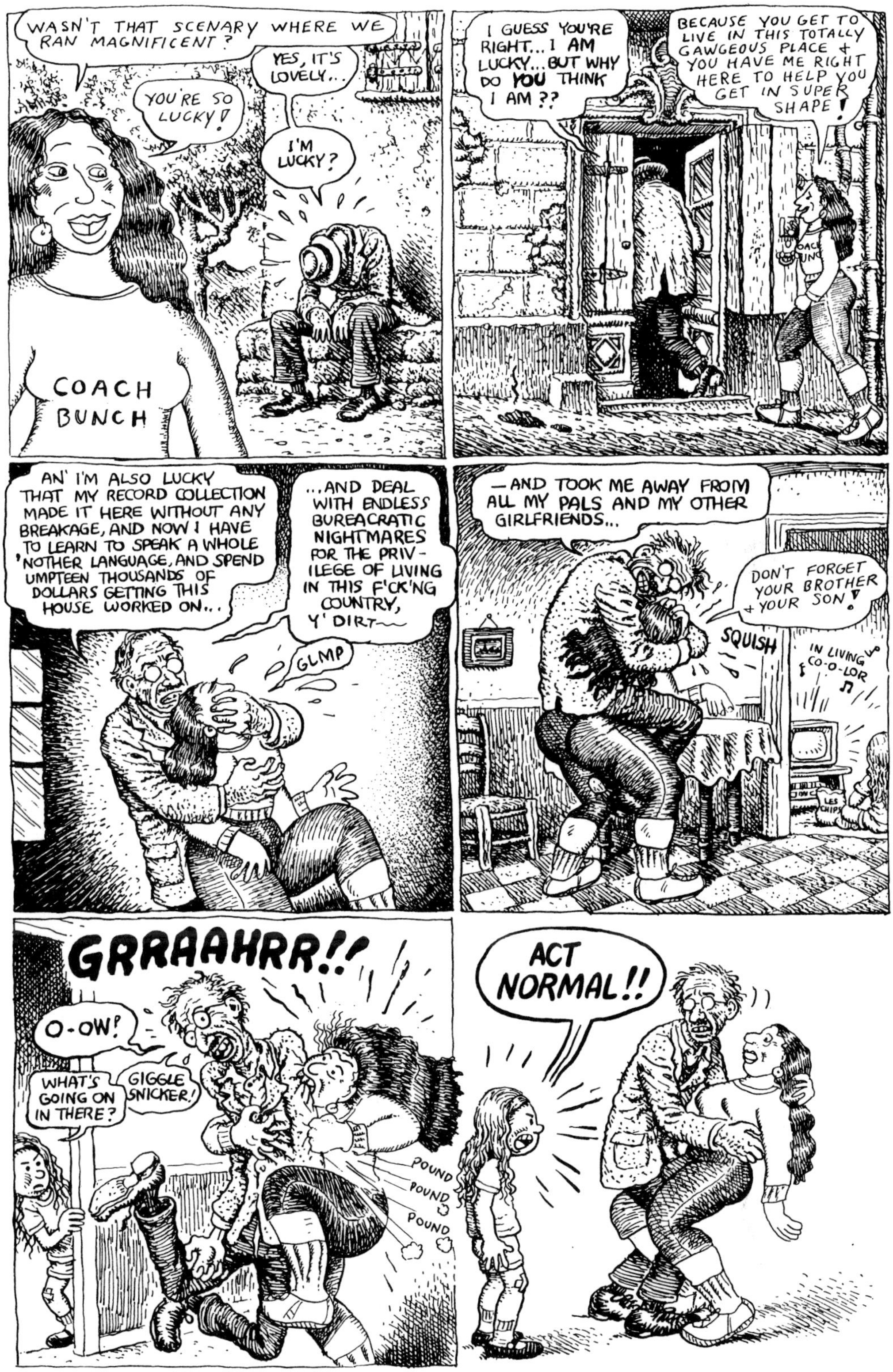
WASN'T THAT SCENARY WHERE WE RAN MAGNIFICENT?
YOU'RE SO LUCKY!
YES, IT'S LOVELY...
I'M LUCKY?
COACH BUNCH
I GUESS YOU'RE RIGHT... I AM LUCKY... BUT WHY DO YOU THINK I AM??
BECAUSE YOU GET TO LIVE IN THIS TOTALLY GAWGEOUS PLACE + YOU HAVE ME RIGHT HERE TO HELP YOU GET IN SUPER SHAPE!
AN' I'M ALSO LUCKY THAT MY RECORD COLLECTION MADE IT HERE WITHOUT ANY BREAKAGE, AND NOW I HAVE TO LEARN TO SPEAK A WHOLE 'NOTHER LANGUAGE, AND SPEND UMPTEEN THOUSANDS OF DOLLARS GETTING THIS HOUSE WORKED ON...
...AND DEAL WITH ENDLESS BUREACRATIC NIGHTMARES FOR THE PRIV-ILEGE OF LIVING IN THIS F'CK'NG COUNTRY, Y' DIRT~
GLMP
—AND TOOK ME AWAY FROM ALL MY PALS AND MY OTHER GIRLFRIENDS...
DON'T FORGET YOUR BROTHER + YOUR SON!
SQUISH
IN LIVING CO-O-LOR
LES CHIPS
GRRAAHRR!!
O-OW!
WHAT'S GOING ON IN THERE?
GIGGLE SNICKER!
POUND
POUND
POUND
ACT NORMAL!!

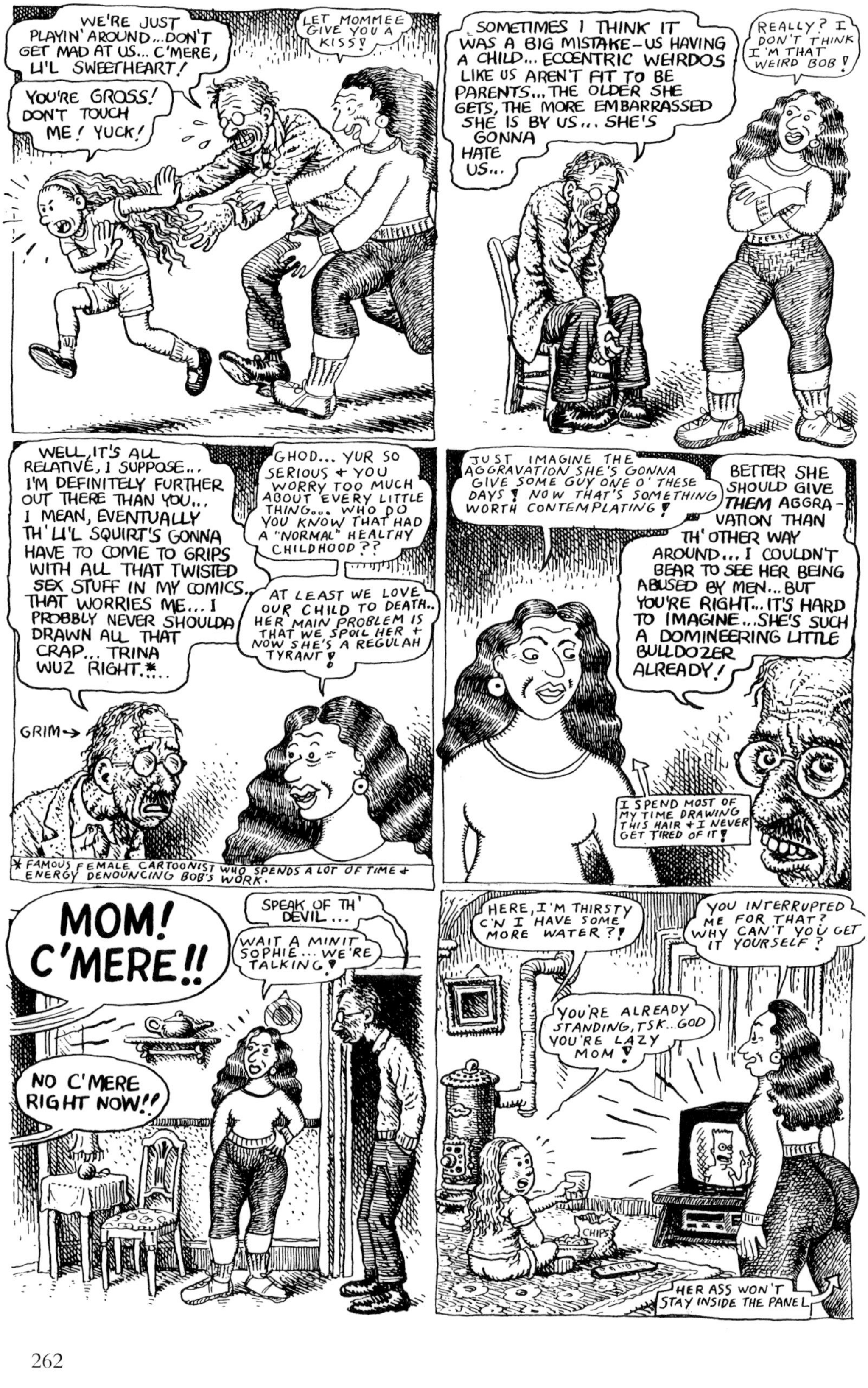
WE'RE JUST PLAYIN' AROUND... DON'T GET MAD AT US... C'MERE, LI'L SWEETHEART!
LET MOMMEE GIVE YOU A KISS!
YOU'RE GROSS! DON'T TOUCH ME! YUCK!
SOMETIMES I THINK IT WAS A BIG MISTAKE—US HAVING A CHILD... ECCENTRIC WEIRDOS LIKE US AREN'T FIT TO BE PARENTS... THE OLDER SHE GETS, THE MORE EMBARRASSED SHE IS BY US... SHE'S GONNA HATE US...
REALLY? I DON'T THINK I'M THAT WEIRD BOB!
WELL, IT'S ALL RELATIVE, I SUPPOSE... I'M DEFINITELY FURTHER OUT THERE THAN YOU... I MEAN, EVENTUALLY TH' LI'L SQUIRT'S GONNA HAVE TO COME TO GRIPS WITH ALL THAT TWISTED SEX STUFF IN MY COMICS.. THAT WORRIES ME... I PROBBLY NEVER SHOULDA DRAWN ALL THAT CRAP... TRINA WUZ RIGHT.*...
GHOD... YUR SO SERIOUS + YOU WORRY TOO MUCH ABOUT EVERY LITTLE THING... WHO DO YOU KNOW THAT HAD A "NORMAL" HEALTHY CHILDHOOD??
AT LEAST WE LOVE OUR CHILD TO DEATH.. HER MAIN PROBLEM IS THAT WE SPOIL HER + NOW SHE'S A REGULAH TYRANT!
GRIM→
*FAMOUS FEMALE CARTOONIST WHO SPENDS A LOT OF TIME + ENERGY DENOUNCING BOB'S WORK.
JUST IMAGINE THE AGGRAVATION SHE'S GONNA GIVE SOME GUY ONE O' THESE DAYS! NOW THAT'S SOMETHING WORTH CONTEMPLATING!
BETTER SHE SHOULD GIVE THEM AGGRAVATION THAN TH' OTHER WAY AROUND... I COULDN'T BEAR TO SEE HER BEING ABUSED BY MEN... BUT YOU'RE RIGHT... IT'S HARD TO IMAGINE... SHE'S SUCH A DOMINEERING LITTLE BULLDOZER ALREADY!
I SPEND MOST OF MY TIME DRAWING THIS HAIR + I NEVER GET TIRED OF IT!
MOM! C'MERE!!
SPEAK OF TH' DEVIL...
WAIT A MINIT SOPHIE... WE'RE TALKING!
NO C'MERE RIGHT NOW!!
HERE, I'M THIRSTY C'N I HAVE SOME MORE WATER?!
YOU INTERRUPTED ME FOR THAT? WHY CAN'T YOU GET IT YOURSELF?
YOU'RE ALREADY STANDING, TSK... GOD YOU'RE LAZY MOM!
CHIPS
HER ASS WON'T STAY INSIDE THE PANEL

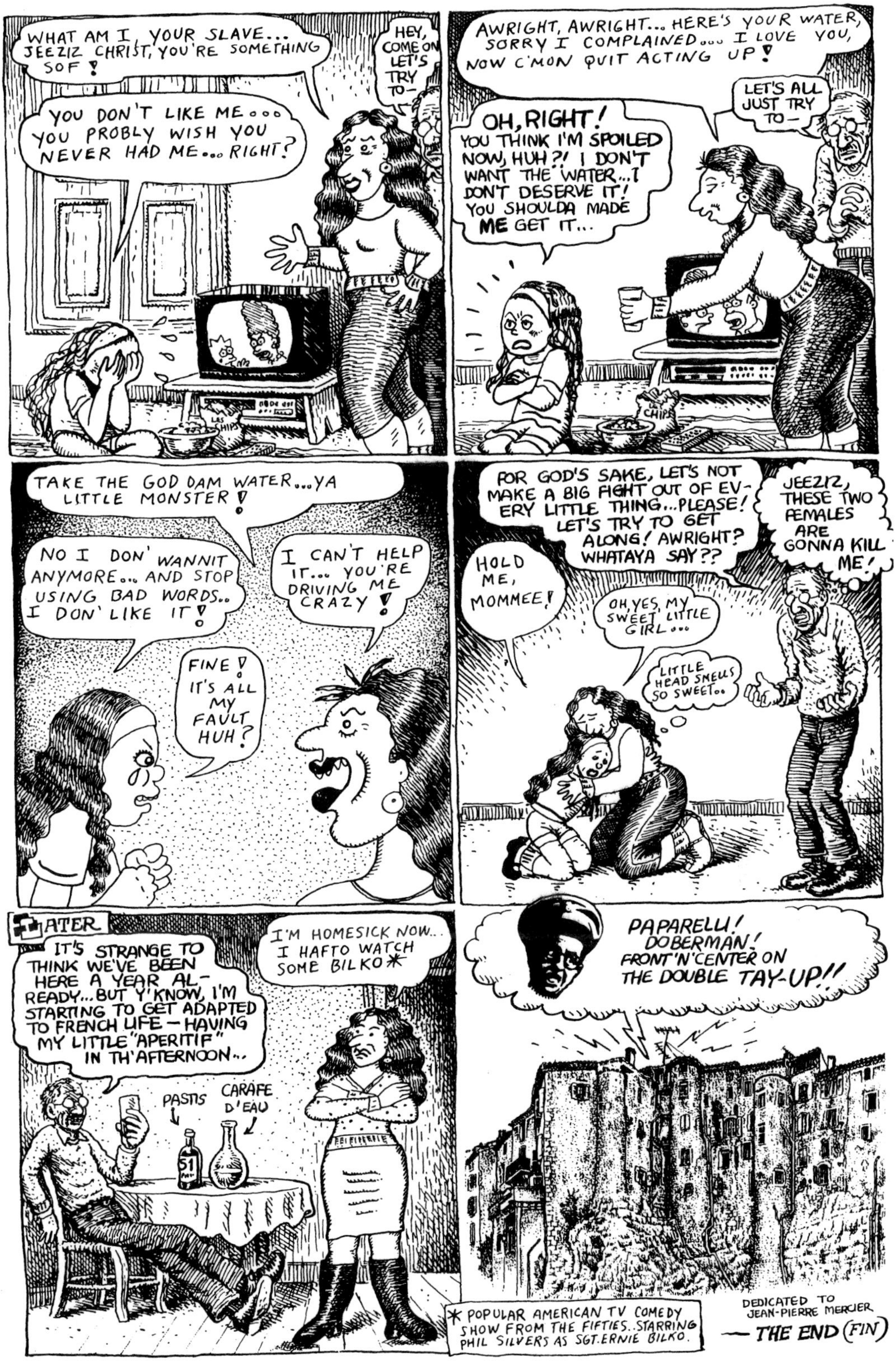

WHAT AM I, YOUR SLAVE... JEEZIZ CHRIST, YOU'RE SOMETHING SOF!
HEY, COME ON LET'S TRY TO-
YOU DON'T LIKE ME... YOU PROBLY WISH YOU NEVER HAD ME... RIGHT?
LAS CHIPS
AWRIGHT, AWRIGHT... HERE'S YOUR WATER, SORRY I COMPLAINED... I LOVE YOU, NOW C'MON QUIT ACTING UP!
LET'S ALL JUST TRY TO-
OH, RIGHT! YOU THINK I'M SPOILED NOW, HUH?! I DON'T WANT THE WATER... I DON'T DESERVE IT! YOU SHOULDA MADE ME GET IT...
CHIPS
TAKE THE GOD DAM WATER... YA LITTLE MONSTER!
NO I DON' WANNIT ANYMORE... AND STOP USING BAD WORDS.. I DON' LIKE IT!
I CAN'T HELP IT... YOU'RE DRIVING ME CRAZY!
FINE! IT'S ALL MY FAULT HUH?
FOR GOD'S SAKE, LET'S NOT MAKE A BIG FIGHT OUT OF EVERY LITTLE THING... PLEASE! LET'S TRY TO GET ALONG! AWRIGHT? WHATAYA SAY??
JEEZIZ, THESE TWO FEMALES ARE GONNA KILL ME!
HOLD ME, MOMMEE!
OH, YES, MY SWEET LITTLE GIRL...
LITTLE HEAD SMELLS SO SWEET..
LATER
IT'S STRANGE TO THINK WE'VE BEEN HERE A YEAR ALREADY... BUT Y'KNOW, I'M STARTING TO GET ADAPTED TO FRENCH LIFE - HAVING MY LITTLE "APERITIF" IN TH'AFTERNOON..
I'M HOMESICK NOW.. I HAFTO WATCH SOME BILKO*
PASTIS
CARAFE D'EAU
51
PAPARELLI! DOBERMAN! FRONT 'N' CENTER ON THE DOUBLE TAY-UP!!
* POPULAR AMERICAN TV COMEDY SHOW FROM THE FIFTIES.. STARRING PHIL SILVERS AS SGT. ERNIE BILKO.
DEDICATED TO JEAN-PIERRE MERCIER
— THE END (FIN)

Adjusting to our new life

When Sophie entered the local elementary school, she was faced with the difficulty of total immersion. The principal and teachers were very kind and patient, but the small-town kids lived sheltered lives and were not sympathetic to outsiders. They teased and tormented Sophie, who had been accustomed to being very popular and on top of everything. Our poor child had stomach aches for a whole year. She did master the French language with remarkable speed, but learning how to act French was a more subtle and complicated process.

Ironically, Sophie came to see Robert and me as embarrassing immigrant parents. We never mastered the language very well, particularly Robert. Worse than that, we did everything wrong, from eating our salade before the main course to drinking weak coffee and failing to spend enough time sitting in the Café du Commerce with the other parents. She complained I was overly protective, a mother hen who insisted on driving her and her friends to various activities instead of letting them hitchhike along the mountain roads. (Believe me, they're dangerous! The number of traffic deaths in these parts is incredibly high, and French drivers, especially anorexic French women drivers, could take up an entire chapter of this book.) I also talk too loud and dress too flamboyantly for any teenager, so I'm sure I would have been almost as embarrassing a mother if we had stayed in the States.

By the time Sophie was in high school, she was smoking a lot of hash—or shit as they call it in France—and had lost interest in studying. She started a rock band which was pretty good and did manage to pass her baccalauréat exam at the lycée, but just barely. After high school, she stayed in Paris for a while, and went to Circus school for a year before heading for the USA to rediscover what she had left behind. She has become a serious cartoonist and a highly skilled tattoo artist. She also plays 1920s Jazz on the piano, and can play several string instruments as well. Yes I'm a proud, anxiety-ridden Jewish mother, and of course I hope she'll settle down here one day near us!

Right: **Sophie playing the piano, Hamburg, 2003**
The guitar next to her is being played by Robert and I'm cringing in the background with my violin (better known as my "squawkbox").

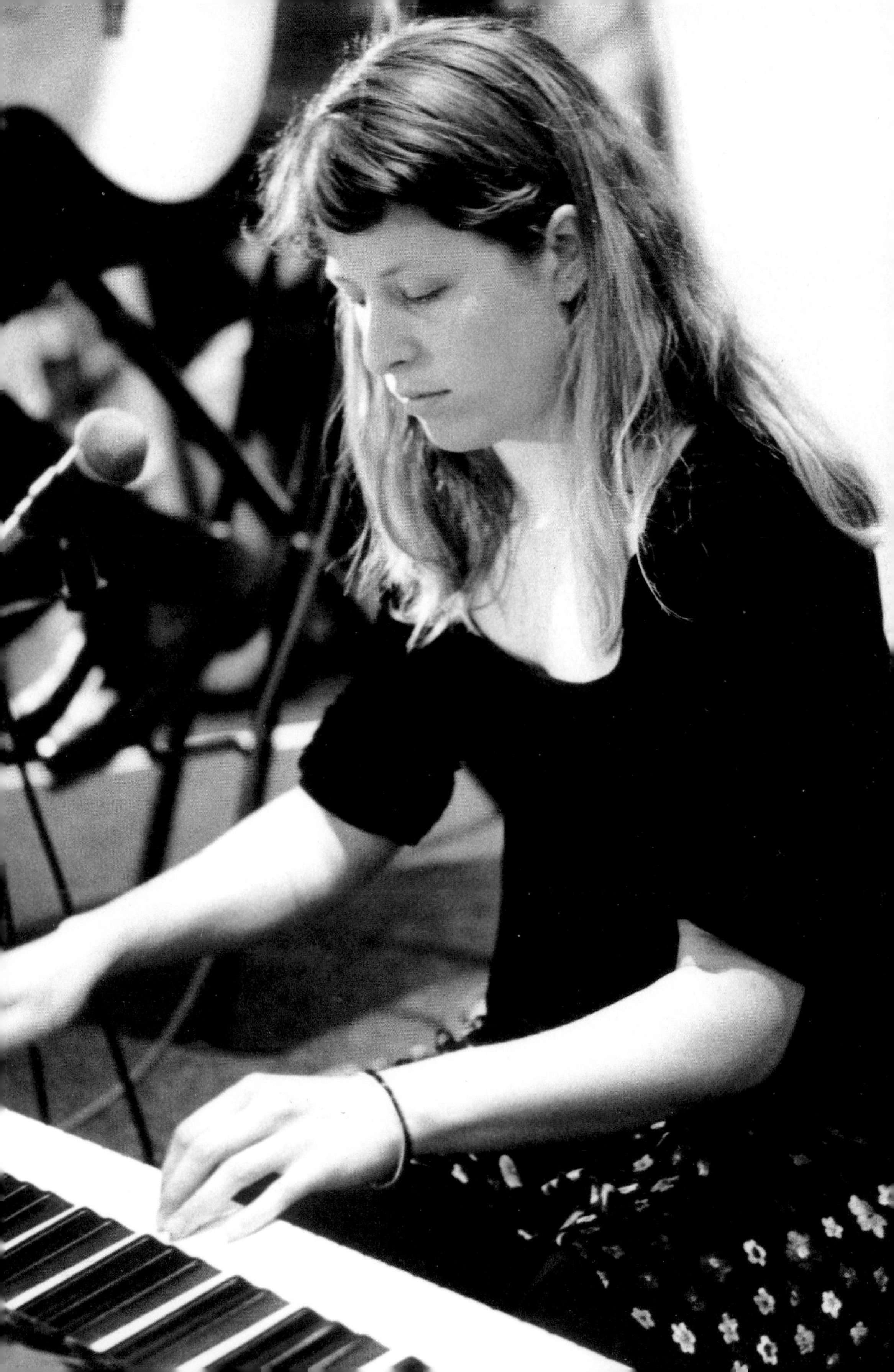

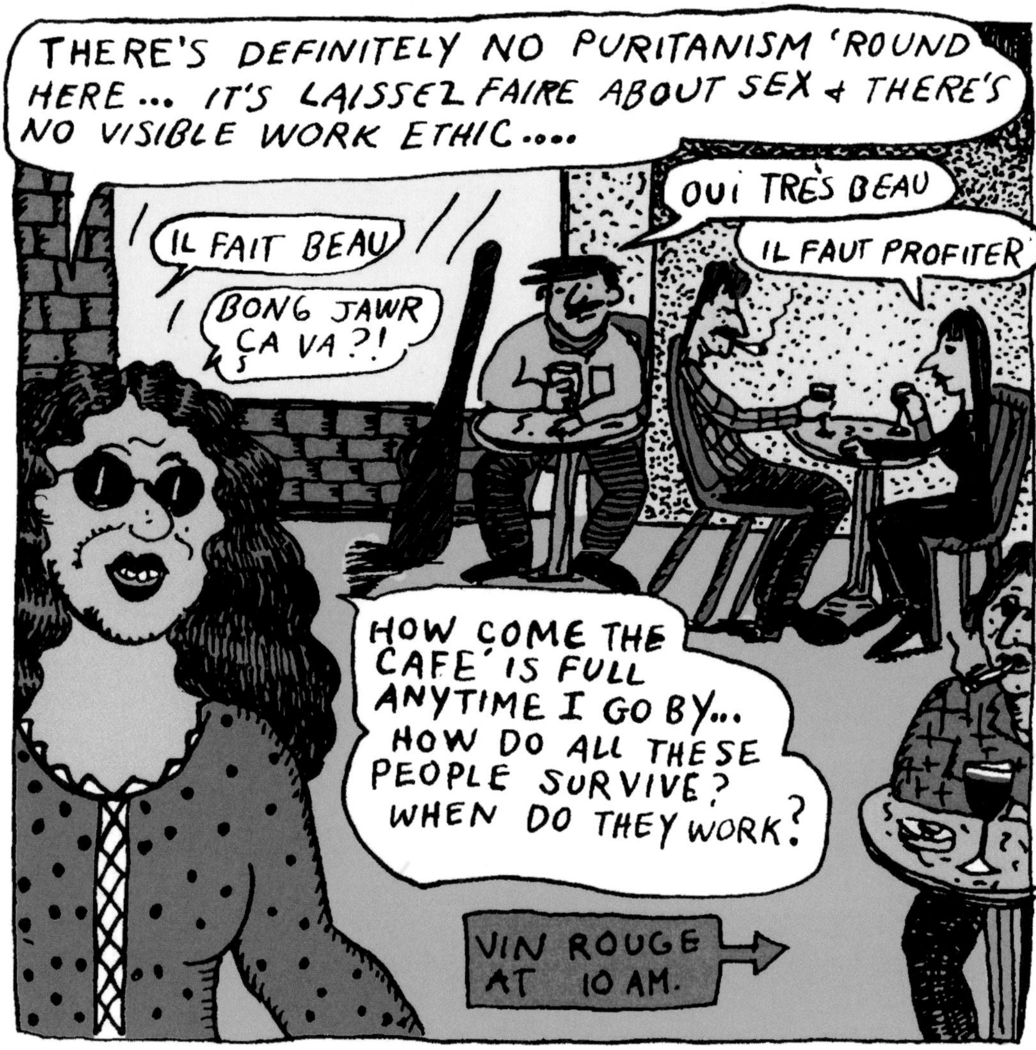
THERE'S DEFINITELY NO PURITANISM 'ROUND HERE... IT'S LAISSEZ FAIRE ABOUT SEX & THERE'S NO VISIBLE WORK ETHIC....
IL FAIT BEAU
BONG JAWR ÇA VA ?!
OUI TRÈS BEAU
IL FAUT PROFITER
HOW COME THE CAFÉ IS FULL ANYTIME I GO BY... HOW DO ALL THESE PEOPLE SURVIVE? WHEN DO THEY WORK?
VIN ROUGE AT 10 AM.

THE LOCALS SURE KNOW HOW TO LIVE!

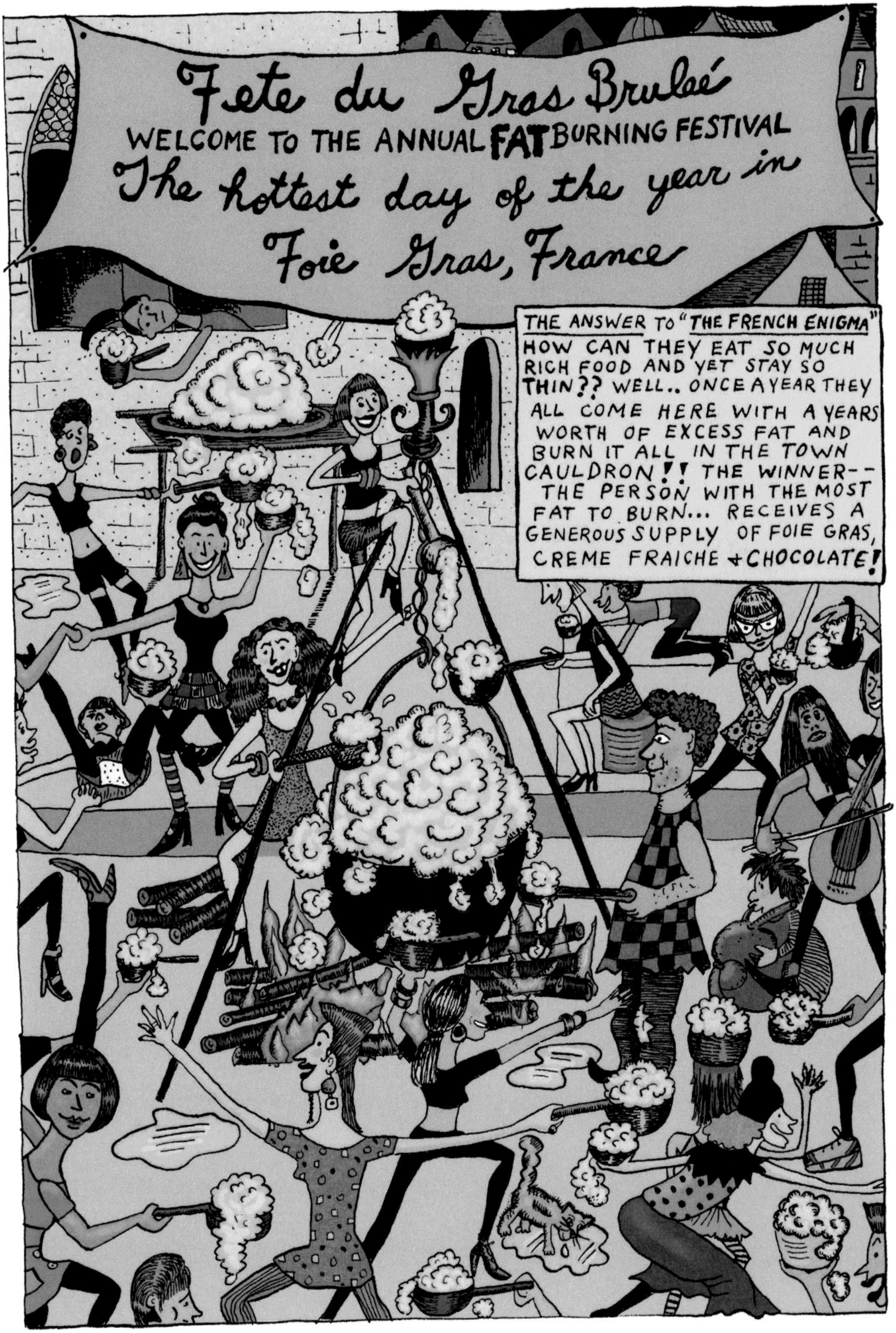

Fete du Gras Brulée
WELCOME TO THE ANNUAL FAT BURNING FESTIVAL
The hottest day of the year in Foie Gras, France
THE ANSWER TO "THE FRENCH ENIGMA" HOW CAN THEY EAT SO MUCH RICH FOOD AND YET STAY SO THIN?? WELL.. ONCE A YEAR THEY ALL COME HERE WITH A YEARS WORTH OF EXCESS FAT AND BURN IT ALL IN THE TOWN CAULDRON!! THE WINNER-- THE PERSON WITH THE MOST FAT TO BURN... RECEIVES A GENEROUS SUPPLY OF FOIE GRAS, CREME FRAICHE + CHOCOLATE!

AND WE DO OUR OWN THING ...

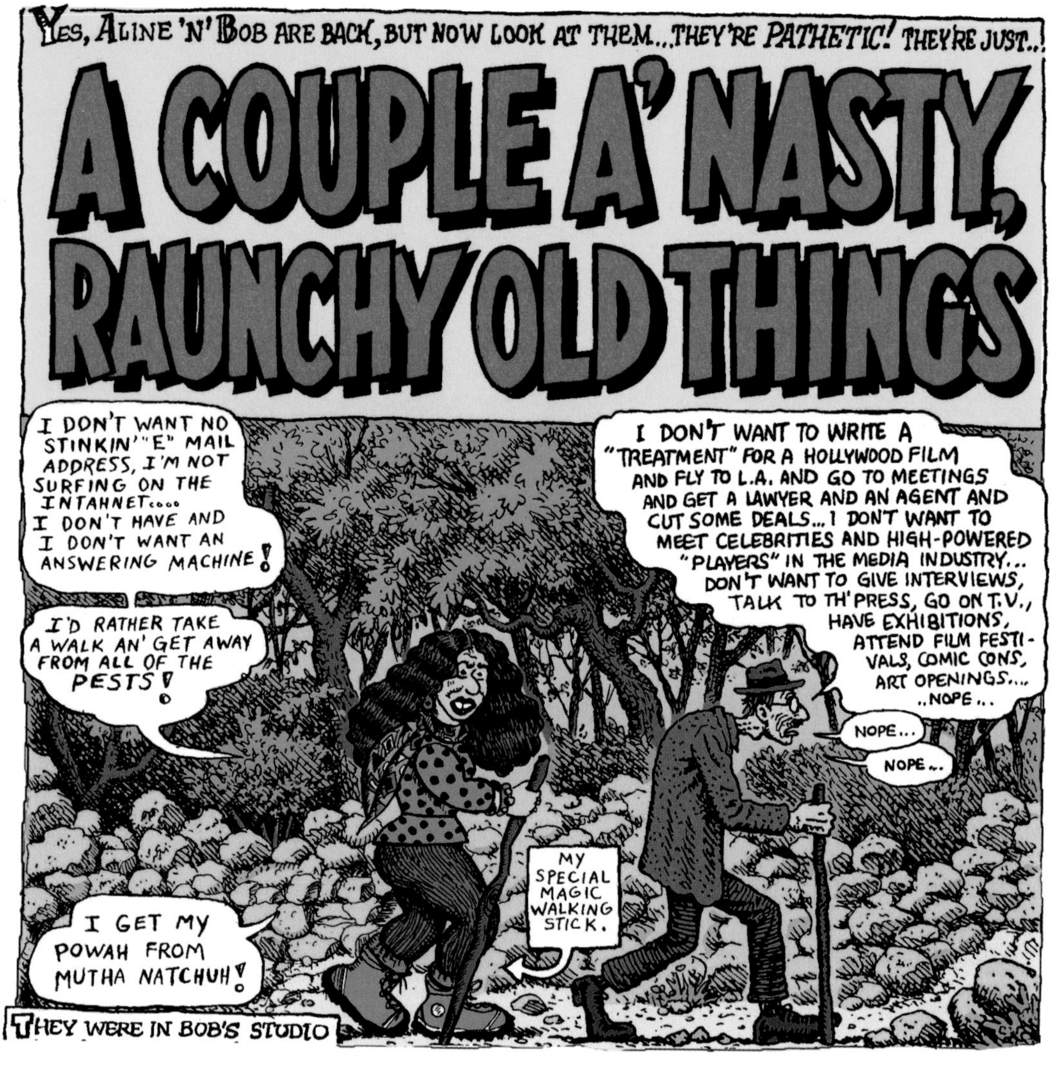
YES, ALINE 'N' BOB ARE BACK, BUT NOW LOOK AT THEM...THEY'RE PATHETIC! THEY'RE JUST..!
A COUPLE A' NASTY, RAUNCHY OLD THINGS
I DON'T WANT NO STINKIN' "E" MAIL ADDRESS, I'M NOT SURFING ON THE INTAHNET.... I DON'T HAVE AND I DON'T WANT AN ANSWERING MACHINE!
I'D RATHER TAKE A WALK AN' GET AWAY FROM ALL OF THE PESTS!
I DON'T WANT TO WRITE A "TREATMENT" FOR A HOLLYWOOD FILM AND FLY TO L.A. AND GO TO MEETINGS AND GET A LAWYER AND AN AGENT AND CUT SOME DEALS... I DON'T WANT TO MEET CELEBRITIES AND HIGH-POWERED "PLAYERS" IN THE MEDIA INDUSTRY... DON'T WANT TO GIVE INTERVIEWS, TALK TO TH' PRESS, GO ON T.V., HAVE EXHIBITIONS, ATTEND FILM FESTIVALS, COMIC CONS, ART OPENINGS.... ..NOPE...
NOPE...
NOPE...
MY SPECIAL MAGIC WALKING STICK.
I GET MY POWAH FROM MUTHA NATCHUH!
THEY WERE IN BOB'S STUDIO

Above and right: **Two pages from *Self Loathing* comics No. 2, by me & Robert, 1997**

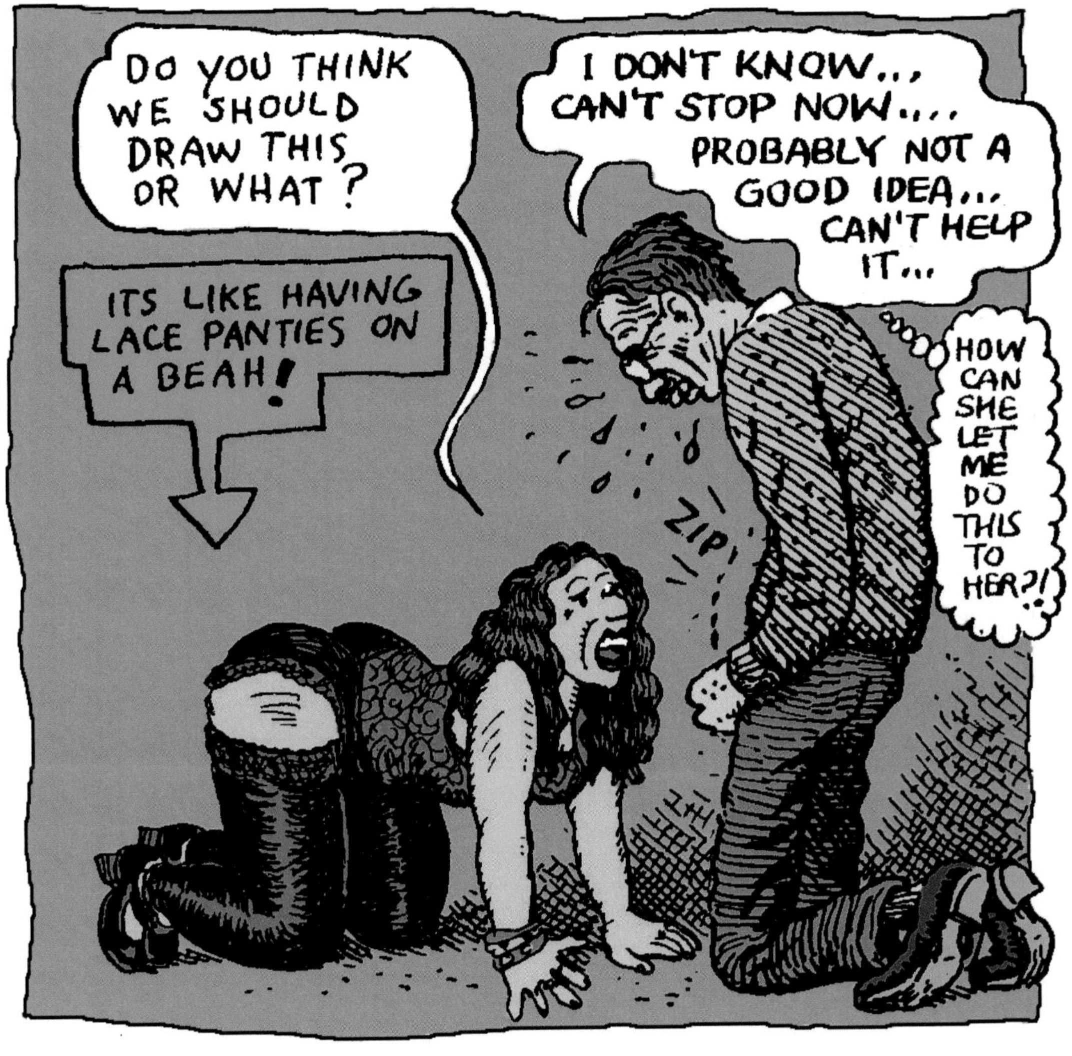
DO YOU THINK WE SHOULD DRAW THIS OR WHAT?
I DON'T KNOW... CAN'T STOP NOW.... PROBABLY NOT A GOOD IDEA... CAN'T HELP IT...
ITS LIKE HAVING LACE PANTIES ON A BEAH!
HOW CAN SHE LET ME DO THIS TO HER?!
ZIP

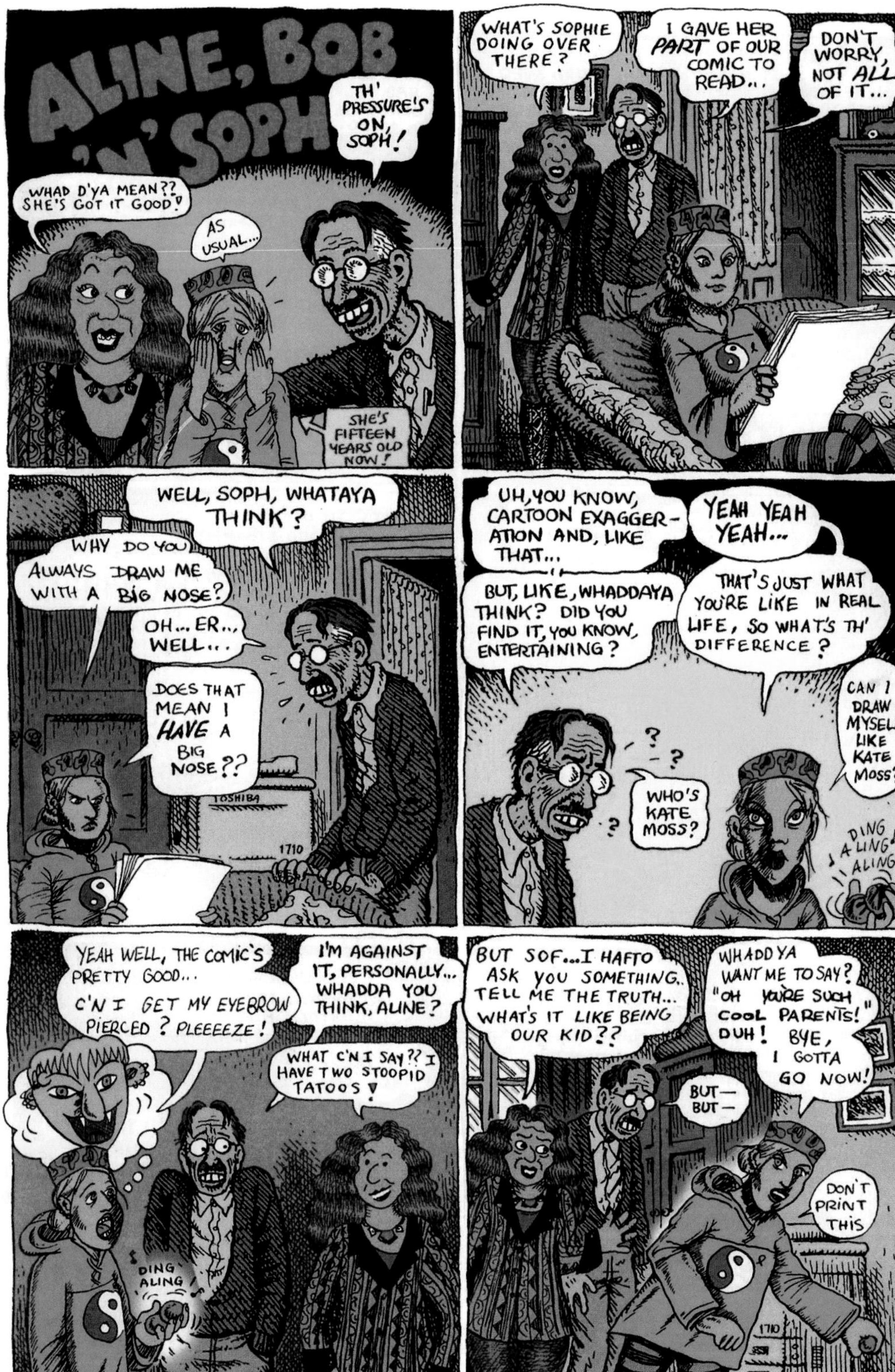
ALINE, BOB 'N' SOPH
TH' PRESSURE'S ON, SOPH!
WHAD D'YA MEAN?? SHE'S GOT IT GOOD!
AS USUAL...
SHE'S FIFTEEN YEARS OLD NOW!
WHAT'S SOPHIE DOING OVER THERE?
I GAVE HER PART OF OUR COMIC TO READ...
DON'T WORRY, NOT ALL OF IT...
WELL, SOPH, WHATAYA THINK?
WHY DO YOU ALWAYS DRAW ME WITH A BIG NOSE?
OH... ER.., WELL...
DOES THAT MEAN I HAVE A BIG NOSE??
TOSHIBA
1710
UH, YOU KNOW, CARTOON EXAGGER-ATION AND, LIKE THAT...
YEAH YEAH YEAH...
BUT, LIKE, WHADDAYA THINK? DID YOU FIND IT, YOU KNOW, ENTERTAINING?
THAT'S JUST WHAT YOU'RE LIKE IN REAL LIFE, SO WHAT'S TH' DIFFERENCE?
CAN I DRAW MYSELF LIKE KATE MOSS?
? ? ?
WHO'S KATE MOSS?
DING A LING ALING
YEAH WELL, THE COMIC'S PRETTY GOOD... C'N I GET MY EYEBROW PIERCED? PLEEEEZE!
I'M AGAINST IT, PERSONALLY... WHADDA YOU THINK, ALINE?
WHAT C'N I SAY?? I HAVE TWO STOOPID TATOOS!
DING ALING
BUT SOF...I HAFTO ASK YOU SOMETHING.. TELL ME THE TRUTH... WHAT'S IT LIKE BEING OUR KID??
WHADDYA WANT ME TO SAY? "OH YOU'RE SUCH COOL PARENTS!" DUH! BYE, I GOTTA GO NOW!
BUT— BUT—
DON'T PRINT THIS
1710

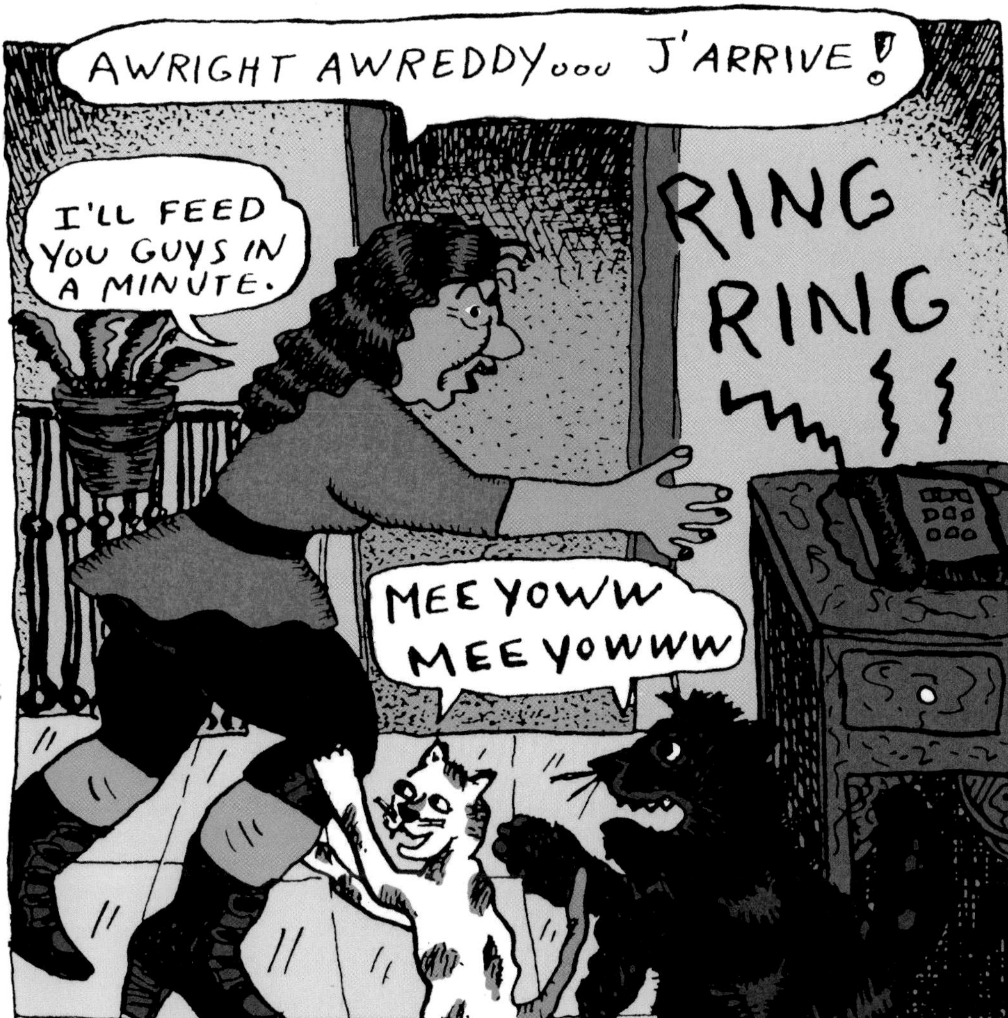
AWRIGHT AWREDDY... J'ARRIVE!
I'LL FEED YOU GUYS IN A MINUTE.
RING RING
MEE YOWW MEE YOWWW

THERE'S NEVER A DULL MOMENT ...

Above: **Panel by me from "A Day In The Life" *Self Loathing* comics No. 1, 1955**
Left: **Back cover of *Self Loathing* comics No. 2, by me, Robert & Sophie**

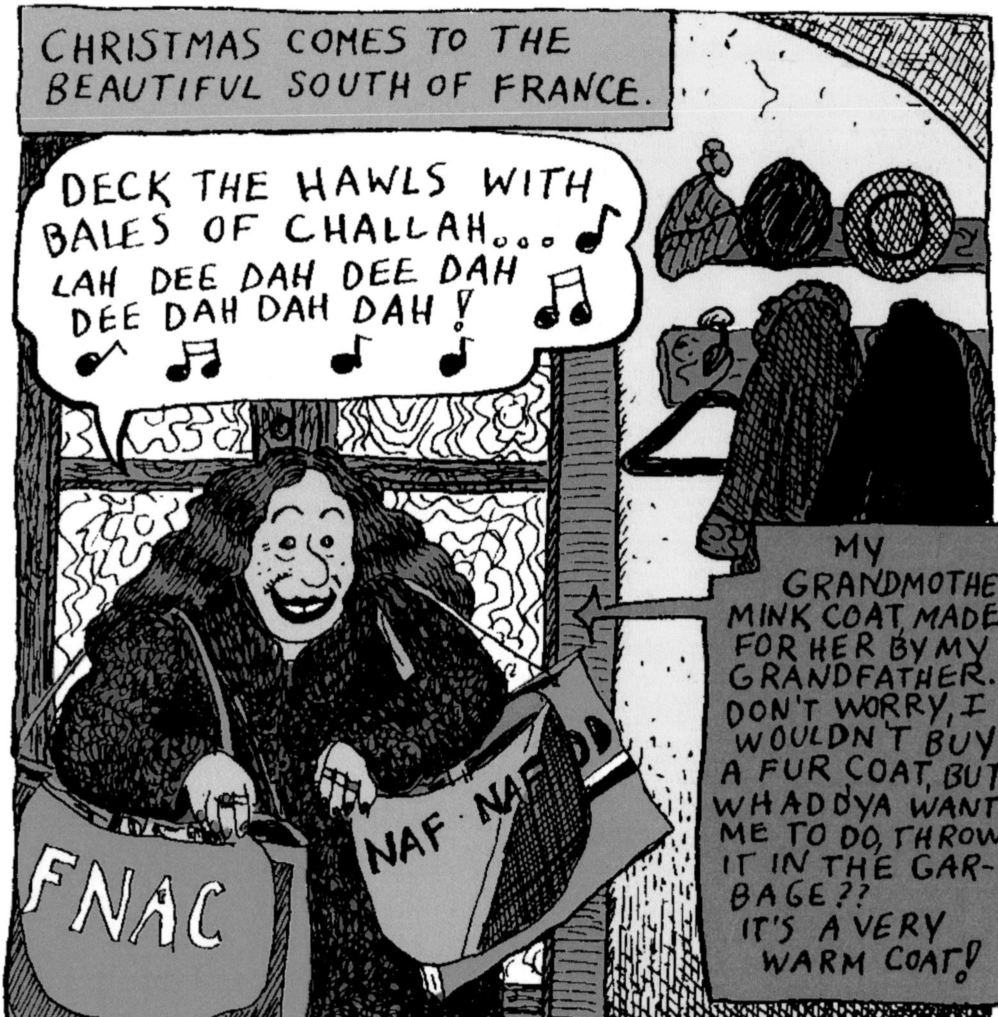
CHRISTMAS COMES TO THE BEAUTIFUL SOUTH OF FRANCE.
DECK THE HAWLS WITH BALES OF CHALLAH... LAH DEE DAH DEE DAH DEE DAH DAH DAH!
FNAC
NAF NAF
MY GRANDMOTHERS MINK COAT, MADE FOR HER BY MY GRANDFATHER. DON'T WORRY, I WOULDN'T BUY A FUR COAT, BUT WHADDYA WANT ME TO DO, THROW IT IN THE GARBAGE?? IT'S A VERY WARM COAT!

I ENTERTAIN AT HOME ...

Above: **Panel by me from *Self Loathing* comics No. 2**
Right: **Hand-colored comic page by me ... never seen before ... rejected by publisher**

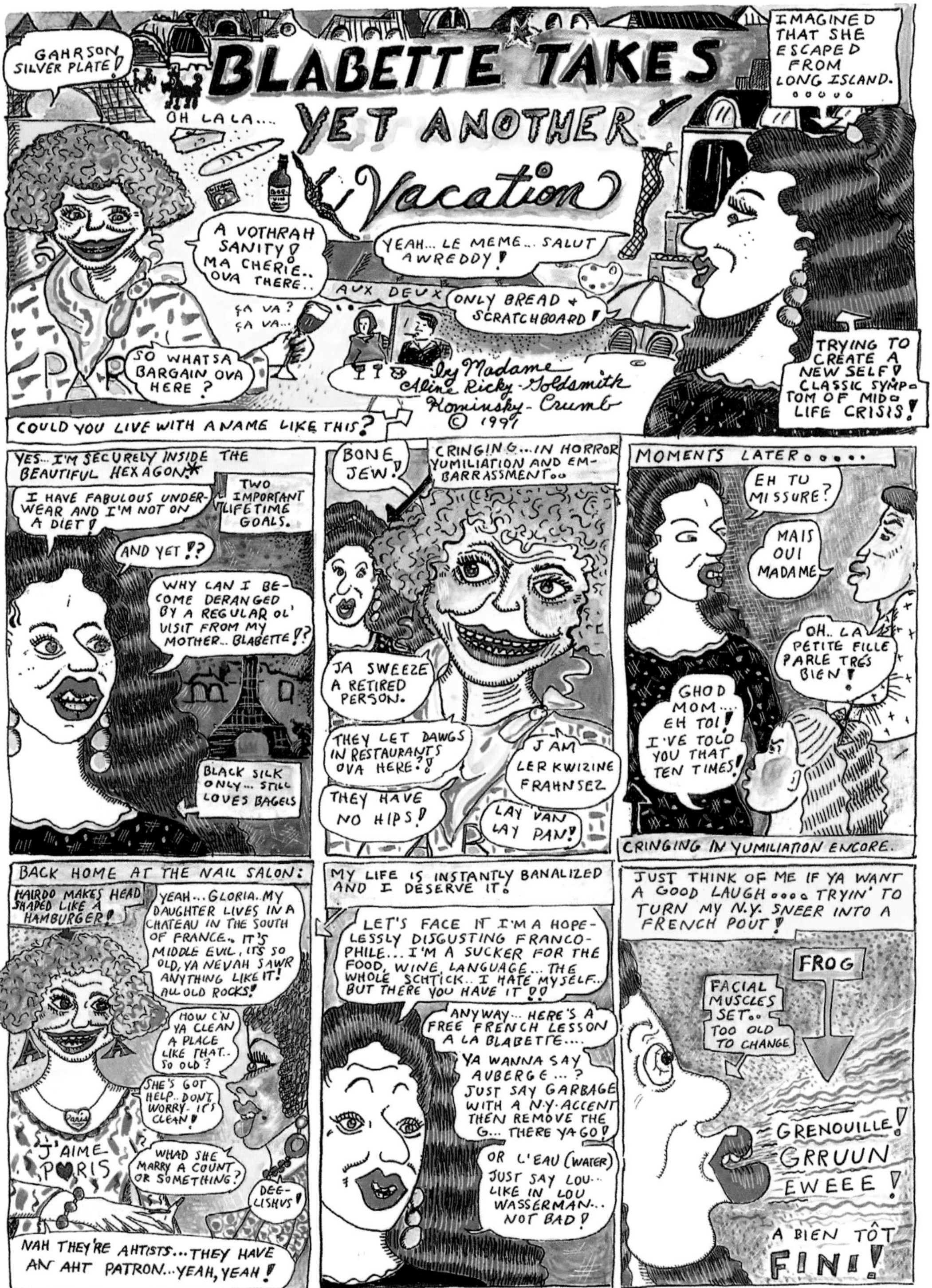
BLABETTE TAKES YET ANOTHER VACATION
GAHRSON SILVER PLATE!
OH LA LA....
IMAGINED THAT SHE ESCAPED FROM LONG ISLAND......
A VOTHRAH SANITY! MA CHERIE.. OVA THERE..
YEAH... LE MEME... SALUT AWREDDY!
AUX DEUX
ONLY BREAD + SCRATCHBOARD!
ÇA VA? ÇA VA...
SO WHATSA BARGAIN OVA HERE?
TRYING TO CREATE A NEW SELF! CLASSIC SYMPTOM OF MID-LIFE CRISIS!
by Madame Aline Ricky-Goldsmith Kominsky-Crumb © 1991
COULD YOU LIVE WITH A NAME LIKE THIS?
YES... I'M SECURELY INSIDE THE BEAUTIFUL HEXAGON.*
I HAVE FABULOUS UNDERWEAR AND I'M NOT ON A DIET!
TWO IMPORTANT LIFETIME GOALS.
AND YET!?
WHY CAN I BECOME DERANGED BY A REGULAR OL' VISIT FROM MY MOTHER... BLABETTE!?
BLACK SILK ONLY... STILL LOVES BAGELS
BONE JEW!
CRINGING... IN HORROR YUMILIATION AND EMBARRASSMENT...
JA SWEEZE A RETIRED PERSON.
THEY LET DAWGS IN RESTAURANTS OVA HERE?!
J'AM LERKWIZINE FRAHNSEZ
THEY HAVE NO HIPS!
LAY VAN LAY PAN!
MOMENTS LATER......
EH TU MISSURE?
MAIS OUI MADAME
OH.. LA PETITE FILLE PARLE TRES BIEN!
GHOD MOM... EH TOI! I'VE TOLD YOU THAT TEN TIMES!
CRINGING IN YUMILIATION ENCORE.
BACK HOME AT THE NAIL SALON:
HAIRDO MAKES HEAD SHAPED LIKE A HAMBURGER!
YEAH... GLORIA. MY DAUGHTER LIVES IN A CHATEAU IN THE SOUTH OF FRANCE. IT'S MIDDLE EVIL, IT'S SO OLD, YA NEVAH SAWR ANYTHING LIKE IT! ALL OLD ROCKS!
HOW C'N YA CLEAN A PLACE LIKE THAT.. SO OLD?
SHE'S GOT HELP.. DON'T WORRY.. IT'S CLEAN!
J'AIME PARIS
WHAD SHE MARRY A COUNT OR SOMETHING?
DEE-LISHUS!
NAH THEY'RE AHTISTS... THEY HAVE AN AHT PATRON... YEAH, YEAH!
MY LIFE IS INSTANTLY BANALIZED AND I DESERVE IT!
LET'S FACE IT I'M A HOPELESSLY DISGUSTING FRANCOPHILE... I'M A SUCKER FOR THE FOOD, WINE, LANGUAGE... THE WHOLE SCHTICK.. I HATE MYSELF.. BUT THERE YOU HAVE IT!!
ANYWAY... HERE'S A FREE FRENCH LESSON A LA BLABETTE....
YA WANNA SAY AUBERGE...? JUST SAY GARBAGE WITH A N.Y. ACCENT THEN REMOVE THE G... THERE YA GO!
OR L'EAU (WATER) JUST SAY LOU.. LIKE IN LOU WASSERMAN.. NOT BAD!
JUST THINK OF ME IF YA WANT A GOOD LAUGH.... TRYIN' TO TURN MY N.Y. SNEER INTO A FRENCH POUT!
FROG
FACIAL MUSCLES SET.. TOO OLD TO CHANGE
GRENOUILLE! GRRUUN EWEEE!
A BIEN TÔT
FINI!

★ JUST IN CASE YOU DON'T KNOW HER... SHE'S A 59 YR. OLD JEWISH AMERICAN PRINCESS... NOW RETIRED FROM THE N.Y. AD. BUSINESS.. SHE DEVOTES TIME TO GOLF, AEROBICS, SHOPPING, PLANNED LEISURE + VISITING ME!

✳ HOW THE FRENCH LOVINGLY REFER TO THE SHAPE OF THEIR COUNTRY.

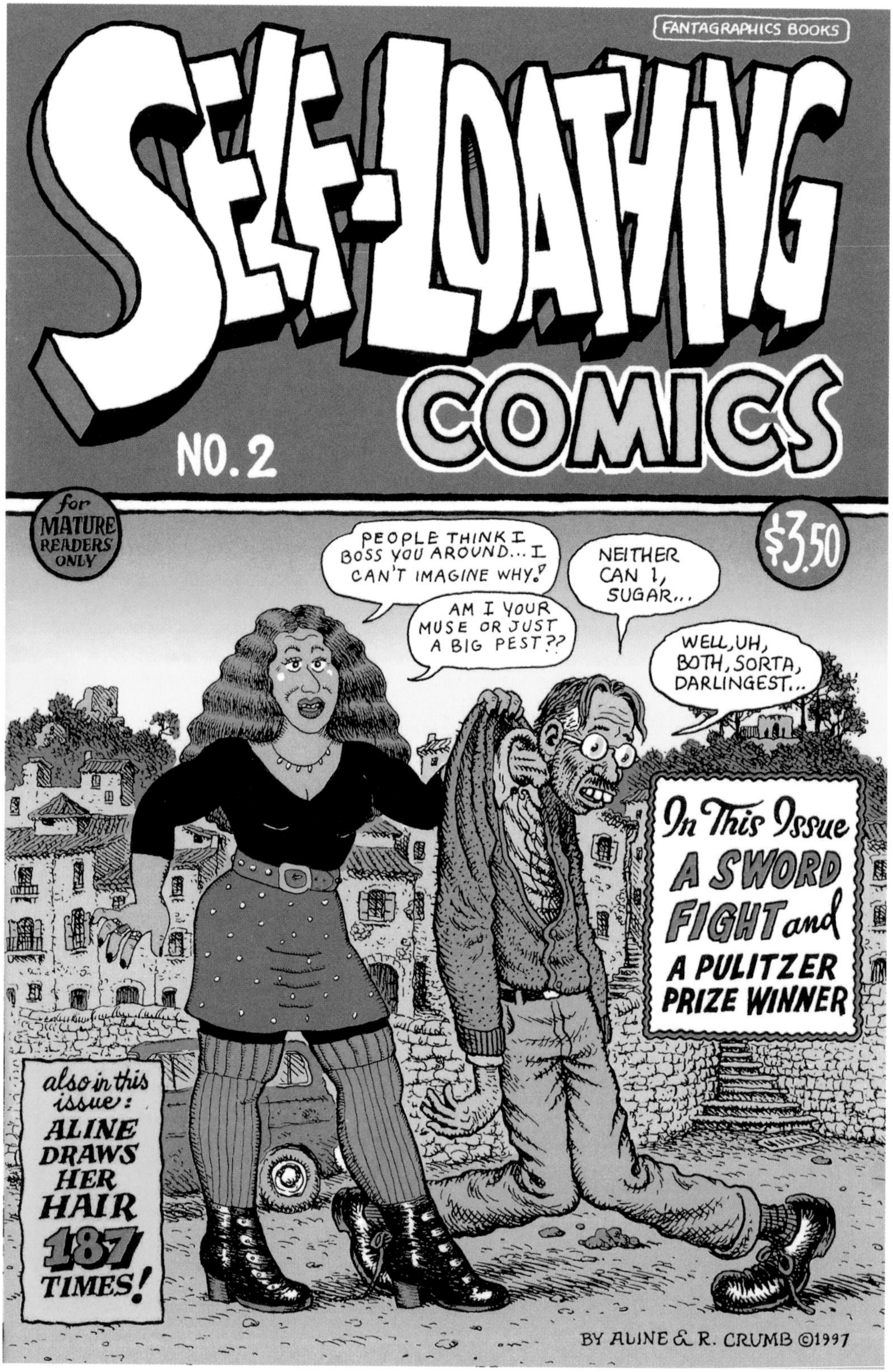
FANTAGRAPHICS BOOKS
SELF-LOATHING COMICS
NO. 2
for MATURE READERS ONLY
$3.50
PEOPLE THINK I BOSS YOU AROUND... I CAN'T IMAGINE WHY!
AM I YOUR MUSE OR JUST A BIG PEST??
NEITHER CAN I, SUGAR...
WELL, UH, BOTH, SORTA, DARLINGEST...
In This Issue A SWORD FIGHT and A PULITZER PRIZE WINNER
also in this issue: ALINE DRAWS HER HAIR 187 TIMES!
BY ALINE & R. CRUMB ©1997

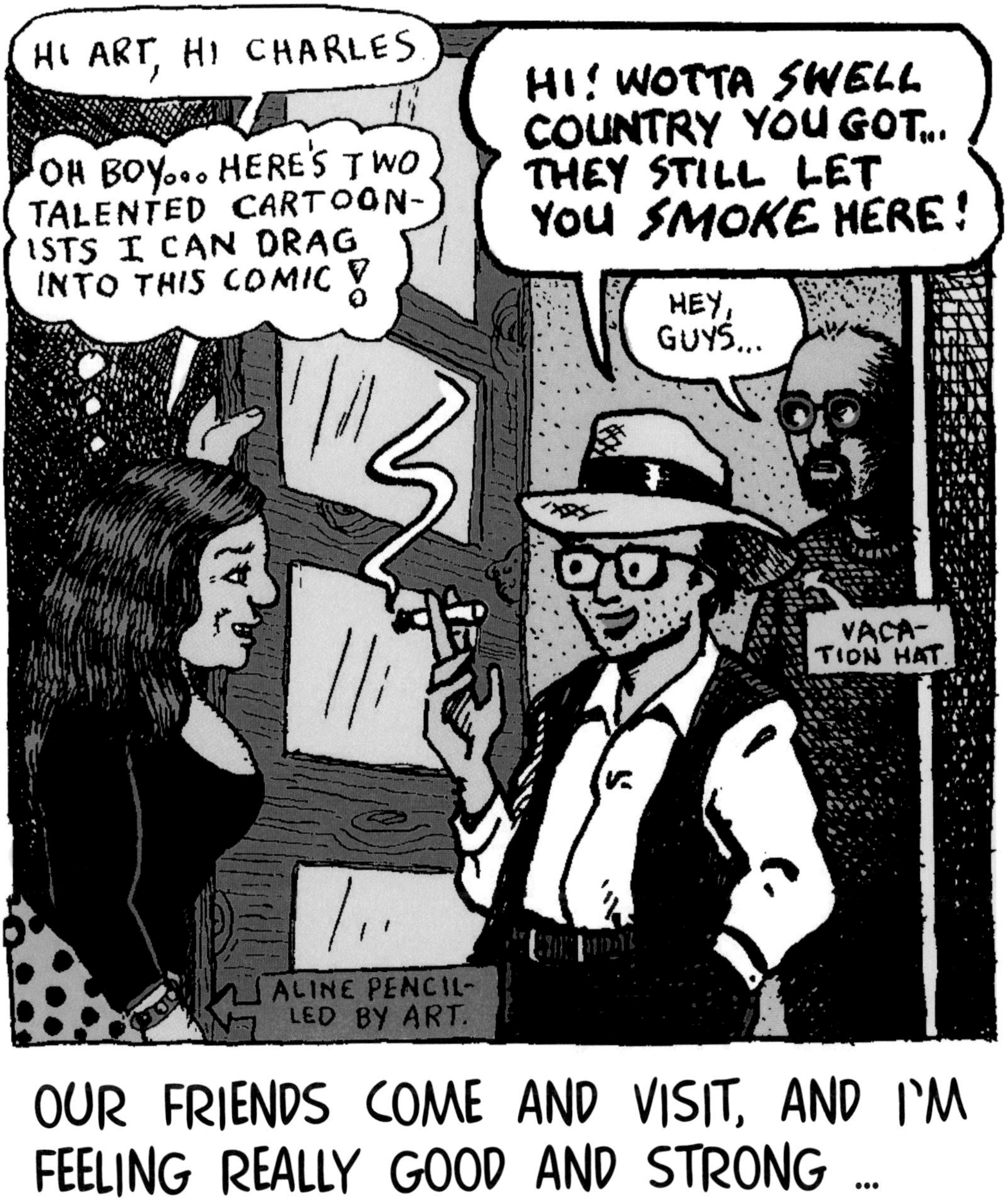
HI ART, HI CHARLES
OH BOY... HERE'S TWO TALENTED CARTOON-ISTS I CAN DRAG INTO THIS COMIC
HI! WOTTA SWELL COUNTRY YOU GOT... THEY STILL LET YOU SMOKE HERE!
HEY, GUYS...
VACA-TION HAT
ALINE PENCIL-LED BY ART.
OUR FRIENDS COME AND VISIT, AND I'M FEELING REALLY GOOD AND STRONG ...

Above: **Panel from *Self Loathing* comics No. 2 by me, Art Spiegelman, & Charles Burns, 1997**
Left: ***Self Loathing* cover**
Next page: **Center spread by me, *Self Loathing* comics No. 1**

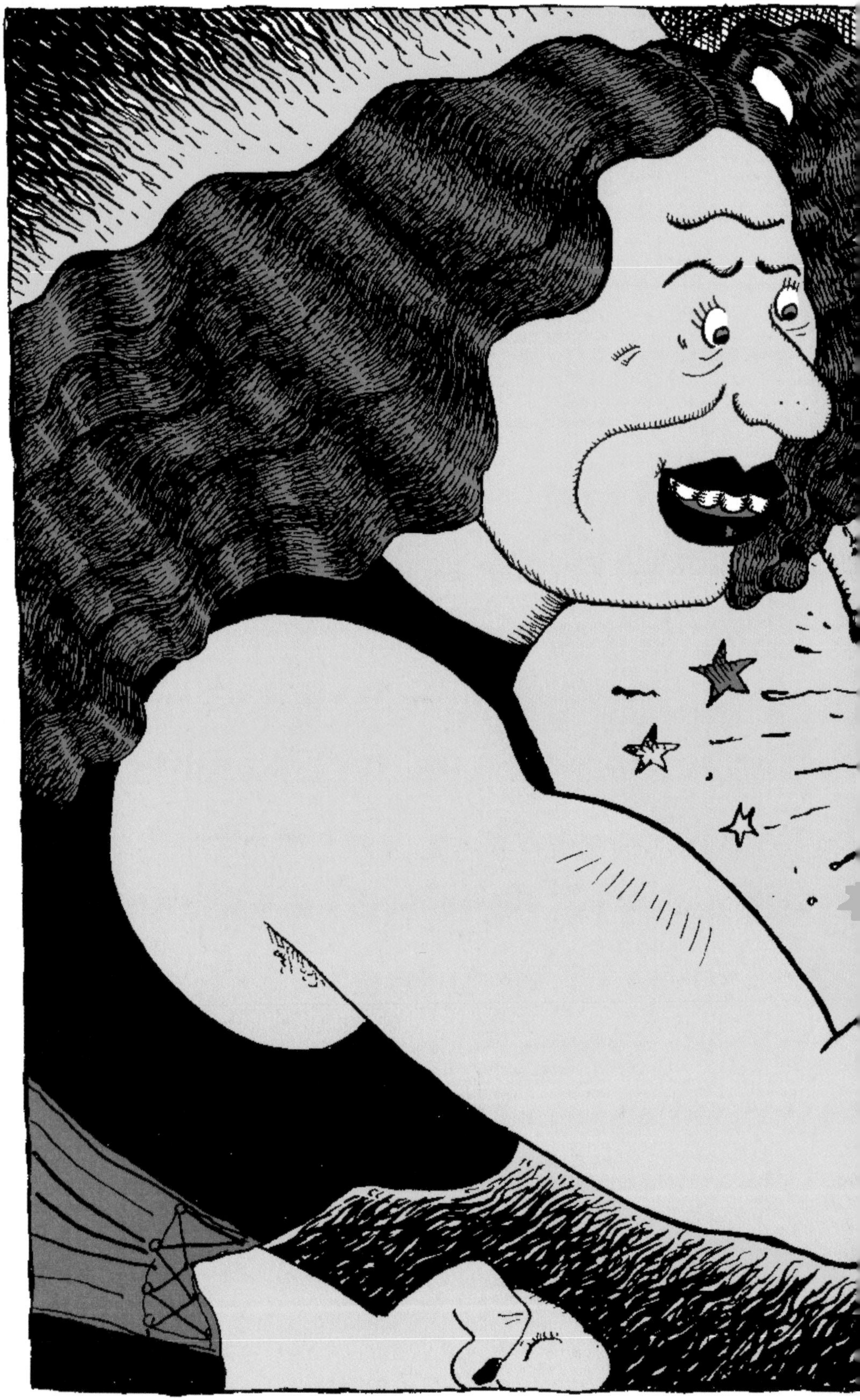

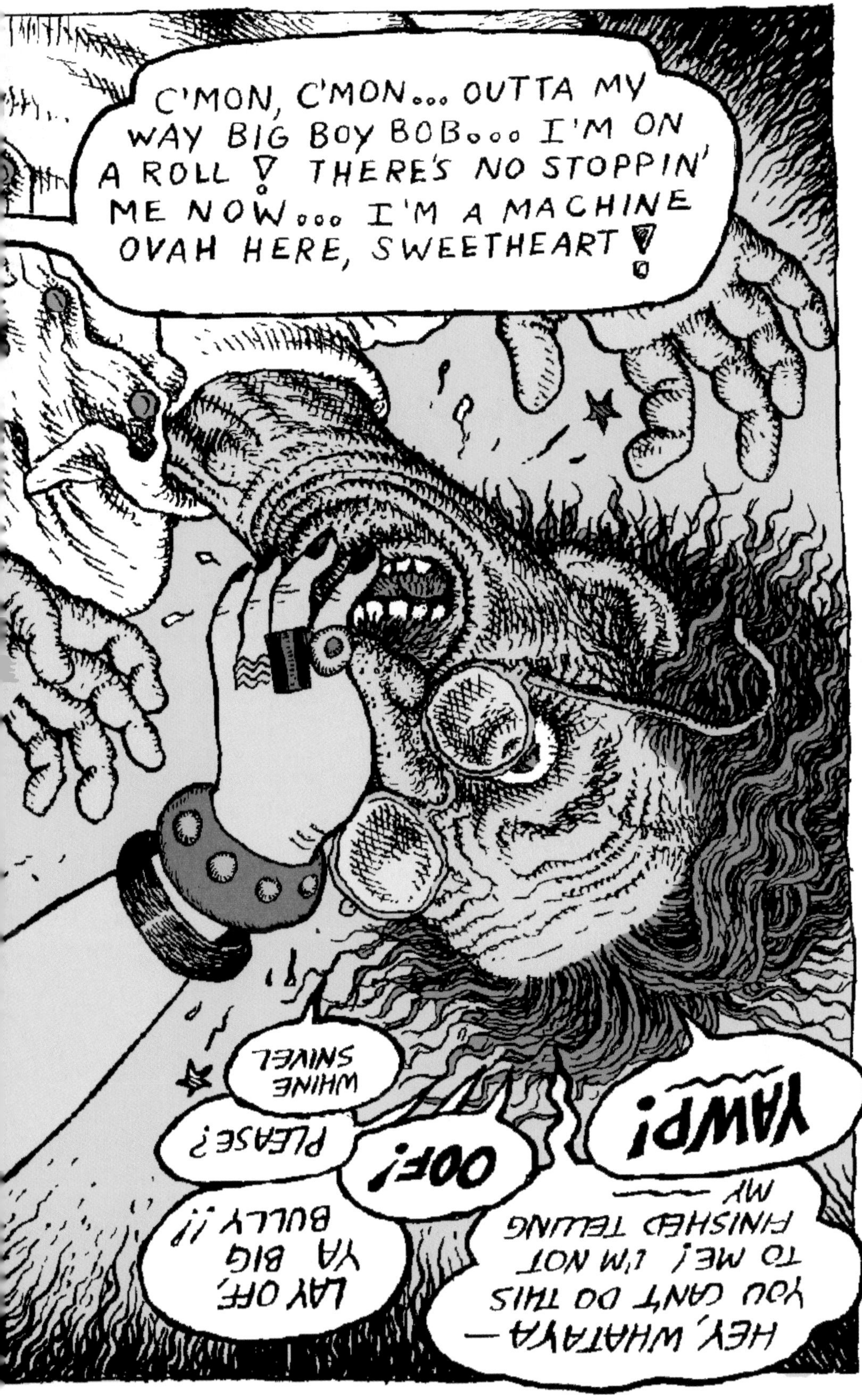
C'MON, C'MON... OUTTA MY WAY BIG BOY BOB... I'M ON A ROLL! THERE'S NO STOPPIN' ME NOW... I'M A MACHINE OVAH HERE, SWEETHEART!
YAWP!
OOF!
WHINE SNIVEL
PLEASE?
LAY OFF, YA BIG BULLY!!
HEY, WHATAYA— YOU CAN'T DO THIS TO ME! I'M NOT FINISHED TELLING MY ——

My husbands and I ...

Back to us crazy adults and our mid-life adventures! Before we left California, Robert had warned me that when we moved to France, he would spend at least six weeks each year back in the U.S. He has done so every year since we've been here. He's traveled all over the States visiting friends and family, and especially spending time with several intense girlfriends he has had over the years. Since there have been several Carols, I call them "The Legion of Carols." I have no complaints, since they are all really nice, and haven't in any way trodden on my personal territory.

While Robert was away and I was alone for different periods of time, I became very close to our local printer. To simplify an impossibly complicated story, I will merely describe the ensuing relationship as "the other husband!" Over the years, Robert, Christian (husband number two) and I have become a kind of eccentric extended family. Christian's beautiful daughters and grandchildren have enriched our lives, and somehow it all works. In addition to being a printer, Christian is good at plumbing and likes to drive. Robert and I generate projects that supply work, and the family around us keeps busy. We exchange skills and everyone earns a living. However I don't recommend that everyone tries this route because it rarely turns out so well, and you have to be prepared to handle a lot of ambiguity.

The set-up between me and my two husbands works, mainly because Robert is a little autistic emotionally, Christian has been married enough times to value his independence and not to desire more from me than I am able to give, and I seem to have the knack of not getting overly romantic and emotional about things. Also, I think that Robert feels less guilty because he's always had other girlfriends and now he knows I won't be lonely if he's gone for a long time. Whew! Ironically, we're too old now to get over-excited about sexual affairs, so these extracurricular relationships fulfill other needs. I doubt this would have worked when we were younger and more sex-driven.

Right: **Aline Kominsky Crumb, drawing. Postcard from series "6 Nudes With Baguettes" printed by Christian Coudures in Sauve, 1997**
Next page: **Agathe Coudurés-McCamy with baby Alistair (left) and Eva Coudurés (right), France, 1996**

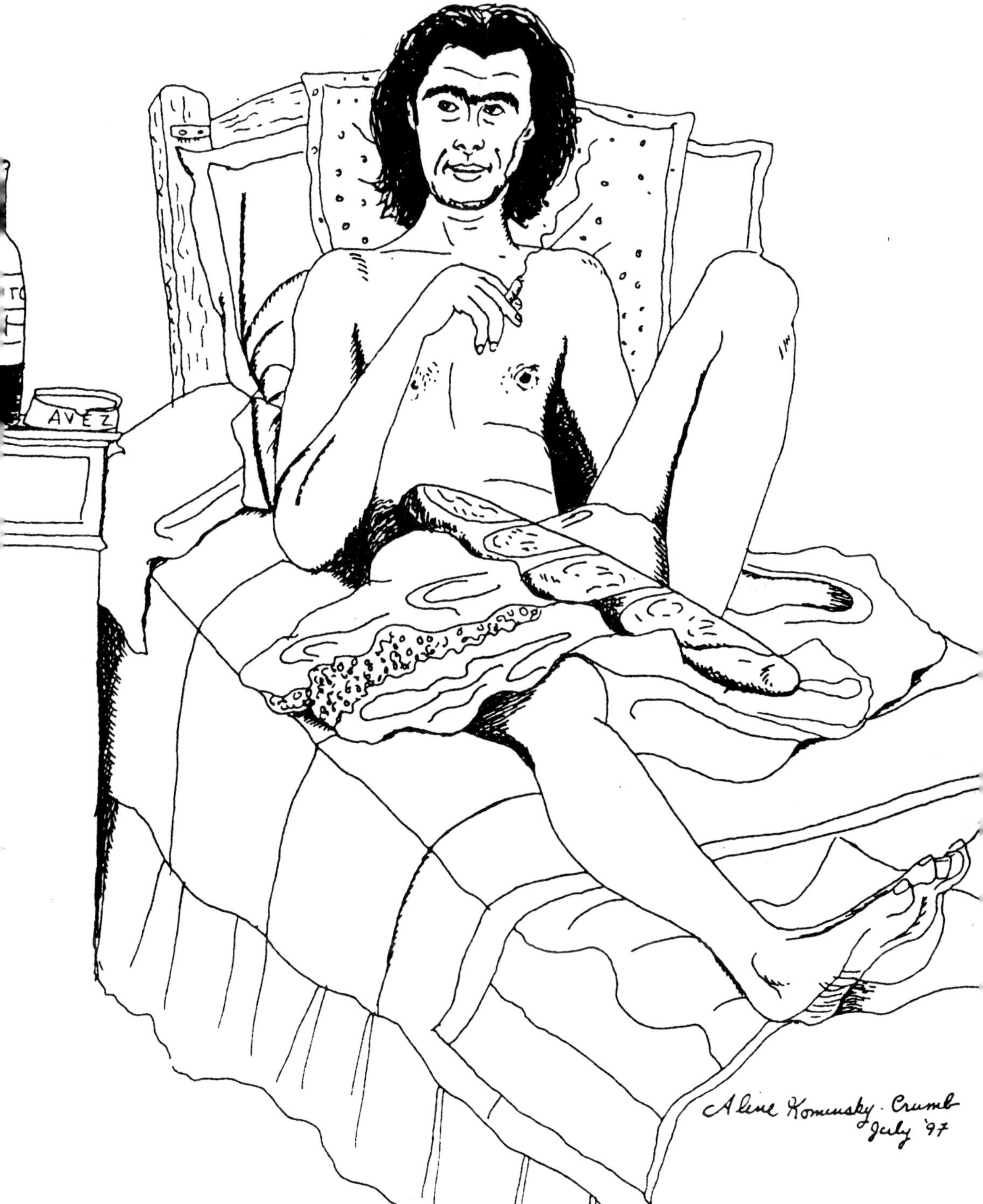
AVEZ
Aline Kominsky-Crumb
July '97

CUTE
NUDE
FRENCH GUY
WITH WINE AND
BAGUETTE

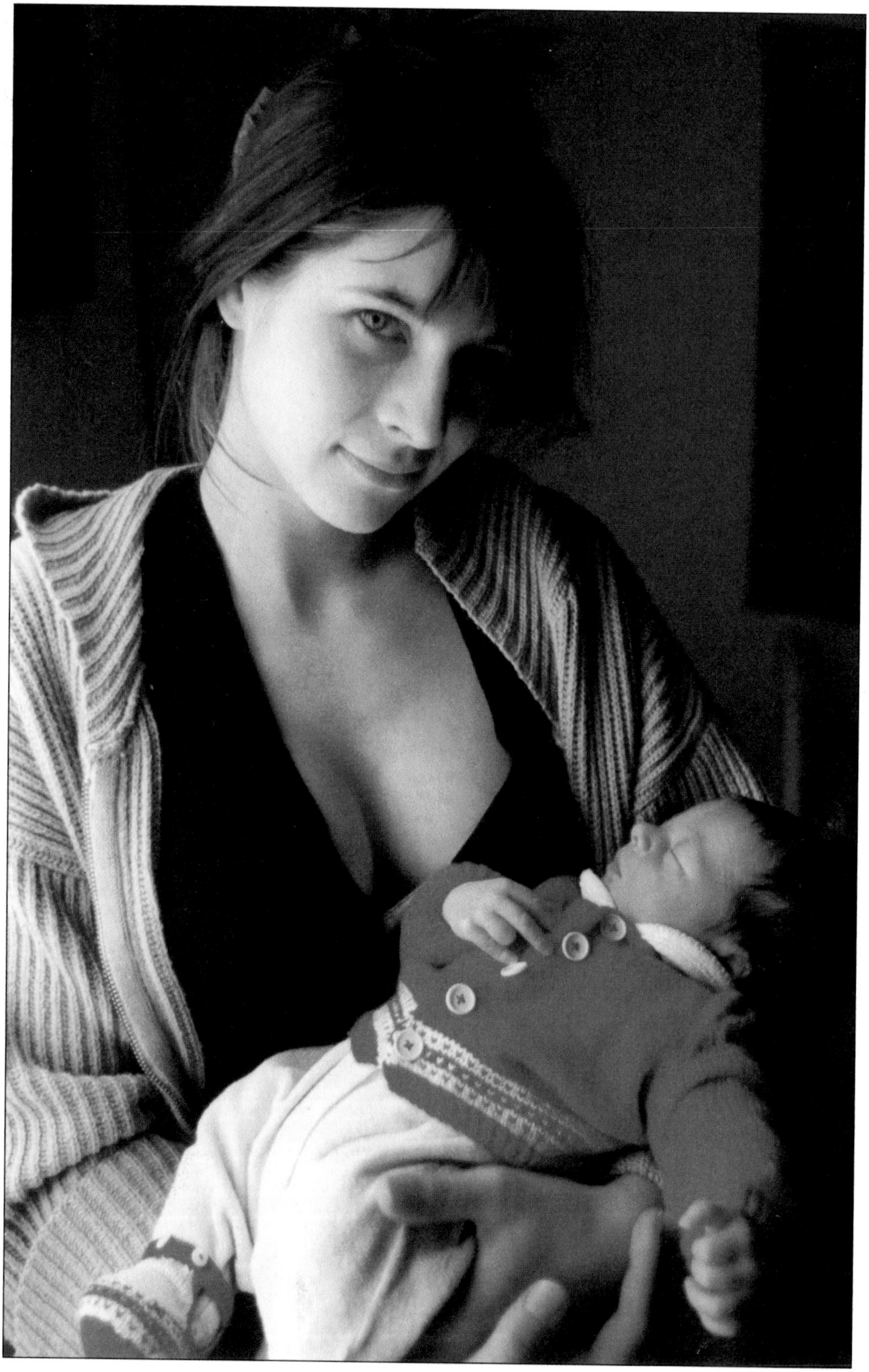

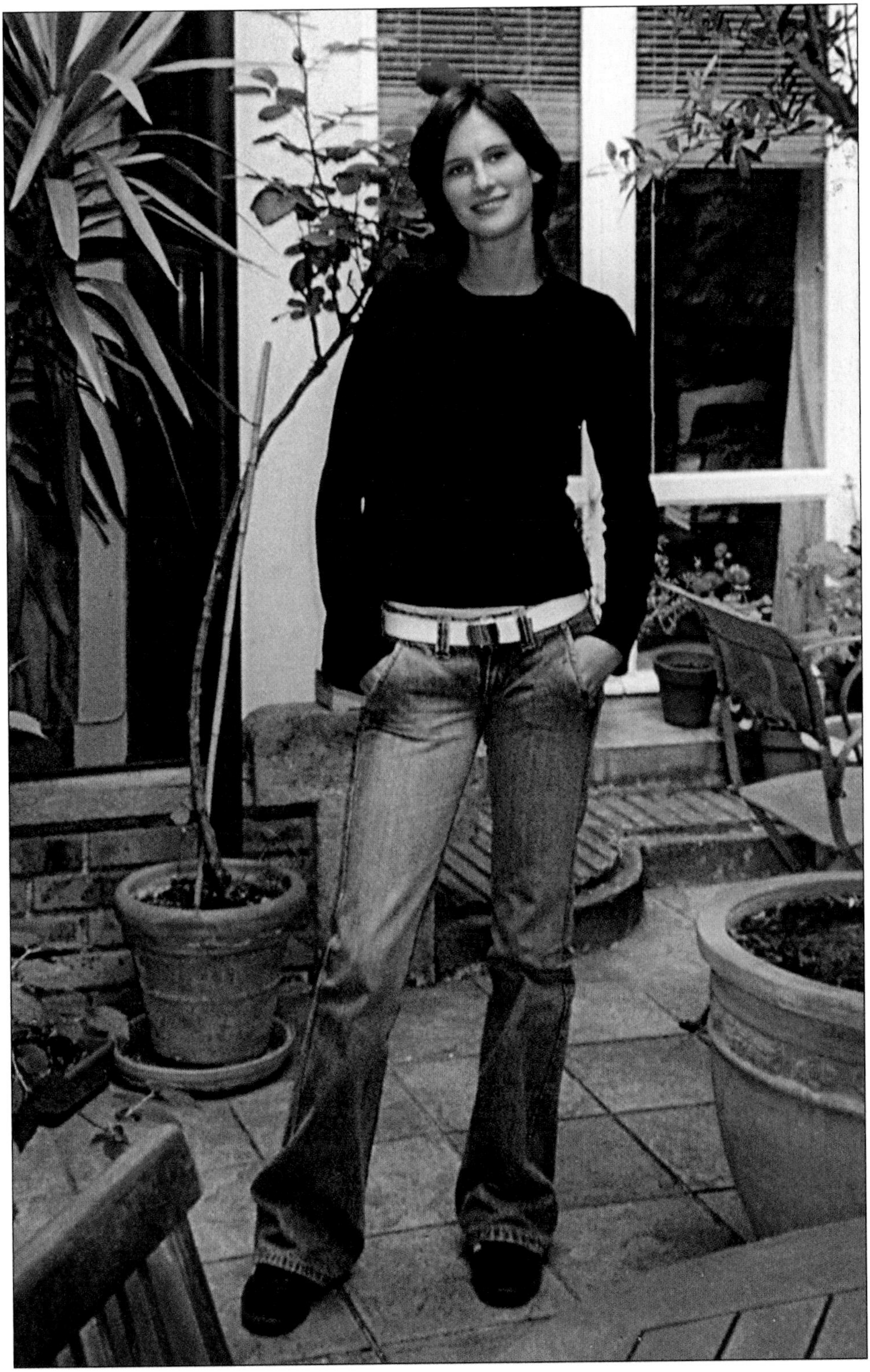

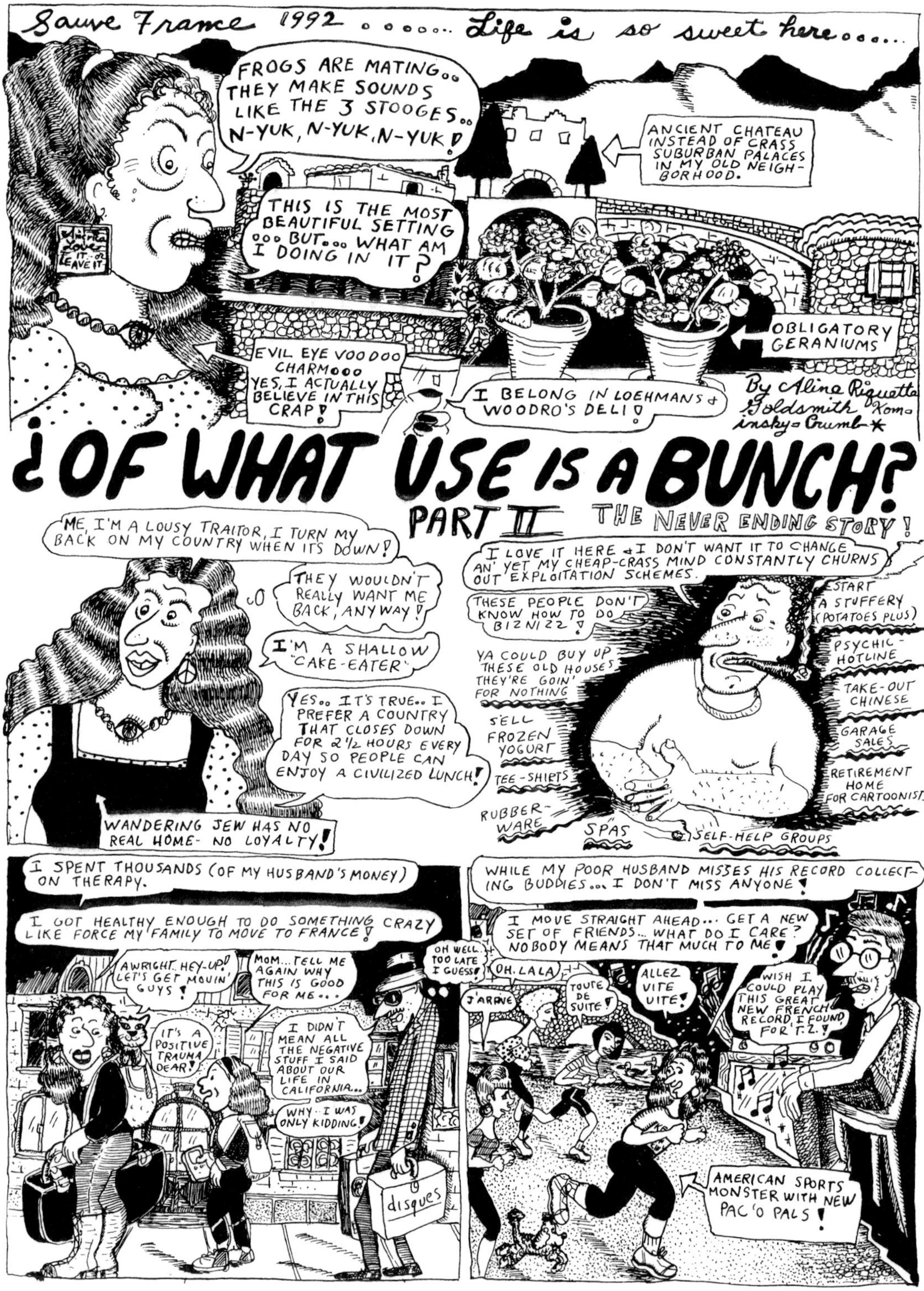
Sauve France 1992 ...... Life is so sweet here......
FROGS ARE MATING.. THEY MAKE SOUNDS LIKE THE 3 STOOGES.. N-YUK, N-YUK, N-YUK!
ANCIENT CHATEAU INSTEAD OF CRASS SUBURBAN PALACES IN MY OLD NEIGH-BORHOOD.
THIS IS THE MOST BEAUTIFUL SETTING ... BUT... WHAT AM I DOING IN IT?
OBLIGATORY GERANIUMS
EVIL EYE VOODOO CHARM... YES, I ACTUALLY BELIEVE IN THIS CRAP!
I BELONG IN LOEHMANS & WOODRO'S DELI!
By Aline Riquette Goldsmith Kominsky-Crumb *
¿OF WHAT USE IS A BUNCH?
PART II
THE NEVER ENDING STORY!
ME, I'M A LOUSY TRAITOR, I TURN MY BACK ON MY COUNTRY WHEN ITS DOWN!
THEY WOULDN'T REALLY WANT ME BACK, ANYWAY!
I'M A SHALLOW "CAKE-EATER"
YES.. IT'S TRUE.. I PREFER A COUNTRY THAT CLOSES DOWN FOR 2½ HOURS EVERY DAY SO PEOPLE CAN ENJOY A CIVILIZED LUNCH!
WANDERING JEW HAS NO REAL HOME- NO LOYALTY!
I LOVE IT HERE & I DON'T WANT IT TO CHANGE AN' YET MY CHEAP-CRASS MIND CONSTANTLY CHURNS OUT EXPLOITATION SCHEMES.
THESE PEOPLE DON'T KNOW HOW TO DO BIZNIZZ!
YA COULD BUY UP THESE OLD HOUSES THEY'RE GOIN' FOR NOTHING
SELL FROZEN YOGURT
TEE-SHIRTS
RUBBER-WARE
SPAS
SELF-HELP GROUPS
START A STUFFERY (POTATOES PLUS)
PSYCHIC-HOTLINE
TAKE-OUT CHINESE
GARAGE SALES
RETIREMENT HOME FOR CARTOONISTS
I SPENT THOUSANDS (OF MY HUSBAND'S MONEY) ON THERAPY.
I GOT HEALTHY ENOUGH TO DO SOMETHING CRAZY LIKE FORCE MY FAMILY TO MOVE TO FRANCE!
AWRIGHT.. HEY-UP! LET'S GET MOVIN' GUYS!
MOM... TELL ME AGAIN WHY THIS IS GOOD FOR ME...
OH WELL.. TOO LATE I GUESS!
IT'S A POSITIVE TRAUMA DEAR!
I DIDN'T MEAN ALL THE NEGATIVE STUFF I SAID ABOUT OUR LIFE IN CALIFORNIA...
WHY.. I WAS ONLY KIDDING!
disques
WHILE MY POOR HUSBAND MISSES HIS RECORD COLLECT-ING BUDDIES... I DON'T MISS ANYONE!
I MOVE STRAIGHT AHEAD... GET A NEW SET OF FRIENDS... WHAT DO I CARE? NOBODY MEANS THAT MUCH TO ME!
OH, LALA
J'ARRIVE
TOUTE DE SUITE!
ALLEZ VITE VITE!
WISH I COULD PLAY THIS GREAT NEW FRENCH RECORD I FOUND FOR T.Z.!
AMERICAN SPORTS MONSTER WITH NEW PAC 'O PALS!

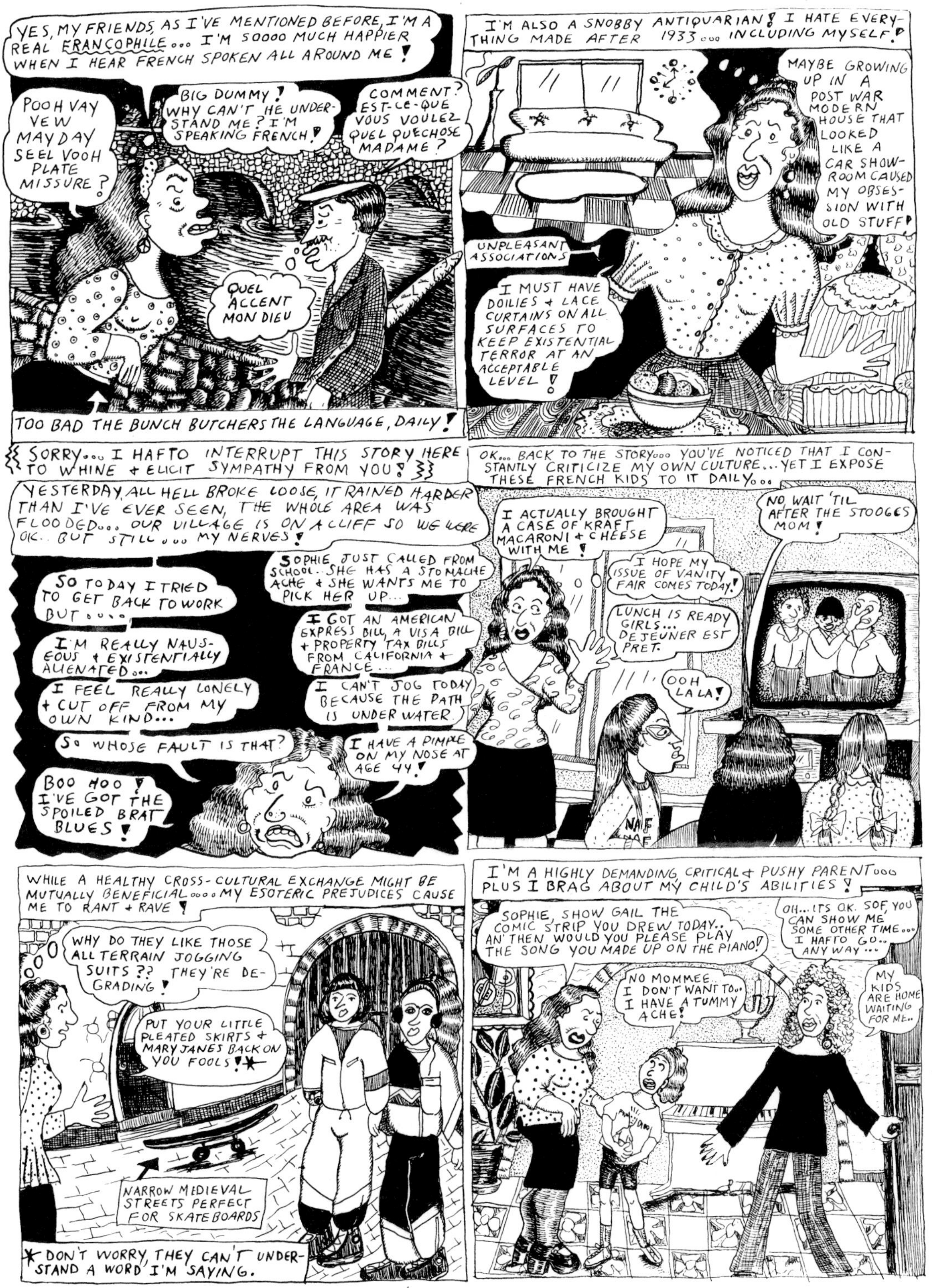
YES, MY FRIENDS, AS I'VE MENTIONED BEFORE, I'M A REAL FRANCOPHILE... I'M SOOOO MUCH HAPPIER WHEN I HEAR FRENCH SPOKEN ALL AROUND ME!
POOH VAY VEW MAY DAY SEEL VOOH PLATE MISSURE?
BIG DUMMY! WHY CAN'T HE UNDERSTAND ME? I'M SPEAKING FRENCH!
COMMENT? EST-CE-QUE VOUS VOULEZ QUEL QUECHOSE MADAME?
QUEL ACCENT MON DIEU
TOO BAD THE BUNCH BUTCHERS THE LANGUAGE, DAILY!
I'M ALSO A SNOBBY ANTIQUARIAN! I HATE EVERYTHING MADE AFTER 1933... INCLUDING MYSELF!
MAYBE GROWING UP IN A POST WAR MODERN HOUSE THAT LOOKED LIKE A CAR SHOWROOM CAUSED MY OBSESSION WITH OLD STUFF!
UNPLEASANT ASSOCIATIONS
I MUST HAVE DOILIES + LACE CURTAINS ON ALL SURFACES TO KEEP EXISTENTIAL TERROR AT AN ACCEPTABLE LEVEL!
SORRY... I HAFTO INTERRUPT THIS STORY HERE TO WHINE + ELICIT SYMPATHY FROM YOU!
YESTERDAY, ALL HELL BROKE LOOSE, IT RAINED HARDER THAN I'VE EVER SEEN, THE WHOLE AREA WAS FLOODED... OUR VILLAGE IS ON A CLIFF SO WE WERE OK.. BUT STILL... MY NERVES!
SO TODAY I TRIED TO GET BACK TO WORK BUT....
I'M REALLY NAUSEOUS + EXISTENTIALLY ALIENATED...
I FEEL REALLY LONELY + CUT OFF FROM MY OWN KIND...
SOPHIE JUST CALLED FROM SCHOOL.. SHE HAS A STOMACHE ACHE + SHE WANTS ME TO PICK HER UP...
I GOT AN AMERICAN EXPRESS BILL, A VISA BILL + PROPERTY TAX BILLS FROM CALIFORNIA + FRANCE...
I CAN'T JOG TODAY BECAUSE THE PATH IS UNDER WATER
SO WHOSE FAULT IS THAT?
I HAVE A PIMPLE ON MY NOSE AT AGE 44!
BOO HOO! I'VE GOT THE SPOILED BRAT BLUES!
OK... BACK TO THE STORY... YOU'VE NOTICED THAT I CONSTANTLY CRITICIZE MY OWN CULTURE... YET I EXPOSE THESE FRENCH KIDS TO IT DAILY...
I ACTUALLY BROUGHT A CASE OF KRAFT MACARONI + CHEESE WITH ME!
I HOPE MY ISSUE OF VANITY FAIR COMES TODAY!
NO WAIT 'TIL AFTER THE STOOGES MOM!
LUNCH IS READY GIRLS... DEJEUNER EST PRET.
OOH LA LA!
NAF NAF
WHILE A HEALTHY CROSS-CULTURAL EXCHANGE MIGHT BE MUTUALLY BENEFICIAL.... MY ESOTERIC PREJUDICES CAUSE ME TO RANT + RAVE!
WHY DO THEY LIKE THOSE ALL TERRAIN JOGGING SUITS?? THEY'RE DEGRADING!
PUT YOUR LITTLE PLEATED SKIRTS + MARY JANES BACK ON YOU FOOLS!*
NARROW MEDIEVAL STREETS PERFECT FOR SKATEBOARDS
* DON'T WORRY, THEY CAN'T UNDERSTAND A WORD I'M SAYING.
I'M A HIGHLY DEMANDING CRITICAL + PUSHY PARENT... PLUS I BRAG ABOUT MY CHILD'S ABILITIES!
SOPHIE, SHOW GAIL THE COMIC STRIP YOU DREW TODAY.. AN' THEN WOULD YOU PLEASE PLAY THE SONG YOU MADE UP ON THE PIANO!
NO MOMMEE.. I DON'T WANT TO... I HAVE A TUMMY ACHE!
OH... ITS OK. SOF, YOU CAN SHOW ME SOME OTHER TIME... I HAFTO GO.. ANY WAY...
MY KIDS ARE HOME WAITING FOR ME..

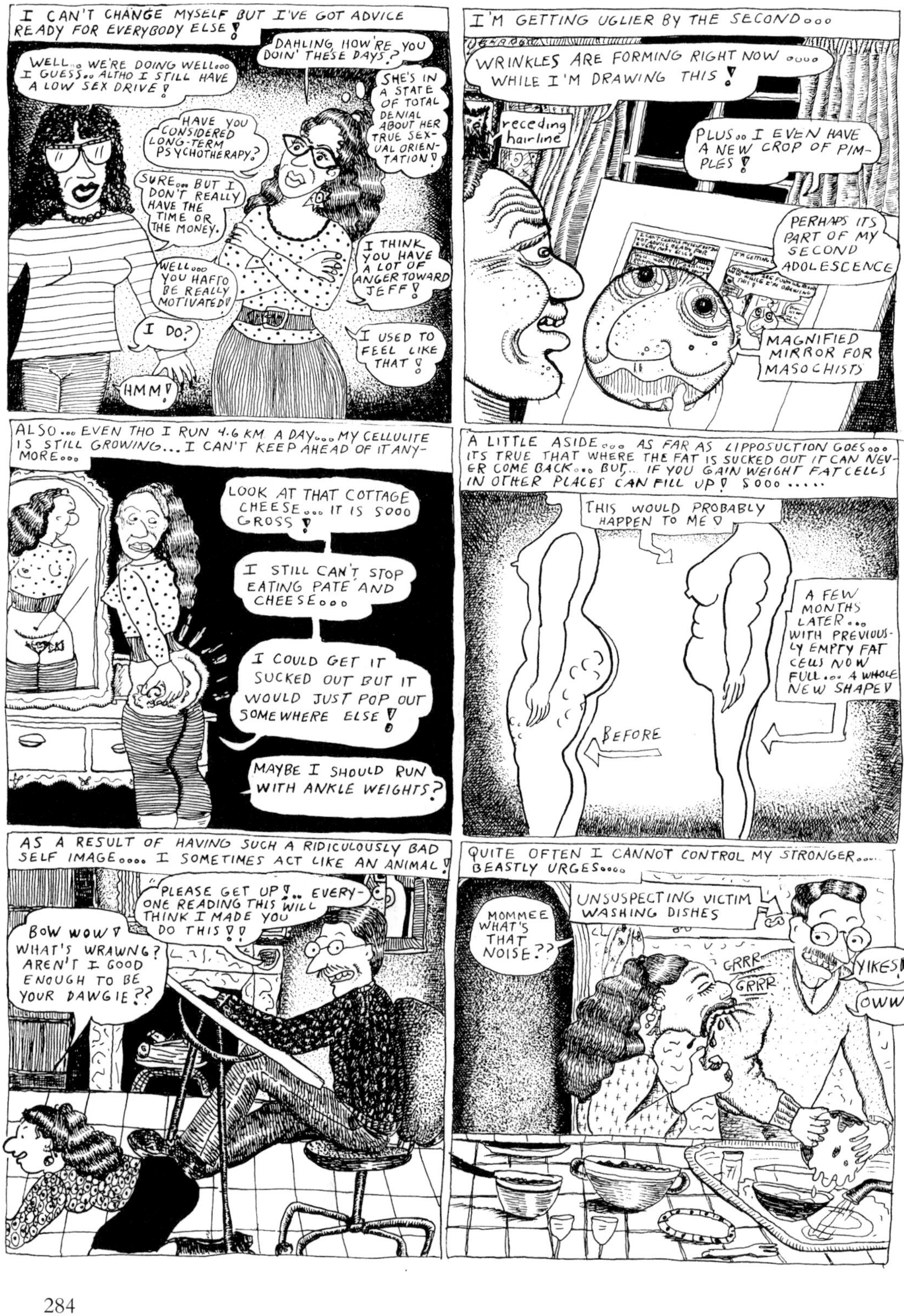
I CAN'T CHANGE MYSELF BUT I'VE GOT ADVICE READY FOR EVERYBODY ELSE!
WELL.. WE'RE DOING WELL... I GUESS.. ALTHO I STILL HAVE A LOW SEX DRIVE!
DAHLING HOW'RE YOU DOIN' THESE DAYS?
SHE'S IN A STATE OF TOTAL DENIAL ABOUT HER TRUE SEXUAL ORIENTATION!
HAVE YOU CONSIDERED LONG-TERM PSYCHOTHERAPY?
SURE... BUT I DON'T REALLY HAVE THE TIME OR THE MONEY.
I THINK YOU HAVE A LOT OF ANGER TOWARD JEFF!
WELL... YOU HAFTO BE REALLY MOTIVATED!
I DO?
I USED TO FEEL LIKE THAT!
HMM!
I'M GETTING UGLIER BY THE SECOND...
WRINKLES ARE FORMING RIGHT NOW.... WHILE I'M DRAWING THIS!
receding hairline
PLUS.. I EVEN HAVE A NEW CROP OF PIMPLES!
PERHAPS ITS PART OF MY SECOND ADOLESCENCE
MAGNIFIED MIRROR FOR MASOCHISTS
ALSO... EVEN THO I RUN 4.6 KM A DAY... MY CELLULITE IS STILL GROWING... I CAN'T KEEP AHEAD OF IT ANYMORE...
LOOK AT THAT COTTAGE CHEESE... IT IS SOOO GROSS!
I STILL CAN'T STOP EATING PATE AND CHEESE...
I COULD GET IT SUCKED OUT BUT IT WOULD JUST POP OUT SOMEWHERE ELSE!
MAYBE I SHOULD RUN WITH ANKLE WEIGHTS?
A LITTLE ASIDE... AS FAR AS LIPPOSUCTION GOES... ITS TRUE THAT WHERE THE FAT IS SUCKED OUT IT CAN NEVER COME BACK... BUT... IF YOU GAIN WEIGHT FAT CELLS IN OTHER PLACES CAN FILL UP! SOOO.....
THIS WOULD PROBABLY HAPPEN TO ME!
A FEW MONTHS LATER... WITH PREVIOUSLY EMPTY FAT CELLS NOW FULL... A WHOLE NEW SHAPE!
BEFORE
AS A RESULT OF HAVING SUCH A RIDICULOUSLY BAD SELF IMAGE.... I SOMETIMES ACT LIKE AN ANIMAL!
"PLEASE GET UP!.. EVERYONE READING THIS WILL THINK I MADE YOU DO THIS!!
BOW WOW! WHAT'S WRAWNG? AREN'T I GOOD ENOUGH TO BE YOUR DAWGIE??
QUITE OFTEN I CANNOT CONTROL MY STRONGER... BEASTLY URGES....
MOMMEE WHAT'S THAT NOISE??
UNSUSPECTING VICTIM WASHING DISHES
GRRR
GRRR
YIKES!
OWW!

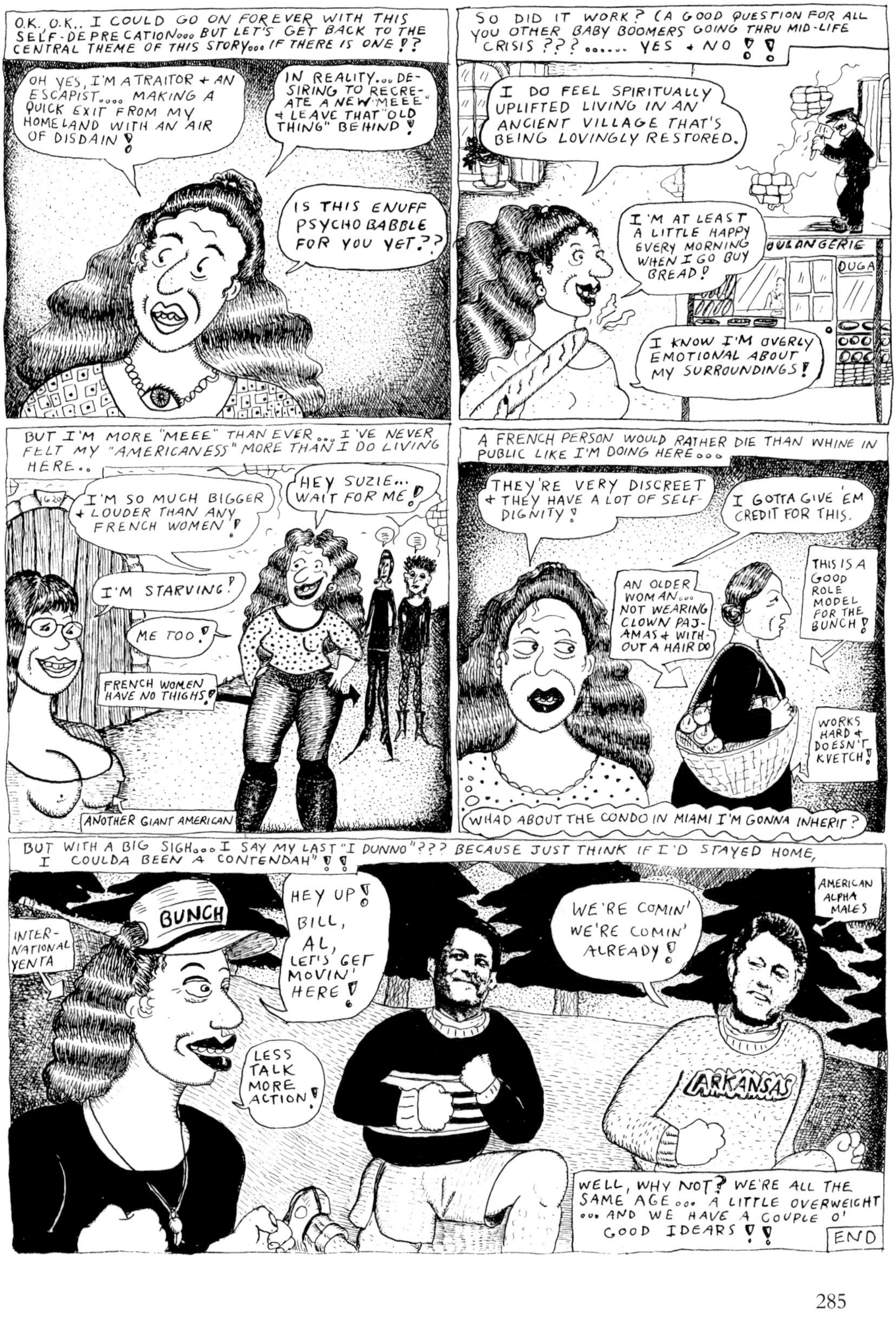
O.K. O.K.. I COULD GO ON FOREVER WITH THIS SELF-DEPRECATION... BUT LET'S GET BACK TO THE CENTRAL THEME OF THIS STORY... IF THERE IS ONE!?
OH YES, I'M A TRAITOR + AN ESCAPIST.... MAKING A QUICK EXIT FROM MY HOMELAND WITH AN AIR OF DISDAIN!
IN REALITY... DESIRING TO RECREATE A NEW "MEEE" + LEAVE THAT "OLD THING" BEHIND!
IS THIS ENUFF PSYCHO BABBLE FOR YOU YET??
SO DID IT WORK? (A GOOD QUESTION FOR ALL YOU OTHER BABY BOOMERS GOING THRU MID-LIFE CRISIS??? ...... YES + NO!!
I DO FEEL SPIRITUALLY UPLIFTED LIVING IN AN ANCIENT VILLAGE THAT'S BEING LOVINGLY RESTORED.
I'M AT LEAST A LITTLE HAPPY EVERY MORNING WHEN I GO BUY BREAD!
BOULANGERIE
DUGA
I KNOW I'M OVERLY EMOTIONAL ABOUT MY SURROUNDINGS!
BUT I'M MORE "MEEE" THAN EVER... I'VE NEVER FELT MY "AMERICANESS" MORE THAN I DO LIVING HERE..
1620
I'M SO MUCH BIGGER + LOUDER THAN ANY FRENCH WOMEN!
HEY SUZIE... WAIT FOR ME!
I'M STARVING!
ME TOO!
FRENCH WOMEN HAVE NO THIGHS!
ANOTHER GIANT AMERICAN
A FRENCH PERSON WOULD RATHER DIE THAN WHINE IN PUBLIC LIKE I'M DOING HERE...
THEY'RE VERY DISCREET + THEY HAVE A LOT OF SELF-DIGNITY!
I GOTTA GIVE 'EM CREDIT FOR THIS.
AN OLDER WOMAN... NOT WEARING CLOWN PAJAMAS + WITHOUT A HAIR DO
THIS IS A GOOD ROLE MODEL FOR THE BUNCH!
WORKS HARD + DOESN'T KVETCH!
WHAD ABOUT THE CONDO IN MIAMI I'M GONNA INHERIT?
BUT WITH A BIG SIGH... I SAY MY LAST "I DUNNO"??? BECAUSE JUST THINK IF I'D STAYED HOME, I COULDA BEEN A CONTENDAH"!!
INTER-NATIONAL YENTA
BUNCH
HEY UP! BILL, AL, LET'S GET MOVIN' HERE!
WE'RE COMIN' WE'RE COMIN' ALREADY!
AMERICAN ALPHA MALES
LESS TALK MORE ACTION!
ARKANSAS
WELL, WHY NOT? WE'RE ALL THE SAME AGE... A LITTLE OVERWEIGHT ... AND WE HAVE A COUPLE O' GOOD IDEARS!!
END

Our friends and neighbors

For the first time since we moved here, Robert won't be going back to the U.S. this year because he's too immersed in his *Genesis* book, a colossal project which will take him at least two years to finish. I have also changed a lot in the last few years, and since I quit drinking and socialize less, I derive more satisfaction from my creative activities such as painting, drawing and writing.

But during our early days in France, Robert and I drank a lot of wine (especially me) and did a lot of entertaining. Our dear friend, the artist Pete Poplaski, showed up here one year after the Comics Festival in Angoulême.

I found him a house where he could stay for free, and he's since moved here permanently. Later, my brother Alex arrived in pretty bad shape. We gave him our downstairs studio apartment to live in, and he's still here and doing really well. Tony Baldwin, a great jazz piano player and 78 rpm record collector, has bought the house across the street. There are numerous other characters around, enough to make some very wild parties. Our friend Raoul Phillip makes a great local wine, Domaine de Baubiac, so there's no reason to run out of wine, and this great old stone house of ours has seen many memorable celebrations.

A few years back, there was a plan to create a giant toxic waste dump near our village. We mobilized local people and outsiders like ourselves, and managed to squelch this scheme. One of the positive outcomes of this near-disaster was that we met Zaro Weil and Gareth Jenkins, who have since become very dear friends. They are the publishers of this book, and of Robert's books *The R. Crumb Handbook* and *The Sweeter Side of R. Crumb*. It's really amazing that Zaro and I met here in the South of France, because we both come from the New York area, are the same age, and have very similar backgrounds. It was Zaro who encouraged me to write this book, and she cried when she read the first chapters. As I get older I find that life becomes a thicker and richer soup: we just keep adding more spices …

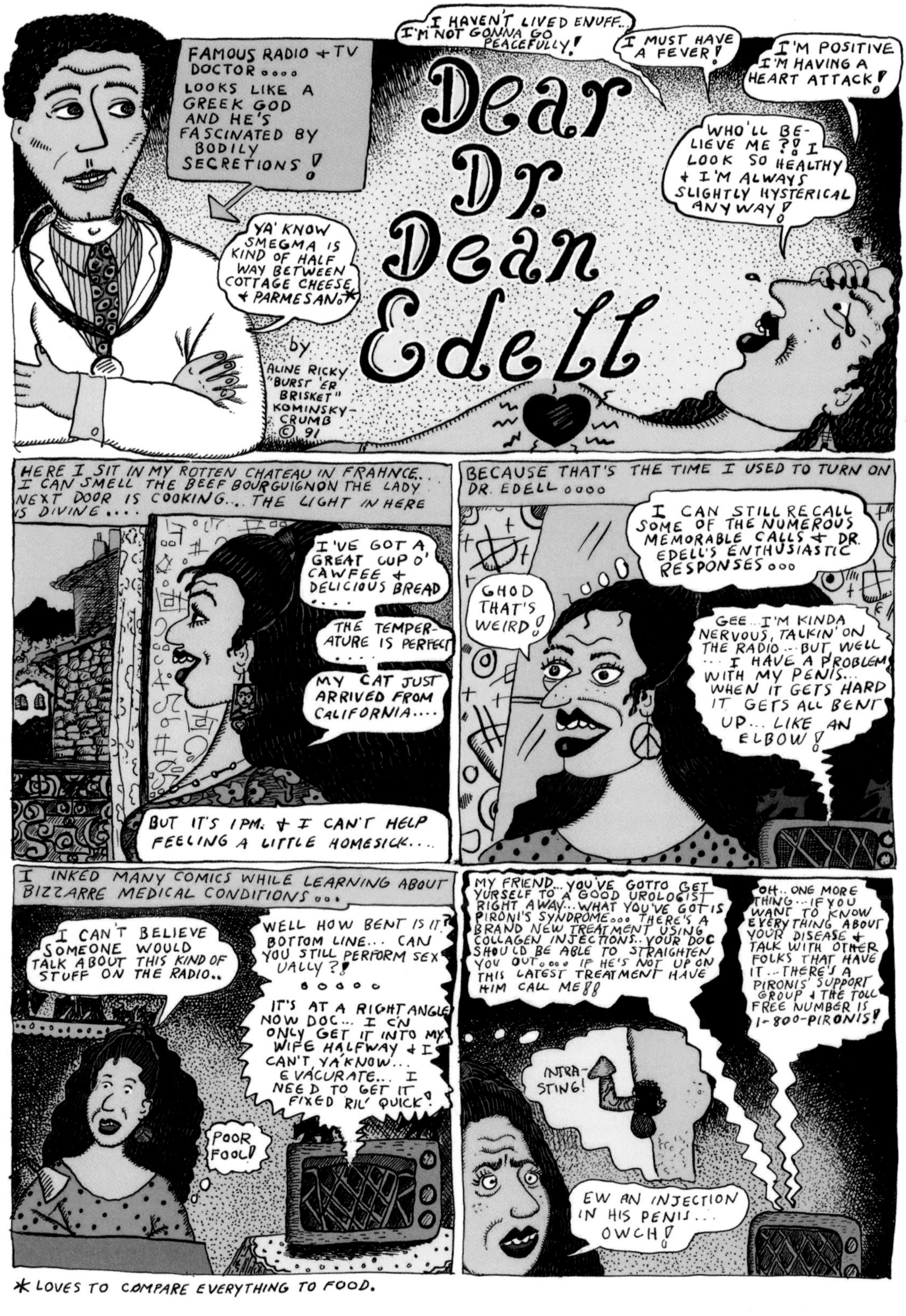
I HAVEN'T LIVED ENUFF.. I'M NOT GONNA GO PEACEFULLY!
I MUST HAVE A FEVER!
I'M POSITIVE I'M HAVING A HEART ATTACK!
FAMOUS RADIO + TV DOCTOR.... LOOKS LIKE A GREEK GOD AND HE'S FASCINATED BY BODILY SECRETIONS!
Dear Dr. Dean Edell
WHO'LL BELIEVE ME?! I LOOK SO HEALTHY + I'M ALWAYS SLIGHTLY HYSTERICAL ANYWAY!
YA' KNOW SMEGMA IS KIND OF HALF WAY BETWEEN COTTAGE CHEESE + PARMESAN.*
by ALINE RICKY "BURST 'ER BRISKET" KOMINSKY-CRUMB © 91
HERE I SIT IN MY ROTTEN CHATEAU IN FRAHNCE.. I CAN SMELL THE BEEF BOURGUIGNON THE LADY NEXT DOOR IS COOKING... THE LIGHT IN HERE IS DIVINE....
I'VE GOT A GREAT CUP O' CAWFEE + DELICIOUS BREAD...
THE TEMPERATURE IS PERFECT...
MY CAT JUST ARRIVED FROM CALIFORNIA....
BUT IT'S 1PM. + I CAN'T HELP FEELING A LITTLE HOMESICK...
BECAUSE THAT'S THE TIME I USED TO TURN ON DR. EDELL....
I CAN STILL RECALL SOME OF THE NUMEROUS MEMORABLE CALLS + DR. EDELL'S ENTHUSIASTIC RESPONSES...
GHOD THAT'S WEIRD!
GEE.. I'M KINDA NERVOUS, TALKIN' ON THE RADIO -- BUT, WELL ... I HAVE A PROBLEM WITH MY PENIS... WHEN IT GETS HARD IT GETS ALL BENT UP... LIKE AN ELBOW!
I INKED MANY COMICS WHILE LEARNING ABOUT BIZZARRE MEDICAL CONDITIONS...
I CAN'T BELIEVE SOMEONE WOULD TALK ABOUT THIS KIND OF STUFF ON THE RADIO..
WELL HOW BENT IS IT? BOTTOM LINE... CAN YOU STILL PERFORM SEXUALLY?!
IT'S AT A RIGHT ANGLE NOW DOC... I C'N ONLY GET IT INTO MY WIFE HALFWAY + I CAN'T, YA'KNOW... EVACURATE... I NEED TO GET IT FIXED RIL' QUICK!
POOR FOOL!
MY FRIEND... YOU'VE GOTTO GET YERSELF TO A GOOD UROLOGIST RIGHT AWAY... WHAT YOU'VE GOT IS PIRONI'S SYNDROME... THERE'S A BRAND NEW TREATMENT USING COLLAGEN INJECTIONS.. YOUR DOC SHOULD BE ABLE TO STRAIGHTEN YOU OUT.... IF HE'S NOT UP ON THIS LATEST TREATMENT HAVE HIM CALL ME!!
OH.. ONE MORE THING -- IF YOU WANT TO KNOW EVERYTHING ABOUT YOUR DISEASE + TALK WITH OTHER FOLKS THAT HAVE IT... THERE'S A PIRONIS' SUPPORT GROUP + THE TOLL FREE NUMBER IS 1-800-PIRONIS!
INTRA-STING!
EW AN INJECTION IN HIS PENIS... OWCH!
* LOVES TO COMPARE EVERYTHING TO FOOD.

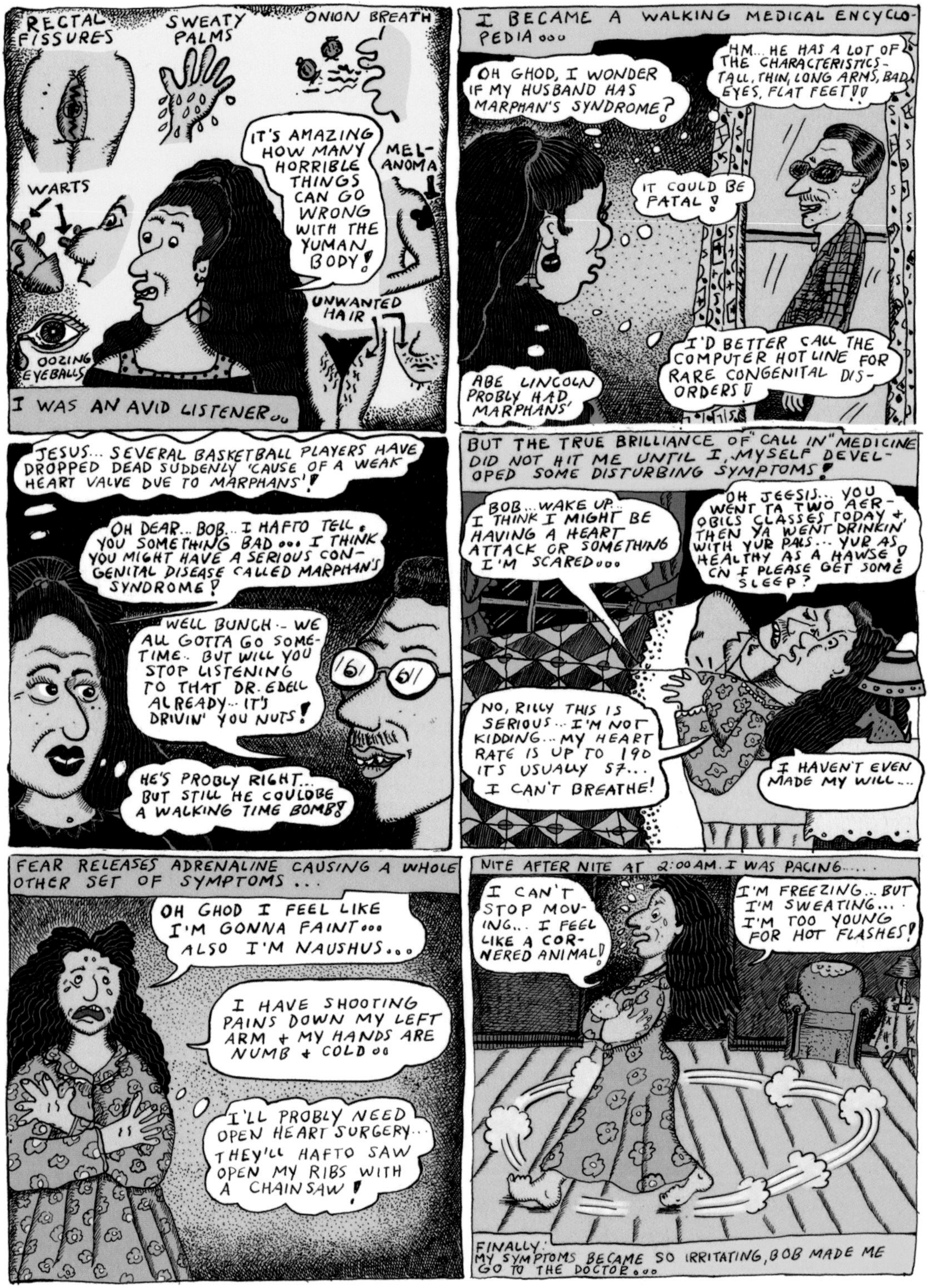
RECTAL FISSURES
SWEATY PALMS
ONION BREATH
WARTS
MEL-ANOMA
IT'S AMAZING HOW MANY HORRIBLE THINGS CAN GO WRONG WITH THE YUMAN BODY!
UNWANTED HAIR
OOZING EYEBALLS
I WAS AN AVID LISTENER...
I BECAME A WALKING MEDICAL ENCYCLOPEDIA...
OH GHOD, I WONDER IF MY HUSBAND HAS MARPHAN'S SYNDROME?
HM... HE HAS A LOT OF THE CHARACTERISTICS - TALL, THIN, LONG ARMS, BAD EYES, FLAT FEET!!
IT COULD BE FATAL!
I'D BETTER CALL THE COMPUTER HOT LINE FOR RARE CONGENITAL DISORDERS!
ABE LINCOLN PROBLY HAD MARPHANS'
JESUS... SEVERAL BASKETBALL PLAYERS HAVE DROPPED DEAD SUDDENLY 'CAUSE OF A WEAK HEART VALVE DUE TO MARPHANS'!
OH DEAR.. BOB.. I HAFTO TELL YOU SOMETHING BAD... I THINK YOU MIGHT HAVE A SERIOUS CONGENITAL DISEASE CALLED MARPHAN'S SYNDROME!
WELL BUNCH.. WE ALL GOTTA GO SOMETIME.. BUT WILL YOU STOP LISTENING TO THAT DR. EDELL ALREADY.. IT'S DRIVIN' YOU NUTS!
HE'S PROBLY RIGHT... BUT STILL HE COULDBE A WALKING TIME BOMB!
BUT THE TRUE BRILLIANCE OF "CALL IN" MEDICINE DID NOT HIT ME UNTIL I, MYSELF DEVELOPED SOME DISTURBING SYMPTOMS!
BOB... WAKE UP.. I THINK I MIGHT BE HAVING A HEART ATTACK OR SOMETHING I'M SCARED...
OH JEESIS.. YOU WENT TA TWO AEROBICS CLASSES TODAY + THEN YA WENT DRINKIN' WITH YUR PALS... YUR AS HEALTHY AS A HAWSE! CN I PLEASE GET SOME SLEEP?
NO, RILLY THIS IS SERIOUS... I'M NOT KIDDING... MY HEART RATE IS UP TO 190 IT'S USUALLY 57... I CAN'T BREATHE!
I HAVEN'T EVEN MADE MY WILL....
FEAR RELEASES ADRENALINE CAUSING A WHOLE OTHER SET OF SYMPTOMS...
OH GHOD I FEEL LIKE I'M GONNA FAINT... ALSO I'M NAUSHUS...
I HAVE SHOOTING PAINS DOWN MY LEFT ARM + MY HANDS ARE NUMB + COLD..
I'LL PROBLY NEED OPEN HEART SURGERY.. THEY'LL HAFTO SAW OPEN MY RIBS WITH A CHAINSAW!
NITE AFTER NITE AT 2:00 AM. I WAS PACING.....
I CAN'T STOP MOVING.. I FEEL LIKE A CORNERED ANIMAL!
I'M FREEZING... BUT I'M SWEATING... I'M TOO YOUNG FOR HOT FLASHES!
FINALLY: MY SYMPTOMS BECAME SO IRRITATING, BOB MADE ME GO TO THE DOCTOR...

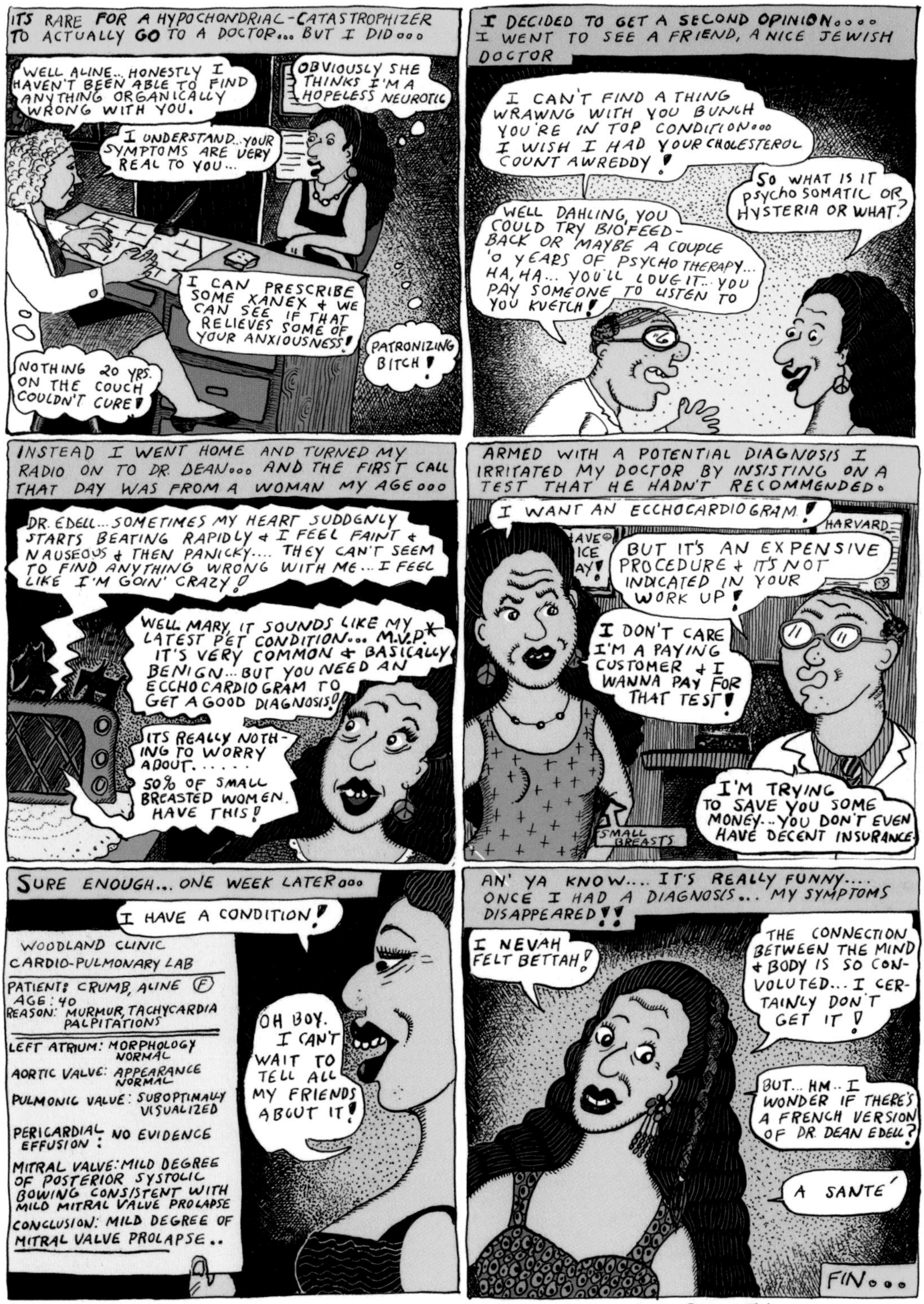
ITS RARE FOR A HYPOCHONDRIAC-CATASTROPHIZER TO ACTUALLY GO TO A DOCTOR... BUT I DID...
WELL ALINE... HONESTLY I HAVEN'T BEEN ABLE TO FIND ANYTHING ORGANICALLY WRONG WITH YOU.
OBVIOUSLY SHE THINKS I'M A HOPELESS NEUROTIC
I UNDERSTAND... YOUR SYMPTOMS ARE VERY REAL TO YOU...
I CAN PRESCRIBE SOME XANEX & WE CAN SEE IF THAT RELIEVES SOME OF YOUR ANXIOUSNESS!
PATRONIZING BITCH!
NOTHING 20 YRS. ON THE COUCH COULDN'T CURE!
I DECIDED TO GET A SECOND OPINION.... I WENT TO SEE A FRIEND, A NICE JEWISH DOCTOR
I CAN'T FIND A THING WRAWNG WITH YOU BUNCH YOU'RE IN TOP CONDITION... I WISH I HAD YOUR CHOLESTEROL COUNT AWREDDY!
SO WHAT IS IT PSYCHO SOMATIC OR HYSTERIA OR WHAT?
WELL DAHLING, YOU COULD TRY BIOFEED-BACK OR MAYBE A COUPLE 'O YEARS OF PSYCHO THERAPY... HA, HA... YOU'LL LOVE IT... YOU PAY SOMEONE TO LISTEN TO YOU KVETCH!
INSTEAD I WENT HOME AND TURNED MY RADIO ON TO DR. DEAN... AND THE FIRST CALL THAT DAY WAS FROM A WOMAN MY AGE...
DR. EDELL... SOMETIMES MY HEART SUDDENLY STARTS BEATING RAPIDLY & I FEEL FAINT & NAUSEOUS & THEN PANICKY.... THEY CAN'T SEEM TO FIND ANYTHING WRONG WITH ME... I FEEL LIKE I'M GOIN' CRAZY!
WELL MARY, IT SOUNDS LIKE MY LATEST PET CONDITION... M.V.P.* IT'S VERY COMMON & BASICALLY BENIGN... BUT YOU NEED AN ECCHOCARDIOGRAM TO GET A GOOD DIAGNOSIS!
ITS REALLY NOTHING TO WORRY ABOUT...... 50% OF SMALL BREASTED WOMEN HAVE THIS!
ARMED WITH A POTENTIAL DIAGNOSIS I IRRITATED MY DOCTOR BY INSISTING ON A TEST THAT HE HADN'T RECOMMENDED.
I WANT AN ECCHOCARDIOGRAM!
HARVARD
BUT IT'S AN EXPENSIVE PROCEDURE & IT'S NOT INDICATED IN YOUR WORK UP!
I DON'T CARE I'M A PAYING CUSTOMER & I WANNA PAY FOR THAT TEST!
I'M TRYING TO SAVE YOU SOME MONEY... YOU DON'T EVEN HAVE DECENT INSURANCE
SMALL BREASTS
SURE ENOUGH... ONE WEEK LATER...
I HAVE A CONDITION!
WOODLAND CLINIC
CARDIO-PULMONARY LAB
PATIENT: CRUMB, ALINE (F)
AGE: 40
REASON: MURMUR, TACHYCARDIA PALPITATIONS
LEFT ATRIUM: MORPHOLOGY NORMAL
AORTIC VALVE: APPEARANCE NORMAL
PULMONIC VALVE: SUBOPTIMALLY VISUALIZED
PERICARDIAL EFFUSION: NO EVIDENCE
MITRAL VALVE: MILD DEGREE OF POSTERIOR SYSTOLIC BOWING CONSISTENT WITH MILD MITRAL VALVE PROLAPSE
CONCLUSION: MILD DEGREE OF MITRAL VALVE PROLAPSE..
OH BOY. I CAN'T WAIT TO TELL ALL MY FRIENDS ABOUT IT!
AN' YA KNOW.... IT'S REALLY FUNNY.... ONCE I HAD A DIAGNOSIS... MY SYMPTOMS DISAPPEARED!!
I NEVAH FELT BETTAH!
THE CONNECTION BETWEEN THE MIND & BODY IS SO CON-VOLUTED... I CER-TAINLY DON'T GET IT!
BUT... HM.. I WONDER IF THERE'S A FRENCH VERSION OF DR. DEAN EDELL?
A SANTÉ
FIN...

*MVP - MITRAL VALVE PROLAPSE - A BENIGN CONGENITAL HEART ABNORMALITY.

The traveling "ahtist!"

Living in Europe has made it much easier to travel to other exotic places. Thanks to my friend Ulla Rowohlt, I've spent time in a remote village in Greece, journeyed through southern India, explored the volcanic island of Ischia, and made friends in Vienna. I've traveled all over Western Europe and know people in almost every capital. I've visited Morocco, Corsica and Jerusalem. Thanks to my dahling Christian, I've also come to know and love Marseille, and we often go to Barcelona, just four hours away by car.

These travels have inspired my painting and shrine-making over the last ten years—the vivid colors of India, the dripping Virgins of Italy, the *iconostases* that mark death and miracles in Greece, the turquoise and ochre hues of Morocco … And like most clichés, there is some truth about the magical light in southern France.

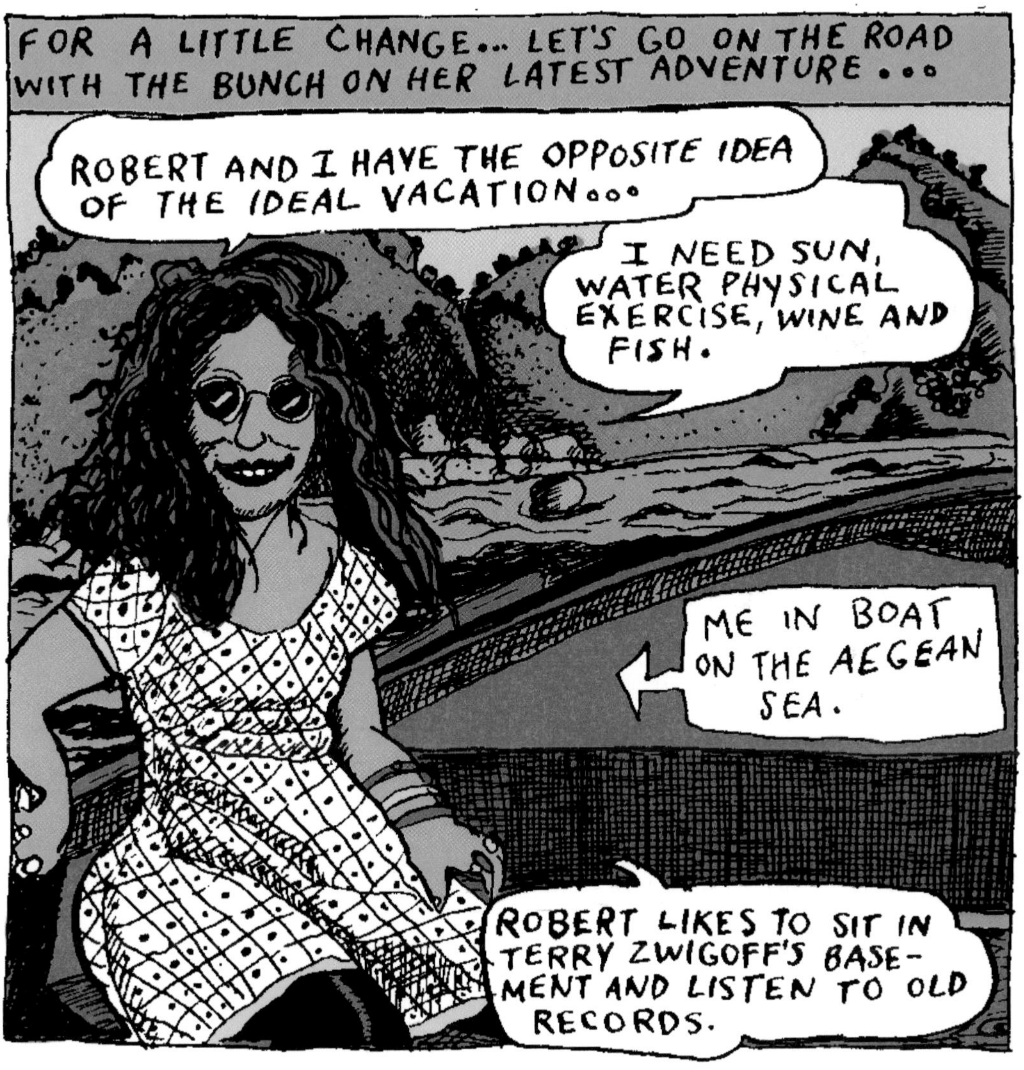
FOR A LITTLE CHANGE... LET'S GO ON THE ROAD WITH THE BUNCH ON HER LATEST ADVENTURE...
ROBERT AND I HAVE THE OPPOSITE IDEA OF THE IDEAL VACATION...
I NEED SUN, WATER PHYSICAL EXERCISE, WINE AND FISH.
ME IN BOAT ON THE AEGEAN SEA.
ROBERT LIKES TO SIT IN TERRY ZWIGOFF'S BASE-MENT AND LISTEN TO OLD RECORDS.

Above: **Color panel by me from *Self Loathing* comics No. 2**
Left: **Aline Kominsky Crumb, drawing, 2005**
Ulla Rowohlt and me in her shop in Hamburg
Next page: **Dominique Sapel (my painting partner) and me in Kerala, India 2003**

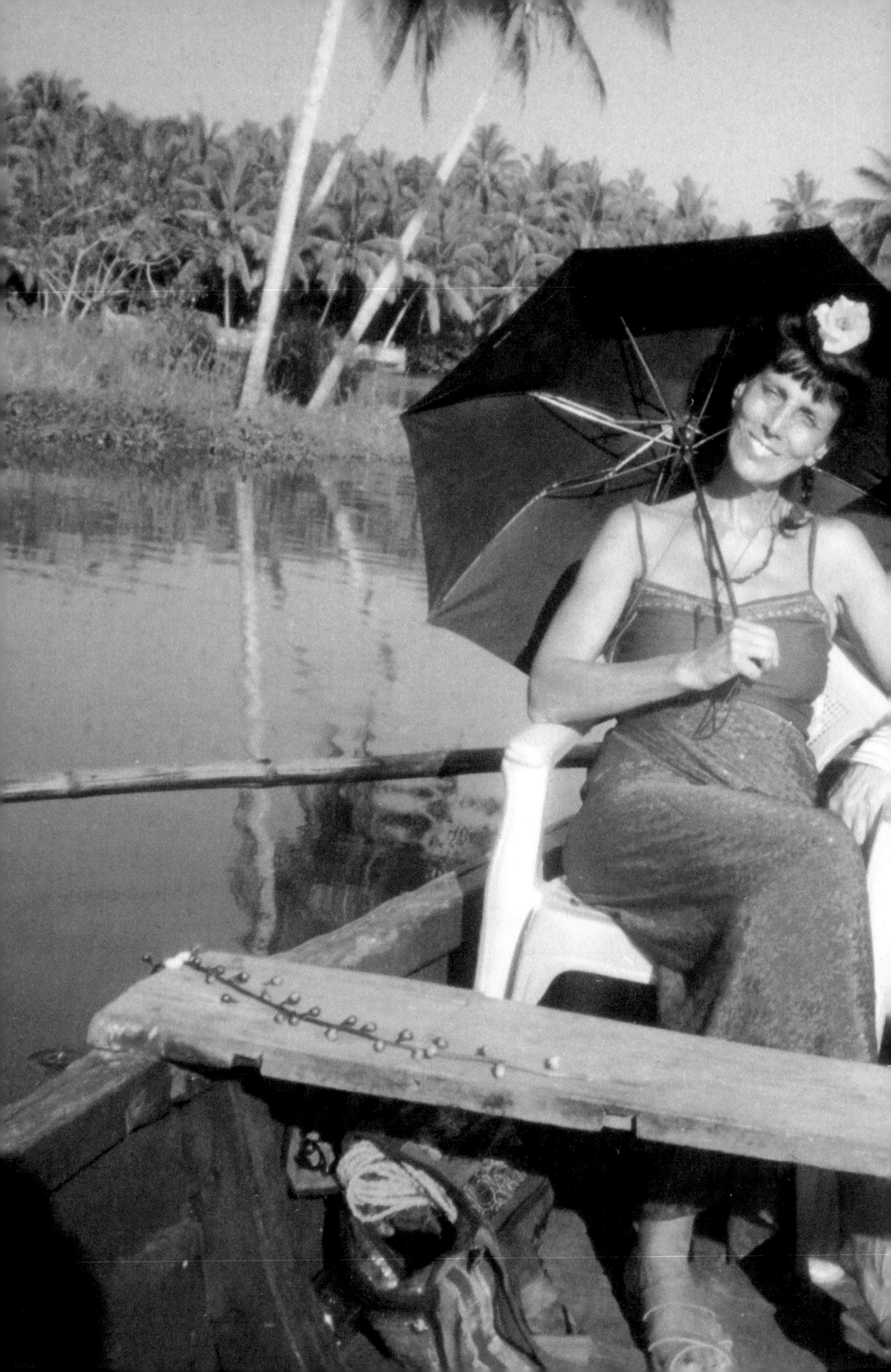

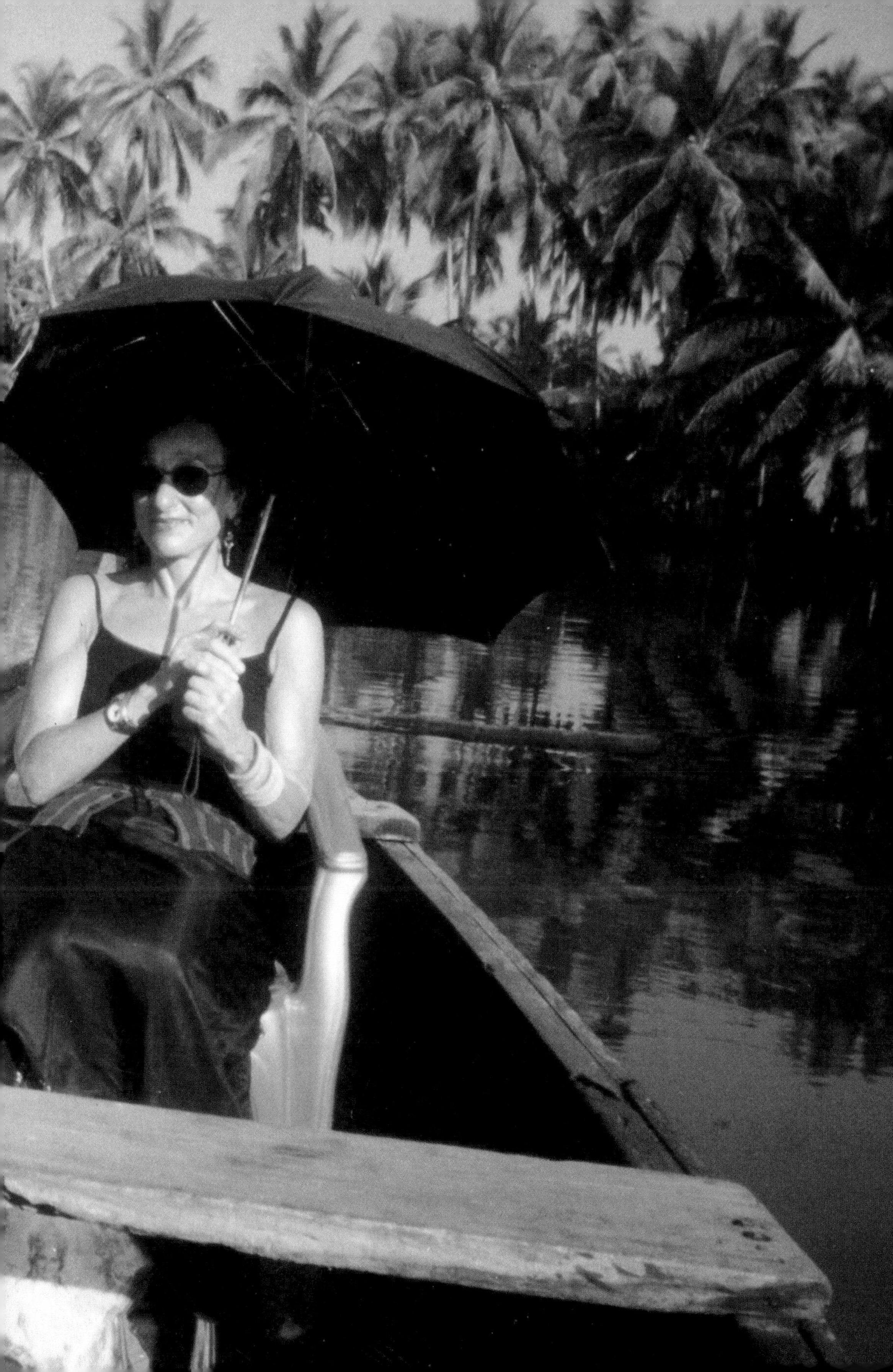

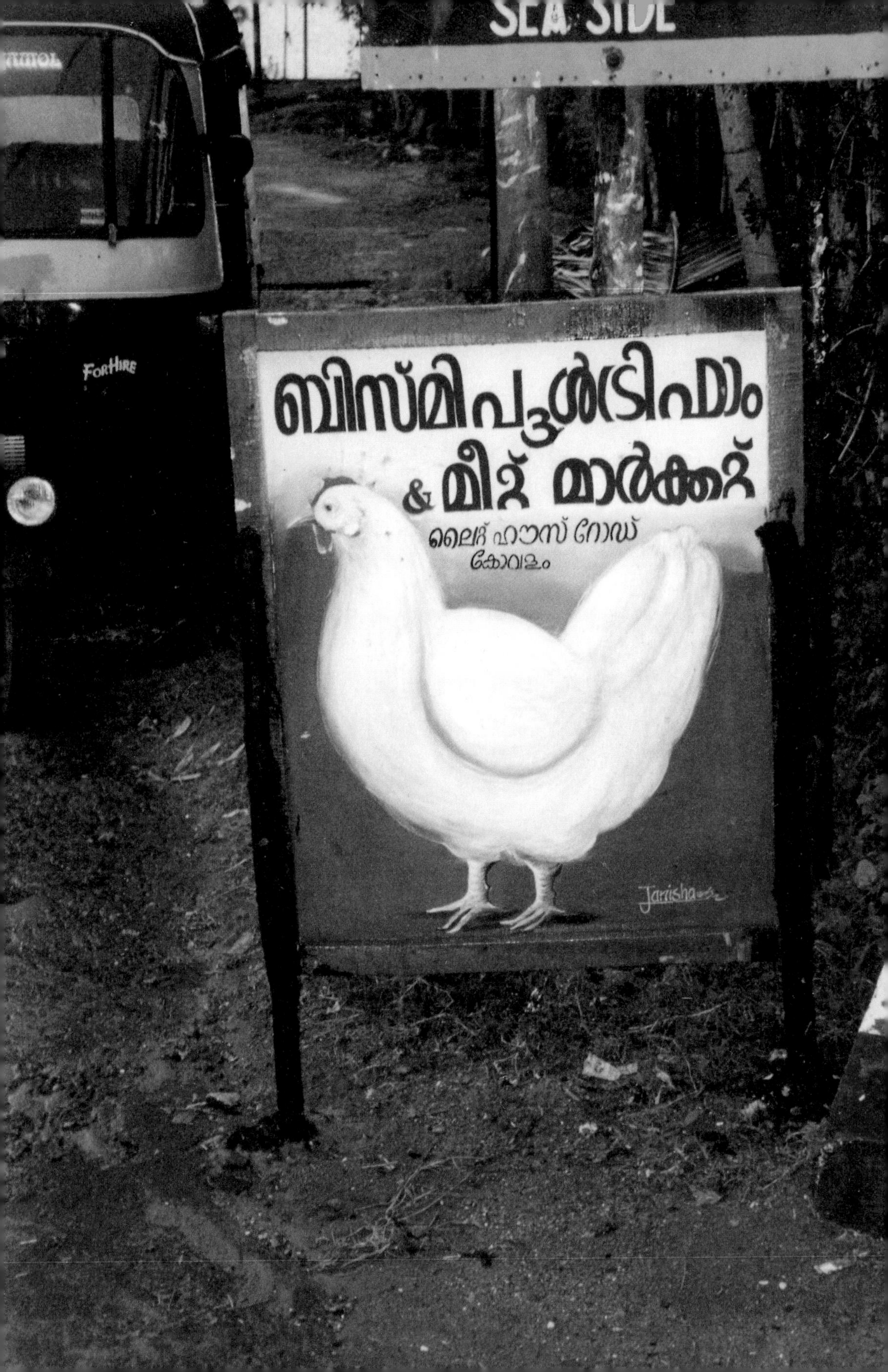
SEA SIDE
FORHIRE
ബിസ്മി പൗൾട്രി ഫാം
& മീറ്റ് മാർക്കറ്റ്
ലൈറ്റ് ഹൗസ് റോഡ്
കോവളം
Jarisha

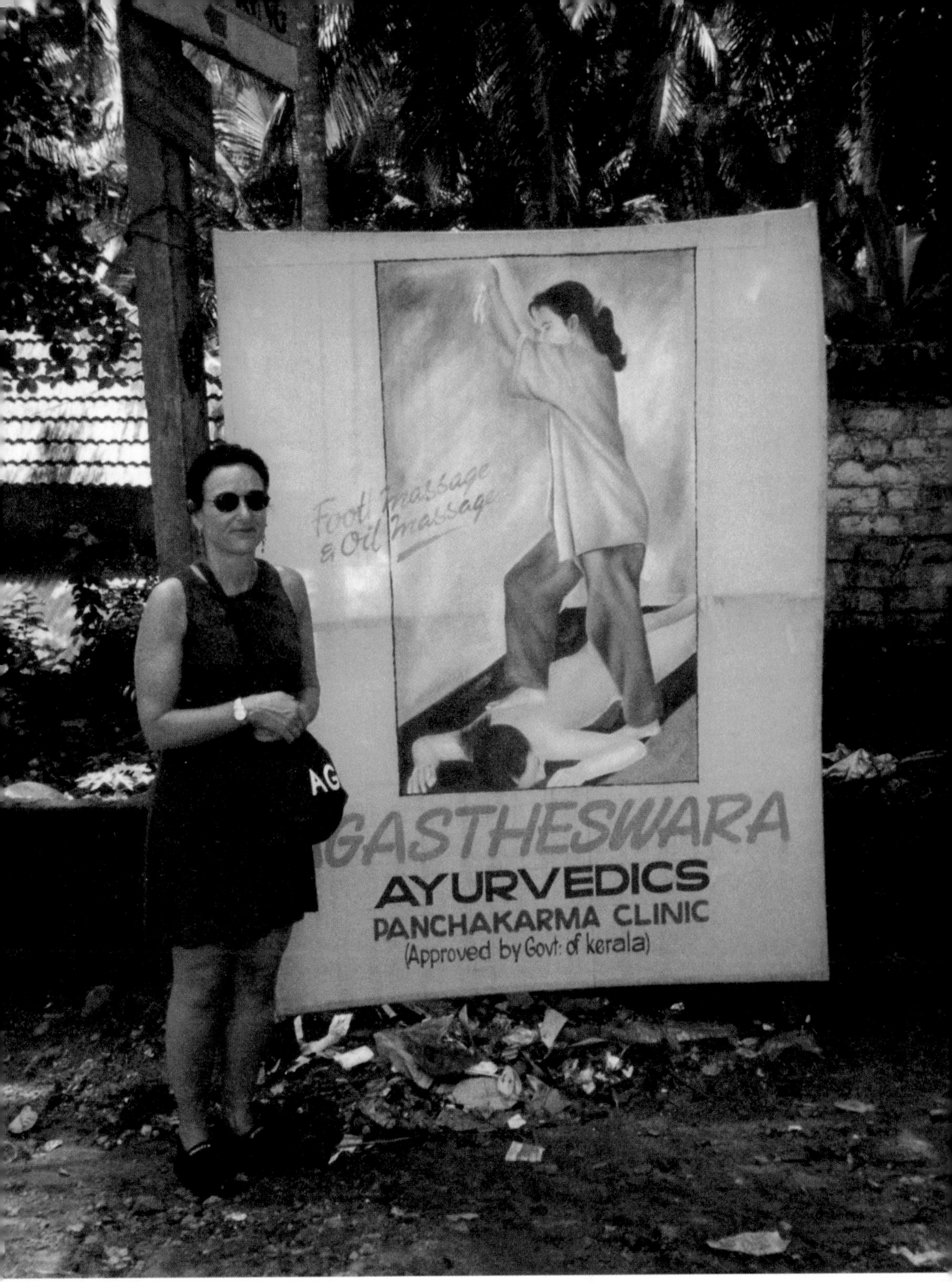
Foot massage
& Oil massage
AGASTHESWARA
AYURVEDICS
PANCHAKARMA CLINIC
(Approved by Govt: of kerala)

Above and left: **Hand-painted signs in India, 2000**

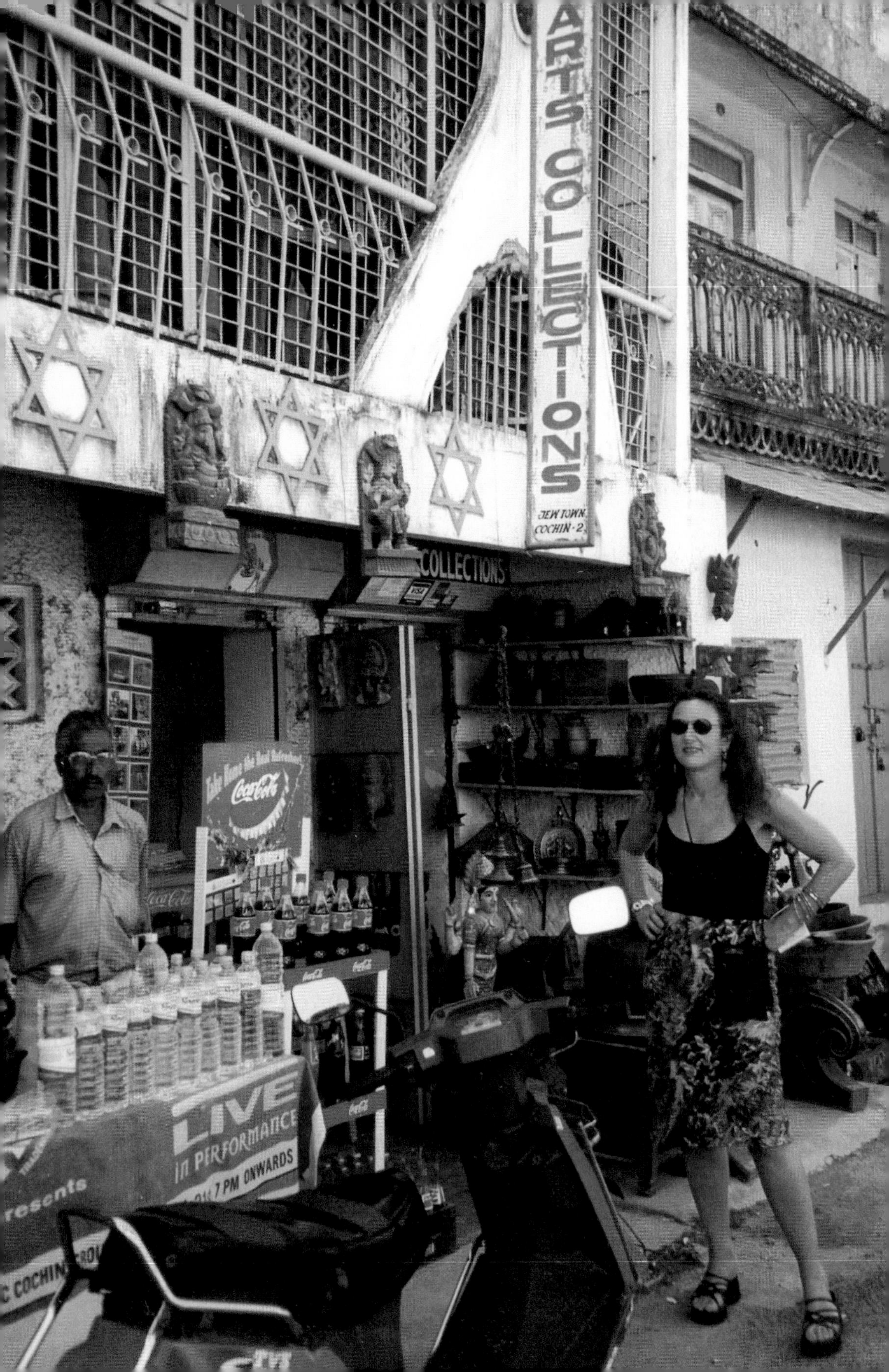

ARTS COLLECTIONS
JEW TOWN
COCHIN - 2
COLLECTIONS
Take Home the Real Refresher!
Coca-Cola
LIVE
in PERFORMANCE
7 PM ONWARDS
presents
COCHIN

Left: **Me in Cochin, India, 2000**
Below: **Right at home in "Jew Town" Cochin**
Next pages: **Me, inside the Synagogue in Cochin, 2000**

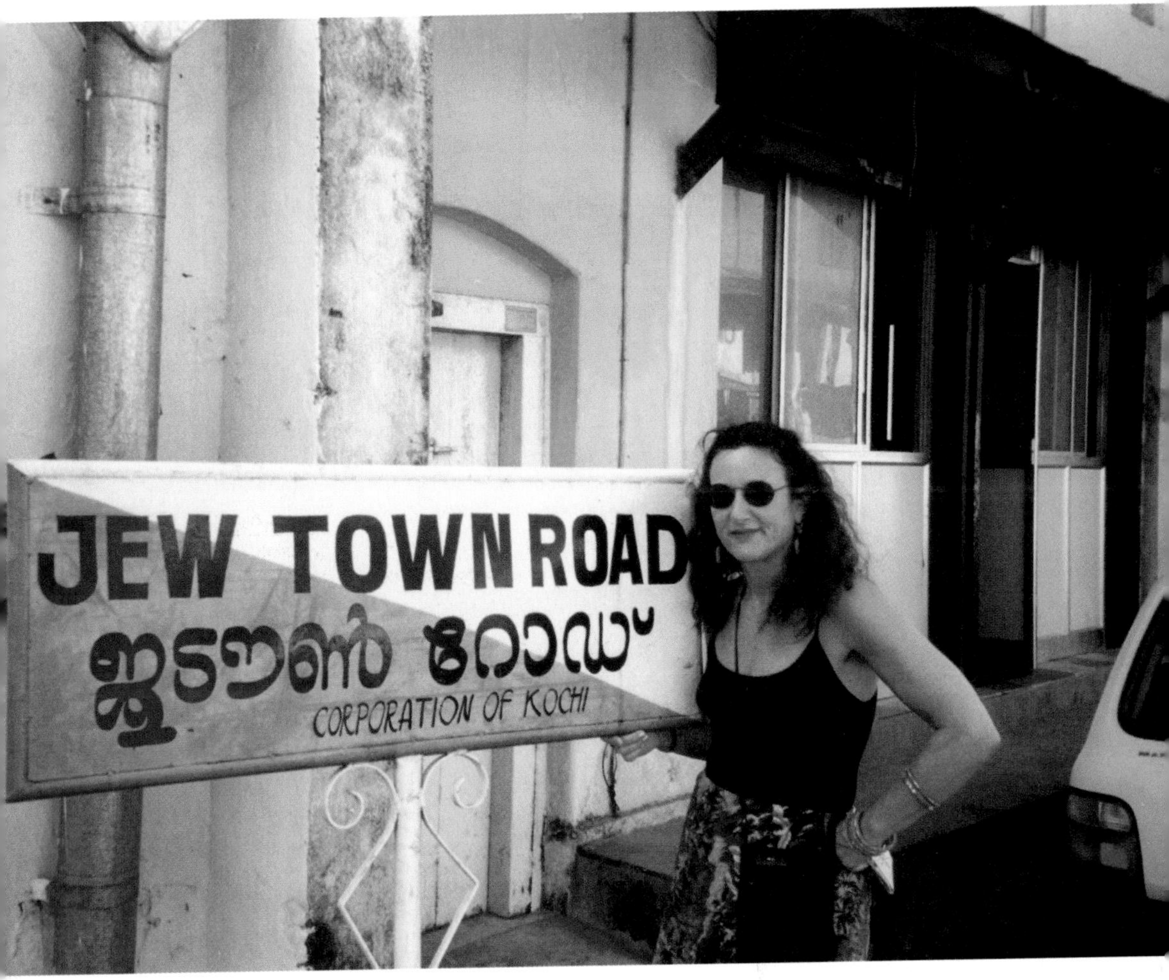
JEW TOWN ROAD
CORPORATION OF KOCHI

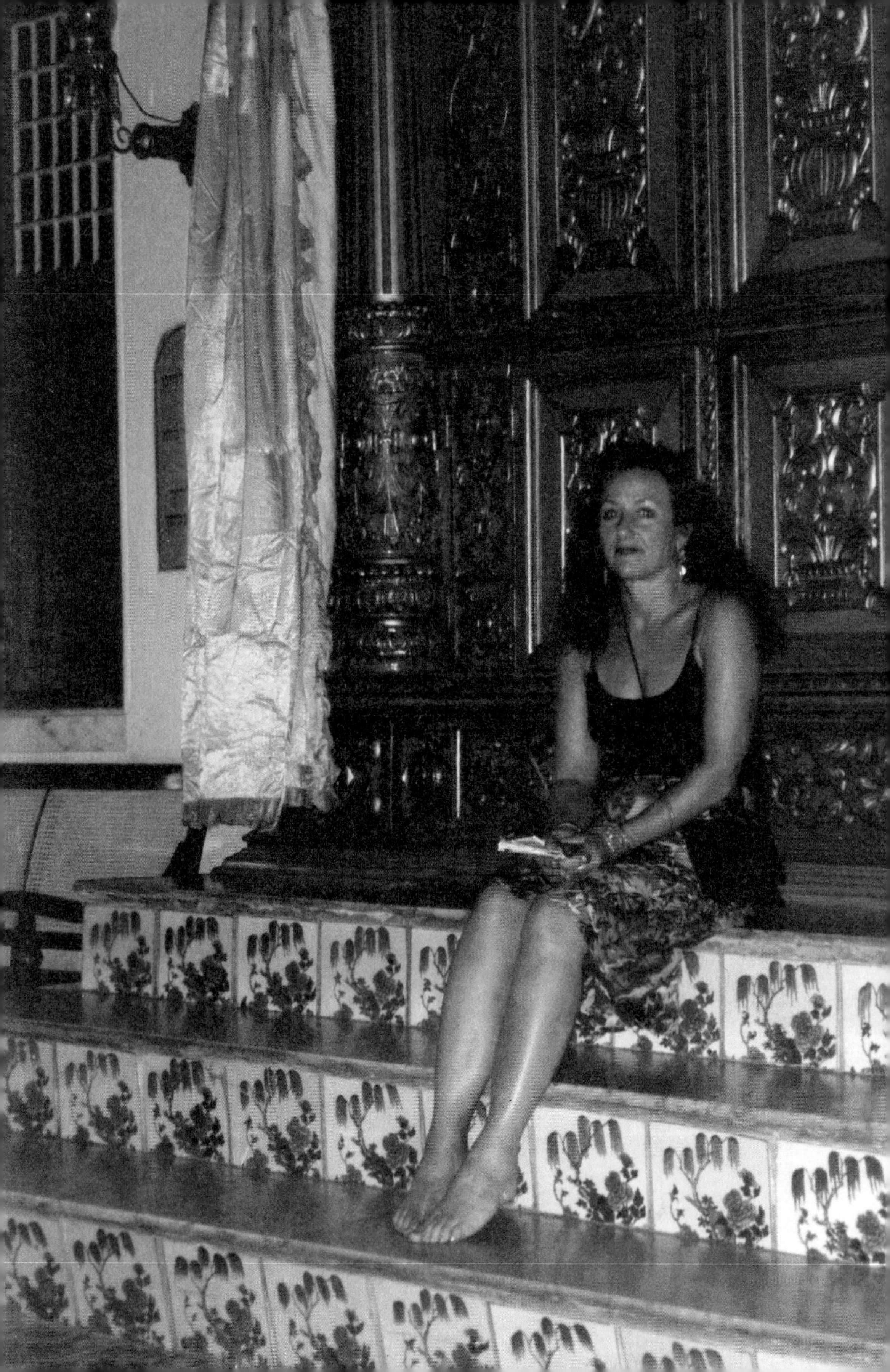

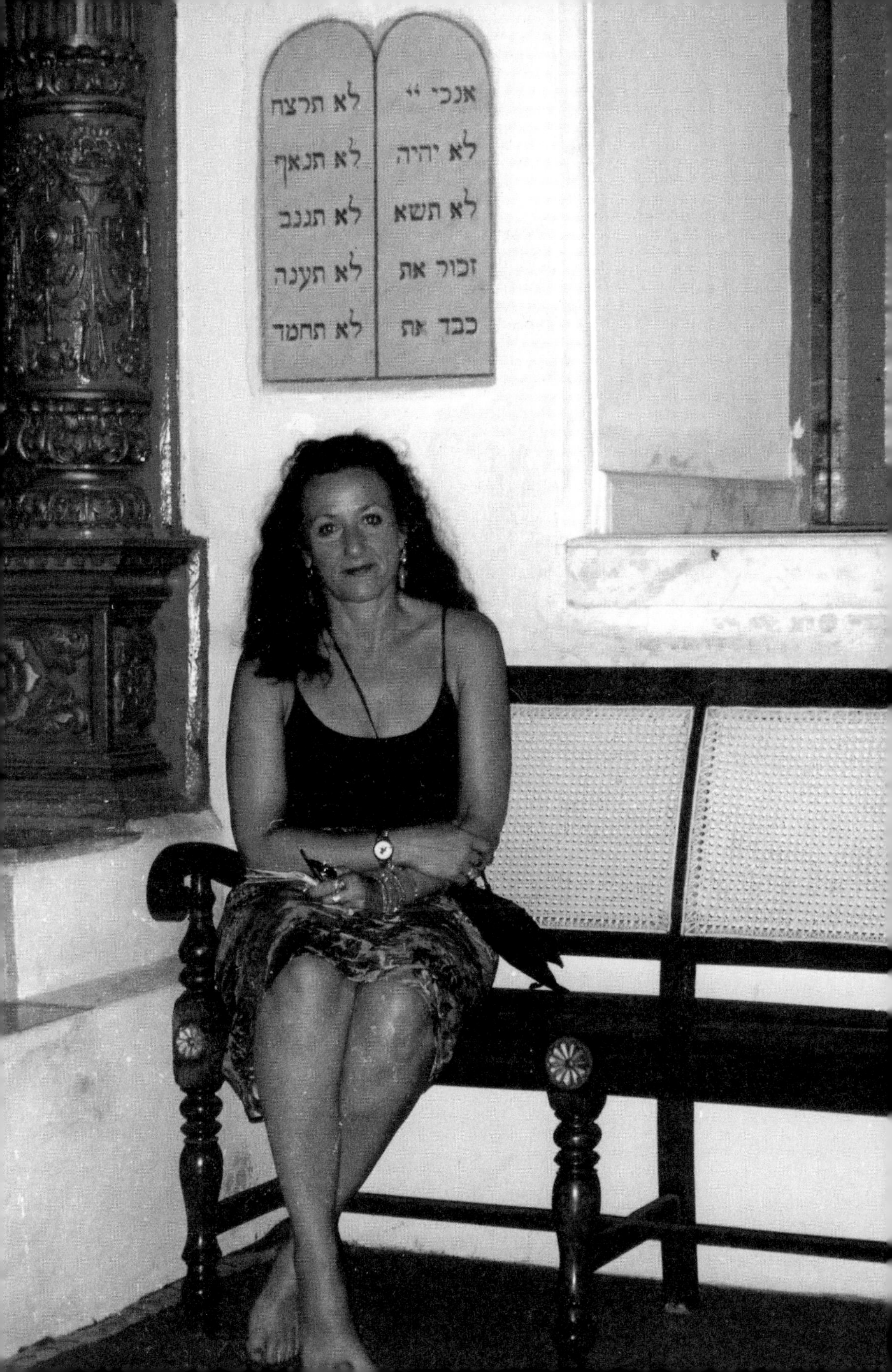
אנכי ״
לא יהיה
לא תשא
זכור את
כבד את
לא תרצח
לא תנאף
לא תגנב
לא תענה
לא תחמד

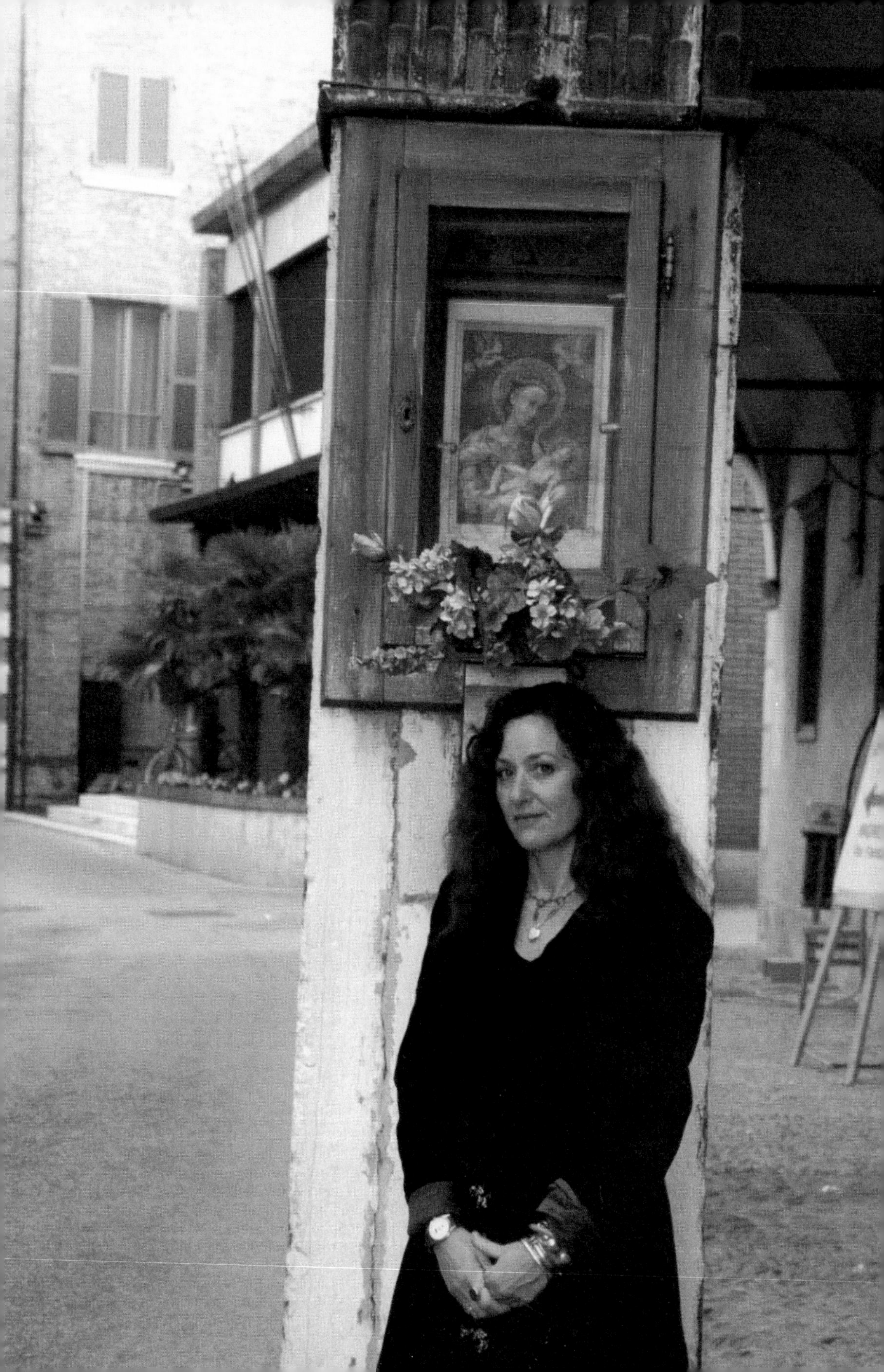

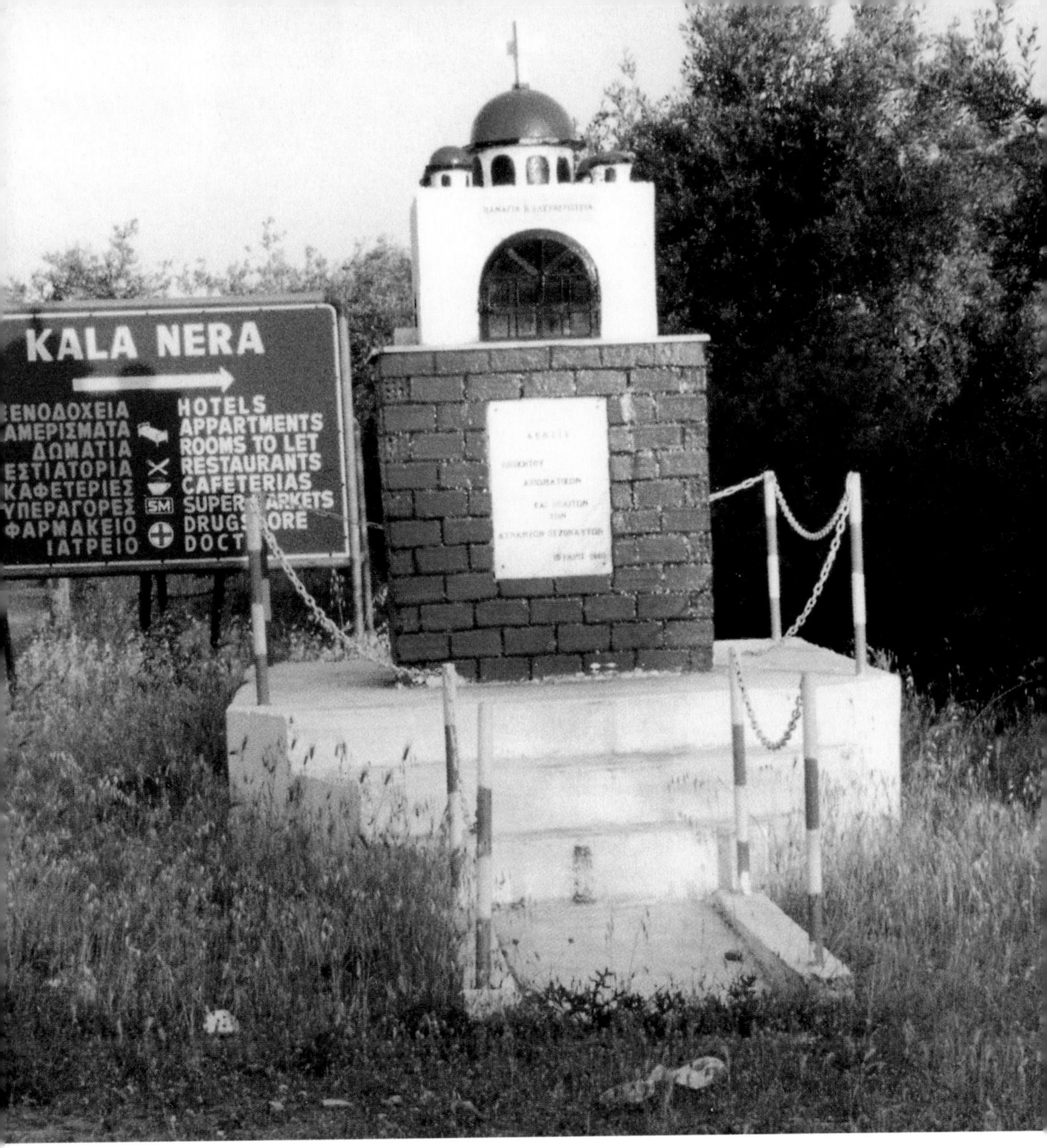
KALA NERA
ΕΝΟΔΟΧΕΙΑ HOTELS
ΑΜΕΡΙΣΜΑΤΑ APPARTMENTS
ΔΩΜΑΤΙΑ ROOMS TO LET
ΕΣΤΙΑΤΟΡΙΑ RESTAURANTS
ΚΑΦΕΤΕΡΙΕΣ CAFETERIAS
ΥΠΕΡΑΓΟΡΕΣ SM SUPER ARKETS
ΦΑΡΜΑΚΕΙΟ DRUGS ORE
ΙΑΤΡΕΙΟ DOCT

Above: **Yet another "gawgeous" shrine in Greece, 1996**
Left: **Me in Greece in front of a typical *iconostasi* (which literally means icon station) 1996**

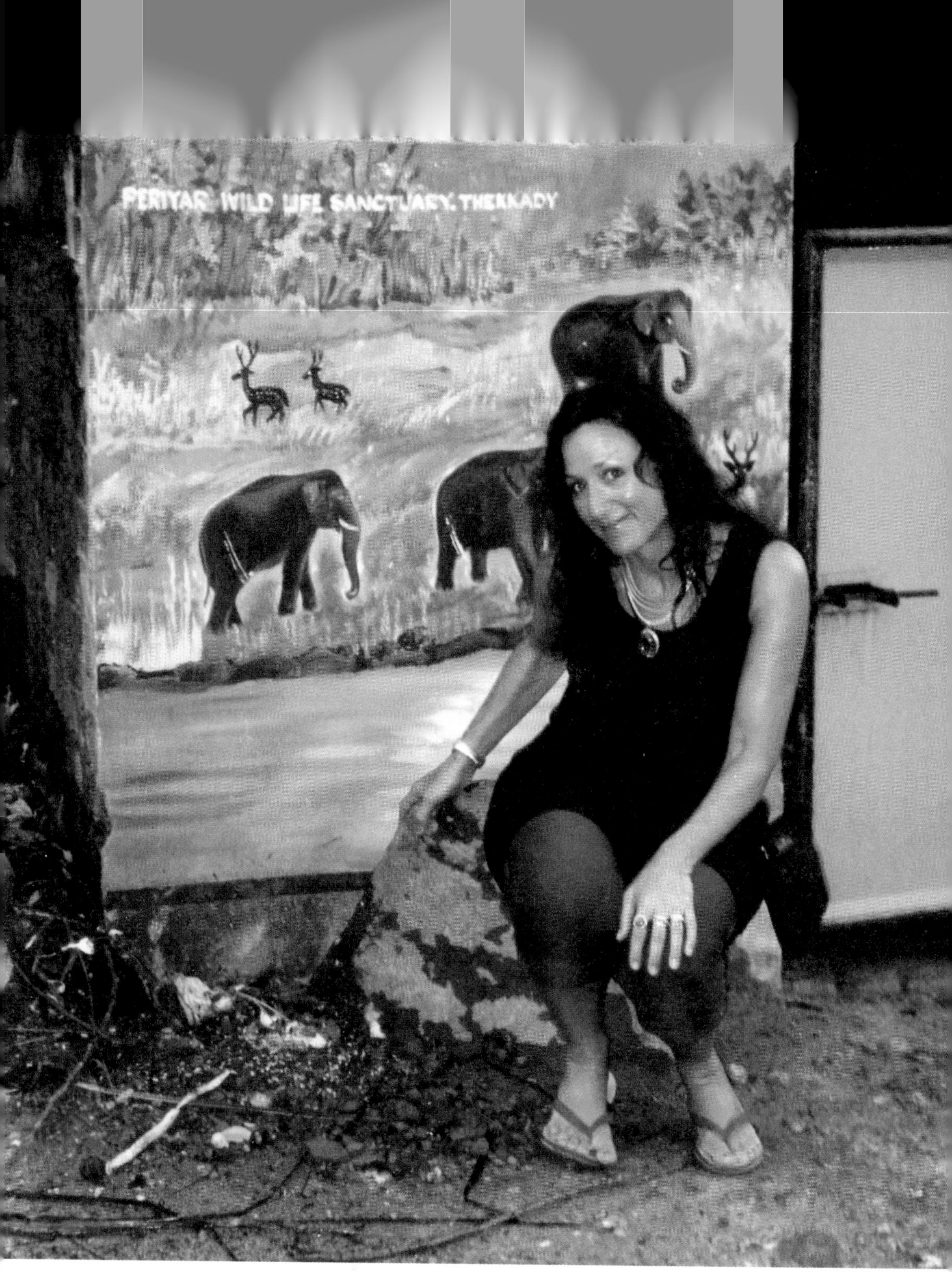
PERIYAR WILD LIFE SANCTUARY. THEKKADY

Above: **Me in Thekadyn India with another hand-painted sign, 2003**
Right: **Reflection of me in the glass of this beautiful shrine near Paltsi, Greece, 2001**

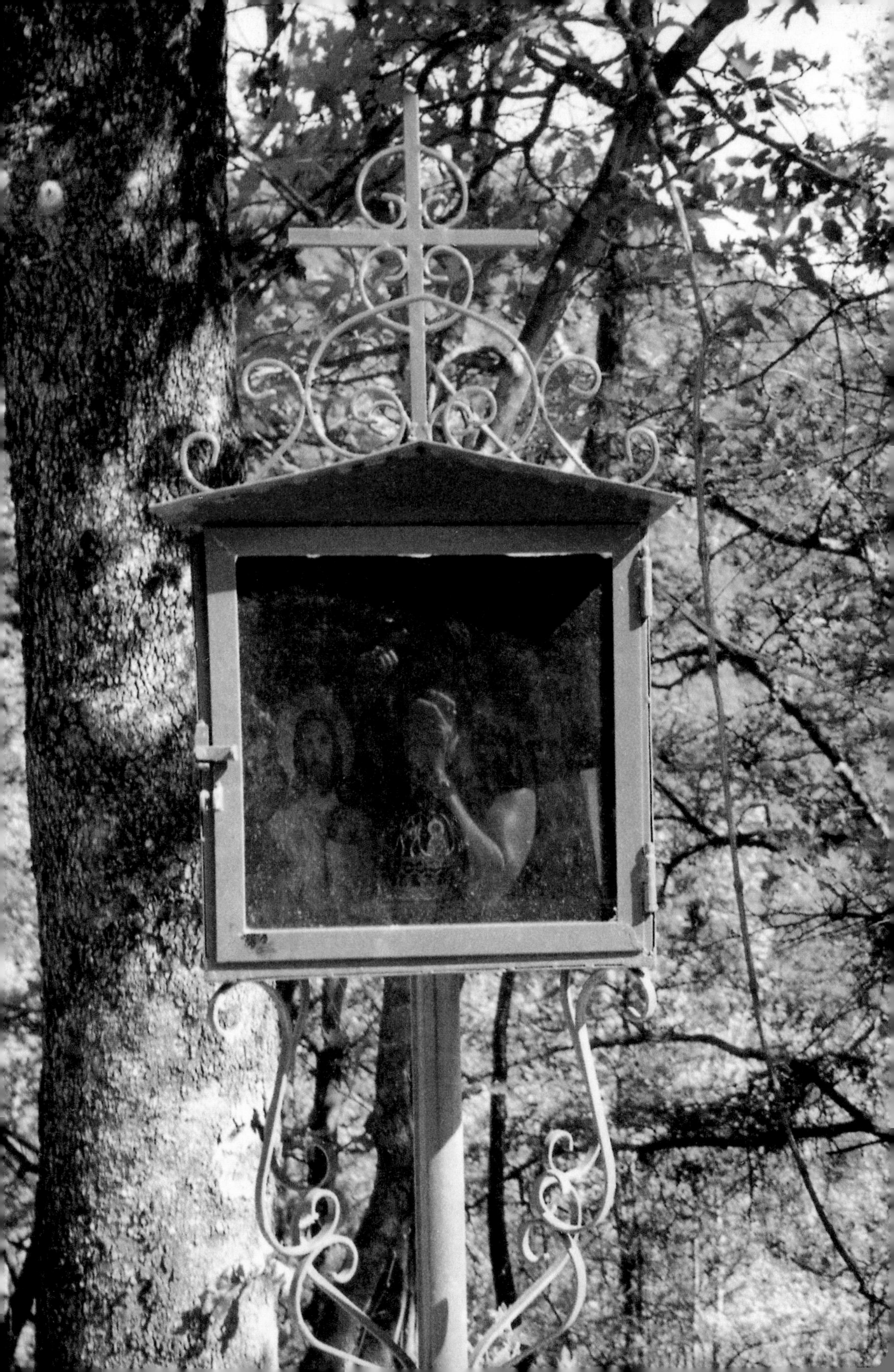

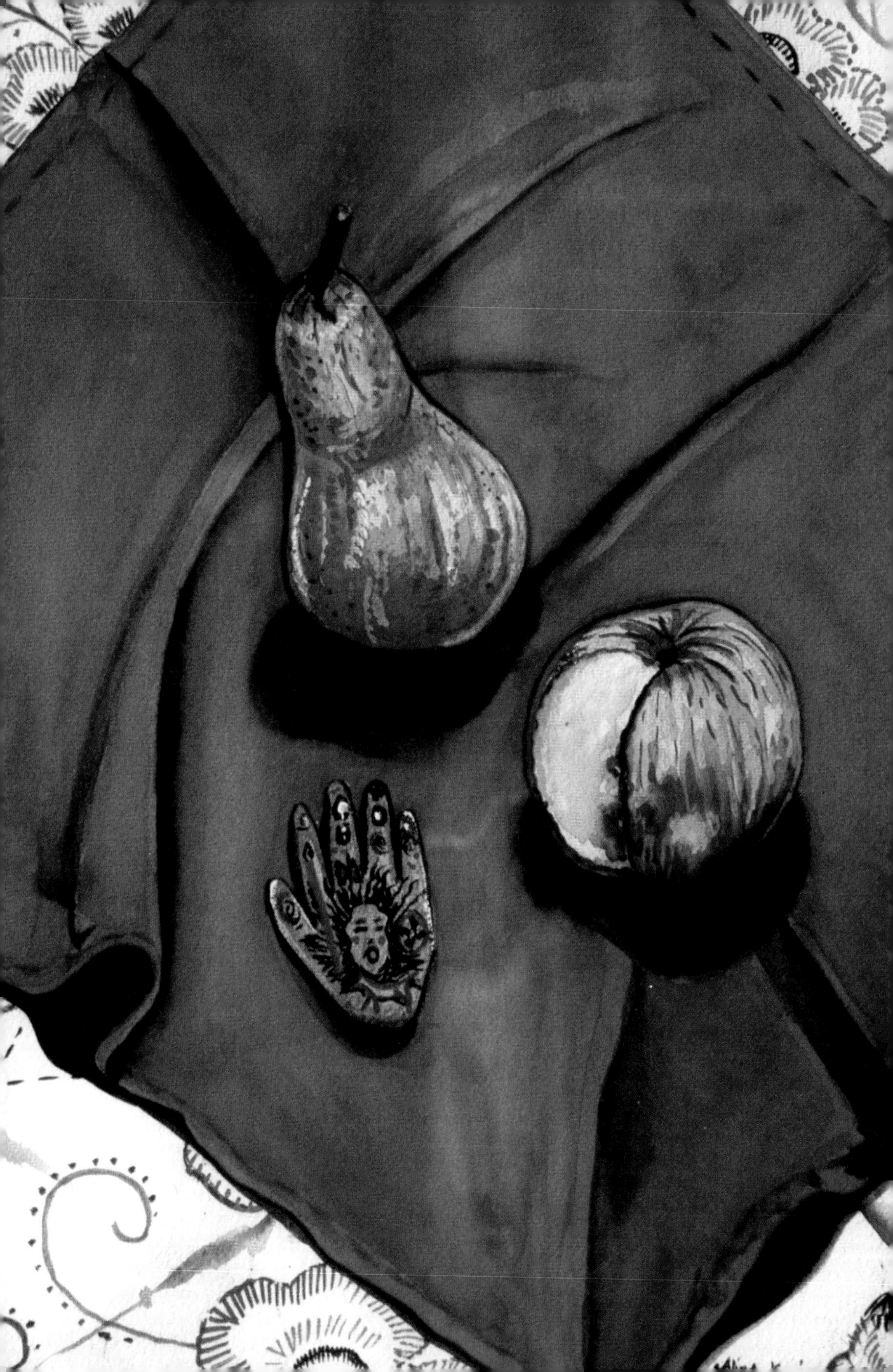

Light and color...

The painting opposite and those on the following pages were inspired by my trips to India, Greece, Italy, Corsica, Morocco, Lourdes, and France in general. I pushed the watercolor paint to get maximum color possible … I discovered Goddesses everywhere, and I put myself in many of these pictures with miniature self-portraits on candles, virgins, mermaids and other semi-sacred objects.

Pages 312–315: **Watercolor/collages from a series I made in India while traveling, using materials found there—I'm not sure how long they will last**
Page 314: Three women in Trivandrum (Dominique Sapel is the one in the middle.)
Page 315: Collage done on a boat in the "Backwaters" of Kerala, India 2003

Page 316: **Painting of my departed friend Diane Callum, as the Sensual Goddess that she was … done in honor of her daughter Oceana, 2002**
Page 317: **Watercolor with self-portrait as "Virgin On The Halfshell," 2002**
Pages 320–321: **Watercolor, Christian in a Café in Sumene, France, 2002**
Page 322–323: **Self-portrait, in front of bar in Marseille, France**
Two weeks after I did this painting they completely changed the front of this bar!

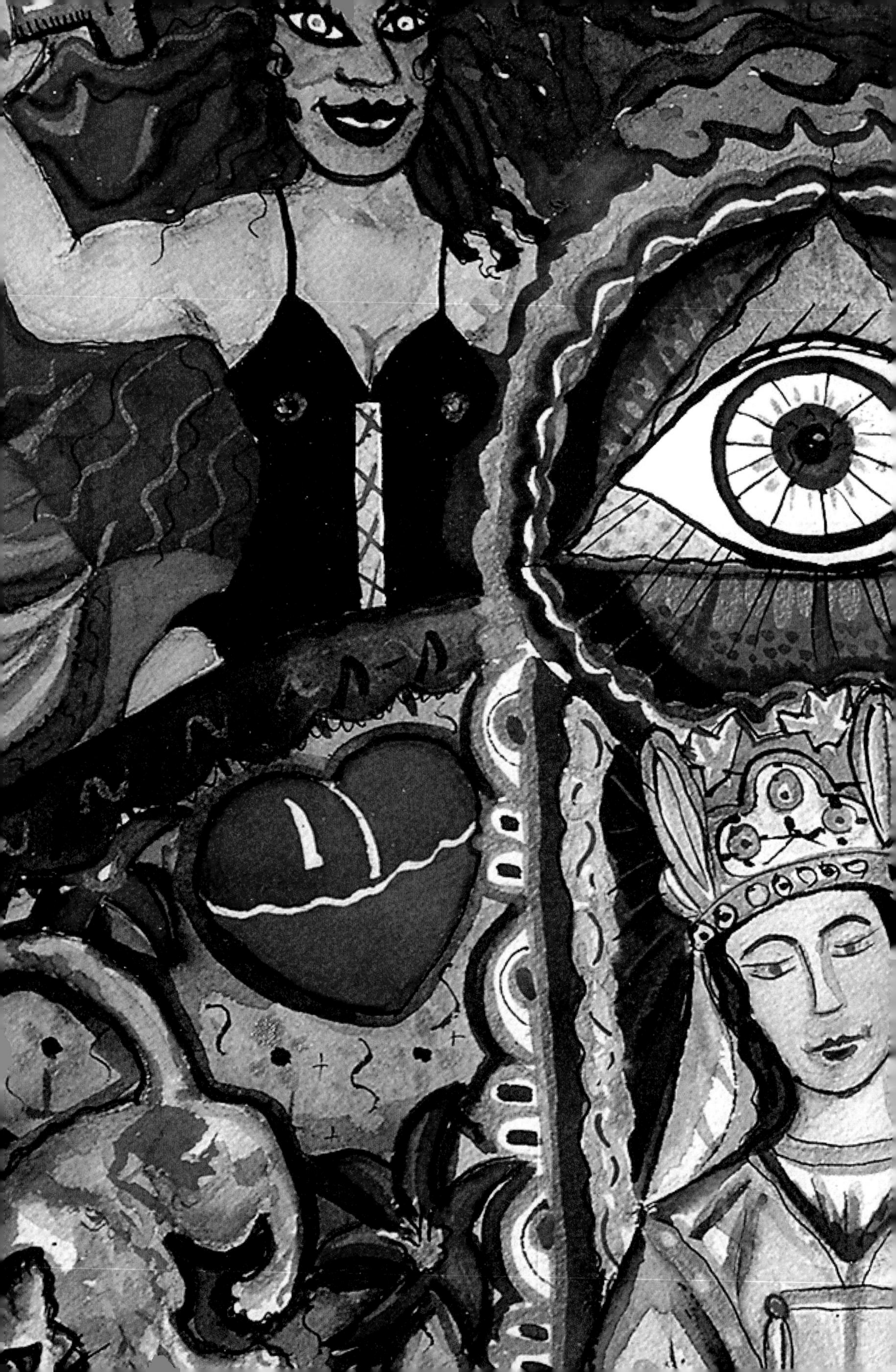

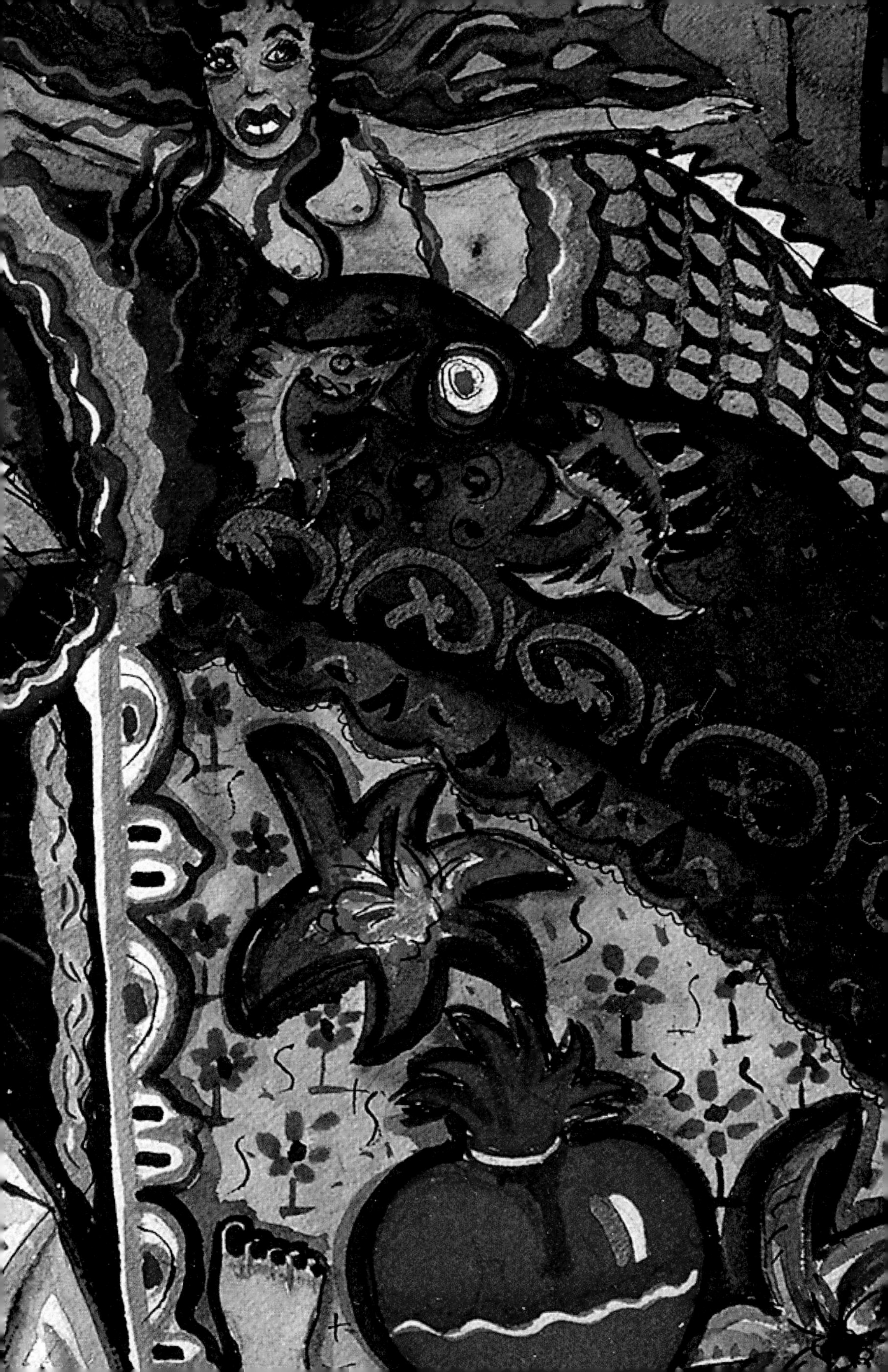

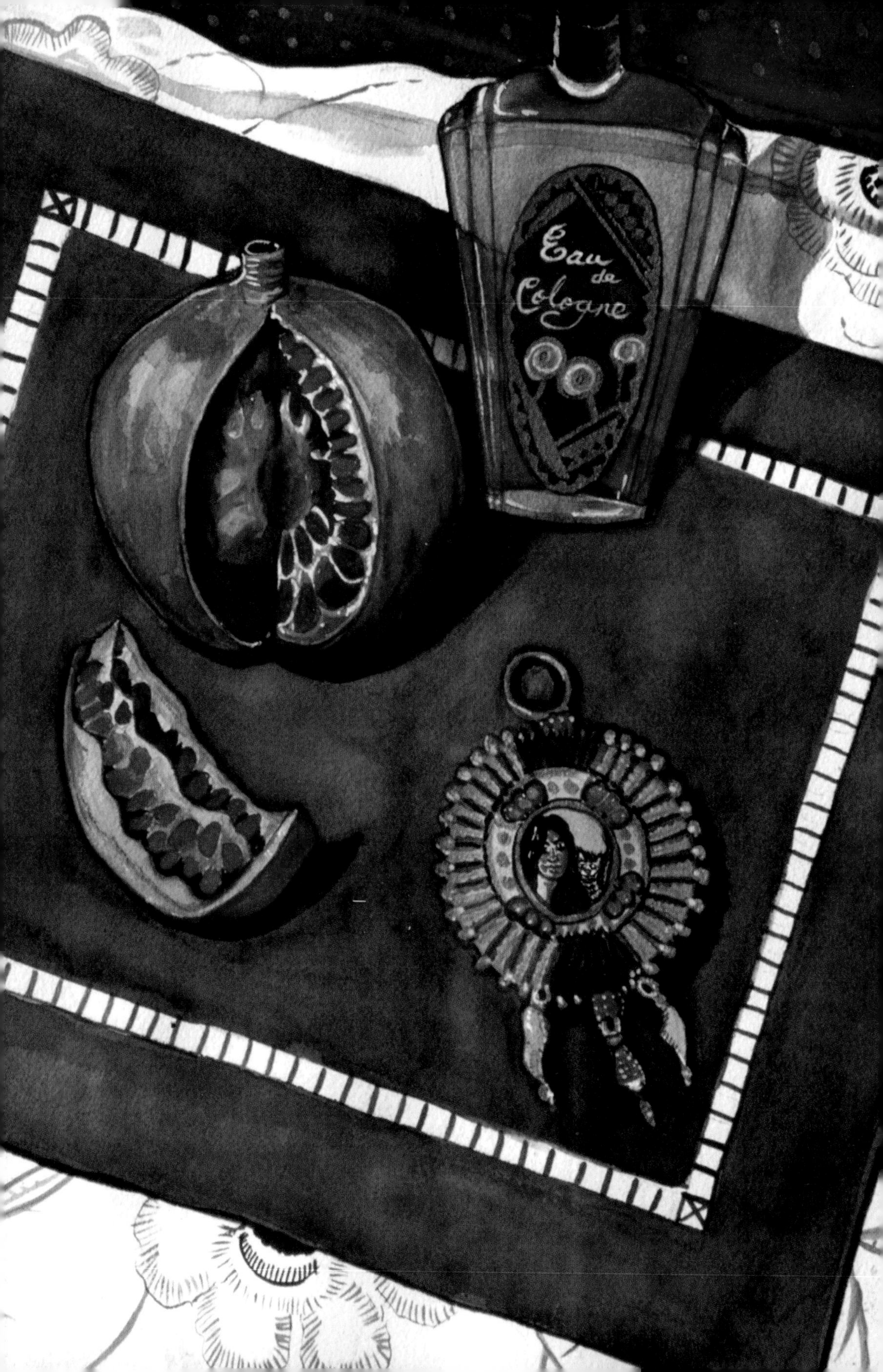
Eau de Cologne

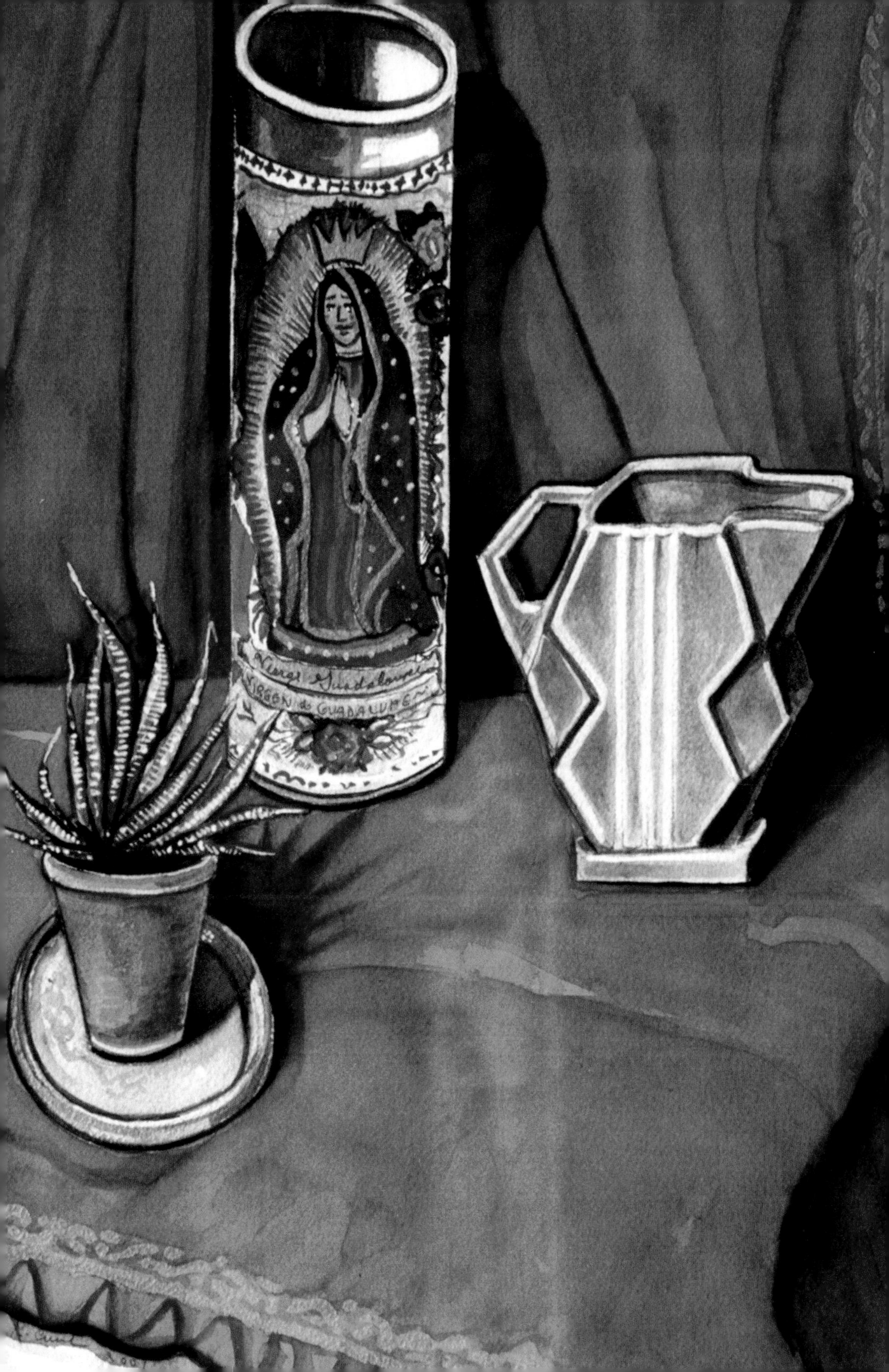

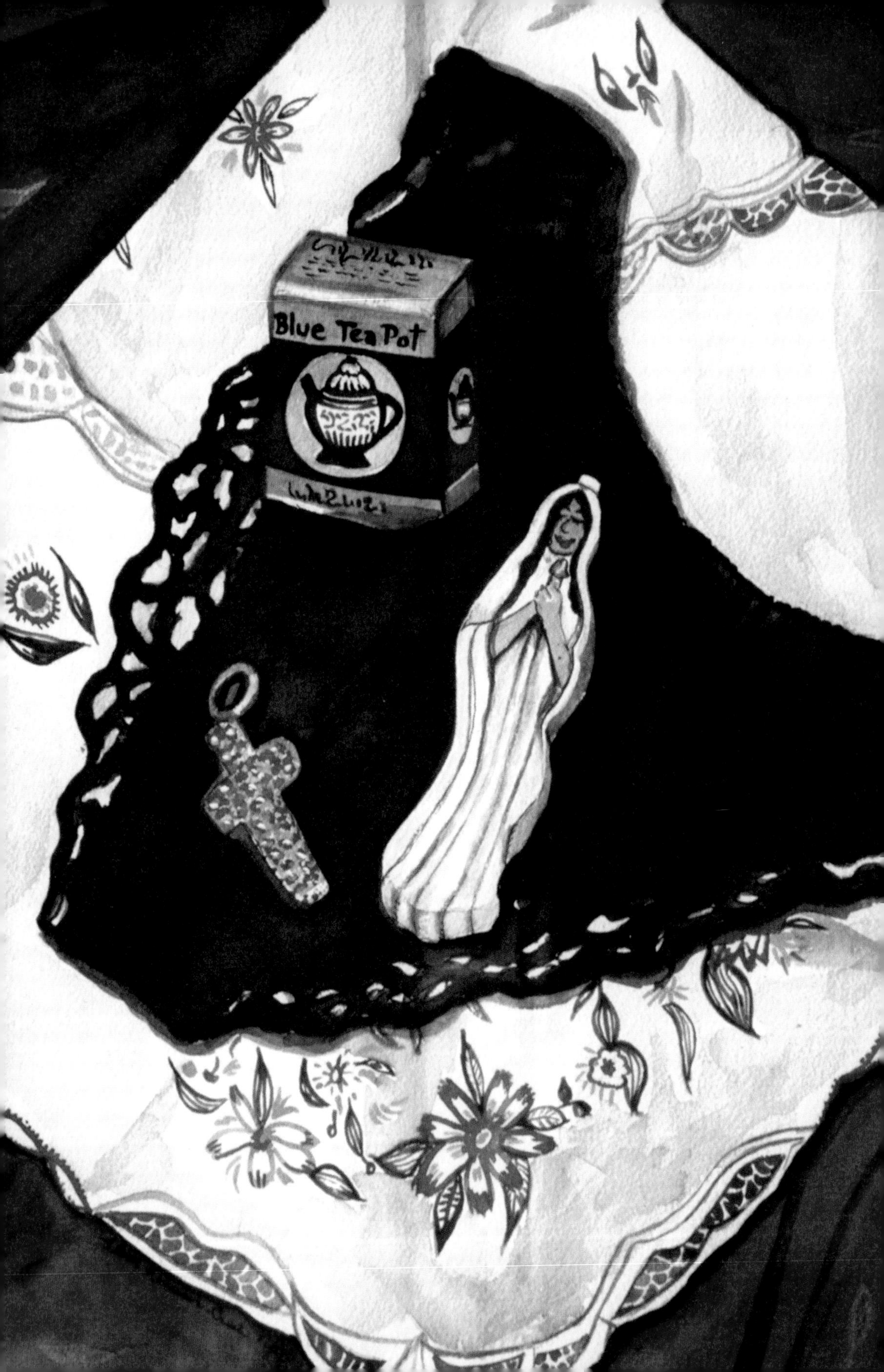
Blue Tea Pot

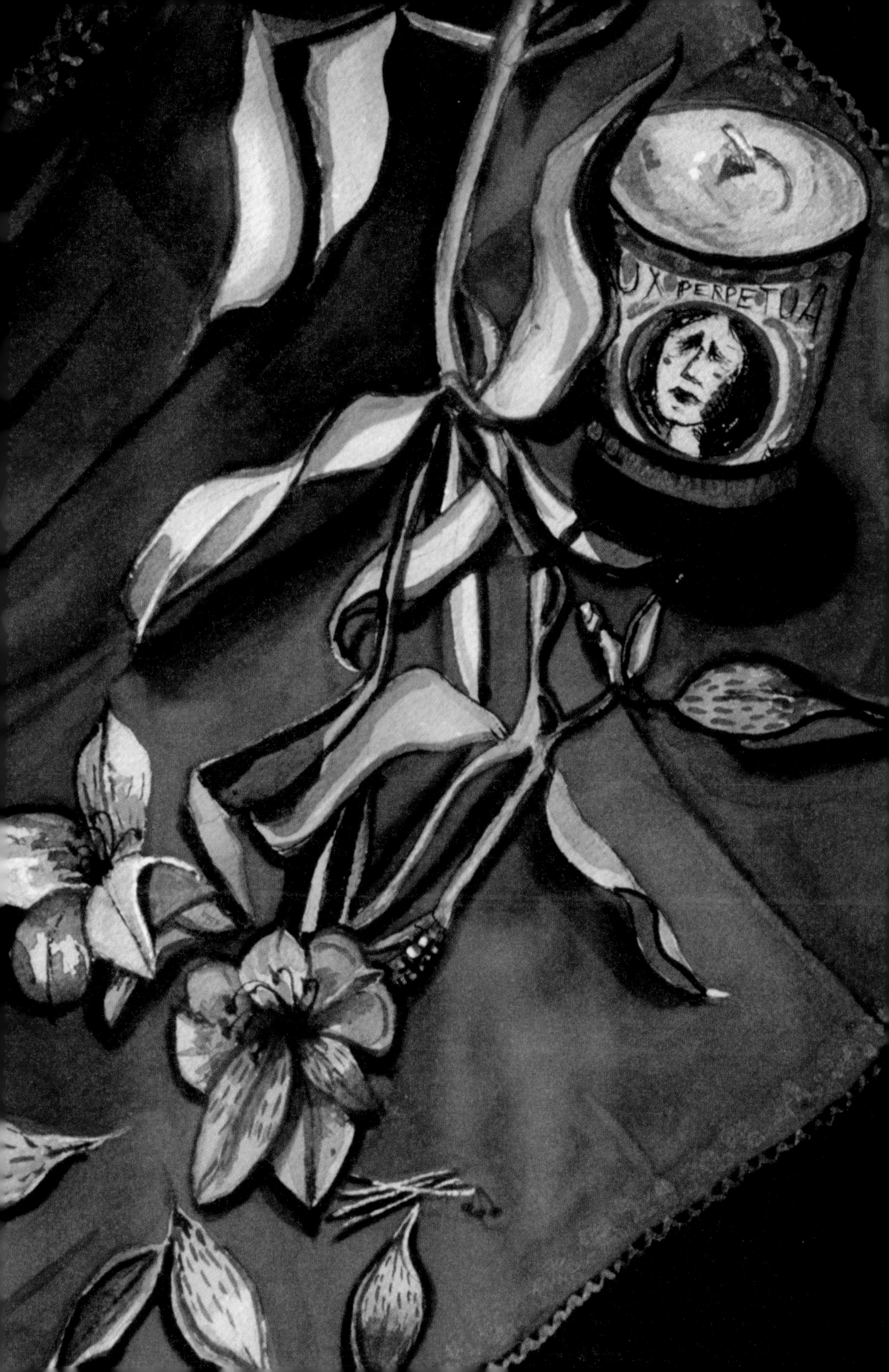
UX PERPETUA

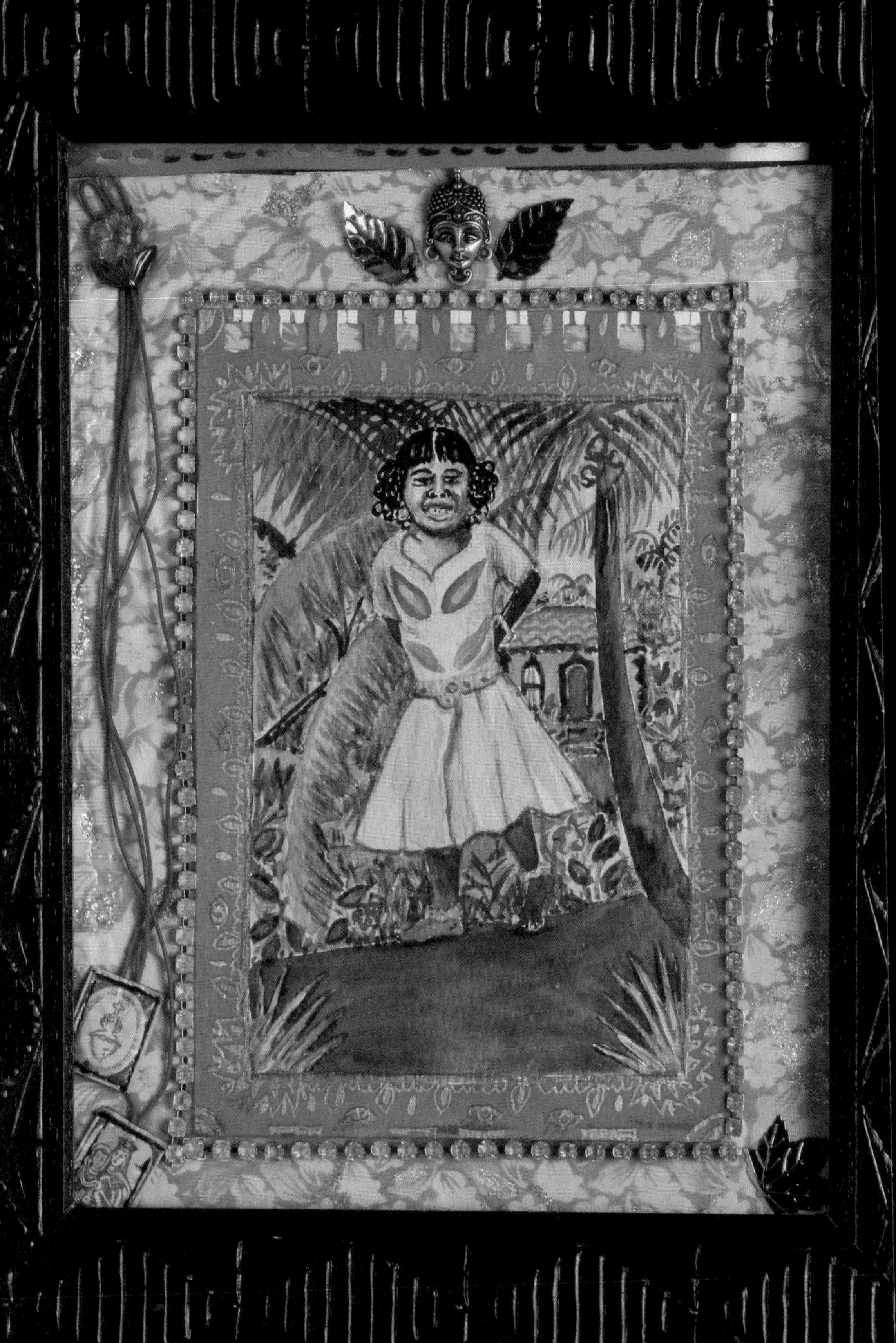

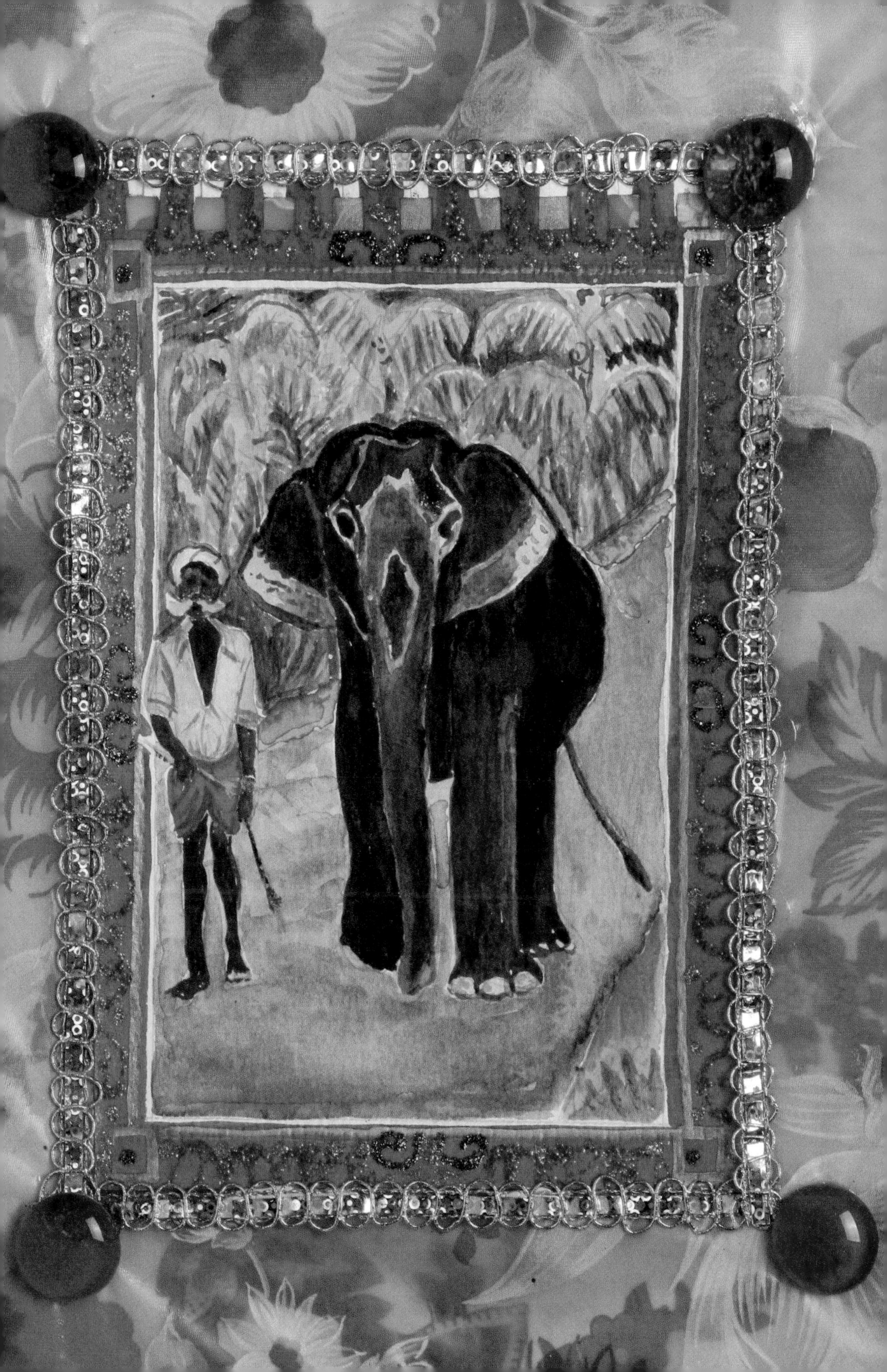

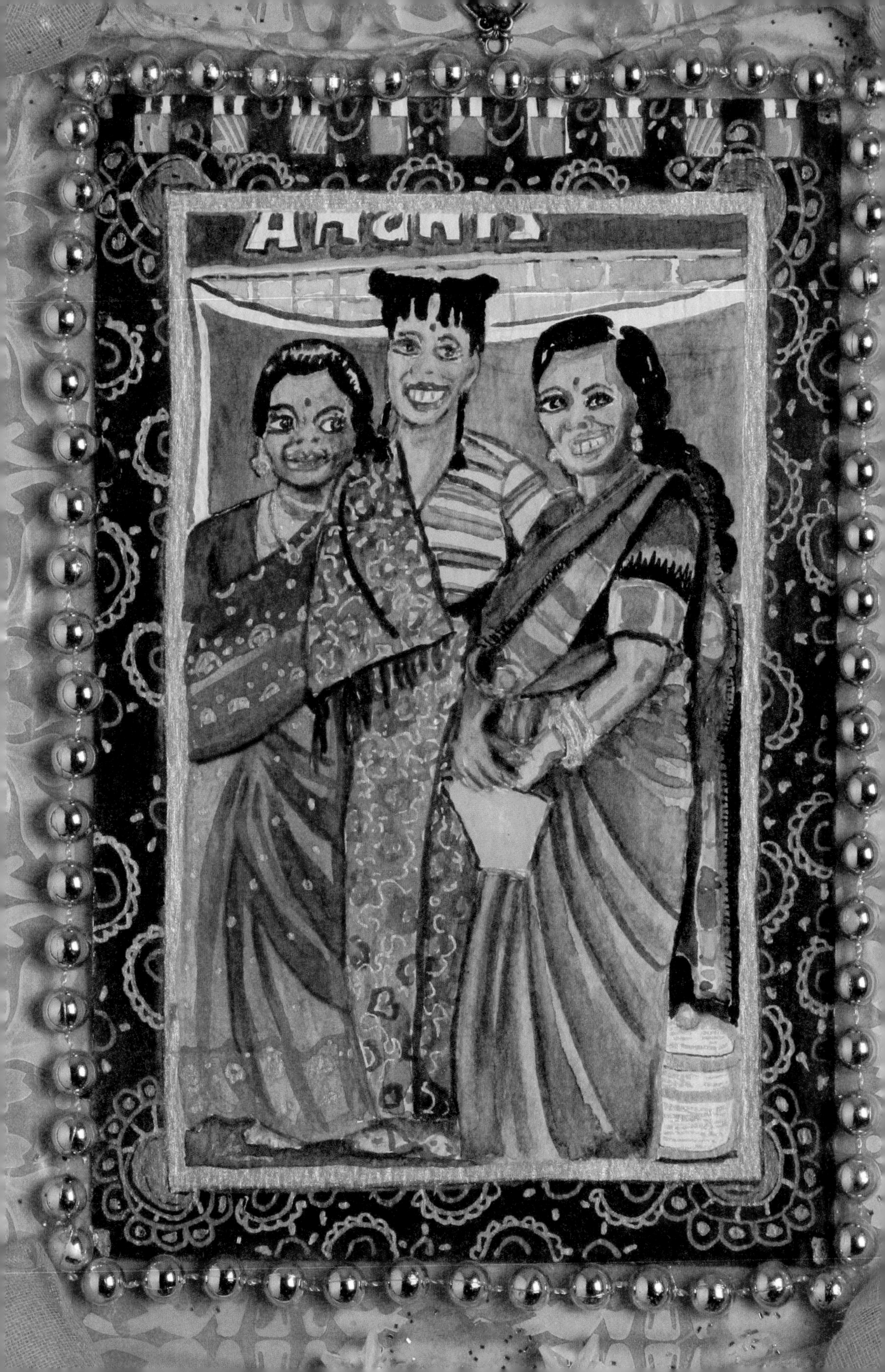

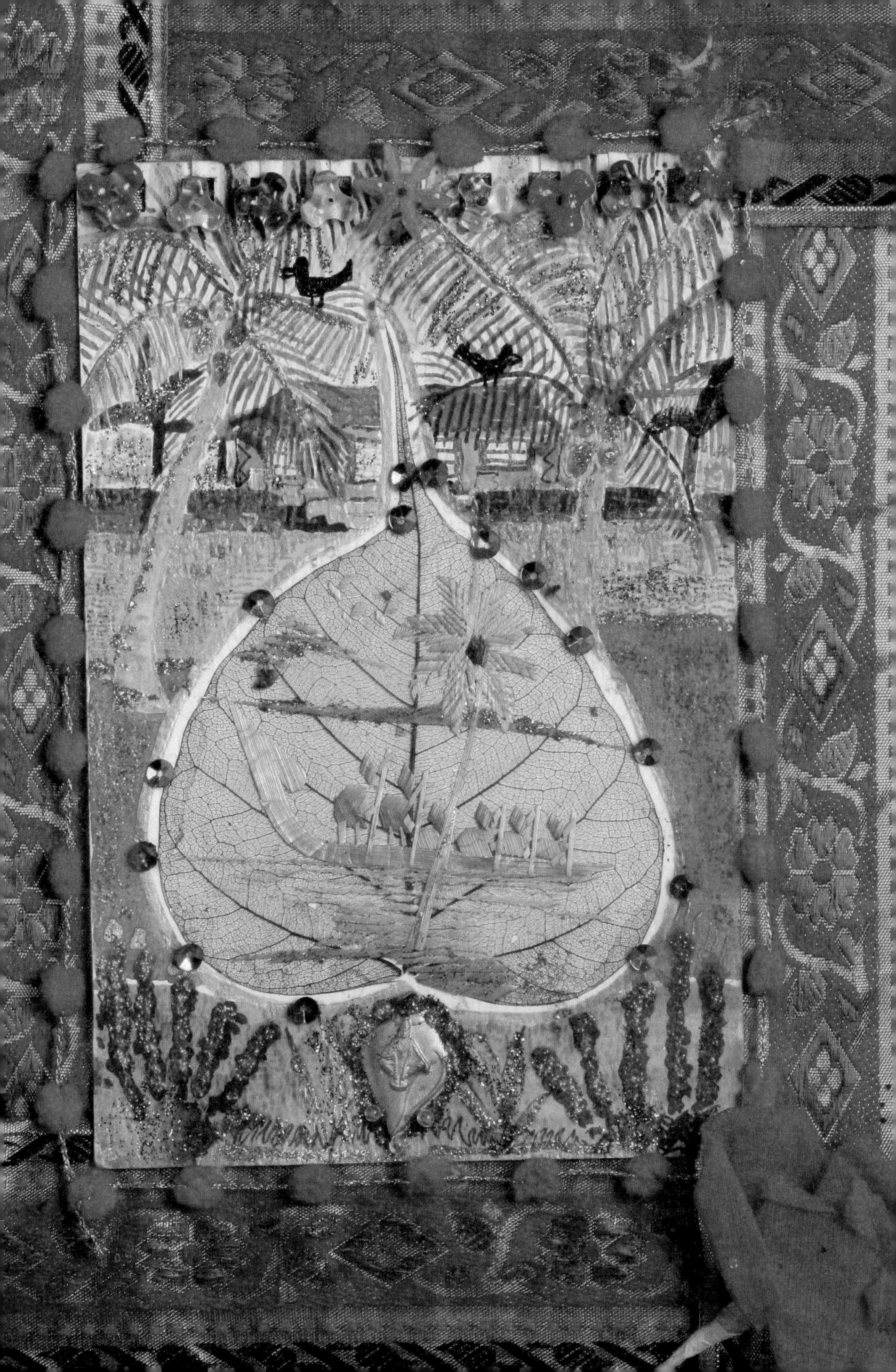

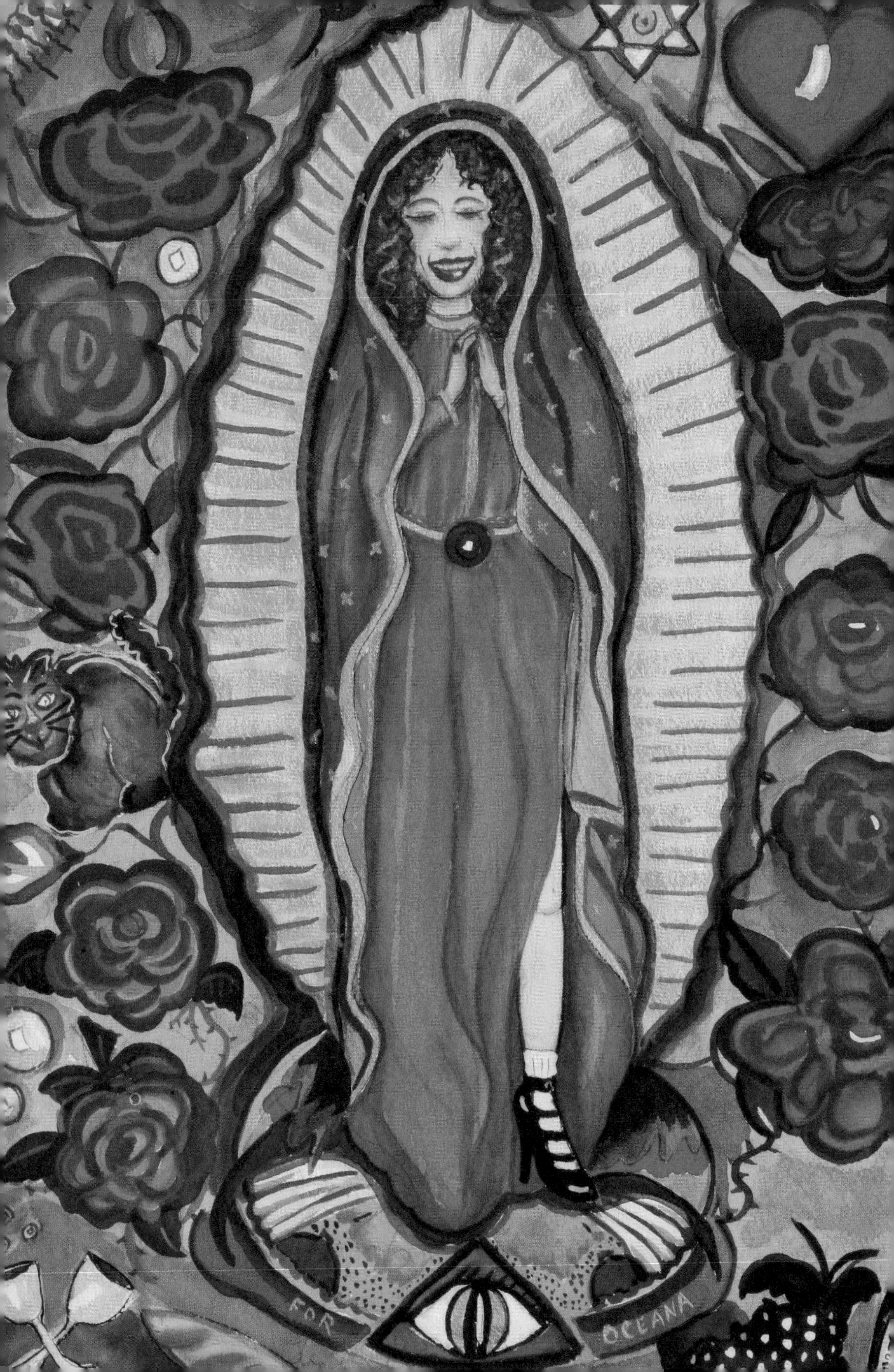
FOR
OCEANA

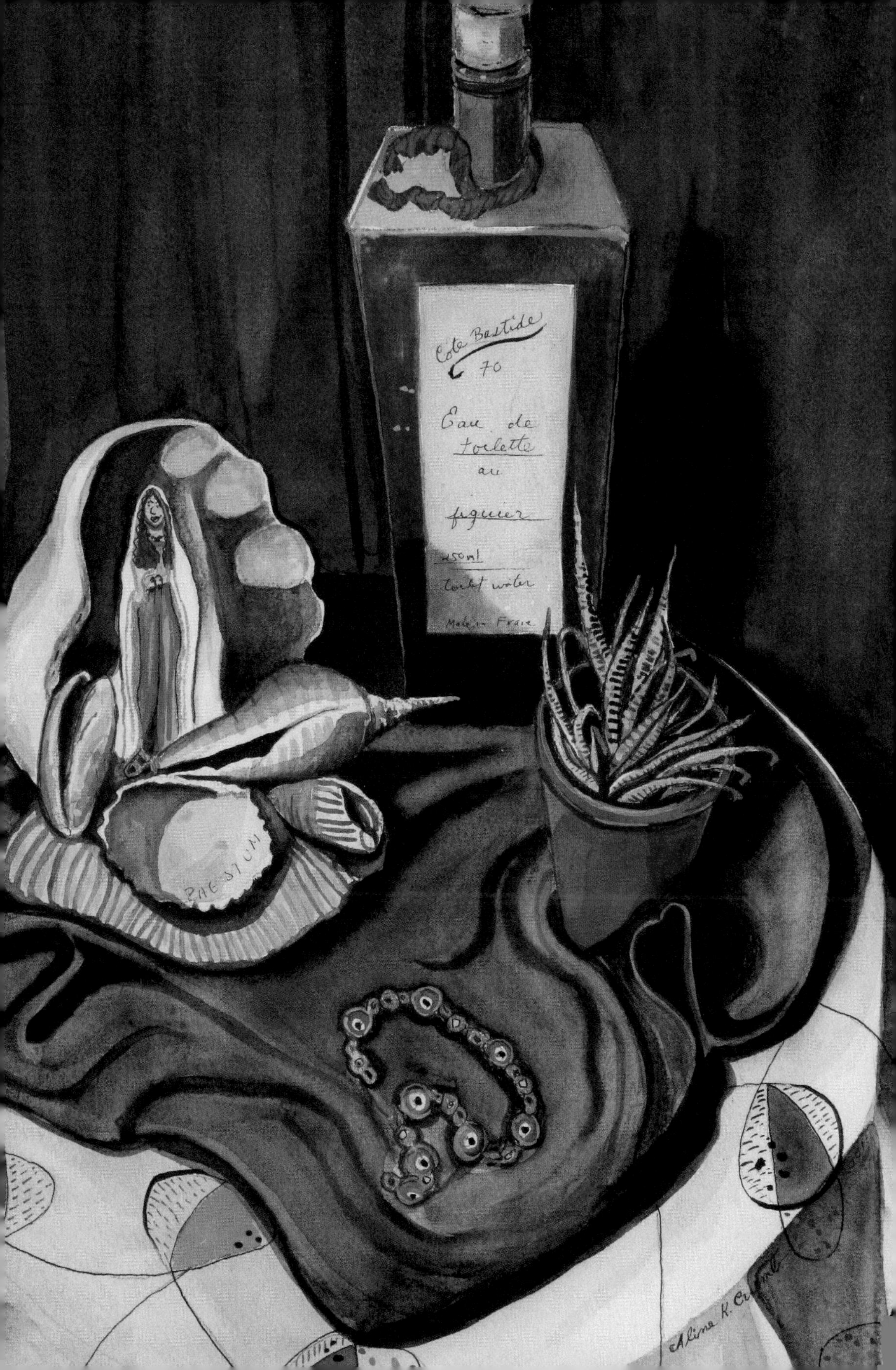
Côte Bastide
70
Eau de toilette
au
figuier
250ml
Toilet water
PAESTUM

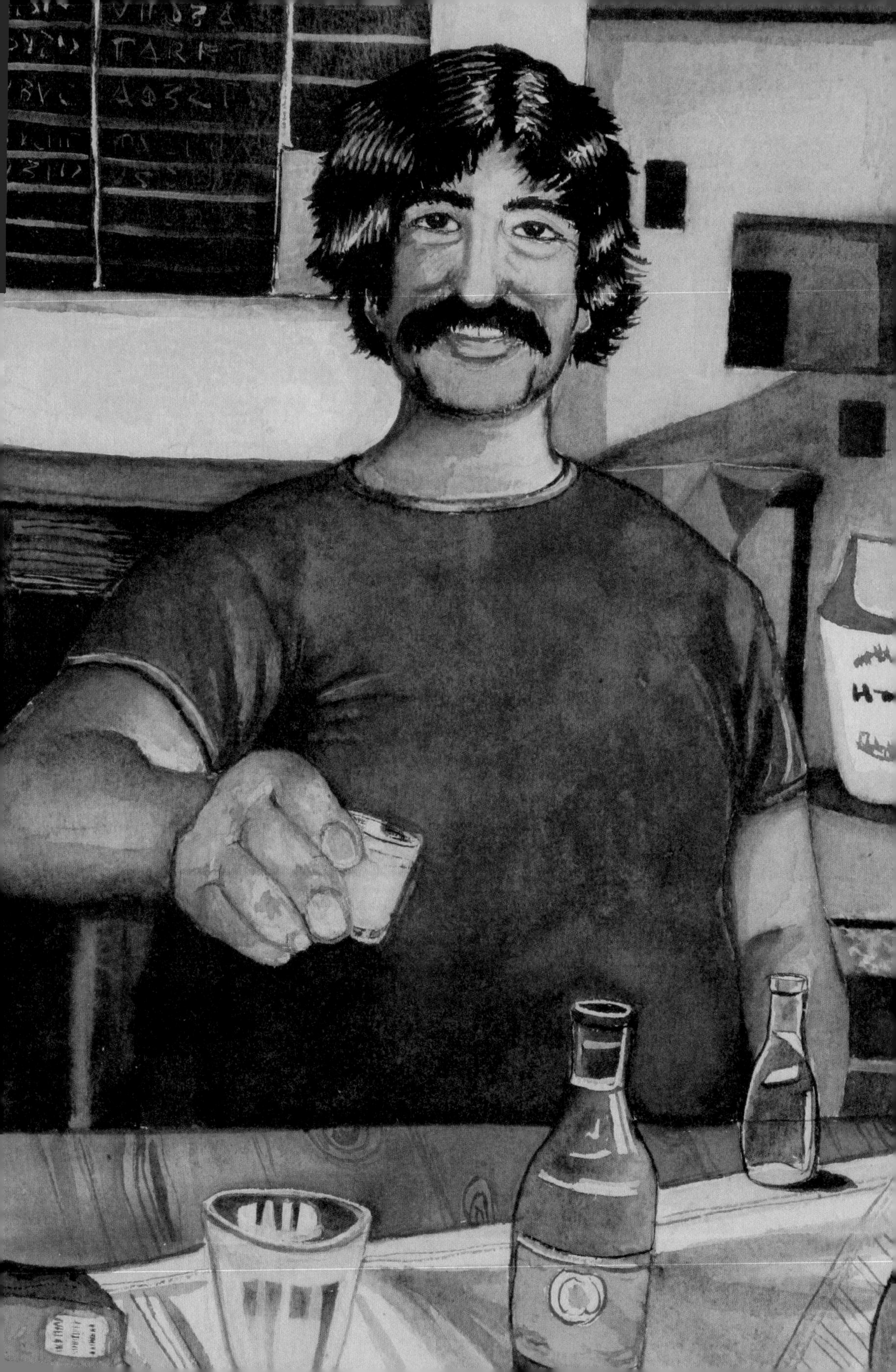

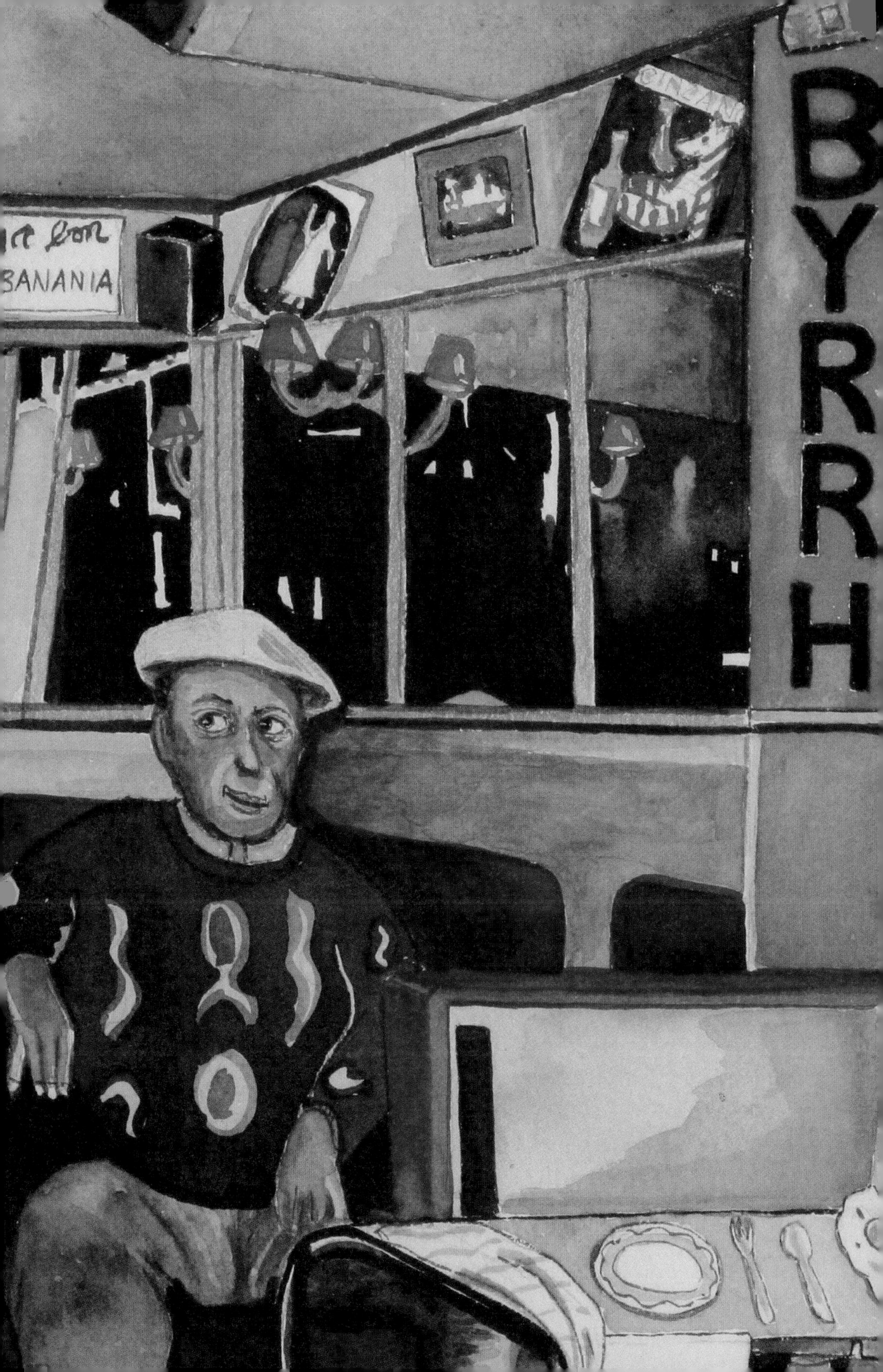
BANANIA
BYRRH

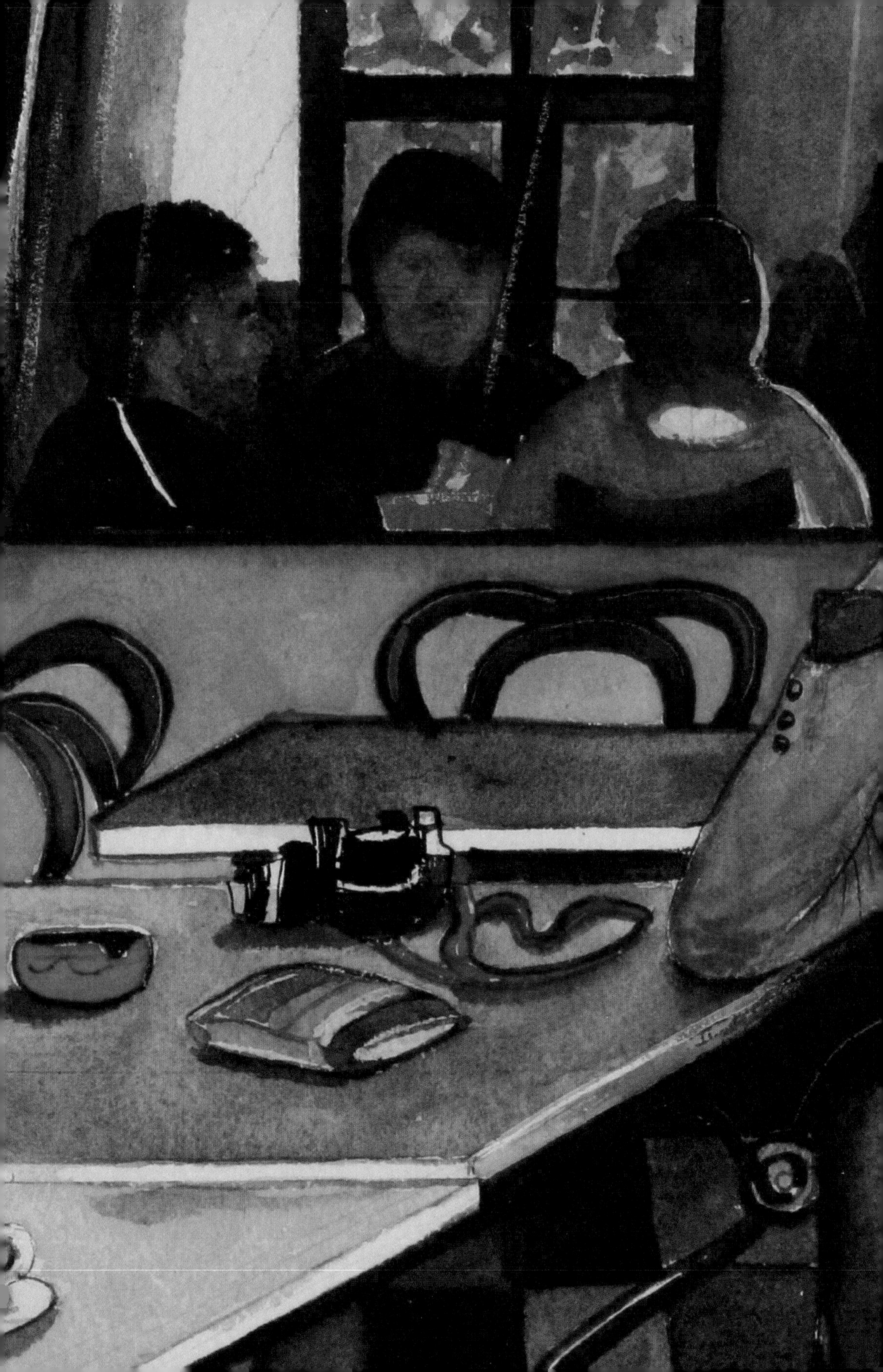

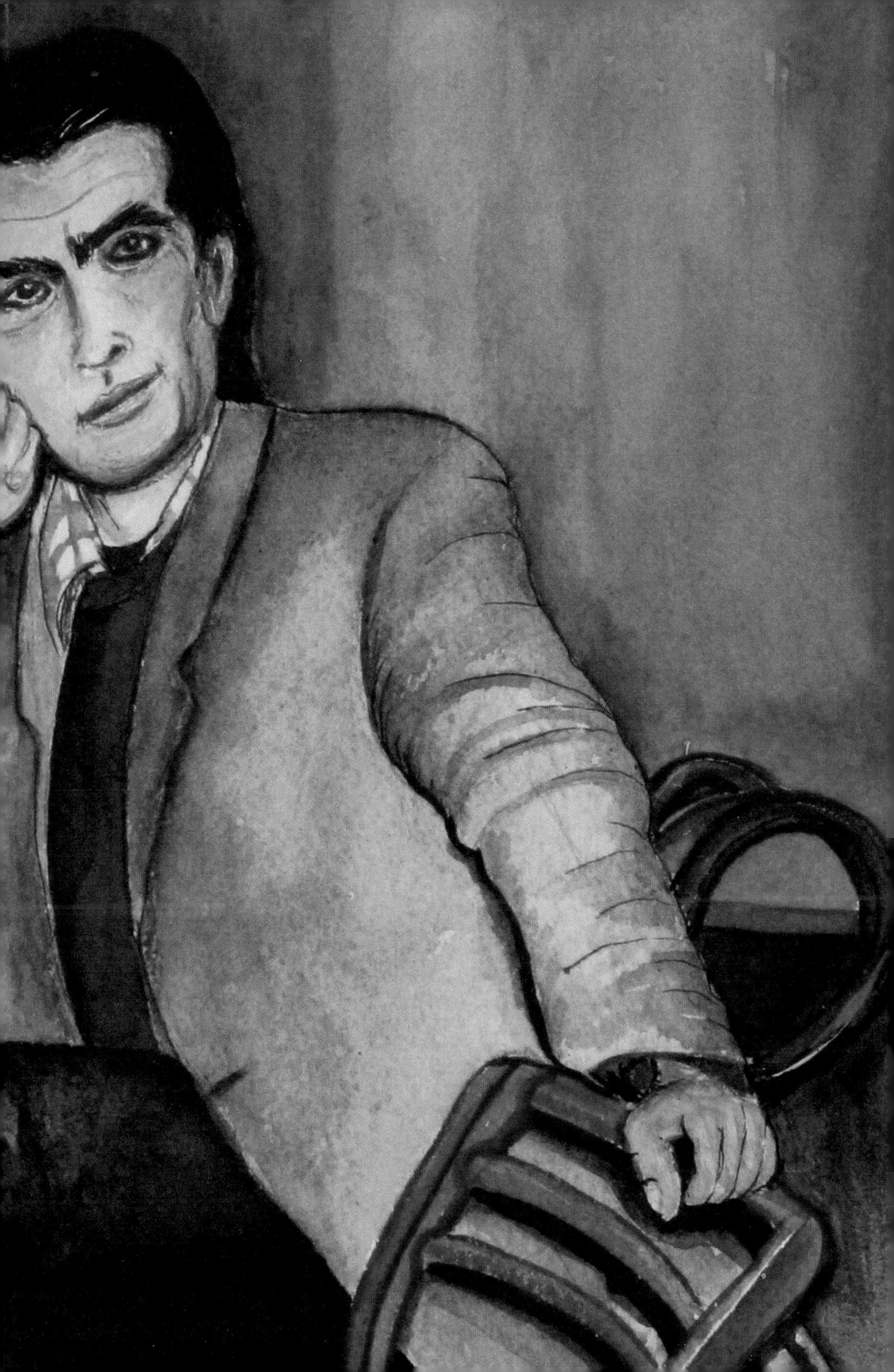

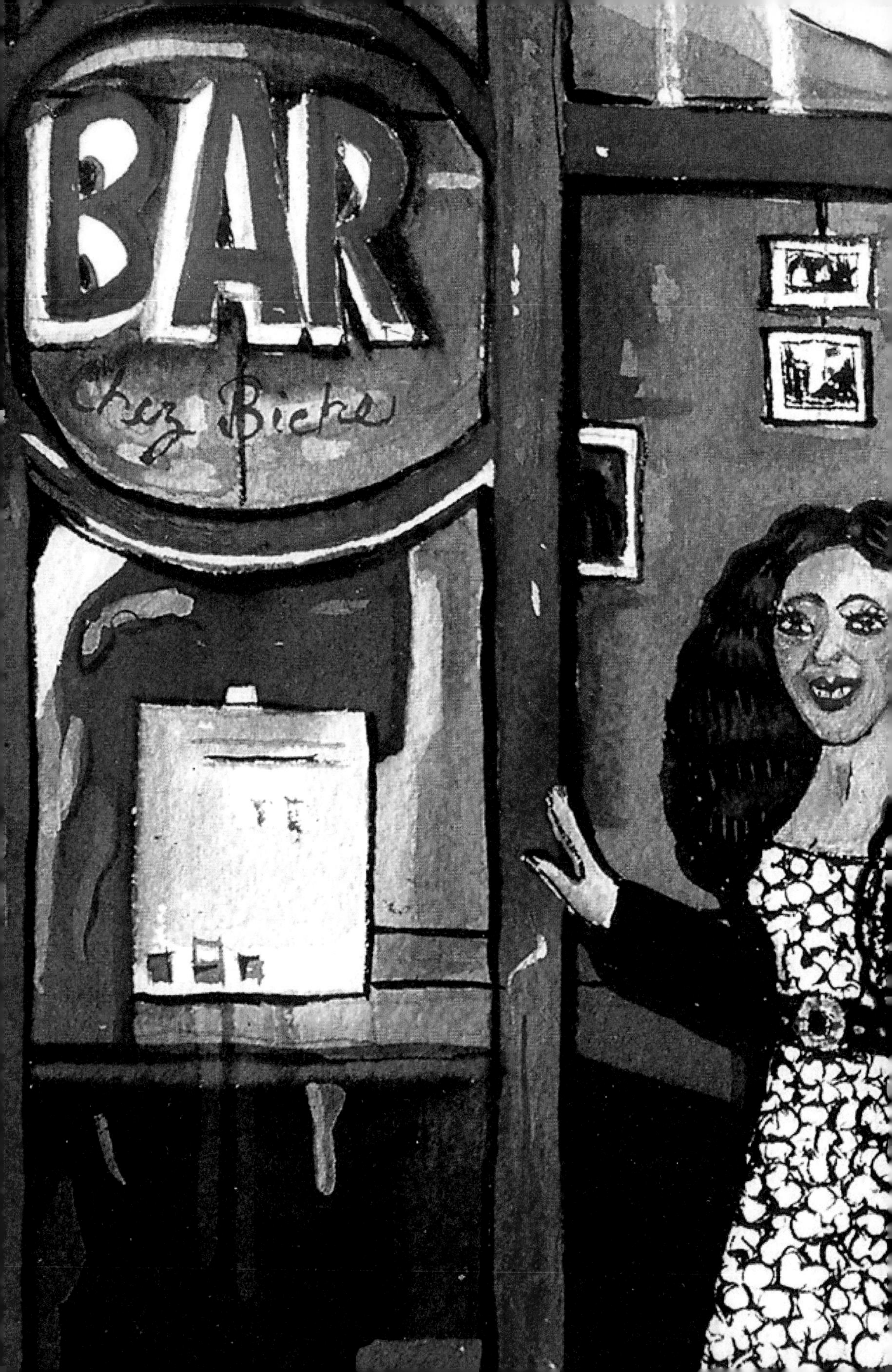
BAR
Chez Biche

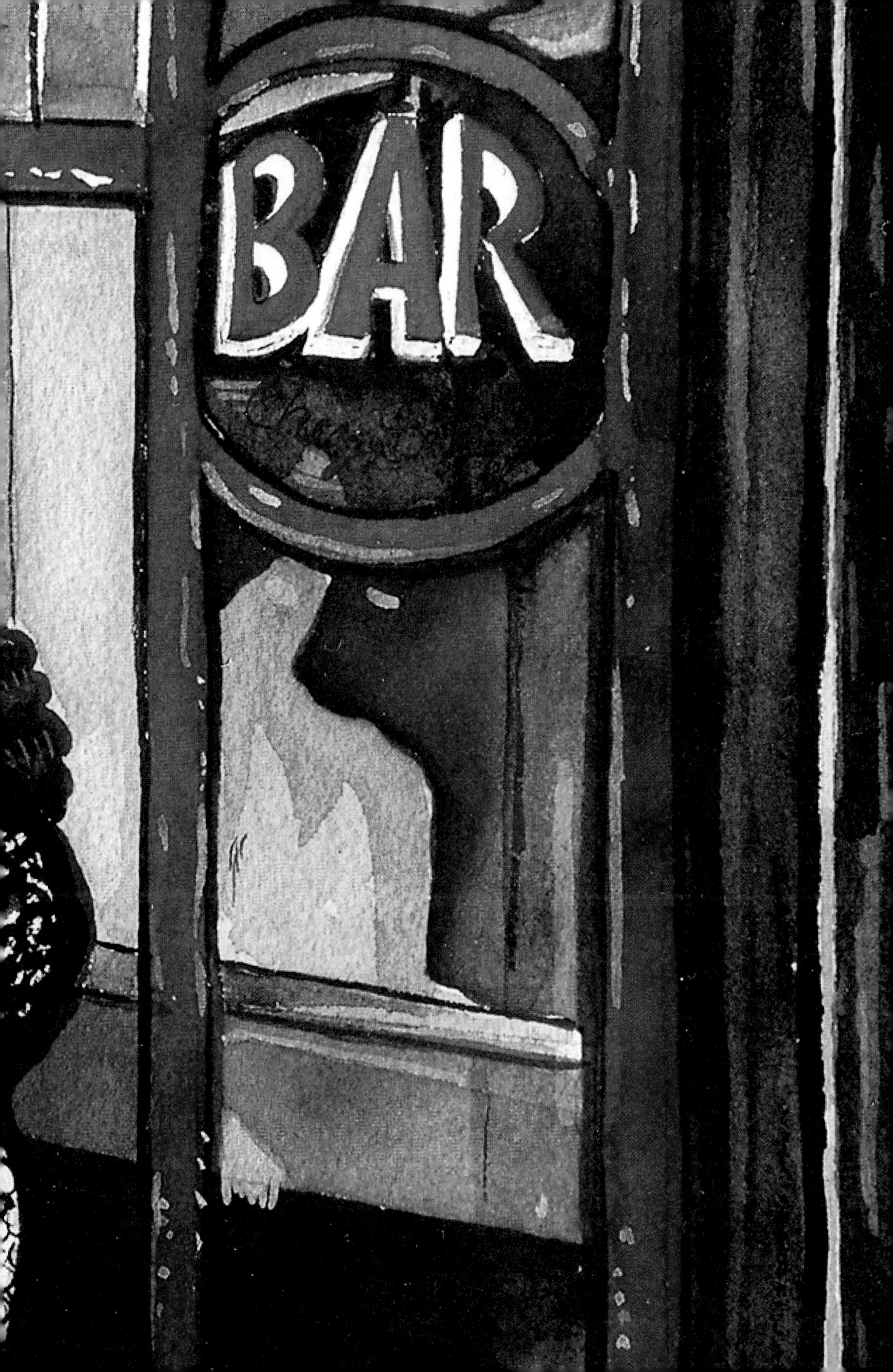
BAR

CHAPTER FIVE
The Kominsky Code

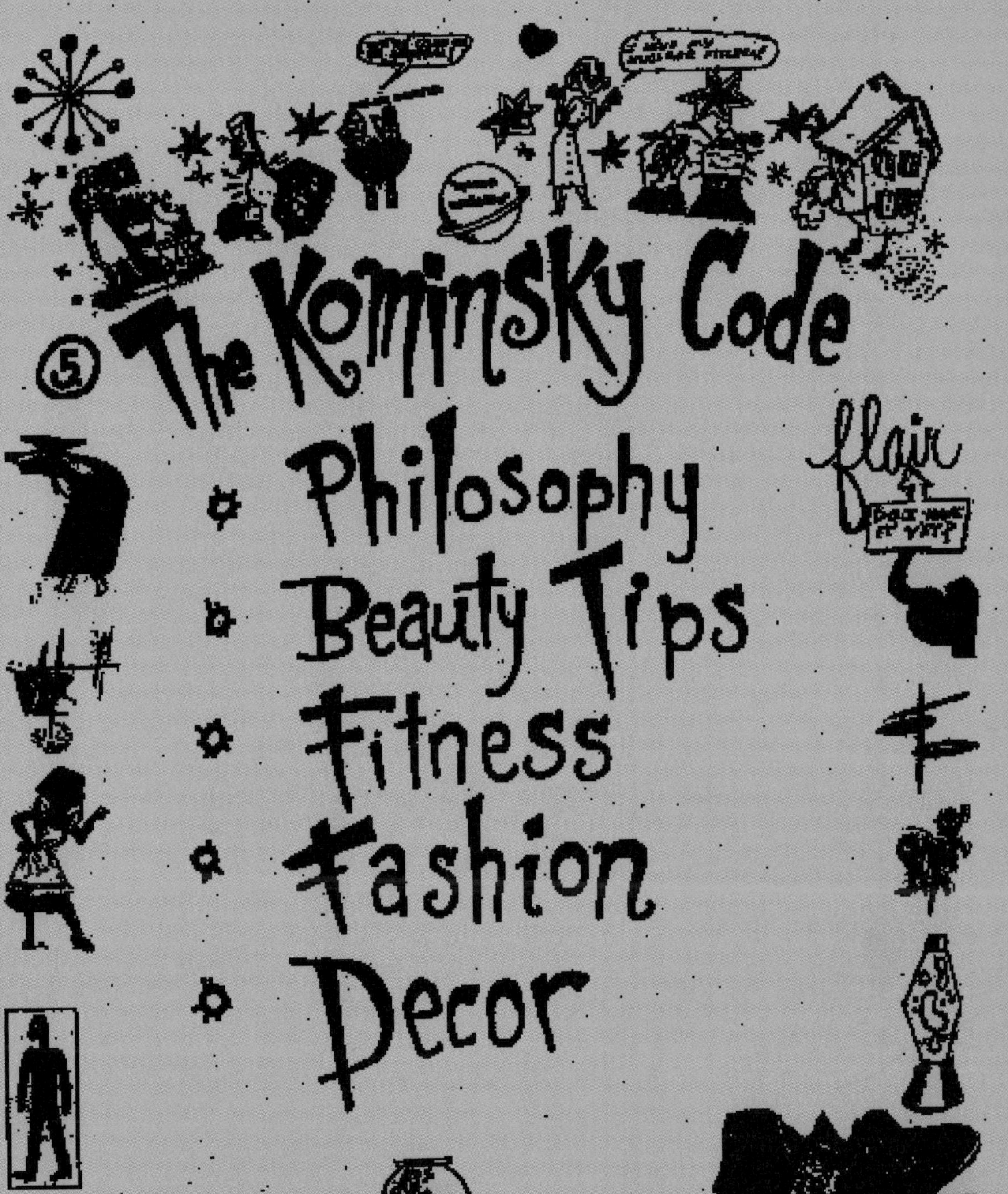
5
The Kominsky Code
Philosophy
Beauty Tips
Fitness
Fashion
Decor
flair

Unlocking the Kominsky Code

Now that you've read about all my adventures over the years, my publisher Zaro Weil (she's here on the left) thought it would make a great last chapter to interview me at my home in France, so I can talk about what's happening with the REAL me right now. In our talk I shall reveal the true secrets of the Da Vinci (OOPS!) I mean the KOMINSKY Code ...

Zaro: So, let's talk about your Kominsky Code. What do you mean by that? I know that Kominsky was your first husband's name ... because you talk about him in the book.

Aline: Yes, it's my name, and it rhymes with the Da Vinci Code—it's catchy and funny and plays on popular culture. Hey, c'mon, I'm just trying to capitalize on one of the biggest money-making hypes out there!

Zaro: Do you mean that when I read this book I shouldn't take it seriously? How are people going to see it, and how do you want them to react to it?

Aline: Well, I don't take myself all that seriously, but at the same time, I think I have figured some things out. After age 50, lots of things become more obvious, and I'm sure that's true for other people too. But many people are still looking for a way to get themselves there. So yes, I hope the book's funny, because I laugh at myself all the time—and I'm pretty self-deprecating. I have a black sense of humor about my life, the good and the bad. Maybe it'll help at least someone out there get a better perspective on everything.

As for the Kominsky Code, well, it's a somewhat satirical commentary on women's magazines, fashion, beauty, diet, health tips—the whole deal. Usually, that stuff's treated so terribly seriously, and it's all very repetitive—we all know what diet's about, we all know what we're supposed to do. But in your 50s, you've lived through a lot, so how do you get to benefit from your personal experience? That's what I'm talking about—in a way seriously, but at the same time I hafto laugh at the absurdity of it all and in a way, laughing, is the best medicine in the end.

Zaro: You always look amazing, and wear the most inventive, witty, colorful outfits—is that part of the Kominsky Code?

Right: **In London, 2004, 56 years old**

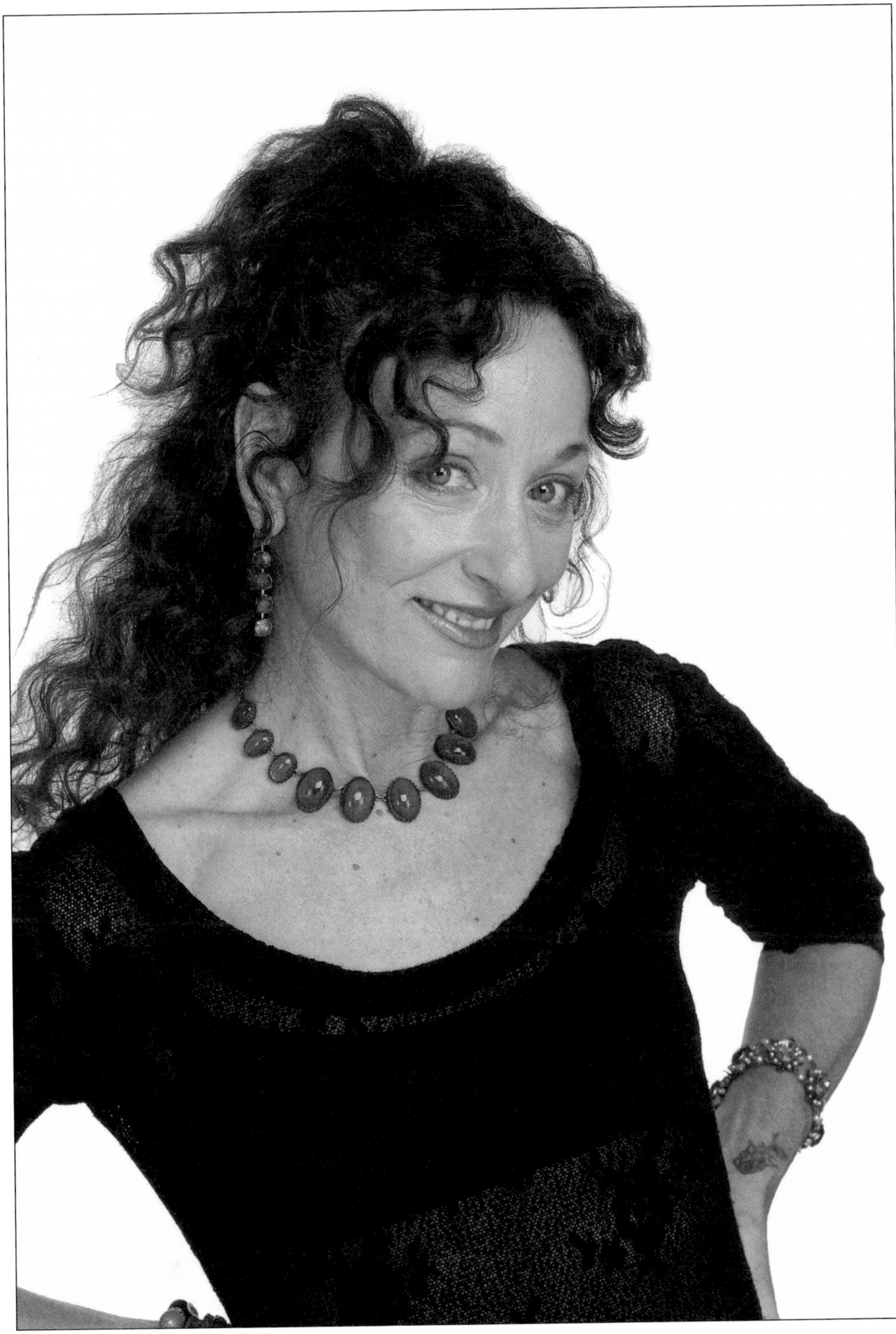

Aline: Well, I think that at a certain age you stop caring so much about what's supposed to be in style, and you kind of figure out what you can get away with. You have certain weaknesses and certain strengths, and hopefully, at this point in time, you will have confronted those. You'll know what your style is and then you can go with that and develop it to its extreme. Since I'm a painter—I need to have color everywhere, in my painting, in my house, and in my clothes. When I get dressed in the morning, I feel a certain color attracting me really strongly, and I go with that theme, and decorate myself the same way you would decorate a Christmas tree.

Zaro: Robert refers to you as "my little Christmas tree."

Aline: Yes! I am my own Christmas tree, and I always like to look and feel festive. I want to be always ready for a great party, I love excess! On the other hand, I always stop when the color reaches a point that feels perfect. That's the positive side of being old and experienced—I have stopped worrying about what people will think and about being in style. This gives me the freedom to "play."

Zaro: How would you describe your personal style?

Aline: I pick and choose from various things and take what I like, without having to justify or rationalize everything that I do. It might be a designer item that looks good on me: I'll mix that with a dress I made from a bedspread, and something else I found in a clothing swap meet, then another thing I bought in a mid-price store, and I'll use all those elements to create my particular "look." I know exactly where I'm going with it, the picture is already formed in my mind—I have a very definite style. I know what I can do, and what I need—colors, shape, everything.

Zaro: A lot of people might say, well I'm not an artist, and I don't have that brilliant color sense, so I'll just take what's on offer in chain stores.

Aline: Actually, I think everybody does have some color sense, and I think you can find ways to develop that. I'm not saying that you have to wear Day-Glo orange, but surely there are flowers in your garden that delight you, there are beautiful art objects and paintings that you love? Everyone responds to color—you just have to find out which ones turn you on. If it's beige, so be it, if it's totally white, that's okay too. But I do think, at this point in your life, you need to know exactly what color does for you. If you don't know, look at art, and beautiful things in nature to find forms and colors and shapes that appeal to you. Then incorporate all that into your personal style, and into your daily life, in as many ways as you can.

328

The end result is different for everybody, but you should feel liberated enough to do your own thing. When you dress that way you're viewing yourself in a completely new light. You go with what you have—you're not trying to look like a model or a movie star. You're playing with your image in a very different way. As you get older you have the liberty to be yourself. Younger people love to be different, but they're being different as a group. Like you see these Japanese kids who dress in incredible fantasy styles, that's great, but they're just part of a whole bunch of kids doing that. Then you'll see the amazing urban looks that kids put together. But there are constraints on that too—mainly about whether it's cool or not cool. But me, I don't care. I don't have a cool or not cool. I don't have to go by that anymore. I'm free of it and that is the advantage of getting older, I think.

When someone has found their personal style, I feel very comfortable with them, even if it's not at all my taste! In fact, it can be completely the opposite of what I like, but if they're doing exactly what they want, I really enjoy it. When I meet someone who hasn't found their own look I have an urge to do a makeover on them, and that's how I can tell. If people are wearing bad fashion choices, it makes me really uncomfortable.

It has nothing to do with whether they're a great beauty, or if they have a fabulous figure—it's about whether they have found their distinctive look, their inner essence. Take someone who is dressed completely in white—maybe white linen with a hat and flat shoes and incredibly geometric lines, something like that—that's kind of the opposite of me but if it works on them, I can thoroughly appreciate it. I can't pull that look off at all, but it's nice to see someone else do it right. By now I know myself so well, that I can tell right away if something stands a chance of looking good on me … I can see some totally gawgeous item and know that I will look horrible in it, I can also look at something in a pile of rags and envision immediately how to make it work for me.

Zaro: Where do you get your design ideas?

Aline: I get inspired by nature—there's nothing more perfect and beautiful than the geometric forms in nature, in flowers, in seashells—if that sounds trite, take another look at the natural forms around you. Quite often I'm inspired by children's clothes and their fable/fairytale connections. Also, of course, it's art that inspires me, and crass popular culture as well; I don't keep these elements separate, try to incorporate them more pervasively into my life and my look.

329

Zaro: How do you stay a size 2? I mean, your body is like a 22 year-old.

Aline: Oh darling! I was always a chunky, athletic girl in high school and I did a lot of sports. But that was in the 1950s and being sporty just wasn't cool for girls. So I gradually suppressed my physicality and wore a girdle and pointy shoes. Later, during the liberated 60s, I discovered dance, yoga, hiking, and other ways to be physical. In my twenties I settled down with my husband in rural California. I started cooking and baking for fun, and also to try and fatten up my skinny mate. He stayed the same weight and I gained 30 pounds! We were isolated in the country—there were no gyms close by—so I started to run around a field of tomatoes. This was neither hi-tech nor glamorous, but it worked. (I later found that the farm workers were betting on my times around the field—just like a horse!)

Over the years I have done Jazzercise, Jane Fonda, weight training, high intensity aerobics, African dance—you name it, I've enjoyed it all. A lot depends on what's available, who is teaching, and who's participating.

I love to move my body, and I have a lot of energy, but if you're not naturally athletic you'll find it more of a challenge to stay fit. I've been teaching my own classes for the last eight years in my village in France. I have a wide variety of students in terms of age and fitness levels. I now concentrate on a short dance warm-up and do mainly Pilates for abs and butt, and yoga for everything else. I end with meditation and breathing.

One thing I must say: if you hate sports but know that you must do something to stave off total deterioration, yoga is best for you. Remember, it's been around for thousands of years. And forget about age being a negative factor. At 58, I've never looked better: I have a trimmer body and more energy and stamina than when I was 25. If you're walking and breathing then there's hope for you! You don't have to be perky, or sporty, or politically correct to be in shape: you can be bohemian, eccentric, artistic, intellectual, left-wing or right-wing, or even existentially alienated and still benefit from becoming totally fit.

If you've reached middle age without any serious health problems, you need to keep strong, avoid osteoporosis, and build muscle. That way, you have a chance to continue to do all kinds of incredible things in the world with all the wisdom that you have acquired in your life. Our generation is incredibly healthy. My grandmother looked about 100 at my age—but people of our age look incredible because we've figured a few things out.

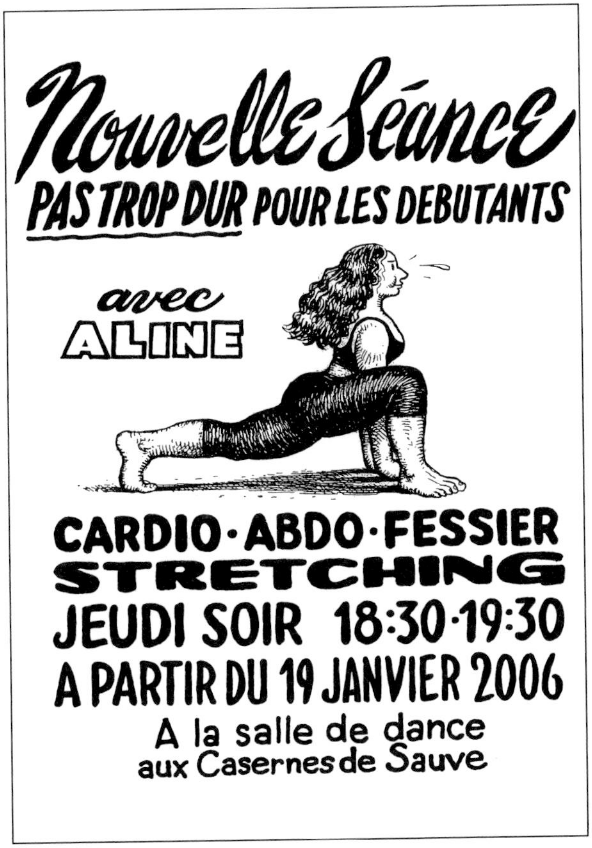
Nouvelle Séance
PAS TROP DUR POUR LES DEBUTANTS
avec
ALINE
CARDIO·ABDO·FESSIER
STRETCHING
JEUDI SOIR 18:30·19:30
A PARTIR DU 19 JANVIER 2006
A la salle de dance
aux Casernes de Sauve

Left: **Poster made by Robert for my exercise class in France**

Below: **My class, in our medieval gym**

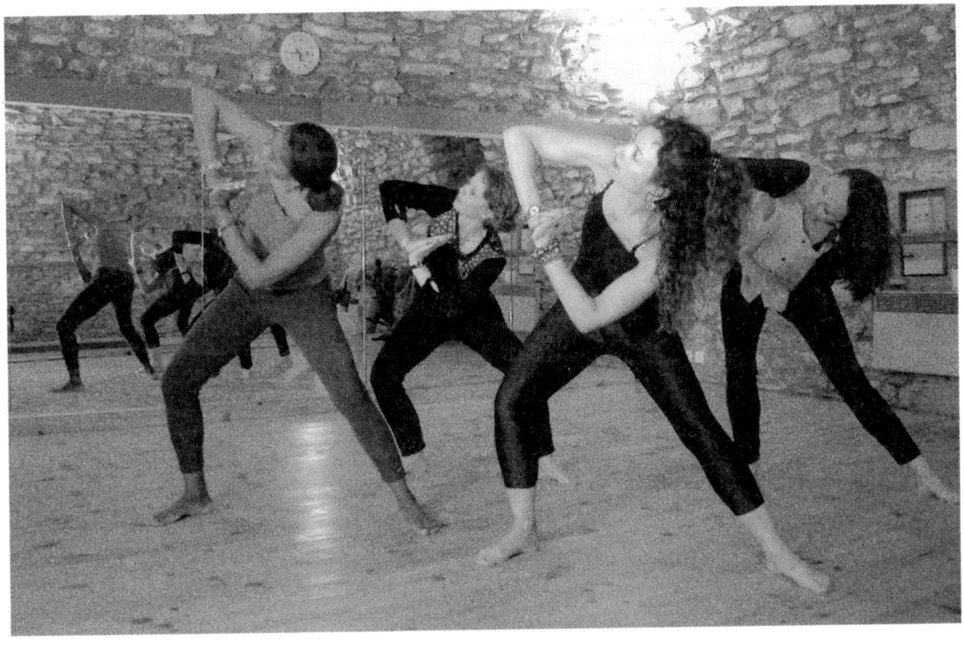

Zaro: Some people will read this interview, and look at the book, and look at your pictures and say, "oh my God, I can't be like her, she's too perfect." So do you feel perfect?

Aline: Okay, I have cellulite on my outer thighs … and I've very small breasts and I'm sort of pear-shaped naturally. I have inherited my grandma Fanny's dewlaps, which we call "Jew laps," and that goes along with the positive side of being an Ashkenazi Jew. You have a very high IQ. The negative side is that you get dewlaps and jowls. So anyway, what else? Oily skin … which was bad as a teen but now it's helpful and big knees, which can go either way!

Zaro: Well that's all physical—is there anything else, or do we sail through?

Aline: No, I'm completely pushy and overbearing and I'm a know-it-all, and I'm not too tolerant of laziness, and I have also been through periods of being very overweight. There have been times in my life when I've been a total slob, not caring about things. I've also been through periods of alcohol excess, and I've smoked, so it's not like I'm this pure, saintly person who hasn't done anything. I've done it all, and to excess. I'm a person of excess, but I've just realized recently: that's it! All that's over for this lifetime. I have to be serious now or it's all over! That's what I'm dealing with in the comic strip on the following pages!

Life's actually more tolerable now. I find that lucidity, and clear-headedness is enjoyable, as compared to being drunk, or stoned, or addicted to sex, over-eating or obsessively collecting stuff. Lucidity is actually amazing. I'm able to access my ideas faster and my vision is clearer. It's all in there: I've spent my life acquiring knowledge, whether I knew it or not. I've stopped messing myself up, stopped being neurotic, and freed myself from addictive behavior, so I can actually see straight! I think to myself: "You've lived a whole life already, and you're still here. You're healthy, you're breathing, you're moving around, and there's an incredible resource there within you." That's pretty much true for everyone, I think.

Zaro: That self-deprecating thing you mentioned earlier—I remember talking to Calvin Reid from *Publisher's Weekly* in America, he said that I should do a book with your work, because some of Robert's work was influenced by you—the fact that you could look closely at every pimple. Also, this self-deprecating aspect, the real baldness, was so brave, and it's something that a number of other cartoonists, both male and female, picked up on.

Aline: Yeah, well I don't like to take credit for all of that, I think that comic art was already going in that direction, and certainly Justin Green, who did *Binky Brown Meets the Holy Virgin Mary,* and inspired me, was as honest as you can get. But I was raised on a certain kind of Jewish fatalistic humor, like the stand-up comics of the 1950s, and the storytelling in my family, where you make fun of yourself, to make other people laugh. You exaggerate in a certain way, and it's all to make a philosophical point, and also to get people to relax and to respond to you. I was raised with that kind of east coast Jewish humor, and it has pervaded my entire life. And certainly, in my comic storytelling, there's my grandpa Joe, who was a great storyteller. And his style comes from a very old tradition of Jewish storytelling, and Jewish writing. So I sort of took that tradition of Jewish self-deprecating humor, and applied it to comics, and perhaps that was unique.

Right: **Ready for action with my basket of free weights, London, 2003**
I'm wearing my Scotty dog dress that I bought at a flea market in Sacramento, California, in the 1970s.
Next page: **A painful comic strip, 2004**
Inspired by a dream I had after I quit drinking wine

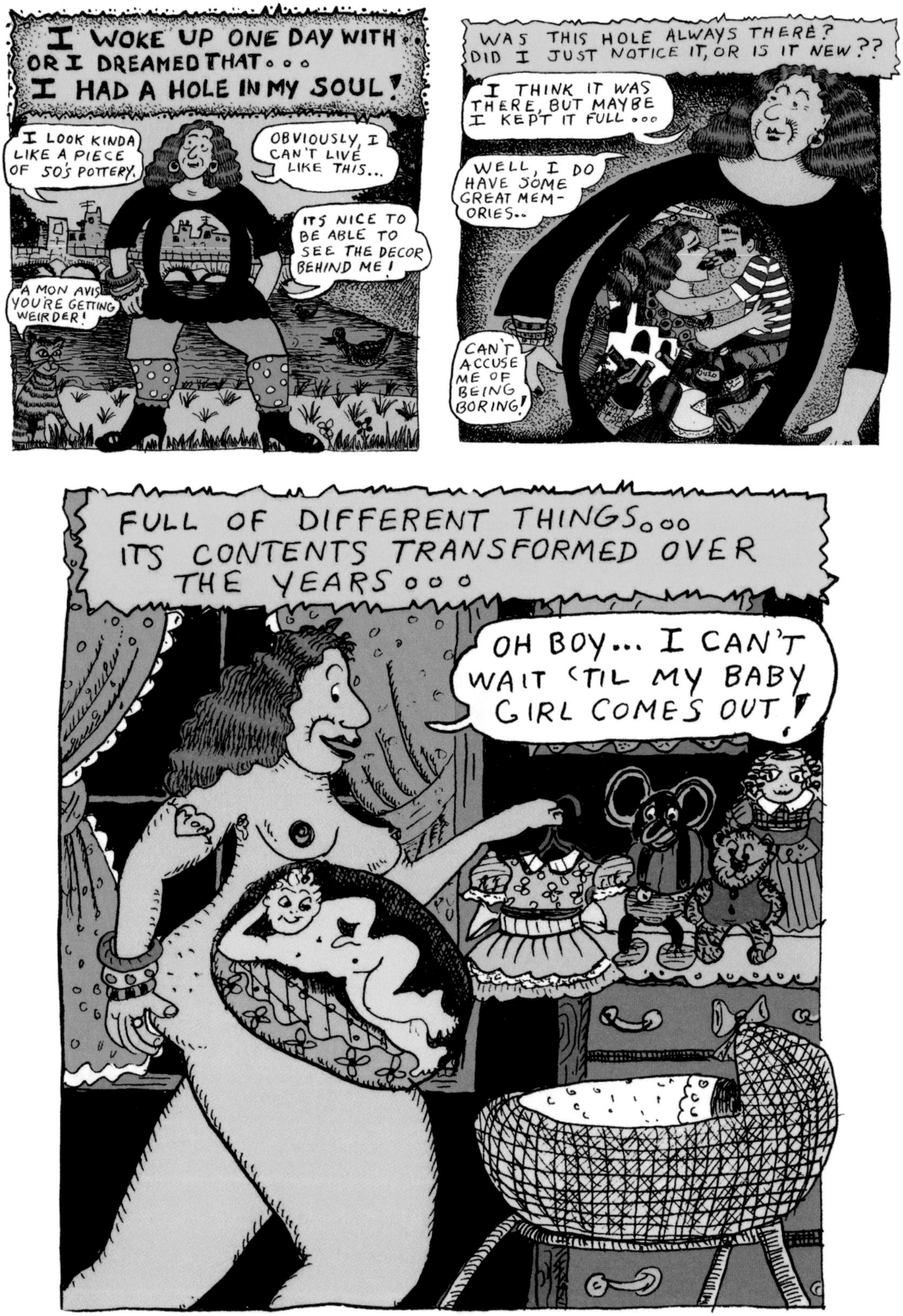
I WOKE UP ONE DAY WITH OR I DREAMED THAT... I HAD A HOLE IN MY SOUL!
I LOOK KINDA LIKE A PIECE OF 50'S POTTERY.
OBVIOUSLY, I CAN'T LIVE LIKE THIS...
ITS NICE TO BE ABLE TO SEE THE DECOR BEHIND ME!
A MON AVIS YOU'RE GETTING WEIRDER!
WAS THIS HOLE ALWAYS THERE? DID I JUST NOTICE IT, OR IS IT NEW??
I THINK IT WAS THERE, BUT MAYBE I KEPT IT FULL...
WELL, I DO HAVE SOME GREAT MEMORIES..
CAN'T ACCUSE ME OF BEING BORING!
FULL OF DIFFERENT THINGS... ITS CONTENTS TRANSFORMED OVER THE YEARS...
OH BOY... I CAN'T WAIT 'TIL MY BABY GIRL COMES OUT!

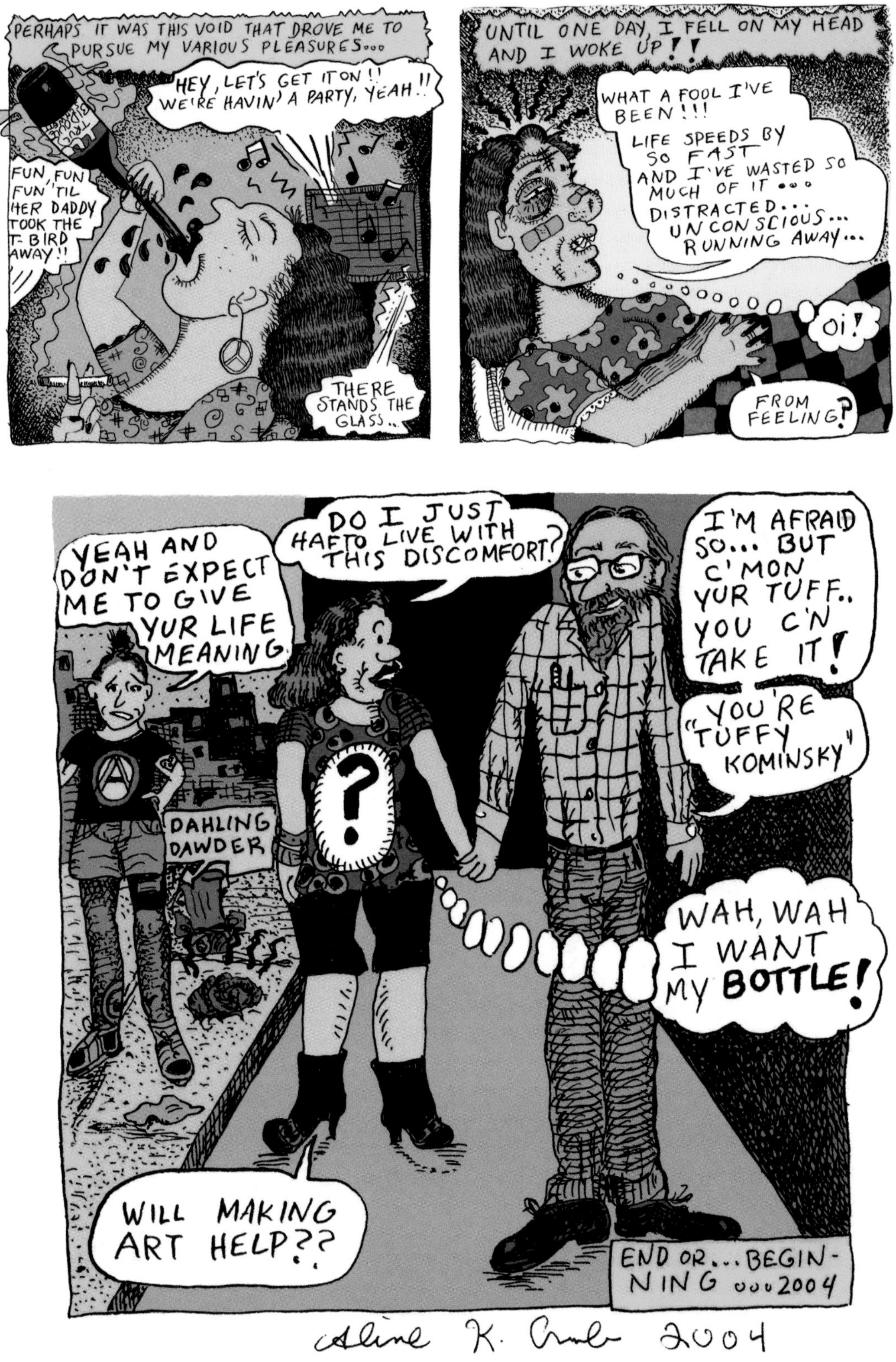
PERHAPS IT WAS THIS VOID THAT DROVE ME TO PURSUE MY VARIOUS PLEASURES...
HEY, LET'S GET IT ON!! WE'RE HAVIN' A PARTY, YEAH!!
FUN, FUN FUN 'TIL HER DADDY TOOK THE T-BIRD AWAY!!
THERE STANDS THE GLASS..
UNTIL ONE DAY, I FELL ON MY HEAD AND I WOKE UP!!
WHAT A FOOL I'VE BEEN!!!
LIFE SPEEDS BY SO FAST AND I'VE WASTED SO MUCH OF IT... DISTRACTED... UNCONSCIOUS... RUNNING AWAY...
OI!
FROM FEELING?
YEAH AND DON'T EXPECT ME TO GIVE YUR LIFE MEANING
DO I JUST HAFTO LIVE WITH THIS DISCOMFORT?
I'M AFRAID SO... BUT C'MON YUR TUFF.. YOU C'N TAKE IT!
"YOU'RE "TUFFY KOMINSKY"
DAHLING DAWDER
WAH, WAH I WANT MY BOTTLE!
WILL MAKING ART HELP??
END OR... BEGINNING ...2004
Aline K. Crumb 2004

Zaro: Has being Robert Crumb's wife made it any harder for you to come forward with your own work?

Aline: It's not made it any harder for me to do the work, but it has made it harder for other people to see me as a separate artist, and take me seriously. Therefore in the long run, it has discouraged me because I had very little response to my work. For example, Robert and I work together in what we call "dirty laundry" style, where he draws himself and writes his own dialogue, and I draw myself and write my own dialogue. And we've been working that way together for 30 years. Recently in the last few years, we've been doing work in the *New Yorker* together, including strips about New York Fashion Week, about the Cannes Film Festival and other aspects of our life.

Zaro: And the response from the *New Yorker* pieces has been phenomenal.

Aline: Absolutely phenomenal, but a lot of people think that Robert draws and writes the whole thing. They don't realize that I'm in there too, and that has completely astounded me, because our drawing styles and our voices are so different. It makes me realize that people aren't very observant, and who knows—all these years, they may have been thinking that Robert's been drawing and writing all my things, I've no idea. So that also makes me want to get my work out there, separately from his. I think it's important to distinguish my art as a body of work in its own right, and I hope people are ready to see that. My work is very different.

You asked me has it been hard living with him? He's been extremely supportive of me as an artist, so as I said, it hasn't been hard for me to work, it's just that it's been difficult to know how to get it out there, and how to deal with people's reactions to me. I've got this huge body of work, but I've never known what to do with it. And I also think that I've been a little bit afraid of success. I've seen what's happened to Robert, and how his life changed as a result of becoming very successful, and I think it made me hold back somewhat also.

Right: **Silkscreen print by Robert, 2005**
In front of Robert's famous 78rpm record collection

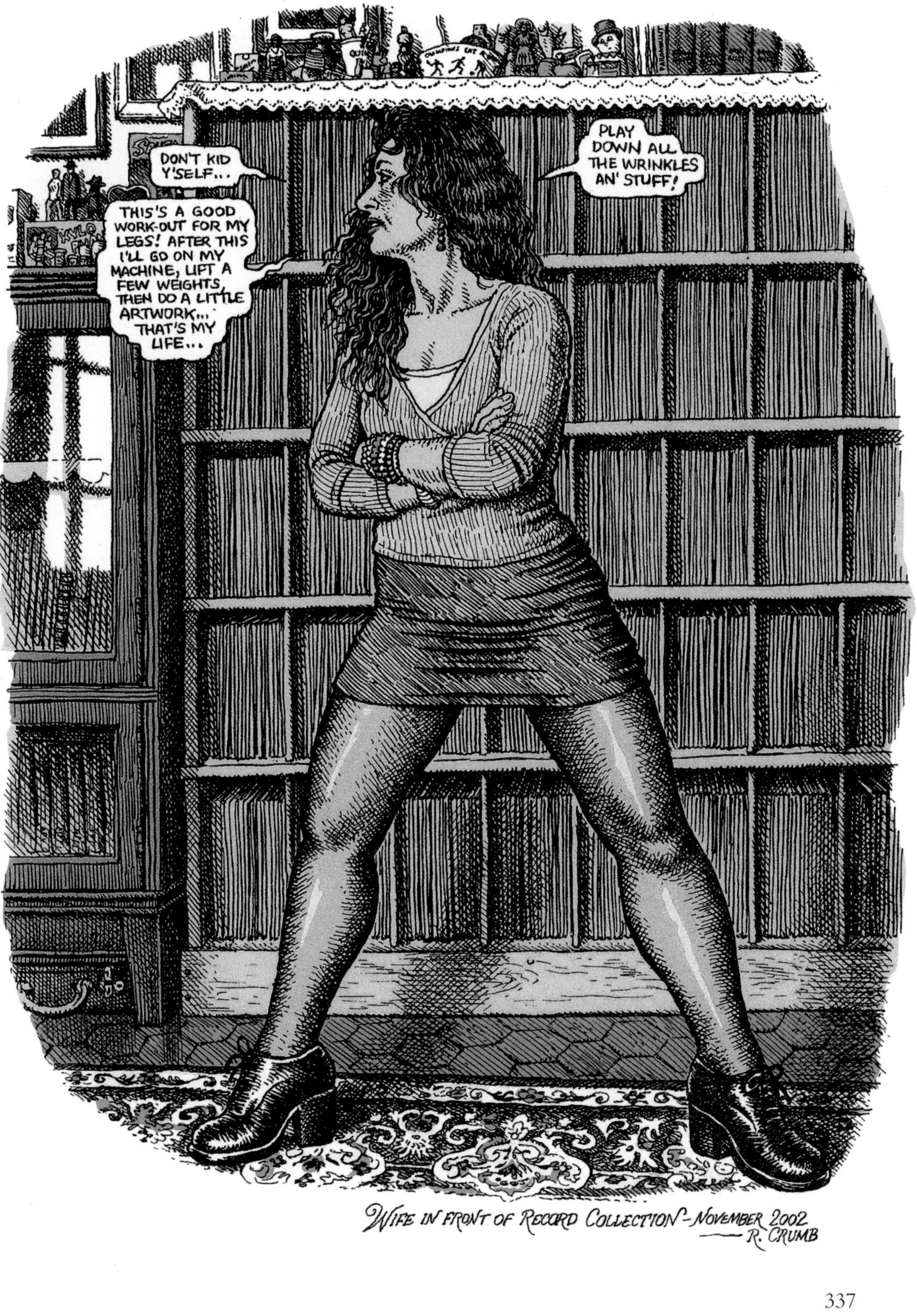
DON'T KID Y'SELF...
THIS'S A GOOD WORK-OUT FOR MY LEGS! AFTER THIS I'LL GO ON MY MACHINE, LIFT A FEW WEIGHTS, THEN DO A LITTLE ARTWORK... THAT'S MY LIFE...
PLAY DOWN ALL THE WRINKLES AN' STUFF!

WIFE IN FRONT OF RECORD COLLECTION - NOVEMBER 2002
— R. CRUMB

Zaro: I'm fascinated that you have so carefully chronicled your life over the years—most people don't save all the things that you've kept and organized.

Aline: I think that's very true—at some level, I've always felt like a pioneer, always one step ahead, breaking ground in some way. I felt like an alien in that Long Island environment where I grew up, and I always felt slightly removed from everything. So I think I chronicled everything because I felt like a witness in a certain way. I was always a little bit detached, so I recorded life around me from very early on. I also felt like I was out there on the cutting edge—I was doing completely crazy things and inventing my life. At the same time, as an artist and writer, I was also keeping track of it, so I always had those two things going on. I also think doing that helped me to keep my sanity: my way of clarifying what was going on was to write about it after something had happened. And that's how I got into doing autobiographical comics too—it was a logical extension of keeping notebooks and painting from the time I was eight years old, and then moving onto the next level of making coherent stories, to communicate to other people. Writing comics is like writing storyboards for films—lots of film-makers actually started as cartoonists, like Federico Fellini, Scorsese … it's very closely related to the way that you set up the whole storyboard, the dialogue and the visuals. It's a similar art form, and also very logical. I never wanted to be a filmmaker, but those stories with words and pictures do have a cinematic atmosphere. But as I say, I've always felt like one step removed from myself. I was the commentator on your shoulder and the actress at the same time.

Zaro: Why do you think your generation—the Baby Boomers—are so important today?

Aline: Well, we are the children of the people I call the "post-war jerks." We became the '60s generation, and are a unique group. Baby boomers worldwide revolutionized everything, nothing's been the same since then. I meet younger people in their twenties who say "You're so lucky you lived during the 1960s!" The post-war period was an incredibly sterile shutdown with McCarthyism, nuclear terror, and the fear of liberal views. And it was driven by a crazed economic striving, capitalist in the extreme—and a sanitized, smug view of life. We kids rebelled against all that in the most violent way. I think that living that out and surviving it is the important story of my generation, and of that post-war period. Many young people now look to us for inspiration, to see how we revolted against that horrible repression, because it's happening again now. We're back in the 1950s again in many ways, with Bush, and his fundamentalist, warlike Christian mentality. Maybe it's even worse than before—and this young generation needs to find ways to evolve beyond that. Of course I think it's an important story.

Zaro: I agree, I often feel that the subsequent generations have kind of let us down, because they haven't fought hard enough. Nobody has been willing to stand up in sufficient numbers. There's been an enormous crisis of faith.

Aline: Well, it's a mess here in France also, but here the people do take to the streets—at least they feel that they have some chance of changing things, and they feel it's their right to demonstrate when they don't think things are okay. The Americans are asleep politically, and it's because material glut has lulled them into a kind of stupor. Americans are always saying "our First Amendment rights, our rights!" I feel that the only right they have left now is to consume 24 hours a day. They've given up all the other freedoms, except the right to consume. Stores are open 24 hours a day, they can eat and buy, they have endless credit, and they mainly exercise the right to keep consuming, consuming, and consuming.

When people feel depressed, or feel empty, they often go out and buy something new—so consuming has become a kind of religion, a spiritual activity, a comfort. And I think part of the reason you have this huge Christian movement in America, is that people know on some level that their lives are empty, and they seek something more. Unfortunately what they've chosen is, I think, not terribly evolved, but people do need an outlet. In America, there's no sense of community any more, there's no center, there's no sense of ordinary belonging, or a culture that you can wrap yourself around, be involved in, and identify with. You go to the mall and you buy things, and you live at home in an isolated island of comfort with every kind of stimulation possible, your computer, your great sound system, whatever, and yet you're more and more cut off from other people.

Zaro: You're an incredibly prolific artist apart from your comics. How do you choose the subjects for this other kind of artwork?

Aline: Well quite often I recycle plastic objects and other junk that I actually find grotesque, or even things I find in the garbage, things that people throw away. There's so much crap produced by rich western societies, I have become perversely fascinated with it. I find the ugliest, weirdest, manufactured items. I put these together to make something that I hope

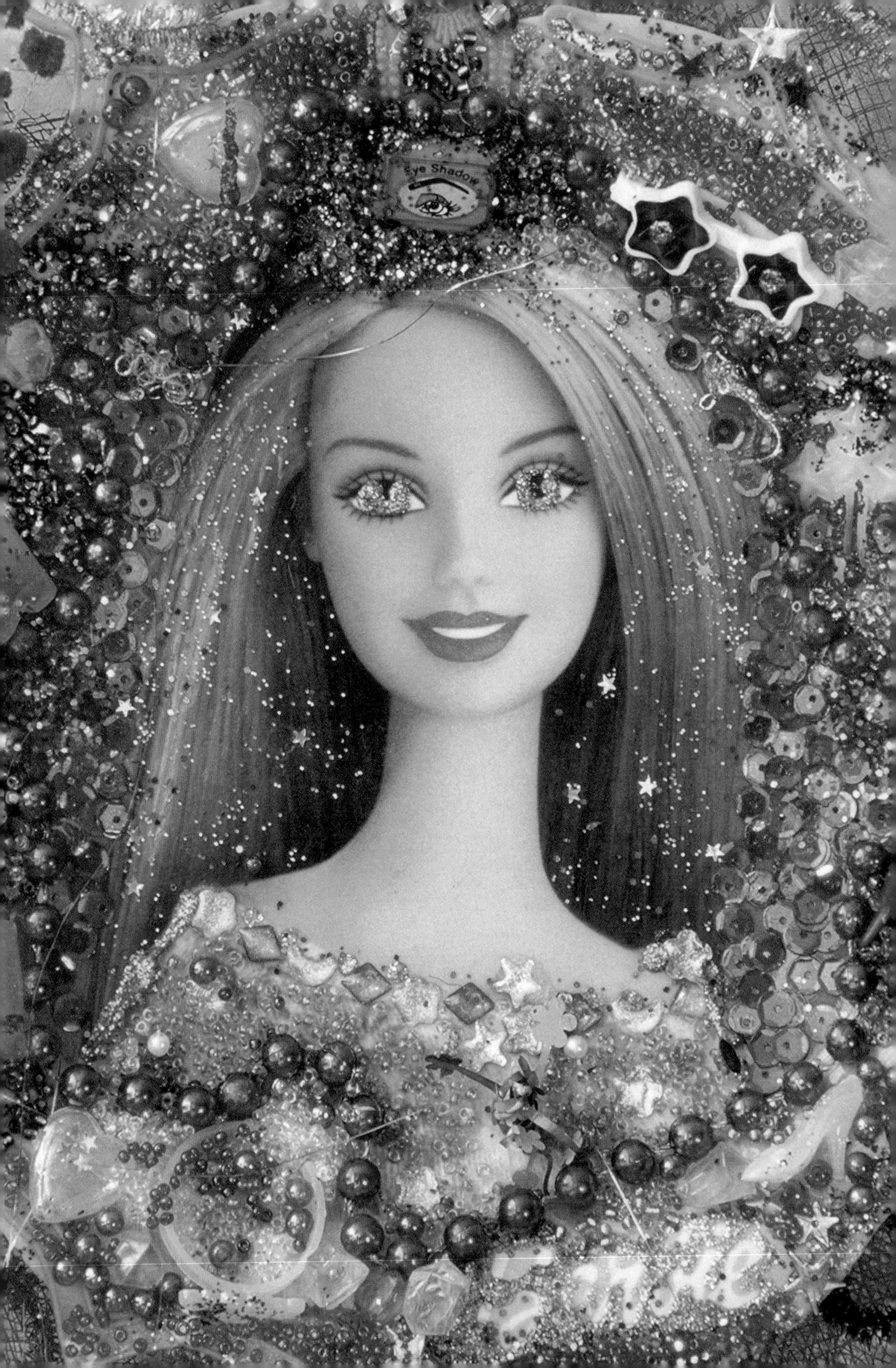
Eye Shadow

becomes a sacred object; I'm trying to recycle the garbage and the horror of the material world around me and turn it into something beautiful, and to put it in a context that hopefully can be provocative.

Zaro: The other theme that runs through your contemporary work is a sort of sexual violence, having to do with fairytale, and a kind of lost Eden.

Aline: I feel that the myths that our society is based on, including religious myths, are a means for people who want power to control us; I think these myths are perverse, as are fairytales, as is the Bible. They are foisted on us from the time we're children.

When I'm painting objects that are supposed to be cute—dolls and other toys designed for children to play with—I feel they're imbued with evil and treachery. They have a terrible quality of fake innocence, manufactured by middle-aged men who just want to make money. So, when I work with these plastic toys, all that perversity is revealed and I'm telling stories about all that in my paintings, and reflecting all the intrinsic phoniness and hypocrisy. In fact, this fake, plastic innocence is so corrupt, that I see it as evil—that's what I read into it—but talking about "Aht" after the fact, is kind of meaningless, 'cause when I'm working I have no idea why I'm doing anything. It comes from the deep, murky unknown!

Zaro: What are you striving for in your life and art?

Aline: I'm trying to create something that is influenced as little as possible by all the commercial forces out there that want to tell me what to buy and what to do. I'm trying to live in a way that keeps my brain from being constantly occupied by what's being thrown out by the media.

I want to pick and choose, and control what I'm taking in, so as not to be controlled by it. And then I want to create art that makes sense to me and that hopefully says something to somebody else as well. I mainly have to please myself and make things I want to look at all the time and live in an environment that continually arouses me!

I want to look in the mirror and laugh, I want to excite myself and I want to feel good. I know that people react to me strongly. I create some kind of force out there, and I even want to be provocative in a way. I'm willing to make myself an object of derision, or admiration, whatever it is. I'm willing to expose myself and provoke a reaction in both life and art.

Left: **Aline Crumb, "The Unobtainable Perfection of Barbie," 2003**
Collage, plastic on plastic
Next page: **"Fashion Week in New York" comic strip, the *New Yorker* magazine, 2003**

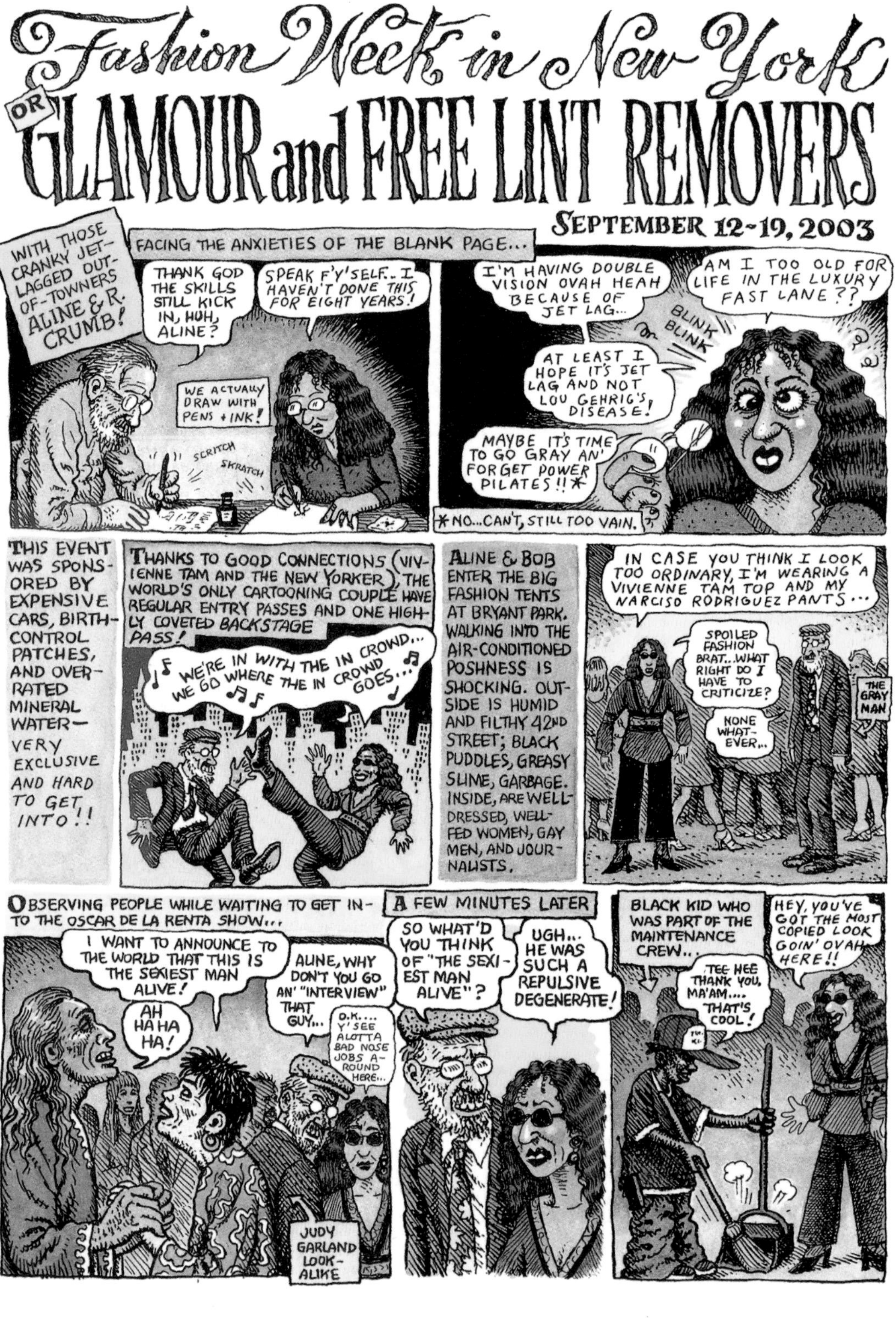

Fashion Week in New York
OR
GLAMOUR and FREE LINT REMOVERS
SEPTEMBER 12~19, 2003
WITH THOSE CRANKY JET-LAGGED OUT-OF-TOWNERS ALINE & R. CRUMB!
FACING THE ANXIETIES OF THE BLANK PAGE...
THANK GOD THE SKILLS STILL KICK IN, HUH, ALINE?
SPEAK F'Y'SELF.. I HAVEN'T DONE THIS FOR EIGHT YEARS!
WE ACTUALLY DRAW WITH PENS + INK!
SCRITCH
SKRATCH
I'M HAVING DOUBLE VISION OVAH HEAH BECAUSE OF JET LAG...
AM I TOO OLD FOR LIFE IN THE LUXURY FAST LANE??
BLINK
BLINK
AT LEAST I HOPE IT'S JET LAG AND NOT LOU GEHRIG'S DISEASE!
MAYBE IT'S TIME TO GO GRAY AN' FORGET POWER PILATES!!*
*NO...CAN'T, STILL TOO VAIN.
THIS EVENT WAS SPONSORED BY EXPENSIVE CARS, BIRTH-CONTROL PATCHES, AND OVER-RATED MINERAL WATER— VERY EXCLUSIVE AND HARD TO GET INTO!!
THANKS TO GOOD CONNECTIONS (VIVIENNE TAM AND THE NEW YORKER), THE WORLD'S ONLY CARTOONING COUPLE HAVE REGULAR ENTRY PASSES AND ONE HIGHLY COVETED BACKSTAGE PASS!
WE'RE IN WITH THE IN CROWD... WE GO WHERE THE IN CROWD GOES...
ALINE & BOB ENTER THE BIG FASHION TENTS AT BRYANT PARK. WALKING INTO THE AIR-CONDITIONED POSHNESS IS SHOCKING. OUTSIDE IS HUMID AND FILTHY 42ND STREET; BLACK PUDDLES, GREASY SLIME, GARBAGE. INSIDE, ARE WELL-DRESSED, WELL-FED WOMEN, GAY MEN, AND JOURNALISTS.
IN CASE YOU THINK I LOOK TOO ORDINARY, I'M WEARING A VIVIENNE TAM TOP AND MY NARCISO RODRIGUEZ PANTS...
SPOILED FASHION BRAT...WHAT RIGHT DO I HAVE TO CRITICIZE?
NONE WHATEVER...
THE GRAY MAN
OBSERVING PEOPLE WHILE WAITING TO GET INTO THE OSCAR DE LA RENTA SHOW...
I WANT TO ANNOUNCE TO THE WORLD THAT THIS IS THE SEXIEST MAN ALIVE!
AH HA HA HA!
ALINE, WHY DON'T YOU GO AN' "INTERVIEW" THAT GUY...
O.K.... Y'SEE ALOTTA BAD NOSE JOBS AROUND HERE...
JUDY GARLAND LOOK-ALIKE
A FEW MINUTES LATER
SO WHAT'D YOU THINK OF "THE SEXIEST MAN ALIVE"?
UGH... HE WAS SUCH A REPULSIVE DEGENERATE!
BLACK KID WHO WAS PART OF THE MAINTENANCE CREW...
HEY, YOU'VE GOT THE MOST COPIED LOOK GOIN' OVAH HERE!!
TEE HEE THANK YOU, MA'AM.... THAT'S COOL!

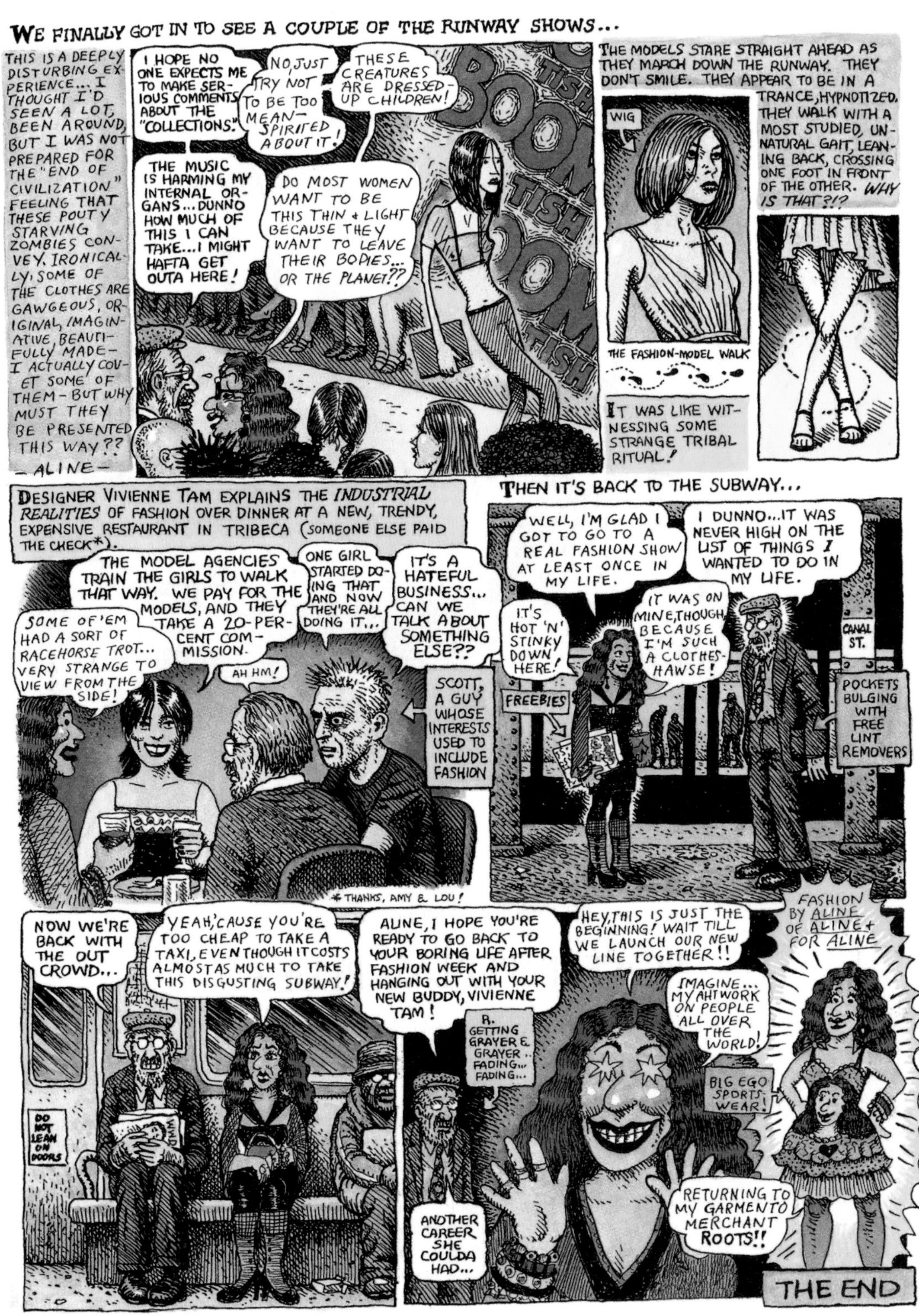
WE FINALLY GOT IN TO SEE A COUPLE OF THE RUNWAY SHOWS...
THIS IS A DEEPLY DISTURBING EXPERIENCE... I THOUGHT I'D SEEN A LOT, BEEN AROUND, BUT I WAS NOT PREPARED FOR THE "END OF CIVILIZATION" FEELING THAT THESE POUTY STARVING ZOMBIES CONVEY. IRONICALLY, SOME OF THE CLOTHES ARE GAWGEOUS, ORIGINAL, IMAGINATIVE, BEAUTIFULLY MADE- I ACTUALLY COVET SOME OF THEM - BUT WHY MUST THEY BE PRESENTED THIS WAY?? -ALINE-
I HOPE NO ONE EXPECTS ME TO MAKE SERIOUS COMMENTS ABOUT THE "COLLECTIONS."
NO, JUST TRY NOT TO BE TOO MEAN-SPIRITED ABOUT IT!
THESE CREATURES ARE DRESSED-UP CHILDREN!
THE MUSIC IS HARMING MY INTERNAL ORGANS... DUNNO HOW MUCH OF THIS I CAN TAKE... I MIGHT HAFTA GET OUTA HERE!
DO MOST WOMEN WANT TO BE THIS THIN & LIGHT BECAUSE THEY WANT TO LEAVE THEIR BODIES... OR THE PLANET??
BOOM TISH BOOM TISH BOOM TISH
THE MODELS STARE STRAIGHT AHEAD AS THEY MARCH DOWN THE RUNWAY. THEY DON'T SMILE. THEY APPEAR TO BE IN A TRANCE, HYPNOTIZED. THEY WALK WITH A MOST STUDIED, UNNATURAL GAIT, LEANING BACK, CROSSING ONE FOOT IN FRONT OF THE OTHER. WHY IS THAT?!?
WIG
THE FASHION-MODEL WALK
IT WAS LIKE WITNESSING SOME STRANGE TRIBAL RITUAL!
DESIGNER VIVIENNE TAM EXPLAINS THE INDUSTRIAL REALITIES OF FASHION OVER DINNER AT A NEW, TRENDY, EXPENSIVE RESTAURANT IN TRIBECA (SOMEONE ELSE PAID THE CHECK*).
THE MODEL AGENCIES TRAIN THE GIRLS TO WALK THAT WAY. WE PAY FOR THE MODELS, AND THEY TAKE A 20-PERCENT COMMISSION.
ONE GIRL STARTED DOING THAT AND NOW THEY'RE ALL DOING IT...
IT'S A HATEFUL BUSINESS... CAN WE TALK ABOUT SOMETHING ELSE??
SOME OF 'EM HAD A SORT OF RACEHORSE TROT... VERY STRANGE TO VIEW FROM THE SIDE!
AH HM!
SCOTT, A GUY WHOSE INTERESTS USED TO INCLUDE FASHION
* THANKS, AMY & LOU!
THEN IT'S BACK TO THE SUBWAY...
WELL, I'M GLAD I GOT TO GO TO A REAL FASHION SHOW AT LEAST ONCE IN MY LIFE.
I DUNNO... IT WAS NEVER HIGH ON THE LIST OF THINGS I WANTED TO DO IN MY LIFE.
IT'S HOT 'N' STINKY DOWN HERE!
IT WAS ON MINE, THOUGH, BECAUSE I'M SUCH A CLOTHES-HAWSE!
CANAL ST.
FREEBIES
POCKETS BULGING WITH FREE LINT REMOVERS
NOW WE'RE BACK WITH THE OUT CROWD...
YEAH, 'CAUSE YOU'RE TOO CHEAP TO TAKE A TAXI, EVEN THOUGH IT COSTS ALMOST AS MUCH TO TAKE THIS DISGUSTING SUBWAY!
DO NOT LEAN ON DOORS
ALINE, I HOPE YOU'RE READY TO GO BACK TO YOUR BORING LIFE AFTER FASHION WEEK AND HANGING OUT WITH YOUR NEW BUDDY, VIVIENNE TAM!
R. GETTING GRAYER & GRAYER... FADING... FADING...
HEY, THIS IS JUST THE BEGINNING! WAIT TILL WE LAUNCH OUR NEW LINE TOGETHER!!
FASHION BY ALINE OF ALINE + FOR ALINE
IMAGINE... MY AHTWORK ON PEOPLE ALL OVER THE WORLD!
BIG EGO SPORTSWEAR!
ANOTHER CAREER SHE COULDA HAD...
RETURNING TO MY GARMENTO MERCHANT ROOTS!!
THE END

Zaro: Why do we love shopping so much?

Aline: Well it's all there in our Long Island genes—I mean we were practically raised in Loehmans and Saks and Macy's. Genetically we've been imprinted, but also we're imprinted for change, we're stimulated by the seasons—we want to change our clothes when the fall comes, we want new sweaters and coats. There's a certain aspect of renewal in getting something new. But shopping isn't necessarily about spending and getting things. It can also be about defining and eliminating. Some of my best shopping days involve looking and trying on and fantasizing, and then deciding that I don't really want anything! I simply realize that, at the moment, there's nothing out there I'd kill for. I'm so relieved that I go home and pull things out of my closet that I've forgotten about, and re-

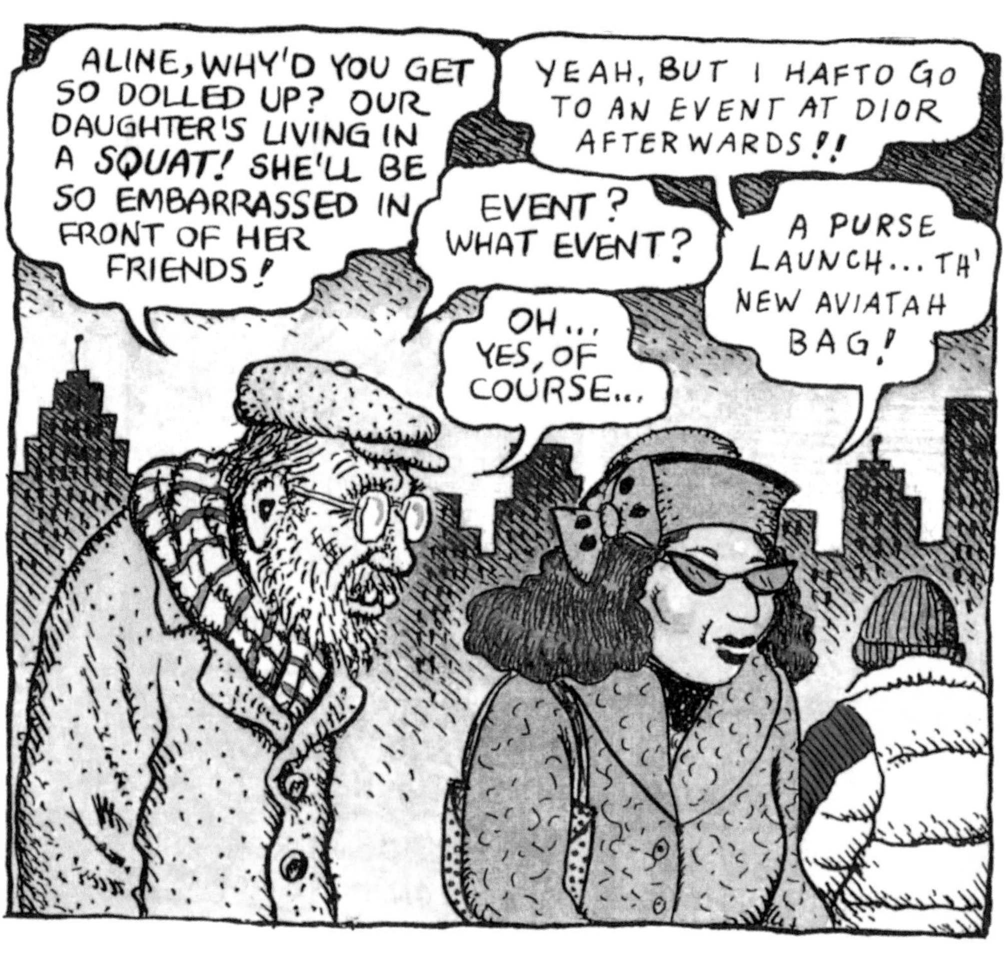

ALINE, WHY'D YOU GET SO DOLLED UP? OUR DAUGHTER'S LIVING IN A SQUAT! SHE'LL BE SO EMBARRASSED IN FRONT OF HER FRIENDS!
YEAH, BUT I HAFTO GO TO AN EVENT AT DIOR AFTERWARDS!!
EVENT? WHAT EVENT?
A PURSE LAUNCH... TH' NEW AVIATAH BAG!
OH... YES, OF COURSE...

make my look with my own clothes and accessories. There are moments when clothes and shoes reach an apex of beauty and I buy in a frenzy because it won't last. If it's a fabulous shoe year I buy multiples, because the cycle changes, and I'll find only hideous shoes for the next five years.

There are these key moments, and they must be recognized. To do this, you must have a very good sense of your own style (as you will, if you listen to me!). Also, I love really good second-hand stores: I get favorites from the good years recycled at bargain prices. I never care about what my mother says "It's what they're wearing!" Don't pay attention to fashion trends—you can easily become a fashion victim!

Below: **Panel from "Winter Wonderland" comic strip, the *New Yorker* magazine, 2006**

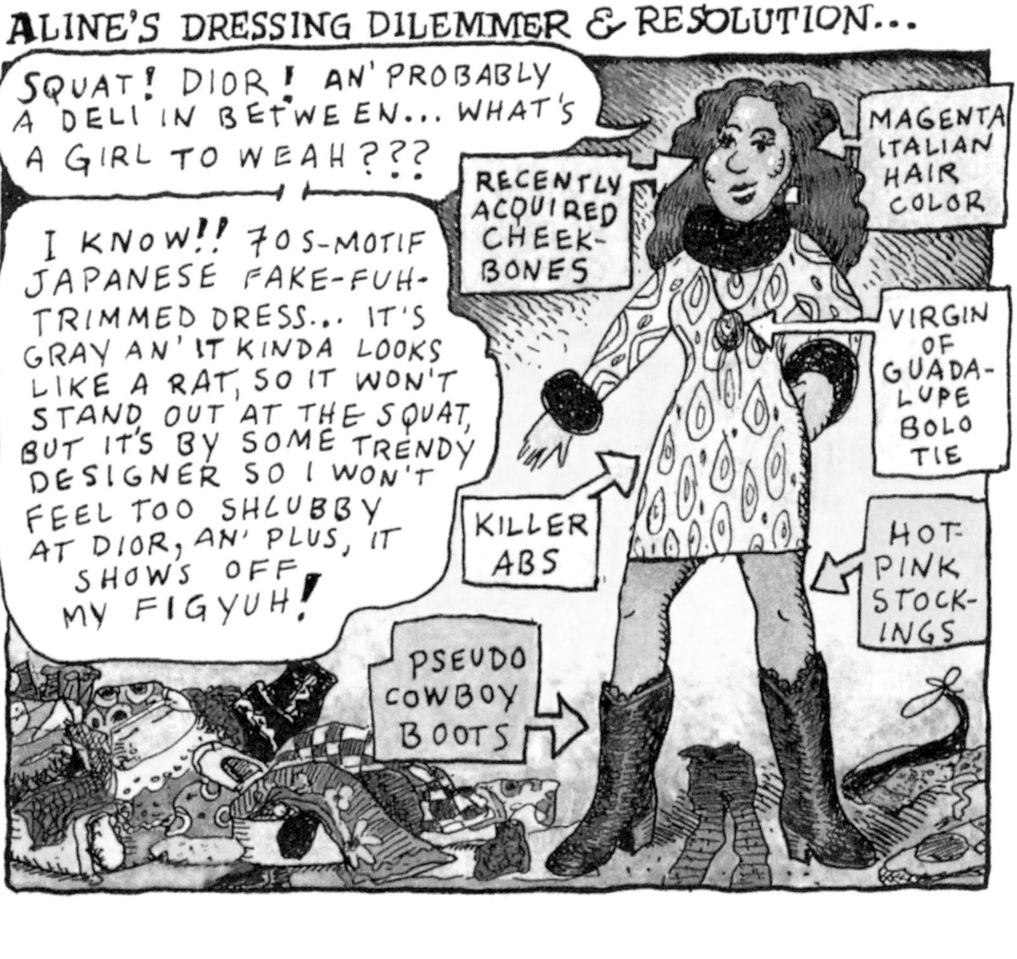
ALINE'S DRESSING DILEMMER & RESOLUTION...
SQUAT! DIOR! AN' PROBABLY A DELI IN BETWEEN... WHAT'S A GIRL TO WEAH???
I KNOW!! 70S-MOTIF JAPANESE FAKE-FUH-TRIMMED DRESS... IT'S GRAY AN' IT KINDA LOOKS LIKE A RAT, SO IT WON'T STAND OUT AT THE SQUAT, BUT IT'S BY SOME TRENDY DESIGNER SO I WON'T FEEL TOO SHLUBBY AT DIOR, AN' PLUS, IT SHOWS OFF MY FIGYUH!
RECENTLY ACQUIRED CHEEK-BONES
MAGENTA ITALIAN HAIR COLOR
VIRGIN OF GUADA-LUPE BOLO TIE
KILLER ABS
HOT-PINK STOCK-INGS
PSEUDO COWBOY BOOTS

Shopping can pick you up, just by distracting you from grim realities that perhaps you can do nothing about. There's an ancient aspect of the "hunt" involved—the satisfaction of finding the right item in a sea of junk. Plus there's the simple hope that an article of clothing, a pair of shoes—even a piece of china—will make life better! And guess what? It does—at least for a little while. That's why they call it retail therapy! Also, don't forget you're doing your bit to keep the good old economy healthy! All this applies to any budget, whether it's flea market or haute couture—the emotional and psychic results are just the same.

Zaro: How has living in France affected you?

Aline: I soon realized that older French women have got it way over older American and English women, in the sense of they know how to be sexy. They're not afraid to show it. You see middle-aged French women wearing sexy stockings and shoes, because they still have good legs, and they look fabulous. They still have bright red hair, and put on red lipstick; they wear the kind of suit or dress that flatters the figure, even if it's no longer perfect. They know how to do all that. French and Italian women also stay sexy way longer than American women. And that was one of the first things I noticed when I moved to France! I thought "Ah, there's still hope for me! I'm over 40, but I can still look sexy!" and it really has had an effect on me—a positive effect.

Zaro: Magazines are always running features about what you should wear at specific ages. And by the time you're in your 50s you might as well be dead because you're wearing beige and your skirts are a bit longer. God forbid you should wear a mini skirt or high-heeled boots. Or tight jeans.

Aline: If you're working out, why not? Personally I have to say that my body is in as good shape now as when I was in my twenties—at least in clothes, I won't talk about being naked—and why shouldn't I take advantage of that? I'm not trying to look like a teenager, but there are some things that I really like, and if I want to wear them, I'm damned well going to. When I see women walking around in what I call "all-terrain pajamas"—that horrible baggy leisurewear clothing that looks as if they've given up—I get depressed, it makes me feel sad. But when I see a woman really dressed and feeling good about herself, strutting her stuff out there, you know, colorful and everything, it totally uplifts my spirit. Actually I think we owe it to other people to make an effort.

Right: **A perk from my *New York Times* modeling job**
Wearing a Narciso Rodríguez outfit. Don't I look totally obnoxious?

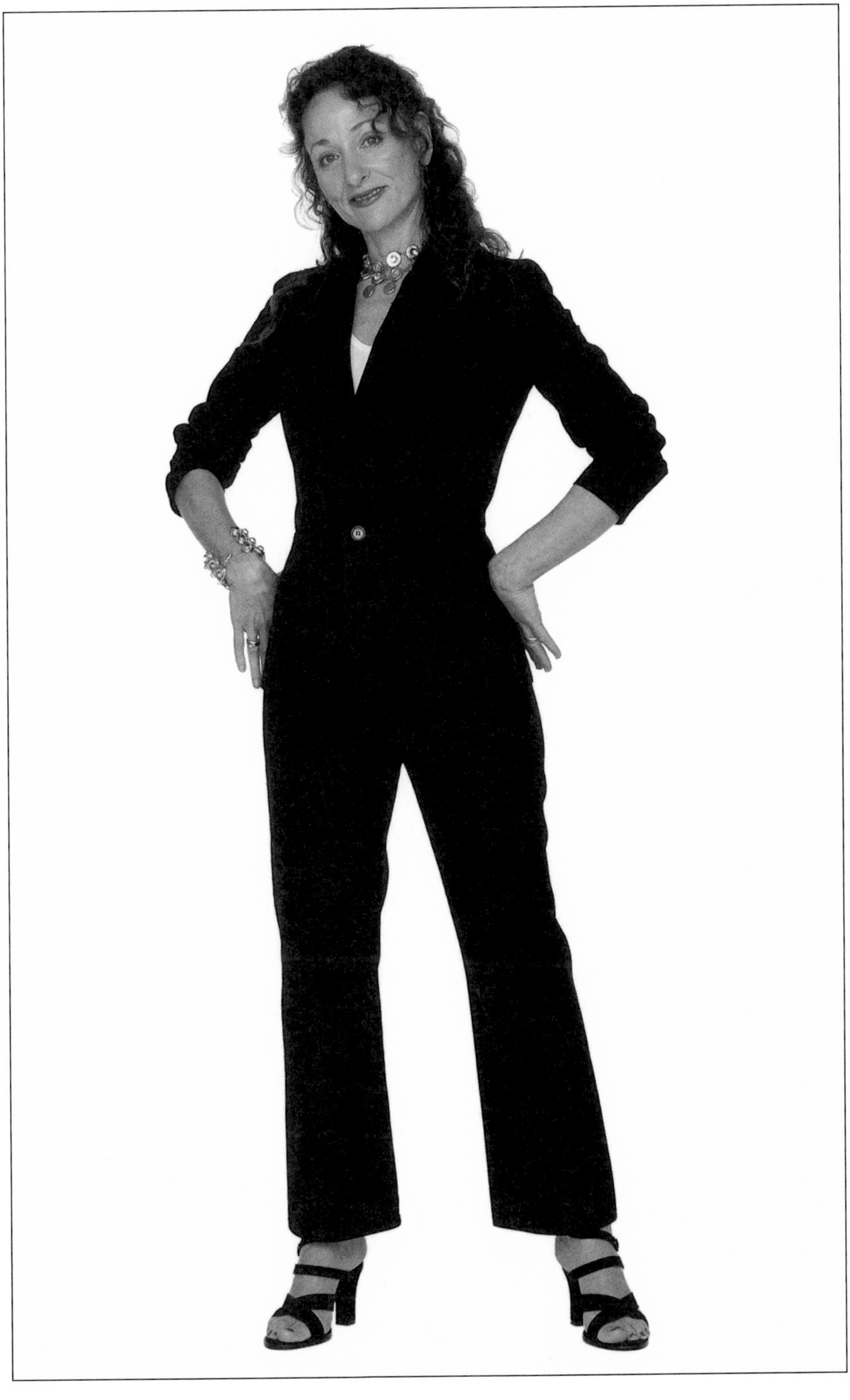

Zaro: What do you mean by that?

Aline: When you're out there and you see other women your age looking really good, it's both a pleasure to see and gives you hope. It makes you realize just how important visual appeal is. Moreover, it proves that being young is not the only phase of life in which you can look exciting. Western culture has made us think that, because it's a consumer ethos obsessed by youth. When I went to India I saw so many beautiful older Indian women: they have this lovely way of dressing and a sense of style that really works for older women. They keep their hair long, they don't have stupid hairstyles, they wear tons of jewelry and they look like queens—even the poorest people—and that was both inspiring and educational. In America, women of a certain age are supposed to become sexless, and cut their hair short because long hair means sexy. You have to wear a jogging suit or something that's baggy.

American society infantilizes older people—those leisurewear outfits that middle-aged Americans wear are just like baby clothes! You should see the difference here in France—there are women in their sixties walking around my village in high heels, mini skirts and lace stockings and I go "Wow, look at that, that looks good, it looks great!" It might not be completely perfect by model standards but it looks damn good, it's sexy, it's appealing, and I love that. I think it's important to share that.

Zaro: I know you've had some experience with designer clothes. I remember one time I was in San Francisco and I got a call from you and you said "You won't believe my job; I have the best job in the whole wide world." I said "What is it?" and you said "All these designers give me their clothes and I get to model them for Robert."

Aline: Yes, and I got to choose them too! I went to the *New York Times* and they had this big closet containing sample clothes of every designer. I had been asked to model them (my muse role) for Robert in his cartoons. They told me to pick out what I wanted to wear for Robert to draw me in. I was amazed that I could fit into a lot of the clothes—that was pretty inspiring to begin with. I couldn't fit into everything, but I chose some things that were really fun. Like I found a really short Dolce & Gabbana mini dress, and a totally beaded tight dress, and a whole bunch of Mark Jacobs, including a satin dress with beads and incredible stuff. My favorite of all the things I wore was this see-through oriental hand embroidered tunic with silk pants that was designed by Vivienne Tam. So Robert drew me in all these outfits and they appeared in the *New York Times* Sunday pages. I loved that particular piece by Vivienne so much I really wanted to have it, so I said to Robert "could I buy this?" He said "Sure!" so I called the *New York Times* and asked them to contact Vivienne to see if I could buy the outfit. She wrote me a letter and said "You don't have to buy it, I'll give you the outfit as soon as we're done with it." A month later I got the outfit and a letter from Vivienne and a book and it was the nicest letter you could imagine—hand written.

Zaro: For the launch of Robert's book last year you wore a lot of Stella McCartney.

Aline: Yes I did, because Robert had done a project with Stella McCartney, a tee-shirt, and she had a party for the book, and her stylists dressed me. That was great fun. Her things were beautiful and exquisitely made—the fabrics are incredible, the tailoring is amazing and I also learnt a lot from just looking at the clothes she made and from getting a few pieces from her. I mixed them with other things I had and found that they made a great look. I couldn't dress completely in her clothes, but picking and choosing pieces from her collection and mixing them with my own worked brilliantly. Stella gave me some really beautiful shoes, which I love. They have very high heels and they're actually wearable for a few hours. They're incredible looking, like high-heeled sneakers, because, while designing sports clothes for Adidas, she incorporated that sports look into her collection, and the shoes were really wonderful.

Left: **With my favorite Stella McCartney shoe, 2006**
Next page, left: **Posing for Robert in his studio, 2003**
I'm wearing a dress by Douglas Hannant and shoes by Manolo Blahnik—sexy but uncomfortable.
Next page, right: **The finished drawing by Robert that appeared in the *New York Times* Sunday Magazine, 2003**
Please notice how enormous he made me look!

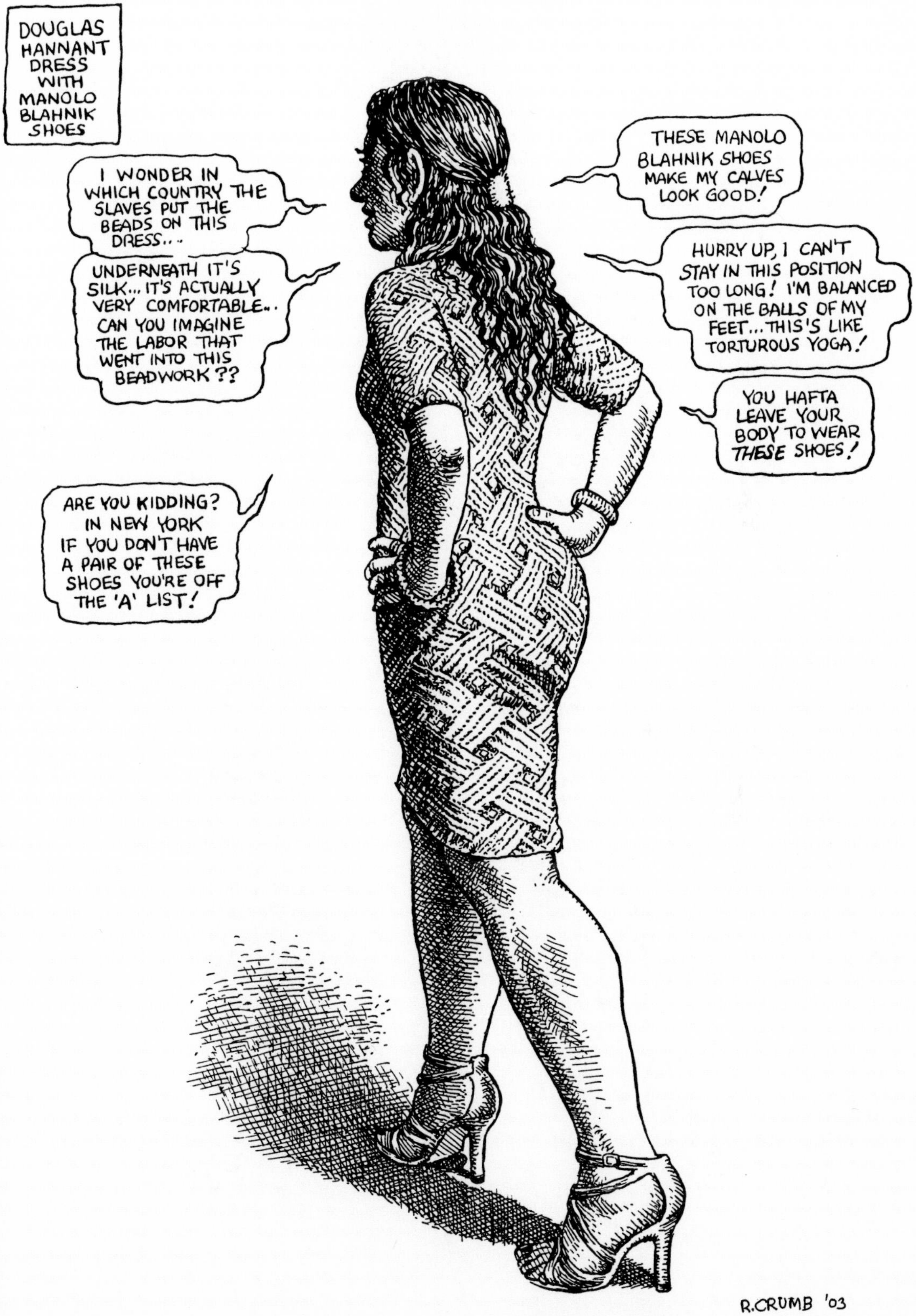
DOUGLAS HANNANT DRESS WITH MANOLO BLAHNIK SHOES
I WONDER IN WHICH COUNTRY THE SLAVES PUT THE BEADS ON THIS DRESS...
UNDERNEATH IT'S SILK... IT'S ACTUALLY VERY COMFORTABLE.. CAN YOU IMAGINE THE LABOR THAT WENT INTO THIS BEADWORK??
THESE MANOLO BLAHNIK SHOES MAKE MY CALVES LOOK GOOD!
HURRY UP, I CAN'T STAY IN THIS POSITION TOO LONG! I'M BALANCED ON THE BALLS OF MY FEET... THIS'S LIKE TORTUROUS YOGA!
YOU HAFTA LEAVE YOUR BODY TO WEAR THESE SHOES!
ARE YOU KIDDING? IN NEW YORK IF YOU DON'T HAVE A PAIR OF THESE SHOES YOU'RE OFF THE 'A' LIST!
R.CRUMB '03

Zaro: Gosh, people would give anything to walk into one of those great designer showrooms and have them say oh, just pick out whatever you want.

Aline: Remember when we were kids there was a TV show called supermarket sweepstakes where you get a certain amount of time and you can run around and fill up your cart with as much food for free? That's what I felt like. It was some kind of incredible, glutinous dream. You're almost overwhelmed and you don't know what to choose, you don't know where to start. I almost felt like someone should pour cold water on my head.

Zaro: What about your home? Do you see any distinction between decorating yourself, your environment and your art?

Aline: For me it's seamless … art, décor, fashion … I don't make a distinction between these different areas of esthetic expression. I mean, look at this medieval French village where I live … it has been my canvas for the last 15 years and it's taken me this long, but little by little I've come to understand how to live as a modern person here. I think you have to listen to your inner voice, be honest with yourself, and understand what things you respond to positively, and what your family needs, also. Of course, you always have practical concerns—everything has to function and work well and hold up and be well made. That goes without saying for any style that you choose.

You have to have confidence in your intuition: do you like bright open spaces with a lot of light, or are you drawn to cozy cave-like interiors? What spaces make you feel good? Each of us is like an animal. Every animal has a different natural habitat where it feels comfortable and where it thrives. You just have to find your natural habitat. You may have to look around a lot of places to discover the kind of ambience that makes you most comfortable.

My husband likes dark, cozy, spaces, so in our house, which is very large, we have several very small, dark, cozy, rooms that are very intimate. Then we have others with a lot of light and glass, airy and open with bright colors— that's the kind of space I like. Often it's the woman who makes these choices, and has to decide what will be the most comforting, relaxing, visually stimulating environment for herself and her family.

You should be able to do everything you need in your home, so use space as well as possible. If you have a small space, you have to think of creative ways to make the most of it. Conversely, if you have a giant space, you have to think of ways of breaking it up into smaller units that are cozy and work on a human scale. But mostly, you have to be aware what kind of animal you are and what your habitat is.

Zaro: That's a good way of expressing it. Now let's say you've kept a note book and know what you want. When I walk into your house, I see that the kitchen is decorated with pieces of saris from India and the tablecloth on the terrace table is a shower curtain from Greece and it looks so great. How could other people get the courage to take what's at hand to recreate it … reuse it and re-purpose everyday items?

Aline: I think all that has to evolve little by little … by taking one step at a time. I think it's too shocking if you redo your whole environment—everyone will have a nervous breakdown. However, you could change one little area at a time—maybe a small corner, your little office, or perhaps a bathroom—and you should do that in the most dramatic manner you want.

That way you can cut loose in one small space and live with it for a while and see how it goes. Or you start adding objects here and there. Maybe you could change your dishes to ones that are much more colorful, or you do your table in a way that really pleases you. Try out things that don't have to be permanent. You'll gradually develop your style—it's something that evolves. But if you buy a designer's look from a showroom, or a store, or a magazine, and superimpose that onto your environment, you'll never be happy. It will eventually end up going back to how it was before.

Zaro: Right. It's very much like fashion or anything else.

Aline: Yes, exactly. Bit by bit you can incorporate what's out there with your own things, including any family heirlooms that you've got. You'll get to see what you're comfortable with. I find cold, clean, modern, lines very off-putting. Maybe it's because I grew up in a 1950s house where everything was so sterile. But my grandparents' house had furniture from the 1920s, and it was a lovely, cozy, warm, place to me because emotionally it was like that too. I love that feeling, and I've worked out that's where it comes from. It's interesting to analyze where your taste originated, because every house has an emotional environment, and every place you've ever lived in has had an emotional impact on you—so perhaps the choices you make go back to that. Exploring all this helps you to develop your style even more. Think about whether you liked the childhood place you grew up in or hated it. Ask yourself why. Go with that feeling, because your early environment had a huge emotional impact on you.

Zaro: What's been the most unusual home that you've ever decorated?

Aline: Well, I lived in a little trailer for while. It was one of those 1950s silver models with wood inside and was a complete, miniature home. It was a perfect little Miss Mouse habitat, and looked incredibly sweet inside. You wouldn't dream that an adult lived in it—and that's what amazed people. From the outside it just looked like a tin can, but inside it was the coziest place you could imagine. I think that really started me on my idea of how to decorate, plus I really had to be very neat in that trailer. It was so small I couldn't make it chaotic. It would have become non-functional very quickly, and it made me understand the importance of order. Even though I'm a very exuberant character, and have lots of color, hundreds of paintings, and masses of stuff in my house, it's really a bit like a museum. It's very precisely organized because otherwise it would be disturbing. I find that order is a powerfully calming and important aspect of my household.

I also need to be able to keep my house in good condition—that's incredibly important. It's an astonishing building—a medieval French house, originally built around the 12th century. Parts of it have been re-done about every hundred years or so. There are 13 rooms with all these different levels. Every one of them has a different shape. There's nothing square in it. We have rounded ceilings and skylights going from one floor to the other. It's wonderfully crazy—and I love it. I've painted it in bright shades of the natural ochre colors that are typical of this region of France, and have all my outrageous artwork displayed up there on the walls. So, I find it's a pretty amazing home.

Zaro: And we get to see your wonderful house and more of your paintings in these pages—thank you for letting us into your life, Aline.

Aline: Hey … No Problem!

Right: **The interior stairway of our house, decorated with some of my artwork**
Next page: **In my studio, 2006**
Pages 358–9: **Continuing down the interior stairway**
My first impression of this house before all our stuff was in it was of a faded old Italian hotel that had seen better days.
Page 360: **One of my disturbing giant doll paintings above the mantel in the living room, 2006**
Sophie is scared of them.
Page 361: **Looking out of the little guest room window into the interior hallway, with skylight above, 2006**
Pages 362–3: **Halloween decorations on the front mantel, 2006**
Pages 364–5: **My inner sanctum—bath, dressing and exercise room**
Pages 366–7: **Little salon, leading onto the kitchen**

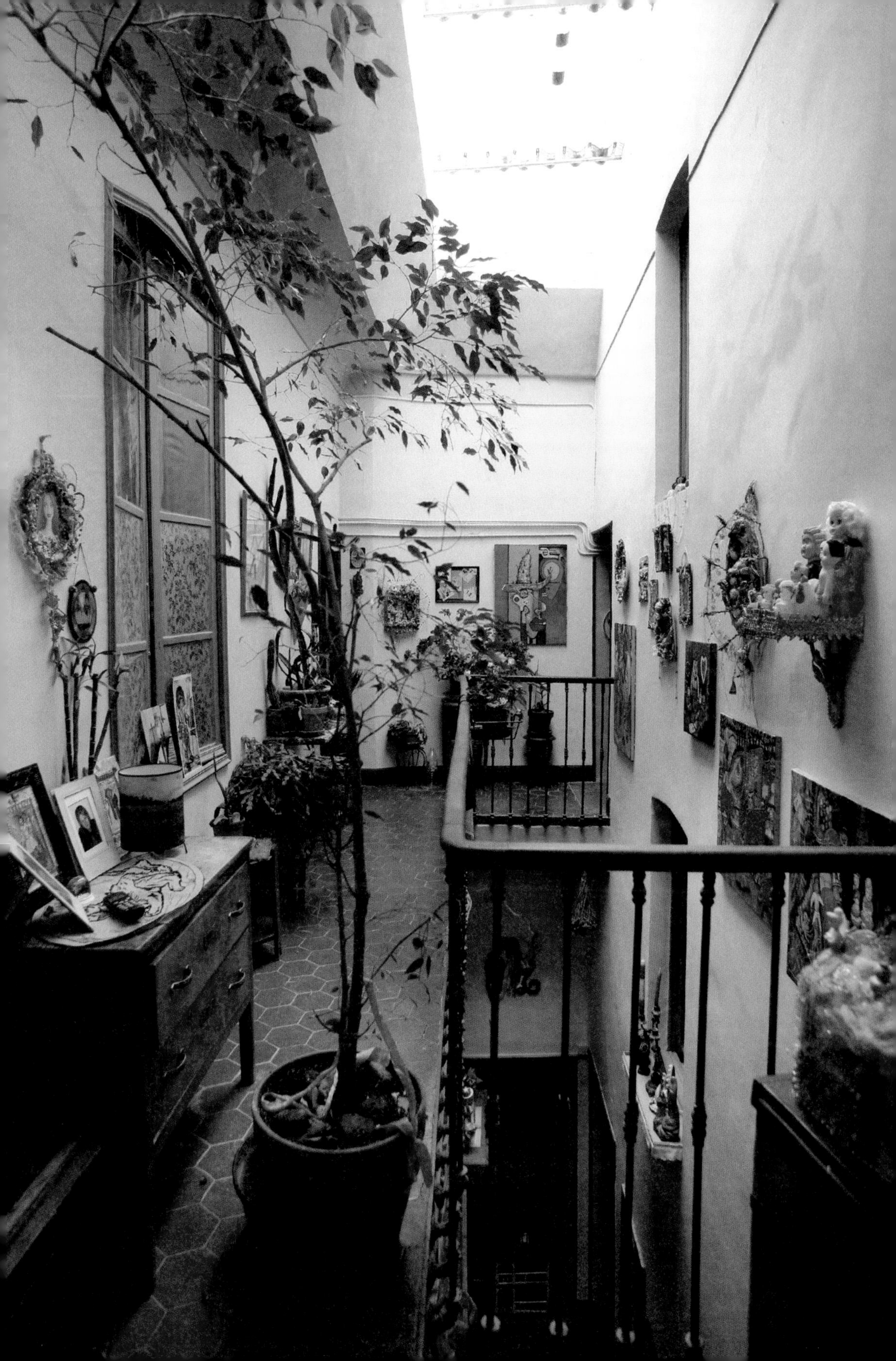

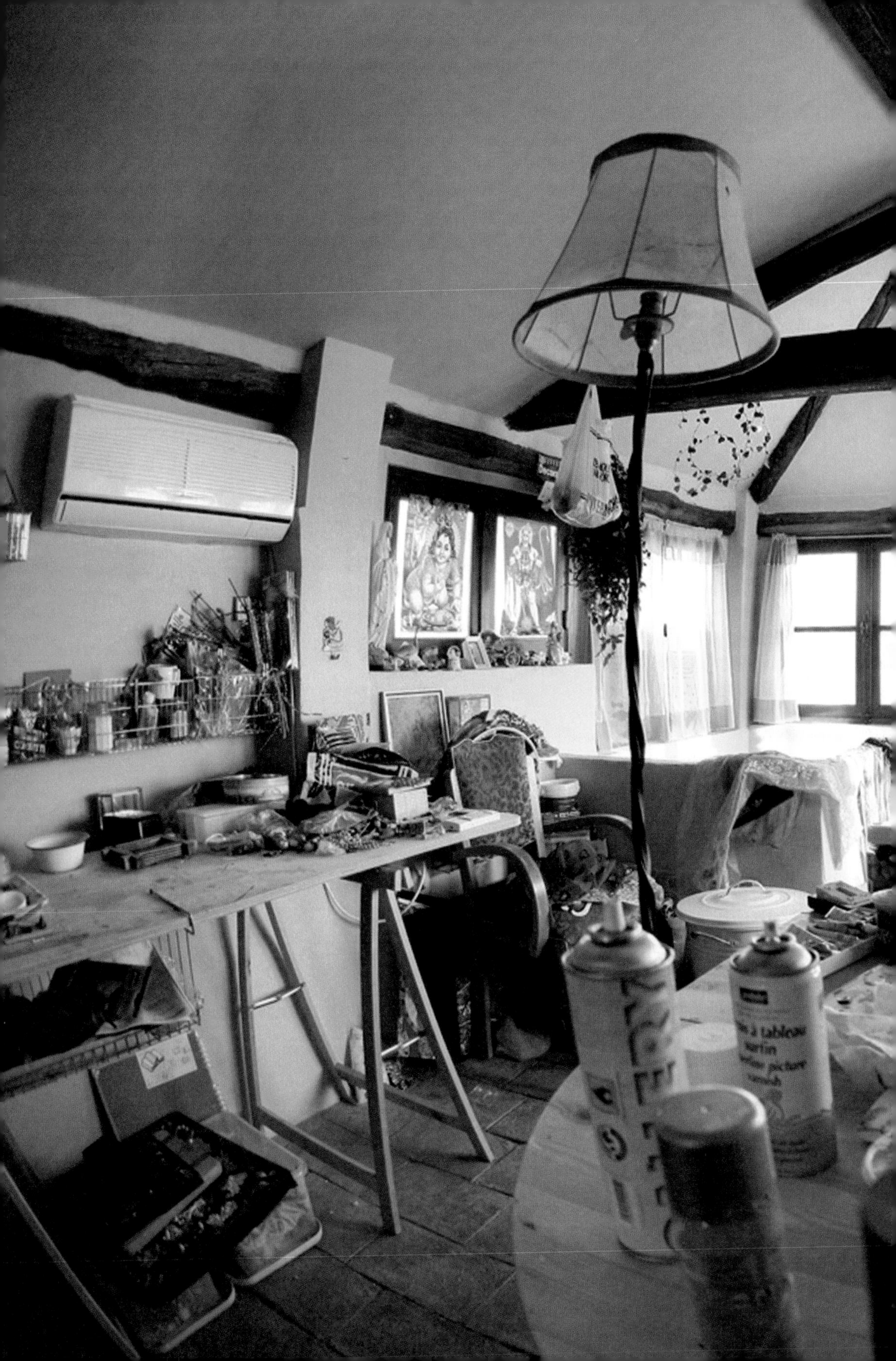
à tableau
satin

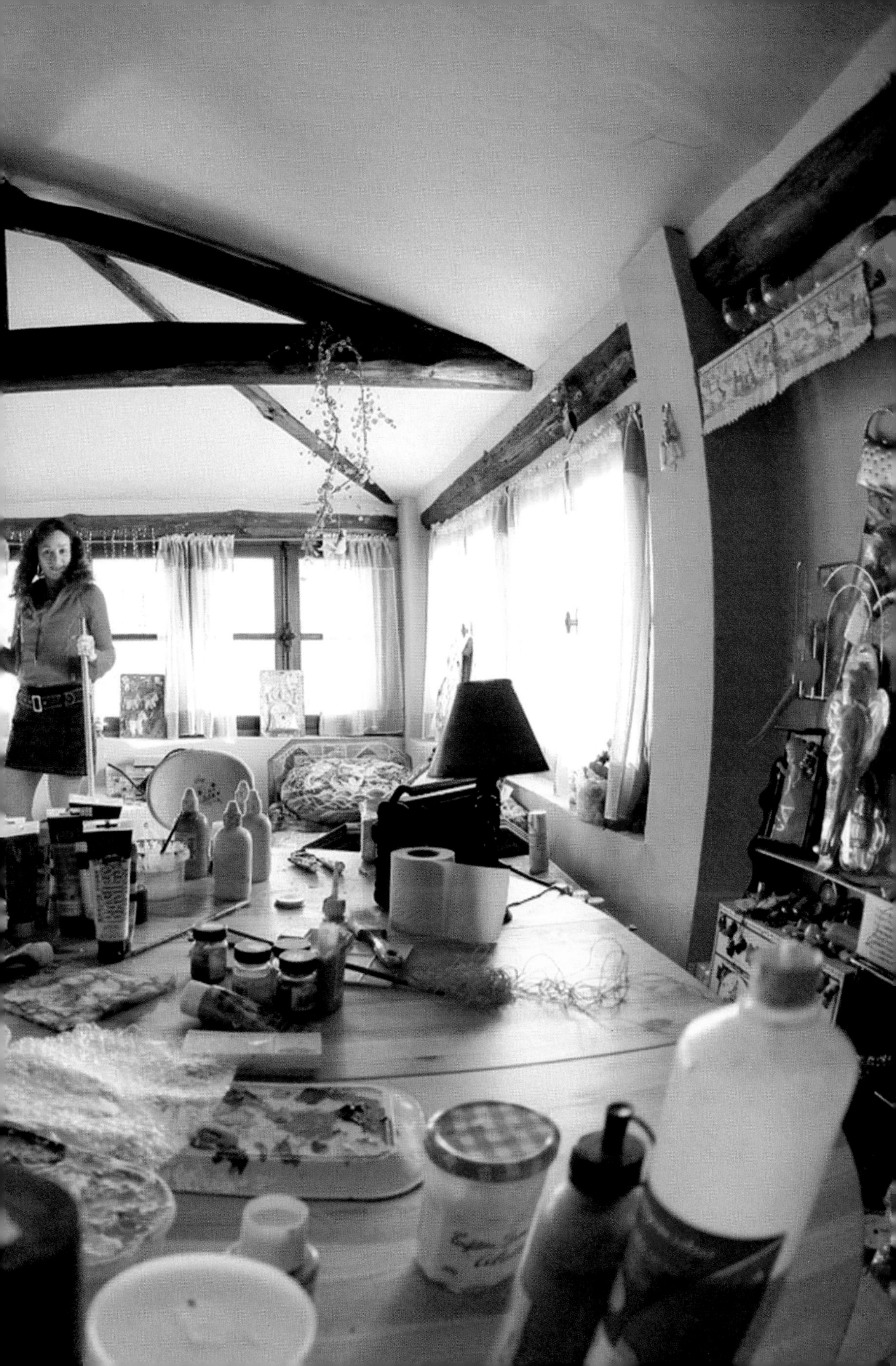

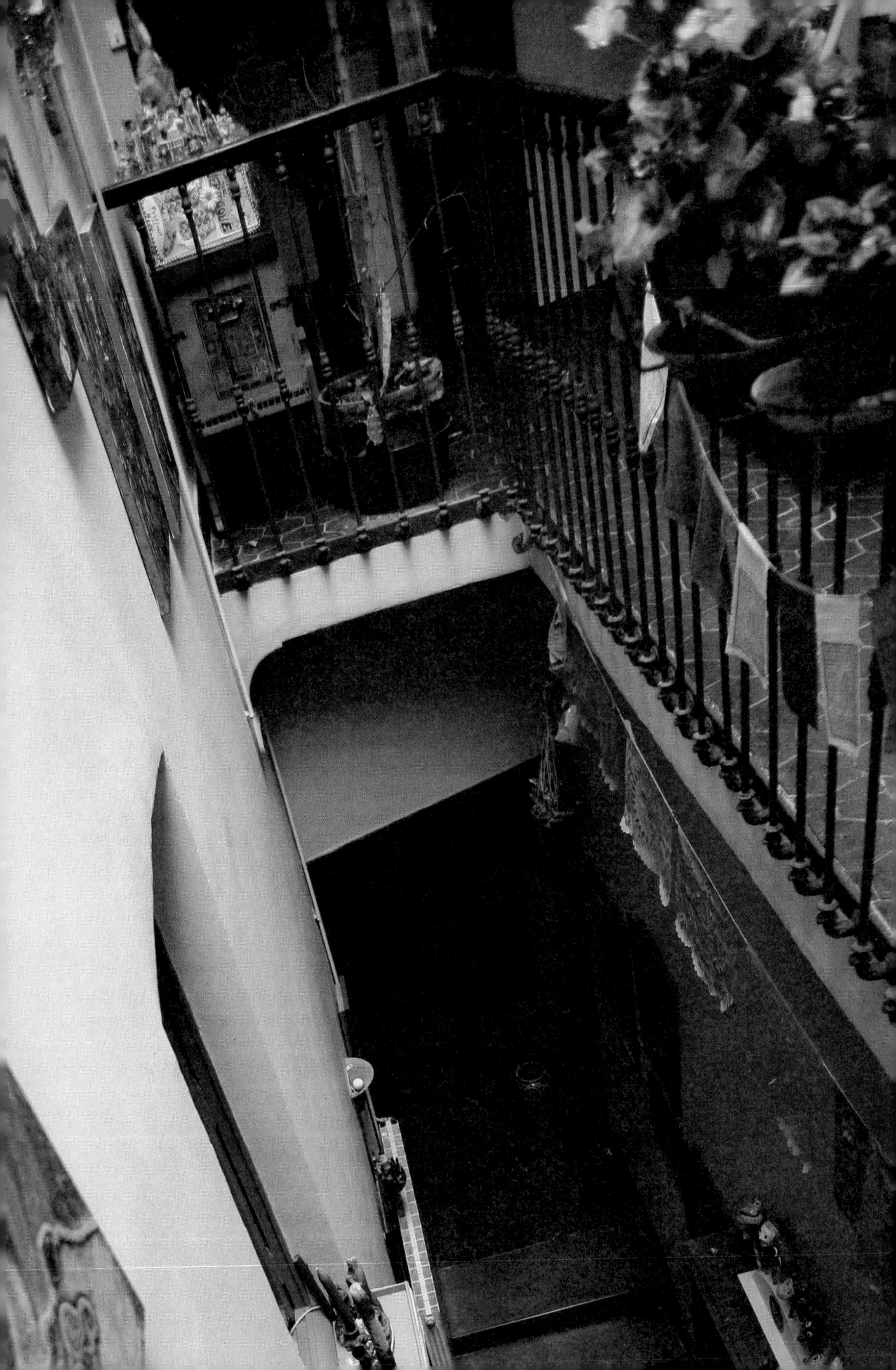

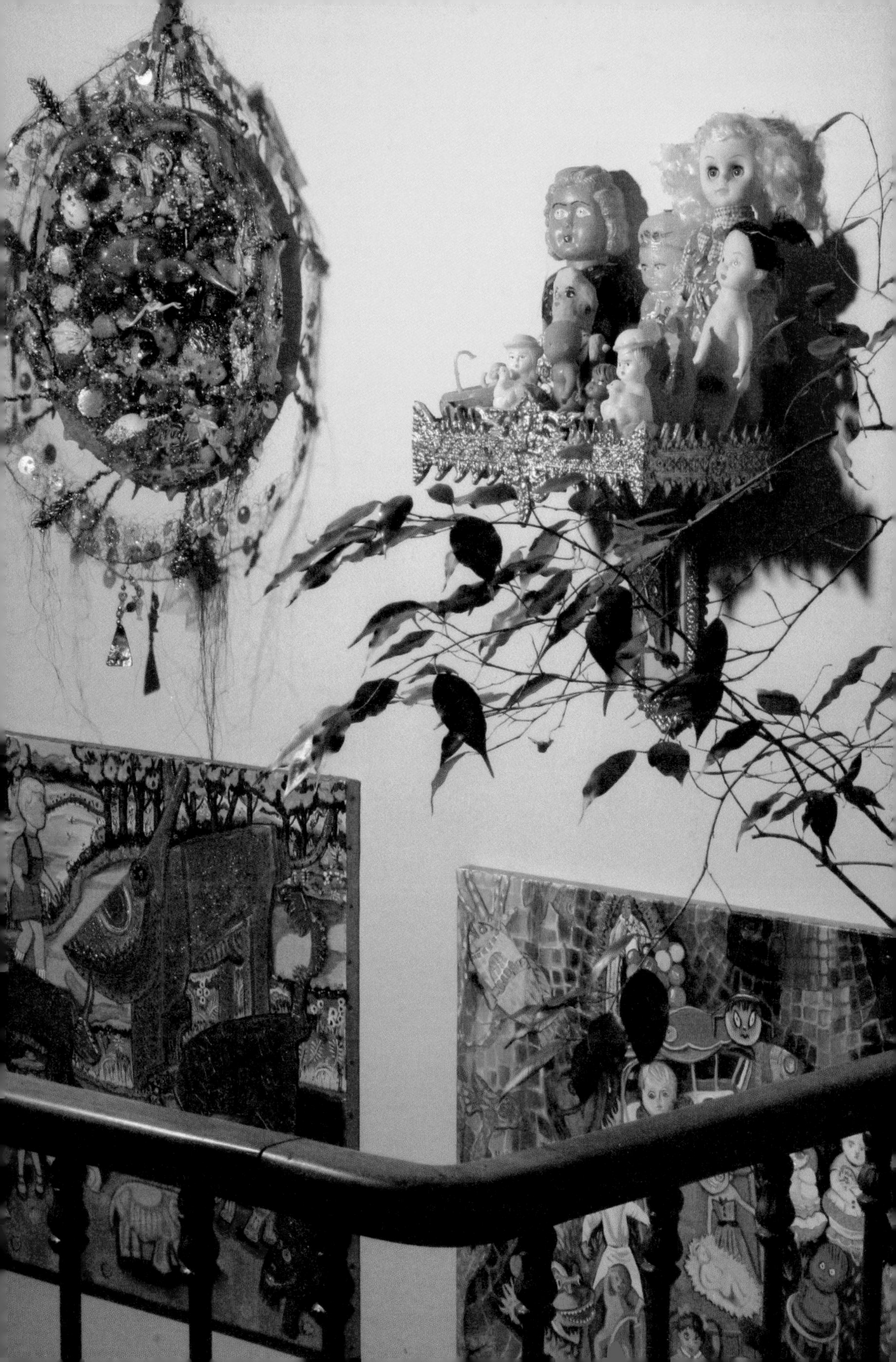

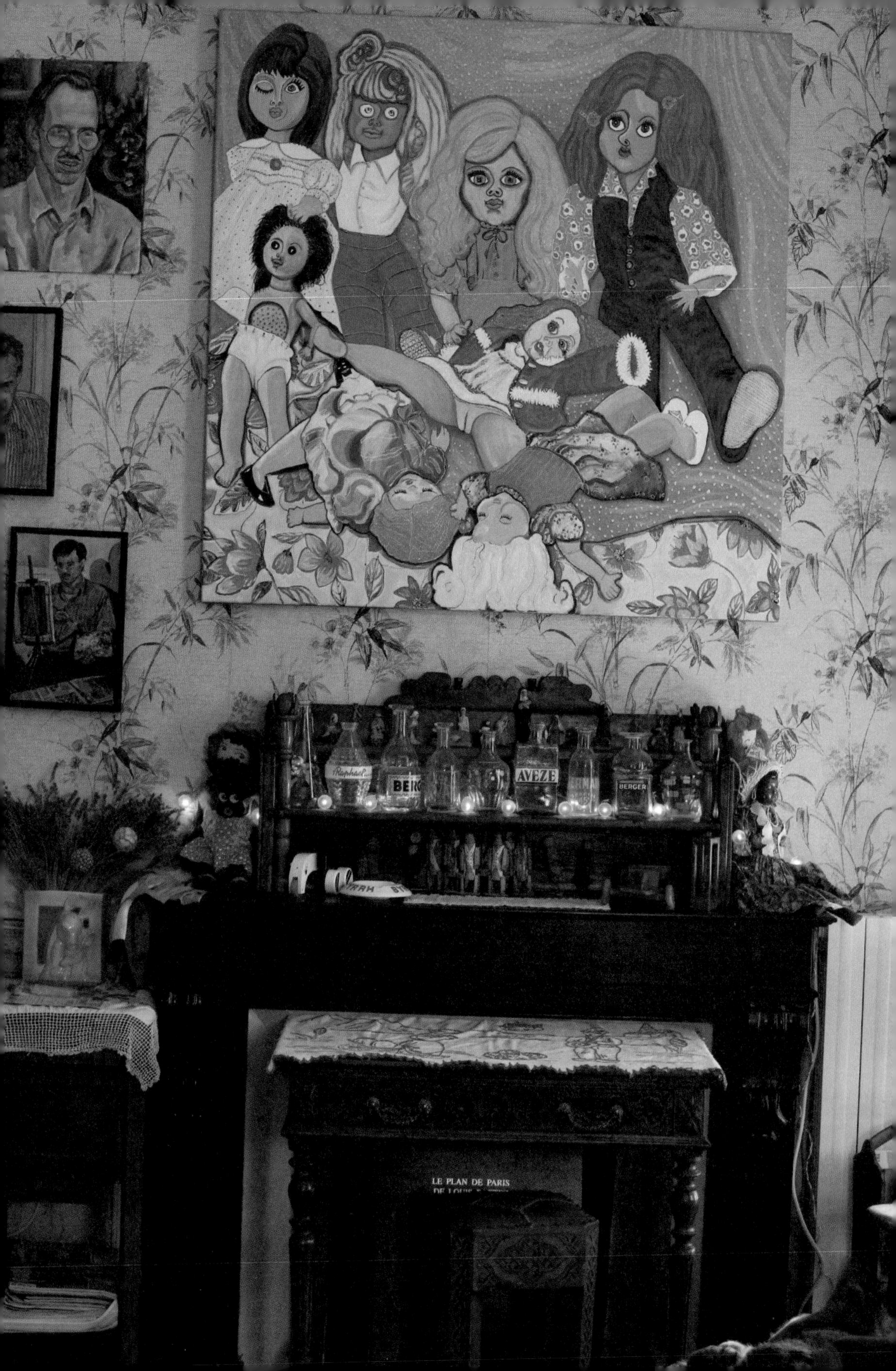
AVEZE
BERGER
LE PLAN DE PARIS

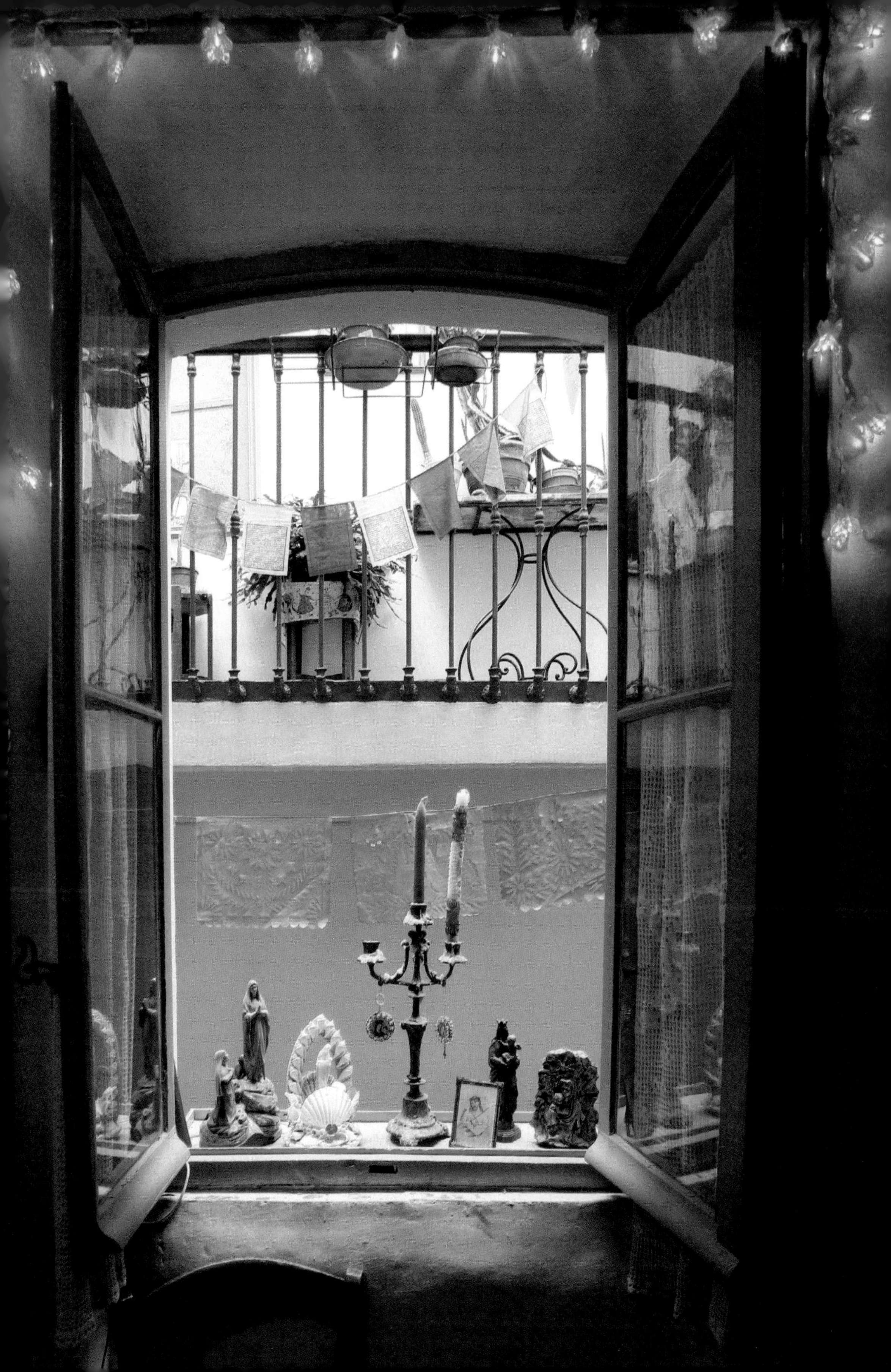

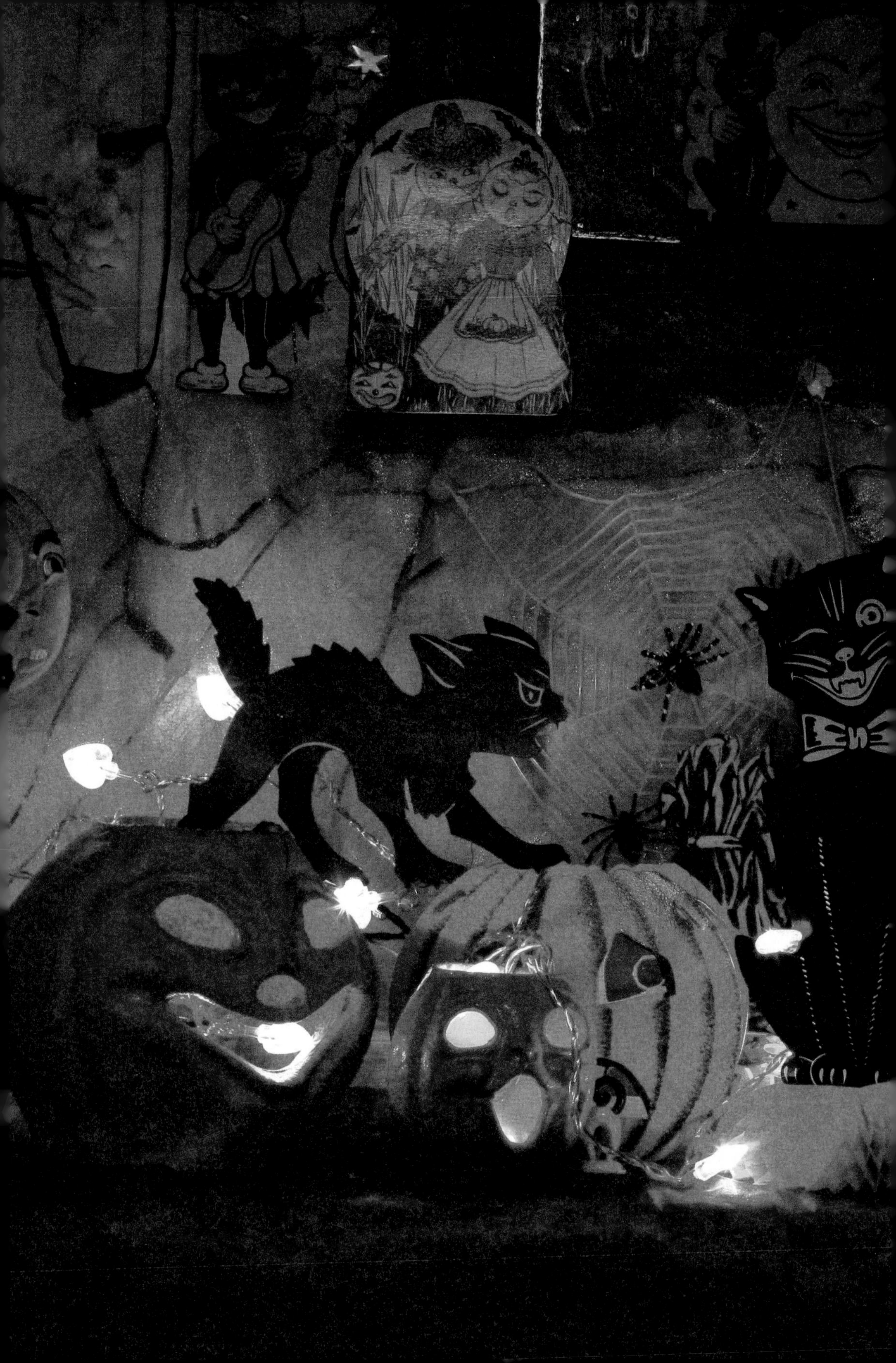

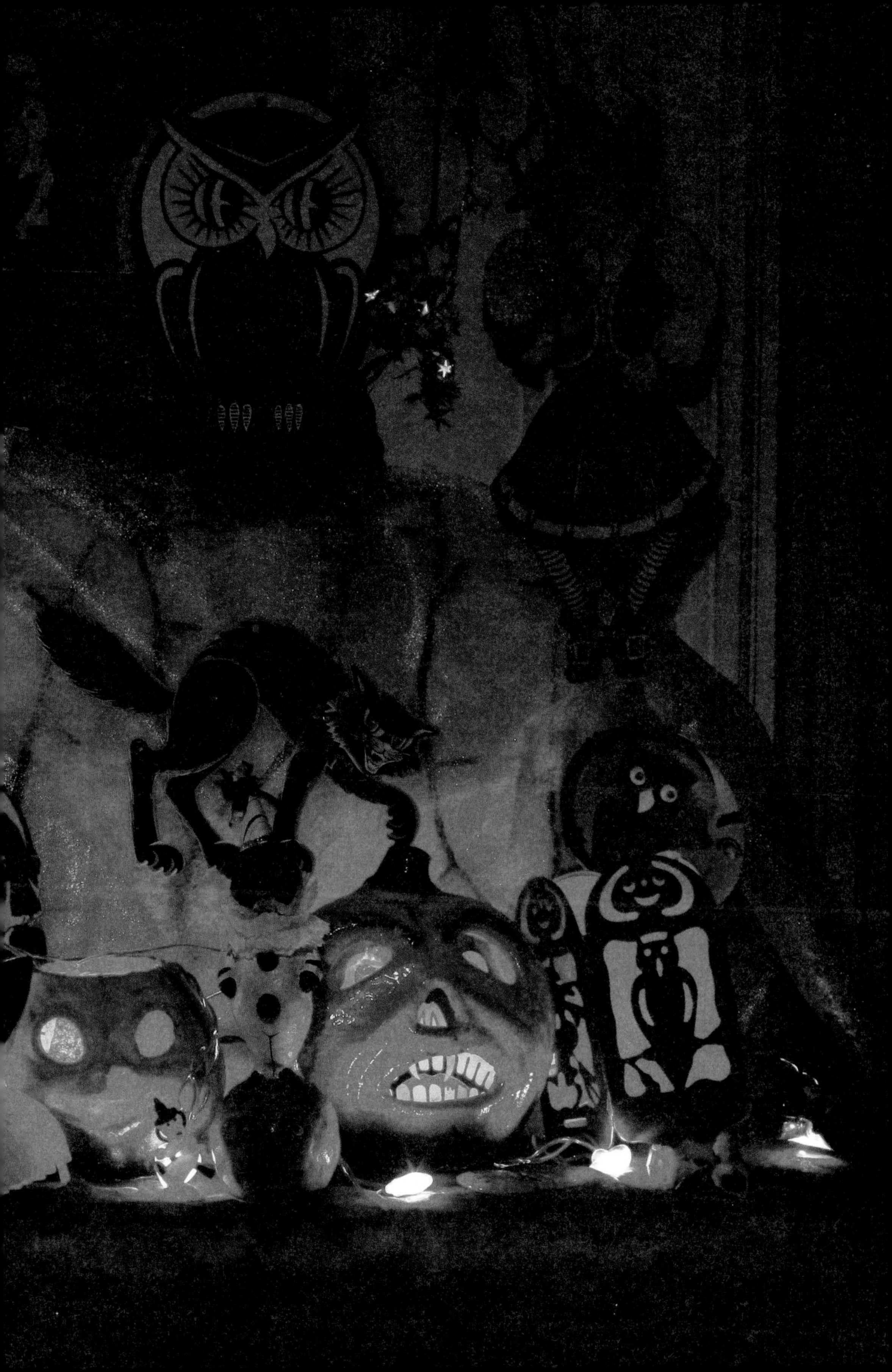

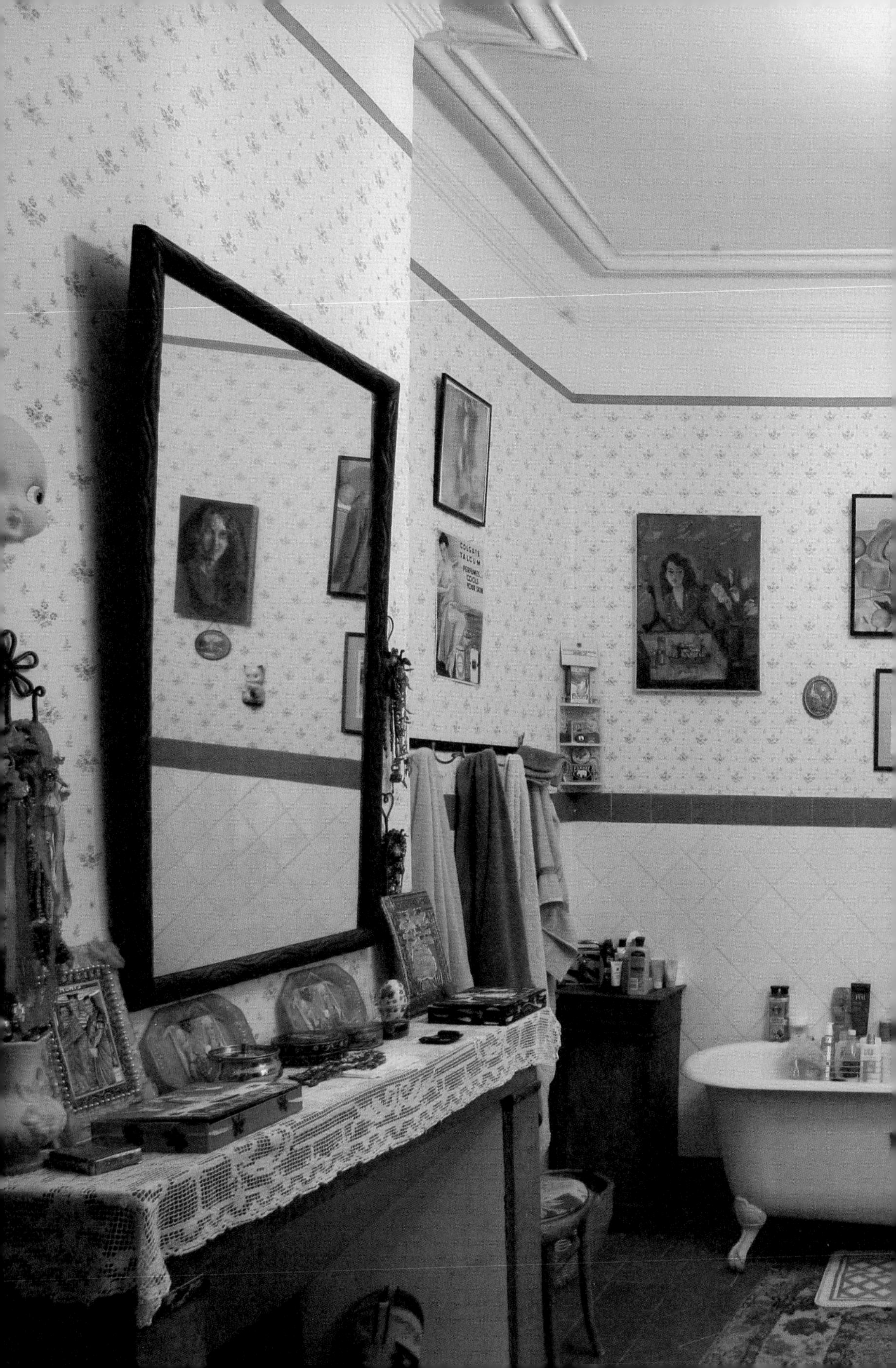
COLGATE
TALCUM
PERFUMES,
COOLS
YOUR SKIN

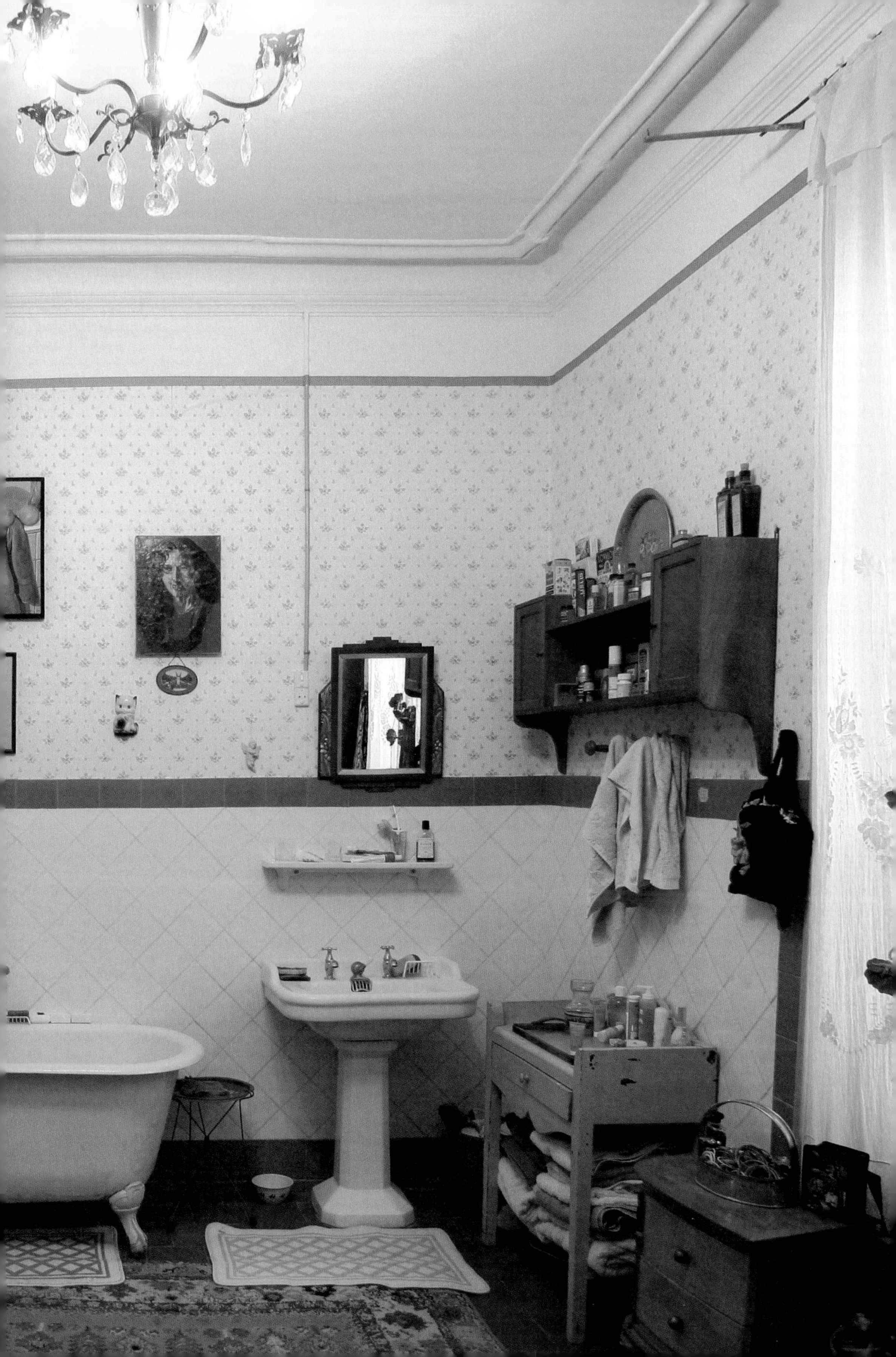

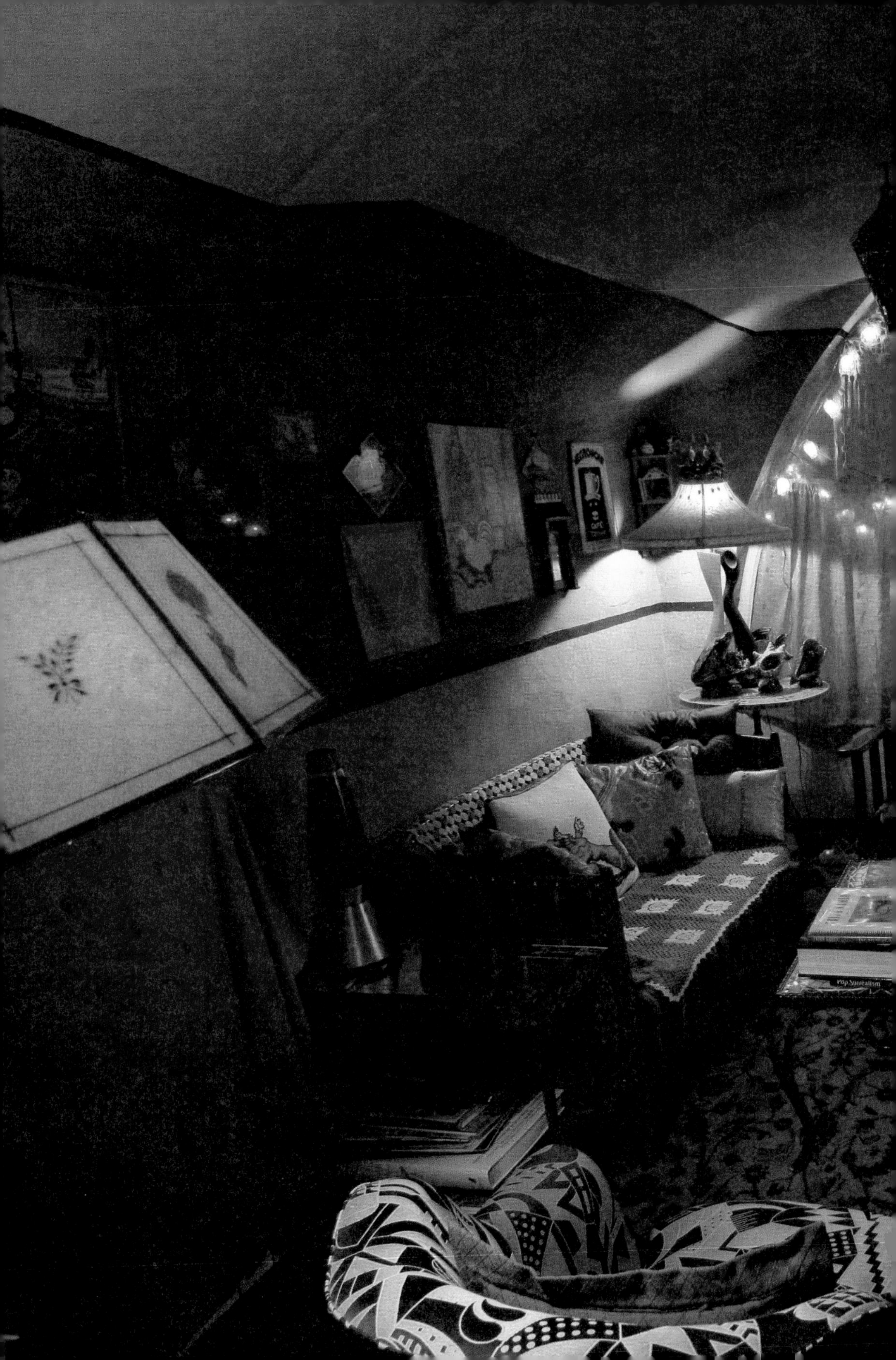
Pop Surrealism

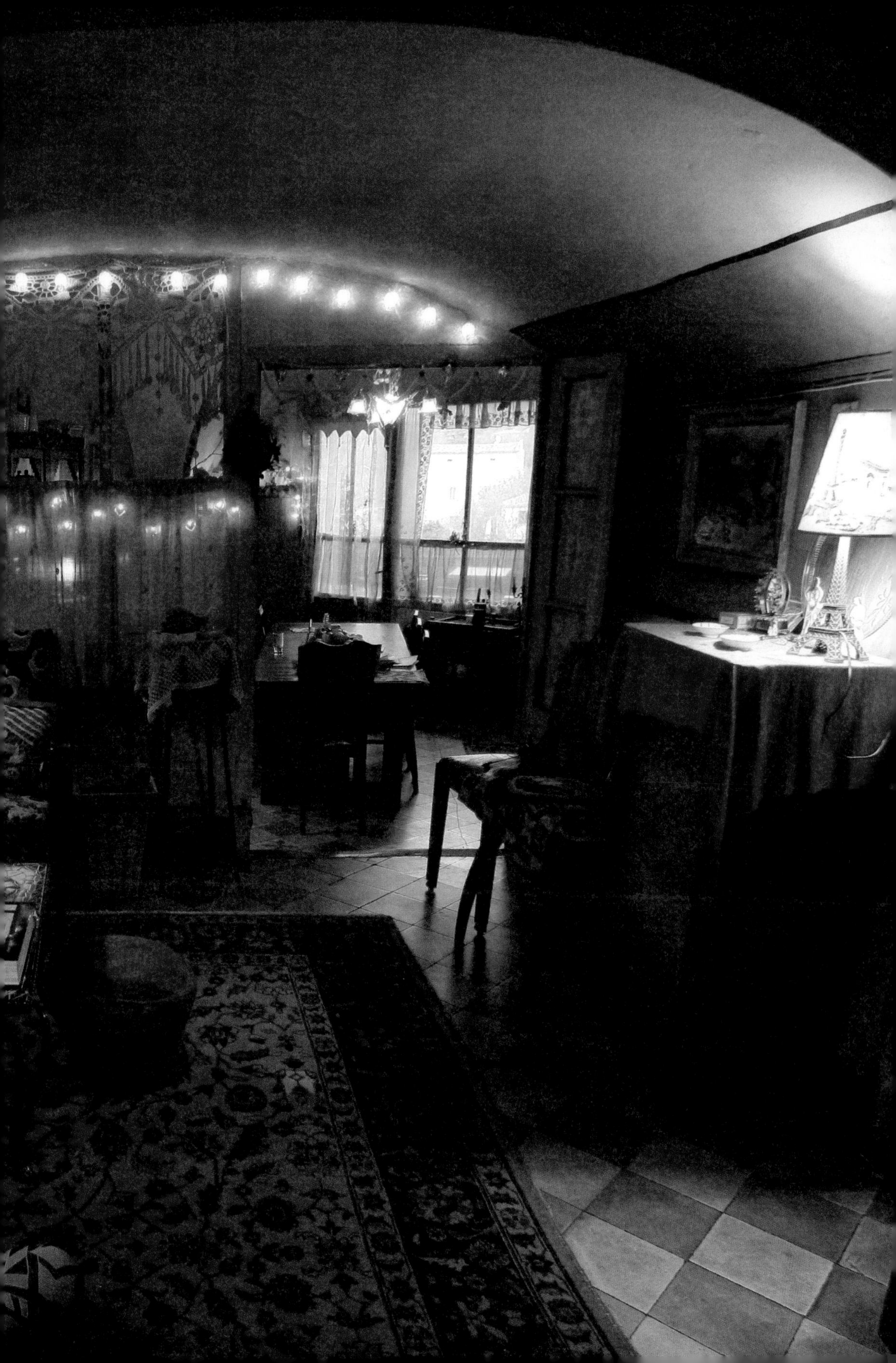

PRAISE FROM THE HUSBAND

THE FIRST TIME I EVER SAW ALINE'S COMICS, IN 1971, I WAS STRUCK BY HOW CRAZY AND INTENSE THEY WERE, BY HOW RAW, PRIMITIVE AND UNSCHOOLED THE ARTWORK WAS. THE DRAWINGS SEEMED TOTALLY IR-RATIONAL, THE WORK OF A DEEPLY DISTURBED INDIVIDUAL. THEY LOOKED TORTURED, UGLY EVEN, DIRECTLY OUT OF THE SUBCONSCIOUS, YET THERE WAS HUMOR, DEEPLY PERSONAL AND VERY SELF-DEPRACATING. WHAT A CRAZY GIRL, I THOUGHT. I WAS DRAWN IN, PULLED IN. I READ THE PAGES CLOSELY. WITHIN THE APPARENTLY CRUDE DRAWING AND BLUNT TEXT, THERE WERE NUANCES, SUBTLETIES, ALOT GOING ON. QUICKLY I SAW THAT THIS WOMAN, 23 YEARS OLD AT THE TIME, WAS NOT JUST A CRAZY, STONED OUT HIPPY CARTOONIST, BUT ALSO A CLASSIC, FATALISTIC JEWISH HUMORIST-COMEDIAN, PUTTING DOWN HER AUTOBIOGRAPHY IN ALL ITS DARK, TRAGIC-COMIC ABSURDITY.

HER GROTESQUE, SCRATCHY NON-STYLE OF DRAWING WAS, AND IS, OFF-PUTTING FOR THE VAST MAJORITY OF COMICBOOK READERS, UNDERGROUND OR OTHERWISE. MOST OF THEM ARE NOT GOING TO MAKE THE EFFORT TO GET PAST THEIR INITIAL REVULSION. CONSEQUENTLY, ALINE HAS ALWAYS HAD ONLY A SMALL BUT DEDICATED AUDIENCE, A SCATTERING OF INDIVIDUALS WHO MANAGED SOME-HOW TO DISCOVER HER COMICS, BADLY DISTRIBUTED THOUGH THEY ARE. THESE ODD PEOPLE ARE NOT USUALLY COMICS READERS PARTICULARLY. IN THE COMICS SUBCULTURE HER WORK HAS BEEN LARGELY OVERLOOKED, BUT UP TO NOW IT'S BEEN ENTIRELY UNAVAILABLE OUTSIDE THE CONFINES OF SMALL COMICBOOK SHOPS AND COMICBOOK PUBLISHERS.

AND LATELY THERE'S A NEW IRONIC TWIST, NOW THAT MILLIONS OF PEOPLE ARE SEEING HER WORK OCCASIONALLY IN THE NEW YORKER, IN THE COLLABORATIVE STRIPS WE'VE DONE TOGETHER. IT AP-PEARS THAT MANY OF THESE READERS, EVEN PROFESSIONAL JOURNALISTS, ASSUME THAT I WRITE AND DRAW THE WHOLE THING BY MYSELF, THAT I DRAW ALINE AND WRITE HER DIALOGUE AS WELL AS MY OWN. THEY'RE COMPLETELY TAKEN ABACK WHEN I INFORM THEM THAT THE NEW YORKER STRIPS ARE 50/50 COLLABORATIONS, THAT ALINE DRAWS HERSELF AND WRITES HER OWN DIALOGUE. "REALLY??" THEY EXCLAIM, "HUH! THAT'S INCREDIBLE!"

IT IS CLEARLY STATED IN THE TITLE PANEL OF EACH OF THESE NEW YORKER STRIPS, "BY ALINE & R. CRUMB", BUT I GUESS "ALINE" MAKES NO IMPRESSION. "R. CRUMB" IS A WELL-KNOWN QUANTITY (GOD HELP ME). THEY'VE SEEN THE MOVIE "CRUMB", PERHAPS. PEOPLE AS A RULE DON'T REALLY LOOK THAT CLOSELY OR PAY THAT CLOSE ATTENTION TO ANYTHING MUCH.

ALINE'S REACTION: SHE'S DOOMED TO BE OVERLOOKED AS AN ARTIST, IGNORED, UNAPPRECIATED. I TRY TO REASSURE HER THAT HER BODY OF WORK HAS A PROMINENT PLACE IN THE HISTORY OF COMIC ART, AND THAT POPULARITY IN YOUR OWN TIME IS NO MEASURE OF THE QUALITY OF AN ARTIST'S WORK. THESE WORDS ARE SMALL CONSOLATION. "EASY FOR YOU TO TALK," SHE SAYS. THEN WE GO ON TO DISCUSS THE PROBLEMATIC POSITION SHE FINDS HERSELF IN BECAUSE OF BEING MARRIED TO ME. PEOPLE SOMETIMES JUDGE HER HARSHLY. THEY LOOK AT HER "UNPROFESSIONAL" DRAWINGS AND ASSUME THAT SHE'S ONLY GETTING PUBLISHED BECAUSE OF MY INFLUENCE, RIDING ON MY COAT TAILS. IT'S AN EXERCISE IN FUTILITY FOR ME OR ALINE TO TRY TO DEFEND HER FROM SUCH CHARGES. THE WORK SPEAKS FOR ITSELF. IN THESE HOMELY DRAWINGS AND ARTLESS STORY TELL-ING, THERE IS INDEED REAL ART; A DIRECT, PLAINSPOKEN TRUTH AND HUMOR. ALINE COULDN'T BE PRETENTIOUS IF SHE TRIED. BUT, YOU KNOW, EITHER YOU SEE IT OR YOU DON'T.

ALINE WAS AMONG THE VERY FIRST ARTISTS TO SHOW, IN THE EARLY 1970s, THAT THE COMIC STRIP IS A POWERFUL MEDIUM FOR PERSONAL, AUTOBIOGRAPHICAL STORY TELLING. SHE MAY WELL HAVE BEEN THE FIRST WOMAN EVER TO DO THAT IN THE COMICS MEDIUM, CLOSELY FOL-LOWING UP ON THE FIRST TO DO IT, JUSTIN GREEN, WHOSE WORK INSPIRED HER TO TRY IT.

AND THEN, TOO, THE COLLABORATIVE STRIPS WE'VE DONE ARE VERY LIKELY THE ONLY SUCH COMICS OF THEIR KIND, IN WHICH A MALE ARTIST AND A FEMALE ARTIST BOUNCE OFF EACH OTHER... A CURIOUS FACT WHEN YOU THINK ABOUT IT... WHY HAVEN'T THERE BEEN OTHERS? I DON'T KNOW OF ANY... IN FACT, DOING THESE COMICS WITH HER IS EASY. ALL WE NEED TO START WITH IS THE GERM OF AN IDEA, A THEME, A SETTING. IF I WANT, I CAN JUST PLAY THE STRAIGHT MAN TO HER COMPULSIVE JEWISH COMEDIAN CHARACTER, WHICH JUST POURS OUT OF HER ALL THE TIME ANYWAY. MY MAIN JOB IN THE STRIP IS TO KEEP US ON SOME KIND OF STORY TRACK. SHE CAN GO OFF ON ENDLESS TANGENTS, SO I HAVE TO BE THE ENGINEER, DO THE STRUCTURAL WORK. USUALLY, IN HONING IT DOWN TO THE ALLOTTED PAGES, WE HAVE TO CUT OUT LARGE AMOUNTS OF DIALOGUE BY ALINE. SHE DOESN'T SEEM TO MIND. THERE'S ALWAYS PLENTY MORE WHERE THAT CAME FROM.

WHAT A CRAZY GIRL!

—— R. CRUMB
SEPT., 2006

Right: **With Robert, 2006**

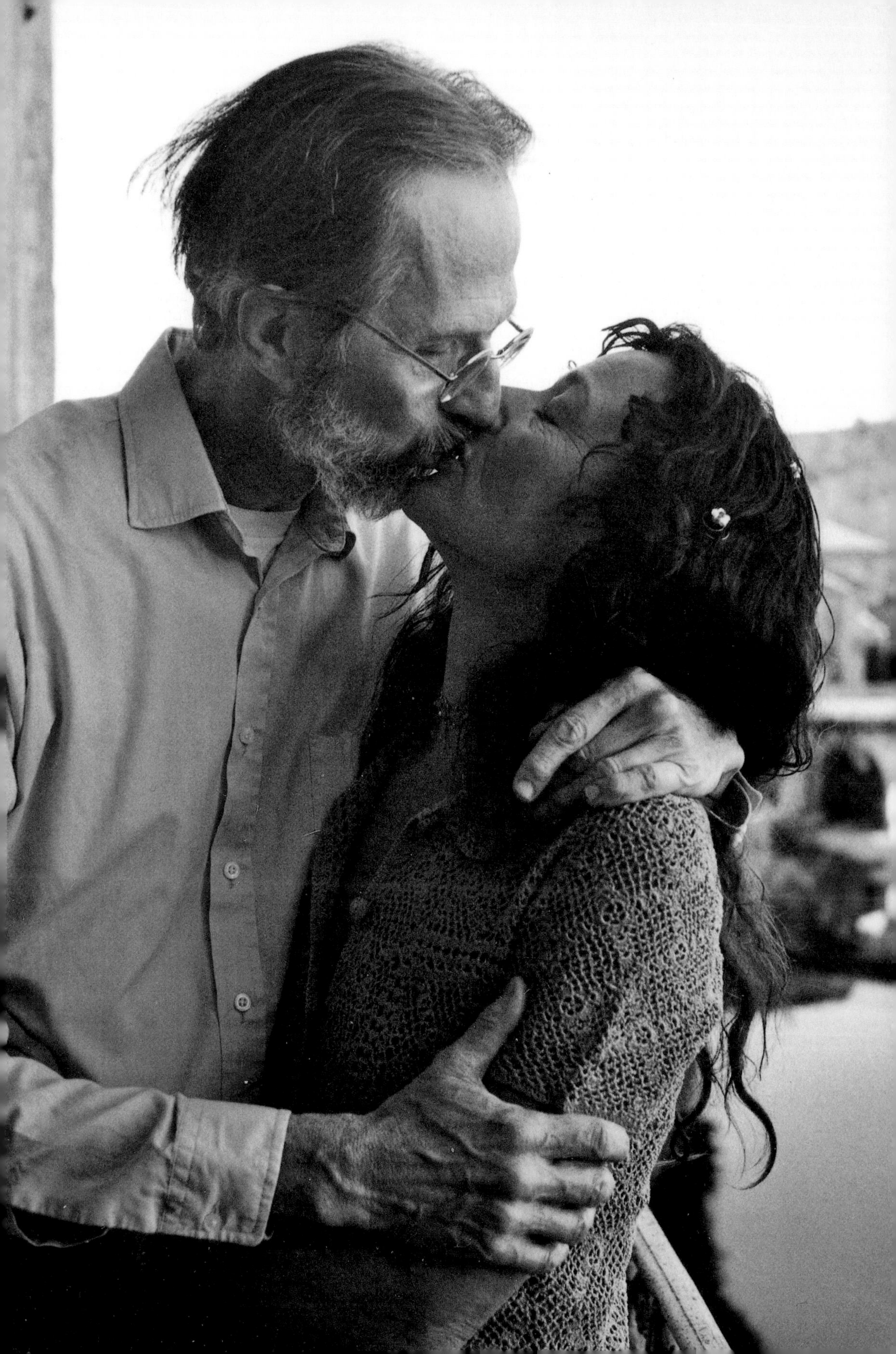

Sophie Crumb
OUR DARLING DAUGHTER AND WORKING CARTOONIST

Zaro: Could you talk a bit about your mother's influence on women's comic artists ... both older and younger generation artists.

Sophie: Her influence is not recognized enough. But if you think about it, there was no female autobiographical cartoonist that came before her. She was the first of her kind, 100% original, 100% unheard of. If she wasn't married to my father, her own fame and influence would stand out more, but since they both did something that nobody did before them, and since they are a couple, of course HE gets all the attention. Men read and draw more comics than women. She has her own fans and people that she influenced. But you have to be able to identify with her stuff ... which means you must be a female, be an underground comic-reader, and have a twisted, voyeuristic, sexually-deviant sense of humor. So that pretty much narrows down the field ... Phoebe Gloeckner, for example, was a messed-up teenager with a messed-up life, but so much artistic potential ... and I guess when she saw the comix produced by my mother and her buddies in San Francisco back then, it was a revelation to her—something made by girls but fucked-up in a way that she could relate to—and she is one of the best cartoonists in the world I think. So is Dori Seda who died young so she didn't produce that much, sadly ... basically without my mother's guts, and humor, and balls (and the balls of all her twisted girlfriends), others would have never had the balls. I feel like now it's my job to recruit female cartoonists just like my mother did, and also, show her old comix to the girls of today. They are quite obscure. No one my age knows of *Twisted Sisters* and *Wimmins Comix.* Check it out, cunts.

Zaro: What about her influence on comic art in general.

Sophie: Well, she is obviously not the hero of the masses like Garfield or the Boondocks or something. Her stuff is pretty hard to digest! If you have read it, you will understand that not everyone can appreciate or laugh at a fat, hairy, big-nosed freaky Jew touching herself while thinking about her dad, or 5 foot-long pink and green fluorescent paintings of psycho killer dolls raping each other ... only a select few have taste that raffiné.

Zaro: How was it growing up and becoming a female cartoonist in your own right with your own style? How did you find your own path?

Sophie: I can't say. I am not beyond it all yet. Maybe, in hindsight, but I

370

am only 24, have only printed a few comics ... I am not my "own cartoonist" in my "own right" yet, but thank you for the compliment. Come back in 10 years and I'm sure I'll bore you for hours with self important statements! But this is about Aline Ricky Goldsmith Kominsky Crumb! Try sleeping in her house, waking up with glittery, hot-pink, bug-eyed, psycho dolls staring at you, a foot away from your head, and then you can just start to imagine what it's like to be me.

Southern France, September 2006

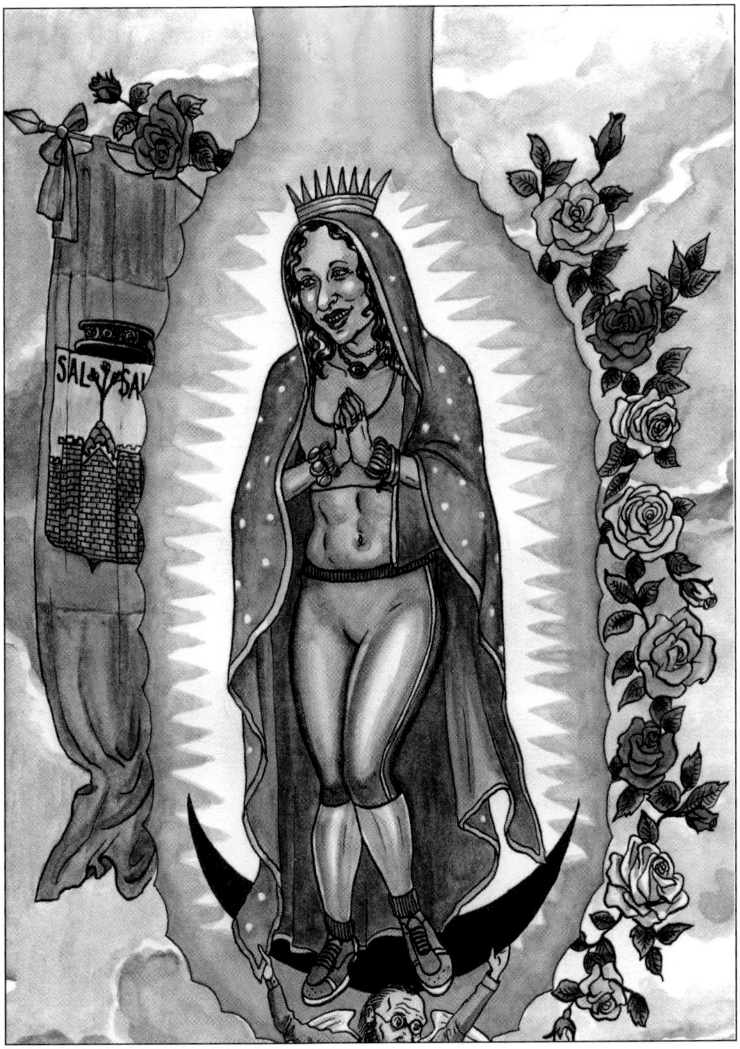
SAL

Above: **Sophie Crumb, ink and watercolor portrait of Aline as "The Virgin of Something," 2006**
Next page: **Aline and Sophie Crumb, comic story, 2005**
Written and drawn together at Fort Lauderdale airport while waiting to go home after a week at my mother's Miami apartment.

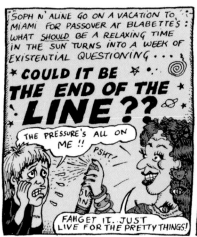

SOPH N' ALINE GO ON A VACATION TO MIAMI FOR PASSOVER AT BLABETTE'S: WHAT SHOULD BE A RELAXING TIME IN THE SUN TURNS INTO A WEEK OF EXISTENTIAL QUESTIONING...

* COULD IT BE *
THE END OF THE LINE??

THE PRESSURE'S ALL ON ME!!

PSHT!

FAHGET IT... JUST LIVE FOR THE PRETTY THINGS!

HERE WE ARE, THE DAY OF THE DEPARTURE, WAITING FOR OUR PLANE AT FORT LAUDERDALE... ...REMINISCING...

MO-OM! DO YOU WANNA DO THIS COMIC OR NOT!?! KEEP IT SIMPLE!

BUT I HAVE SO MANY INTERESTING INSIGHTS!

YOU KEEP GOING OFF ON TANGENTS ABOUT YOURSELF!

TSK!

TRYING TO DO COMIC IN ONE HOUR

BACKTRACK TO ONE WEEK AGO, NYC TO MIAMI...

MOM, SHOULD I TAKE YOUR VALIUM?

NAH, IT'LL MAKE YA FEEL ALL LOGEY.

DON'T WORRY, WE'RE NOT GONNA GET OUTTA DEALIN' WITH BLABETTE!

BUT I'M SCARED...

JEEZ... THE PLANE IS FULL OF HASSIDS!

YEAH... IF THIS CRATE GOES DOWN, IT'LL BE NO GREAT LOSS TO HUMANITY!

FATALISTIC

ANOTHER SELF-HATING JEW

UPON ARRIVAL, FAILED MAKEOVER ATTEMPTS ON SOPH...

THOSE TATTOOS COME OFF, RIGHT??

YEAH, OF COURSE, GRANDMA...

A LITTLE SPRITZ O' THIS STUFF'LL MAKE YOUR HAIR LIGHTER!

BLONDE IS BEAUTIFUL!

FSHHT

YOU'D BE SO MUCH PRETTIER IF YOU WORE LIPSTICK AND HIGH-HEELS!!

YA' WANNA WEAR THIS TOP??

I'M NOT A DRESS-UP DOLL!!!

BUT YOU SHOULD SHOW OFF YER GAWGEOUS FIGYUH! ONE DAY YOU'LL CHANGE!

AT LEAST LET ME BUY YOU A DRESS!

NOPE

NO

SURE, YOU WON'T WEAR THIS?

EVEN SO, AT FIRST SOPH IS TOLERANT AND HAS COMPASSION...

MOM... BE NICER TO GRANDMA... SHE'S REALLY TRYING... AT LEAST THROW HER A BONE...

I JUST TOOK SOME OF POP'S CODEINE... I'M KINDA FUCKED UP...

I HOPE YOU LEFT SOME FOR HIS ARTHRITIS!

ACTUALLY... I HAVE A CONFESSION TO MAKE...

HA HA

I JUST TOOK A VALIUM!

ROOM-MATES FOR A WEEK

BUT HER PATIENCE QUICKLY FADES... NEXT MORNING: THE GYM!

LOOK AT 'ER, ON THE TRAMPOLINE!

OH MY GOD... I CAN'T DO THIS MOM!

SHE'S A MONSTAH!

JUMPING HIGHER THAN ANYONE AT 76!!

DON'T WORRY THIS IS PILATES... IT'S GOOD FOR YOU!

SOPHIE, I WANNA INTRADUCE YEW TO SERRETTA 'N' JAMS!

THE "RINGER"

I FEEL LIKE I'M AT THE GYNECOLOGIST... THIS ISN'T HAPPENING...

HI! NICE TO MEET YOU! WE LOVE YOUR GRANDMA! SHE'S OUR INSPIRATION! SHE PUTS US ALL TO SHAME!

SHE'S SO FANTASTIC.

HOLY FUCK

IN THEIR 70'S

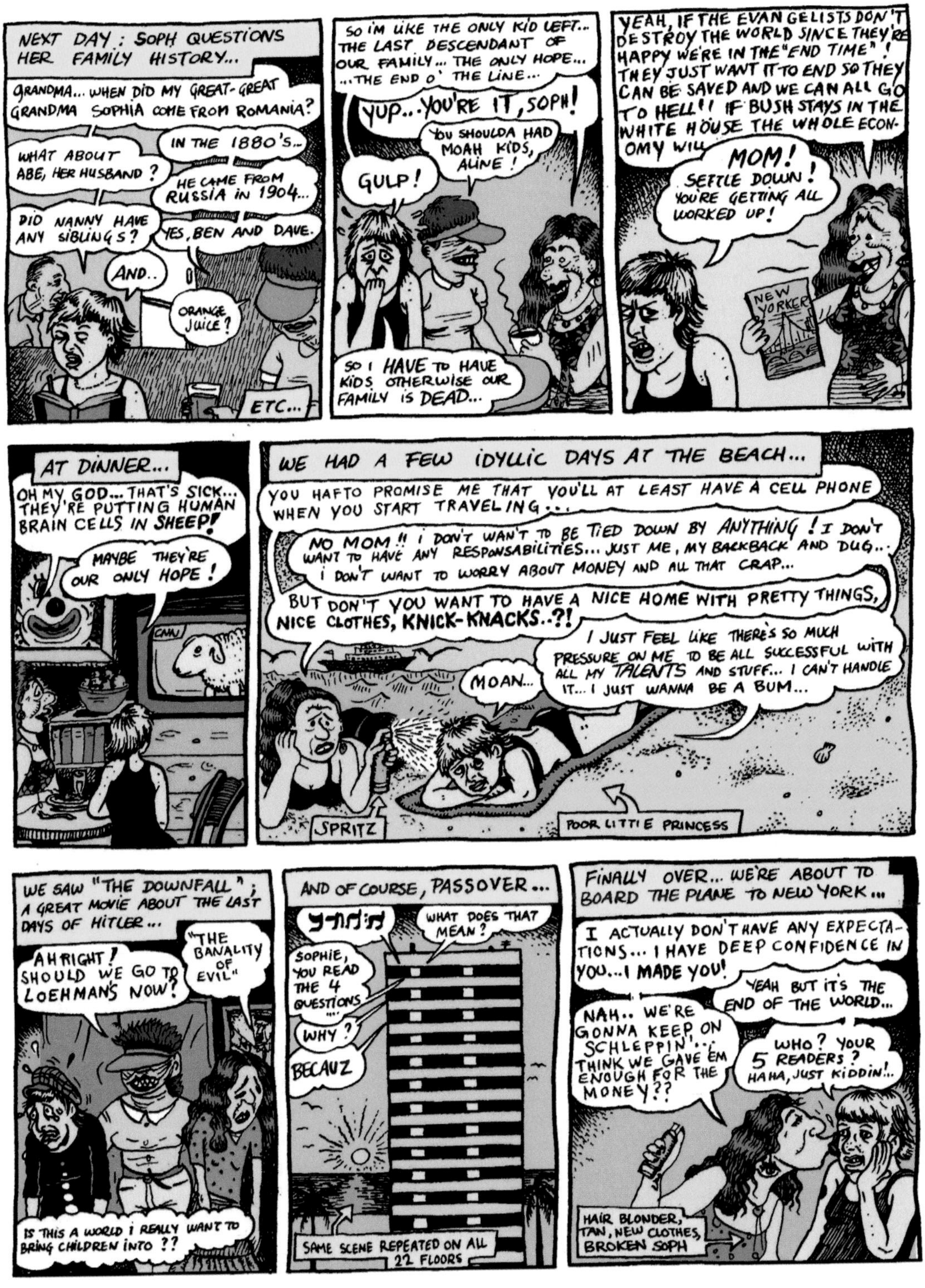
NEXT DAY: SOPH QUESTIONS HER FAMILY HISTORY...
GRANDMA... WHEN DID MY GREAT-GREAT GRANDMA SOPHIA COME FROM ROMANIA?
IN THE 1880's...
WHAT ABOUT ABE, HER HUSBAND?
HE CAME FROM RUSSIA IN 1904...
DID NANNY HAVE ANY SIBLINGS?
YES, BEN AND DAVE.
AND..
ORANGE JUICE?
ETC...
SO I'M LIKE THE ONLY KID LEFT... THE LAST DESCENDANT OF OUR FAMILY... THE ONLY HOPE... ...THE END O' THE LINE...
YUP... YOU'RE IT, SOPH!
YOU SHOULDA HAD MOAH KIDS, ALINE!
GULP!
SO I HAVE TO HAVE KIDS OTHERWISE OUR FAMILY IS DEAD...
YEAH, IF THE EVANGELISTS DON'T DESTROY THE WORLD SINCE THEY'RE HAPPY WE'RE IN THE "END TIME"! THEY JUST WANT IT TO END SO THEY CAN BE SAVED AND WE CAN ALL GO TO HELL!! IF BUSH STAYS IN THE WHITE HOUSE THE WHOLE ECONOMY WILL
MOM! SETTLE DOWN! YOU'RE GETTING ALL WORKED UP!
NEW YORKER
AT DINNER...
OH MY GOD... THAT'S SICK... THEY'RE PUTTING HUMAN BRAIN CELLS IN SHEEP!
MAYBE THEY'RE OUR ONLY HOPE!
CNN
WE HAD A FEW IDYLLIC DAYS AT THE BEACH...
YOU HAFTO PROMISE ME THAT YOU'LL AT LEAST HAVE A CELL PHONE WHEN YOU START TRAVELING...
NO MOM!! I DON'T WANT TO BE TIED DOWN BY ANYTHING! I DON'T WANT TO HAVE ANY RESPONSABILITIES... JUST ME, MY BACKBACK AND DUG... I DON'T WANT TO WORRY ABOUT MONEY AND ALL THAT CRAP...
BUT DON'T YOU WANT TO HAVE A NICE HOME WITH PRETTY THINGS, NICE CLOTHES, KNICK-KNACKS..?!
I JUST FEEL LIKE THERE'S SO MUCH PRESSURE ON ME TO BE ALL SUCCESSFUL WITH ALL MY TALENTS AND STUFF... I CAN'T HANDLE IT... I JUST WANNA BE A BUM...
MOAN...
SPRITZ
POOR LITTLE PRINCESS
WE SAW "THE DOWNFALL", A GREAT MOVIE ABOUT THE LAST DAYS OF HITLER...
AHRIGHT! SHOULD WE GO TO LOEHMAN'S NOW?
"THE BANALITY OF EVIL"
IS THIS A WORLD I REALLY WANT TO BRING CHILDREN INTO??
AND OF COURSE, PASSOVER...
WHAT DOES THAT MEAN?
SOPHIE, YOU READ THE 4 QUESTIONS...
WHY?
BECAUZ
SAME SCENE REPEATED ON ALL 22 FLOORS
FINALLY OVER... WE'RE ABOUT TO BOARD THE PLANE TO NEW YORK...
I ACTUALLY DON'T HAVE ANY EXPECTATIONS... I HAVE DEEP CONFIDENCE IN YOU... I MADE YOU!
YEAH BUT IT'S THE END OF THE WORLD...
NAH.. WE'RE GONNA KEEP ON SCHLEPPIN'... THINK WE GAVE 'EM ENOUGH FOR THE MONEY??
WHO? YOUR 5 READERS? HAHA, JUST KIDDIN'!..
HAIR BLONDER, TAN, NEW CLOTHES, BROKEN SOPH

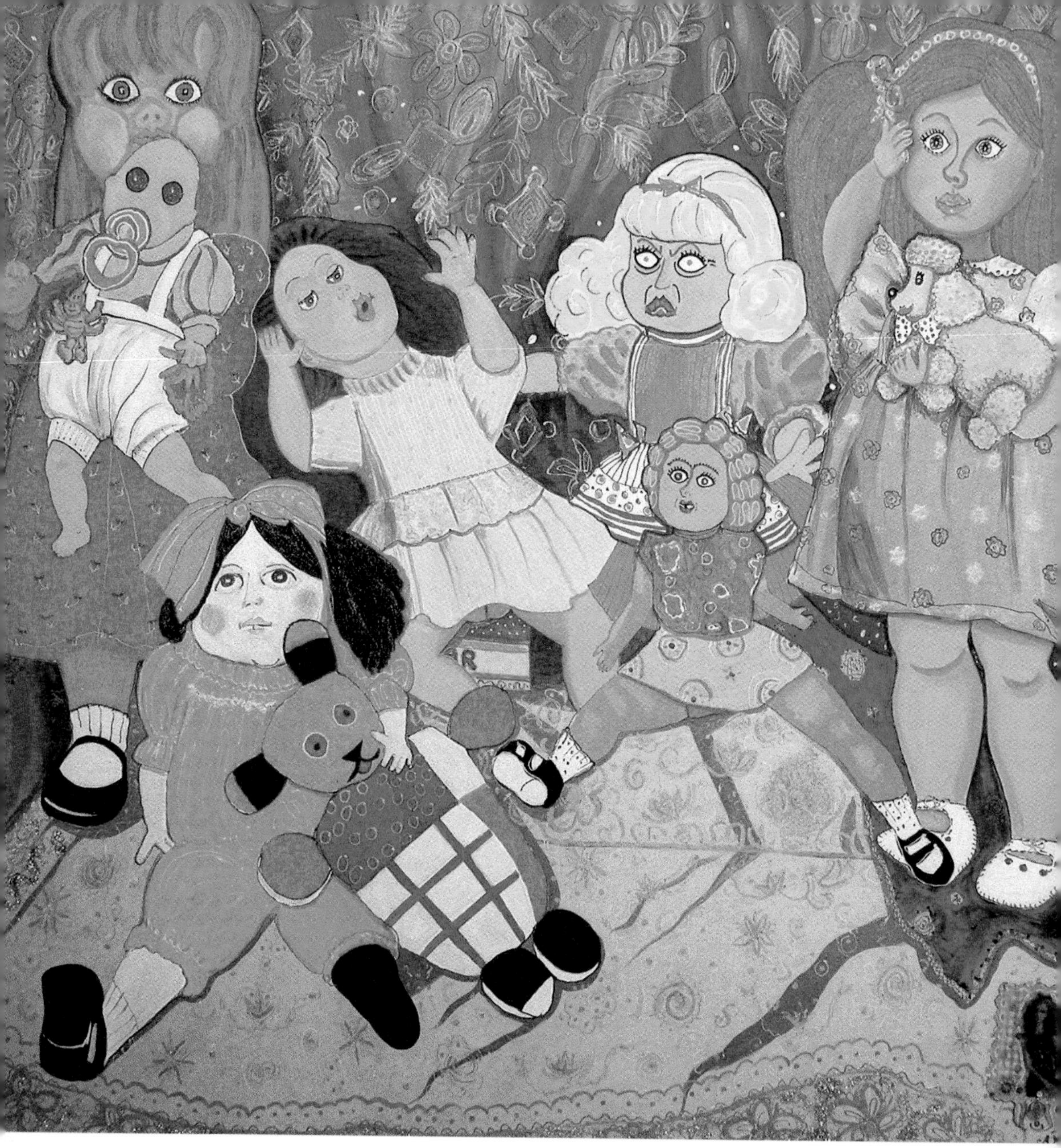

Above: **Aline Crumb, giant psychotic doll painting, acrylic and glitter, 2005**
This is the painting Sophie had to look at when she woke up in the morning. This is part of a large series of paintings of dolls and other strange plastic objects that weave an edgy tale with sexual overtones. Dominique Sapel, her husband Ian, and I worked on this series in their studio for two years.
Right: **Aline Crumb, "Barbie's Bordel," acrylic painting, 2005**
Next page: **Aline Crumb, "Demented Dolls," detail**
Page 378: **Aline Crumb, "Mermaid Shrine" magic box, wood, glass and jewels, 2003**
Page 379: **Aline Crumb, "Mystic Pizza Underwater Mermaid World," 2003**

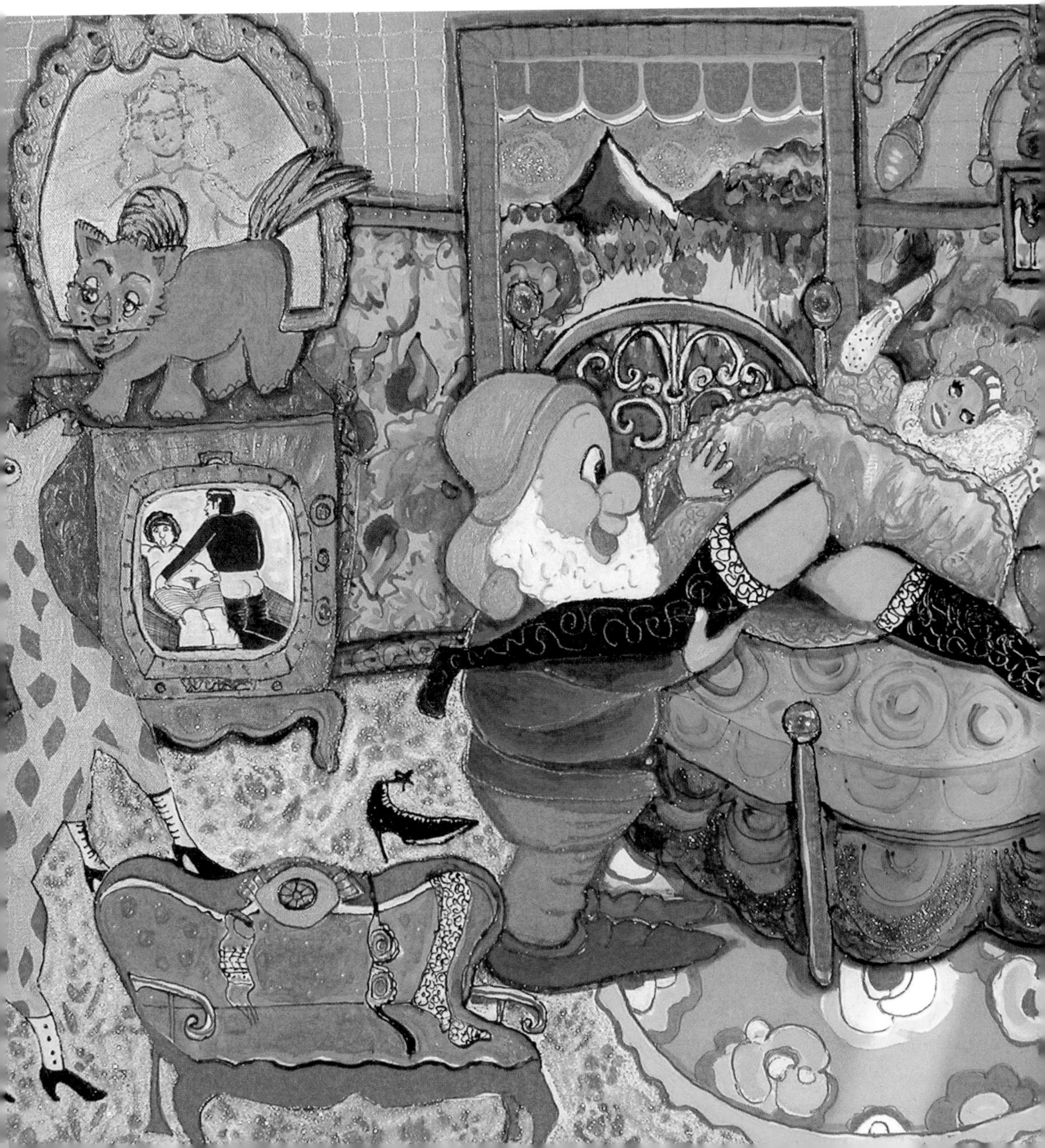

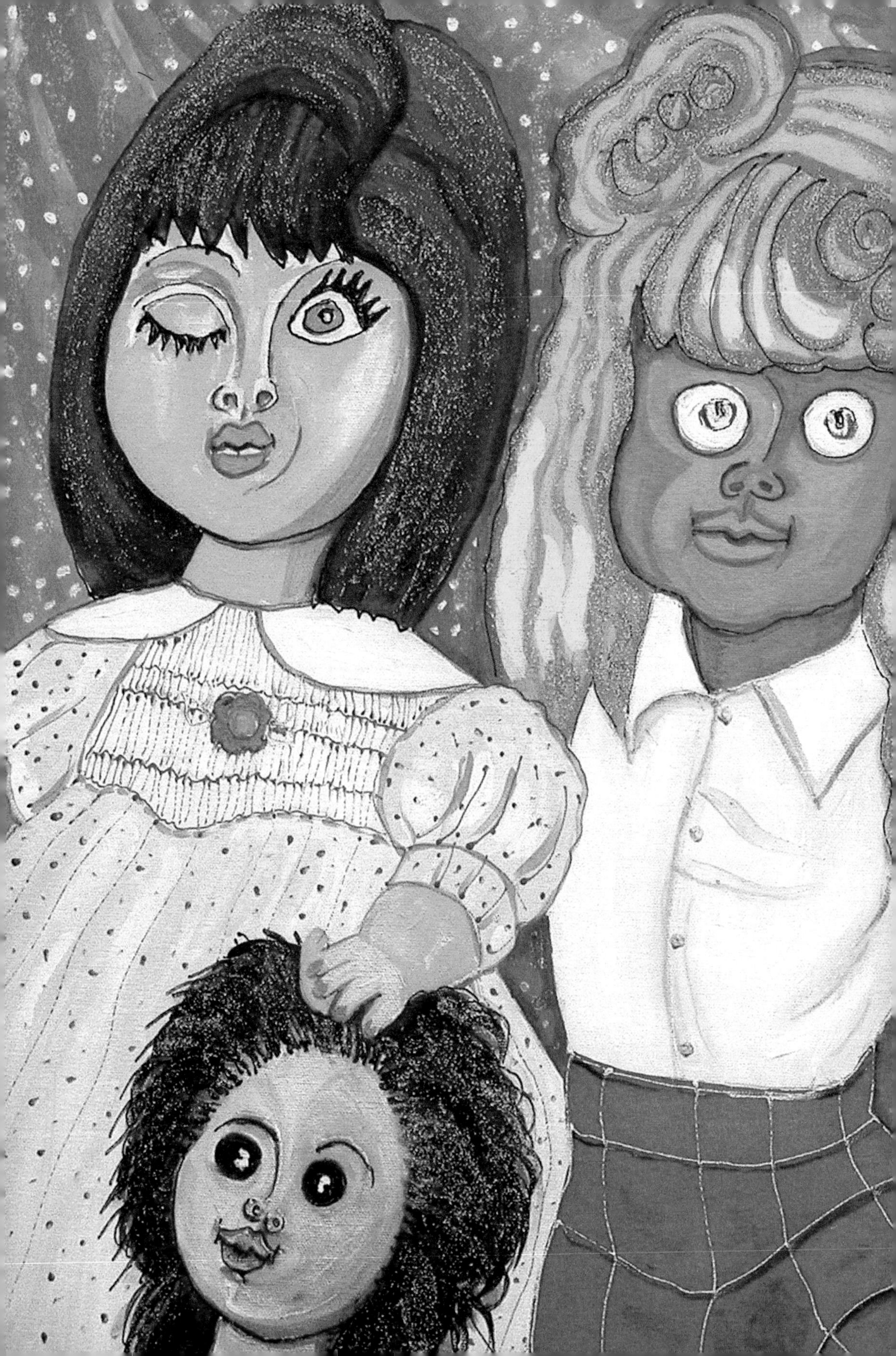

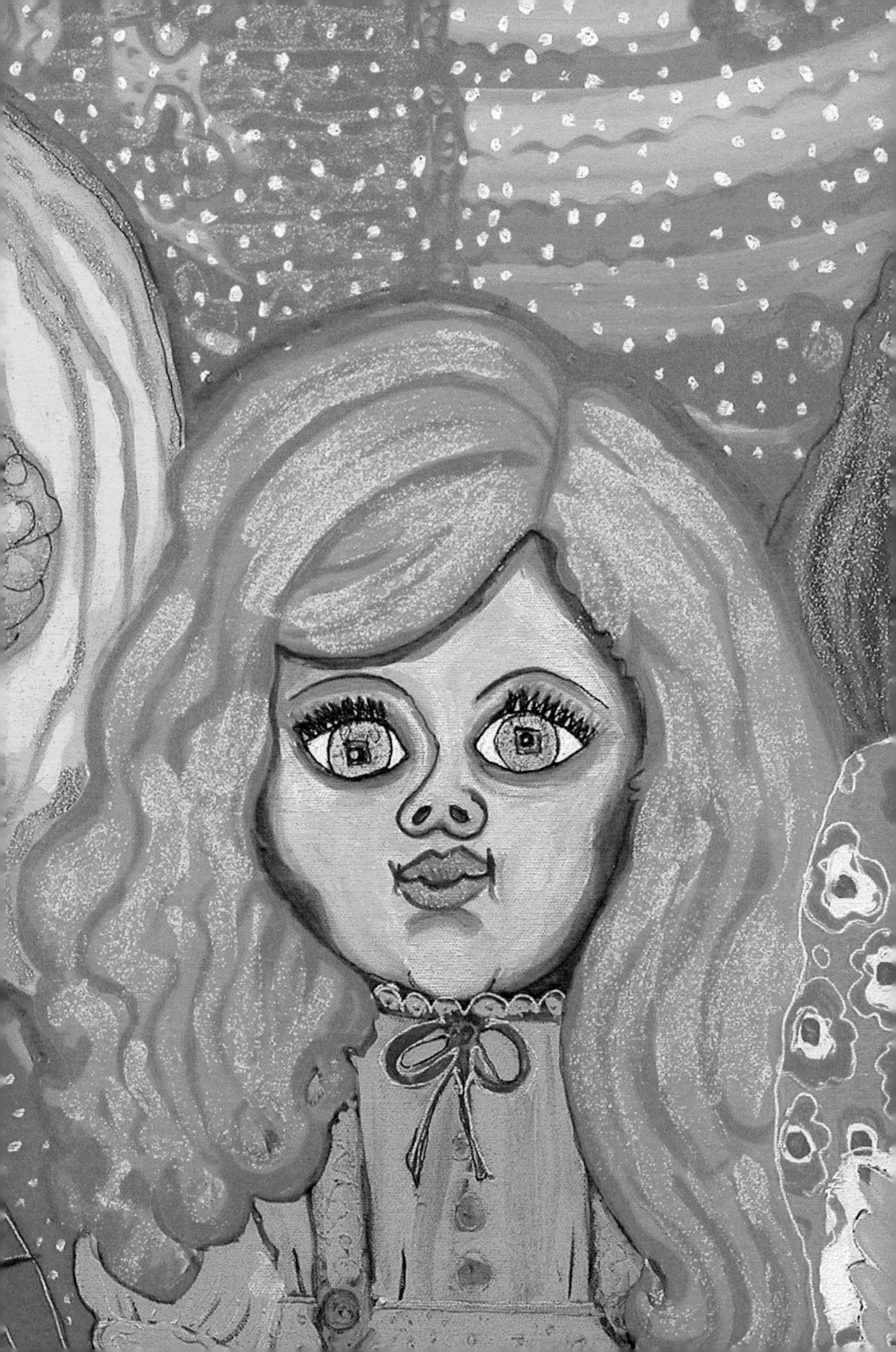

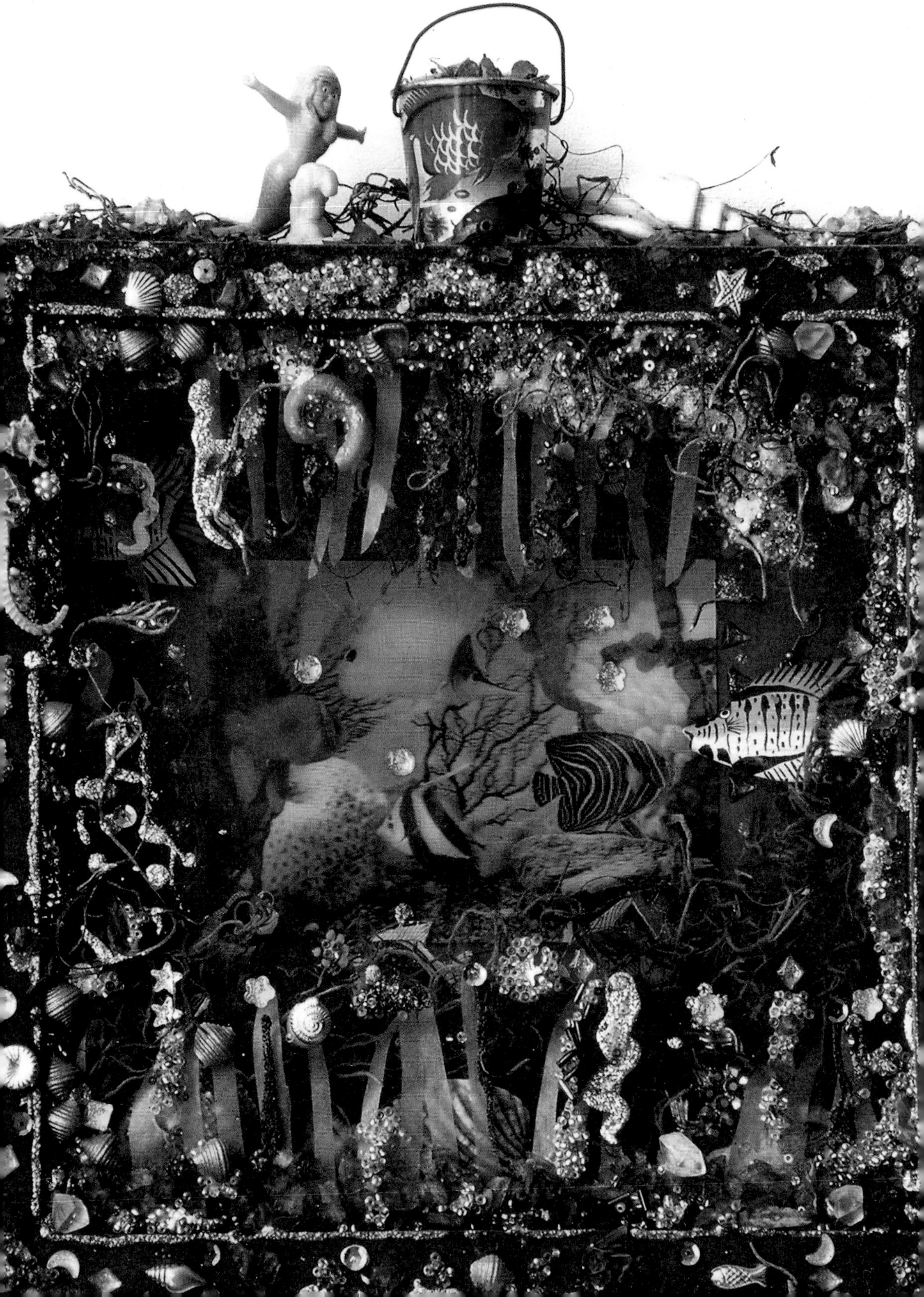

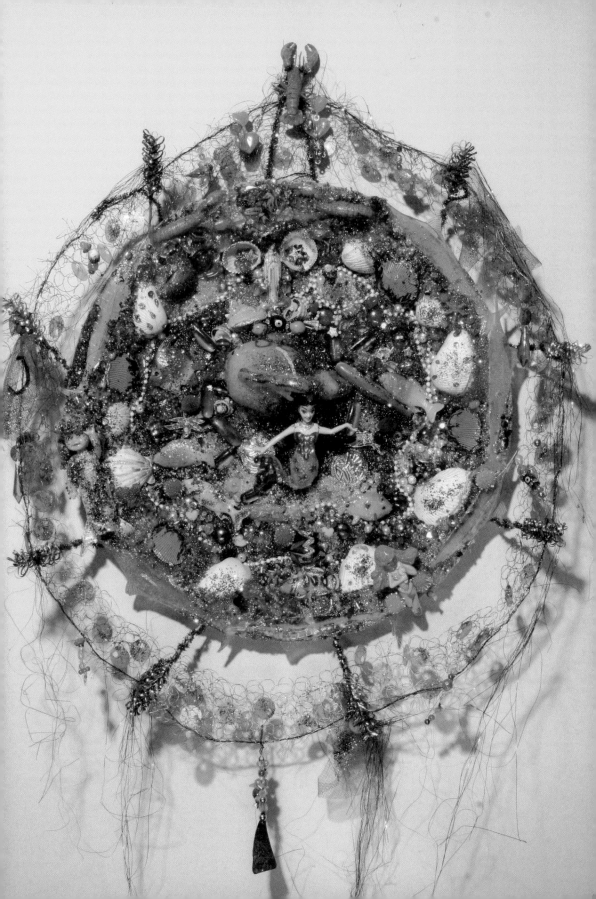

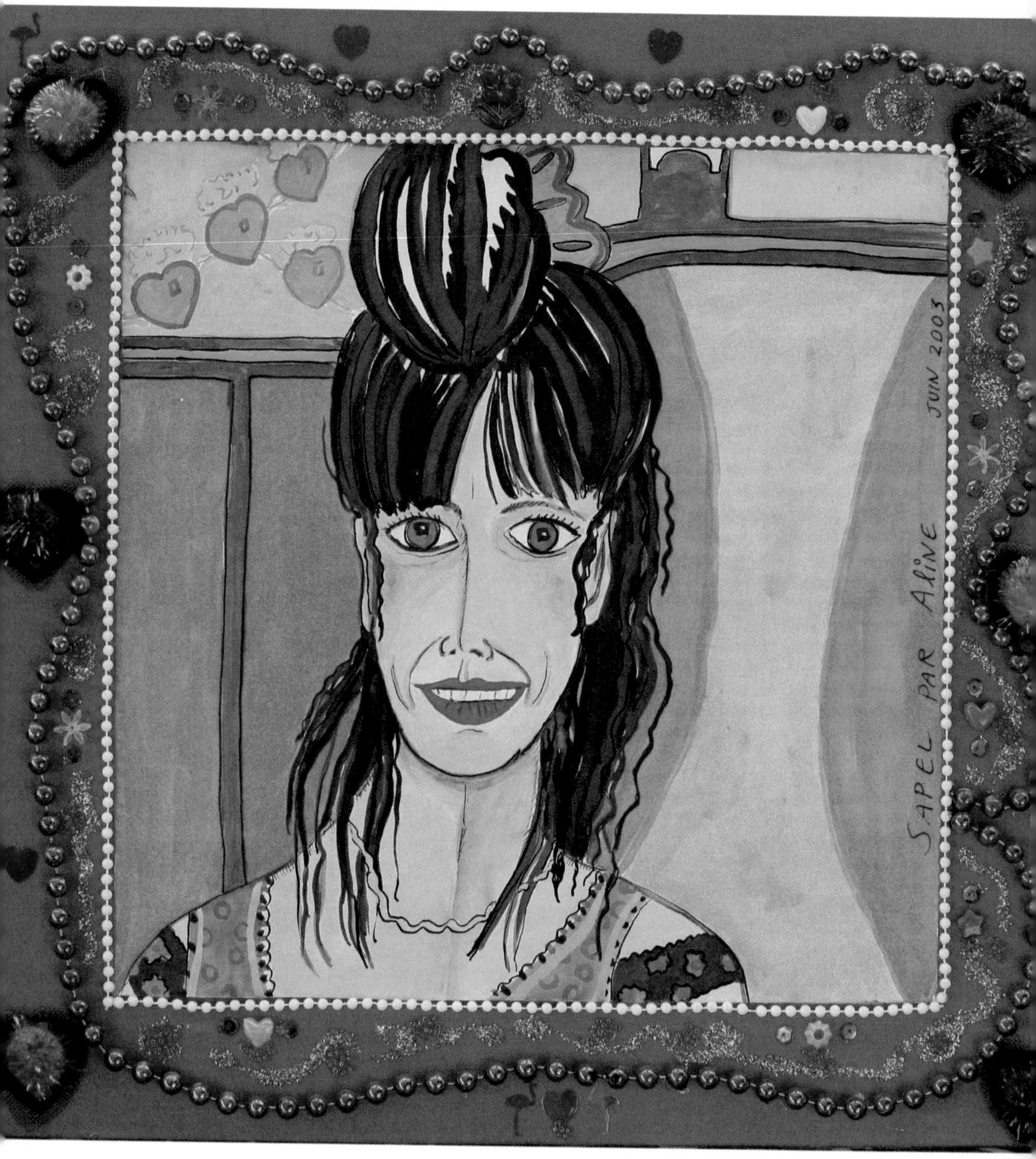
SAPEL PAR Aline
JUIN 2003

Above: **Aline Crumb, portrait of Dominique Sapel, 2003**
Made for the invitation to a joint exhibition.
Right: **Aline Crumb, watercolor with jewels and plastic boots, 2003**
Made for Vivienne Tam. I am wearing a dress she gave me.
Page 382: **My personal shrine in the hallway to my house, with all sort of icons included**
Page 383: **Aline and Sophie Crumb, "The Good Little Girl," plastic tray with jewels**

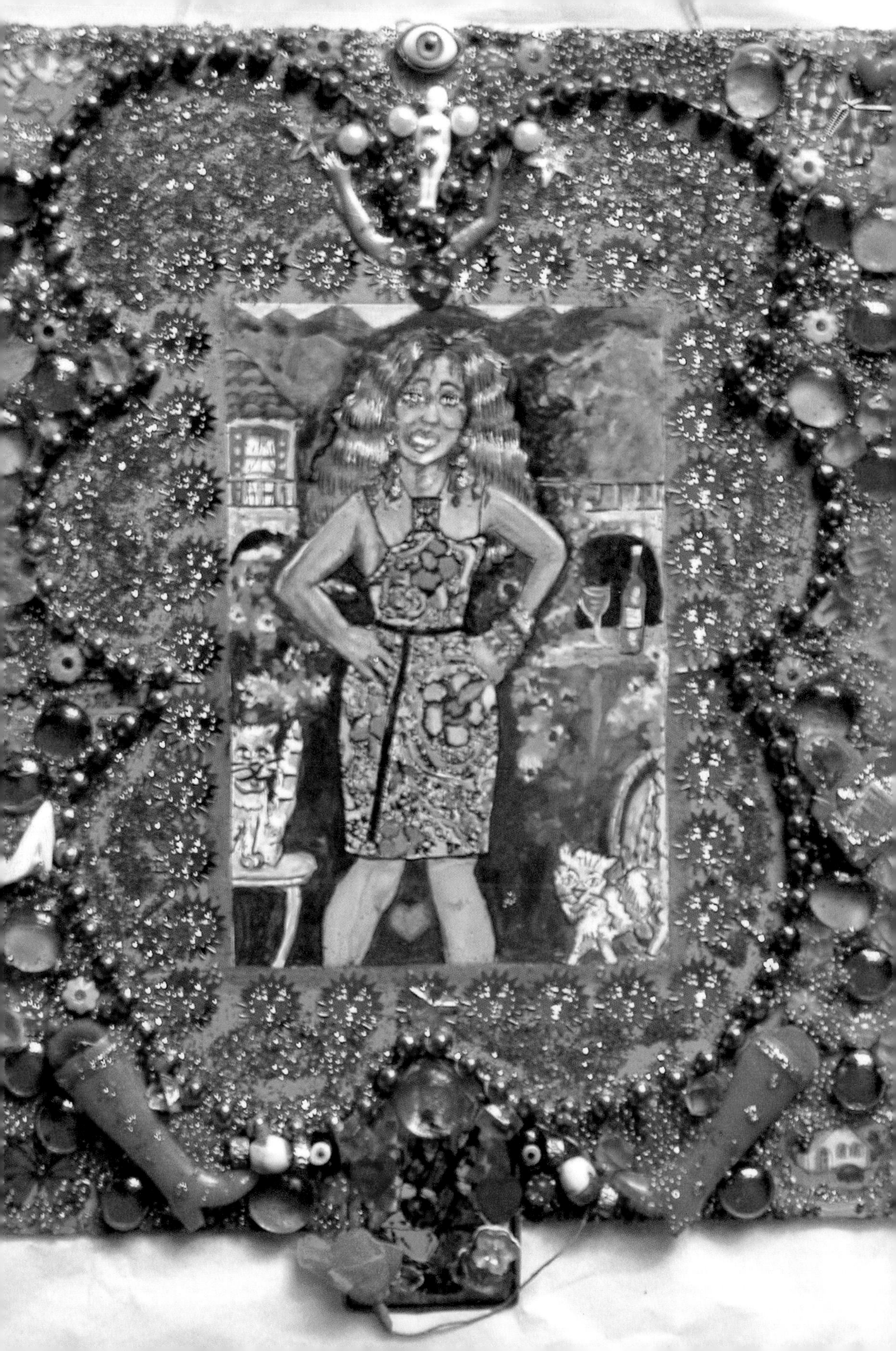

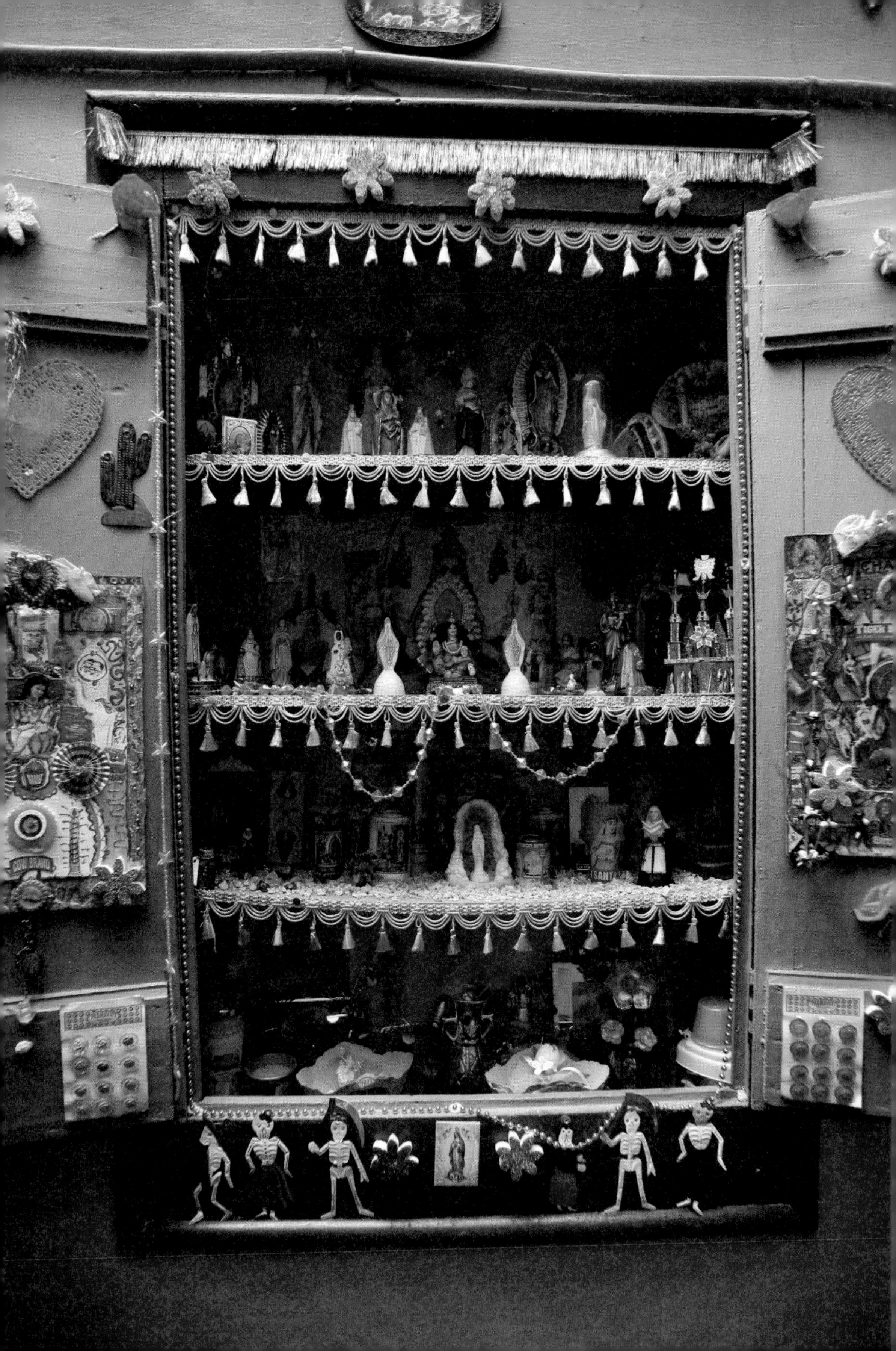
COW BRAND

Acknowledgments

Technical assistance: Christian Coudurès, Laurel Avery, Agathe McCamy
Lettering: Sophie Crumb
Text correction and editing: Maggie DuMiramon
Photos: Gregg Gannon, Christian Coudurès, Olivier Menard
Special help from Diane Noomin, Betsy Sandlin, Lora Fountain
Psychic Twin and Editor at MQ Publications: Yvonne Deutch
Graphic assistance: Graham Saville and Anna Gould
Special thanks to John Casey and Gordon Parker
Moral Support: Sophie Crumb, Joey Zeman, and Robert Crumb
Guardian Angels: Zaro Weil and Gareth Jenkins
Apologies to all the people I have said mean things about (even tho it's all true!)
And thanks to my family and the people I grew up with for providing such rich comic material

First published by MQ Publications Ltd
12 The Ivories
6–8 Northampton Street
London N1 2HY
Tel: 020 7359 2244
Fax: 020 7359 1616
email: mail@mqpublications.com
website: www.mqpublications.com

North American Office:
49 West 24th Street, 8th Floor
New York, NY 10010
email: information@mqpublicationsus.com

MQP Handbooks Director: Gareth Jenkins
MQP Handbooks Series Editor: Yvonne Deutch

ISBN 10: 1-84601-133-7
ISBN 13: 978-1-84601-133-7

10 9 8 7 6 5 4 3 2 1

Printed in the U.S.

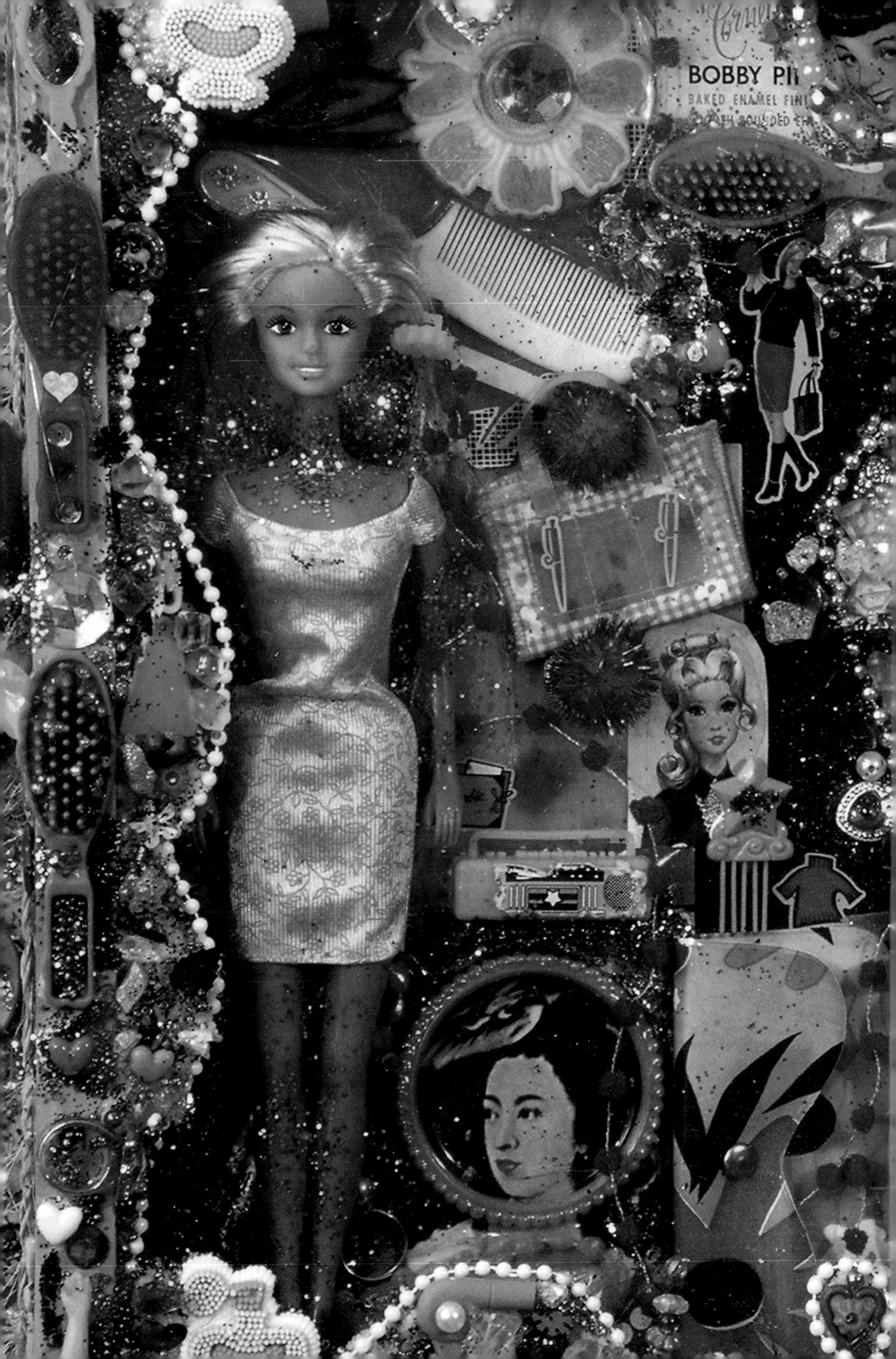
BOBBY PI
BAKED ENAMEL FINI